ASPEN PUBLISHERS

403(b) Answer Book
Seventh Edition

Edited by Donald R. Levy, Barbara N. Seymon-Hirsch, and Janet M. Anderson-Briggs

403(b) Answer Book is the only professional resource that systematically answers hundreds of questions on Section 403(b) and Section 457 plans, 501(c)(3) organizations, and church plans. It provides insight on how to handle complicated issues not yet resolved by the IRS or the courts. *403(b) Answer Book, Seventh Edition*, includes coverage of qualified domestic relations orders, nondiscrimination requirements, contribution limits, correction of plan defects, and Section 403(b)(7) custodial accounts.

Highlights of the Seventh Edition

403(b) Answer Book, Seventh Edition, discusses administrative developments and changes in the past year, including the following:

- The new Section 403(b) plan document requirements and their effect on non-ERISA plans.

- The new responsibilities of employers and providers for administration of the Section 403(b) plan as set forth in information sharing agreements.

- The repeal of IRS Notice 89-23 for satisfying nondiscrimination requirements and how plans must apply universal availability to Section 403(b) salary reduction plans.

- The rules regarding how Section 403(b) contributions are subject to the Section 415(c) limits, the 15-year catch-up limits, and age 50+ catch-up rules.

- The new Code Section 403(b) tax-free transfer rules, information sharing agreements, and when a Section 403(b) plan may not be affected.

- The new distribution restrictions that apply to employer contributions in annuity contracts for contracts issued after December 31, 2008.

- The regulations in Revenue Procedure 2007-71.

Wolters Kluwer
Law & Business

- The changes made to Section 403(b) plans as a result of the Pension Protection Act of 2006.

- Analysis of Roth 403(b) arrangements.

- Treatment and administration of participant loans.

- Duty of plan fiduciary to collect repayments on a participant loan.

- Investment blackout periods, blackout notices, and duration of blackouts.

- Application of securities laws when compiling plan investment information.

- The right of participants to obtain written confirmation of their investment instructions.

- DOL interpretive guidance relating to investment education for participants.

- Gap-fillers and default provisions in beneficiary designation forms.

- Survivor benefits required under ERISA for a spouse.

- Common mistakes with beneficiary designations.

- Special rules that apply when a plan is subject to ERISA and when a plan would fall within the safe harbor exemption from ERISA.

- Special requirements applying to cross-tested Section 403(b) plans.

- When an interest in a pooled or collective investment vehicle should be considered issued directly to eligible employee.

- The SEC's position on the employer's obligation to provide eligible employees with prospectuses and other reports.

In short, *403(b) Answer Book* gives subscribers the most current and comprehensive answers to the issues faced daily by plan administrators, benefits consultants, attorneys, and other pension professionals.

6/08

For questions concerning this shipment, billing, or other customer service matters, call our Customer Service Department at 1-800-234-1660.

For toll-free ordering, please call 1-800-638-8437.

403(b)
Answer Book

Seventh Edition

ASPEN PUBLISHERS

403(b)
Answer Book

Seventh Edition

Edited by

Donald R. Levy
Barbara N. Seymon-Hirsch
Janet M. Anderson-Briggs

Wolters Kluwer

Law & Business

AUSTIN   BOSTON   CHICAGO   NEW YORK   THE NETHERLANDS

© 2008 Aspen Publishers. All Rights Reserved.

No part of this publication may be reproduced or transmitted in any form or by any means, electronic or mechanical, including photocopy, recording, or any information storage and retrieval system, without permission in writing from the publisher. Requests for permission to reproduce content should be directed to the Aspen Publishers website at *www.aspenpublishers.com*, or a letter of intent should be faxed to the permissions department at 212-771-0803.

Printed in the United States of America

ISBN 978-0-7355-7433-5

2 3 4 5 6 7 8 9 0

About Wolters Kluwer Law & Business

Wolters Kluwer Law & Business is a leading provider of research information and workflow solutions in key specialty areas. The strengths of the individual brands of Aspen Publishers, CCH, Kluwer Law International and Loislaw are aligned within Wolters Kluwer Law & Business to provide comprehensive, in-depth solutions and expert-authored content for the legal, professional and education markets.

CCH was founded in 1913 and has served more than four generations of business professionals and their clients. The CCH products in the Wolters Kluwer Law & Business group are highly regarded electronic and print resources for legal, securities, antitrust and trade regulation, government contracting, banking, pension, payroll, employment and labor, and healthcare reimbursement and compliance professionals.

Aspen Publishers is a leading information provider for attorneys, business professionals and law students. Written by preeminent authorities, Aspen products offer analytical and practical information in a range of specialty practice areas from securities law and intellectual property to mergers and acquisitions and pension/benefits. Aspen's trusted legal education resources provide professors and students with high-quality, up-to-date and effective resources for successful instruction and study in all areas of the law.

Kluwer Law International supplies the global business community with comprehensive English-language international legal information. Legal practitioners, corporate counsel and business executives around the world rely on the Kluwer Law International journals, loose-leafs, books and electronic products for authoritative information in many areas of international legal practice.

Loislaw is a premier provider of digitized legal content to small law firm practitioners of various specializations. Loislaw provides attorneys with the ability to quickly and efficiently find the necessary legal information they need, when and where they need it, by facilitating access to primary law as well as state-specific law, records, forms and treatises.

Wolters Kluwer Law & Business, a unit of Wolters Kluwer, is headquartered in New York and Riverwoods, Illinois. Wolters Kluwer is a leading multinational publisher and information services company.

ASPEN PUBLISHERS SUBSCRIPTION NOTICE

This Aspen Publishers product is updated on a periodic basis with supplements to reflect important changes in the subject matter. If you purchased this product directly from Aspen Publishers, we have already recorded your subscription for the update service.

If, however, you purchased this product from a bookstore and wish to receive future updates and revised or related volumes billed separately with a 30-day examination review, please contact our Customer Service Department at 1-800-234-1660, or send your name, company name (if applicable), address, and the title of the product to:

ASPEN PUBLISHERS
7201 McKinney Circle
Frederick, MD 21704

Important Aspen Publishers Contact Information

- To order any Aspen Publishers title, go to *www.aspenpublishers.com* or call 1-800-638-8437.

- To reinstate your manual update service, call 1-800-638-8437.

- To contact Customer Care, e-mail *customer.care@aspenpublishers.com*, call 1-800-234-1660, fax 1-800-901-9075, or mail correspondence to Order Department, Aspen Publishers, PO Box 990, Frederick, MD 21705.

- To review your account history or pay an invoice online, visit *www.aspenpublishers.com/payinvoices*.

To the memory of Beatrice F. Seymon—
devoted mother and grandmother.

Preface

403(b) Answer Book, Seventh Edition, examines all aspects of Sections 403(b) plans (also known as tax-sheltered annuity arrangements), 457 plans, 501(c)(3) organizations, and church plans. This type of defined contribution retirement vehicle involves a host of unique planning and compliance issues, requiring specialized approaches, knowledge, understanding, and experience. *403(b) Answer Book, Seventh Edition,* helps keep pension professionals, accountants, attorneys, financial planners, employers, trustees, brokers, and others up to date on the latest Section 403(b) planning techniques and rulings by examining planning issues and considering changes in legislation and practice. Planning and administrative suggestions are incorporated into the text.

To guide the practitioner through the complexities of establishing and administering these plans, *403(b) Answer Book, Seventh Edition,* covers the full range of Section 403(b) plan topics, plan administration issues, and insurance and investment issues. This edition has been substantially revised and updated to reflect and incorporate the final Code Section 403(b) regulations. It provides clear, practice-oriented coverage of maximum contribution and other discrimination rules; multiple funding alternatives available; fiduciary responsibility; prohibited transactions and exemptions; reporting and other requirements of the Internal Revenue Service (IRS) and the Department of Labor (DOL); and much more.

403(b) Answer Book uses straightforward language and avoids technical jargon whenever possible, yet it provides professionals with the tools to become conversant in the idiom of Section 403(b) plans. Citations to authority are provided as research aids for those who wish to pursue particular items in greater detail, and an extensive system of cross-referencing guides the reader toward related or additional topics of interest.

Format. The question-and-answer format breaks down complex subject areas into concise units. Introductory text provides an overview of the subject that is covered in detail in the questions and answers.

Numbering System. The questions are numbered consecutively within each chapter.

List of Questions. The detailed List of Questions that follows the Table of Contents helps the reader locate areas of immediate interest. A series of subheadings organizes questions by topic within each chapter.

Appendices. For the reader's convenience, supplementary reference materials related to Section 403(b) plans are provided in the appendices that appear at the end of the book.

Index. A detailed topical index is provided to aid in locating specific information. All references are to question numbers.

Donald R. Levy
Barbara N. Seymon-Hirsch
Janet M. Anderson-Briggs
May 2008

Editors and Contributors

Donald R. Levy, Esq., MBA, is an attorney and benefits consultant. A graduate of Harvard Law School and Harvard College, he received an MBA in accounting from New York University. Mr. Levy has more than 30 years of experience as a pension administrator and tax planner. He has practiced law and has served as Vice President and Director of Employee Benefits with United States Tobacco; Vice President, Benefits, with Johnson and Higgins; and Senior Technical Consultant for Prentice Hall, where he authored the *Pension Handbook*. Mr. Levy is co-author of Aspen's *Individual Retirement Account Answer Book* and *Quick Reference to IRAs*. He has taught at the University of Connecticut, has been a panelist for the Practising Law Institute, and has lectured before other professional groups.

Barbara N. Seymon-Hirsch, Esq., is a partner with Davis & Harman LLP, a Washington, DC, law firm specializing in federal tax and legislative matters. Ms. Seymon-Hirsch specializes in federal tax matters, concentrating particularly on issues relating to insurance product tax compliance, individual retirement arrangements, qualified retirement plans, Section 403(b) arrangements, and employment tax. She received her BA from Vassar College, her JD from California Western School of Law, and her LL.M. in Taxation from Georgetown University Law School. Ms. Seymon-Hirsch was previously Assistant Tax Counsel with Metropolitan Life Insurance Company. She was also previously with the Internal Revenue Service in Washington, DC. She is a member of the District of Columbia and New York bars. Ms. Seymon-Hirsch is a member of the Committee on Employee Benefits of the Tax Section of the American Bar Association and has served as a member of the IRS Information Reporting Program Advisory Committee (IRPAC), from 1994 through 1995 and again from 2002 through 2004.

Janet M. Anderson-Briggs, Esq., is an attorney and benefits consultant in the greater Portland, Oregon area. Her practice has covered the tax and pension laws governing Section 403(b) tax deferred annuities and Section 457 nonqualified deferred compensation plans for more than 20 years. She has written and lectured extensively in the area of Section 403(b) tax and ERISA compliance for public and private tax-exempt organizations. She previously served as a senior benefits consultant for Mercer Investment Consulting, both in Richmond,

Virginia, and Seattle, Washington. She is a member of the American Bar Association, where she is a member of the Tax Section's Employee Benefits Committee and its Subcommittee on Section 403(b), Section 457, and Exempt Organization Issues. Before joining Mercer, Ms. Anderson-Briggs was Senior Counsel and Assistant Secretary of The Variable Annuity Life Insurance Company (VALIC). Ms. Anderson-Briggs received her BA, *cum laude*, from Georgian Court College, Lakewood, New Jersey. She received her JD from South Texas College of Law in Houston, Texas, where she received an American Jurisprudence award in Federal Procedure. She is admitted to practice before the U.S. Supreme Court, the U.S. Tax Court, the Fifth Circuit Court of Appeals, and the U.S. District Court for the Southern District of Texas and is a member of the State Bar of Texas. She is an NASD insurance investment products registered principal.

Contributors:

Jason Bortz, Esq., is a partner with Davis & Harman LLP, a Washington, DC, law firm. Mr. Bortz's practice focuses exclusively on employee benefit matters, advising clients on tax, ERISA, and other aspects of tax-favored retirement plans, and executive compensation arrangements. He counsels a broad range of clients including insurance companies and other financial institutions, plan service providers, and tax-exempt organizations. Mr. Bortz is a frequent speaker on employee benefits issues and has authored several articles. He is a contributing author to CRI Publishers' *Complete Guide to Nonprofit Organizations.* Following a clerkship on the U.S. Court of Appeals for the Eighth Circuit, Mr. Bortz was an associate and later a member of Caplin and Drysdale, Chartered. Mr. Bortz holds a BA from Hamilton College and a JD from Cornell Law School, where he was a member of the Order of the Coif and an editor of the *Cornell Law Review*.

Robert A. Browning, Esq., is a partner with Spencer Fane Britt & Brown LLP, a law firm based in Kansas City, Missouri. He is a member of the firm's Employee Benefits Group, and his practice area includes the pension and tax laws governing qualified retirement plans, health and welfare plans, and executive compensation arrangement. Before joining Spencer Fane, Mr. Browning was a shareholder with Polsinelli Shalton Flanigan Suelthaus PC, another Kansas City law firm. Before joining Polsinelli, he was Senior Counsel for The Variable Annuity Life Insurance Company (now known as AIG Retirement), in Houston, Texas. Mr. Browning received his JD, with honors, from the University of Houston in 1989, and he is currently a member of the Employee Benefits Committee of the American Bar Association Section on Taxation, the Employee Benefits Committee of the Kansas City Metropolitan Bar Association, the Employee Benefits Institute of Kansas City, and the Heart of America Employee Benefits Conference.

John P. Curran, Esq., is Associate General Counsel with Teachers Insurance and Annuity Association-College Retirement Equities Fund (TIAA-CREF), where he works in the Individual Client Services Law area. Mr. Curran received his JD from the Fordham University School of Law.

Michael Footer, Esq., is a former principal of Mercer Investment Consulting in Richmond, Virginia. Mr. Footer has started his own consulting firm, focusing exclusively on helping providers improve products and market share. He has written and lectured extensively in the areas of health and welfare plans, pension and profit-sharing plans, and tax-sheltered annuities. For the past 26 years, he was in charge of Mercer's Nonprofit 403(b) Practice in Richmond, Virginia. In his current position, Mr. Footer has had an opportunity to address design, funding, and administrative issues relating to all types of employee benefit plans with special emphasis on nonprofit organizations. Mr. Footer received his JD from George Washington University Law School in 1966 and his designation as a Chartered Life Underwriter in 1973. Mr. Footer is an active member of the American Bar Association's Employee Benefits Committee, serving on the Welfare Benefits Subcommittees and as Chairperson of the Tax Sheltered Annuity/457 Subcommittee. He is a Charter Fellow of the American College of Employee Benefits Counsel.

Evan Giller, Esq., is Vice President and General Counsel, Institutional Client Services, with Teachers Insurance and Annuity Association-College Retirement Equities Fund (TIAA-CREF), where he manages the Pension Law Unit. He is responsible for ERISA, tax, and insurance law issues relating to Section 403(b) plans, qualified plans, and nonqualified defined compensation plans. He has also spent five years as the Chief Compliance Officer for TIAA-CREF's pension business. Mr. Giller has served on the Employee Benefits Committee of the Association of the Bar of the City of New York. He received his JD in 1978 from the State University of New York at Buffalo Law School.

David S. Goldstein, Esq., is a partner in the law firm of Sutherland Asbill & Brennan, LLP, in Washington, DC. Before joining Sutherland in May 1989, he served for three and a half years on the staff of the Securities and Exchange Commission (SEC), where he was Attorney-Adviser and later Special Counsel in the Division of Investment Management. From 1981 through 1985, Mr. Goldstein was Assistant Vice President, Assistant General Counsel, and Assistant Secretary of The Variable Annuity Life Insurance Company. He is also a contributor to Aspen Publishers' *457 Answer Book*. He is a member of the District of Columbia, Texas, and Massachusetts bars; the American Bar Association, Section of Business Law (Committee on Federal Regulation of Securities and Subcommittee on Securities Activities of Insurance Companies); and the District of Columbia Bar Section on Corporation, Finance, and Securities Law. Mr. Goldstein received his BA in 1978 from Hampshire College and his JD in 1981 from Boston University.

Peter Gulia, Esq., is the shareholder of Fiduciary Guidance Counsel, a Philadelphia, Pennsylvania, law firm that advises retirement plans' fiduciaries. After more than 21 years of experience with one of America's largest retirement services businesses, Mr. Gulia now counsels employers that administer retirement plans, and investment advisers, trustees, and other fiduciaries. In addition to ERISA-governed plans, Mr. Gulia has wide experience with church plans and governmental plans, and with how laws beyond ERISA and the Internal Revenue Code affect retirement plans.

Mr. Gulia is a contributing author of Aspen Publishers' *457 Answer Book; Governmental Plans Answer Book, Roth IRA Answer Book,* and *SIMPLE, SEP, and SARSEP Answer Book.* He also contributes to AICPA's *The CPA's Guide to Retirement Plans for Small Businesses.*

Mr. Gulia teaches continuing professional education programs and is a member of the American Bar Association, the American Society of Pension Professionals and Actuaries (as an Associated Professional Member), the American Institute of Certified Public Accountants (as an associate of a member), and the Philadelphia Compliance Roundtable.

Gary E. Herzlich, Esq., is Associate General Counsel with Teachers Insurance and Annuity Association-College Retirement Equities Fund (TIAA-CREF). Mr. Herzlich advises on Section 403(b) plans, Section 401(a) qualified plans, nonqualified deferred compensation arrangements, fiduciary issues, compliance, and general pension and compensation matters. He also spent two years serving as Senior Compliance Officer for TIAA-CREF's pension business. Before joining TIAA-CREF, Mr. Herzlich was a member of the Employee Benefits and Executive Compensation group of Proskauer Rose LLP. Mr. Herzlich received his JD from Boston University School of Law and his LL.M. in Taxation from New York University Law School.

Bryan W. Keene, Esq., is a partner in Davis & Harman LLP, a Washington, DC, law firm specializing in federal tax and legislative matters. Mr. Keene's practice focuses on issues relating to the federal income tax treatment of insurance products and qualified retirement plans, particularly Section 403(b) programs and individual retirement arrangements. Prior to joining Davis & Harman LLP in 1999, Mr. Keene received a BS from the University of Florida in 1994. He received a JD, *cum laude,* from the University of Florida in 1998. While at the University of Florida, Mr. Keene was a senior editor of the *Florida Law Review.* Mr. Keene is a member of the bars of the District of Columbia and Florida and is a frequent author and speaker on issues relating to the taxation of insurance companies and their products.

Danny Miller, Esq., is a partner in the Washington, DC, office of Conner & Winters LLP, a Tulsa, Oklahoma-based law firm and a member of that firm's Employee Benefits practice group. Mr. Miller received his law degree from the Vanderbilt University School of Law in 1974, at which time he began practicing in the employee benefits area. Mr. Miller is a Fellow of the American College of Employee Benefits Counsel and has served as adjunct professor at Southern Methodist University School of Law, where for three years he taught a course on Taxation of Deferred Compensation. Mr. Miller is a member of the Employee Benefits Committee of the Tax Section of the American Bar Association and serves on the Subcommittee on Section 403(b), 457, and Exempt Organization Issues—of which he served as chair from the spring of 1989 until August 1992. Mr. Miller is also a past director and current member of the South West Benefits Association based in Dallas, Texas.

Beverly J. Orth, Esq., FSA, is a principal in the Portland, Oregon, office of Mercer. She has been a consultant with Mercer since 1984, consulting primarily in the area of retirement benefits, with emphasis on compliance with federal legislation and regulations. She is a member of Mercer's Public Sector and Nonprofit Consulting Group, specializing in consulting to Section 403(b) and 457 plan sponsors. Ms. Orth has written a number of articles on employee benefits, recently focusing on the issue of mitigating longevity risk in the defined contribution plan environment. Her background prior to joining Mercer included six years of law practice in the areas of income tax, estate planning, and employee benefits. Ms. Orth received her BS in mathematics, with honors and distinction, from Harvey Mudd College and her JD from Harvard University. She is also a Fellow in the Society of Actuaries.

Glenn Poehler, ASA, MAAA, EA, is a principal at Mercer in the Richmond office. He has over 30 years of experience in qualified and nonqualified plan consulting. Mr. Poehler serves as the co-leader of Mercer's Healthcare Industry Expert Group, an international team of consultants who oversee Mercer's retirement-related services to healthcare clients across North and South America. and is the practice leader in Mercer's Non-profit and Public Sector Consulting Practice. He has extensive experience in the design, administration, and funding of all types of qualified and nonqualified defined contribution and deferred compensation plans including Section 401(k), profit-sharing, thrift savings, Section 403(b), and Section 457 plans. Mr. Poehler specializes in consulting to health care systems, hospitals, and institutes of higher education. He received his BS in mathematics from Virginia Tech. He is an associate of the Society of Actuaries, member of the American Academy of Actuaries, and an enrolled actuary.

David W. Powell, Esq., is a principal in the Washington, DC, tax law firm of Groom Law Group, Chartered. He is a certified public accountant as well as an attorney and is a past President of the Washington Employee Benefits Forum. He received his JD from the University of Texas in 1982. Mr. Powell works with tax and ERISA issues relating to all types of employee pension and welfare benefits plans. Mr. Powell frequently contributes topical articles to and is a member of the Board of Contributors of *Employee Benefits for Nonprofits* and the Editorial Advisory Board of the *Journal of Deferred Compensation*. He is a frequent speaker and writer on employee benefits topics, particularly on the topics of nonqualified deferred compensation plans and employee benefit plans for nonprofit organizations. He is also a contributor to Aspen Publishers' *457 Answer Book.*

Douglas A. Rothermich, Esq., serves as Vice President, Wealth Planning Strategies for TIAA-CREF's Wealth Management Group, where he manages the national delivery of estate planning and wealth transfer planning services. Before joining the Trust Company, Mr. Rothermich practiced law in St. Louis with the firm of Bryan Cave, LLP, a national and international law firm. He has also served as Vice President and Senior Trust counsel at Boatmen's Trust Company (now part of Bank of America).

Michael S. Sirkin, Esq., is a past Chairman of the Tax Department of Proskauer Rose LLP and a co-chair of its Employee Benefits and Executive Compensation Group. Mr. Sirkin serves as benefits and compensation counsel to a large number of tax-exempt organizations. He advises on Section 403(b) plans, Section 401 qualified plans, nonqualified deferred compensation arrangements, fiduciary issues, and prohibited transactions. Mr. Sirkin's practice has also included advising insurance companies and benefits consultants on Section 403(b) plans and other benefit and compensation issues for tax-exempt organizations. He is a 1972 graduate of Columbia Law School. Mr. Sirkin is a member of the IRS Advisory Committee to the TE/GE Division and co-chair of the Liaison Committee to the IRS. He has been an Adjunct Assistant Professor of Law at New York University School of Law, past Chairman of the Employee Benefits Committee, and a past member of the Committee on Nonprofit Organizations of the Association of the Bar of the City of New York, past Co-Chairman of the Employee Benefits Committee of New York County Lawyers' Association, and a past Chairman of the Subcommittee on Tax-Exempt and Governmental Plans of the Employee Benefits and Executive Compensation Committee of the Business Law Section of the American Bar Association. He has written and spoken extensively on Section 403(b) and other benefit and compensation issues for tax-exempt entities.

Henry A. Smith, III, Esq., is a partner of Smith & Downey, a Baltimore, New York, and Washington, DC, law firm that concentrates in the areas of employee benefits, executive compensation, and labor and employment law. He received a BA from Frostburg State College, an MLA from the Johns Hopkins University, and a JD from the University of Maryland School of Law. He is a member of the Maryland and District of Columbia bars, past chair of both the Maryland State Bar Association Section of Taxation and the MSBA Employee Benefits Committee, and former adjunct professor in the University of Baltimore School of Law Graduate Tax Program. Mr. Smith is co-author of Aspen Publishers' *Nonqualified Deferred Compensation Answer Book*.

Robert J. Toth, Jr., Esq., is a partner in Baker & Daniels, a law firm with offices in Indiana, Washington, DC, and China. Mr. Toth counsels national clients in Baker & Daniels' Employee Benefits and Executive Compensation Practice group, having more than 24 years of experience in employee benefits law. His practice focuses on the design, administration, and distribution of financial products and services for retirement plans, and combines elements of ERISA, tax law, insurance law, securities law, and investment law. Mr. Toth's experience includes developing open architecture programs for Section 403(b) plans, designing annuitization programs for defined contribution plans, and developing standards for fiduciary and advisory practices.

Before joining Baker & Daniels, Mr. Toth spent 17 years in the legal division of Lincoln National Corporation in Fort Wayne, Indiana, where he was Associate General Counsel for the last six years. He managed the legal affairs of Lincoln's employer market division, which has nearly 30,000 retirement plan clients. Prior to joining Lincoln National Corporation, he was a Senior Attorney at Kellogg Company in Battle Creek, Michigan, where he provided in-house counsel for all benefit law issues related to the company. He is a Fellow of the American College of Benefits Counsel; active in the Taxation Section of the American Bar Association; an officer of the IRS Great Lakes TE/GE Council;

board member of the Indiana and Purdue Universities' Pension Policy Institute; board member of the ASPPA Benefits Council of Northern Indiana; and is a member of the Indiana and Michigan state bar associations. Mr. Toth has served as a member of the ALI-ABA faculty for the Advanced Law of Pensions, and has chaired the Pension Committee of the American Council of Life Insurers. He is a graduate of the Wayne State University Law School and the University of Michigan.

Richard A. Turner, Esq., is Vice President and Deputy General Counsel for AIG Retirement, where he focuses primarily on retirement plans and related matters affecting public and private tax-exempt employers. At AIG Retirement he leads a team of legal professionals in supporting the products and services of the retirement services companies of American International Group, Inc. He has nearly 20 years of legal and compliance experience working specifically with Section 403(b) plans, beginning in January, 1989. His earlier work with retirement plans and products dates back to 1984 and includes roles as a marketing representative and as an actuarial analyst. Mr. Turner is a frequent speaker on retirement plan matters. He has served as moderator and contributor for many Web casts and presentations on the final Code Section 403(b) regulations, and on other plan-related topics. He also has previously served on ALI-ABA conference faculty discussing Section 403(b) issues, including regulatory and audit developments, and on the Practitioner Panel for IRS 403(b)/457 Examination Workshop. Mr. Turner has authored several articles on retirement plan topics for internal and external distribution, including for associations comprised of plan sponsors. Mr. Turner graduated with honors from Capital University Law School, where he served as a Notes Editor on the Law Review, and from Capital University, from which he received a BA in Economics.

Regina M. Watson Esq., is Vice President and Associate Legal Counsel of T. Rowe Price Associates, where she specializes in retirement plan matters. Ms. Watson previously served as Vice President and Senior Counsel at Merrill Lynch Pierce Fenner & Smith in New York, where she focused on retail retirement products. Before joining Merrill Lynch, Ms. Watson was with the law firm of Groom & Nordberg in Washington, DC, where she provided ERISA advice to the firm's clients, including Fortune 100 corporations, pension plans, broker-dealers, and mutual fund companies. As Senior Associate Counsel of the United Mine Workers Health and Retirement Funds, Ms. Watson provided ERISA advice to the Fund's officials regarding more than $6 billion in fund assets. From 1987 to 1990, Ms. Watson was a federal investigator with the U.S. Department of Labor, Pension and Welfare Benefits Administration, Office of Enforcement. Ms. Watson received her BA from Fairfield University and her JD from the National Law Center at George Washington University. She also studied international law at Oxford University.

Catherine W. Wilkinson, CPA, is a member of the tax practice at the law firm of Steptoe & Johnson LLP in Washington, DC. Ms. Wilkinson provides tax planning and advice to tax-exempt organizations and represents corporations, including publicly traded corporations, closely-held entities, and tax-exempt organizations and individuals in designing and negotiating executive compensation arrangements. This advice includes use of incentive and performance-based compensation and deferred compensation, stock options, and other forms of equity compensation; compensation paid in connection with a change in control; and the application of the intermediate sanction rules to compensation of executives of tax-exempt organizations. In addition, Ms. Wilkinson represents corporations, partnerships, tax-exempt organizations, and individuals in complex federal and state tax audits and investigations. These include routine civil audits of domestic and international organizations and investigations relating to tax shelters and charges of tax fraud and evasion.

Lori Z. Wright, CEBS, CMS, is a principal in Mercer's Public Sector and Nonprofit Consulting group in Richmond, Virginia. She provides retirement plan consulting for Section 403(b), 401(a), 401(k), and 457 plans and vendor management and selection services to employers, as well as design and technical assistance to other consultants within the Mercer organization.

Ms. Wright joined Mercer in 1988. She has previously served as recording clerk for the South Carolina House of Representatives. She also has administrative defined contribution plan experience with the South Carolina Deferred Compensation Plan. She has provided consulting services to major not-for-profit, public sector, and church plan sponsors, including health care systems, universities, public school systems, and research institutions.

Ms. Wright received her BA in political science from the College of Charleston, Charleston, South Carolina. She has obtained the Certified Employee Benefits Specialist (CEBS) and the Compensation Management Specialist (CMS) designations offered by the International Foundation of Employee Benefit Plans in conjunction with the Wharton School of the University of Pennsylvania. She is also a fellow in the International Society of Certified Employee Benefit Specialists (ISCEBS).

Acknowledgments

403(b) Answer Book, Seventh Edition, is the product of the hard work and dedication of many people. Special thanks are due to the authors of the chapters. Don also thanks his coeditors, Barbara N. Seymon-Hirsch and Janet M. Anderson-Briggs, who are also contributors, for their great expertise and tireless dedication to reviewing all the chapters, as well as raising some questions that they subsequently helped to answer. He is profoundly grateful to his children, Daryl and Cathy, for their advice, encouragement, patience, and understanding.

Barbara thanks her daughter, Sydney Roth (who demonstrated patience beyond her six years of age), and husband, Jerry (whose extraordinary patience was sometimes tested).

Last, but not least, Janet wishes to acknowledge her husband, Mike Briggs, with whom she has reconnected after 30 years, thanks to the Internet.

Donald R. Levy
Barbara N. Seymon-Hirsch
Janet M. Anderson-Briggs
May 2008

Contents

CHAPTER 13

Contents

List of Questions

Chapter 2   Section 501(c)(3) Organizations

Chapter 3   Contribution Limits

Overview of Section 403(b) Contribution Limits

Section 402(g) Contribution Limits

Years of Service

Section 414(v) Catch-up Limit

Coordination of Deferrals and Contributions

Correction of Excess Amounts

Correction of Excess Deferrals

Chapter 5   Investments

Retirement Income Accounts

Grandfathered Investments

Participant Loans

Trusts to Hold Section 403(b) Accounts

Employer Responsibility for Section 403(b) Investments

Chapter 6   Annuities

Chapter 7   Section 403(b)(7) Custodial Accounts

Chapter 8 Application of Federal Securities Laws to Section 403(b) Arrangements

Chapter 9   ERISA Requirements

Chapter 10   Distributions

Requirements Governing Timing and Amount of Benefit Distributions

Tax Withholding and Reporting

Chapter 11   Loans, Life Insurance, and Plan Termination

Loans

Loans as Distribution

Loan Availability

Limitation on Amounts

Interest Rates

Repayment Requirements

Principal-Residence Loans

Correction of Defects under IRS Correction Programs

Consequences of Failure to Repay

Transfers

When a Loan Is Treated as a Distribution

Life Insurance

Underwriting

Insurance on Family Members

Limitations on Amount of Premiums

Correction of Defects under the IRS Voluntary Correction Program

Transfers of Assets to a Section 403(b) Annuity

Taxation of Estimated Insurance Cost

Chapter 12 Beneficiary Designations

About Beneficiary Designations

Elective-Share Rights

Community Property

Tenancy by the Entirety

Who Can Give Advice

Common Mistakes

Chapter 13   Qualified Domestic Relations Orders

Overview

Requirements of a Qualified Domestic Relations Order

Special Provisions

Plan Administration Procedures

Chapter 14   Tax Aspects of Church Plans

Church Retirement Income Accounts

Special Definitions and Rules for Section 403(b)Church Plans

Final Code Section 403(b) Regulations Issues for Church Section 403(b) Arrangements

Rules Applicable to Nonelecting Church Qualified Plans

Failure to Qualify as a Church Plan or a Church 403(b) or 401(a) Plan

ERISA Coverage of Church Plans

Miscellaneous Church Plan Provisions

Impact of New Tax-Exempt Controlled Group Rules on Church Section 403(b) Plans

Chapter 15   Section 457 Plans

Overview

ERISA Considerations

Miscellaneous

Intermediate Sanctions Rules

Three-Party Nonqualified Arrangements

Code Section 409A

Chapter 16 Mergers and Acquisitions

Chapter 19 Retirement and Estate Planning for Section 403(b) Participants

Chapter 1

Overview of Section 403(b) Plans

Jason Bortz, Esq.
Davis & Harman LLP

A Section 403(b) plan is a form of defined contribution retirement plan that is comparable to a Section 401(k) plan or a governmental Section 457(b) plan. However, a Section 403(b) plan may be offered only by employers that are educational and charitable organizations. Subject to various limitations and restrictions, Section 403(b) of the Internal Revenue Code allows tax-deferred contributions to be made for employees of educational and charitable organizations through an employer-funded plan or through an employee's voluntary salary reduction contributions. Section 403(b) requires that the contributions be invested in an annuity contract issued by a life insurance company (a Section 403(b)(1) annuity contract), shares of regulated investment companies (generally mutual fund shares) held in a custodial account (a Section 403(b)(7) custodial account) or a retirement income account maintained for employees of certain church-affiliated organizations.

Introduction to Section 403(b) Plans

Q 1:1   How are Section 403(b) plans used?

The character and use of Section 403(b) plans range widely. Many employers maintain Section 403(b) plans purely on a salary reduction basis. That type of Section 403(b) plan is simply a voluntary retirement savings arrangement for employees, and the employer incurs no funding cost. This use of Section 403(b) is common for public school employees, who typically participate in a qualified defined benefit pension plan as their primary retirement plan, and for employees of small charities, who do not participate in any other type of retirement plan. Other eligible employers, including many colleges, universities, and tax-exempt hospitals, use Section 403(b) plans as the primary retirement plans for some or all of their employees. In such cases, where the Section 403(b) plan is the primary retirement plan for employees, employer contributions may be made on a nonelective basis as a percentage of each eligible employee's compensation or on a matching basis as a percentage of each eligible employee's salary reduction contributions. Under almost all employer-funded plans, employees are also allowed to make supplemental (unmatched) salary reduction contributions.

Q 1:2   What is the general tax treatment of a Section 403(b) plan?

In general, contributions to a Section 403(b) plan are excluded from an employee's gross income under the Internal Revenue Code (Code) and most state income tax laws as long as the contributions satisfy certain conditions and limits discussed below. The earnings credited to the employee under the Section 403(b) plan accumulate on a pre-tax basis. Both contributions and earnings become taxable only when distributed. Once distributed, these amounts are taxable as ordinary income unless rolled over to another Section 403(b) program, an individual retirement arrangement (IRA), a qualified plan, or a Section 457(b) plan maintained by a governmental employer.

For FICA tax purposes, contributions made pursuant to a salary reduction agreement under a Section 403(b) program are treated as "wages." Therefore, these contributions are subject to both employer and employee FICA taxes when contributed. [I.R.C. § 3121(a)(5)(D)] However, amounts distributed from a Section 403(b) plan are not subject to FICA taxes, regardless of whether the distributions are attributable to salary reduction contributions or an employer's nonelective contributions. This is the same rule that applies to voluntary pre-tax contributions to a Section 401(k) plan subject to one exception. Contributions made to a Section 401(k) plan pursuant to a one-time irrevocable election made at or before the time of initial eligibility to participate are not subject to FICA taxes. However, so-called one-time irrevocable contributions made to a Section 403(b) plan on or after November 16, 2004, are subject to FICA taxes. [Treas. Reg. § 31.3121(a)(5)-2] This distinction is apparently based on legislative history indicating that a different rule was intended to apply to Section 403(b) plans.

Q 1:3   What is the tax treatment of a Section 403(b) plan that permits salary reduction Roth contributions?

Beginning in 2006, a Section 403(b) plan may permit employees who make salary reduction contributions to designate some or all of those contributions as Roth contributions.

Designated Roth contributions are currently included in an employee's gross income under the Code and most state tax laws. [I.R.C. § 402A] The earnings credited to the employee and attributable to the designated Roth contributions accumulate on a tax-free basis. In contrast to pre-tax salary reduction contributions, however, a qualified distribution of an amount attributable to designated Roth contributions, including earnings, is entirely excluded from the employee's gross income under the Code and most state laws. That is, unlike pre-tax salary reduction contributions, designated Roth contributions are included in gross income, but distributions attributable to designated Roth contributions generally are tax-free. However, the same FICA tax rules that apply to pre-tax salary reduction contributions under a Section 403(b) plan also apply to designated Roth contributions. [I.R.C. § 3121(a)(5)(D)]

A designated Roth contribution to a Section 403(b) plan must be a contribution made pursuant to a salary reduction agreement. However, one-time irrevocable contributions may not be designated Roth contributions. [I.R.C. § 402A(e)(2)] To be a designated Roth contribution, a salary reduction contribution must be irrevocably designated by the employee as such at the time of the deferral, must be treated by the employer as includible in the employee's income, and must be maintained by the Section 403(b) plan in a separate account apart from pre-tax salary reduction contributions. Otherwise, a designated Roth contribution is subject to the same rules (e.g., contribution limits) that apply to pre-tax salary reduction contributions to a Section 403(b) plan. Employer nonelective contributions and matching contributions may not be designated Roth contributions.

In order to be nontaxable, a distribution from a Roth contribution account must be a "qualified distribution." In general, a qualified distribution is a distribution that is made on or after the earliest of the date the employee attains age 59½, dies, or becomes disabled. [I.R.C. §§ 402A(d)(2)(A), 408A(d)(2)(A)] However, a distribution is not considered a qualified distribution, in which case a portion of the distribution may be taxable, if it is made within a period of five years from the date the employee first made a designated Roth contribution.

Eligible Employers

Q 1:4   What types of employers may maintain Section 403(b) plans?

Section 403(b) plans may be maintained by organizations that are exempt from tax under Code Section 501(c)(3) or that are public educational organizations. Section 403(b) plans may also be maintained by a duly ordained, commissioned, or licensed minister of a church who is self-employed or by an organization that, although not exempt from tax under Code Section 501(c)(3), shares common religious bonds with such a minister whom it employs. [I.R.C. § 403(b)(1)(A)]

Q 1:5   What is a Section 501(c)(3) organization?

Tax-exempt Section 501(c)(3) organizations are nonprofit organizations organized and operated exclusively for religious, charitable, scientific, literary, educational, or safety testing purposes. Ordinarily, an organization must have received a Section 501(c)(3) determination letter from the IRS to be so classified. However, an organization created on or before October 9, 1969, may qualify as a Section 501(c)(3) organization without a determination letter, provided that it has the requisite organizational attributes. [I.R.C. § 508(a)]

Q 1:6   What public educational organizations may maintain Section 403(b) plans?

A public educational organization described in Code Section 170(b)(1)(A)(ii) may maintain a Section 403(b) plan for its employees without regard to whether it qualifies as a Section 501(c)(3) organization. Such an educational organization must be a teaching institution with a faculty, curriculum, and enrolled students. This category of eligible employers includes public primary and secondary schools, state colleges and universities, and public junior colleges.

Q 1:7   May public employers other than educational organizations maintain Section 403(b) plans?

Certain public institutions, such as government-operated hospitals, libraries, and museums, may be recognized as Section 501(c)(3) organizations and, thus, generally may maintain Section 403(b) plans on that basis, although they are otherwise exempt from federal income tax as governmental entities. [Rev. Rul. 67-290, 1967-2 C.B. 183; Rev. Rul. 74-15, 1974-1 C.B. 126] For such a public employer to qualify as a Section 501(c)(3) organization, it must have the same basic attributes as a nongovernmental Section 501(c)(3) organization. In the view of the IRS, this means that the employer must not be an integral part of the government (i.e., must have some degree of separate organization) and must not have significant enforcement or regulatory powers. [Rev. Rul. 60-384, 1960-2 C.B. 172] Such a public employer may apply for a determination letter recognizing its Section 501(c)(3) status, and, as in the case of private charitable institutions, it may legally qualify as a Section 501(c)(3) organization without a determination letter if it has the necessary organizational attributes and was organized on or before October 9, 1969.

At times, questions have been raised about these dual-status entities, including how the retirement plan rules that differ for Section 501(c)(3) employers and governmental employers should apply. For example, questions have arisen over whether dual-status entities may maintain both a governmental Section 457(b) plan and a Section 403(b) plan, and whether dual-status plans are entitled to relief from the nondiscrimination requirements of Section 403(b) as governmental plans. The preamble to the proposed regulations under Code Section 403(b) supports an affirmative answer to both questions although this preamble language was not included in the final Code Section 403(b) regulations. [T.D. 9159]

Q 1:8   If an eligible employer is affiliated with a noneligible employer, may employees of the noneligible employer participate in the Section 403(b) plan?

Generally, no. For example, if a Section 501(c)(3) hospital has a for-profit taxable subsidiary, or if a Section 501(c)(3) charity is affiliated with another tax-exempt organization that is not a Section 501(c)(3) organization, employees of the non-Section 501(c)(3) organization may not participate in the Section 403(b) plan. However, where an individual is jointly employed by both a Section 501(c)(3) organization and a non-Section 501(c)(3) organization, there is no reason Section 403(b) contributions cannot be made by or for the individual based on the compensation earned as an employee of the Section 501(c)(3) organization, assuming that a bona fide allocation of compensation is made. In addition, the IRS has privately ruled that employees of an LLC, where the sole member is a Section 501(c)(3) organization, may participate in the organization's Section 403(b) plan so long as the LLC's separate status is disregarded for federal tax purposes. [Ltr. Rul. 200334040]

Q 1:9   May American Indian tribal governments maintain Section 403(b) plans for their employees?

Generally, no. American Indian tribal governments are usually treated as governmental entities for retirement plan purposes. [*Cf.* I.R.C. § 414(d)] As a result, only educational organizations associated with American Indian tribal governments are typically eligible to offer Section 403(b) plans to their employees. However, the treatment of American Indian tribal governments has not always been clear and, under a grandfather rule, American Indian tribal governments may maintain Section 403(b) plans with respect to annuity contracts purchased before 1995 and such contracts may be rolled over into Section 401(k) plans maintained by American Indian tribal governments. [Pub. L. No. 104-188 § 1450(b)]

Eligible Employees

Q 1:10   May individuals participate in a Section 403(b) plan if they perform services for an eligible employer other than as employees?

No. Only common law employees may participate in a Section 403(b) plan. Thus, for example, outside lawyers and accountants, physicians engaged as independent contractors, and paid trustees who are not otherwise employees cannot have Section 403(b) contributions made with respect to their fees. However, if an individual works for an eligible employer both as an employee and as an independent contractor (e.g., an officer who also serves as a director), Section 403(b) contributions may be made with respect to that individual's compensation as an employee.

Q 1:11 May leased employees participate in a Section 403(b) plan?

The IRS has not specifically addressed the treatment of leased employees under Code Section 403(b), but it would appear that individuals who perform services for an eligible employer as employees of a leasing organization are not eligible to participate in a Section 403(b) plan. Code Section 414(n) provides that certain leased employees are treated as common law employees for some statutory purposes, but Code Section 403(b) is not among these. Accordingly, since leased employees are not common law employees of an eligible employer, they would apparently be barred from participation. Thus, even though the nondiscrimination rules that apply to employer-funded Section 403(b) arrangements generally treat leased employees as employees, it appears that leased employees are not so treated for Code Section 403(b) purposes. [I.R.C. §§ 401(a)(4), 410(b), 414(n)(3)]

Q 1:12 May government employees participate in a Section 403(b) plan if they provide support services for an educational organization but are not directly employed by such an institution?

Code Section 403(b)(1)(A)(ii) allows Section 403(b) contributions to be made on behalf of an "employee" who performs services for a public educational institution, without expressly requiring an employment relationship between the employee and the institution. The IRS has interpreted this to mean that employees of a state department of education (and, implicitly, employees of a local board of education) may participate in Section 403(b) plans because they indirectly perform services for an educational organization. On the other hand, appointed or elected officials of a state board who are not education professionals may not participate. [Treas. Reg. § 1.403(b)-2(b)(10); Rev. Rul. 73-607, 1973-2 C.B. 145] The IRS has also ruled that employees of a state teachers' retirement system [Rev. Rul. 80-139, 1980-1 C.B. 88] and employees of a financial management agency that supervises the payroll functions of certain public schools are not eligible for Section 403(b) plans. [Rev. Rul. 72-390, 1972-2 C.B. 227] One limitation is that the employee's compensation must be paid by the state. The IRS rulings in this area are not a model of clarity.

Q 1:13   May nonresident aliens working abroad participate in a Section 403(b) plan?

It appears that nonresident alien employees working abroad may participate in a Section 403(b) plan even though compensation paid to such employees is generally not subject to U.S. income taxation. [*Cf.* Treas. Reg. § 1.415(c)-2(g)(5)] It is, however, relatively uncommon to cover nonresident alien employees working abroad because it appears that such employees would be taxable by the United States on the earnings portion of any distributions at a flat 30 percent rate, unless an income tax treaty exemption applies. [*Cf.* I.R.C. § 1441; Rev. Rul. 79-388, 1979-2 C.B. 270]

Plan Requirement

Q 1:14   Must a Section 403(b) plan be maintained by an employer pursuant to a written plan?

Yes. One of the most prominent changes in the final 403(b) regulations is to provide that Section 403(b) annuity contracts and custodial accounts must be maintained pursuant to a written plan, which, in both form and operation, satisfies the applicable requirements. [Treas. Reg. § 1.403(b)-3(b)(3)] The only exception to the plan requirement is for church plans that are funded through annuity contracts (and, apparently, custodial accounts) that are not part of a retirement income account. [Treas. Reg. § 1.403(b)-3(b)(3)(iii)]

Q 1:15   Must the employer adopt a formal plan document in order to satisfy the written plan requirement?

No. A Section 403(b) plan may be comprised of a variety of writings and need not be a single plan document. [T.D. 9340] In fact, virtually all Section 403(b) plans will be comprised of at least two writings, an employer-maintained document and the provider-maintained annuity contracts or custodial agreements that fund the plan. Moreover, the employer-maintained document need not be a formal plan document. In this regard, for example, a Section 403(b) plan may comply with the final regulations without any formal plan document beyond the individual salary-reduction agreements and the group or individual annuity contracts or custodial accounts that are purchased under the program, provided that the combined writings contain all of the material terms of the plan.

There are, however, a number of reasons for employers to adopt formal written plan documents. First, the IRS has published a model plan document for governmental salary-reduction plans. The model plan is a formal plan document and many employers will choose to adopt plans that closely track the model plan document. [Rev. Proc. 2007-71, 2007-51 I.R.B. 1184] Second, a formal plan document typically encourages employers to think through the operation and administration of their Section 403(b) plans before questions (and potentially problems) arise, and also provide a useful tool for employees trying to understand their rights. Third, a formal plan document can clearly document the allocation of administrative responsibility among the employer, any third-party administrator, and the financial institutions that provide contracts and accounts under the plan. In this regard, the IRS anticipates that allocations of administrative responsibility will be reflected in the plan document. [Treas. Reg. § 1.403(b)-3(b)(3)(ii)]

Q 1:16   Does a Section 403(b) plan document need to contain certain provisions?

Yes. The plan document required under the final regulations must set forth all of the material terms of the arrangement including, among others, eligibility, benefits, available investment alternatives, and the time and form of payments. [Treas. Reg. § 1.403(b)-3(b)(3)]

As mentioned in Q 1:15, most plans will be comprised of an employer-maintained document and a provider-maintained document, such as an annuity contract or custodial account. The employer-maintained plan document will ordinarily contain provisions related to eligibility to participate, contribution limits, and available contracts and/or custodial accounts to which employees may direct contributions and investment changes. The provider-maintained document will often include provisions related to loans, eligibility for distributions, and available payout forms. However, some employer-maintained plan documents will be more expansive and may include provisions that might also be included in the provider-maintained annuity contracts and/or custodial accounts that fund the plan. In such cases, care should be taken to ensure that provisions in the employer-maintained document are consistent with terms in the plan's funding vehicles. Similarly, to the extent that a plan allows plan amounts to be contributed or invested with more than one provider, care should be taken to ensure consistency and coordination between the contract and account terms of the different providers. In this regard, the IRS has indicated that where a plan is funded through multiple providers, the employer should adopt a "wrap" plan document that coordinates administration among the different providers. [T.D. 9340]

Under the statute, the terms of the annuity contract or other funding vehicles must include specific terms. Contributions to purchase an annuity contract or custodial account will not qualify for tax deferral under Code Section 403(b) unless the contract or account:

1. Is nontransferable by the employee in the case of an annuity contract [I.R.C. § 401(g)];

2. Specifies the dollar limit on salary reduction contributions [I.R.C. §§ 403(b)(1)(E), 401(a)(30)];

3. Requires minimum distributions after age 70½ in accordance with Code Section 401(a)(9) and otherwise satisfies the incidental benefit requirement [I.R.C. § 403(b)(10)];

4. Limits withdrawals of accumulations attributable to salary reduction contributions [I.R.C. § 403(b)(11)]; and

5. Provides for the direct rollover of "eligible rollover distributions." [I.R.C. §§ 403(b)(10), 401(a)(31)]

These requirements also generally apply to Section 403(b)(7) custodial accounts and life insurance contracts purchased under Code Section 403(b). In addition, a Section 403(b)(7) custodial account must satisfy the requirements of Code Section 401(f), which means that a bank or other IRS-approved person must serve as custodian of the account.

To some extent, the plan requirement blurs the line between terms that must be contained in the annuity contract or custodial account and the employer-maintained plan document. In this regard, for example, the terms of an annuity contract or custodial account may incorporate plan terms by reference or provide that the terms of the employer-maintained plan document govern in the event of a conflict with the terms of the annuity contract or custodial account.

Q 1:17   How does the written plan requirement affect administrative responsibilities?

The final Code Section 403(b) regulations provide that the plan may allocate responsibility for performing administrative functions to persons other than the employer, such as third-party administrators or the providers of annuity contracts or custodial accounts that fund the plan. [Treas. Reg. § 1.403(b)-3(b)(3)] As a result, for example, a plan may assign to a provider responsibility for determining whether hardship distributions are available.

One limitation in the final regulations is that a plan generally cannot be administered on the basis of participant representations. In this regard, the regulations provide that a plan cannot assign compliance responsibilities to participants (other than employees whose job entails plan administration). [Treas. Reg. § 1.403(b)-3(b)(3)(ii)] As a result, for example, a provider generally cannot rely on a participant's representation that he or she is eligible for a distribution by reason of severance from employment. Instead, the provider must coordinate with the employer to confirm that the participant has had a severance from employment. The line between permitted and impermissible participant representations is not entirely clear. It is reasonably clear, for example, that a plan may rely on a participant's representation as to age. However, it is not clear whether, for example, a provider can rely on representations, in connection with a loan request, as to whether a participant has a loan outstanding under another contract or account under the plan. Such a representation is arguably a permitted representation; however, it closely implicates compliance responsibilities. [*Cf.* T.D. 9021 (preamble to I.R.C. § 72(p) regulations permitting reliance on participant representations on existing loans)]

Q 1:18   Can an employer get a ruling that the form of its plan meets the 403(b) requirements?

A Section 403(b) plan must satisfy the applicable requirements of Code Section 403(b) in both form and operation. The IRS issues determination letters for pension, profit-sharing, and stock bonus plans that the form of the plan meets the applicable qualification requirements of Code Section 401(a) or 403(a). Although a Section 403(b) plan is subject to many of the same requirements, it is not classified as a qualified plan, and thus a determination letter may not be obtained with respect to a Section 403(b) plan.

An employer may, however, apply to the National Office of the IRS for a private letter ruling with respect to its Section 403(b) program, but the overwhelming majority of Section 403(b) programs operate without a ruling. To minimize the need for a private letter ruling, the IRS has issued a model plan document for governmental plans that are funded entirely through salary reduction contributions. [Rev. Proc. 2007-71, 2007-51 I.R.B. 1184] A governmental employer that adopts the terms of the model plan (or substantially similar terms in all material respects) is entitled to the same level of reliance as an employer that receives a private letter ruling. [Rev. Proc. 2007-71 § 4, 2007-51 I.R.B. 1184]

Governmental employers that adopt different plan terms and all nongovernmental employers may only look to the model as a useful guide in drafting plan terms.

Q 1:19   When is the plan requirement effective?

The plan requirement is generally effective as of January 1, 2009. As a result, employers will generally need to have a plan in place by January 1, 2009. [Rev. Proc. 2007-71, 2007-51 I.R.B. 1184] However, there is relief from the plan requirement for certain contracts or accounts that were issued prior to January 1, 2009 (see Q 1:32).

Requirements Relating to Contributions

Q 1:20   Do the requirements for a Section 403(b) plan differ based on the manner in which contributions are made?

The rules for salary reduction contributions differ in a number of ways from the rules for employer nonelective contributions under Code Section 403(b). These differences relate to:

1. FICA tax treatment of the contributions (see Q 1:2);
2. Contribution limits (see chapter 3);
3. Applicable nondiscrimination rules (see chapter 4);
4. Applicability of ERISA (see chapter 9); and
5. Availability of withdrawals (see chapter 10).

Q 1:21   What Section 403(b) contributions are classified as salary reduction contributions?

Generally, salary reduction contributions are those that result from an employee's agreement to reduce his or her regular salary payments in exchange for the employer's agreement to contribute such amounts to the Section 403(b) plan. The overwhelming majority of salary reduction contributions are readily identifiable as voluntary contributions made under an explicit salary reduction agreement. In addition, however, contributions may be classified as salary reduction contributions if they result from individual negotiation between the employer and employee, as might occur if an employer agreed to make a specified level of Section 403(b) contributions on behalf of a particular employee as part of an employment agreement.

Contributions to a Section 403(b) plan will also be classified as salary reduction contributions if they are made under a so-called "negative election" procedure. By contrast to a conventional election procedure under which an employee makes an affirmative election to have a specific amount or percentage of pay contributed to a Section 403(b) plan rather than paid in cash, a negative election procedure provides for an automatic contribution to the Section 403(b) plan unless the employee elects to receive it as a cash payment. A negative election procedure must give the employee an "effective opportunity" to elect to receive the contribution in cash.

Except for FICA tax purposes, Section 403(b) contributions that are effectuated through a reduction of an employee's salary are not classified as salary reduction contributions if such contributions are made pursuant to an employee's one-time, irrevocable election to participate in a plan. [I.R.C. §§ 402(g)(3), 403(b)(12)(A)] For example, if an employer's plan provides that employees must contribute 5 percent of compensation on a salary reduction basis in order to participate in a plan under which the employer will contribute an additional 5 percent, the employee's 5 percent contribution will not be treated as a salary reduction contribution if the employee has a one-time opportunity to participate in the plan (or is required to participate as a condition of employment) and may not withdraw from participation in any later year. In effect, the plan would be treated as the equivalent of a plan under which the employer made 10.5 percent nonelective contributions ($10 for each $95 of salary).

Q 1:22   Are salary reduction contributions also referred to as "elective deferrals"?

Salary reduction contributions under Section 403(b) plans are one of the categories of "elective deferrals" under Code Section 402(g)(3). Voluntary pre-tax contributions under Section 401(k) plans, Section 408(p) SIMPLE IRAs, and Section 408(k)(6) salary reduction simplified employee pension (SARSEP) arrangements are also classified as elective deferrals. The term "elective deferrals" refers to contributions that are made at an employee's election out of amounts that would otherwise be received as taxable compensation but that are treated as tax-deferred "employer" contributions for income tax purposes.

Q 1:23   What rules apply to salary reduction agreements under Code Section 403(b)?

The rules concerning the frequency with which participants in a Section 403(b) plan may enter into salary reduction agreements, the compensation to which those agreements can apply, and the revocability of those agreements are the same as the rules that apply to participants in a Section 401(k) plan. Therefore, a Section 403(b) participant may make, modify, or revoke a salary reduction election at any time before the compensation to which it relates would otherwise become payable.

Q 1:24   Must all contributions under a Section 403(b) plan be fully vested when made?

Code Section 403(b)(1)(C) provides that an employee's interest in a Section 403(b) contract must be nonforfeitable, except for failure to pay future premiums. Nonetheless, it has long been clear under the regulations that a Section 403(b) plan may incorporate a vesting schedule, that is, an employee's interest in employer contributions may be forfeitable until a minimum service requirement is satisfied. If an employer's contributions under a Section 403(b) plan are not vested when made, the contributions and any earnings thereon were counted as contributions for purposes of the Section 403(b)(2) exclusion allowance (which has been repealed) when the employee satisfied the service requirement and became vested in such amounts. [Treas. Reg. § 1.403(b)-1(b)(2)] For purposes of the contribution limits under Code Section 415(c), unvested Section 403(b) contributions are counted as annual additions when allocated to an employee's account.

Though permitted, deferred vesting can pose substantial administrative burdens under a Section 403(b) plan and thus is generally avoided. Eligible employers that want to have vesting requirements for employer contributions are more apt to use a plan that is qualified under Code Section 401(a) or 403(a). For example, where employer matching contributions are subject to a vesting requirement, the matching contributions may be made under a qualified plan based on the amount of each eligible employee's salary reduction contributions under a Section 403(b) contract.

Q 1:25   May an employee make after-tax contributions under a Section 403(b) plan?

After-tax contributions are simply employee contributions that are made to a Section 403(b) plan out of after-tax compensation. After-tax contributions are to be distinguished from designated Roth contributions, which are taxed much more favorably than ordinary after-tax contributions. A participant is generally taxed on the earnings of a distribution that is attributable to after-tax distributions. In contrast, a qualified distribution of amounts attributable to designed Roth contributions is entirely excludible from gross income.

Because the primary operative effect of Code Section 403(b) is to provide a limited exclusion from gross income for "employer" (including salary reduction) contributions, historically, there has been some uncertainty whether after-tax employee contributions can be regarded as made under Code Section 403(b). Nonetheless, after-tax contributions are permitted under some Section 403(b) plans, and the IRS has apparently acknowledged that such contributions may be made. Among other complications, after-tax contributions by highly compensated employees, if considered made under Code Section 403(b), may be subject to the nondiscrimination rule of Section 401(m). In any case, after-tax employee contributions to Section 403(b)(7) custodial accounts should be avoided because a penalty tax applies to any such contributions that exceed the amount excludable from gross income under Code Section 403(b)(2). [I.R.C. § 4973]

In lieu of allowing after-tax contributions, the same tax effect (after-tax savings with tax-deferred earnings) can be achieved with fewer compliance burdens by allowing employees to purchase nonqualified annuity contracts on a payroll deduction basis; where this is done, it is advisable to use separate annuity contracts to avoid any appearance that the nonqualified annuities are part of the Section 403(b) plan.

Q 1:26   May an employer automatically enroll participants in a Section 403(b) plan?

The majority of Section 403(b) plans provide that an employee will receive cash unless the employee makes an affirmative election to have salary reduction contributions made on his or her behalf. However, a Section 403(b) plan may provide that salary reduction contributions are made at a specified rate unless the employee elects otherwise (i.e., elects not to make contributions or to make contributions at a different rate). Arrangements that operate in this manner are sometimes referred to as "automatic enrollment" or "negative election" programs.

For ERISA-covered Section 403(b) plans, the Pension Protection Act of 2006 (PPA) includes a number of special rules designed to encourage employers to include automatic enrollment features. In this regard, the new law creates a fiduciary safe harbor for investments made pursuant to an automatic enrollment feature that satisfy certain requirements and creates slightly more relaxed nondiscrimination tests for matching contributions if an employer maintains a qualified automatic enrollment arrangement. In addition, the PPA provides that state anti-wage garnishment laws that generally prohibit deductions from an employee's paycheck, unless the employee consents, are inapplicable if the automatic enrollment arrangement meets certain minimum requirements.

The special rules designed to encourage automatic enrollment features in a Section 403(b) plan generally do not apply to non-ERISA Section 403(b) plans, including governmental and church plans. As a result, unless a particular state has favorable laws, it may be difficult for a non-ERISA Section 403(b) program to include an automatic enrollment feature in light of fiduciary responsibilities relating to investing contributions and state anti-wage-garnishment laws. One unanswered question as of the date of this writing is whether including an automatic enrollment feature in a pure salary reduction program that is designed to be exempt from ERISA, because the tax-exempt employer's involvement is very limited, will cause the program to become subject to ERISA.

Q 1:27 Are contributions to an employer's Section 403(b) plan subject to nondiscrimination rules?

Yes. There are nondiscrimination requirements set forth in Code Section 403(b)(12). There are two sets of these nondiscrimination requirements: one for employer contributions (i.e., contributions not made under a salary-reduction agreement) and one for salary reduction contributions. The requirements for employer contributions apply differently to governmental and nongovernmental eligible employers.

Requirements Relating to Investments

Q 1:28 Are there rules governing the investment of amounts held under a Section 403(b) plan?

Yes. Contributions to a Section 403(b) plan must be invested in an annuity contract issued by a life insurance company, a custodial account or, in the case of certain church plans, a retirement income account. Life insurance is not a permitted investment. However, there is a grandfather rule for life insurance contracts issued before September 24, 2007, provided that the life insurance is merely incidental. [Treas. Reg. § 1.403(b)-11(f)] Grandfathered life insurance contracts may continue to receive premium payments on or after September 24, 2007. The prohibition is against the issuance of new contracts.

Q 1:29 Are there rules regarding what types of investments may be offered under an annuity contract or a custodial account for a Section 403(b) plan?

An annuity contract may be either fixed or variable, and the Code generally does not regulate the underlying investments of an annuity contract for purposes of Code Section 403(b). For example, the IRS has stated that contributions held under a Section 403(b)(1) annuity contract may be invested in publicly available securities (such as retail mutual fund shares), as long as the investment is one that, if it had been made instead under a Section 403(b)(7) custodial account, would not have generated additional federal tax liability (such as the tax on unrelated business taxable income under Code Section 511). [Rev. Proc. 99-44, 1999-48 I.R.B. 598] Amounts held in a Section 403(b)(7) custodial account must be invested in shares of investment companies (mutual funds). The custodian of the account must be a bank or another entity approved by the IRS to act as custodian. [I.R.C. § 401(f)(2)]

Additionally, if the Section 403(b) program is subject to ERISA, the general fiduciary, plan asset, and prohibited transaction rules of ERISA will apply to the program. These rules generally require that amounts held under an ERISA-covered Section 403(b) program be invested prudently and for the exclusive benefit of employees and their beneficiaries (see chapter 5).

Q 1:30 Does the employer decide the investments that are available under the plan?

Many Section 403(b) plans allow employees to direct contributions to one or more providers that are authorized to receive contributions. Similarly, many Section 403(b) plans allow employees to direct the investment of amounts attributable to contributions (i.e., among different mutual funds within a custodial account and between different custodial accounts and/or annuity contracts).

The extent to which an employer allows for investment control is a question of plan design. The final Code Section 403(b) regulations make clear that an employer can choose whether or not to allow participants to move their plan amounts to a provider that is not authorized to receive contributions. Some employers will choose to limit investment changes to providers that are authorized to receive contributions. Others will allow plan amounts to migrate to a select group of providers that are not authorized to receive contributions or to migrate to any provider that is willing to meet certain basic criteria. In such instances, the employer will generally need to enter into an information sharing agreement with any providers that are not authorized to receive contributions but are authorized to receive exchanges. [Treas. Reg. § 1.403(b)-10(b)(2)]

Q 1:31 Does the plan requirement affect the investments that may be available to employees?

Prior to the final Code Section 403(b) regulations, it was not uncommon for Section 403(b) plans, particularly arrangements of governmental employers, to allow participants to "transfer" their plan amounts to providers that were not authorized to receive contributions but that met certain minimum requirements. These "transfers" are often called "90-24" transfers after the IRS guidance that authorized transfers. [Rev. Prov. 90-24, 1990-1 C.B. 97] The providers that received 90-24 transfers often had no relationship with the employer and typically did not coordinate with the employer or other providers in administering contracts and accounts.

One aspect of the plan requirement is that each contract or account needs to be maintained under the plan. This generally means that there needs to be a connection between the financial institution that provides the contract or account and the employer that maintains the plan. The final regulations provide two basic ways that a contract or accounts can be connected to the employer that maintains the plan. First, the employer can include the provider in its plan, which ordinarily means that employees may direct contributions to the provider. Second, if the provider is not authorized to receive contributions, the employer and the provider can enter into an agreement to share information necessary to satisfy the Section 403(b) requirements (an "information sharing agreement"). [Treas. Reg. § 1.403(b)-10(b)(2)] The information that needs to be shared is generally information necessary to determine whether a participant is eligible for a distribution based on severance from employment, whether a loan is taxable, and whether a participant is entitled to a hardship distribution. An information sharing agreement might be appropriate where the employer decides that it will not make contributions to a particular provider, but the employer will allow employees or other participants to move all or a portion of their plan amounts to the provider (referred to in the final 403(b) regulations as an "exchange").

Q 1:32   Are there any plan transition rules that affect investments?

Yes. One of the biggest challenges under the final 403(b) regulations is moving from the old world of 403(b) arrangements that are comparable to individual retirement arrangements to the new world of employer-maintained arrangements. The general rule is that all contracts and accounts must be maintained under a plan when the final regulations are effective. However, to facilitate an orderly transition, the IRS has published a number of different transition rules that affect annuity contracts and custodial accounts that are outstanding before the regulations are generally effective.

There are two broad categories of contracts and accounts that are eligible for transition relief. The first category is comprised of (1) contracts and accounts that were issued by providers that ceased receiving contributions before January 1, 2005, and (2) contracts and accounts that were issued by providers in 90-24 transfers that were complete on or before September 24, 2007. [Treas. Reg. § 1.403(b)-11(g); Rev. Proc. 2007-71 § 8, 2007-51 I.R.B. 1184] Although not entirely clear from the face of the guidance, the IRS views this category of contracts and accounts as entirely exempt from the plan requirement.

The second category of contracts or accounts that are eligible for transition relief is comprised of (1) contracts and accounts that were issued by providers that ceased receiving contributions on or after January 1, 2005 and before January 1, 2009, and (2) contracts and accounts that were issued in a 90-24 transfer after September 24, 2007 (the end of the grandfather in the final regulations) and before January 1, 2009. [Rev. Proc. 2007-71 § 8, 2007-51 I.R.B. 1184] For this category, the transition relief provides that a contract or account will continue to be tax-compliant on January 1, 2009 (assuming the contract or account otherwise satisfies all of the applicable Section 403(b) requirements) if either the employer or the provider of the contract or account makes reasonable, good-faith efforts to include the contract or account in the employer's plan. This relief generally has two components—establishing a connection between the employer and the provider of the contract or account and sharing information.

For the employer, a reasonable, good-faith effort to connect with a provider generally means identifying the providers to which it made contributions on or after January 1, 2005 and reaching out to those providers. By way of example, one approach might be for an employer to sweep its payroll records to identify all of the providers that received employee salary reduction or employer contributions on or after January 1, 2005. Similarly, employers may ask each of the providers that are authorized to receive contributions whether the provider has made a 90-24 transfer to another provider after September 24, 2007.

For the provider, a reasonable, good-faith effort to connect to the employer generally means contacting the employer before making a distribution or loan to a participant. Under a helpful exception, a provider is entitled to rely on a participant's representation that they have had a severance from employment if such severance occurs prior to January 1, 2009. This exception means that coordination between a provider and an employer will ordinarily not be necessary in order for contracts or accounts to get the benefit of the good-faith exception unless the former employee or beneficiary is seeking a loan.

The transition relief does not shed much light on what the employer and the provider should do once a connection has been established. The guidance states that any contracts covered by the good-faith relief should be "included" in the employer's plan. However, the good-faith relief for providers makes clear that the contract or account need not be reflected in the employer's written plan document. Similarly, it is clear that the relief need not involve a formal information sharing agreement but may instead involve a more informal and transactional sharing of information. As a result, it appears that the IRS generally expects the employer and the provider to share information necessary for the contracts to be administered in a manner that satisfies Code Section 403(b).

There is one other special rule under the rubric of "good faith" transition relief. This special rule is available only to contracts or accounts issued in a 90-24 transfer after September 24, 2007. It provides that a contract or account will be treated as tax-compliant even if good-faith efforts are not made by either the employer or the issuer if the participant holding such a contract moves their plan savings back to a provider that is authorized to receive contributions. Under the transition relief, the participant will not have any adverse tax consequences as long as the move occurs by July 1, 2009.

If these good-faith standards are satisfied, then the IRS will continue to treat any affected contracts or accounts (even ones not covered by information sharing agreements or otherwise included in the employer's plan) as tax-compliant under Code Section 403(b). If good-faith efforts are not attempted by either the employer or the provider, participants with these types of contracts or accounts may suffer adverse tax consequences. One caveat on all of the transition relief is that the relief may be lost if contributions resume or are otherwise made to a contract that would otherwise be eligible for relief.

Requirements Relating to Distributions

Q 1:33 Are there distribution restrictions that apply to a Section 403(b) plan?

Yes. The distribution restrictions generally preclude a participant from making a withdrawal of salary reduction contributions and allocable earnings until the participant's attainment of age 59½, severance from employment, disability, or death. There is an exception for hardship, but earnings on salary reduction contributions may not be withdrawn in the event of hardship.

These same rules apply to amounts that are attributable to employer contributions in the case of a Section 403(b)(7) custodial account. [Treas. Reg. § 1.403(b)-6(b)] However, amounts that are attributable to employer contributions are subject to more liberal distribution rules in the case of a Section 403(b)(11) annuity contract. These rules generally permit distributions of amounts attributable to employer contributions upon the participant's severance from employment or upon the prior occurrence of some event, such as after a fixed number of years, the attainment of a stated age or the disability. [Treas. Reg. § 1.403(b)-6(b); *see also* Treas. Reg. § 1.401-1(b)(1)(ii)] There is also a grandfather rule for annuity contracts issued prior to January 1, 2009, which allows for distributions of amounts attributable to employer contributions (including contributions made after 2008) without limitation.

The distribution restrictions of Code Sections 403(b)(7) and 403(b)(11) do not apply to amounts attributable to rollovers that are maintained in separate accounts. As a result, unless a restriction is imposed by the issuer or the employer, participants generally may withdraw amounts attributable to rollover contributions at any time, even though distribution of other amounts under the Section 403(b) plan may be restricted. [*See* Rev. Rul. 2004-12, 2004-7 I.R.B. 478 (Feb. 17, 2004)]

Q 1:34 Can distributions from a Section 403(b) plan be rolled over to another employer plan or an IRA?

Yes. Any distribution that is an "eligible rollover distribution" is subject to the direct rollover rules of Code Section 401(a)(31). A distribution from a Section 403(b) plan can be rolled over to another Section 403(b) plan, an IRA, a qualified plan, or a governmental Section 457(b) plan (subject to special recordkeeping requirements for the Section 457(b) plan). Also, a Section 403(b) plan generally can receive a rollover from another Section 403(b) plan, a qualified plan, a governmental Section 457(b) plan, or an IRA (although the Section 403(b) plan is not required to accept a rollover). An "eligible rollover distribution" includes any distribution from a Section 403(b) plan other than a distribution that is one of a series of substantially equal periodic payments, a minimum distribution required under Code Section 401(a)(9), a distribution not includible in gross income, or a hardship distribution (see chapter 10). [I.R.C. §§ 403(b)(10), 402(c)(4); Notice 2000-32, 2000-26 I.R.B. 1274; Notice 99-5, 1999-3 I.R.B. 10]

Additionally, certain direct trustee-to-trustee transfers from Section 403(b) programs to governmental defined benefit plans are permitted. Such transfers are excludable from the employee's income if used for the purchase of permissive service credit under Code Section 415(n)(3)(A) or for the repayment of a benefit under Code Section 415(k)(3). [I.R.C. § 403(b)(13)]

Q 1:35 Do the automatic rollover requirements apply to mandatory distributions from a Section 403(b) plan?

Yes. Effective for distributions made on or after March 28, 2005, a Section 403(b) plan, including a governmental or church program, must provide that a mandatory distribution will be rolled over to an IRA, unless the employee affirmatively elects to have the distribution paid in cash or rolled over to another employer plan or IRA. [Notice 2005-5, 2005-3 I.R.B. 337] For this purpose, a mandatory distribution is any distribution that is more than $1,000 and that is made without the employee's consent and before the employee attains normal retirement age. Ordinarily, these are small sum cashouts of no more than $5,000. As a practical matter, the automatic rollover requirement generally means that a Section 403(b) plan will need to select an IRA provider and an investment fund that will receive mandatory distributions subject to the automatic rollover requirements. Rather than assume this administrative burden, some employers have elected instead to simply eliminate mandatory distributions from their Section 403(b) plans, thereby allowing employees to defer payouts until normal retirement age.

For ERISA-covered arrangements, the selection of an IRA provider and the default investment fund are fiduciary decisions. The Department of Labor, however, has established a safe harbor pursuant to which a plan fiduciary will be deemed to have satisfied his or her fiduciary duties with respect to both the selection of the IRA provider and the investment of funds in connection with an automatic rollover. [DOL Reg. § 2550.404a-2]

Q 1:36 Is a Section 403(b) plan subject to required minimum distributions under Section 401(a)(9) when a participant reaches age 70½?

Yes. The minimum distribution requirements of Code Section 401(a)(9) apply to all amounts accruing under a Section 403(b) plan after December 31, 1986. Therefore, a participant in a Section 403(b) plan who has both reached the age of 70½ and terminated employment must begin to receive annual minimum distributions. Except for the fact that distributions do not have to be made at age 70½ if the participant has not terminated employment, the rules for Section 403(b) programs are essentially the same as those for IRAs. [See I.R.C. § 403(b)(10)] Final regulations issued in 2004 address certain issues that are unique to Section 403(b) plans that are invested in annuity contracts. [Treas. Reg. § 1.401(a)(9)-6] For example, these regulations require that the actuarial present value of certain benefits in addition to the account balance, such as a guaranteed death benefit, be taken into account in applying the minimum distribution requirements. The final regulations also expand the annuity forms of distribution that satisfy the minimum distribution requirements.

Q 1:37   Can a participant in a Section 403(b) plan take a loan from the program?

Although certain amounts held under a Section 403(b) plan are subject to in-service distribution restrictions, those (and other) amounts may be borrowed by a participant under the rules of Code Section 72(p). The availability of loans provides employees with significant access to their Section 403(b) savings and, in many cases, can be an important inducement to employee participation in the program. However, many custodial accounts do not provide loans to employees (although the IRS has stated that loans from custodial accounts are permitted).

Application of ERISA

Q 1:38   When is a Section 403(b) program considered to be an ERISA plan?

Section 403(b) programs are authorized by the Code. ERISA is a separate statute, generally administered by the Department of Labor that imposes separate and distinct requirements on ERISA-covered "pension plans," including some Section 403(b) programs.

The Section 403(b) programs of governmental employers, such as public schools, are completely exempt from ERISA. Section 403(b) plans that qualify as church plans (which include certain plans maintained for church-controlled tax-exempt organizations) are also exempt from ERISA, unless an election has been made to have the program become subject to certain requirements of the Code and ERISA.

The Section 403(b) programs of nongovernmental, nonchurch employers are subject to ERISA, except for pure salary reduction programs under which employees' rights under the annuity contracts are solely enforceable by the employees, employees are offered a reasonable choice of Section 403(b) investments, and the employer's role is essentially limited to the transmission of salary reduction contributions to the issuers. [DOL Reg § 2510.3-2(f)]

In connection with issuance of the final Code Section 403(b) regulations, the DOL published guidance that addresses whether tax-exempt employers will be able to comply with the final Code Section 403(b) regulations and remain within the safe harbor exemption from ERISA. [Field Assistance Bulletin 2007-02] The guidance provides that a plan of a tax-exempt employer may satisfy the requirements of the final Code Section 403(b) regulations and remain exempt from ERISA. The guidance notes, however, that there will be different approaches to compliance with the final Code Section 403(b) regulations and, depending on the facts and circumstances, some approaches may involve a level of employer involvement that will cause a plan to fall outside of the safe harbor.

Failure and Correction

Q 1:39 What are the tax consequences if a Section 403(b) plan fails to satisfy the applicable Code Section 403(b) requirements?

A contract or account that fails to satisfy the Code Section 403(b) requirements is not a Section 403(b) contract or account. In the IRS view, this means that the participant that is the beneficial owner of a contract or account is taxable on the fair market value of his or her interest (to the extent vested). [Treas. Reg. § 1.403(b)-3(d)(iii)] The tax treatment of subsequent investment earnings depends on whether the funding vehicle is an annuity contract or a custodial account. In this regard, in the case of a Section 403(b)(7) custodial account (but not an annuity contract), the tax benefits provided by Code Section 403(b) includes the exemption from income tax for the custodial account itself. As a result, the failure of the program to satisfy Code Section 403(b) will cause the employee to become taxable on the fair market value of the custodial account and cause the future income of the custodial account to become subject to income tax.

Q 1:40 Does a failure affect all contracts and accounts under the plan?

It depends. A failure to operate in accordance with the Code Section 403(b) requirements only affects the contracts and accounts with respect to which the failure occurred. [Treas. Reg. § 1.403(b)-3(d)] As a result, for example, an impermissible in-service distribution will only affect the contract or account from which the distribution is made. However, if a participant has more than one contract or account, all contracts or accounts of the participant under the plan will be adversely affected.

A failure to meet the plan requirement, an employer eligibility failure, or a nondiscrimination failure affects all contracts or accounts of all participants under the plan. [Treas. Reg. § 1.403(b)-3(d)]

Q 1:41 Has the IRS established any correction procedures for situations in which the requirements of Code Section 403(b) have not been satisfied?

Yes. The Employee Plans Compliance Resolution System (EPCRS) provides comprehensive guidance for correcting a "403(b) failure."

EPCRS for Section 403(b) programs has three components: the Self-Correction Program (SCP), the Voluntary Correction Program with Service Approval (VCP), and the Audit Closing Agreement Program (Audit CAP). Almost any tax compliance problem affecting a Section 403(b) program may be corrected under one of these three programs, often at relatively modest cost.

SCP permits self-correction of an operational failure if there are established practices and procedures for general compliance with Section 403(b) and if the failure is corrected by the end of the second year after the year in which it occurred (and prior to any IRS audit) or is insignificant, in which case there is no correction deadline. Self-correction under SCP does not require IRS review of the correction. In addition, SCP is available even if there is a pending IRS audit.

VCP provides for the issuance by the IRS of a compliance statement covering an operational, demographic, or employer eligibility failure. Under VCP, an employer submits an application to the IRS and agrees to pay a negotiated compliance correction fee that varies (in accordance with a published schedule) with the number of employees and the severity of the compliance failure. VCP is not available if there is a pending IRS audit. Correction under VCP can be initiated on an anonymous (or "John Doe") basis.

Finally, Audit CAP permits an employer undergoing an IRS audit whose Section 403(b) program has a Section 403(b) failure that cannot be corrected under SCP to pay a negotiated sanction to the IRS (determined as a percentage of the income tax that the IRS could collect as a result of the compliance failure) and to enter into a closing agreement for correction of the failure.

Comparison to Other Plan Types

Q 1:42   How do Section 403(b) salary reduction plans compare to Section 401(k) salary reduction arrangements?

Except for certain grandfathered plans, governmental employers may not maintain Section 401(k) plans. [I.R.C. § 401(k)(4)(B)(ii)] However, since 1996, nongovernmental tax-exempt employers have been permitted to maintain Section 401(k) salary reduction arrangements. Previously, the only permissible Section 401(k) plans of tax-exempt organizations were those established before July 2, 1986. As a result, nongovernmental employers eligible to maintain Section 403(b) programs may maintain a Section 401(k) plan instead.

Although Section 403(b) plans are subject to a number of the requirements that apply to Section 401(k) plans, Section 403(b) plans are generally subject to fewer technical requirements and somewhat lesser administrative burdens than are Section 401(k) plans. Although all plans, including Section 403(b) plans, present greater compliance burdens than existed in prior years, there are fewer ways to make plan-wide "disqualifying" mistakes under a Section 403(b) plan than under a Section 401(k) plan. In addition, the providers of Section 403(b) annuity contracts as custodial accounts often assume responsibility for certain compliance matters (especially relating to distributions) that typically are the responsibility of the plan administrator under a Section 401(k) plan.

Moreover, Section 403(b) plans have certain distinct advantages over Section 401(k) plans. Most important, the rate at which highly compensated employees may make salary reduction contributions under a Section 401(k) plan in any year generally is limited by the average rate at which non-highly compensated employees make such contributions, but no such limitation applies to salary reduction contributions under Section 403(b). Rather, Section 403(b) plans must make salary reduction contributions available to all employees subject to certain exceptions. In addition, the contribution limits under Section 403(b) can be higher, even for non-highly compensated employees, because of a special "catch-up" rule applicable to Section 403(b) plans.

Q 1:43   When might a tax-exempt employer prefer a Section 401(k) plan to a Section 403(b) plan?

Section 403(b) plans may only cover employees of organizations that are exempt from tax under Section 501(c)(3) or that are public educational organizations. Section 401(k) plans, however, may generally cover employees of any organization other than a governmental employer. As a result, where an eligible tax-exempt employer has one or more taxable subsidiaries or tax-exempt affiliates that cannot maintain a Section 403(b) plan, it may make sense to maintain a single Section 401(k) plan rather than a Section 403(b) plan for eligible employees and a Section 401(k) plan for ineligible employees.

One consideration in maintaining both types of plans is ensuring that the Section 401(k) plan will satisfy the minimum coverage and nondiscrimination requirements that apply to such a plan. In this regard, special rules apply in testing the Section 401(k) plan if the tax-exempt employer maintains both a Section 401(k) plan and a Section 403(b) plan. [Treas. Reg. § 1.410(b)-6(g)]

Q 1:44   How do Section 403(b) salary reduction plans compare to Section 457(b) eligible deferred compensation plans?

Governmental employers cannot maintain Section 401(k) plans. However, governmental employers may offer Section 457(b) eligible deferred compensation plans. The general tax treatment of Section 457(b) plans is comparable to the general tax treatment of Section 403(b) plans (although Section 457(b) plans may not permit designated Roth contributions). In addition, many of the basic rules are the same. For example, the basic limit on pre-tax salary reduction contributions for both a Section 403(b) plan and a Section 457(b) plan is $15,500 in 2008 (although each type of plan still has its own particular "catch-up" limit for longer-service or older participants). In addition, distributions from a governmental Section 457(b) plan or a Section 403(b) plan can be rolled over to another employer plan or IRA.

There are, however, some differences in the rules applicable to Section 403(b) plans and governmental Section 457(b) plans. For example, distributions from Section 403(b) programs but not Section 457(b) plans are potentially subject to the 10 percent tax on early distributions. [I.R.C. § 72(t)(1)] By way of another example, in-service distributions from Section 403(b) programs are permitted in certain circumstances. [I.R.C. §§ 403(b)(7), (11); 457(d)(1)] Further, Section 403(b) plans, but not Section 457(b) plans, are subject to rules that govern who must be eligible to participate, usually referred to as the "universal availability requirement."

Rather than choose between a Section 403(b) plan and a governmental Section 457(b) plan, many governmental employers that are eligible to offer Section 403(b) plans offer both types of plans. Contributions under a Section 403(b) plan do not count against the limits under Section 457(b) and vice versa. As a result, offering both types of plans allows many covered employees to double the limit on their pre-tax salary reduction contributions. (Nongovernmental, tax-exempt employers are permitted to offer Section 457(b) plans only to a "select group of management or highly compensated employees.")

Chapter 2

Section 501(c)(3) Organizations

Catherine W. Wilkinson, CPA
Steptoe & Johnson, LLP

> A Section 501(c)(3) organization is a type of tax-exempt organization that is eligible to maintain a Section 403(b) arrangement. This chapter discusses the formation and operation of Section 501(c)(3) organizations and the federal and state requirements for obtaining and maintaining tax-exempt status as a Section 501(c)(3) organization.

Introduction to Section 501(c)(3) Organizations

Q 2:1   What is a Section 501(c)(3) organization?

A Section 501(c)(3) organization is a nonprofit organization (i.e., corporation, community chest, fund, or foundation) that qualifies for exemption from federal income tax under Section 501(c)(3) of the Internal Revenue Code of 1986, as amended (the Code). To qualify under Code Section 501(c)(3), the organization must meet the following requirements:

1. It is organized and operated exclusively for religious, charitable, scientific, testing for public safety, literary, or educational purposes, or to foster national or international amateur sports competition, or for the prevention of cruelty to children or animals;

2. No part of the net earnings of the organization inures to the benefit of a private shareholder or individual;

3. No substantial part of the activities of the organization includes the carrying on of propaganda or otherwise attempting to influence legislation (except as otherwise permitted under Code Section 501(h)); and

4. The organization does not participate in, or intervene in, any political campaign on behalf of or in opposition to any candidate for public office.

Q 2:2 What are the advantages of 501(c)(3) status?

The primary advantage of 501(c)(3) status is that the organization is generally exempt from federal income tax. Although the organization is subject to the unrelated business income tax on any unrelated business income (see Qs 2:38–2:42), any income derived from the organization's exempt activities is not subject to the federal income tax. [I.R.C. § 501(a)] Generally, Section 501(c)(3) organizations are eligible for a similar exemption from state income or franchise tax, and certain states also provide an exemption from sales, use, and property taxes. Section 501(c)(3) organizations also enjoy other favorable tax treatment. Although such organizations and their employees are generally subject to the Social Security tax imposed by the Federal Insurance Contribution Act, they are exempt from the employment tax imposed by the Federal Unemployment Tax Act. [I.R.C. § 3306(c)(8)] In addition, contributions to Section 501(c)(3) organizations are generally deductible by the donor for income, estate, and gift tax purposes. [I.R.C. §§ 170(a), 2055(a)(2), 2522(a)(2)] Thus, Section 501(c)(3) organizations tend to receive greater public support than other tax-exempt organizations, contributions to which are not deductible or are deductible only to a lesser extent.

Q 2:3 What are the disadvantages of 501(c)(3) status?

The primary disadvantage of 501(c)(3) status is that the organization becomes subject to various operational restrictions. A Section 501(c)(3) organization may participate in lobbying activities only to a limited extent and is prohibited from participating in any political campaign activities on behalf of or in opposition to a candidate for public office (see Qs 2:35, 2:36). In addition, because of the prohibition against private inurement, a Section 501(c)(3) organization may not make any payments or give anything of value, other than for reasonable consideration, to any insider of the organization and must structure its dealings so as not to benefit any insider. [Rev. Rul. 73-126, 1973-1 C.B. 220] If a Section 501(c)(3) organization violates any of these proscriptions, it will be subject to various excise taxes and may lose its tax-exempt status (see Qs 2:26–2:28).

Q 2:4 What is the difference between a public charity and a private foundation?

Code Section 509(a) creates two classes of Section 501(c)(3) organizations: private foundations and public charities. A private foundation is defined as any organization described in Code Section 501(c)(3) that does not meet any of the following four exceptions:

1. Organizations engaged in certain legislatively favored activities defined in Code Section 170(b)(1)(A);
2. Organizations that receive broad public support as defined in Code Section 509(a)(2);
3. Organizations that have a supporting relationship to organizations described in (1) and (2) above; and
4. Organizations organized and operated for public safety testing.

[I.R.C. § 509(a)]

An organization that falls within one of these four exceptions is a public charity.

Private foundations are, under certain circumstances, subject to various excise taxes and restrictions under Chapter 42 of the Code that do not apply to public charities. [I.R.C. §§ 4940–4945] In addition, contributions to private foundations are deductible to a lesser extent than contributions to public charities. [I.R.C. § 170(b)(1)(B)]

Q 2:5   Can a private foundation maintain a 403(b) plan?

Yes. Any organization described in Code Section 501(c)(3) and exempt from federal tax under Code Section 501(a), including a private foundation, can maintain a 403(b) plan. [I.R.C. § 403(b); Treas. Reg. § 1.403(b)-1(a)(1)(i)]

Basic Requirements

Q 2:6   How is a Section 501(c)(3) organization established?

A Section 501(c)(3) organization is established by forming a nonprofit entity under the applicable state law and obtaining recognition of federal tax exemption under Code Section 501(c)(3). In order to be an organization described in Code Section 501(c)(3), the entity must be organized and operated exclusively for one or more exempt purposes described in Code Section 501(c)(3). [Treas. Reg. § 1.501(c)(3)-1(a)(1)]

Q 2:7   What is the organizational test?

To meet the organizational test, the organization's articles of organization (i.e., trust instrument, articles of incorporation, articles of association, or other organizing documents) must specifically limit the organization's purposes to one or more of the exempt purposes stated in Code Section 501(c)(3). [Treas. Reg. § 1.501(c)(3)-1(b)(1)(i)(a)] If the organization's purposes are broader than those stated in Code Section 501(c)(3), the organization will not qualify. [Treas.

Reg. § 1.501(c)(3)-1(b)(1)(iv)] Furthermore, if the organizing document expressly allows the organization to engage, other than as an insubstantial part of
its activities, in activities that are not in furtherance of its exempt purposes, the
organization will not meet the organizational test. [Treas. Reg. § 1.501(c)(3)-
1(b)(1)(iii)] To ensure that the organization's assets are dedicated to an exempt
purpose, the organization's articles of organization should further provide that,
upon dissolution or liquidation, the organization's assets will be distributed for
one or more exempt purposes or to one or more other tax-exempt organizations
described in Code Section 501(c)(3). [Treas. Reg. § 1.501(c)(3)-1(b)(4)] Although it is not expressly required to be included in the articles of organization,
the organizing documents should include the following language to guard
against violations of the restrictions imposed on lobbying and political activities
of Section 501(c)(3) organizations:

> No substantial part of the activities of the [organization] shall be the
> carrying on of propaganda, or otherwise attempting to influence legis-
> lation, and the [organization] shall not participate in, or intervene in
> (including publishing or distribution of statements), any political cam-
> paign on behalf of or in opposition to any candidate for public office.
> [See I.R.S. Pub. 557 at 20]

In addition to the above requirements, the organizing documents of a private
foundation must include certain statements related to the excise taxes imposed
under Chapter 42 of the Code. [I.R.C. § 508(e)] A private foundation is not
required to include this language if the state law under which it is formed either
(1) requires the private foundation to act in a manner that will not subject it to
the Chapter 42 excise taxes or (2) treats the private foundation's organizing
documents as containing the required language. [Treas. Reg. § 1.508-3(d)(1);
see also Rev. Rul. 75-38, 1975-1 C.B.161]

Q 2:8   What is the operational test?

To meet the operational test, the organization must engage primarily in
activities that accomplish one or more of the exempt purposes described in Code
Section 501(c)(3), and no part of the organization's net earnings can inure to the
benefit of a private shareholder or individual. [Treas. Reg. §§ 1.501(c)(3)-
1(c)(1), 1.501(c)(3)-1(c)(2)] An organization will not meet the operational test
if more than an insubstantial part of its activities do not further its exempt
purposes. [Treas. Reg. § 1.501(c)(3)-1(c)(1)] On March 28, 2008, the IRS
published final regulations under Code Section 501(c)(3) to clarify what types of
behavior fail to meet the operational test and result in revocation of an
organization's tax-exempt status. [Treas. Reg. § 1.501(c)(3)-1(d)(1)(iii)]

> **Example.** O is an educational organization that trains individuals in a
> program developed by P, O's president. Company K, a for-profit entity, owns
> all of the rights to P's program. P owns Company K. Before O, Company K
> conducted all of the program training exercises. O licenses the right to use a
> reference to the program and the right to teach the program from Company
> K. Under the license agreement, Company K provides O with trainers and

course materials on the program. O pays Company K royalties for these services. Because O's sole activity is conducting seminars and lectures on P's program, it is operated solely for the benefit of P and Company K in violation of the private benefit restriction in Treasury Regulations Section 1.501(c)(3)-1(d)(ii), regardless of whether O's payments are reasonable. O is not operated exclusively for exempt purposes; therefore, O is not a 501(c)(3) organization. [*See* Treas. Reg. § 1.501(c)(3)-1(d)(1)(iii), Ex. 3]

This example suggests that prohibited private benefits may arise regardless of whether payments made to private interests are reasonable or excessive.

Q 2:9   What types of entities may obtain Section 501(c)(3) status?

A Section 501(c)(3) organization can be formed as a corporation, a trust, an unincorporated association, a community fund, a foundation, or a limited liability company (LLC). [I.R.C. § 501(c)(3)] The IRS will treat an unincorporated association as a corporation for tax purposes. [Treas. Reg. §§ 301.7701-2(a), 301.7701-2(b)] Neither an individual nor a partnership will qualify as a Section 501(c)(3) organization.

Q 2:10   What are the advantages of forming a corporation as opposed to an association or a trust?

While unincorporated associations and trusts are typically simpler to create, less expensive, and subject to less extensive state regulation, the corporate form generally provides (1) better protection from liability for the managers and decision-makers of the organization and (2) a clearer legal framework in which to operate.

Corporation versus Unincorporated Association. The law governing unincorporated associations is limited and often unclear. Under common law, the unincorporated association is not a legal entity and has no legal existence apart from its membership. Thus, the association's governing instrument defines its structure, the duties and authority of its directors and officers, the liability of its members, and the procedures for undertaking various actions. Although this lack of a clear legal framework affords the unincorporated association certain flexibility, it also creates uncertainty where the organizing document does not specifically authorize or address particular actions. Courts will typically resolve such uncertainty by looking to principles of agency law. The result, however, may be contrary to the intentions of the association members.

By contrast, the laws governing nonprofit corporations are generally well defined by state statute. Many state nonprofit corporation statutes define the scope of the rights, duties, authority, and liability of members, directors, and officers. [*See, e.g.,* D.C. Code Ann. §§ 29-301.12, 29-301.14–29-301.25, 29-301.113–29-301.114] Thus, depending on the state in which the organization is formed, incorporation generally reduces the risk of uncertainty as to the treatment of actions taken by the corporation and its authorized officers and directors.

Because the unincorporated association is not a *legal entity,* it does not afford its members, officers, and directors the same protections against personal liability as a corporation. However, Congress enacted the Volunteer Protection Act of 1997 (VPA), which preempts state law and provides volunteers of nonprofit organizations with protection from certain liability arising as a result of their actions. [42 U.S.C. §§ 14501–14505] As of August 1997, this federal law protects a volunteer from liability if: (1) the volunteer was acting within the scope of the volunteer's responsibilities; (2) the volunteer was properly licensed by the state, if such licensing is required; (3) the harm was caused by ordinary negligence; and (4) the harm was not caused by the volunteer's operating certain vehicles, vessels, and aircraft. [42 U.S.C. § 14503(a)] Thus, to the extent that officers and directors of an unincorporated association serve in a voluntary capacity and receive no compensation for their services, they will be protected by the VPA from liability arising from certain acts performed within the scope of their responsibilities. However, to the extent that there is a lack of clarity in the organization's articles of organization or bylaws regarding the scope of the officers' and directors' authority and duties, the officers and directors could be personally liable for actions undertaken on behalf of the association. Thus, although the VPA minimizes many of the liability concerns that traditionally existed with respect to unincorporated associations, it does not completely eliminate potential liability. Liability still exists for volunteers who act outside the scope of their authority. Because the scope of a volunteer's authority is defined only by the organizing documents, rather than by a body of well-developed law, and is thus often unclear, the risk of liability arising from actions taken outside the scope of the volunteer's authority is real. Therefore, even with the VPA, incorporation provides better protection from liability.

Corporation versus Trust. Although state laws governing trusts are generally more extensive than those governing unincorporated associations, the laws governing corporations are generally better defined, particularly with respect to management's liability. Even in those states that have adopted statutes to govern charitable trusts, these statutes tend to be more limited and less flexible than the state corporation statutes. Although trusts, like corporations, provide the benefit of centralized management, the fiduciary duties imposed on trustees are often more onerous than those imposed on corporate officers and/or directors.

Costs of Incorporation. There are advantages to incorporation, but there are also costs and administrative burdens associated with incorporation, such as filing fees and state filing requirements. Each state has its own rules regarding fees and filing requirements for corporations incorporated in the state and for corporations incorporated in one state but qualified to operate in another state. Generally, states require a corporation to file articles of incorporation with the secretary of state, maintain a registered agent in the state, and submit annual reports to the state's corporation regulatory arm. Although, generally, the costs of incorporating are outweighed by the advantages afforded by the corporate form, discussed above, the question of whether to incorporate will nevertheless depend on the facts and circumstances and the intentions of the individuals forming the organization.

Q 2:11   What are the advantages of using LLC status?

Many of the benefits from LLC status are not allowed by the tax-exempt framework. LLCs blend the limited liability protections granted to corporations with the pass-through tax advantages of partnerships. However, if an LLC files for tax exemption, it will automatically be treated as a corporation rather than as a partnership for tax purposes. An LLC should not file an exemption application if it wants to be treated as a disregarded entity by its tax-exempt member. Unlike other pass-through entities, LLCs typically have fewer restrictions on membership. However, in order to qualify for tax exemption, an LLC may only have 501(c)(3) members. [*See* Form 1023 Instructions]

Q 2:12   What organizational documents are required?

The organizational documents required to establish a Section 501(c)(3) organization depend on the type of entity established. If the organization is created as a trust, a trust agreement is required. [*See* IRS Pub. 557 at 19–21] The trust agreement will set forth the exempt purposes of the organization and the management structure. The trustees of the trust will control the assets and activities of the organization.

If the organization is created as an unincorporated association, articles of association will be required. These are similar to a corporation's articles of incorporation but contain less formality, as state law does not generally impose statutory requirements on unincorporated associations.

If the organization is established as a corporation, articles of incorporation and bylaws will be required. [*See* IRS Pub. 557 at 19–21] The articles of incorporation must contain the information required in the state's corporation statutes. To formally establish a corporation, articles of incorporation must be filed with and approved by the appropriate state authority, usually the secretary of state, and generally, the corporation must hold an organizational meeting at which the initial directors adopt bylaws and appoint officers of the corporation. The moment at which a corporation comes into legal existence is determined by the law of the state in which the corporation is incorporated.

If the organization is created as an LLC, articles of organization (sometimes referred to as the certificate of formation or the certificate of organization) and an operating agreement, if it has adopted such an agreement, will be required. [*See* IRS Pub. 557 at 19–21] In addition to the other operational test requirements under Code Section 501(c)(3), the organizational language must require that any amendments to the LLC's articles of organization and operating agreement be consistent with Code Section 501(c)(3). Furthermore, the organizational language must prohibit the LLC from merging with, or converting into, a for-profit entity. Finally, the organizational language must contain an acceptable contingency plan in the event one or more members ceases, at any time, to be an organization described in Code Section 501(c)(3) or a governmental unit or instrumentality. [Richard A. McCray and Ward L. Thomas, "Limited Liability Companies as Exempt Organizations—Update," EO CPE 2001-B]

Regardless of the entity structure, the organizing documents should include the statements discussed in Q 2:7 in order to meet the organizational test under Code Section 501(c)(3).

Q 2:13   How does an organization obtain 501(c)(3) status?

Any organization formed after October 9, 1969, must file an application for tax exemption with the IRS in order to obtain 501(c)(3) status. [I.R.C. § 508(a); Treas. Reg. § 1.508-1(a)(1)] The application, along with a certified copy of the organization's organizational documents, must be filed with the IRS Service Center at the following address:

Internal Revenue Service Center
P.O. Box 192
Covington, KY 41012-0192

The application must be submitted with the appropriate user fee made payable to the United States Treasury. The user fee for an initial application for exemption is $750. [IRS Form 1023] If the organization had gross annual receipts averaging $10,000 or less during the preceding four taxable years, or if a new organization anticipates average gross annual receipts of $10,000 or less during its first four years, the user fee is only $300. [IRS Form 1023] Before it can submit an application for exemption, the organization is required to have filed an application for an employer identification number (EIN) (Form SS-4). Every organization must file for an EIN whether or not it has employees. Organizations can no longer submit Form SS-4 with their applications for tax exemption. If the organization will be represented by an attorney, accountant, or other agent, it should file a power of attorney (Form 2848) authorizing the person or persons to represent the organization before the IRS.

The staff of the Joint Committee on Taxation of the U.S. Congress issued a report recommending that, every five years, each Section 501(c)(3) organization (other than churches) be required to file with the IRS information sufficient to demonstrate that the organization continues to qualify for 501(c)(3) status. The proposal would exempt organizations that were recognized as exempt more than 10 years prior to enactment of the requirement. [See "Options to Improve Tax Compliance and Reform Tax Expenditures," JCS-02-05, Jan 27, 2005, at pp. 220–229] It is not presently clear whether the Joint Committee staff recommendation will be incorporated into formal legislation or ultimately adopted as law.

Q 2:14   What is Form 1023?

Form 1023 is the application for tax exemption that must be filed with the IRS by organizations seeking 501(c)(3) status. [Treas. Reg. § 1.508-1(a)(1)]

In 2004, the IRS issued a new, expanded version of Form 1023 that requires applicants to supply significantly more information than was previously required. The form was redesigned in an effort to capture all the information the IRS is likely to need to assess an organization's qualification for 501(c)(3) status.

In 2006, the IRS updated Form 1023 to reflect an increase in the initial application for recognition of exemption user fee for most organizations from $500 to $750, and $150 to $300 for organizations anticipating average gross annual receipts of $10,000 or less during its first four years. [*See* Rev. Proc. 2008-8, 2008-1 I.R.B. 233 (updated annually)]

Q 2:15   When should an organization apply for 501(c)(3) status?

An organization should file Form 1023 within 15 months after the end of the month in which the organization was formed, so that, if approved by the IRS, the organization will be treated as tax exempt retroactively to the date it was established. [Treas. Reg. § 1.508-1(a)(2)(i)] Upon obtaining its tax exemption, the organization may apply for a refund for any income tax paid during the period covered by its determination letter.

Generally, if the organization files its Form 1023 more than 15 months after the end of the month in which it was established, it will not qualify for retroactive tax-exempt treatment. Instead, if the IRS approves the application, the organization will be treated as tax exempt on a prospective basis from the date on which the Form 1023 was filed. Thus, any contributions received by such an organization during the first 15 months of its existence, and up until the time it files Form 1023, will be nondeductible. [I.R.C. § 508(d)(2)(B)] Churches, organizations that are not private foundations and that normally have annual gross receipts of less than $5,000, and certain subordinate organizations covered by group exemption letters are not required to file Form 1023 within 15 months of formation. [Treas. Reg. § 1.508-1(a)(3)(i)]

Under Form 1023 and pursuant to Treasury Regulations Section 301.9100-2(a)(2)(iv), organizations are allowed an automatic 12-month extension as long as the application for recognition of tax exemption is filed within the extended (i.e., 27-month) period. The IRS also may grant an extension beyond the 27-month period if the organization is able to establish that it acted reasonably and in good faith and that granting relief will not prejudice the interests of the government. [Treas. Reg. §§ 301.9100-1, 301.9100-3] Schedule E, "Organizations Not Filing Form 1023 Within 27 Months of Formation," was added to Form 1023 to consolidate questions and financial data in one place that relates to whether an exemption can be made retroactive to the organization's date of formation.

Q 2:16   How long does it take to obtain 501(c)(3) status?

The Internal Revenue Code and the regulations thereunder do not prescribe a period of time within which the IRS must rule on an organization's application for tax exemption. Generally, the application process takes approximately four to six months. Currently applications are separated into three groups: (1) those that are processed immediately based on the submitted information; (2) those that require minimal additional information to be resolved; and (3) those that require additional development. If an application falls into the first or second group, an organization can expect to receive its determination letter or request for additional information within two months. If an application falls into the third group, an organization will not be contacted until its application has been assigned to an EO specialist. As this supplement goes to press, the IRS had a backlog of three months in assigning applications in the third group to an EO specialist for review. [*See* "Where Is My Exemption Application?" available at http://www.irs.gov/charities] The IRS resumed processing exemption applications from 509(a)(3) functionally integrated Type III supporting organizations after it suspended the issuance of determination letters to these organizations in February 2007. [*See* "Memorandum for Manager, EO Determinations," dated Sept. 24, 2007]

If the application is approved, the IRS will issue a determination letter stating that the organization will be treated for tax purposes as an organization described in Code Section 501(c)(3). If an organization receives an adverse determination letter from the IRS, the organization may appeal by filing a sworn written protest with the key IRS district director within 30 days of receiving the adverse ruling. If the organization receives an adverse ruling from the IRS Appeals Office, the decision may be appealed to the courts after exhaustion of the organization's administrative remedies.

Q 2:17   What is an advance ruling?

An organization may receive an advance ruling from the IRS that it will be treated as a public charity, rather than as a private foundation, for tax purposes for its first five taxable years. In the event of an advance ruling, a final determination as to the public support of the organization will be based on the support the organization actually receives during its first five taxable years. Thus, an organization that has not received significant public support during its first taxable year, but that expects to receive significant public support by the end of its fifth taxable year, should consider requesting an advance ruling. In order to obtain an advance ruling, the organization must voluntarily consent, as part of its Form 1023 filing, to extend the statute of limitations period for the tax years covered by the five-year advance ruling period to eight years, four months, and 15 days beyond the end of its first taxable year. By doing so, the organization, in effect, agrees to be subject to the private foundation taxes under Chapter 42 of the Code in the event that it fails to qualify as a public charity at the expiration of the advance ruling period.

Q 2:18   Can a new organization obtain a definitive ruling that it is a public charity and not a private foundation?

No. A new organization that has not completed at least eight months of a taxable year may not obtain a definitive ruling regarding its status as a public charity. [Treas. Reg. § 1.509(a)-3(d)(1)] Such an organization must instead request an advance ruling regarding its public charity, nonprivate foundation status.

Q 2:19   How does an organization obtain a definitive ruling?

To receive a definitive ruling from the IRS regarding its status as a public charity, the organization must have completed at least eight months of a taxable year and must meet the public support test based on the support it has received as of the date of filing Form 1023. [Treas. Reg. § 1.509(a)-3]

An organization that has previously received an advance ruling may receive a definitive ruling regarding its status as a public charity by filing financial information with the IRS at the expiration of its five-year advance ruling period, showing that it has met the public support test. The organization generally has 90 days following the last day of its fifth taxable year in which to file Form 8734, "Support Schedule for Advance Ruling Period," submitting this information.

Q 2:20   How does an organization meet the public support test?

For an organization described in Code Section 501(c)(3) to be treated as a public charity rather than a private foundation by reason of its public support, it must meet the public support test under one of two statutory alternatives. Either the organization must pass the *one-third public support test* or, if it fails this test, it may qualify as publicly supported under the "facts and circumstances test."

Under the one-third public support test, the organization must show that it normally receives at least one-third of its support from governmental units, from contributions made directly by the general public, or from a combination of these sources. [Treas. Reg. § 1.509(a)-3(a)(2)] An organization will be treated as *normally* receiving one-third of its support from these sources for the current tax year and the following tax year if for the preceding four tax years the organization has met the one-third public support test in the aggregate. [Treas. Reg. § 1.509(a)-3(c)(1)(i)]

An organization that cannot meet the one-third public support test may nevertheless qualify as a public charity under the facts and circumstances test if it receives a substantial portion of its support: (1) from governmental units; (2) directly or indirectly from the general public; or (3) from a combination of these sources. [I.R.C. § 170(b)(1)(A)(vi); Treas. Reg. § 1.170A-9(e)(3)] To qualify, the organization must: (1) show that at least 10 percent of the total support it receives is from governmental units and/or from contributions from the general public and (2) be organized to attract new and additional public and governmental support. [Treas. Reg. §§ 1.170A-9(e)(3)(i), 1.170A-9(e)(3)(ii)] The organization meets the second requirement if it either maintains a continuous and bona fide program for solicitation of funds from new and additional public and/or governmental sources or carries on activities designed to attract support from governmental units or other public charities. [Treas. Reg. § 1.170A-9(e)(3)(ii)] To make the determination as to whether the organization meets the facts and circumstances test, the IRS will consider all relevant facts and circumstances, including five particular factors set forth in the regulations. [Treas. Reg. § 1.170A-9(e)(3)(ii)]

The purpose of these public support tests is to ensure that an organization that is treated as a public charity rather than a private foundation "is responsive to the general public, rather than to the private interests of a limited number of donors or other persons." [Treas. Reg. § 1.509(a)-3(a)(4)]

Q 2:21   What are the annual filing requirements with the Internal Revenue Service?

With limited exceptions, Section 501(c)(3) organizations are required to file an annual information return with the IRS each year. [I.R.C. § 6033(a)(1)] To meet this requirement, an organization must file Form 990, "Return of Organization Exempt From Income Tax," along with Schedules A and B, with the IRS each year. An organization whose exempt status is still pending must also file a Form 990 indicating that its status is pending. [Treas. Reg. § 1.6033-2(c)]

Schedule A is used to report the following:

1. Compensation of the five highest paid employees other than officers, directors, and trustees;

2. Compensation of the five highest paid independent contractors for professional services and other services;

3. Information about the organization's lobbying activities;

4. Information about the organization's transactions with insiders and certain other organizations;

5. Information about the organization's scholarship programs; and

6. Financial information showing the organization's public support.

Schedule B is used to report names, addresses, and the amount and type of contribution for each donor who contributed to the organization money or property aggregating $5,000 or more for the year.

A Section 501(c)(3) organization with annual gross receipts of less than $100,000 and total assets at year end of less than $250,000 may file a short form return—Form 990-EZ (see Q 2:22 for information regarding the filing of a Form 990-EZ for the 2008 tax year and beyond). Private foundations are required to file a more detailed information return known as Form 990-PF. If the organization has $1,000 or more in gross income from unrelated trades or businesses (defined in Q 2:39), the organization must file Form 990-T in addition to an annual information return (i.e., Form 990, Form 990-EZ, or Form 990-PF).

Certain Section 501(c)(3) organizations, such as churches and church-affiliated schools below college level, are exempt from the annual filing requirement. [I.R.C. § 6033(a)(2); Treas. Reg. § 1.6033-2(g)(1)] Nevertheless, such organizations are required to notify the IRS of any changes to the organization's charitable purposes, operations, or activities. [Treas. Reg. § 1.6033-2(i)(1)] The following Section 501(c)(3) organizations qualify for this exemption:

- A church, an interchurch organization of local units of a church, a convention or association of churches, or an integrated auxiliary of a church (such as a men's or women's organization, religious school (such as a seminary), mission society, or youth group)
- An exclusively religious activity of any religious order
- An organization (other than a private foundation) that normally has gross receipts in each taxable year of not more than $25,000 (but see Q 2:22)
- A mission society sponsored by or affiliated with one or more churches or church denominations, more than one-half of the activities of which society are conducted in, or directed at persons in, foreign countries
- A state institution whose income is excluded from gross income under Code Section 115
- An instrumentality of the United States
- A school below college level that (1) is affiliated with a church or operated by a religious order, and (2) normally maintains a regular faculty and curriculum and normally has a regularly enrolled student body in attendance at the place where educational activities are regularly held
- An organization that is operated, supervised, or controlled by one or more churches, integrated auxiliaries, or conventions or associations of churches
- An organization that is operated, supervised, or controlled by one or more religious orders and is engaged in financing, funding, or managing assets used for exclusively religious activities
- A governmental unit or an affiliate of a governmental unit (except that if such unit has any unrelated business income, it may need to file Form 990-T)

[Treas. Reg. § 1.6033-2(g)(1); Rev. Proc. 83-23, 1983-1 C.B. 687; Rev. Proc. 96-10, 1996-1 C.B. 517; Rev. Proc. 95-48, 1995-2 C.B. 418]

These filing exceptions do not apply to private foundations.

Q 2:22   Is there an exception from the filing requirements for smaller organizations?

No. Although certain Section 501(c)(3) organizations that do not normally have more than $25,000 in gross receipts each year are not required to file Form 990, such organizations must now file with the IRS an annual notice, also known as an e-Postcard, containing basic contact and financial information. [I.R.C. § 6033(i)] Beginning in 2008, small tax-exempt organizations that previously were not required to file returns must file an annual electronic notice, Form 990-N, "Electronic Notice (e-Postcard) for Tax-Exempt Organizations not Required To File Form 990 or 990-EZ." This filing requirement applies to tax periods beginning after December 31, 2006. If a small organization fails to meet its annual filing requirement for three consecutive years, the IRS must revoke that organization's tax-exempt status. [I.R.C. § 6033(j)] These provisions were added to the Code by PPA Section 1223. The IRS issued Temporary Treasury Regulations Section 1.6033-6T to provide further guidance on the time and manner in which certain tax-exempt organizations are required to file an e-Postcard. [*See* 72 Fed. Reg. 64,147 (Nov. 15, 2007)]

Q 2:23   What is Form 990?

Form 990 is the annual information return that most tax-exempt organizations, including most Section 501(c)(3) organizations, must file with the IRS each year. Generally, the financial and operational information required to be furnished on Form 990 is intended to allow the IRS to assess whether the organization is continuing to operate as a charitable organization described in Code Section 501(c)(3).

Employer contributions to 403(b) plans are reported on Part II (Statement of Functional Expenses) and Part V-A (Current Officers, Directors, Trustees, and Key Employees) and Part V-B (Former Officers, Directors, Trustees, and Key Employees) of Form 990. These contributions are also reported on Part I (Compensation of the Five Highest Paid Employees Other Than Officers, Directors and Trustees) of Schedule A to Form 990. Schedule A also questions whether the organization had a Section 403(b) annuity plan for its employees. [Form 990, Sch A, line 3b] Form 990 and Schedule A do not require reporting of employee salary reduction contributions.

On December 20, 2007, the IRS released an updated version of the Form 990 effective for the 2008 tax year (returns filed in 2009). To assist smaller organizations' transition to the new form, the IRS announced a graduated phase-in period that allows certain organizations to file a Form 990-EZ for up to three years. For more information on the updated Form 990, go to http://www.irs.gov/charities/index.html.

Q 2:24   When and where must Form 990 be filed?

Form 990 must be filed by the fifteenth day of the fifth month following the close of the organization's accounting period. Thus, if the organization follows a calendar year, its Form 990 will be due May 15 of each year. An organization can obtain an automatic three-month extension of time for filing Form 990 by filing Form 8868, "Application for Extension of Time to File an Exempt Organization Return." Form 8868 may also be used to file for an additional three-month extension of time. This additional extension, however, is subject to the discretion of the IRS for reasonable cause. No further extensions of time to file are allowed. A penalty of $20 per day not to exceed the lesser of $10,000 or 5 percent of the organization's gross receipts for the year may be imposed on an organization that files late. For organizations with gross receipts exceeding $1 million for any year, the penalty is $100 per day and the maximum penalty is $50,000. [I.R.C. § 6652(c)(1)(A)]

Prior to July 1, 1996, an organization filed its Form 990 with the IRS district office in charge of the state in which the organization's principal office was located. However, on July 1, 1996, the IRS began to centralize the processing of certain exempt organization information and tax returns. As of January 1, 1997, all Section 501(c)(3) organizations should file their Forms 990 with the IRS Service Center in Ogden, Utah, at the following address:

Internal Revenue Service Center
Ogden, UT 84201-0027

[Ann. 96-63, 1996-29 I.R.B. 18]

The IRS encourages all non-profit organizations to take advantage of new electronic filing, or e-filing, procedures. In fact, certain large tax-exempt organizations are required to e-file. [Treas. Reg. § 1.6033-4] For taxable years ending on or after December 31, 2006, organizations with $10 million or more in assets that make at least 250 filings must e-file. [Treas. Reg. § 301.6033-4] In addition, beginning with taxable years ending on or after December 31, 2006, private foundations making 250 or more filings will be required to file their Forms 990-PF electronically, regardless of size.

Tax-exempt organizations may be able to request waiver of the electronic filing requirement. On November 11, 2005, the IRS issued Notice 2005-88 to establish criteria under which tax-exempt organizations may request waivers. For instance, waivers may be requested if the tax-exempt organization cannot meet electronic filing requirements due to technology constraints or if compliance with the requirements would result in undue financial burden on the filer. [Notice 2005-88] The notice also allows for a rejected electronically-filed return (which is transmitted on or before the due date) to be considered timely filed, and any elections attached to the return will be considered valid. For taxable years 2005 or after, the IRS will allow 20 calendar days from the date of first transmission of an electronic return to perfect the return for electronic resubmission. If the electronic return cannot be accepted for processing electronically, the taxpayer must file a paper return with the IRS by the later of the due date, or five calendar days after the last rejection notification from the IRS.

Q 2:25   Are Forms 990 filed with the IRS confidential?

Generally, no. Code Section 6104 provides that certain information filed by tax-exempt organizations is *open for public inspection.* Specifically, the statute provides for public disclosure of applications for exemption and their supporting documents and annual information returns. This means, for example, that salary information about directors, trustees, officers, and key employees of tax-exempt organizations reported on Part V of Form 990 or Part I of Schedule A to Form 990 is subject to public disclosure.

A controversy exists regarding the extent of disclosure of donor information reported on Schedule B to Form 990, *Schedule of Contributors.* Schedule B was introduced for tax years beginning in 2000. Prior to introduction of Schedule B, Form 990 filers were required to provide an attachment of their own design identifying large donors in connection with reporting total contributions on Line 1d of Form 990. Information provided as an attachment to Line 1d of Form 990 was not subject to public disclosure. After a number of inadvertent releases of donor information, Schedule B was introduced as a means for the IRS to capture the nonpublic donor information separately from the otherwise public Form 990 data, and to withhold such data from public inspection. When first introduced, Schedule B bore a prominent legend: "This form is generally not open to public inspection except for section 527 organizations."

In November 2001, the IRS reversed its position regarding public disclosure of information on Form 990, Schedule B. The current Schedule B provides that only the names and addresses of contributors to Section 501(c)(3) organizations (other than private foundations) are not subject to disclosure. All other information, including the amount of contributions, the description of noncash contributions and any other information provided is open to public inspection, unless it clearly identifies the donor. The tax-exempt community greeted the revised Schedule B with alarm due to a concern that, in some cases, the amount of a contribution, and particularly the description of a noncash contribution, may indirectly identify the donor and thus deter some donors. In November 2002, in response to complaints from the tax-exempt community, the IRS stated that it will no longer include Schedule B on CD sets or other media generally made available to the public through third parties such as GuideStar (a Web site that posts information about tax-exempt organizations, including Forms 990). If a Schedule B is requested directly from the IRS, the requests will be handled on a case-by-case basis, and information released will be carefully reviewed to ensure that it does not identify individual donors. [See IRS to Protect Privacy of Contributors to EOs, 2002 TNT 218-4 (Nov. 8, 2002)]

Some donor information is also reported on Schedule A, Part IV-A. Lines 26b, 27a and b, and 28 of Schedule A, Part IV-A each call for an attachment providing a list of names of certain types of donors to the organization. Although the form provides that this information is not subject to public disclosure, the IRS apparently released a number of donor lists that were submitted with Schedule A, with only the names and addresses redacted. As with donor information reported on Schedule B, the public availability of the donor lists submitted with Schedule A raised privacy concerns. Beginning in 2001, the IRS no longer requires submission of these lists with organizations' returns. Each filing organization should, however, prepare the list and keep it in its records instead of submitting it to the IRS. [Cheryl Chasin, Susan L. Paul & Paul W. Jones, Form 990, Schedule A and Schedule B, IRS EO CPE Text for FY03]

(For more information on filing Form 990 returns, see http://www. stayexempt.org (a recently launched IRS web-based version of its Exempt Organizations Workshop).)

State Filing Requirements

Q 2:26   Is an organization that is exempt from federal tax as a Section 501(c)(3) organization automatically exempt from state tax?

No. In many states, an organization that is exempt from federal income tax under Code Section 501(c)(3) generally must also apply for exemption under the applicable state statute(s). Moreover, depending on the jurisdiction, there could be several types of state taxes from which a charitable organization could seek exemption, including income, franchise, property, and sales and use taxes. A charitable organization generally will be required to apply for exemption from each type of state tax from which it wishes to be exempt.

Q 2:27   What are the state filing requirements for Section 501(c)(3) organizations?

The filing requirements for charitable organizations vary widely from state to state. Generally, however, a charitable organization must file its organizational documents and an application for exemption with the appropriate state authorities. A charitable organization that wishes to file an application for exemption from state taxes should consult the applicable state statutes for information concerning required application content. In addition, most states have annual tax reporting requirements. Certain states provide that filing requirements can be satisfied by filing a copy of the federal Form 990 with the appropriate state regulator. A corporation may also be required to file a periodic corporate report listing the names and addresses of its current officers, directors, and registered agent.

Q 2:28   If an organization solicits charitable contributions, what are the state filing requirements?

In many states and in the District of Columbia, an organization that solicits charitable contributions must apply for and receive a license from the jurisdiction before soliciting charitable contributions within that jurisdiction. [*See, e.g.,* D.C. Code Ann. § 44-1701 *et seq.*; D.C. Mun. Regs. Tit. 16, ch. 13] Such an organization might also be required to file periodic reports concerning contributions received. [*See* D.C. Code Ann. § 44-1701 *et seq.*; D.C. Mun. Regs. Tit. 16, ch. 13]

Maintaining 501(c)(3) Status

Q 2:29   What is *private inurement*?

Private inurement occurs when any portion of the net earnings of a Section 501(c)(3) organization is paid to or used for the benefit of "any private shareholder or individual." [I.R.C. § 501(c)(3)] This private inurement proscription generally applies to transactions that benefit persons having a personal and private interest in the activities of the organization (sometimes referred to as *insiders* of the organization). [*See* Treas. Reg. § 1.501(a)-1(c)] If an organization violates the private inurement proscription, it is not "operated exclusively for one or more exempt purposes," as the regulations issued pursuant to Code Section 501(c)(3) require. [Treas. Reg. § 1.501(c)(3)-1(c)(2)]

Similarly, a Section 501(c)(3) organization cannot be organized or operated for the benefit of private interests. [Treas. Reg. § 1.501(c)(3)-1(d)(1)(ii)] This prohibition against *private benefit* is broader than the private inurement proscription, reaching transactions that benefit not only insiders but also other private individuals, such as members or beneficiaries of the organization. [*See* Rev. Rul. 77-111, 1977-1 C.B. 144] If an organization engages in a transaction that results in "more than incidental" private benefit, it is not "operated exclusively for one or more exempt purposes."

Although the regulations issued pursuant to Section 501(c)(3) state that an organization may engage in a transaction that results in merely *incidental* private benefit without risking loss of its tax exemption, the statutory language prohibiting private inurement is absolute. [*See* I.R.C. § 501(c)(3); Rev. Rul. 74-146, 1974-1 C.B. 129; GCM 37166 (June 15 1977); GCM 35701 (Mar. 4, 1974)] Some courts, however, have held that an organization may engage in a transaction that results in only incidental private inurement without risking loss of its tax exemption. [*See* Easter House v. Comm'r, 87-1 U.S.T.C. 9359 (Ct. Cl. 1987), *aff'd* 846 F.2d 78 (Fed. Cir. 1988); Founding Church of Scientology v. United States, 412 F.2d 1197, 1200 (Ct. Cl. 1969), *cert. denied*, 397 U.S. 1009 (1970)] An organization that violates the private inurement proscription or the private benefit proscription could face loss of its tax exemption or the imposition of *intermediate sanctions* (see Q 2:30). The IRS has recently published final regulations on the standards of recognizing tax-exempt status if an organization benefits any private interest or if an exempt organization has engaged in excess benefit transactions. [*See* Treas. Reg. § 1.501(c)(3)-1(f)].

Q 2:30   What are *intermediate sanctions*?

Code Section 4958 provides for the imposition of a series of excise taxes—referred to as *intermediate sanctions*—on *disqualified persons* and certain officers and directors of Section 501(c)(3) organizations (other than private foundations), where such an organization enters into a transaction that confers an *excess benefit* on a disqualified person. [I.R.C. § 4958] The intermediate sanctions provisions in the Code thus allow the IRS to impose a penalty that is less severe than revocation of an organization's exemption in the event that the private inurement proscription is violated. However, the final regulations under Code Sections 501(c)(3) and 4958, published by the IRS on March 28, 2008, clarify that the IRS has the discretion to revoke the exemption of any organization that violates the provisions of Code Section 501(c)(3) in addition to imposing the intermediate sanctions in Code Section 4958.

Notwithstanding the foregoing, the intermediate sanctions provisions do not apply to governmental entities that have obtained 501(c)(3) status if such entities are exempt from taxation without regard to Code Section 501(a). [Treas. Reg. § 53.4958-2(a)(1)]

The taxes imposed on an excess benefit transaction apply to transactions occurring on or after September 14, 1995. [Treas. Reg. § 53.4958-1(f)]

Q 2:31   Who is a *disqualified person*?

A *disqualified person* is any person who was, at any time during the five-year period preceding a transaction, in a position to exercise *substantial influence* over the affairs of the organization, a member of that person's family, or a 35 percent controlled entity. [I.R.C. § 4958(f)(1)] For example, in TAM 200244028 (June 21, 2002), the IRS ruled that the spouse of the president and chief executive officer of a nonprofit health care group was a disqualified person within the meaning of Code Section 4958.

Q 2:32   What is an *excess benefit transaction*?

An *excess benefit transaction* is a transaction in which the economic benefit to the disqualified person exceeds the value of the consideration received by the organization. [I.R.C. § 4958(c)(1)(A)] The payment of excessive compensation to a disqualified person, for example, can constitute an excess benefit transaction under Code Section 4958. For purposes of determining whether a disqualified person's compensation package is reasonable under Code Section 4958, benefits provided pursuant to a qualified pension, profit-sharing, or stock bonus plan are deemed received on the date the benefit is vested. [Treas. Reg. § 53.4958-1(e)(2)]

The regulations generally provide that the parties to a challenged transaction will receive the benefit of a rebuttable presumption that the transaction was reasonable if the parties satisfy the following three-part test:

1. The transaction is approved in advance by an authorized body of the organization, composed entirely of individuals who do not have a conflict of interest with respect to the arrangement;

2. Appropriate data as to comparability was obtained and relied upon by the authorized body in making the determination that the transaction was reasonable; and

3. Such determination is adequately and contemporaneously documented.

[Treas. Reg. § 53.4958-6(a)]

If the parties to the transaction satisfy the three-part test, the burden of proof shifts to the IRS to develop evidence that the transaction was an excess benefit transaction. [Treas. Reg. § 53.4958-6(b)] However, the IRS may overcome the presumption of reasonableness if it develops sufficient contrary evidence to rebut the probative value of the data relied upon by the authorized body. No adverse inference is to be drawn from an organization's failure to meet the three-part test. [Treas. Reg. § 53.4958-6(e)] In other words, an organization may be unable to satisfy the three-part test, but it may nevertheless escape the imposition of intermediate sanctions if consideration for the transaction is found to have been reasonable.

Example. A used car salesman created a Section 501(c)(3) organization, the purpose of which was to allow individuals to donate their used cars for a tax deduction and at the same time choose the charity to which they wanted the proceeds to go. The organization's board of directors consisted of the founder, his wife, his father-in-law, and a CPA. The founder was the president and executive director of the organization. He was in control of the organization's activities. The organization maintained no records of the number of hours the founder worked, no documentation of the services he provided, and no evidence of comparable salaries. The organization repaid several loans purportedly extended to it by the founder and his family. The loans were not documented. The founder is a disqualified person with respect to the organization because he is in a position to exercise substantial influence over the organization's affairs. The repayment of undocumented loans is an excess benefit. Moreover, the founder's salary is also presumptively an excess benefit because it was not approved by an authorized body composed entirely of disinterested individuals, appropriate data as to comparability was not obtained, and the transaction was not properly documented. [TAM 200243057 (July 2, 2002)]

The staff of the Joint Committee on Taxation of the U.S. Congress has issued a report recommending that the rebuttable presumption of reasonableness contained in the intermediate sanctions regulations be eliminated. Under the recommendation, the procedures currently used to obtain a rebuttable presumption of reasonableness would be recast as "minimum standards of due diligence with respect to an arrangement or transfer involving a disqualified person." [See "Options to Improve Tax Compliance and Reform Tax Expenditures," JCS-02-05, Jan. 27, 2005, pp. 254–269] Organizations not adhering to such procedures would be required to disclose the procedures, if any, that were followed to ensure that no excess benefit was conferred. It is not presently clear whether this Joint Committee staff recommendation will be incorporated into formal legislation or ultimately adopted as law.

Q 2:33 How has the IRS been targeting allegedly abusive executive compensation arrangements?

On March 1, 2007, the Exempt Organizations Office (EO) of the Tax Exempt and Government Entities Division (TE/GE) of the IRS released results from its Executive Compensation Compliance Initiative (the Project). EO initiated the Project in 2004 to review compensation practices of exempt organizations, identify tax administration concerns, and uncover potential areas of abuse in the exempt sector. The Project was divided into three parts: Part I, involved sending compliance check letters to 1,233 organizations; Part II, resulted in the separate examination of 782 organizations; and Part III, initiated further information gathering on loans made by tax-exempt organizations to key employees, directors, officers, and other insiders, the results of which will be released later.

The IRS found that significant reporting issues existed as nearly 30 percent of compliance check recipients were required to amend their Forms 990. Where excess benefit transactions and self-dealing were found, excise penalties were assessed (25 examinations resulted in proposed excise tax assessments under Chapter 42, aggregating in excess of $21 million, against 40 disqualified persons or organization managers). Although high compensation amounts were found in many cases, generally they were substantiated and deemed to be reasonable based on appropriate comparability data.

The IRS concluded that additional education and guidance, as well as training for agents, is needed in the areas of reporting requirements and the rebuttable presumption procedures, which may be relied upon by public charities to establish reasonable compensation. Also, the IRS concluded that it must change Form 990 to reduce errors in reporting and provide sufficient information to enable the IRS to identify compensation issues. [Additional information regarding the Project's findings, as well as "Lessons Learned and Recommendations," may be found at http://www.irs.gov/pub/irs-tege/exec._comp._final.pdf]

Q 2:34 What penalty is imposed in the event of an excess benefit transaction?

If a transaction is found to have been an excess benefit transaction, the following excise taxes may be imposed:

1. On the disqualified person, a tax equal to 25 percent of the excess benefit;
2. On any organization manager who knowingly, and not due to reasonable cause, participated in the excess benefit transaction, a tax equal to 10 percent of the excess benefit; and
3. On the disqualified person, an additional tax equal to 200 percent of the excess benefit if the excess benefit is not corrected within the taxable period.

[I.R.C. §§ 4958(a), 4958(b)]

Imposition of intermediate sanctions under Code Section 4958 does not foreclose revocation of an organization's tax-exempt status by the IRS in appropriate cases, as emphasized by recent regulations. The regulations highlight numerous factors the IRS Commissioner will consider when determining whether to revoke an organization's tax-exempt status or to assess Code Section 4958 excise taxes. Although all relevant facts and circumstances will be considered, the following five factors are specifically enumerated:

1. The size and scope of the organization's regular and ongoing exempt activities before and after the excess benefit(s) occurred;

2. The size and scope of the excess benefit transaction(s) in relation to the size and scope of the organization's regular and ongoing exempt activities;

3. Whether the organization has been involved in repeated excess benefit transactions;

4. Whether the organization has implemented safeguards reasonably calculated to prevent future violations; and

5. Whether the excess benefit transaction has been corrected (as defined by Code Section 4958(f)(6) and Treasury Regulations Section 53.4958-7), or the organization has made a good faith effort to seek correction.

[*See* Treas. Reg. § 1.501(c)(3)-1(f)(2)(ii)] As noted in the examples to the regulations, the IRS looks favorably on self-correction.

As indicated above, present-law intermediate sanctions are not imposed against the entity that confers an excess benefit, but only against the disqualified person and, in some instances, organization managers. However, the staff of the Joint Committee on Taxation of the U.S. Congress has issued a report recommending an entity-level tax. [*See* "Options to Improve Tax Compliance and Reform Tax Expenditures," JCS-02-05, Jan. 27, 2005, pp. 254–269] Under the recommendation, if a tax is imposed against a disqualified person, the organization itself would be subject to a tax equal to 10 percent of the excess benefit, unless the organization can demonstrate that it operated consistent with minimum standards of due diligence with respect to the transaction (see Q 2:32). Similar new penalties were also recommended in the case of a self-dealing transaction involving a private foundation. It is not presently clear whether these Joint Committee staff recommendations will be incorporated into formal legislation or ultimately adopted as law.

Q 2:35   Can a Section 501(c)(3) organization engage in lobbying and/or political campaign activities?

A Section 501(c)(3) organization may engage in limited lobbying activities, but it is strictly prohibited from engaging in any political campaign activity. [*See* I.R.C. § 501(c)(3)] To the extent a Section 501(c)(3) organization exceeds the permissible level of lobbying activities or engages in any political campaign activity, the organization risks classification as an *action organization*, the imposition of excise taxes under Code Section 4911 or 4912 on excess lobbying expenditures, and loss of its tax exemption. [*See* I.R.C. §§ 501(c)(3), 4911, 4912; Treas. Reg. § 1.501(c)(3)-1(c)(3)]

"No substantial part" of a Section 501(c)(3) organization's activities can involve "carrying on propaganda, or otherwise attempting, to influence legislation." [I.R.C. § 501(c)(3)] To determine the permissible level of lobbying activities for a Section 501(c)(3) organization, one of two different tests will be applied. If a Section 501(c)(3) organization has made an election under Code Section 501(h) (see Q 2:36), the organization will be subject to an *expenditure test*, which involves the application of statutory dollar limits on lobbying expenditures. [I.R.C. § 501(h); Treas. Reg. § 1.501(h)-1] If the organization has not made an election under Code Section 501(h), however, it will be subject to the *substantial part test*. [Treas. Reg. § 1.501(c)(3)-1(c)(3)(ii)] The substantial part test is a less precise facts and circumstances test under which no fixed percentages or formulas are applied. [*See, e.g.,* Haswell v. Comm'r, 500 F.2d 1133, 1142 (Ct. Cl. 1974); League of Women Voters v. United States, 180 F. Supp. 379 (Ct. Cl. 1960), *cert. denied,* 364 U.S. 882 (1960)]

Code Section 501(c)(3) also provides that a Section 501(c)(3) organization may "not participate in, or intervene in (including the publishing or distributing of statements), any political campaign on behalf of (or in opposition to) any candidate for public office." [I.R.C. § 501(c)(3)] An organization that violates this absolute prohibition on political campaign activities will be denied exemption under Code Section 501(c)(3). [Treas. Reg. § 1.501(c)(3)-1(c)(3)(iii)] To illustrate under what facts and circumstances an organization will be considered to have participated or intervened in a political campaign, the IRS published Revenue Ruling 2007-41. [*See* IR-2007-190 (Nov. 19, 2007), available at http://www.irs.gov/newsroom/article/0,,id = 175818,00.html (reminding 501(c)(3) organizations that they may not directly or indirectly become involved in the campaigns of political candidates)]

Recently, the IRS has focused increasing resources on stemming political intervention activities by tax-exempt organizations. Educational and enforcement efforts have included the release of a fact sheet to provide charities with advance notice of the statutory rules involving political activity in order to help them remain in compliance with federal tax law as enacted by Congress, Treasury Regulations, and court decisions. [*See* FS-2006-17]

Q 2:36   How does an organization make the election under Code Section 501(h) to be subject to the expenditure test for lobbying activities?

An eligible organization can elect to be subject to the *expenditure test* under Code Section 501(h) by filing Form 5768, "Election/Revocation of Election by an Eligible Section 501(c)(3) Organization to Make Expenditures to Influence Legislation," with the Internal Revenue Service Center in Ogden, Utah, at the following address:

Internal Revenue Service Center
Ogden, UT 84201-0027

[Treas. Reg. § 1.501(h)-2(a)]

A new organization may submit Form 5768 together with Form 1023 at the time it applies for Section 501(c)(3) status. The election is effective for the year in which the form is filed and for all subsequent years, unless and until the organization voluntarily revokes its election. [Treas. Reg. § 1.501(h)-2(a)]

Q 2:37   Can a Section 501(c)(3) organization operate any portion of its business for profit?

Yes. A Section 501(c)(3) organization can operate a portion of its business for profit without risking imposition of the unrelated business income tax, discussed below, and without losing its tax exemption. [Treas. Reg. § 1.501(c)(3)-1(e)(1)] A Section 501(c)(3) organization may even operate a substantial portion of its business for profit if the profit-making activities are in furtherance of the organization's exempt purposes and the organization is not organized for the *primary purpose* of carrying on an *unrelated trade or business* (see Q 2:38). [Treas. Reg. § 1.501(c)(3)-1(e)(1)]

If the organization is organized for the *primary purpose* of carrying on an unrelated trade or business, the IRS may revoke the organization's tax exemption under Code Section 501(c)(3). [Treas. Reg. § 1.501(c)(3)-1(e)(1)] For purposes of the *primary purpose* analysis, the IRS considers all the facts and circumstances surrounding the profit-making activities, including the size and extent of the organization's activities. [Treas. Reg. § 1.501(c)(3)-1(e)(1)]

Q 2:38   What is an *unrelated trade or business*?

An *unrelated trade or business* is "any trade or business the conduct of which is not substantially related" to the exercise or performance of the organization's exempt functions. [I.R.C. § 513(a)] An activity that shares the following three characteristics will constitute an unrelated trade or business:

1. The activity is a "trade or business";
2. The trade or business is regularly carried on by the organization; and
3. The conduct of the trade or business is not substantially related to the performance of the organization's exempt functions.

[Treas. Reg. § 1.513-1(a)]

For purposes of Code Section 513 of the Code, a "trade or business" is generally defined as "any activity carried on for the production of income from the sale of goods or performance of services." [Treas. Reg. § 1.513-1(b)] An activity is "regularly carried on" if it is undertaken with the frequency and continuity of, and in a manner similar to, comparable commercial activities of a nonexempt entity. [Treas. Reg. § 1.513-1(c)(1)] Finally, an activity is "substantially related" to an organization's exempt functions only if there is a substantial causal relationship between the performance of the activity and the achievement of the organization's exempt purpose, other than simply through the production of income. [Treas. Reg. § 1.513-1(d)(2)]

Q 2:39   What is *UBIT*?

The *unrelated business income tax* (*UBIT*) is the tax an exempt organization must pay on income generated through unrelated trades or businesses, often referred to as an organization's unrelated business taxable income (UBTI). UBTI is computed by excluding certain types of investment and other income, enumerated in Code Section 512(b), from the organization's gross income from unrelated trades or businesses and deducting those expenses and other items related to the production of the unrelated income. [I.R.C. § 512(a)(1)] Section 501(c)(3) corporations that have UBTI will be taxed at the regular corporate rates set forth in Code Section 11. [I.R.C. § 511(a)] For this purpose, the IRS will treat an unincorporated association as a corporation. [Treas. Reg. §§ 301.7701-2(a), 301.7701-2(b)] Section 501(c)(3) trusts will be taxed like taxable trusts. [I.R.C. § 511(b); Sherwin-Williams Co., Employee Health Plan Trust v. United States, 403 F.3d 793 (6th Cir. 2005)]

Q 2:40   How much unrelated business income is too much?

A Section 501(c)(3) organization that derives too large a portion of its income through unrelated trades or businesses may lose its exemption if the IRS finds that the organization is organized or operated for the "primary purpose" of carrying on an unrelated trade or business. [Treas. Reg. § 1.501(c)(3)-1(e)(1)]

It is unclear how much unrelated business income an organization may earn before it risks losing its exemption. To determine whether a Section 501(c)(3) organization derives excessive income from unrelated trades or businesses, the IRS generally considers whether the organization's charitable activities are "commensurate in scope with its financial resources." [*See* Rev. Rul. 64-182, 1964-1 (Part I) C.B. 186] Unfortunately, there are no categorical rules or percentage limitations that an organization can use to determine whether it passes the "commensurate" test.

Q 2:41   What is *unrelated debt-financed income*?

Under Code Section 514(a)(1), an exempt organization's income from debt-financed property is generally subject to UBIT in the proportion to which the property is financed by debt. [I.R.C. § 514(a)(1)] Debt-financed property is defined as any property held to produce income with respect to which there is *acquisition indebtedness* (e.g., a mortgage) at any time during the taxable year. [I.R.C. §§ 514(b)(1)(A), 514(b)(1)(B)] Exceptions include property used for purposes substantially related to the organization's exempt purposes and property the income from which is already taxable as unrelated business income. [I.R.C. § 514(b)(1)]

Q 2:42   If an organization must pay UBIT, what tax return must be filed?

Every Section 501(c)(3) organization that receives $1,000 or more of gross income from unrelated trades or businesses in a given year must file Form 990-T, "Exempt Organization Business Income Tax Return," with the IRS. [I.R.C. § 6012(a)(2)] The form must be filed by the fifteenth day of the fifth month following the close of the organization's fiscal year. [I.R.C. § 6072(e); IRS Pub. 598] As discussed in Q 2:44, Section 501(c)(3) organizations that file Form 990-T after August 17, 2006 are required to make that Form 990-T available for public inspection. [I.R.C. § 6104(d)(1)(A)(ii)]

For more information regarding unrelated business income, see http://www. stayexempt.org.

Recordkeeping and Disclosure Requirements

Q 2:43   What recordkeeping requirements are imposed on a Section 501(c)(3) organization?

Pursuant to Code Section 6104(d), Section 501(c)(3) organizations are required to maintain copies of their applications for exemption indefinitely and copies of their annual information returns filed with the IRS for each of the previous three years. [I.R.C. § 6104(d)] Such copies must be retained at the organization's principal office and at certain regional or district offices with three or more employees. [I.R.C. § 6104(d)(1)(A)]

Q 2:44   What public disclosure requirements apply to Section 501(c)(3) organizations?

An organization exempt from tax under Code Section 501(c)(3) is required to make available for public inspection copies of its application for exemption and its annual information returns filed with the IRS for each of the previous three years. [I.R.C. § 6104(d)] Such an organization is also required to provide copies of these documents to persons who request them either in person or in writing. [I.R.C. § 6104(d)(1)(B)] An organization may charge a "reasonable fee" for any copies provided. [I.R.C. § 6104(d)(1)(B)]

A Section 501(c)(3) organization is not required to provide the copies described above, however, if the documents are "widely available" or if the request for copies is deemed by the IRS to be made as part of a "harassment campaign" targeted at the organization. [I.R.C. § 6104(d)(4)] An organization that posts copies of its applications for exemption and annual information returns on an appropriate World Wide Web page likely will satisfy the "widely available" requirement. [*See* Treas. Reg. § 301.6104(d)-3(b)]

For more information on required disclosures and public inspection rules, see http://www.stayexempt.org.

Q 2:45   What excise penalties apply to Section 501(c)(3) organizations that become parties to prohibited tax-shelter transactions?

New Section 4965, added to the Code by TIPRA, imposes penalty excise taxes on certain tax-exempt entities that are parties to "prohibited tax-shelter transactions" and also adopts new disclosure requirements. These penalties apply without regard to whether the entity is aware that it is participating in a prohibited tax-shelter transaction. Entities that may be affected by the new provisions include, but are not limited to, charities, churches, state and local governments, Indian tribal governments, qualified pension plans, individual retirement accounts, and similar tax-favored savings arrangements. Managers of these entities that knowingly approve the entity's participation in a prohibited tax-shelter transaction may also be subject to $20,000 in excise taxes for each approval or other act causing the entity to be a party to the prohibited tax-shelter transaction.

On July 6, 2007, the IRS issued proposed regulations providing guidance under Code Section 4965. [72 Fed. Reg. 36,927 (July 6, 2007)] The proposed regulations define *tax-exempt party to a prohibited tax shelter* as an entity that: (1) facilitates a prohibited tax shelter transaction by reason of its tax-exempt, tax-indifferent or tax-favored status; (2) enters into a listed transaction and the tax-exempt entity's tax return (whether an original or an amended return) reflects a reduction or elimination of its liability for applicable federal employment, excise or unrelated business income taxes that is derived directly or indirectly from tax consequences or tax strategy described in the published guidance that lists the transaction; or (3) is identified in published guidance, by type, class or role, as a party to a prohibited tax shelter transaction. [Prop. Treas. Reg. § 53.4965-4] Prohibited tax-shelter transactions include: (1) *listed* transactions and (2) prohibited *reportable* transactions. [*See* Prop. Treas. Reg. § 53.4965-3]

Q 2:46 What disclosure requirements apply to Section 501(c)(3) organizations that become parties to prohibited tax-shelter transaction?

TIPRA amended Code Section 6033 by adding new disclosure requirements for tax-exempt entities that are parties to prohibited tax-shelter transaction. Under Code Section 6033, a tax-exempt entity that is a party to a prohibited tax-shelter transaction is required to disclose, to the IRS, that it is a party to a prohibited tax-shelter transaction and the identity of any other party to the transaction of which it has knowledge. [I.R.C. § 6033(a)(2)] TIPRA also amended Code Section 6652(c) to impose a $100 per day penalty for each failure by a tax-exempt entity to file the required disclosure under Code Section 6033(a)(2). Under new Code Section 6652(c)(3)(A), the amount of the penalty is $100 for each day during which the tax-exempt organization's failure continues, not to exceed $50,000 with respect to any one disclosure. [I.R.C. § 6652(c)(3)(A)] The IRS issued temporary regulations under Code Section 6033 to provide further guidance on that section's disclosure requirements. [*See* 72 Fed. Reg. 36,871 (July 6, 2007)]

Chapter 3

Contribution Limits

Janet M. Anderson-Briggs, Esq.

In 1958, Congress enacted Code Section 403(b)(2), setting the first of the annual limits on the maximum amounts that could be excluded from taxable income under a Section 403(b) tax-deferred annuity. In 1974, Congress enacted the Employee Retirement Income Security Act (ERISA), imposing additional limits under Code Section 415(c). The Tax Reform Act of 1986 (TRA '86) added a third limit, governing salary reduction contributions. The Economic Growth and Tax Relief Reconciliation Act of 2001 (EGTRRA) repealed the Section 403(b)(2) maximum exclusion allowance, the Section 415(c)(4)(A), (B), and (C) alternative catch-up limits, and added a new catch-up limit under Code Section 414(v). This chapter has been revised to reflect the EGTRRA changes and those of the Pension Protection Act of 2006 (PPA). Finally, this chapter has also been revised for the changes reflected in the final Code Sections 403(b) and 415 regulations.

Overview of Section 403(b) Contribution Limits

Q 3:1   What is the effect of the repeal of the Code Section 403(b)(2) maximum exclusion allowance under the Economic Growth and Tax Relief Reconciliation Act of 2001?

The Economic Growth and Tax Relief Reconciliation Act of 2001 ("EGTRRA") repealed the maximum exclusion allowance under Code Section 403(b)(2) for contributions and deferrals made to a 403(b) program beginning January 1, 2002. The Code Section 415(c) limit replaced the exclusion allowance in Code Section 403(b)(1), but compensation under the Code Section 415(c) limit will be determined under the Code Section 403(b)(3) definition of includible compensation instead of the definition of compensation under Code Section 415(c). The repeal of the maximum exclusion allowance under EGTRRA was scheduled to expire in 2010, but the Pension Protection Act of 2006 (PPA) made this repeal permanent. [EGTRRA, Pub. L. No. 107-16, §§ 632(a)(2)(B) and 632(a)(3)(D), 115 Stat. 38 (2001); PPA, Pub. L. No. 109-280, § 811 (2006)]

Q 3:2   What limits govern contributions to a Section 403(b) tax-deferred annuity program?

Contributions to a Section 403(b) tax-deferred annuity program are subject to three different limits. These limits are prescribed under Code Sections 415(c), 402(g), and 414(v). [EGTRRA, Pub. L. No. 107-16, §§ 632(a)(2)(B) and 631, 115 Stat. 38 (2001)]

Q 3:3   Are these limits imposed on a calendar-year basis or on a plan-year basis?

Generally, all of these limits are on a calendar-year, not a plan-year, basis. If the individual on whose behalf the Section 403(b) annuity is being purchased does not "own or control" an outside employer, as defined under Code Sections 414(b), 414(c), and 415(h), the Section 415(c) limitation year is the calendar year. [Treas. Reg. §§ 1.415-2(b)(7)(i), 1.415-2(b)(7)(ii)] If the individual does "own or control" an outside employer, the Section 415(c) limitation year is the same limitation year as that used by the outside employer. [Treas. Reg. § 1.415-2(b)(7)(iii)] Notwithstanding this, participants may elect to change the Section 415(c) limitation year to another 12-month period by attaching a statement to their income tax return filed for the taxable year in which the change was made. [Treas. Reg. § 1.415-2(b)(7)(ii)] However, most contribution limit calculations for a Section 403(b) program remain on a calendar-year basis so that all contribution limits are consistent.

Q 3:4   How are contributions made to a 403(b) tax-deferred annuity contract?

All amounts contributed to a Section 403(b) tax-deferred annuity contract are considered to be made by the employer for the employee. These contributions can be made either as an employer contribution (i.e., actually from the employer without a reduction in employee salary), as a result of a salary reduction agreement entered into by the employee, or as a designated Roth contribution that is treated as an elective deferral, but is not excludable from gross income. Regardless of the actual source of the contributions, employees may not exceed their maximum limits for any taxable year. Treasury Regulations Section 1.403(b)-4(c)(4) refers to the regulations under Code Section 402A for rules on determining whether an elective deferral is a pre-tax elective deferral or a designated Roth contribution. The Roth 403(b) features were enacted by EGTRRA and effective for plan years beginning on or after January 1, 2006. The addition of Roth 403(b) contributions was made permanent through the PPA. [PPA, Pub. L. No. 109-280, § 811 (2006)]

Q 3:5   What forms of contributions may be made to a Section 403(b) program?

Contributions to a Section 403(b) program may be made either as elective deferrals or as employer contributions that are classified as nonelective contributions or as matching contributions. For purposes of this chapter, all employer contributions other than elective deferrals are referred to as nonelective contributions. As noted in Q 3:4, designated Roth contributions may also be made by an employee, and these are treated as elective deferrals but are not excludable from gross income. Transfers and rollovers are not subject to the contribution limits.

Q 3:6   What is an elective deferral under a Section 403(b) program?

An elective deferral occurs when participants, through salary reduction agreements, elect to have an employer contribute compensation to a Section 403(b) program that would otherwise have been payable to them in cash in their paychecks. If a Section 403(b) retirement plan includes a qualified Roth contribution program, "any designated Roth contribution made by the employees pursuant to the program shall be treated as an elective deferral . . . , except that such contributions shall not be excludable from gross income." [I.R.C. §§ 402(g)(1), 402A(a)(1); Treas. Reg. § 1.402(g)-1(b)(3)] The salary reduction agreement must be legally binding and irrevocable with respect to the amounts earned while the agreement is in effect.

Q 3:7   Are non-salary reduction contributions counted against the Section 403(b) contribution limits?

Yes. All contributions made by the employer, whether an employer contribution or one made pursuant to a salary reduction agreement or made as a designated Roth contribution, must be counted against the Section 415(c) contribution limits. [I.R.C § 403(b)(1)]

Q 3:8   Are salary reduction contributions ever treated as nonelective contributions?

Yes. Under Code Section 402(g)(3) and Treasury Regulation Section 1.402(g)-1(c)(1), a Section 403(b) contribution is not treated as an elective deferral under a salary reduction agreement if the contribution is made pursuant to a one-time irrevocable election made by the employee at the time of initial eligibility to participate in the salary reduction agreement. However, beginning January 1, 2009, a Section 403(b) contribution is not treated as an elective deferral under a salary reduction agreement if the contribution is made pursuant to an employee's one-time irrevocable election made on or before the employee's first becoming eligible to participate under the employer's plans or a contribution made as a condition of employment that reduces the employee's compensation. However, if a participant has the right or ability to terminate or modify an election, the contributions are treated as elective deferrals even if the participant never exercises this right. Irrevocability relates to the election to participate rather than to terminate participation. A viable, one-time irrevocable election salary reduction contribution would not be subject to the Section 402(g)(1) elective deferral limit of $15,500 (for 2008) or the higher expanded limit under Code Section 402(g)(7). [H.R. Conf. Rep. No. 99-841, 99th Cong., 2d Sess., 405 (1986); Joint Committee on Taxation, General Explanation of the Tax Reform Act of 1986, H.R. 3838, 99th Cong., Pub. L. No. 99-514, at 662 (May 4, 1987); EGTRRA, Pub. L. No. 107-16 §§ 611(d)(1) and (3), 115 Stat. 38 (2001); Treas. Reg. § 402(g)(3)-1(a) and (b)]

Q 3:9   Are nonelective contributions ever treated as elective deferrals?

Yes. If an employer nonelective contribution is deemed to be "individually negotiated," it will be subject to the elective deferral limits under Code Sections 402(g)(1) and 402(g)(7). In other words, if, on an individual basis, an employee negotiates with an employer to have the employer make a contribution for the employee in an effort to circumvent the Section 402(g) limit, then such contribution is treated as an elective deferral subject to the Section 402(g) limit. [I.R.C. §§ 402(g)(3)(C), 3121(a)(5)(D); H.R. Conf. Rep. No. 99-841, 99th Cong., 2d Sess., 405 (1986); H.R. Conf. Rep. No. 98-47, 98th Cong., 1st Sess., 147 (1983)]

Q 3:10   Are elective deferrals forfeitable?

No. Elective deferrals are 100 percent nonforfeitable (vested) immediately.

Section 415(c) Contribution Limits

Q 3:11   What is the Section 415(c) limit?

Code Section 415(c) provides that annual additions to defined contribution plans on behalf of a participant cannot exceed 100 percent of compensation up to $40,000 (which is indexed in $1,000 increments). A Section 403(b) annuity contract is treated as a defined contribution plan for purposes of the limit on contributions imposed by Code Section 415. A technical correction to EGTRRA contained in the Job Creation and Worker Assistance Act of 2002 (JCWAA) clarified that the Section 415(c) limit applies to contributions in the year contributions are made without regard to vesting. [I.R.C. § 403(b)(6); Treas. Reg. § 1.403(b)-1(b)(2); EGTRRA, Pub. L. No. 107-16 §§ 632(a)(2)(A), 605, 115 Stat. 38 (2001); JCWAA, Pub. L. No. 107-147, § 411(p)(1), 116 Stat. 21 (2002)]

Q 3:12   What contribution sources comprise Section 415(c) annual additions?

Annual additions are the sum of:

1. Employer contributions;

2. Employee (after-tax) contributions; and

3. Forfeitures.

[I.R.C. § 415(c)(2); Treas. Reg. § 1.415(c)-1(b)(1)]

Q 3:13   Will the $40,000 limit on annual additions increase?

Yes. The $40,000 limit in Code Section 415(c)(1)(A) will be adjusted annually for increases in cost of living pursuant to regulations prescribed by the Secretary of the Treasury. The $40,000 limit will be indexed in increments of $1,000 (i.e., rounded down to the next lowest multiple of $1,000). The limit for 2008 is $46,000. [I.R.C. § 415(d); Treas. Reg. § 1.415(d)-1(b); Uruguay Round Agreements Act, Pub. L. No. 103-465, § 732, 108 Stat. 4809 (1994); EGTRRA, Pub. L. No. 107-16 §§ 611(b)(1) and (2)]

Q 3:14   Are Roth 403(b) contributions subject to the Section 415(c) limits?

There is no Code section specifically applying Code Section 415(c) to Roth 403(b) contributions. However, since Roth 403(b) contributions are treated as elective deferrals under Code Section 402(g)(1), which are treated as "employer contributions," and there is no specific exception for Roth 403(b) contributions under the "annual additions" definition in Code Section 415(c) (as there is for age-50+ catch-up contributions), this author believes the Section 415(c) limits apply to Roth 403(b) contributions that are treated as elective deferrals under Code Section 402(g)(1). [I.R.C. § 402(g)(1); Treas. Reg. § 1.415(c)-1(b)]

Includible Compensation

Q 3:15   How is compensation defined under Code Section 415(c) for Section 403(b) plans?

Compensation is to be determined under the Code Section 403(b)(3) definition of includible compensation. [EGTRRA, Pub. L. No. 107-16 §§ 611(b)(1) and (2) and 632(a)(3)(D), 115 Stat. 38 (2001); I.R.C. § 415(c)(3)(E); Treas. Reg. § 1.415(c)-2(g)(1)]

Q 3:16   How is *includible compensation* defined under Code Section 403(b)(3)?

Generally, *includible compensation* is the amount of compensation received from the employer currently sponsoring the Section 403(b) program that is includible in the employee's gross income for the most recent period that may be counted as one year of service. Includible compensation does not include (1) any amount contributed directly by the employer (non-salary reduction) to any Section 403(b) annuity contract, or (2) any amount that is made through a salary reduction agreement but treated as a nonelective contribution to any Section 403(b) annuity contract. [Taxpayer Relief Act of 1997, Pub. L. No. 105-34, § 1504(a), 111 Stat. 1063 (1997); I.R.C. § 403(b)(3); Treas. Reg. § 1.403(b)-2(b)(11)]

Q 3:17   Is includible compensation calculated on a calendar-year basis?

Yes. In most cases, includible compensation is calculated on a calendar-year basis. If an employee's includible compensation has been, or is reasonably anticipated to be, increased or decreased during the current year, includible compensation should properly reflect the increase or decrease. [Treas. Reg. § 1.403(b)-2(b)(11)]

Q 3:18   How is includible compensation determined for a part-time or retiring employee?

Since includible compensation is determined for the employee's last full year of service, in the case of part-time employees and employees who retire during a calendar year, includible compensation must include amounts received over two or more calendar years.

To determine includible compensation for the last full year of service of a part-time or retiring employee, a participant may go back into the previous year or years of service to make up one full year of service, and includible compensation for purposes of contribution limit should reflect the includible compensation for that last full year of service.

Beginning January 1, 2002, includible compensation excludes any amount received by a former employee after the fifth year in which the employee terminated employment. This means that Section 403(b) contributions can be made for an employee for up to five years after employment is terminated, based upon includible compensation for the last year of service before retirement. For purposes of applying the Code Section 415(c) limit, a former employee is deemed to have monthly includible compensation for the period through the end of the taxable year of the employee in which he or she ceases to be an employee and through the end of each of the next five taxable years. The amount of the monthly includible compensation is equal to one twelfth of the former employee's includible compensation during the former employee's most recent year of service. Accordingly, nonelective employer contributions for a former employee must not exceed the limitation of Code Section 415(c)(1) up to the lesser of the dollar amount in Code Section 415(c)(1)(A) and the former employee's annual includible compensation based on the former employee's average monthly compensation during his or her most recent one year of service. If a former employee dies during the first five years after termination, the contributions must stop. [Technical Amendments Act of 1958, Small Business Tax Revision Act of 1958, Pub. L. No. 85-866, U.S. Code Cong. & Admin. News (72 Stat.) 4939, 4940; EGTRRA, Pub. L. No. 107-16, § 632(a)(2)(C), 115 Stat. 38 (2001); JCWAA, Pub. L. No. 107-147, § 411(p)(2), 116 Stat. 21 (2002); I.R.C. § 403(b)(3); Treas. Reg. §§ 1.403(b)-4(d)((1) & (2)]

Q 3:19   Are salary reduction amounts included in includible compensation?

Yes. Includible compensation includes any elective deferrals or other amount contributed or deferred by the eligible employers at the election of the employee that would be includible in gross income of the employee but for the rules of Code Sections 125, 132(f)(4), 402(e)(2), 402(h)(1)(B), 402(k), or 457(b). The amount of includible compensation is determined without regard to community property laws. Code Section 414(h) employer "picked-up" contributions under a government pension system, or Code Section 457(f) contributions made on a salary reduction basis, are excluded from includible compensation. Non-salary reduction contributions (such as nonelective basic or matching contributions) are never included in includible compensation. [Taxpayer Relief Act of 1997, Pub. L. No. 105-34, § 1504(a), 111 Stat. 1063 (1997); I.R.C. § 403(b)(3); Rev. Rul. 79-221, 1979-2 C.B. 188; Treas. Reg. § 1.403(b)-2(b)(11)]

Q 3:20   Does includible compensation include nontaxable benefits?

No. Includible compensation does not include nontaxable benefits, such as a minister's tax-free parsonage allowance. [Ltr. Rul. 200135045; Treas. Reg. § 1.415(c)-2(c)]

Q 3:21   May certain payments paid after severance from employment be included in includible compensation?

Separating employees often receive payments of bonuses, accumulated unused sick or vacation pay, or taxable payments of nonqualified deferred compensation. Participants are permitted to defer such amounts under a Section 403(b) plan if (1) the payments would have to be paid to the employee had the employee continued to work; (2) the payments are made within a limited period after severance from employment (within 2½ months after severance from employment); and (3) the deferral election is made before the amounts are paid. Deferral during this limited period applies to regular pay (i.e., salary, bonuses, overtime, commissions), unused sick, vacation or other leave, or taxable payments due under nonqualified deferred compensation plans. However, these amounts must meet the three criteria for deferral outlined above. Severance from employment means the date on which an employee ceases to be employed by the employer maintaining the plan. [Treas. Reg. § 1.415(c)-2(e)(3)]

> **Example.** Jane Doe terminates employment on December 31, 2007. Her accumulated sick leave, totaling $15,000, is payable on March 15, 2008, unless deferred under her employer's Section 403(b) plan. On January 31, 2008, Jane elects to defer all of the sick pay to the Section 403(b) plan. The deferral election is valid because (1) she would have been able to use the sick leave if employment had continued, (2) the sick pay was payable within 2½ months after the last day of work, and (3) Jane's election was made before the sick pay was payable to her. Jane's includible compensation for 2008 includes the $15,000 payable for the accrued sick pay.

Q 3:22   Is sabbatical pay treated as part of includible compensation?

Yes. University employees are commonly provided paid sabbatical leaves for research or other purposes. Employees who receive full pay while on sabbatical may treat this as a full year's worth of includible compensation. Employees who receive half pay (or any other fraction of full pay) while on sabbatical would treat it as includible compensation during the last full year of service.

Q 3:23   May a self-employed minister's earned income be included in includible compensation?

Yes. Since January 1, 1997, a self-employed minister is considered a church employee, and the minister's earned income (as defined under Code Section 401(c)(2)) from the ministry rather than the amount of compensation received from an employer is his or her includible compensation under Code Section 403(b)(3). Includible compensation for a minister who is self-employed means the minister's earned income as defined in Code Section 401(c)(2) (computed without regard to Code Section 911) for the most recent period that is a year of service. [Small Business Job Protection Act of 1996, Pub. L. No. 104-188, § 1461, 110 Stat. 1755 (1996); Treas. Reg. § 1.403(b)-2(b)(11)]

Q 3:24   May certain salary continuation payments be includible in an employee's includible compensation?

Yes. Salary continuation payments to an individual in qualified military service may be included in includible compensation if the plan provides, but only to the extent they do not exceed the amount that would otherwise have been paid as compensation. Salary continuation payments to a participant who is totally disabled may be included in includible compensation if the plan so provides. A plan may limit this availability to participants who were not highly compensated before they became disabled. However, a plan may provide this right to all totally disabled participants, but only if the salary continuation is provided to all such participants for a fixed or determinable period. [Treas. Reg. § 1.415(c)(2)(e)(4)]

Q 3:25   How are Section 403(b) plans treated for purposes of combining and aggregating plans under Code Section 415?

Although under the general rule governing Section 415(c) defined contribution plans, all defined contribution plans maintained by the employer (and employers under common control) are treated as one defined contribution plan subject to the Section 415(c) limit, the participant under a Section 403(b) annuity contract—not the actual employer—is deemed to maintain the Section 403(b) contract, regardless of the form of contributions (nonelective or salary reduction) or degree of actual control maintained by the employer. Thus, if the actual employer maintains a Section 401(a) or 403(a) qualified plan, the Section 415(c) limit is determined separately for the Section 403(b) contract, and another Section 415(c) limit applies to the Section 401(a) or 403(a) defined contribution plan. Consequently, it is conceivable, although unlikely, that employer contributions of up to $40,000 (indexed) (not through salary reduction) could be made on behalf of a participant to the Section 403(b) plan and the employer could contribute up to an additional $40,000 (indexed) to the Section 401(a) or 403(a) plan. This provision was codified by EGTRRA and made permanent through the PPA. [I.R.C. § 415(k)(4); Treas. Reg. § 1.415(f)-1(f)(1); EGTRRA, Pub. L. No. 107-16, § 632(b)(1) (2001); PPA, Pub. L. No. 109-280, § 811 (2006)]

Q 3:26   How is the Section 415(c) limit applied if the participant is deemed to maintain the plan of another employer?

If a Section 403(b) participant controls another business that maintains another Section 403(b) contract or a qualified plan, the Section 403(b) annuity contract is treated as a defined contribution plan maintained by both the employer that purchased the annuity contract and the participant on whose behalf it was purchased. For example, if the participant maintains a Section 401(a) or 403(a) Keogh plan with respect to self-employment income, or if he or she participates in a Section 401(a) or 403(a) plan of a partnership or corporation in which the participant has a more than 50 percent ownership interest, the aggregation rules will apply. The aggregation rules will also apply if the participant has a Section 403(b) contract through another employer. If a Section 403(b) annuity contract is aggregated with a qualified plan of a controlled employer in accordance with the requirements of Treasury Regulations Section 1.415(f)-1(f)(2), then in applying the limitations of Code Section 415(c) in connection with the aggregation of the Section 403(b) annuity with a qualified plan, the total compensation from both employers is permitted to be taken into account. [Treas. Reg. §§ 1.415(c)-2(g)(3), 1.415(f)-1(f)(2) and (3)]

Q 3:27   What is the special alternative limit under Code Section 415(c)(7) for church employees?

An alternative Section 415(c) limit is available to church employees of an organization as defined in Q 3:28. The alternative limit for such a church employee who elects it is the lesser of $10,000 and the Section 415(c) annual additions limit. This alternative church limit is subject to the Section 402(g) limit if contributions are based on elective deferrals and the maximum lifetime limit on this special church limit is $40,000. Of course, any church employee whose Section 415(c) limit for the year otherwise exceeds $10,000 would have no reason to use this special limit. This provision was made permanent through the PPA. [I.R.C. § 415(c)(7); PPA, Pub. L. No. 109-280, § 811 (2006)]

Q 3:28   What is the definition of a church for purposes of the special alternative limit under Code Section 415(c)(7)?

A church organization must be a Section 501(c)(3) organization, which is one of the following:

1. A church;
2. A convention or association of churches;
3. An organization (whether a civil law corporation or otherwise) whose principal purpose or function is the administration or funding of a plan or program for the provision of retirement benefits or welfare benefits, or both, for employees of (1) and (2) above, if such organization is controlled or associated with either (1) or (2). This organization must share common religious bonds and convictions with (1) and (2); or
4. An elementary or secondary school that is controlled, operated, or principally supported by (1) or (2) above.

Section 402(g) Contribution Limits

Q 3:29   What is the Section 402(g) limit?

Code Section 402(g)(3)(C) and Treasury Regulations Section 1.402(g)-1(b)(3) define a Section 403(b) elective deferral as an employer contribution to a Section 403(b) program made under a salary reduction agreement (within the meaning of Code Section 3121(a)(5)(D)).

Beginning January 1, 2002, the Section 402(g)(1)(B) limit is increased each year as follows:

Year	Deferral Amount
2002	$11,000
2003	$12,000
2004	$13,000
2005	$14,000
2006	$15,000

Thereafter, the deferral limit will be indexed in $500 increments. The limit for 2008 is $15,500. This was made permanent through the PPA. [EGTRRA, Pub. L. No. 107-16, § 611(d)(1), (2), and (3), 115 Stat. 38 (2001); PPA, Pub. L. No. 109-280, § 811 (2006)] Code Section 402(g)(7) and Treasury Regulations Section 1.402(g)-1(d)(2) increase this $15,500 amount (for 2008) for employees (with at least 15 years of service with the current employer) of qualified organizations by no more than an extra $3,000 per taxable year, for a maximum of $20,500 (for 2008).

Q 3:30 Are designated Roth contributions to a Section 403(b) (or 401(k)) plan treated as elective deferrals under Code Section 402(g)?

Yes. If an applicable retirement plan includes a qualified Roth contribution program, "any designated Roth contribution made by an employee pursuant to the program shall be treated as an elective deferral . . . , except that such contribution shall not be excludable from gross income. . . ." [I.R.C. § 402A(a)(1)]

Q 3:31 Are nonelective contributions subject to the elective deferral limit under Code Section 402(g)?

Generally, nonelective contributions are not subject to the Section 402(g) limitation governing Section 403(b) elective deferrals, unless the exception (as discussed in Q 3:9) applies.

Q 3:32 What is the 15-year cap expansion under Code Section 402(g)(7)?

wrong!

Under Code Section 402(g)(7), the "15-year cap expansion" option allows a participant to make elective deferrals of up to $20,500 (for 2008) if certain conditions are met. Generally, employees who have completed at least 15 years of service with the current qualifying employer purchasing the Section 403(b) annuity contract may increase the $15,500 limit (for 2008) by the least of (1) $3,000; (2) $15,000, reduced by amounts not included in gross income for prior taxable years by reason of this cap expansion option, plus the aggregate amount of designated Roth contributions (as defined in Code Section 402A(c)) or (3) $5,000 multiplied by years of service, minus all amounts of prior years' contributions that were due to prior elective deferrals. The IRS has indicated that the breadth of the language which requires the aggregate amount of designated Roth contributions for prior taxable years to be subtracted from the $15,000 is in error and will be corrected through a technical correction to the Gulf Opportunities Zone Act of 2005. [GOZA, Pub. L. No. 109-135, § 407(a)(1); I.R.C. § 402(g)(7); Treas. Reg. § 1.403(b)-4(c)(3)] Treasury Regulations Section 1.403(b)-4(c)(5) contains numerous examples outlining the proper use of the catch-up rules under Code Sections 402(g)(7) and 414(v).

Q 3:33   Who is eligible to use the 15-year cap expansion?

Employees of qualified employers that are defined as tax-exempt educational institutions, hospitals, home health service agencies, certain churches, and health and welfare organizations are eligible to use the 15-year cap expansion. In other words, those participants with at least 15 years of service with their current qualified employers, who may have used the special alternative limits under Code Section 415(c)(4) as they were in effect before they were repealed by EGTRRA, may use the 15-year cap expansion. The years of service with the current employer do not have to be consecutive, but they must all have been with this current employer and not with multiple Section 403(b) eligible employers. [I.R.C. § 402(g)(7); Treas. Reg. §§ 1.403(b)-4(c)(3)(i), (ii) & (iii)]

Q 3:34   Is there a lifetime limitation on the use of the 15-year cap expansion?

Yes. The 15-year cap expansion provision contains a $15,000 lifetime limit. In other words, no more than $15,000 of the cap expansion amount may be used by any participant (regardless of Section 403(b) employer) for 1987 or any later year. Participants who exhaust their $15,000 limit may never use the 15-year cap expansion again; their limit then will be $10,500 for 2001, $11,000 for 2002, $12,000 for 2003, $13,000 for 2004, $14,000 for 2005, $15,000 for 2006, and indexed thereafter. [I.R.C. § 402(g)(7)(A)(ii); Treas. Reg. § 1.403(b)-4(c)(3)(i)]

Q 3:35   May a participant contribute elective deferrals up to the Section 402(g) limit and ignore the Section 415(c) limit?

No. In no event may the maximum elective deferral exceed the lesser of the Section 402(g)(1) or 402(g)(7) limits or the limit under Section 415(c).

Years of Service

Q 3:36 How are years of service defined under Code Section 403(b) for purposes of includible compensation and the Section 402(g)(7)(A)(iii) limit?

For purposes of determining includible compensation and years of service under the Code Section 402(g)(7) catch-up rule, in determining years of service, one should include the following:

- One year for each full year during which an individual was a full-time employee of the organization purchasing the annuity for the individual;
- A fraction of a year for each full year during which such individual was a part-time employee of the organization; and
- A fraction of a year for each part of a year during which such individual was a full-time or part-time employee of the organization.

[I.R.C. §§ 403(b)(3) and (4); Treas. Reg. §§ 1.403(b)-2(11), 1.403(b)-4(e)]

Q 3:37 How are years of service determined for an employee under Code Section 403(b) for purposes of includible compensation and the Section 402(g)(7)(A)(iii) limit?

An employee's total number of years of service for the employer is determined as of the close of the taxable year. [Treas. Reg. § 1.403(b)-1(f)(1)]

Q 3:38 In determining years of service, may an employee have less than one year of service?

No. The number of years of service for an employee shall never be counted as less than one year of service. [I.R.C. § 403(b)(4); Treas. Reg. § 1.403(b)-1(e)(8)]

Q 3:39 How is a full year of service determined?

To determine a full year of service, the employer's annual work period, and not the employee's taxable year, is used as the standard of measurement. Each annual work period during which an individual is employed full time by the eligible employer shall be considered one year of service. In considering whether an employee is employed full time, the amount of work that the employee is required to perform shall be compared with the amount of work that is normally required of individuals who hold the same position with the same employer and who generally derive the major portion of their annual compensation from such position. However, in no case may an employee accumulate more than one year of service in a 12-month period. [Treas. Reg. § 1.403(b)-4(e)(2)]

Q 3:40   How are fractional years determined under years of service?

Fractional years should be calculated as the number of weeks or months of service divided by the number of weeks or months in the employer's annual work period. For example, if an employer's annual work period is 10 months (August to May), and an employee is employed for the spring semester only (January 1 to May 31), the employee has one-half year of service. [Treas. Reg. § 1.403(b)-4(e)(5)]

Q 3:41   How are years of service determined for church employees?

All years of service by a duly ordained, commissioned, or licensed minister of a church or a layperson who is an employee of a church or a convention or association of churches shall be considered as years of service for one employer. All amounts that are contributed for annuity contracts by such a church during these years for a minister or layperson shall be considered to have been contributed by one employer. However, any period during which an individual is not an employee of a church-related organization or is an employee of a church-related organization that does not have an association with that eligible employer is not counted as years of service for this aggregated purpose. [JCWAA, Pub. L. No. 107-147, § 411(p)(4), 116 Stat. 21 (2002); Treas. Reg. § 1.403(b)-4(e)(3)(ii)]

Q 3:42   May a self-employed minister's years of self-employment be included in years of service?

Yes. Since January 1, 1997, under Code Section 414(e)(5)(B), years of service for purposes of Code Section 403(b)(4) for a self-employed minister are those years (or portions of years) in which he or she was a self-employed individual (within the meaning of Code Section 401(c)(1)(B). [Small Business Job Protection Act of 1996, Pub. L. No. 104-188, § 1461, 110 Stat. 1755 (1996)]

Q 3:43   What are some examples of different time periods employees might work?

The following are examples of how years of service would be computed:

Example 1. Janet Jones works full time for the Oshkosh school district. She ordinarily works 10 months of the year and therefore will receive one year of service for every 10-month period that she works full time.

Example 2. Jack Pollack teaches art full time in the fall semester each year. Since he works only five months of the above 10-month year, he will receive only one-half year of service for every year that he works.

Example 3. Glenda Gould teaches three music appreciation classes each day. Although she works 10 months of the year, she works only half a day each day and therefore will receive only one-half year of service for every year that she works.

Example 4. Bill Buckley teaches two speech classes and coaches the debating team each spring semester. He works only five months of the 10-month year, and only half a day each day. Bill therefore will receive one-quarter year of service for every year that he works.

Q 3:44   Which entity is the eligible employer for determining years of service?

An eligible employer is defined as:

(A) A State, but only with respect to an employee of the State performing services for a public school;

(B) A Section 501(c) organization with respect to any employee of the Section 501(c)(3) organization;

(C) Any employer of a minister described in Code Section 414(e)(5)(A), but only with respect to the minister; or

(D) A minister described in Code Section 414(e)(5)(A), but only with respect to the retirement income account established for that minister.

> An entity is not an eligible employer under (A) above if it treats itself as not being a State for any other purpose of the Internal Revenue Code, and a subsidiary or other affiliate of an eligible employer is not an eligible employer under (A-D) above if the subsidiary or other affiliate is not an entity described in (A-D) above.

[Treas. Reg. § 1.403(b)-2(b)(8)(i) and (ii)]

Q 3:45   How are an employee's years of service counted if the employer merges or consolidates with another employer?

If an employer is absorbed by or consolidated with another employer and the employee continues performing essentially the same services for the "successor" employer, years of service include years with both the predecessor and the successor organizations provided the employee did not have any severance from service in connection with the acquisition. Of course, years of service with an employer that is ineligible to sponsor a Section 403(b) program may not be included as years of service for Section 403(b) purposes. This is true even if the employee has always been employed by the same employer and that employer subsequently becomes ineligible to sponsor a Section 403(b) program. [Ltr. Rul. 7739065 (June 30, 1977); Treas. Reg. § 1.403(b)-4(c)(5), Example 5]

Q 3:46   How are years of service determined for an employee who is receiving sabbatical pay?

If it is part of the normal work pattern for employees to go on sabbatical and to receive full pay while on sabbatical, the employee is considered to be earning a regular, full year of service. If the employee receives half pay (or any other fraction of full pay), the employee would be considered to be earning a fractional year of service.

Q 3:47   What is the special minimum exclusion allowance available to church employees?

Employees of churches, conventions or associations of churches, or church-controlled organizations who earn an adjusted gross income equal to or less than $17,000 may exclude the lesser of (1) $3,000 and (2) the amount of compensation includible in gross income for the taxable year. EGTRRA repealed this rule beginning in 2002. However, the technical correction to EGTRRA, contained in the Job Creation and Worker Assistance Act of 2002, restored this rule for contributions of foreign missionaries beginning in 2002 as the lesser of $3,000 and the employee's includible compensation under Code Section 403(b)(3). [I.R.C. § 403(b)(2)(D); JCWAA, Pub. L. No. 107-147, § 411(p)(4), 116 Stat. 21 (2002)]

Q 3:48   For purposes of the Section 402(g)(7) limit, what is an *educational organization*?

For purposes of the Section 402(g)(7) limit, an *educational organization*, as described in Code Section 170(b)(1)(A)(ii), is one that normally maintains a regular faculty and curriculum and normally has a regularly enrolled body of pupils or students in attendance at the place where its educational activities are regularly carried on. [I.R.C. §§ 402(g)(7)(B), 170(b)(1)(A)(ii); Treas. Reg. § 1.403(b)-4(c)(3)(ii)]

Q 3:49   For purposes of the Section 402(g)(7) limit, what is a *home health service agency*?

A *home health service agency* is an organization described in Code Section 501(c)(3) that is exempt from tax under Code Section 501(a) and that has been determined by the Secretary of Health, Education, and Welfare to be a home health agency (as defined in Code Section 1861(o) of the Social Security Act). [I.R.C. § 402(g)(7)(B); Treas. Reg. §§ 1.403(b)-4(c)(3)(ii)(A) & (C)]

Q 3:50   For purposes of the Section 402(g)(7) limit, what is a *church or convention or association of churches*?

The terms *church* and *convention or association of churches* have the same meaning as those ascribed to them in Code Section 414(e)(3)(B)(ii) (see Q 3:28). [I.R.C. § 402(g)(7)(B); Treas. Reg. §§ 1.403(b)-4(c)(3)(ii)(A) & (B)]

Section 414(v) Catch-up Limit

Q 3:51   What is the Section 414(v) catch-up limit?

Beginning January 1, 2002, participants who are age 50 or more by the end of the plan year can contribute an additional deferral amount each year up to the amounts in the following table:

Year	Catch-up Amount
2002	$1,000
2003	$2,000
2004	$3,000
2005	$4,000
2006	$5,000

Thereafter, the catch-up limit will be indexed in $500 increments. The limit for 2008 is $5,000. This catch-up limit was made permanent through the PPA. [EGTRRA, Pub. L. No. 107-16, § 631(a), 115 Stat. 38 (2001); JCWAA, Pub. L. No. 107-147, § 411(o)(7), 116 Stat. 21 (2002); PPA, Pub. L. No. 109-280, § 811 (2006)]

Q 3:52   When is a participant eligible to use the age-50+ catch-up provision?

The participant must be at least age 50 during the plan year and must also first make elective deferrals up to the Section 402(g) limit or the plan-imposed limit, whichever applies. Such an employee is eligible to use the age 50 catch-up provision as of the beginning of the taxable year. The IRS has determined that a participant must exhaust the 15-year cap expansion (if eligible) before using the age-50+ catch-up. [EGTRRA, Pub. L. No. 107-16, § 631(a), 115 Stat. 38 (2001); Treas. Reg. § 1.403(b)-4(c)(3)(iv)] Treasury Regulations Section 1.403(b)-4(c)(5) contains numerous examples outlining the proper use of the catch-up rules.

Q 3:53   How does an employee who is participating in both a Section 403(b) program and a Section 401(k) plan in the same calendar year meet the Section 402(g) limit for eligibility to use the age-50+ catch-up?

An employee who is participating in both a Section 403(b) program and a Section 401(k) plan in the same calendar year can meet the Section 402(g) limit for eligibility to use the age-50+ catch-up by contributing to both plans up to the Section 402(g) limit. In other words, in 2008, a participant can contribute $8,500 to the Section 403(b) plan and $7,000 to the Section 401(k) plan, for a total of $15,500, to become eligible for the age-50+ catch-up. In such a situation, there is no guidance on whether the age-50+ catch-up amount should be made to the Section 401(k) plan or the Section 403(b) plan. However, the full amount cannot be made to both plans. [Treas. Reg. § 1.414(v)-1(g)]

Q 3:54   Can a participant take advantage of the 15-year cap expansion and the age-50+ catch-up in the same year?

Yes. Currently, a participant can use both the 15-year cap expansion and the age-50+ catch-up in the same year. The IRS has determined that a participant must exhaust the 15-year cap expansion (if eligible) before using the age-50+ catch-up. [Treas. Reg. § 1.403(b)-4(c)(3)(iv)]

Q 3:55   Are age-50+ catch-up contributions subject to the Section 415(c) limits?

No, age-50+ catch-up contributions are specifically exempted from the Section 415(c) limits and do not count against them when determining a participant's contribution limits. [I.R.C. § 414(v)(3)(A)(i); Treas. Reg. § 1.414(v)-1(d)]

Coordination of Deferrals and Contributions

Q 3:56   Must other elective deferrals be coordinated with Section 403(b) elective deferrals?

Yes. Code Section 402(g) applies to elective deferrals under Sections 401(k), 403(b), 402A designated Roth contributions to Sections 403(b) and 401(k) plans and Section 408(k)(6) salary reduction simplified employee pension plans (SARSEPs). Additionally, deferrals to a Section 501(c)(18) plan or a Section 7701(j) Federal Thrift Savings Plan must be coordinated with the Section 403(b) elective deferrals. Elective deferrals to Section 401(k) plans, SARSEPs, or Section 403(b) contracts may not exceed $15,500 for 2008) (or higher, under the Section 402(g)(7) limit for Section 403(b) plans).

The ability to establish Section 408(k)(6) SARSEPs was eliminated on January 1, 1997, but current plans were grandfathered. In general, savings incentive match plans for employees (SIMPLEs) have been enacted to take the place of SARSEPs. It appears that SIMPLE employee contributions made to a Section 401(k) plan may have to be coordinated with other elective deferrals under Code Section 402(g). [TRA 1986, Pub. L. No. 99-514, Title XI, § 1147(a), at 410 (Oct. 22, 1986); H.R. Conf. Rep. No. 99-841, 99th Cong., 2d Sess., at 497 (1986); General Explanation of the Tax Reform Act of 1986, H.R. 3838, 99th Cong., Pub. L. No. 99-514, at 776 (May 4, 1987); I.R.C. § 7701(j)(1)(A); Small

Business Job Protection Act of 1996, Pub. L. No. 104-188, § 1422, 110 Stat. 1755 (1996)]

Q 3:57   Will the Section 402(g)(1)(B) limit on Section 403(b) elective deferrals be subject to inflation indexing?

Yes. The Section 402(g)(1)(B) limit is indexed beginning after December 31, 2006. When indexed, Section 403(b) deferrals will be rounded down to the next lowest multiple of $500. [I.R.C. § 402(g)(4)]

Q 3:58   Are salary reduction contributions under a Section 125 cafeteria plan treated as elective deferrals under Code Section 402(g)?

No. Section 125 salary reduction contributions are not defined as elective deferrals under Code Section 402(g)(3). Consequently, Section 125 contributions do not count against the Section 402(g)(1) or 402(g)(7) limits governing Section 403(b) elective deferrals.

Q 3:59   Are Section 414(h) salary reduction picked-up contributions subject to the elective deferral limitations under Code Section 402(g)?

No. Section 414(h) salary reduction picked-up contributions are not defined as elective deferrals under Code Section 402(g)(3). Consequently, these contributions do not count against the Section 402(g)(1) or 402(g)(7) limits governing Section 403(b) elective deferrals.

Q 3:60   How are contributions to Section 403(b) and 457(b) plans coordinated?

A deferral to a Section 457(b) plan is not defined as an elective deferral under Code Section 402(g)(3). Consequently, it is not subtracted from the Section 403(b) elective deferral limit.

As of January 1, 2002, elective deferrals under Section 401(k) plans or Section 403(b) programs do not have to be coordinated with deferrals under Section 457(b) plans. For example, in 2008, a participant in a Section 403(b) program can make full deferrals of up to $15,500 to a Section 403(b) program and full deferrals of up to an additional $15,500 in a Section 457(b) plan. Since contributions to a Section 7701(j) Federal Thrift Savings Plan are treated as Section 401(k) deferrals, these Section 7701(j) contributions will no longer have to be coordinated with Section 457(b) deferrals. This provision was made permanent by the PPA. [EGTRRA, Pub. L. No. 107-16, § 615(a), 115 Stat. 38 (2001); PPA, Pub. L. No. 109-280, § 811 (2006)]

Q 3:61   How are age-50+ catch-up contributions coordinated between Section 403(b) and governmental 457(b) plans?

Age-50+ catch-up contributions do not have to be coordinated between Section 403(b) and governmental Section 457(b) plans. An employee who is eligible to make the age-50+ catch-up contributions may contribute the full amount in each plan. In 2008, that would mean $5,000 in age-50+ catch-up contributions to the Section 403(b) plan and another $5,000 in age-50+ catch-up contributions to the governmental Section 457(b) plan. [JCWAA, Pub. L. No. 107-147, § 411(o)(9), 116 Stat. 21 1(2002)]

Q 3:62   How is participation in multiple Section 403(b) annuity contracts or Section 403(b) investments treated for an employee of one employer?

Code Section 403(b)(5) and Treasury Regulations Section 1.403(b)-2(b)(16) state that if an employee has more than one annuity contract with an employer, these contracts are treated as one annuity contract. This means that all Section 403(b) contributions to other investment vehicles for the current year or prior years must be taken into account.

Q 3:63   How are contributions to multiple Section 403(b) employers treated under the Section 415(c) limit?

For Section 415(c) purposes, Section 403(b) contributions with all employers must be taken into account. Where this is done, compensation from all Section 403(b) employers is also taken into account for purposes of determining the Section 415(c)(1)(B) percentage limit.

Q 3:64   How are contributions to either multiple employers or one employer with multiple contracts treated under the Section 402(g) limit?

The Section 402(g) limit on Section 403(b) elective deferrals applies to the participant on a calendar-year basis, regardless of the employer or Section 403(b) provider. This means that all deferrals with all employers or Section 403(b) providers are subject to one Section 402(g) limit.

Correction of Excess Amounts

Q 3:65   What are excess contributions or deferrals?

Any contribution made for a participant to a Section 403(b) contract for the taxable year that either exceeds the Code Section 415(c) limit or the maximum annual Section 403(b) elective deferral limit constitutes an excess contribution that is includible in gross income of the participant for that taxable year. [Treas. Reg. § 1.403(b)-4(f)(1)]

Q 3:66   How are amounts that are in excess of the Section 415(c) contribution limits to be treated within a Section 403(b) annuity contract or custodial account?

A contract to which a contribution is made that exceeds the Code Section 415(c) annual additions limit is not a Section 403(b) contract unless the excess contribution is held in a separate account which constitutes a separate account for purposes of Code Section 72. If an excess annual addition is made to a Section 403(b) contract that otherwise satisfies the Section 403(b) requirements, then the portion of the contract that includes such excess annual addition fails to be a Section 403(b) contract and the remaining portion of the contract is a Section 403(b) contract. Treasury Regulations Section 1.403(b)-3(b)(2) is not satisfied unless, for the year of the excess and each year thereafter, the issuer of the contract maintains separate accounts for each such portion. Thus, the entire contract fails to be a Section 403(b) contract if an excess annual addition is made and a separate account is not maintained with respect to the excess. In other words, the annuity contract or custodial agreement must be bifurcated into a nonqualified annuity under Code Section 403(c) (comprised of the excess and earnings thereon) and a qualifying Section 403(b) annuity contract. A Section 403(b) contract does not fail the requirements of Section 403(b)'s distribution or funding rules solely by reason of a distribution made from a separate account of the excess amounts. [Treas. Reg. §§ 1.403(b)-3(b)(2), 1.403(b)-4(f)(2), 1.403(b)-4(f)(3)]

Q 3:67   How may amounts contributed in excess of the Section 415 contribution limit be corrected?

Contributions made in excess of the applicable contribution limits may be corrected (1) through self-correction as "Excess Amounts" under the Self-Correction Program (SCP), or (2) as "Excess Amounts" under the Voluntary Correction Program with Service Approval (VCP) or the Audit Closing Agreement Program (Audit CAP). The correction of Excess Amounts is part of the application of the Employee Plans Compliance Resolution System (EPCRS) to Section 403(b) plans as defined under Revenue Procedure 2006-27. [Rev. Proc. 2006-27, 2006-22 I.R.B. 945, § 6.06(2)]

Q 3:68   What are *Excess Amounts*?

Excess Amounts means any amount returned to ensure that the plan satisfies the requirements of Code Section 401(a)(30), 415, or 403(b)(2) (for plan years prior to January 1, 2002). In addition, the term *Excess Amount* includes (for all plan years) any distributions required to ensure that the plan complies with the applicable requirements of Code Section 403(b). [Rev. Proc. 2006-27, 2006-22 I.R.B. 945, § 5.02(3)]

Q 3:69   How may Excess Amounts be corrected?

Excess Amounts may be corrected by distributing the Excess Amounts. A distribution of Excess Amounts is generally treated in the manner described in Section 3 of Revenue Procedure 92-93 [1992-2 C.B. 505] relating to corrective disbursement of elective deferrals. [Rev. Proc. 2006-27, 2006-22 I.R.B. 945, § 6.06(2)]

Q 3:70   How may Excess Amounts be self-corrected?

Excess Amounts that are self-corrected through SCP may be corrected through distribution of excess amounts. [Rev. Proc. 2006-27, 2006-22 I.R.B. 945, §§ 4.01(1), 5.02, 6.06(2)]

Q 3:71   May Excess Amounts be corrected through VCP or Audit CAP?

Yes. Under VCP or Audit CAP, correction may be made by distribution of excess amounts. [Rev. Proc. 2006-27, 2006-22 I.R.B. 945, §§ 4.01(2) & (3), 5.02, 6.06(2)]

Q 3:72   Are distributed Excess Amounts reported?

Yes. The distribution must be reported on IRS Form 1099-R for the year of distribution with respect to each participant or beneficiary receiving such a distribution. [Rev. Proc. 2006-27, 2006-22 I.R.B. 945, § 6.06(2)]

Q 3:73   Are distributed Excess Amounts eligible for rollover?

No. The distribution of Excess Amounts is not an eligible rollover distribution within the meaning of Code Section 403(b)(8). In addition, the plan sponsor must inform affected participants and beneficiaries that an Excess Amount has been or will be distributed and that the distribution of the Excess Amount is not eligible for rollover. [Rev. Proc. 2006-27, 2006-22 I.R.B. 945, § 6.06(2)]

Correction of Excess Deferrals

Q 3:74   What are *excess deferrals*?

Excess deferrals are salary reduction contributions to a Section 403(b) program that exceed the applicable Section 402(g) limits in any taxable year. A designated Roth contribution is treated as an excess deferral only to the extent that the total amount of designated Roth contributions for an individual exceeds the applicable limit for the taxable year or the designated Roth contributions are identified as excess deferrals and the individual receives a distribution of the excess deferrals and allocable income under Treasury Regulations Section 1.402(g)-1(e)(2) or 1.402(g)-1(e)(3). [I.R.C. §§ 402(g)(1), 402(g)(2), 402A(d)(2)(C), 402A(d)(3); Treas. Reg. § 1.402(g)-1(e)(1)(iii)]

Q 3:75   What are the tax consequences for the Section 403(b) program in which excess deferrals have occurred?

For deferrals made before 1996, Code Section 401(a)(30), which is applicable to Section 403(b) plans under Code Section 403(b)(1)(E), mandated that elective deferrals under a plan could not exceed the applicable Section 402(g) limit. For deferrals made beginning on or after January 1, 1996, Code Section 403(b)(1)(E) was amended to require "a contract purchased under a salary reduction agreement to meet the requirements of Section 401(a)(30)." In other words, each tax-sheltered annuity contract, not the tax-sheltered annuity plan, must provide that elective deferrals made under the contract may not exceed the applicable Section 402(g) limit. The legislation indicates that it is intended that the contract terms be given effect in order for this requirement to be satisfied and states that an annuity contract is not required to meet any change in any provision before the 90th day after the date of enactment. However, the IRS provided a transition for including such language in annuity contracts and custodial agreements until the first day of the first plan year beginning on or after January 1, 1998 (or for a Section 403(b) contract of a governmental employer the later of (1) the first day of the first plan year beginning on or after January 1, 2000, or (2) the last day of the first plan year beginning on or after the 1999 legislative date, provided there is retroactive compliance. Treasury Regulations Section 1.403(b)-3(a)(4) states that a contract does not satisfy Code Section 401(a)(30) as required under the Code Section 403(b) regulations unless the contract requires that all elective deferrals for an employee not exceed the limits of Code Section 402(g)(1), including elective deferrals for the employee under the contract and any other elective deferrals under the plan under which the contract is purchased and under all other plans, contracts, or arrangements of the employer. [I.R.C. § 401(a)(30); Treas. Reg. § 1.401(a)-30; Small Business Job Protection Act of 1996, Pub. L. No. 140-188, § 1450, 110 Stat. 1755 (1996); Rev. Proc. 97-41]

Q 3:76   Is there a requirement to distribute excess deferrals?

No. There is no requirement that mandates distribution of excess deferrals from a plan. However, excess deferrals are treated as employer contributions for purposes of Code Section 415 unless distributed under Treasury Regulations Section 1.402(g)-1(e)(2) or 1.402(g)-1(e)(3). [Treas. Reg. §§ 1.402(g)-1(e)(4), 1.402(g)-1(e)(1)(ii)]

Q 3:77   Is it permissible to distribute excess deferrals?

Yes. Up until April 15 of the year following the year of deferral, excess deferrals may be distributed from the Section 403(b) program. If excess deferrals are not distributed by then, they may only be distributed when permitted under Code Section 403(b)(7) or 403(b)(11). [Treas. Reg. §§ 1.402(g)-1(e)(2), 1.402(g)-1(e)(3), 1.402(g)-1(e)(8)(iii)]

Q 3:78   How are excess deferrals corrected before the end of the taxable year?

The plan may provide that the participant may receive a corrective distribution of excess deferrals during the same year, if the following conditions are met:

- The participant designates the distribution as an excess deferral. If any designated Roth contributions were made to a plan, the notification must identify the extent, if any, to which the excess deferrals are comprised of designated Roth contributions. However, the plan may provide that the participant is deemed to have designated his or her excess deferrals under the plan and all other plans of the employer (including the portion of excess deferrals that are comprised of designated Roth contributions). Alternatively, the plan may provide that the employer may make the designation on behalf of the participant;

- The correcting distribution is made after the date on which the plan received the excess deferral; and

- The plan designates the distribution as a distribution of excess deferrals.

[I.R.C. § 402(g)(2)(A)(i); Treas. Reg. § 1.402(g)-1(e)(3)]

Q 3:79   How are excess deferrals corrected after the taxable year?

The plan may provide that if any amount of an excess deferral is includible in the participant's gross income for the taxable year, excess deferrals can be corrected in one of the following ways:

1. Not later than the first April 15 (or an earlier date specified in the plan) following the end of the participant's taxable year, the participant may notify the plan of the amount of excess deferrals. If any designated Roth contributions were made to a plan, the notification must also identify the extent, if any, to which the excess deferrals are comprised of designated Roth contributions. The plan may provide that the participant is deemed to have notified the plan of his or her excess deferrals under the plan and all other plans of the employer (including the portion of excess deferrals that are comprised of designated Roth contributions). Alternatively, a plan may provide that the employer may notify the plan on behalf of the participant.

2. Not later than the first April 15 following the end of the participant's taxable year, the plan may distribute the excess deferral amount (and any income allocable to the excess deferral).

[Treas. Reg. § 1.403(b)-4(f)(4); I.R.C. § 402(g)(2)(A)(ii); Treas. Reg. §§ 1.402(g)-1(e)(2)(i), 1.402(g)-1(e)(2)(ii)]

Q 3:80   Is there any other permissible self-correction method for excess deferrals?

Yes. Excess deferrals that are considered insignificant or significant operational failures may be corrected (i.e., distributed and reported) under SCP until the end of the second calendar year following the year the excess deferrals were made. However, the IRS has indicated that if the correction is made after April 15 following the end of the participant's taxable year, the double taxation still applies. [Rev. Proc. 2007-26, 2006-22 I.R.B. 945, §§ 4.01(1), 5.02, 6.06(2)]

Q 3:81 How is the income identified for distribution from a 403(b) program?

A refund of excess deferrals must include allocable investment earnings, including gains or losses for the *gap* period. The *gap* period is from the close of the taxable year until the distribution is made. These are called "gap period earnings." To determine the allocable investment earnings, the plan may use an alternative method of allocating income under Treasury Regulations Section 1.402(g)-1(e)(5)(iii) and the safe harbor method for allocating gap period earnings under Treasury Regulations Section 1.402(g)-1(e)(5)(iv) or use the alternative method for allocating taxable year and gap period earnings under Treasury Regulations Section 1.402(g)-1(e)(5)(v). The gap period earnings rule is effective for excess deferrals attributable to the tax years beginning on or after January 1, 2007. As a consequence, excess deferrals made in 2007 and refunded in early 2008 must include gap period earnings for the period between December 31, 2007 and the distribution date.

The investment earnings may be allocated using any reasonable method that does not violate Code Section 401(a)(4), is used consistently for all participants and for all corrective distributions under the Section 403(b) program for the year, and is used by the Section 403(b) program for allocating income to participants' accounts [Treas. Reg. § 1.402(g)-1(e)(5)(iii)]

The IRS recently clarified when plan documents and plan operations must comply with the gap period earnings requirement (i.e., for excess deferrals attributable to tax years beginning on or after January 1, 2007). The plan document requirement does not apply to Section 403(b) plans, but since Section 403(b) plans will have to have a plan beginning January 1, 2009 to comply with the final Code Section 403(b) regulations, it would seem appropriate to include investment earnings (and gap period earnings) excess deferral provisions in the plan. [Notice 2008-30, 2008-12, I.R. B. 638, Part V]

Q 3:82 May excess deferrals be corrected under VCP or under Audit CAP?

Yes. An operational failure to satisfy the limit on elective deferrals under Code Section 403(b)(1)(E) may be corrected under VCP or under Audit CAP (see chapter 18 for more information). [Rev. Proc. 2006-27, 2006-22 I.R.B. 945, § 5.02]

Q 3:83   What is the tax treatment of corrective distributions on or before the first April 15 after the end of the taxable year?

A corrective distribution of excess deferrals by the first April 15 after the end of the participant's taxable year is includible in the participant's gross income for the taxable year of deferral. However, the income allocable to the excess deferral is includible in the participant's gross income in the year of distribution. The corrective distribution of excess deferrals and income is not subject to the Section 72(t) 10 percent penalty tax or the excise tax under Code Section 4980A. [I.R.C. § 402(g)(2)(C); Treas. Reg. §§ 1.402(g)-1(a), 1.402(g)-1(e)(8)(i)]

Q 3:84   What is the tax treatment of corrective distributions of excess deferrals after the correction period?

If excess deferrals and income are not distributed by the first April 15 after the end of the taxable year, they may be distributed only when permitted under Code Section 403(b)(7) or 403(b)(11). These amounts are includible in gross income when distributed and are treated as elective deferrals and income that were excludable from the participant's gross income under Code Section 402(g). These amounts are not treated as investment in the contract under Code Section 72. In other words, amounts not distributed on or before the first April 15 following the close of the tax year are subject to double income taxation: once at the time of deferral and again at the time of actual distribution. [Treas. Reg. § 1.402(g)-1(e)(8)(iii)]

Q 3:85   What is the tax treatment of distributions of excess deferrals from a designated Roth account?

If a designated Roth account described in Code Section 402A includes any excess deferrals, any distribution of amounts attributable to those excess deferrals are includible in gross income (without adjustment for any return of investment in the contract under Code Section 72(e)(8)). In addition, such distributions cannot be qualified distributions under Code Section 402A(d)(2) and are not eligible rollover distributions within the meaning of Code Section 402(c)(4). If a designated Roth account includes any excess deferrals, any distributions from the account are treated as attributable to those excess deferrals until the total amount distributed from the designated Roth account equals the total of such deferrals and attributable income. [Treas. Reg. § 1.402(g)-1(e)(8)(iv)]

Q 3:86   How is a partial corrective distribution of excess deferrals treated?

A partial corrective distribution of excess deferrals of less than the entire amount of excess deferrals and income is treated as a pro rata distribution of excess deferrals and income. [I.R.C. § 402(g)(2)(D); Treas. Reg. § 1.402(g)-1(e)(10)]

Q 3:87   What provisions must the plan contain?

To allow for distribution of excess deferrals, a plan should contain language permitting distribution of excess deferrals. A plan may require that the notification be in writing and may require the participant to certify or otherwise establish that the amount is an excess deferral. [Treas. Reg. § 1.402(g)-1(e)(4)]

Q 3:88   Is a corrective distribution of an elective deferral treated as an amount that meets the minimum distribution requirements under Code Section 401(a)(9)?

No. A corrective distribution of excess deferrals and income is not treated as a distribution for purposes of determining whether the plan meets the minimum distribution requirements of Code Section 401(a)(9). [Treas. Reg. § 1.402(g)-1(e)(9)]

Q 3:89   Is employee or spousal consent required for making a corrective distribution of an excess deferral?

No. A corrective distribution of excess deferrals and income may be made pursuant to the terms of the plan without regard to any notice or consent otherwise required under Code Section 411(a)(11) or 417 (or comparable ERISA sections). [Treas. Reg. § 1.402(g)-1(e)(7)]

Contributions That Exceed All Limits

Q 3:90   What limits take precedence when all three limits have been exceeded?

There are no rules that mandate what rules take precedence when all three contribution limits have been exceeded. However, it would seem that because the consequence of exceeding Section 402(g) limits is contract disqualification, any amounts over the Section 402(g) limits would take precedence.

Excess Contributions Under Section 403(b)(7) Custodial Accounts

Q 3:91   Is an excise tax imposed on excess contributions to a Section 403(b)(7) custodial account?

Yes. Under Code Section 4973(a)(2), a 6 percent excise tax is imposed on excess contributions to Section 403(b)(7) custodial accounts. The 6 percent excise tax is imposed on excess contributions relating to the Section 415(c) limit.

Q 3:92 May these excess contributions be distributed?

No rules allow for distribution of these amounts. The 6 percent excise tax is imposed annually until the excess amount has been absorbed by unused contribution limits for subsequent years or is actually distributed at the time a participant meets a distributable event.

Q 3:93 Does this excise tax apply to Section 403(b)(1) annuity contracts?

No. The 6 percent excise tax does not apply to Section 403(b)(1) tax-deferred annuity contracts.

Chapter 4

Nondiscrimination in Coverage and Benefits

Robert A. Browning, Esq.
Spencer Fane Britt & Browne LLP

Code Section 403(b) provides that eligible employers may make current contributions toward the purchase of an annuity contract, but employees will not be taxed on such contributions or earnings until the amounts are distributed to them. However, in order to receive this tax-favored treatment, the contract must be purchased under a plan that meets certain coverage and nondiscrimination requirements. These rules generally require that the salary reduction feature of the plan, if any, must be made available to any employee of the organization willing to contribute more than $200 per year, and that employer contributions under the plan satisfy the same coverage and nondiscrimination requirements that apply to qualified Section 401(a) plans. Compliance with the rules is important, since the effect of violating the nondiscrimination requirements of Code Section 403(b)(12) is loss of Section 403(b) status for the employer's entire Section 403(b) program. This chapter gives an overview of the coverage and nondiscrimination requirements applicable to Section 403(b) programs.

Overview of Nondiscrimination Requirements

Q 4:1   What coverage and nondiscrimination rules apply to Section 403(b) programs?

There are separate rules with respect to contributions made pursuant to a salary reduction agreement (i.e., employee pre-tax contributions and/or Roth 403(b) contributions) and all other types of contributions. [I.R.C. § 403(b)(12)(A)]

With respect to salary reduction contributions, a plan meets the nondiscrimination requirements of Code Section 403(b)(12) so long as all employees of the employer (other than certain excludable employees) may elect to make salary reduction contributions of more than $200 per year. This is sometimes referred to as the *universal availability* requirement of Code Section 403(b)(12), and it is unique to Section 403(b) programs. [I.R.C. § 403(b)(12)(A)(ii)]

With respect to contributions other than salary reduction contributions, Section 403(b) programs are generally subject to the same nondiscrimination rules as qualified plans. These rules apply to plan coverage, contributions, and other benefits, and are contained in Code Sections 401(a)(4), 401(a)(5), 401(a)(17), 401(m), and 410(b). [I.R.C. § 403(b)(12)(A)(i)]

For tax years prior to January 1, 2009, Notice 89-23 [1989-1 C.B. 654] provides that the nondiscrimination requirements of Code Section 403(b)(12) are satisfied if the employer operates its Section 403(b) plan in accordance with a reasonable, good-faith interpretation of Code Section 403(b)(12). The Notice also sets forth certain transitional safe harbors to facilitate compliance with Code Section 403(b)(12). When IRS Notice 89-23 was issued in 1989, it was intended to apply for a limited period to alleviate compliance problems for tax-exempt employers. It has since been extended several times. However, under the final Code Section 403(b) regulations, both the "reasonable, good-faith" standard of compliance and the safe harbors set forth in Notice 89-23 are eliminated. Therefore, Notice 89-23 will generally not apply after December 31, 2008.

Q 4:2   Are all Section 403(b) programs subject to these nondiscrimination requirements?

No. Plans maintained by churches and certain church-controlled organizations, as described under Code Section 3121(w)(3), are totally exempt from the nondiscrimination rules. [I.R.C. § 403(b)(1)(D)]

In addition, plans maintained by governmental employers are deemed to satisfy many (but not all) of the nondiscrimination requirements applicable to non-salary reduction contributions. It must be noted that certain church plans, as defined in Code Section 414(e), may be sponsored by church-affiliated tax-exempt organizations (such as colleges, hospitals, retirement homes, or day care centers) that do not qualify as church-controlled organizations under Code

Section 3121(w)(3). As a result, these plans are subject to the nondiscrimination rules of Code Section 403(b)(12).

Q 4:3   When must Section 403(b) programs comply with the nondiscrimination rules?

The coverage and nondiscrimination requirements of Code Section 403(b)(12), including the universal availability requirement for salary reduction contributions, generally apply to plan years beginning on or after January 1, 1989. However, as a result of delays in finalizing the IRS regulations governing the nondiscrimination requirements applicable to qualified plans, the compliance date for many of the nondiscrimination rules applicable to non-salary reduction Code Section 403(b) contributions was deferred until the first day of the first plan year commencing after October 1, 1997 (for tax-exempt employers), or the first day of the first plan year commencing after December 31, 1998 (for governmental employers and nonelecting Section 414(e) church plans). [Ann. 95-48, I.R.B. 1995-23 (May 11, 1995); Notice 96-47, 1996-2 C.B. 213] Until those dates, governmental plans were deemed to satisfy and tax-exempt employers (including nonelecting Section 414(e) church plan sponsors) could rely on a reasonable, good-faith interpretation of many of the nondiscrimination requirements.

The Taxpayer Relief Act of 1997 (TRA '97) permanently exempted plans of state and local governments (including Section 403(b) arrangements) from many of the nondiscrimination requirements. [I.R.C. § 401(a)(5)(G)] As a result, the only nondiscrimination requirements applicable to Section 403(b) programs maintained by state or local governments (such as those sponsored by public schools) are the universal availability requirement for salary reduction contributions and the requirement that non-salary reduction contributions satisfy the limit on considered compensation under Code Section 401(a)(17). [I.R.C. § 403(b)(12)(C)]

There are special effective dates for the application of certain nondiscrimination rules for "nonelecting" church plans (church plans that have not elected, pursuant to Code Section 410(d), to be subject to the participation, vesting, and funding requirements of the Employee Retirement Income Security Act of 1974 (ERISA)). As indicated in Q 4:2, certain church plans sponsored by church-affiliated tax-exempt organizations may not qualify as church-controlled organizations under Code Section 3121(w)(3) and therefore are generally subject to the nondiscrimination rules under Code Section 403(b)(12). As noted above, the coverage and nondiscrimination regulations are generally applicable to tax-exempt employers on the first day of the first plan year commencing after October 1, 1997. However, Notice 2001-46 [2001-32 I.R.B. 122] provides that the effective date of regulations under Code Sections 401(a)(4), 401(a)(5), 401(l), and 414(s) for nonelecting church plans have been extended until further notice, but not earlier than the first plan year beginning on or after January 1, 2003. As of January 1, 2008, the IRS had not provided any additional guidance on the effective date of these regulations for nonelecting church plans.

As noted above, for tax years prior to 2009, Notice 89-23 provides several alternatives to demonstrate compliance with the nondiscrimination requirements of Code Section 403(b)(12). However, Notice 89-23 will no longer apply once the final Code Section 403(b) regulations become effective in 2009.

Application of Nondiscrimination Requirements for Different Types of Contributions

Q 4:4   What types of contributions may be made to a Section 403(b) program?

A Section 403(b) program may include the following types of contributions:

1. Salary reduction contributions (i.e., employee pre-tax deferrals and/or Roth 403(b) contributions);

2. After-tax employee contributions;

3. Nonmatching (discretionary or nonelective) employer contributions (sometimes referred to as "employer basic" contributions); and

4. Employer matching contributions.

The nondiscrimination rules vary for each type of contribution. The rules that apply to salary reduction contributions (see Q 4:6) are designed to provide "universal" coverage, regardless of the employee's income. The rules that apply to non-salary reduction contributions (see Qs 4:7–4:10) are designed to provide broad coverage and to prevent discrimination in favor of highly compensated employees (HCEs), as that term is defined in Code Section 414(q).

Q 4:5   Who is a highly compensated employee?

For plan years beginning after December 31, 1996, an HCE is any employee who:

1. Was a 5 percent owner at any time during the plan year or the preceding year; or

2. Received compensation from the employer during the preceding plan year in excess of $105,000 (indexed for inflation, 2008 figure) and, *if elected by the employer,* was among the top 20 percent of the most HCEs during the preceding plan year when ranked on the basis of compensation during that year. [I.R.C. § 414(q)(1)]

Notice 97-45 [1997-2 C.B. 296] describes how the employer may make this "top paid group" election and also describes a method for determining HCEs on a calendar-year basis rather than a plan-year basis. Note that the 2008 compensation limit of $105,000 is used to determine HCEs for plan years beginning in 2009. The 2007 compensation limit (which was $100,000) is used to determine HCEs for plan years beginning in 2008.

All members of a controlled group or affiliated service group associated with an employer are taken into account in determining HCEs. When the Section 403(b) regulations were finalized in 2007, the IRS also issued final regulations addressing how the controlled group rules under Code Sections 414(b), (c), (m) and (o) are to be applied to tax-exempt organizations. These regulations, which are effective for plan years beginning after December 31, 2008, do not apply to governmental employers, and they generally do not apply to churches or qualified church-controlled organizations described in Code Section 3121(w)(3). The IRS had previously indicated that tax-exempt and governmental employers could rely on a reasonable, good-faith interpretation of the controlled group and affiliated service group rules under Code Sections 414(b), (c), (m) and (o) until further guidance is issued. [I.R.S. Notice 96-64, 1996-2 C.B. 229] The final Code Section 414(c) regulations provide that tax-exempt employers may rely on a reasonable, good-faith interpretation of the controlled group and common control rules for plan years prior to 2009. The regulations also provide that reliance on the final regulations will be deemed to constitute a reasonable, good-faith interpretation of the rules for that purpose. It would appear that the previous *good-faith* standard will continue to apply to governmental employers and Section 3121(w)(3) churches.

Notice 89-23 [1989-1 C.B. 654] includes a special definition of HCE that may be used for purposes of the rules in that notice. This alternative definition, which basically limits HCEs to 5 percent owners or individuals who receive compensation in excess of $50,000, as adjusted in the manner described in Code Section 415(d), was only useful before 1997, when the Section 414(q) definition described above became more liberal than the special definition provided in Notice 89-23.

Q 4:6   What nondiscrimination rules apply to salary reduction contributions?

Generally, the right to make salary reduction contributions must be universally available. This means that if an eligible employer (other than a Section 3121(w)(3) church or church-controlled organization) allows any employee to make salary reduction contributions under a Section 403(b) plan, the employer may not exclude any eligible employee from participating in the salary reduction arrangement except to require that annual contributions be greater than $200. [I.R.C. § 403(b)(12)(A)(ii)] However, the following categories of employees may be excluded:

1. Nonresident aliens with no U.S.-source income;
2. Employees who normally work less than 20 hours per week (or such lower number of hours per week as may be set forth in the plan);
3. Students providing services described in Code Section 3121(b)(10); and
4. Employees eligible to make salary reduction contributions to other employer plans maintained under Code Sections 401(k), 457(b), or 403(b).

[I.R.C. § 403(b)(12)]

With regard to categories 2 and 3 above, such employees may be excluded for discrimination testing purposes only if the plan or program excludes *all* employees in that category. Therefore, in order to exclude employees who normally work fewer than 20 hours per week, the plan cannot allow any employee who normally works less than that amount to participate in the salary deferral arrangement. For purposes of this exclusion, an employee normally works fewer than 20 hours per week if and only if:

1. For the 12-month period beginning on the date of employment, the employer reasonably expects the employee to work fewer than 1,000 hours of service (as defined in Code Section 410(a)(3)(C)) in such period; and

2. For each plan year ending after the close of the 12-month period described above (or, if the plan so provides, for each subsequent 12-month period), the employee worked fewer than 1,000 hours of service in the preceding 12-month period.

With regard to category 4 above, coverage under another plan is permitted to be taken into account only if the right to make elective deferrals with respect to that coverage would satisfy the "effective opportunity" requirement (discussed below) if that coverage were provided under the Section 403(b) plan. In addition, coverage under a Section 457(b) plan of the employer is limited to governmental Section 403(b) arrangements.

The final Code Section 403(b) regulations clarify that an employee is not treated as being permitted to make Section 403(b) salary reduction contributions unless the employee is provided an "effective opportunity" to defer. The regulations provide that whether an employee has an "effective opportunity" to defer depends on the facts and circumstances, including notice of the opportunity to defer, the period of time during which an election to defer may be made, and any other conditions on elections.

In order to satisfy the "effective opportunity" requirement, the plan must provide the employee an effective opportunity to make or change a cash-or-deferred election (as defined in Treasury Regulations Section 1.401(k)-1(a)(3)) at least once during each plan year. In addition, the employee must be allowed to defer up to the applicable dollar limit under Code Section 402(g) (including any permissible catch-up deferrals) or up to the applicable limit under the Section 403(b) arrangement. An effective opportunity will not be considered to exist if any other rights or benefits (other than the right to receive employer matching contributions or other benefits described in Treasury Regulations Section 1.401(k)-1(e)(6)(i)(B) and (D)) are conditioned (directly or indirectly) upon the participant making or failing to make a cash-or-deferred election.

In the case of a Section 403(b) plan that covers more than one Section 501(c)(3) organization, the universal availability requirement applies separately to each common law entity. In the case of a Section 403(b) plan that covers more than one State entity, the universal availability requirement applies separately to each entity that is not part of a common payroll. In addition, an employer that has historically treated one or more of its various geographically distinct units as separate for employee benefit purposes may treat each unit as a separate organization if the unit is operated independently on a day-to-day basis. Units are not "geographically distinct" if they are located within the same Standard Metropolitan Statistical Area (SMSA).

It is important to note that salary reduction contributions under a Section 403(b) plan that are the result of a one-time irrevocable election made at the time of initial eligibility to participate in the salary reduction arrangement are deemed to be employer contributions, not salary reduction contributions. [I.R.C. § 403(b)(12)]

Therefore, mandatory employee contributions are not treated as salary reduction contributions for purposes of the nondiscrimination requirements of Code Section 403(b). Instead, they are subject to the discrimination rules otherwise applicable to non-salary reduction amounts.

Pursuant to Notice 89-23, for plan years prior to 2009, employers may apply a reasonable, good-faith interpretation of the nondiscrimination requirements of Code Section 403(b)(12) (or a safe harbor set forth in the Notice) for purposes of satisfying the universal availability requirement with respect to salary reduction contributions to a Section 403(b) arrangement. (See Qs 4:37–4:41 for more details on the relief provided by Notice 89-23, including additional categories of employees that may be excluded from a Section 403(b) salary reduction arrangement without violating the discrimination requirements.)

Under the final Code Section 403(b) regulations, for plan years after 2008, salary reduction contributions must be made pursuant to a plan, and the terms of the plan must satisfy the nondiscrimination requirements of Code Section 403(b)(12) and Treasury Regulations Section 1.403(b)-5.

The average deferral percentage (ADP) test applicable to salary reduction contributions under Section 401(k) plans does not apply to salary-reduction contributions under Section 403(b) arrangements. For HCEs, this can be a significant advantage. Conversely, the universal availability requirement of Code Section 403(b)(12)(A)(ii) does not apply to salary reduction contributions under a Section 401(k) plan.

Q 4:7 What nondiscrimination rules apply to employee after-tax contributions?

Since no rules (other than the universal availability requirement described in Q 4:6) prohibit discrimination in salary reduction (i.e., pre-tax or Roth 403(b)) contributions) one might expect a similar treatment for after-tax contributions to Section 403(b) plans, but that is not the case. Employee after-tax contributions are considered non-salary reduction contributions for purposes of Code Section 403(b)(12), and are therefore subject to the same coverage and nondiscrimination rules that apply to after-tax contributions to qualified plans. For nongovernmental Section 403(b) arrangements, employee after-tax contributions and employer matching contributions are subject to the Section 410(b) coverage test and the actual contribution percentage (ACP) test under Code Section 401(m).

[I.R.C. § 401(m)(1)] Governmental Section 403(b) arrangements are deemed to satisfy the coverage test and the ACP test for employee after-tax and employer matching contributions. However, for nongovernmental employers, the right to make such after-tax contributions is a "benefit, right, or feature" that must be tested under the regulations of Code Section 401(a)(4). Therefore, not only must after-tax contributions to a nongovernmental Section 403(b) plan satisfy the coverage test and the numerical ACP test, but the right to make such contributions must be currently and effectively available to a nondiscriminatory group of employees.

Q 4:8   What rules apply to matching contributions?

For nongovernmental employers, employer matching contributions (as well as employee after-tax contributions) are subject to the coverage test under Code Section 410(b) and the ACP test under Code Section 401(m).

In addition, the right to receive matching contributions at a specific rate or percentage is itself a "benefit, right, or feature" that must be tested under Code Section 401(a)(4).

To satisfy the ACP test, the average contribution rate (expressed as a percentage of compensation) of the HCEs for the testing year cannot exceed the *greater of*:

1. 125 percent of the average contribution rate for all eligible non-highly compensated employees (NHCEs) for the prior year; or
2. The lesser of
   (a) 200 percent of the average contribution rate for all eligible NHCEs for the prior year, or
   (b) the average contribution rate for all eligible NHCEs for the prior year, plus 2 percent.

[I.R.C. § 401(m)(2)]

The following table illustrates which of the three contribution limit rules applies, depending on the range of average matching and after-tax contributions for NHCEs:

Average NHCE (%)	*Applicable Rule*
Less than 2	200%
2 to 8	+2%
Over 8	125%

For example, if the average matching and after-tax contributions rate for NHCEs for the prior year was 1 percent of compensation, then the maximum average for HCEs is 2 percent (200% × 1%). If the average rate for NHCEs for the prior year was 3 percent, then the maximum average for HCEs is 5 percent

(3% + 2%). If the average rate for NHCEs for the prior year was 9 percent, then the maximum average for HCEs is 11.25 percent (9% × 125%).

All HCEs who are *eligible for* after-tax or matching contributions during the testing year, and all NHCEs who were eligible during the prior year, are counted, including those who make no after-tax contributions and those who receive no matching contributions. The employer may elect to perform the Section 401(m) ACP test by using current year NHCE contributions instead of prior year NHCE contributions. However, once the employer elects to use current year contribution data, the employer cannot revert to "prior year" testing unless certain requirements are met. [Treas. Reg. § 1.401(m)-2(c)(1)]

If the average Section 401(m) contribution rate for HCEs exceeds the limit, the excess contributions must generally be returned (to the extent the participant is vested in such contributions) or forfeited (if the participant is not vested in such contributions). Specific timing requirements must be met to avoid excise taxes. [I.R.C. § 401(m)(6)] Alternatively, the employer may make additional qualified nonelective contributions (QNECs) to satisfy the Section 401(m) test. Note, however, that the Section 401(m) regulations that were finalized in 2004 impose certain restrictions on *targeted* or *bottom-up* QNECs, effective for the 2006 plan year and future years.

Governmental Section 403(b) arrangements are deemed to satisfy the non-discrimination requirements with respect to matching contributions. Therefore, they are not subject to the Section 401(m) ACP test, the Section 410(b) coverage test, or the Section 401(a)(4) test for benefits, rights, and features.

Q 4:9   What is a safe-harbor 403(b) plan?

Nongovernmental Section 403(b) plans may also satisfy the requirements of Code Section 401(m) through the use of a "design-based" safe harbor. Just as Section 401(k) plans may be structured as safe-harbor plans to avoid the ADP and ACP tests, Section 403(b) arrangements may be structured as safe-harbor arrangements that are "deemed" to satisfy the ACP test. However, the safe harbor only applies with respect to matching contributions (i.e., it does not apply to employee after-tax contributions).

Code Section 401(m)(11) provides that a plan shall be treated as satisfying the requirements of Section 401(m) with respect to matching contributions (i.e., it is treated as satisfying the ACP test for matching contributions) if the plan meets certain minimum contribution requirements, certain notice requirements, and certain additional limitations. The IRS provided guidance on the application of this design-based safe harbor in Notice 98-52 and Notice 2000-3. Additional guidance was provided in the Code Section 401(m) regulations that were finalized in 2004. The Code Section 401(m) regulations are effective for plan years beginning on or after January 1, 2006.

The contribution requirement may be satisfied by (1) a basic matching formula, (2) an enhanced matching formula, or (3) a nonelective contribution formula. Regardless of the formula, all *safe-harbor* contributions must be

100 percent vested, and they must be subject to withdrawal restrictions that are similar to those that otherwise apply to salary reduction contributions.

Under the basic matching formula, the plan will be deemed to satisfy the ACP test if, under the terms of the plan, the employer is required to make matching contributions on behalf of each eligible NHCE equal to 100 percent of the elective contributions that do not exceed 3 percent of the employee's compensation, and 50 percent of the elective contributions that exceed 3 percent of compensation but do not exceed 5 percent of compensation. The enhanced matching formula requires that the employer make matching contributions on behalf of each eligible NHCE that, for any rate of elective contributions, provides an aggregate amount of matching contributions at least equal to the aggregate matching contributions that would have been provided under the basic matching formula. Under either formula, the rate of matching contributions may not increase as the employee's rate of elective contributions increases, and the rate of matching contributions that applies to any HCE must not be greater than the rate of matching contributions that would apply to any NHCE who has the same rate of elective contributions. The employee's right to matching contributions cannot be subject to an allocation condition, such as a requirement that the participant be employed on the last day of the plan year or a requirement to work at least 1,000 hours during the plan year.

Under the nonelective contribution formula, the plan will be deemed to satisfy the ACP test if, under the terms of the plan, the employer is required to make a safe harbor nonelective contribution on behalf of each eligible NHCE equal to at least 3 percent of the employee's compensation. This contribution must be based on a nondiscriminatory definition of compensation, and the employee's right to the contribution must not be subject to any "last day" or "1,000 hours of service" allocation condition.

The notice requirement is satisfied if each eligible employee for the plan year is given written notice of his or her rights and obligations under the plan, and the notice satisfies both a content requirement and a timing requirement.

The content requirement is satisfied if the notice is sufficiently accurate and comprehensive to inform the employee of his or her rights and obligations under the plan and is written in a manner calculated to be understood by the average employee eligible to participate in the plan. The timing requirement is satisfied if the notice is provided within a reasonable period before the beginning of the plan year (or, in the year an employee first becomes eligible, within a reasonable period before the employee becomes eligible). The timing requirement is deemed to be satisfied if the notice is provided at least 30 days (and no more than 90 days) before the beginning of each plan year. In the case of a newly established plan or a newly eligible employee, the notice may be provided within the 90-day period ending on the date the employee becomes eligible for the plan.

In addition to the contribution requirement and the notice requirement, the plan must satisfy certain other limitations and restrictions on matching contributions. These include the following:

1. If the plan uses the basic matching formula, there may not be any other matching contributions under the plan;

2. If the plan uses an enhanced matching formula or the nonelective contribution formula, matching contributions may not be made with respect to employee contributions or elective deferrals in excess of 6 percent of compensation; and

3. If the plan uses an enhanced matching formula or the nonelective contribution formula, and the plan provides for matching contributions at the employer's discretion, the plan must limit such discretionary matching contributions to an amount which, in the aggregate, will not exceed 4 percent of the employee's compensation.

4. The final 401(m) regulations also provide that any additional matching contributions, whether fixed or discretionary, cannot be subject to a "last day" or "1,000 hours" allocation condition.

The final Code Section 401(m) regulations also provide that safe harbor contributions may be made to another defined contribution plan. Therefore, the nondiscrimination requirement for matching contributions under a Section 403(b) arrangement could be satisfied, for example, by *safe-harbor* nonelective contributions to another Section 401(a) plan of the employer (such as a profit-sharing or money purchase plan).

For plan years beginning after December 31, 2007, a Section 403(b) arrangement will also be deemed to satisfy the Section 401(m) ACP test if the plan is a "qualified automatic contribution arrangement," as defined in Code Section 401(k)(13). Such plans must provide for *automatic* salary deferrals with an auto-increase feature, the employer must make matching contributions equal to 100 percent of the first 1 percent of compensation deferred, plus 50 percent of the next 5 percent of compensation deferred, and such employer contributions must be 100 percent vested after two years. The IRS issued proposed regulations regarding qualified automatic contribution arrangements in November 2007.

Q 4:10   What rules apply to employer nonmatching contributions?

With respect to Section 403(b) arrangements of nongovernmental employers, nonmatching contributions that are not made pursuant to a salary reduction agreement (i.e., employer discretionary or nonelective contributions) must meet the requirements of Code Sections 401(a)(4), 401(a)(5), 401(a)(17), and 410(b) in the same manner as if the plan were a qualified plan under Code Section 401(a). For purposes of these tests, students performing services described in Code Section 3121(b)(10) and employees who normally work fewer than 20 hours per week may be excluded (provided that all such employees are excluded from participation in the Section 403(b) program). For plan years prior to 2009, Notice 89-23 [1989-1 C.B. 654] allows additional employees to be excluded for purposes of the safe harbors set forth in that notice. Governmental Section 403(b) arrangements are deemed to satisfy the nondiscrimination requirements under Code Sections 401(a)(4), 401(a)(5), and 410(b), but they must satisfy the requirements of Code Section 401(a)(17), which limits the amount of compensation that can be taken into account for purposes of contributions or benefits. This limit, which is $230,000 for plan years beginning in 2008, is indexed for inflation. Under a special transition rule, certain grandfathered employees of certain governmental employers may be permitted to take into account more than $230,000 of compensation. [Treas. Reg. § 1.401(a)(17)-1]

Pursuant to Notice 89-23, for plan years prior to 2009, employers may apply a reasonable, good-faith interpretation of the nondiscrimination requirements of Code Section 403(b)(12). The Notice also provides three safe-harbor formulas (and many special definitions) for satisfying the requirements of Code Section 403(b)(12) that apply to non-salary reduction contributions (see Q 4:37). As previously noted, however, this good-faith standard of compliance, as well as the safe harbors and the special definitions, are not available for plan years beginning after December 31, 2008.

Minimum Participation Rules

Q 4:11   Which employees must be allowed to participate in the plan?

Code Section 401(a)(26) generally provides that a plan must benefit at least the lesser of 50 employees or 40 percent of all employees. However, effective for plan years beginning on or after January 1, 1997, the requirements of Code Section 401(a)(26) apply solely to defined benefit plans. Because Section 403(b) arrangements are limited, under the final regulations, to defined contribution plans, the requirements of Code Section 401(a)(26) do not affect the determination of which employees must be allowed to participate in a Section 403(b) arrangement. Therefore, there is generally no requirement that employer contributions under a Section 403(b) defined contribution arrangement be made for any minimum number, or percentage, employees.

Code Section 410(a), which sets forth the minimum age and service requirements that can be imposed by plans that are intended to be "qualified" under Code Section 401(a), does not apply to Section 403(b) plans. However, if an employer-sponsored Section 403(b) arrangement is subject to ERISA, similar provisions apply. Section 202(a) of ERISA provides that, in general, employees may not be excluded from a plan on account of age or service if they have attained age 21 and have completed at least one year of service. Employees must generally be allowed to participate within six months after they have met those requirements. Normally, a year of service means a 12-month period during which an employee has completed at least 1,000 hours of service, although other methods of determining a year of service may be used. Regulations issued by the IRS and the Department of Labor (DOL) set forth myriad requirements and alternatives for measuring years and hours of service. [*See, e.g.,* DOL Reg. §§ 2530.200b-3(c), 2530.200b-3(d), and 2530.200b-3(e)]

It should be noted that the age and service rules described in Section 202(a) of ERISA do not preempt the universal availability requirement that applies to salary reduction contributions to Section 403(b) arrangements. Therefore, for Section 403(b) plans that are subject to ERISA, regardless of any age or service requirements applicable to employer contributions under the plan, employees who are under age 21 or have less than one year of service must be permitted to make salary reduction contributions unless they fall into one of the four categories of excludable employees described in Q 4:6. Also, the rule under Code Section 403(b)(12) that permits the exclusion from nondiscrimination testing of employees who "normally work less than 20 hours per week" does not preempt the rule under Section 202(a) of ERISA that prohibits the exclusion of "part-time" employees who may otherwise complete at least 1,000 hours of service in a year and become eligible to participate in the plan. Therefore, for an ERISA-covered Section 403(b) arrangement, the exclusion of employees who normally work less than 20 hours per week may violate Section 202(a) of ERISA, even though it is permissible under the nondiscrimination requirements of Code Section 403(b)(12).

Q 4:12   Are there exceptions to the one-year-of-service and minimum age rules for ERISA-covered Section 403(b) arrangements?

If an ERISA-covered plan provides that all participants shall be 100 percent vested from the commencement of participation, a two-year eligibility requirement may be substituted for the one-year requirement (for purposes of the right to participate in non-salary reduction contributions). A plan maintained by a tax-exempt educational institution that provides 100 percent vesting at all times may increase the age-21 requirement to age 26, although if an age older than 21 is specified, the two-year service requirement cannot be applied.

Q 4:13   May a Section 403(b) program that is subject to ERISA set maximum age limits?

No. ERISA Section 202(a)(2) provides that no employee may be excluded under a maximum age requirement. This rule applies both to newly hired employees and to others already participating in a plan.

Q 4:14   May an ERISA-covered Section 403(b) program exclude employees for other reasons?

The rules discussed above merely define certain age and service-related conditions that may be applied to exclude employees from non-salary reduction contributions under an ERISA-covered Section 403(b) program. For purposes of non-salary reduction contributions, an employer may exclude employees or groups of employees by criteria other than age or service, as long as the plan will satisfy the coverage requirements of Code Section 410(b). For example, the employees entitled to employer contributions could be defined by pay status (e.g., salaried or hourly), job classification (e.g., professional, administrative, or maintenance), geographic location, or any other reasonable basis. However, if a nongovernmental plan does not cover all of the nonunion employees of an employer who are not excluded for failure to meet age or service requirements, it must pass one of the coverage tests under Code Section 410(b). Those tests are applied to the plan in its entirety, although if different benefit or contribution levels are provided for different participants under the plan, the plan must also demonstrate that benefits or contributions are not discriminatory under Code Section 401(a)(4).

Coverage Rules

Q 4:15   What coverage rules apply to non-salary reduction contributions to Section 403(b) plans?

Code Section 410(b) regulations determine who must be covered by the non-salary reduction contribution portion of a Section 403(b) arrangement. In order to satisfy the Section 410(b) coverage test, the Section 403(b) plan (or the relevant component of the plan) must satisfy either the ratio percentage test (see Q 4:16) or the average benefits test (see Q 4:17). The term *plan*, as used in this chapter, may refer to an individual plan, an aggregated group of plans, or disaggregated components of a plan. An aggregated group of plans can include defined contribution and defined benefit plans, although certain types of plans cannot be aggregated for purposes of nondiscrimination testing. For example, the salary deferral portion of a Section 401(k) plan can be aggregated with other plans of the same type, but it cannot be aggregated with any other defined contribution or defined benefit plan maintained by an employer. The same is true for the matching contribution portion of a plan covered under Code Section 401(m). [Treas. Reg. § 1.410(b)-7] The matching contribution portion of a Section 403(b) plan and the nonmatching employer contributions must be tested for coverage separately.

As previously indicated, the Section 410(b) coverage test applies only to non-salary reduction contributions (i.e., employer matching and nonmatching contributions and employee after-tax contributions) made under nongovernmental Section 403(b) arrangements. Pursuant to Notice 89-23, for plan years prior to 2009, Section 403(b) plans may rely on a reasonable, good-faith interpretation of Code Section 403(b)(12), including the coverage rules of Code Section 410(b). Notice 89-23 provides three safe-harbor formulas for satisfying the coverage (and nondiscrimination) requirements applicable to non-salary reduction contributions (see Q 4:37).

Q 4:16   How does the Section 410(b) ratio percentage test work?

Under the ratio percentage test defined in Code Section 410(b)(1), a plan satisfies coverage requirements if the percentage of nonexcludable NHCEs covered by the plan is at least 70 percent of the percentage of nonexcludable HCEs covered. Nonexcludable employees are all employees other than the "excludable" employees. Under Code Section 410(b)(3), the following employees are "excludable" employees:

1. Employees covered by a collective bargaining agreement (i.e., union employees), if there is evidence that retirement benefits were the subject of good-faith bargaining;

2. Employees who are non-resident aliens and who receive no U.S.-source earned income; and

3. Employees who do not meet the minimum age and service requirements set forth in the plan (so long as such minimum age/service requirements do not exceed the maximum permissible age/service requirements under Code Section 410(a)), but only if the plan excludes all such employees.

Under the final Code Section 403(b) regulations, excludable employees also include students performing services described in Code Section 3121(b)(1) and employees who normally work fewer than 20 hours per week, but only if the plan excludes all such employees. However, these exclusions are subject to the conditions applicable under Code Section 410(b)(4). Thus, if any employee who normally works less than 20 hours per week receives an employer contribution under the plan, then no employee working less than 20 hours per week may be treated as an excludable employee for discrimination testing. However, if a plan covers employees who do not meet the statutory age or service requirements of ERISA Section 202(a), then, for purposes of meeting the coverage and nondiscrimination rules for non-salary reduction contributions, it can be tested as two separate plans: one covering employees who meet the statutory requirements and a second covering employees who do not. To be deemed covered under a plan for a year for purposes of Code Section 410(b), a participant must actually be receiving a contribution (or be eligible to receive a matching contribution or an after-tax contribution). Inactive or terminated participants (who do not receive a contribution) are not counted. [Treas. Reg. § 1.410(b)-6]

The following table illustrates the application of the ratio percentage test to an employer's Section 403(b) plan:

| Plan | Nonexcludable Employees | | |
Status	NHCEs	HCEs	Total
Covered	180 (67%)	27 (90%)	207 (69%)
Not covered	90 (33%)	3 (10%)	93 (31%)
Total	270 (100%)	30 (100%)	300 (100%)

Here, 300 nonunion employees are nonexcludable due to age, service, or other factors. Of those, 270 are NHCEs and 30 are HCEs. The plan covers 67 percent of the NHCEs and 90 percent of the HCEs. Because 67 percent divided by 90 percent equals 74 percent, which exceeds 70 percent, the plan passes the ratio percentage test. In fact, if 28 of the 30 HCEs (or 93 percent) were covered, the plan would still pass (67% ÷ 93% = 72%). However, if 29 HCEs (or 97 percent) were covered, the plan would not pass (67% ÷ 97% = 69%).

Q 4:17   How does the Section 410(b) average benefits test work?

If a plan cannot pass the ratio percentage test, it may still satisfy the coverage requirements under Code Section 410(b) by passing the average benefits test. Under that test, the ratio percentage required for a plan to pass can be reduced below 70 percent, provided two other requirements are met:

1. The group of employees covered by the plan represents a nondiscriminatory classification that is reasonable; and

2. The average benefit percentage (determined for all nonexcludable employees) for NHCEs is at least 70 percent of the average benefit percentage for HCEs.

[Treas. Reg. § 1.410(b)-2(b)(3)]

Although for purposes of simplicity, requirement (1) will be addressed first. In practice it may often be desirable to test for requirement (2) first, since that test is performed once for the employer's entire employee population and its outcome will dictate whether any plan of the employer will be able to use the average benefits test.

Q 4:18   What is a reasonable classification?

The regulations issued by the IRS under Code Section 410(b) provide that, to be reasonable, a classification must be established under objective business criteria that identify the category of employees who benefit under the plan. A reasonable classification can be based on pay status, job classification, and other similar bona fide business criteria. A designation of employees by name or other criteria having a similar effect is not considered reasonable. For example, naming specific job titles that can be filled by only one individual at a time may cause a plan to fail this requirement. [Treas. Reg. § 1.410(b)-4(b)]

Q 4:19   How does a reasonable classification affect the ratio percentage test?

If a classification is reasonable, then the ratio percentage required for a plan to satisfy the coverage requirements under Code Section 410(b) is reduced. To determine the revised ratio percentage requirement, a safe-harbor percentage must be calculated. The safe-harbor percentage is equal to 50 percent, reduced by 0.75 percent for each 1 percent that the concentration of NHCEs among nonexcludable employees exceeds 60 percent. Using the example in Q 4:16, 270 of the 300 employees, or 90 percent, are NHCEs. Therefore, the safe-harbor percentage is 27.5 percent (50% − .75 × 30%).

The following table illustrates coverage under a different plan maintained by the same employer used in Q 4:16:

Plan	Nonexcludable Employees		
Status	NHCEs	HCEs	Total
Covered	70 (26%)	27 (90%)	97 (32%)
Not covered	200 (74%)	3 (10%)	203 (68%)
Total	270 (100%)	30 (100%)	300 (100%)

Note that the plan covers 26 percent of the NHCEs and 90 percent of the HCEs. The ratio percentage for the plan is 29 percent (26% ÷ 90%), which exceeds the safe harbor of 27.5 percent. Therefore, assuming that the categories selected for coverage are reasonable, the plan would pass the nondiscriminatory classification leg of the average benefits test.

Q 4:20   What is an unsafe harbor percentage?

A plan can also be deemed to cover a nondiscriminatory classification if the ratio of covered NHCEs to HCEs is at least equal to the unsafe harbor percentage as calculated below, provided that the IRS approves the classification based on the facts and circumstances. The regulations indicate that the IRS will base its decision on the underlying business reason for the classification, the percentage of all employees of the employer benefiting under the plan, whether a representative number of employees benefit under the plan in each salary range of the employer's workforce, and the margin by which the plan fails to satisfy the safe-harbor percentage. [Treas. Reg. § 1.410(b)-4(c)(3)] As of the publication date of this book, there is no precedent to suggest how the IRS will interpret those requirements.

The unsafe harbor percentage is equal to 40 percent reduced by 0.75 percent for each 1 percent that the NHCE concentration percentage exceeds 60 percent, but the unsafe harbor percentage can never be less than 20 percent. Using the example in Q 4:19, the unsafe harbor percentage would be 17.5 percent (40% − .75 × 30%), so the minimum unsafe harbor percentage of 20 percent would apply.

Q 4:21   How does the average benefits percentage requirement apply?

It is not sufficient under the average benefits test to show that the plan passes the reasonable and nondiscriminatory classification requirement. The plan must also pass the average benefits percentage requirement. In general, the average benefits percentage calculation must be performed taking into account all nonexcludable employees and all plans the employer maintains. The salary reduction portion of a Section 401(k) plan is included, but it is not clear whether the salary reduction portion of a Section 403(b) plan is likewise included. [Treas. Reg. § 1.410(b)-5(d)]

Q 4:22 How is the average benefits percentage calculated?

An average benefits percentage can be calculated for each employee on either a defined contribution or a defined benefit basis. If the average benefits percentage is being determined on a contributions basis, then the rate of contribution as a percentage of compensation applicable to each nonexcludable employee is calculated. For a defined contribution plan, this rate would be equal to the amount of contributions and forfeitures allocated to the employee for the year, divided by his or her compensation (limited for the year as provided in Code Section 401(a)(17)—$230,000 for 2008). If a defined benefit plan is maintained by the employer, the amount of benefit accruing under that plan is converted to an equivalent rate of contribution using actuarial assumptions. [Treas. Reg. § 1.401(a)(4)-8] Nonexcludable employees not receiving allocations or accruing benefits are credited with zero. However, for purposes of the average benefits percentage test, the only employees who can be excluded on the basis of age or service requirements are those who do not meet the lowest age and service eligibility requirements of any plan of the employer. [Treas. Reg. § 1.410(b)-6(b)(2)]

1. For employees whose compensation does not exceed the Social Security Wage Base, the lesser of (1) 5.7 percent or (2) the total percentage rate of contributions, or equivalent contributions, that is applicable to total compensation under all eligible plans; or

2. For employees whose compensation exceeds the Social Security Wage Base, a contribution rate (not to exceed 5.7 percent) applicable under the eligible plans to compensation up to the Wage Base equal to (1) the employees' contribution under the plans, divided by (2) the excess of twice the employees' compensation over the Social Security Wage Base for the year.

[Treas. Reg. § 1.401(1)-2(b)]

Q 4:23 What is *permitted disparity?*

The term *permitted disparity* was introduced with the Tax Reform Act of 1986 (TRA '86). It replaces the term *Social Security integration,* which had been used for over 25 years. A credit for permitted disparity can be incorporated for each employee based on the regulations under Code Section 401(l). The additional contribution credit for permitted disparity under the average benefits test is derived taking into account all plans of the employer that are eligible for permitted disparity under Code Section 401(l). Salary reduction plans under Code Sections 401(k) and 403(b) are the most common types of plans not eligible for permitted disparity under Code Section 401(l). The contribution credit for permitted disparity is equal to:

1. For employees whose compensation does not exceed the Social Security Wage Base, the lesser of (1) 5.7 percent or (2) the total percentage rate of contributions, or equivalent contributions, that is applicable to total compensation under all eligible plans; or

2. For employees whose compensation exceeds the Social Security Wage Base, a contribution rate (not to exceed 5.7 percent) applicable under the eligible plans to compensation up to the Wage Base equal to (1) the employees' contribution under the plans, divided by (2) the excess of twice the employees' compensation over the Social Security Wage Base for the year.

[Treas. Reg. § 1.401(l)-2(b)]

Example. Employer E's plans provide a contribution rate of 5 percent of compensation. Under (1) above, Employee C, earning under the Social Security Wage Base, would receive a permitted disparity credit of 5 percent of compensation, which would give him or her a total credited amount of 10 percent of compensation.

Under (2) above, an employee earning $90,900 in 1994, when the Social Security Wage Base was $60,600, would receive a permitted disparity Nondiscrimination in Coverage and Benefits credit of 3.75 percent of $60,600, or $2,272.50. This is determined as (1) 5% × $90,900, divided by (2) (2 × $90,900) – $60,600. The total credited amount for the employee would be $6,817.50 ($2,272.50 + 5% × $90,900), or 7.5 percent ($6,817.50 ÷ $90,900) of compensation. Note that the inclusion of permitted disparity in determining the average benefits percentage will always benefit HCEs.

If the average benefits percentage is to be determined based on defined benefit accruals, then in most instances, for all defined benefit plans of the employer the actual benefit accruing under the plan is used in the calculation, and for defined contribution plans the annual rate of contribution is converted to an equivalent accrued benefit. The credit for permitted disparity is determined using the defined benefit rules under Code Section 401(l), as modified by Code Section 401(a)(4).

Q 4:24   What other factors affect the average benefits test?

In calculating the average benefits percentage for defined benefit plans, numerous adjustments are made to reflect early retirement provisions, optional forms of benefit payments, and other plan features. The specific requirements are beyond the scope of this book and are best left to the plan actuary.

The average benefits percentage can be determined based on either contributions or benefits, and the choice can be complex. If the HCEs tend to be older than the NHCEs, the results will usually be more favorable if testing is based on benefits. Sometimes it is necessary to perform the calculations both ways to be certain that the optimum results are obtained. It is also permissible to test all defined contribution plans of an employer separately from all defined benefit plans.

Q 4:25   What other coverage rules may apply?

Many other features of the coverage tests can be important in certain situations. Some of these features apply only to testing Section 401(a) plans.

Some, however, could be significant to employers testing Section 403(b) plans, such as the following:

- Treasury Regulations Section 1.410(b)-7(f) provides that, in performing the average benefits test to determine whether a Section 403(b) plan meets the coverage requirements under Code Section 410, plans of the employer qualified under Code Section 401(a) can (but need not) be included. However, in testing a Section 401(a) plan, a Section 403(b) plan may not be used. This rule makes it difficult for an employer to provide a Section 401(a) plan of any type primarily for HCEs and a Section 403(b) plan for other employees or to maintain a Section 401(a) plan offset by the value of amounts accumulated under a Section 403(b) plan (usually called a *floor plan arrangement*).

- If a single controlled group contains both taxable and tax-exempt entities, and the taxable entities maintain a Section 401(k) plan, the Section 401(k) plan is allowed to exclude (for coverage testing purposes) those employees who are eligible to make salary reduction contributions to a Section 403(b) plan if (1) no employee of the tax-exempt organization is eligible to participate in the Section 401(k) plan, and (2) at least 95 percent of the nonexcludable employees of the taxable entities are eligible for the Section 401(k) plan. [Treas. Reg. § 1.410(b)-6(g), as modified by Section 664 of the Economic Growth and Tax Relief Reconciliation Act of 2001 (EGTRRA)] Without this rule, it would be difficult for the Section 401(k) plan to pass the coverage test if the taxable entities had a disproportionately higher percentage of HCEs than the tax-exempt entities.

- If employer organizations are merged, then a plan that satisfies Code Section 410(b) prior to the merger will be deemed to continue to satisfy Code Section 410(b) until the last day of the first plan year beginning after the merger takes place. A similar rule applies on disposition. [I.R.C. § 410(b)(6)]

- If a plan covers both union and nonunion employees, the portion of the plan covering nonunion employees is tested as a separate plan. [I.R.C. § 410(b)(5)(e)]

- If an employer has two or more separate lines of business (SLOBs), then each SLOB can be tested for coverage as though it were a unique employer. Final SLOB regulations make it very difficult for any employer to establish that it has SLOBs because of rules requiring totally separate management and separate financial statements as well as numerous other restrictions. It is likely that only a few tax-exempt entities can demonstrate that SLOBs exist within the organization.

As stated earlier, even though a plan may pass coverage requirements using the ratio percentage test or the average benefits test, it must still not discriminate with respect to the contributions or benefits provided to participants (see Qs 4:27, 4:29).

Q 4:26   How often must plans be tested?

The requirement of nondiscrimination in coverage and benefits must be met on at least one day in each plan year. The last day of the plan year may be used if all employees who terminated during the year are included in the testing. Plan provisions must be applied as of the last day of the plan year. Plans under which coverage or benefits do not significantly change can be tested every three years. [Rev. Proc. 93-42, 1993-2 C.B. 540]

Nondiscrimination Rules

Q 4:27   How is it determined whether employer contributions to nongovernmental Section 403(b) arrangements are discriminatory under Code Section 401(a)(4)?

A plan can meet the coverage rules of Code Section 410(b) and still be discriminatory. As a simple example, a plan could cover 100 percent of all statutorily eligible employees but provide substantial contributions for HCEs and de minimis contributions for NHCEs. To prohibit this, Code Section 401(a)(4) provides that a plan cannot discriminate in favor of HCEs with respect to the benefits or contributions provided. Compliance can be demonstrated by testing an individual plan or aggregating that plan with any other eligible plans of the employer. If an aggregated group of plans is demonstrated to be nondiscriminatory with respect to benefits or contributions, then each of the plans contained in the group is deemed to be nondiscriminatory. [Treas. Reg. § 1.410(b)-7(d)]

The regulations under Code Section 401(a)(4) are extremely voluminous and complex, extending to over 300 pages. They deal not only with the quantitative value of the benefits or contributions provided under a plan, but also the qualitative provisions that cover the eligibility for, and distribution of, benefits from a plan. This latter category is generally referred to as the *benefits, rights, and features* of a plan (see Q 4:36).

Virtually all Section 403(b) plans are of the defined contribution type. Therefore, this section of the chapter will deal with the rules governing compliance of defined contribution plans. However, because employers sponsoring Section 403(b) plans may also sponsor defined benefit plans, this section will also cover the rules applicable to defined benefit plans with which it is necessary to comply to aggregate such plans with a Section 403(b) plan to demonstrate compliance of the Section 403(b) plan.

Q 4:28   What definition of compensation must be used under Code Section 403(b)(12)(A)(1)?

For the purposes of the ACP test under Code Section 401(m), the average benefits test under Code Section 410(b) and the nondiscrimination requirements of Code Section 401(a)(4), the plan must use a definition of compensation that satisfies Code Section 414(s). Code Section 414(s) provides that *compensation* may be defined as either (1) Section 415(c)(3) compensation, or (2) an alternative definition permissible under applicable Treasury Regulations, so long as such alternative definition does not discriminate in favor of HCEs. The final Code Section 403(b) regulations clarify that for this purpose, Code Section 415(c)(3)(E) (which defines *compensation* by reference to *includible compensation* under Code Section 403(b)(3)) does not apply. Therefore, although *includible compensation* is used to determine the contribution limits under Code Section 403(b), it is not used for purposes of discrimination testing. Treasury Regulations Sections 1.414(s)-1 and 1.415(c)-2 set forth several definitions of compensation that are deemed to satisfy Code Section 414(s), and Treasury Regulations Section 1.414(s)-1 sets forth the requirements for determining whether an alternative definition of compensation will be considered nondiscriminatory under Code Section 414(s).

It should be noted that under any of the definitions of compensation that are deemed to satisfy Code Section 414(s), the employer may elect to exclude certain *elective* amounts (i.e., amounts contributed by the employer pursuant to a salary reduction agreement and that are not includible in the employee's gross income under Code Sections 125, 132(f)(4), 402(e)(3), 402(h), 403(b) or 457(b)). In addition, any of the definitions of compensation that are deemed to satisfy Code Section 414(s) may be modified to exclude the following items (even if they are includible in gross income):

- Reimbursements or other expense allowances
- Fringe benefits (cash and noncash)
- Moving expenses
- Deferred compensation
- Welfare benefits

The following definitions of compensation are deemed to satisfy Code Section 414(s):

Section 415 "long form" compensation—includes all remuneration described in Treasury Regulations Section 1.415(c)-2(b) and excludes all other compensation, including the items specifically listed as excludable in Treasury Regulations Section 1.415(c)-2(c).

Section 415 "short form" or "safe-harbor" compensation—includes *only* the remuneration described in Treasury Regulations Section 1.415(c)-2(b)(1) and (2) and excludes all other compensation, including items listed as excludable in Treasury Regulations Section 1.415(c)-2(c).

W-2 compensation—includes wages (as defined in Code Section 3401(a)) and all other payments for which the employer is required to furnish the employee a written statement under Code Sections 6041(d), 6051(a)(3), and 6052.

Section 3401(a) wages—includes wages, as defined in Code Section 3401(a), but determined without regard to rules limiting the remuneration to be included on the basis of the nature or location of the employment or the services performed.

Section 414(s) safe-harbor compensation—technically, this is Section 415 *long form* compensation reduced by reimbursements or expense allowances, fringe benefits, moving expenses, deferred compensation, and welfare benefits. As previously indicated, however, any of the definitions of compensation listed above (including Section 415 safe-harbor compensation, W-2 compensation, or Section 3401(a) wages) may also be modified to exclude these items, and such modified definition will be considered a Section 414(s) safe-harbor definition of compensation.

Q 4:29   What safe harbors are provided under Code Section 401(a)(4)?

There are several design-based safe harbors provided under the Section 401(a)(4) regulations that will allow a Section 403(b) plan to comply without any complicated testing. Furthermore, for plan years beginning prior to 2009, Notice 89-23 [1989-1 C.B. 654] allows employers to apply a *reasonable good-faith interpretation* of Code Section 401(a)(4) and alternatively provides three additional design-based safe harbors that allow a Section 403(b) plan to comply with the nondiscrimination requirements applicable to non-salary reduction contributions under Code Section 403(b)(12). However, after 2008, the *good-faith* interpretation and the safe harbors set forth in Notice 89-23 will no longer be effective, and the regulations under Code Section 401(a)(4) will be applied. Therefore, the safe harbor rules of both Code Section 401(a)(4) and Notice 89-23 are explained.

The Section 401(a)(4) rules limit discrimination in contributions or benefits in favor of HCEs. There are no restrictions on disparities in contributions or benefits among NHCEs. For example, a contribution formula providing 15 percent of compensation for NHCEs earning more than $50,000 and 1 percent of compensation for NHCEs earning less than $50,000 is not prohibited by the rules. However, a formula that provides a greater percent of compensation for HCEs than for NHCEs will be subject to the limitations of Code Section 401(a)(4).

The following types of contribution formulas meet a Section 401(a)(4) safe harbor and require no testing:

1. A formula that provides the same contribution percentage or a flat dollar amount for all employees, or one that provides higher contributions for employees earning over a dollar breakpoint that complies with the permitted disparity rules of Code Section 401(1); and

2. A formula that provides contributions based on a uniform points formula taking into account the age, service, and/or compensation of the employee, provided that the average contribution (as a percentage of compensation) for all NHCEs is at least as great as the average contribution for all HCEs.

Permitted disparity under Code Section 401(1) cannot be taken into account for this purpose.

[Treas. Reg. § 1.401(a)(4)-2]

Under the permitted disparity rules, employees earning above the Social Security Wage Base are allowed to receive an additional percentage contribution on compensation above the wage base equal to the lesser of (1) the percentage of total compensation contributed to the plan or (2) 5.7 percent. [I.R.C. § 401(1)] For example, a contribution formula of 4 percent of compensation plus 4 percent of compensation in excess of the wage base would meet the safe harbor. However, formulas of (1) 4 percent of compensation plus 5 percent above the wage base or (2) 7 percent of compensation plus 6 percent above the wage base would not meet the safe harbor. The "5.7 percent" in (1) will be adjusted to conform with any increase in the contribution rate for the retirement insurance portion of an employer's Social Security contributions.

In designing a contribution formula with permitted disparity, it is permissible to reduce the breakpoint where the change in contribution rate takes place relative to an amount as low as 20 percent of the current wage base. If the breakpoint is 80 percent of the wage base or less, the maximum percentage is reduced from 5.7 percent to 4.3 percent; if it is above 80 percent of the wage base, the maximum is reduced to 5.4 percent.

To use these safe harbors, certain other applicable plan provisions must be uniform for all eligible employees. These include the provisions for determining eligibility, crediting service, vesting, and defining compensation.

Q 4:30   Why and how are plans restructured?

If a plan has different contribution rates for different groups of employees, the simplest method of demonstrating that the contributions are not discriminatory is through restructuring. When a plan is restructured, it is separated into two or more component plans, each of which is evaluated separately with respect to discrimination.

Example. Suppose that an employer provides a plan covering all of its employees, and the plan specifies different contribution rates for employees in each of three groups, as follows:

Group	Contribution Rate (%)	NHCEs	HCEs	Total
A	3	250	15	265
B	5	70	10	80
C	8	180	25	205
		500	50	550

The plan can be restructured into three different component plans, the first covering all employees at a contribution rate of 3 percent, the second covering Group B and Group C employees at a rate of 2 percent, and the third covering Group C employees at a rate of 3 percent. Each of these plans would individually satisfy the 70 percent ratio percentage test under Section 410(b):

Plan	Contribution Rate (%)	Coverage Percentage NHCEs	Coverage Percentage HCEs	Ratio Percentage
1	3	100	100	100
2	2	50	70	71
3	3	36	50	72

Note that if only one HCE were moved from Group A to Group B, the ratio percentage under Plan 2 would fall below 70 percent. However, it is also permissible to apply the average benefits test under Code Section 410(b) to these plans. For this purpose, because all employees are covered under a single plan, the reasonable classification requirement is satisfied. To take advantage of a lower required ratio percentage, it would be necessary only to show that the average benefits percentage for NHCEs is at least 70 percent of that for HCEs.

The average benefits percentage (measured using contributions and, for simplicity, ignoring permitted disparity) would be determined as follows:

Group	Contribution Rate (%)	NHCEs No.	NHCEs Total	HCEs No.	HCEs Total
A	3	250	750	15	45
B	5	70	350	10	50
C	8	180	1,440	25	200
Totals		500	2,540	50	295
Average			5.08		5.90

The average benefits percentage is 86 percent (5.08% ÷ 5.90%), which is well above the 70 percent requirement. If the result were below 70 percent, the inclusion of permitted disparity (which always increases rates more for NHCEs) could bring the result above 70 percent. Therefore, the shifting of one HCE from Group A to Group B would merely require that a slightly more difficult test be performed.

In restructuring a plan, it is not permissible to split an employee between two or more plans. In other words, if an employee is receiving a contribution rate of 6 percent, he or she cannot be considered as two separate employees, each receiving 3 percent. [Treas. Reg. § 1.401(a)(4)-9(c)(2)] This rule leads to a unique situation under Code Section 401(a)(4) rules: a multiple rate structure that is not permitted in a single plan could be allowed if provided in multiple plans.

Example. Consider the following rate structure for an employer with 700 statutorily eligible employees:

Group	Contribution Rate (%)	Number in Group	
		NHCEs	HCEs
A	0	0	55
B	5	600	0
C	15	0	45
		600	100

The above plan clearly cannot meet the requirements of Section 410(b) through restructuring because there would be no NHCEs in the highest contribution rate group. However, consider providing this rate structure in three separate plans, each with a 5 percent contribution rate and covering 200 of the NHCEs and all 45 of the HCEs that are receiving contributions. Each of the plans would have a uniform contribution rate and would cover 33 percent of the NHCEs and 45 percent of the HCEs. The ratio percentage for each plan would be 73 percent (33% ÷ 45%), which exceeds the 70 percent requirement—the safest of safe harbors. It is clear under the law and the regulations that a multiple plan approach works in this situation where restructuring would not.

Q 4:31   How is the general test under Code Section 401(a)(4) used to demonstrate nondiscrimination?

The general test, because of its complexity, is used as a last resort to demonstrate that contributions or benefits under a plan are not discriminatory. The test uses the principles of restructuring. However, unlike normal restructuring, it is not based on assigning employees to different rate categories using plan contribution classifications, but rather on assigning each individual employee to a rate group based on the specific contributions or benefits being provided to that employee.

The general test can be performed on either a defined contribution or a defined benefit basis, regardless of the actual form of the plan being tested. The contribution rates for each employee under a defined contribution plan can be converted to equivalent annual defined benefit accruals using actuarial assumptions in accordance with Treasury Regulations Section 1.401(a)(4)-8. Alternatively, annual defined benefit accruals can be converted to equivalent annual contribution rates based on the same regulation. However, for plan years beginning on or after January 1, 2002, the ability to *cross-test* a defined contribution plan on a benefits basis is subject to additional restrictions and limitations (see Q 4:33). [Treas. Reg. § 1.401(a)(4)-8(b)]

Q 4:32   Can plans be aggregated for the general test?

The general test can be performed by aggregating multiple plans of either the defined contribution or defined benefit type. Conversely, the test can also be performed by disaggregating plans into several components. Any aggregated group of plans or component plan tested must meet the coverage requirements of Code Section 410(b). [Treas. Reg. § 1.410(b)-7(c)] Certain types of plans cannot be aggregated with other plans. These include the salary reduction portion of Section 401(k) plans and the matching and/or after-tax contribution portion of Section 401(m) plans. [Treas. Reg. § 1.410(b)-7(c)] Because the salary reduction contributions under Section 403(b) plans are analogous to those under Section 401(k) plans, it is likely that such contributions cannot be aggregated with other plans, although the regulations do not deal specifically with this point (except to stipulate that Section 403(b) plans cannot support the qualification of Section 401(a) plans).

An important rule for aggregating plans for testing is that they must have the same plan year. Therefore, a plan with a July 1 to June 30 plan year cannot be aggregated with a plan that has a calendar plan year. However, under the good-faith compliance standards in effect for tax-exempt employers, this rule applies only to plan years commencing after October 1, 1997. [Treas. Reg. § 1.410(b)-7(d)]

Q 4:33   How is cross-testing used?

The general test can be applied to any plan on a defined contribution or defined benefit basis (see Q 4:31). It may be advantageous to test defined contribution plans on a benefits basis. This is generally called cross-testing of the plans.

The general test is used only in situations where all other methods for demonstrating that a plan does not discriminate in favor of HCEs have failed. These situations will always involve plans with contribution or accrual rates that are higher for HCEs than for NHCEs. Generally, if the HCEs with the highest rates tend to be older than the NHCEs, testing based on benefits will produce the best results. If some very young HCEs have high rates, testing based on contributions may be more favorable.

A common approach to Section 403(b) plan contribution design is to have higher rates of contribution for older or longer service employees. For example, the following schedule of contribution rates might apply:

Age	Contribution Rate (%)
Below 35	1
35–44	4
45–54	6
55–59	8
60 and over	10

In a typical employee group, the HCEs are likely to be older than the NHCEs. Therefore, based on the contribution rates, the schedule above might produce discrimination in favor of HCEs. However, it requires a significantly higher contribution rate for older employees to provide a given amount of retirement benefits at age 65 than it does for younger employees. Therefore, if the contribution rates in the above schedule are converted to equivalent annual benefit amounts payable at age 65, it is very likely that there would be no resulting discrimination in favor of HCEs.

To demonstrate that the above schedule of contributions is not discriminatory, it is necessary to convert, for each individual participant, the amount of contribution to an equivalent annual pension benefit payable at age 65 using actuarial assumptions in accordance with Treasury Regulations Section 1.401(a)(4)-8. The allowable permitted disparity is added to the benefit rate. Each employee is then assigned to a rate group based on his or her specific annual accrual rate as a percentage of compensation. The rate groups must be set up so that all employees within a range of no more than 5 percent (not 5 percentage points) above and below the midpoint are included in the same rate group. [Treas. Reg. § 1.401(a)(4)-2(c)(2)(v)] For example, if the midpoint of a rate group were 2 percent, then the range of the rate group would be 1.9 percent to 2.1 percent. All employees for whom the annual contribution rate plus permitted disparity converts to an equivalent benefit accrual rate of 1.9 percent to 2.1 percent would be included in that rate group. A plan with a contribution formula similar to that illustrated above could easily have 25 to 50 independent rate groups that must be evaluated.

Once the rate groups are established and each individual is assigned to a group based on an equivalent rate of benefit accrual, then the general test can be applied to the entire array of rate groups. For this purpose, each rate group is assumed to include all employees in that group and all higher groups. [Treas. Reg. § 1.401(a)(4)-2(c)(1)]

Example. The table below illustrates a simplified rate group analysis based on a plan in which the equivalent accrual rates range from 1 percent to 1.5 percent. All statutorily eligible employees of the employer are included in the plan.

| Rate Group (%) | Covered Employees | | Ratio Percentage |
	NHCEs (%)	HCEs (%)	
0.95–1.05	300 (100)	50 (100)	100
1.06–1.16	250 (83)	50 (100)	83
1.17–1.28	200 (67)	40 (80)	84
1.29–1.41	150 (50)	35 (70)	71
1.42–1.56	100 (33)	30 (60)	55

Note that 100 of the 300 NHCEs (33 percent) and 30 of the 50 HCEs (60 percent) received the highest rate of benefit accrual. The ratio percentage for this rate group is 55 percent (33% ÷ 60%), which is below the 70 percent required to pass the ratio percentage test. Thus, the plan fails that test. However, if the plan can pass the average benefits percentage leg of the average benefits test by demonstrating that the average benefit (including permitted disparity) for NHCEs is at least 70 percent of that for HCEs, then it could still pass the general test. In fact, because 86 percent (300 ÷ 350) of the employees are NHCEs, the ratio percentage to pass the average benefits test is reduced to 25 percent (for this purpose, the average of the safe and unsafe harbors described in Qs 4:19 and 4:20 can be used). An individual rate group is exempt from the reasonable classification requirement of the average benefits test. The lowest ratio percentage of any rate group is 55 percent—well in excess of the 25 percent ratio percentage required if the average benefits test is to be used.

Even if the plan did not pass the general test, either because there was a rate group below 25 percent or because the plan could not pass the average benefits percentage leg of the average benefits test, alternative methods might be tried before significant revisions to the plan are made. For instance, there is some flexibility in the rate groups identified, provided that the rates for HCEs are not consistently higher than those for NHCEs within all rate groups. [Treas. Reg. § 1.401(a)(4)-2(c)(2)(v)(A)] Because the range of accrual rates was between 1 percent and 1.5 percent, the first rate group could be 0.9 percent to 1 percent, or could be 1 percent to 1.1 percent. Revising the starting point in this manner would revise all subsequent rate groups. A small change of this type could move some NHCEs and HCEs into different rate groups, which could permit the plan to pass, particularly if it had failed by a small amount.

If changing rate groups does not work, a small change in contribution rates for some HCEs could be made. In the above example, only the highest rate group fails the ratio percentage test. If the number of HCEs in that group were reduced from 30 to 23, then the rate group would pass. It might not be too disruptive to reduce the contribution percentage slightly for seven of the HCEs. Of course, any revision in contribution rates should be designed so that the plan will continue to pass the general test in the future. Ad hoc adjustments designed merely to get through the current year may be undesirable.

Q 4:34   What special requirements apply to cross-tested 403(b) plans?

The general test works in the same way when annual benefit accruals are converted to equivalent contribution rates, and when plans of different types are aggregated. This can be a very complex process if multiple plans of different types are included in the test.

The IRS has issued final regulations that restrict the types of defined contribution plans that can be cross-tested on a benefits basis. [Treas. Reg. § 1.401(a)(4)-8 and 1.401(a)(4)-9] Under the cross-testing regulations, which are effective for plan years beginning on or after January 1, 2002, in order for a defined contribution plan to use cross-testing, it must first satisfy a threshold requirement. Except for certain plans that are aggregated with defined benefit plans, a defined contribution plan must do one of the following:

1. Provide broadly available allocation rates, as defined in the regulations;
2. Provide certain age-based allocation rates that are based on either a gradual age and service schedule or a uniform target benefit allocation; or
3. Satisfy a minimum allocation gateway.

A plan provides *broadly available* allocation rates for a plan year if each allocation rate under the plan is currently available during the plan year to a group of employees that satisfies the ratio percentage test under Code Section 410(b). A plan has age-based allocation rates that are based on either a gradual age or service schedule if the schedule of allocation rates under the plan's formula is available to all employees in the plan and provides for allocation rates that increase *smoothly* and at *regular intervals*. These terms have specific meanings, as defined in the regulations.

Finally, a plan will satisfy the minimum allocation gateway if either (1) each NHCE receives a minimum allocation that is at least one-third of the allocation rate of the HCE with the highest allocation rate, or (2) each NHCE receives a minimum allocation of at least 5 percent of his or her Code Section 415(c)(3) compensation, measured over a period of time permitted under the definition of plan year compensation.

Therefore, unless a plan satisfies the *broadly available* test or the *age-based* or *service-based* allocation test, then in order to apply cross-testing, the plan must provide a minimum allocation for NHCEs equal to at least the lesser of 5 percent of Section 415(c) compensation or one-third of the allocation rate of the HCE with the highest allocation rate. There are special rules for defined contribution plans that are aggregated with defined benefit plans.

Q 4:35   What other factors affect the general test?

Many complex rules deal with specific situations that can be encountered when performing the general test. Some of the most common are the following:

- If a defined benefit plan is included in the testing, special *gateway* tests apply, and rate groups must be analyzed based on both normal benefits and most valuable benefits. [Treas. Reg. § 1.401(a)(4)-3(c)(1)] The normal benefits are those payable at the normal retirement date and under the standard form of benefit payment (typically a life annuity). The most valuable rates are those that take into account subsidies for early retirement and optional payment forms (including lump sums based on the Section 417(e) rates). Under a defined contribution plan, regardless of whether contribution rates or accrual rates are being analyzed, the normal and most valuable rates are virtually always identical.

- With the exception of the 5 percent minimum allocation gateway, contribution or accrual rates under the general test are always determined relative to compensation as defined under Code Section 414(s). This rule applies even if a particular plan's contributions or benefits are determined by reference to base salary or some other limited form of pay.

Q 4:36 What are nondiscriminatory benefits, rights, and features?

Non-salary reduction contributions under a nongovernmental Section 403(b) arrangement must be provided under a plan that does not discriminate in favor of HCEs with respect to certain "benefits, rights, and features." [Treas. Reg. § 1.401(a)(4)-4] These include all optional forms of benefit (such as the right to an annuity form of payment) and all rights and features made available to employees under the plan (such as the right to make after-tax contributions, the right to receive a specific rate or percentage of matching contributions, or the right to take a hardship withdrawal).

Benefits, rights, and features (or BRFs, as they are often called) will be considered to be provided in a nondiscriminatory manner only if they satisfy both the current availability test and the effective availability test. The *current availability* test is satisfied if the group of employees to whom a particular BRF is available satisfies the Section 410(b) ratio percentage test. The *effective availability* test is satisfied if, based on all the relevant facts and circumstances, the group of employees to whom a BRF is effectively available does not substantially favor HCEs.

Therefore, if a Section 403(b) program provides for a 50 percent match for some employees and a 100 percent match for other employees, both matching percentages must be available to a group of employees that will satisfy the Section 410(b) ratio percentage test. In other words, each matching rate must be available to a percentage of nonexcludable NHCEs that is at least 70 percent of the percentage of nonexcludable HCEs who are eligible for that rate of matching contributions.

Q 4:37 How is Notice 89-23 applied?

As previously noted, Notice 89-23 will no longer apply when the final Code Section 403(b) regulations become effective. However, until that time, Notice 89-23 [1989-1 C.B. 654] provides that employers may rely on a reasonable, good-faith interpretation of Code Section 403(b)(12). This means that, with respect to non-salary reduction amounts (i.e., employer contributions and after-tax contributions), sponsors of nongovernmental Section 403(b) plans may rely on a reasonable, good-faith interpretation of Code Sections 401(a)(4), 401(a)(5), and 401(a)(17) as well as Code Sections 401(m) and 410(b). Alternatively, Section 403(b) plans that satisfy one of the three safe harbors described below (and that satisfy the requirements of Code Section 401(m), if applicable) are deemed to satisfy the underlying requirements of Code Section 403(b)(12). However, for plan years after December 31, 1995, Section 403(b) plans must independently satisfy Code Section 401(a)(17). [Ann. 95-48, I.R.B. 1995-23 (May 11, 1995)] Therefore, beginning with the 1996 plan year, Section 403(b) plans (including governmental plans) with employer contributions must comply with the compensation limit under Code Section 401(a)(17) and the regulations thereunder. (Code Section 401(a)(17) does not apply to Section 403(b) salary reduction contributions.)

With respect to salary reduction amounts, Notice 89-23 provides that an employer may rely on a reasonable, good-faith interpretation of Code Section 403(b)(12). Alternatively, Notice 89-23 provides a safe harbor for salary reduction contributions. Under the safe harbor, salary reduction contributions will be deemed to satisfy Code Section 403(b)(12) so long as (1) each employee of the common-law employer sponsoring the plan is eligible to defer annually more than $200 pursuant to a salary reduction agreement, and (2) the opportunity to make such contributions is available to all employees on the same basis. (See Q 4:38 for the definition of common-law employer.)

Three special safe harbors are permitted solely for non-salary reduction contributions to Section 403(b) plans under Notice 89-23. Under these safe harbors, the IRS will deem all *nonmatching* employer contributions under any of the Section 403(b) plans included in the employer's "aggregated 403(b) annuity program" (see Q 4:39) to satisfy the coverage requirements of Code Section 410(b) and the nondiscrimination requirements of Code Section 401(a)(4) if the aggregated Section 403(b) program satisfies one of the following three safe harbors:

1. *Maximum disparity safe harbor.* If at least 50 percent of all statutorily eligible NHCEs of the employer are receiving contribution allocations under the Section 403(b) plan, and at least 70 percent of all participants receiving allocations are NHCEs, then a safe harbor is satisfied if the highest contribution rate (as a percentage of compensation) for any HCE is no greater than 180 percent of the lowest contribution rate for any NHCE.

2. *Lesser disparity safe harbor.* If at least 30 percent of all statutorily eligible NHCEs of the employer are receiving contribution allocations under the Section 403(b) plan, and at least 50 percent of all participants receiving allocations are NHCEs, then a safe harbor is satisfied if the highest contribution rate (as a percentage of compensation) for any HCE is no greater than 140 percent of the lowest contribution rate for any NHCE.

3. *No disparity safe harbor.* If at least 20 percent of all statutorily eligible NHCEs of the employer are receiving contribution allocations under the Section 403(b) plan, and at least 70 percent of all participants receiving allocations are NHCEs, then a safe harbor is satisfied if the contribution rate for all NHCEs is at least as great as that for any HCE. Alternatively, 80 percent can be substituted for 20 percent, and 30 percent for 70 percent, and the safe harbor will be satisfied.

Example. Assume that a not-for-profit employer has 1,000 statutorily eligible employees of which 960 are NHCEs and 40 are HCEs. A plan of the employer that covers 480 NHCEs and all 40 HCEs and provides a contribution rate of 9 percent for HCEs and 5 percent for NHCEs would satisfy the first safe harbor. In fact, any variation in contribution rates among the covered group would be permitted, as long as the highest HCE contribution did not exceed 9 percent and the lowest NHCE contribution was not less than 5 percent. If the plan covered fewer than 480 NHCEs, but at least 288, and provided a 5 percent contribution for NHCEs, then HCEs could receive a contribution as high as 7 percent (140% × 5%) under the second safe harbor. The provisions of the third safe harbor do not allow disparate contribution rates.

For purposes of Notice 89-23, HCEs are generally identified by reference to the definition of HCE under Code Section 414(q) and the regulations thereunder. However, Notice 89-23 provides that the employer may elect to include in its class of HCEs only those employees who, during the plan year, are 5 percent owners of any entity within the same controlled group as the employer or who receive compensation in excess of $50,000 (indexed for inflation). (It is unclear whether this alternative definition of HCEs is still available, because the most recent Code Section 414(q) definition of HCE, which became effective in 1997, is now more liberal than this *alternative definition.*) The requirements of Notice 89-23 are applied as of the last day of the plan year, but any HCE participating in the Section 403(b) plan who terminates in the final quarter of the year must be included.

Compensation, for purposes of Notice 89-23, has the same meaning as in Code Section 414(s), and as limited by Code Section 401(a)(17), *except* that it includes only compensation paid by a Section 403(b) eligible employer.

If the vesting schedules applicable to employee accounts are not uniform for all employees in the testing group, then an adjustment in contribution rates must be made in accordance with the principles of Revenue Ruling 74-166. [1974-1 C.B. 97]

If a contribution by an employee is made as a result of a one-time irrevocable election when first eligible for the plan, it is considered an employer contribution for purposes of Code Section 401(a)(4) and Notice 89-23. Also, contributions *picked up* for employees by government entities (as permitted under Code Section 414(h)) are treated as employer contributions.

Q 4:38   Who is the employer for purposes of Notice 89-23?

For purposes of the safe harbor for salary reduction contributions, the *employer* refers to the common law employer (not the controlled group) sponsoring or maintaining the plan. If the common law employer has historically treated its various geographically distinct units as separate for employee benefit purposes, each unit, rather than the entire common law employer, may be considered a separate organization for purposes of the safe harbor, so long as the units are operated independently on a day-to-day basis. However, Notice 89-23 provides that for purposes of this rule, units of the same employer are generally not considered to be "geographically distinct" if they are located within the same Standard Metropolitan Statistical Area.

With respect to the safe harbors applicable to non-salary reduction contributions, the *employer* is deemed to be the entity contributing to or maintaining the Section 403(b) program, and each entity in the same controlled group (as determined pursuant to the rules of Code Sections 414(b), (c), (m), and (o)), which is a Section 403(b) eligible employer. For these purposes, the controlled group is deemed to include each entity of which at least 80 percent of the directors, trustees, or other individual members of the entity's governing body are either representatives of, or directly or indirectly control or are controlled by, the contributing employer. In addition, an entity is included in the same controlled group as the contributing employer if it directly or indirectly provides at least 80 percent of the contributing employer's operating funds, and there is a degree of common management or supervision between the entities. The latter exists if the entity providing the funds has the power to appoint or nominate officers, senior management, or members of the board of directors of the entity receiving the funds, or if the entity providing the funds is involved in the day-to-day operations of the entity receiving the funds.

Notice 89-23 also provides specific guidance for determining which governmental entities must be considered a single *employer* for purposes of the safe harbors for non-salary reduction contributions. This is the sole aspect of Notice 89-23 that will be applicable after 2008.

Q 4:39   What is an *aggregated 403(b) annuity program* for purposes of Notice 89-23?

The term *aggregated 403(b) annuity program* refers to all of the annuity contracts described in Code Section 403(b)(1), all of the custodial accounts described in Code Section 403(b)(7), and all of the retirement income accounts described in Code Section 403(b)(9) to which an employer makes contributions. In addition, the employer may elect to include any one or more of the employer's plans described in Code Section 401(a) (including defined benefit plans), annuity plans described in Code Section 403(a), governmental plans described in Code Section 414(d), and church plans described in Code Section 414(e) to which the employer contributes (to the extent that such plans cover the employer's employees), as long as each plan that the employer decides to include in the program satisfies Code Sections 410(b) and 401(a)(4).

Q 4:40 Which categories of employees may be excluded under Notice 89-23?

Notice 89-23 provides that, for purposes of applying any of the safe harbors under the Notice, the following employees may be excluded (but only if all similarly situated employees are not eligible to participate):

- Nonresident aliens, as described in Code Section 410(b)(3)(C)
- Students performing services described in Code Section 3121(b)(10)
- Employees who normally work less than 20 hours per week
- Employees who made a one-time irrevocable election to participate in a Section 414(d) governmental plan instead of the Section 403(b) plan
- Employees covered by a collective bargaining agreement (if retirement benefits were the subject of good-faith bargaining)
- Certain professors providing services on a temporary basis to another institution (if certain conditions apply)
- Certain individuals who have taken a vow of poverty, if their religious order provides for their retirement
- Certain other employees of governmental entities

In addition to the employees listed above, the following employees may be excluded for purposes of the safe harbor regarding salary reduction contribution (but only if all similarly situated employees are not eligible to participate):

- Employees who are participants in a Section 457(b) deferred compensation plan
- Employees who are eligible to participate in a Section 401(k) plan or another Section 403(b) program of the employer that provides for salary reduction contributions
- Employees whose contributions to the plan under its maximum deferral percentage would be $200 or less

For purposes of the safe harbors applicable to non-salary reduction contributions, a Section 403(b) plan may also exclude employees who have not satisfied the minimum age and service requirements set forth in the plan (so long as such requirements are permissible under Code Section 410(a), applied as if Code Section 410(a) were applicable to Section 403(b) plans), but only if all employees not meeting those requirements are excluded from participation in such non-salary reduction contributions. Notice 89-23 also allows for separate testing of "otherwise excludable employees" (i.e., employees who would be excludable under the previous sentence but for the fact that they, or other employees of the same or lower age, or with the same or fewer years of service, are not excluded from coverage under the plan).

The final Code Section 403(b) regulations provide that, for plan years beginning after December 31, 2008, Section 403(b) plans may no longer exclude the following groups of employees:

- Employees covered by a collective bargaining agreement;
- Professors providing services on a temporary basis to another institution;
- Employees who made a one-time irrevocable election to participate in a governmental plan; or
- Individuals affiliated with a religious order who take a vow of poverty.

However, for plans that on July 26, 2007 relied on Notice 89-23 to exclude the last three categories of employees above, the final Code Section 403(b) regulations provide that such plans may continue to exclude such employees (for purposes of the universal availability requirement) until plan years beginning on or after January 1, 2010. For plans that on July 1, 2007 relied on Notice 89-23 to exclude collectively bargained employees, such plans may continue to exclude such employees (for purposes of the universal availability requirement) until the later of (1) plan years beginning on or after January 1, 2009, or (2) the earlier of (a) the date on which the collective bargaining agreement terminates (without regard to any extension after July 26, 2007), or (b) July 26, 2010. For governmental plans (as defined in Code Section 414(d)), the plan will not fail to satisfy the universal availability requirement as a result of excluding any of the four groups of employees above before the earlier of (1) the close of the first regular legislative session of the legislative body with the authority to amend the plan that begins on or after January 1, 2009, or (2) January 1, 2011.

Q 4:41   How are defined benefits valued under Notice 89-23?

Notice 89-23 provides that the rules under Treasury Regulations Section 1.403(b)-1(d)(4) should be used for converting benefits under a defined benefit plan to equivalent contributions for purposes of meeting a safe harbor. This regulation was first published in 1956 for the purpose of determining the impact on the maximum exclusion allowance (MEA) calculation of a defined benefit plan, a totally different purpose from the determination of compliance with discrimination rules.

Under the regulation, there are two approaches that can be used to determine the equivalent contribution rate for a defined benefit plan. One approach uses a table published in the regulation. [Treas. Reg. § 1.403(b)-1(d)(4)] The table provides an equivalent rate of contribution for combinations of virtually all possible current ages and retirement ages based on one dollar per year of pension benefit. The table was prepared using an 8 percent interest rate, postretirement mortality, no preretirement mortality, and no assumed salary increases before retirement. The table makes no distinction between past service and future service pension benefits, which is logical for determining the MEA, but not logical for determining the equivalent contribution rate for nondiscrimination testing. For example, using the table would make no sense for determining discrimination when past service benefits are updated to current or future salary levels.

The second approach under Treasury Regulations Section 1.403(b)-1(d)(4) is to calculate equivalent contribution rates "under any other method utilizing recognized actuarial principles which are consistent with the provisions of the plan under which such contributions are made and the method adopted by the employer for funding the benefits under the plan." [Treas. Reg. § 1.403(b)-1(d)(4)] Since the methods and assumptions used for pension valuations are complex and can vary considerably, it is not obvious how to interpret this requirement. It seems clear that the interest rate, the postretirement mortality rate, and, if applicable, the salary increase rate used in the most recent actuarial valuation should be considered. Whether employee turnover and preretirement mortality should be used is not clear because a defined benefit plan provides benefits payable due to termination and mortality, which are funded independently of retirement costs. But, given that the purpose of the regulation was related to the determination of the MEA, it is likely that the use of turnover and preretirement mortality rates is not assumed because the intent of the calculation is to determine the amount of annual contributions that is equivalent in value to a pension benefit, assuming that an employee remains in employment until the normal retirement date.

It also seems clear that the use of a salary increase assumption consistent with the most recent actuarial valuation is not only appropriate but required. First, the regulation specifically requires that the same assumptions be used that were used for the valuation. [Treas. Reg. § 1.403(b)-(1)(d)(4)] Second, ignoring a salary increase assumption, particularly under a final average pay defined benefit plan, is inconsistent with the goal of determining the amount of annual contributions deemed made on behalf of the employee that would accumulate to the value of projected pension benefits. Finally, the legislative history of TRA '86 indicates that it was expected that assumed future salary increases would be taken into account in testing for discrimination.

Chapter 5

Investments

Peter Gulia, Esq.
Fiduciary Guidance Counsel

Section 403(b) of the Internal Revenue Code (Code) permits a participant's retirement savings to be invested in fixed and variable annuity contracts and SEC-registered fund shares. This chapter explains 403(b) investment options, and an employer's responsibility for its selection (if any) of investment options.

Because almost all Section 403(b) plans provide for participant-directed investment, this chapter includes an explanation of Section 404(c) of the Employee Retirement Income Security Act of 1974 (ERISA)—a rule that allows plan fiduciaries to avoid liability for a participant's investment directions, along with similar state law for church plans and governmental plans not governed by ERISA. Most participants need help with retirement plan investment choices, and this chapter explains relevant law and interpretations about providing investment education and advice to participants.

Author's Usage Note

For convenience, this chapter uses several words in a specially defined context.

This chapter sometimes distinguishes between an ERISA plan, a governmental plan, and a church plan. In this context, an ERISA plan refers to a plan that is governed by Title I of ERISA, a governmental plan refers to a plan described in ERISA § 3(32), and a church plan refers to a plan described in ERISA § 3(33) that has not elected to be governed by ERISA. Further, this chapter uses the word "non-ERISA" to refer to a governmental plan, a church plan, or to a plan that meets the conditions for tax treatment under Internal Revenue Code Section 403(b) but is not a plan that is governed by ERISA.

This chapter uses the word "contract" to refer to an annuity contract, a custodial account, or another form of investment that Section 403(b) permits as an eligible investment.

In this chapter, "payer" refers to any custodian, insurer, plan administrator, or other person responsible for deciding or paying a claim under a governmental plan.

This chapter uses the word "state" in its popular meaning to refer to the District of Columbia or any state, commonwealth, territory, possession, or similar jurisdiction within the United States. Because this chapter has many references to state law, this chapter makes parallel references to a "state" (rather than to the lawyers' word "jurisdiction") for reading ease. For example, although the District of Columbia is not a state, law that applies to a person because he or she resides in the District of Columbia is state law, as distinguished from U.S. law or federal law, which applies throughout the United States.

Throughout this chapter, the phrase "investment adviser" is used in its specially defined securities-law sense. Although "advisor" is the usual spelling of the common noun, the statute that defines the term spells it "adviser", and this chapter uses that spelling.

Author's Citations Note

This chapter includes many general explanations of state laws. To support each such statement with citations to more than 50 state laws would be unwieldy in this chapter's summary. Moreover, a pension practitioner usually is interested first in a general sense of the state laws. To these ends, the chapter cites the Uniform Trust Code and other uniform acts recommended by the National Conference of Commissioners on Uniform State Laws [www.nccusl. org]. A reader who wants to find whether a particular state enacted a statute based on a uniform law might begin with this chapter's citations to Uniform Laws Annotated [ULA], which includes citations for states' adoptions of, and variations from, the recommended uniform laws.

Because most employee-benefits practitioners do not use printed volumes to read federal or state statutes or regulations, this chapter's citations to statutes and regulations omit publisher and year references. A reader may find statutes efficiently and inexpensively by using Aspen Publishers' Loislaw service (for more information, visit www.loislaw.com or call 1-877-471-5632).

Specialty citations are in the forms, and with the abbreviations, customary to employee-benefits or tax practitioners, including the abbreviations shown in the book's front matter.

403(b) Investment Options

Q 5:1   What kinds of investments can be used to fund a 403(b) plan?

Unlike a Section 401(a) qualified retirement plan, which may invest in almost any kind of investment available in the United States, a Section 403(b) plan is limited to a few specific kinds of investments specified by the Internal Revenue Code (Code).

For most Section 403(b) participants, there are only two kinds of investments allowed:

1. A custodial account that holds shares of SEC-registered "mutual" funds; and

2. An annuity contract.

A Section 403(b) plan maintained by a church may include these options and retirement income accounts.

Some plans include life insurance or other "grandfathered" investments that might be allowed under a transition rule. For an explanation of whether a Section 403(b) amount can be invested in a stable-value fund, see Q 5:3. For an explanation of whether a Section 403(b) amount can be invested in a collective investment fund, see Q 5:4. For an explanation of whether a Section 403(b) amount can be invested in a "brokerage" account, see Q 5:5.

Practice Pointer. In some circumstances, an employer might be permitted to resolve federal income tax consequences that arise from contributions that were intended as Section 403(b) contributions but were mistakenly invested in something other than a proper Section 403(b) contract.

Q 5:2 May an employer provide different investment options for different classes of employees?

Generally, it may be difficult to provide different investment options for different classes of employees.

For instance, if a Section 403(b) plan includes contributions other than elective contributions, such a plan must meet the same coverage and nondiscrimination requirements that apply to a Section 401(a) qualified retirement plan. [I.R.C. § 403(b)(12)(A)(i); Treas. Reg. § 1.403(b)-5(a)] (A governmental plan has no tax-Code nondiscrimination rules.) [I.R.C. § 401(a)(5)(G)] Under those rules, a right to a particular form of investment is an "other right or feature" that must meet nondiscrimination requirements. [Treas. Reg. § 1.401(a)(4)-4] Therefore, unless the employer is confident that each class or group of employees will meet the nondiscrimination requirement, it might be unwise to limit investment options by class or group.

Note. An exception permits separate testing of those employees who belong to a collective-bargaining unit. [Treas. Reg. § 1.410(b)-7(c)(5)]

Those qualified-plan coverage and nondiscrimination rules for investment options do not apply to a Section 403(b) elective deferrals. [Treas. Reg. § 1.403(b)-5(a)(2)] Nevertheless, some practitioners believe that a similar rule should be applied even to a "voluntary-only" plan to give meaning to the "universal-availability" requirement that every employee has an effective opportunity to make elective contributions. [I.R.C. § 403(b)(12)(A)(ii); Treas. Reg. § 1.403(b)-5(b)(2)]

If an employer limits employees' Section 403(b) investment choices for reasons other than neutral concerns about the administrative burden on the employer, that involvement might cause a "voluntary-only" Section 403(b) plan that otherwise might have avoided ERISA coverage (see chapter 9 and Q 5:35) to become governed by ERISA's design, disclosure, reporting, and fiduciary requirements. [ERISA §§ 3(2), 4(a); D.O.L. Reg. § 2510.3-2(f)] If an employer prefers that ERISA not govern a plan, such an employer might avoid unnecessarily restricting employees' Section 403(b) investment choices.

Q 5:3   Can a Section 403(b) amount be invested in a stable-value fund?

Section 403(b) amounts can be invested in a stable-value fund only if it is an SEC-registered fund, a church plan's retirement income account, or a grandfathered investment.

What most pension consultants mean when they refer to a *stable-value fund* is a portfolio of investments that may include insurance company guaranteed interest contracts (GICs), bank investment contracts (BICs), bonds or bond funds, and similar investments. Sometimes a stable-value fund will include a bank's or an insurance company's guarantee so that the fund can credit a promised return even when the portfolio's actual return (without the guarantee) is lower.

With most employers, Section 403(b) contributions can be invested only in an annuity contract or a custodial account that holds SEC-registered fund shares. (See Q 5:1.) Therefore, Section 403(b) contributions can be invested in a stable-value fund only if the "fund" is an annuity contract. Currently, there is no stable-value fund that is registered with the Securities and Exchange Commission (SEC), so none could be eligible to be a regulated investment company (see Q 5:11) that could offer shares to a custodian for a Section 403(b)(7) custodial account. [See I.R.C. §§ 403(b)(7)(C), 851(a)(1)(A)] Further, accounting standards might make it impractical, if not impossible, for an investment manager to develop an SEC-registered stable-value fund that would both maintain a stable net asset value and also account for the fund's assets in a manner that the SEC would not question, at least for shares available for purchase by Section 403(b)(7) custodial accounts. [See Financial Accounting Standards Board, "Reporting of Fully Benefit-Responsive Investment Contracts Held by Certain Investment Companies Subject to the AICPA Investment Company Guide," FASB Staff Position Nos. AAG INV-1 and SOP 94-4-1 (Dec. 29, 2005), available at http://www.fasb.org/fasb_staff_positions/fsp_aag_inv-1&sop_94-4-1.pdf (visited Jan. 11, 2008)]

Q 5:4   Can a Section 403(b) amount be invested in a collective investment fund?

No. Although a group trust, collective investment fund, collective trust fund, or similar arrangement might be permitted under other laws, such a trust or fund is not an SEC-registered investment company.

Note. A group trust is a commingling of trusts of retirement plans. [Rev. Rul. 81-100, 1981-1 C.B. 326; *see also* Rev. Rul. 2004-67, 2004-28 I.R.B. 28] Although the law of trusts generally requires a trustee to keep separate each trust's money, property, and rights, these commingled funds managed by a bank or trust company are allowed as a regulated exception to that general rule. [*See, e.g.,* 7 Pa. Stat. § 404(b); 10 Pa. Code §§ 15.1 to 15.13; accord 20 Pa. Consol. Stat. § 7780(d)] Securities law describes such a commingled trust for retirement plans as a collective trust fund. [Securities Act of 1933 § 3(a)(2), 15 U.S.C. § 77c(a)(2)] Banking law describes it as a collective investment fund. [12 C.F.R. § 9.18]

Q 5:5   Can Section 403(b) amounts be invested in a "brokerage" account?

Section 403(b) amounts can be invested only in an annuity contract or a custodial account that holds SEC-registered fund shares. (See Q 5:1.) While a Section 403(b) custodial account may hold SEC-registered fund shares (see Qs 5:10–5:11), it cannot hold other securities. Therefore, if an account can include securities other than SEC-registered fund shares, it is not a Section 403(b)(7) custodial account. [I.R.C. § 403(b)(7)(A)(i)]

Practice Pointer. If a "brokerage" or securities account is held by a bank, trust company, or IRS-approved custodian and is restricted to investing in SEC-registered fund shares, it might qualify as part of a Section 403(b)(7) custodial account. Along with other conditions, the restrictions against investments other than SEC-registered fund shares must be legally enforceable against all custodians and broker-dealers that serve concerning these accounts. A safer course would be to obtain an Internal Revenue Service (IRS) ruling that an arrangement's "brokerage" provisions do not cause an otherwise qualifying custodial account to lose the tax treatment of Code Section 403(b)(7).

Custodial Accounts

Q 5:6   What is a custodial account?

A Section 403(b)(7) custodial account is a trust agreement or other contract under a Section 403(b) plan under which the trustee or custodian must invest all contributions only in shares of one or more SEC registered funds (see Qs 5:10–5:11). [I.R.C. § 403(b)(7)(A)(i); Treas. Reg. § 1.403(b)-8(d)(2)]

To obtain Section 403(b) tax treatment, a participant may not hold fund shares directly. [I.R.C. § 403(b)(7)(A)(i)] Instead, the shares must be held in what the Internal Revenue Code calls a *custodial account*. The custodian must be a bank or trust company. [I.R.C. §§ 401(f), 403(b)(7)(B), 408(n), 581] A nonbank trustee, such as a securities broker-dealer, may serve as custodian upon IRS approval. [I.R.C. §§ 401(f)(2), 403(b)(7)(B); Treas. Reg. § 1.401-12(n)] The custodian must apply at least the restrictions on distributions required by Code Section 403(b). [I.R.C. § 403(b)(7)(A)(ii)] A custodial account must provide that its assets cannot be used other than for the exclusive benefit of participants or their beneficiaries. [I.R.C. §§ 401(a)(2), 401(f)(1)]

A Section 403(b)(7) custodial account might provide for investment in funds of one fund "complex" or "family"—that is, funds that have in common an investment manager or group of investment managers. In that case, a participant who wants to redirect a portion of his or her Section 403(b) investment to a fund sponsored by a different complex must redeem such a custodial account's investment in the fund that is no longer desired, wait to receive the proceeds, and then, if permitted under the employer's Section 403(b) plan, effect an exchange, transfer, or rollover. Depending on the diligence of the participant, both custodians' recordkeepers, and any intermediaries, the transaction might take a few business days.

Some providers offer a Section 403(b)(7) custodial account that permits investment in funds of many different fund families. Such an account might provide that both the redemption and purchase aspects of an account investment direction are credited on the same New York Stock Exchange day so that the participant's amounts are not out of the market for even one day.

An account that permits investment in bonds or stocks other than SEC-registered fund shares is not a Section 403(b) investment because Code Section 403(b)(7) permits a custodial account to hold only SEC-registered fund shares that are also regulated investment company shares.

For more information about custodial accounts, see chapter 7.

Q 5:7   Is a custodial account a security that is separate from the fund shares that the account invests in?

Maybe. Several SEC no-action letters suggest that relevant divisions of the U.S. Securities and Exchange Commission would not recommend enforcement action because a Section 403(b) custodial account is offered and sold without SEC registration if:

1. The account is "funded solely by specific mutual fund shares";
2. The fund shares are offered by an SEC-registered prospectus;
3. Each fund's prospectus will include disclosures concerning the Section 403(b) plan and the custodial account;
4. Each fund's prospectus is furnished to each participant, beneficiary, and alternate payee;
5. The plan's and the custodial account's provisions make it impossible (or at least quite unlikely) that a participant's investment results could be affected by anything other than his or her investment directions;
6. There is no significant delay in implementing a participant's, beneficiary's, or alternate payee's directions;
7. The custodial account is used to meet the Section 403(b) tax-qualification requirement, but not to provide an investment benefit;
8. The custodial account provides only "custodial services", and not any investment service;
9. "No custodian or trustee has investment discretion with respect to the plan" or the custodial account;
10. Investment advice (if any) is not a feature of the custodial account, but rather is a separate service provided by a separate investment adviser or broker-dealer that is properly registered for the service that it provides.

[SEC No-Action Letters: Cleveland Clinic Foundation, Fed. Sec. L. Rep. (CCH) ¶ 82,303, 1979 WL 14692 (July 13, 1979, publicly available Aug. 12, 1979); Merrill Lynch, Pierce, Fenner & Smith, Inc., Fed. Sec. L. Rep. (CCH)

¶ 81,025, 1977 WL 14960 (Dec. 29, 1976, publicly available Jan. 28, 1977); National Bank of Georgia, 1976 WL 9082 (June 29, 1976, publicly available July 29, 1976 and Aug. 9, 1976, publicly available Sept. 9, 1976); Investment Company Institute, Fed. Sec. L. Rep. (CCH) ¶ 80,018, 1974 WL 11067 (Sept. 20, 1974, publicly available Oct. 21, 1974); Peoples Pension Plans, Inc., (Aug 29, 1972, publicly available Sept. 28, 1972); *see also* Investment Company Act Release No. 5510 (Oct. 8, 1968); *see generally* SEC v W. J. Howey, 328 U.S. 293 (1946)] In 1974, the Investment Company Institute urged a view that a right or interest concerning a custodial account be treated as not a security separate from that of the fund shares that the account invests in. The SEC staff did not concur (or disagree) with the Institute's view.

Q 5:8   Can a custodian accept compensation from a mutual fund?

When a Section 403(b)(7) custodial account is held under an ERISA plan, the account's custodian can accept compensation from a mutual fund's distributor or transfer agent only if the arrangements are such that all fund compensation benefits the account and not the custodian. Such an arrangement must be disclosed to and approved by an independent plan fiduciary.

If a custodian (or any affiliate) gives investment advice or otherwise is a fiduciary, any fund compensation must be credited to the plan or offset against the custodian's fee in such a manner that the custodian's total fee (for example, fund compensation plus net fee charged) cannot vary based on any person's investment direction. [D.O.L. ERISA Adv. Op. 97-15A (May 22, 1997)]

If, however, the custodian (and any affiliate) is not a fiduciary, does not have power to change the investment menu except upon 120 days' notice, and does not give investment advice, the DOL suggests that the fund compensation need not be leveled as long as the independent plan fiduciary approves the compensation arrangement as reasonable. [D.O.L. ERISA Adv. Op. 97-16A (May 22, 1997)]

Both the custodian and the independent plan fiduciary are at risk of participating in a prohibited transaction if the overall compensation arrangement is either not a reasonable arrangement or provides more than reasonable compensation. [D.O.L. Reg. § 2550.408b-2(e)]

In all cases, the independent plan fiduciary must obtain sufficient information concerning all fees and all other compensation to make an informed decision that the custodian's compensation for services is no more than reasonable. [D.O.L. ERISA Adv. Op. 97-15A (May 22, 1997)]

Note. In late 2006 and in 2007, there were filed in federal courts several ERISA lawsuits, generally alleged as class actions and on behalf of each affected retirement plan. These lawsuits assert that, even with full disclosure to independent plan fiduciaries, indirect or "revenue-sharing" compensation—even if reasonable in amount—is inherently unreasonable so as to result in fiduciary breaches and prohibited transactions. Further, these lawsuits allege that an absence of disclosing all details of the indirect or "revenue-sharing" compensation to participants and others who direct investment under a plan means that they did not receive sufficient information about how expenses might vary between plan investment options (see Qs 5:48, 5:51). Thus, with one of the conditions for ERISA Section 404(c) relief not met, all plan fiduciaries (including the plan sponsor and its directors, executive officers, and plan committee members) remain responsible even for losses that result from a participant's investment direction. The contributing author is tracking this litigation, and posts updates at http://www. FiduciaryGuidanceCounsel.com.

Funds

Q 5:9   What is a *fund*?

A *fund* is a corporation, partnership, or business trust that invests commonly for investors who have selected that fund. [*See, e.g.,* Investment Company Act §§ 2(a)(8), 3(a)(1), 15 U.S.C. §§ 80a-2(a)(8), 80a-3(a)(1)] Pooling is the key aspect of fund investing; by banding together, the shareholders may get diversification and management that they could not get if each investor acted alone.

Q 5:10   What is a *registered investment company*?

A *registered investment company* is a fund (see Q 5:9) that has, as required or permitted by the Investment Company Act, registered with the SEC. [Investment Company Act §§ 7, 8, 15 U.S.C. §§ 80a-7, 80a-8] The *Investment Company Act of 1940* is a federal law that regulates how some funds are operated.

Many people who use the popular name mutual fund are familiar only with the kind of investment company that securities lawyers call an open-end management company. Code Section 403(b)(7) does not preclude a custodial account from holding shares of an exchange-traded fund or a closed-end fund, but some aspects of how these fund shares are sold and traded might make it impractical or inconvenient to use these shares for a Section 403(b) custodial account.

Q 5:11   What is a *regulated investment company*?

Although securities lawyers refer to a *registered investment company*, tax lawyers refer to a *regulated investment company*—the defined term provided by the tax Code. Most (but not all) regulated investment companies are SEC-registered funds. [I.R.C. § 851(a)(1)(A)] A few other kinds of funds could be a regulated investment company for federal income tax purposes. [I.R.C. §§ 851(a)(1)(B), (a)(2)] But shares that are not SEC-registered (or even SEC-registered shares of a fund that is not an SEC-registered investment company) cannot lawfully be sold to a custodian for a Section 403(b)(7) custodial account.

[Securities Act § 3(a)(2), 15 U.S.C. § 77b(a)(2); Investment Company Act §§ 3(c)(3), 3(c)(11), 15 U.S.C. §§ 80a-3(c)(3), 80a-3(c)(11)]

Note. To many people, the popular expression mutual fund (which is not a defined term in either federal securities law or federal tax law) suggests a fund with individual investors' shares that are easily redeemable and, in their understanding, excludes exchange-traded funds, closed-end funds, and some other kinds of funds that, if SEC-registered, could be properly available to Section 403(b)(7) custodial accounts. Because almost all SEC-registered funds also meet the requirements for federal tax treatment as a regulated investment company, this chapter uses "SEC-registered fund" to refer to the kind that can sell its shares to a custodian for a Section 403(b)(7) custodial account.

Caution. A fund that is registered with the SEC under the Securities Act of 1933 but is not registered under the Investment Company Act of 1940 might not meet all of the tax Code's conditions to be a regulated investment company available for Section 403(b) purchases.

Q 5:12 How is a fund invested?

The manager of an SEC-registered fund has a fiduciary duty to invest the fund according to the investment objectives and restrictions stated by the fund's prospectus, and as provided by the manager's investment-advisory agreement with the fund. However, the fund cannot give any assurance that its objective will be achieved.

Q 5:13 Do the assets of an ERISA-governed plan include the assets of a fund that the plan invests in?

No. The assets of a fund do not become plan assets because of the plan's investment in shares of the fund. [ERISA § 401(b)(1); DOL ERISA Interpretive Bulletin 75-2, (Feb. 6, 1975), 51 Fed. Reg. 41280 (Nov. 13, 1986), 61 Fed. Reg. 33847 (July 1, 1996), reprinted in 29 C.F.R. § 2509.75-2]

Caution. A plan's investment in SEC-registered fund shares does not by itself cause the fund or its investment adviser to become a fiduciary or a party-in-interest. [ERISA § 3(21)(B)] But an investment adviser might become a plan fiduciary or a party-in-interest for a reason other than the plan's investment in fund shares. [ERISA § 3(21)(B)); DOL ERISA Interpretive Bulletin 75-3, 40 Fed. Reg. 31599 (July 28, 1975), redesignated 41 Fed. Reg. 1906 (Jan. 13, 1976), reprinted in 29 C.F.R. § 2509.75-3] If a fund's investment adviser, beyond managing the SEC-registered fund, also gives investment advice to the plan, the investment adviser becomes a plan fiduciary. [ERISA § 3(21)]

Q 5:14 How does a mutual fund set its adviser's fee?

As explained above, the assets of a fund are not plan assets, and a fund's adviser is not a fiduciary of a retirement plan that invests in fund shares.

(See Q 5:11.) But a mutual fund's adviser has some fiduciary duties concerning its receipt of compensation for its services. [Investment Company Act § 36(b), 15 U.S.C. § 80a-35(b)] A fund adviser's fee need not be the lowest fee that would have resulted from arms-length bargaining. Instead, it is enough that the fee is not "so disproportionately large that it bears no reasonable relationship to the services rendered" and is "within the range of what would have been negotiated at arm's length." [Gartenberg v. Merrill Lynch Asset Management, Inc., 694 F.2d 923, 928 (2d Cir. 1982); *see also* Krinsk v. Fund Asset Management, Inc., 875 F.2d 404 (2d Cir. 1989)]

Annuity Contracts

Q 5:15   What is an *annuity contract*?

An *annuity contract* is an insurance company's written promise that it will pay to the contract holder, or to one or more annuitants, a specified amount of money on a regular basis over a specified period. It may be one of two kinds: fixed (see Qs 5:16, 5:17) or variable (see Qs 5:18-21).

Although a contract holder need not choose an annuity option, the insurance company must offer annuity options. [*See* Treas. Reg. § 1.403(b)-2(b)(2), 1.403(b)-8(c)(1)] Because under an annuity option an insurer is obligated to keep paying the specified amount no matter how long the annuitant lives, the annuity contract is a form of insurance, and is regulated by state insurance law.

A Section 403(b) annuity contract must be nontransferable; that is, the participant may not assign his or her contract rights to any other person, except to the insurer to secure a contract loan. [I.R.C. §§ 401(g), 403(b)]

For more information on annuity contracts, refer to chapter 6.

Fixed Annuity Contracts

Q 5:16   What is a *fixed annuity contract*?

A *fixed annuity contract* is a form of annuity contract that has guaranteed minimum interest, and typically credits a current interest rate that the insurer declares from time to time (often, each month). The fixed annuity holder hopes that the insurer will continue to declare reasonably market-sensitive interest rates; the insurer, however, has no obligation to do so. A fixed annuity contract is regulated by insurance law, but not by securities law. [Securities Act of 1933 § 3(a)(8), 15 U.S.C. § 77c(a)(8); Securities Act Rule 151]

Q 5:17   How is a fixed annuity invested?

The contributions received under a fixed annuity contract are commingled with the insurer's other assets in its general account. An insurer must invest according to state insurance law. An insurer has a fiduciary duty to invest its general account assets for the benefit of all contract holders (except to the extent that applicable law requires different investments).

An insurance company does not "pass through" to contract holders the results of the investment performance of the general account. Rather, the insurer sets current interest rates that its management believes it can support based on projections of future investment performance.

Variable Annuity Contracts

Q 5:18 What is a *variable annuity contract*?

A *variable annuity contract* is a form of annuity contract (see Q 5:15) in which the "cash value" goes up or down with the investment performance of insurance company separate accounts. A separate account might itself be a registered investment company, or a separate account might invest in a fund's shares.

> **Note.** For ERISA purposes, an insurance company may treat a division of a separate account (if it provides adequate and fair separate accounting) as a separate account. [D.O.L. ERISA Adv. Op. 2005-22A (Dec. 7, 2005)]

As is the case with other SEC-registered funds, there can be no guarantee that a separate account or subaccount will achieve its stated investment objective. A variable annuity contract is regulated by insurance law and securities law.

For information about securities laws, see chapter 8.

Q 5:19 How is a separate account invested?

The manager of an SEC-registered fund has a fiduciary duty to invest the fund according to the investment objective and restrictions stated by the fund's prospectus together with any further restrictions stated by the manager's investment-advisory agreement. However, the fund cannot give any assurance that its objective will be achieved.

An insurance company separate account or subaccount typically invests in the shares or units of just one fund or unit investment trust. At least concerning contracts offered, directly or indirectly, to Section 403(b) participants, the underlying fund is a registered investment company and, therefore, should be invested as stated by that fund's prospectus.

Q 5:20 Can a Section 403(b) annuity contract include publicly-available funds?

Yes. An annuity contract "that is intended to qualify as an annuity contract for purposes of [Code Section] 403(b)" may permit the contract holder to direct investment in publicly available funds if "no additional federal tax liability would have been incurred if the employer . . . had instead paid an amount into a . . . custodial account that satisfied the requirements of [Code Section]

403(b)(7)(A)." [Rev. Proc. 99-44 (Nov. 16, 1999), modifying Rev. Rul. 81-225, 1981-2 C.B. 12, and discussing Rev. Rul. 82-55, 1982-1 C.B. 12; Rev. Rul. 82-54, 1982-1 C.B. 11; Rev. Rul. 80-274, 1980-2 C.B. 27; Rev. Rul. 77-85, 1977-1 C.B. 12; Christofferson v. United States, 749 F.2d 513 (8th Cir. 1984); I.R.C. §§ 817–818; Treas. Reg. § 1.817-5]

Q 5:21   What duties does a broker have to advise a participant about whether an annuity contract is suitable?

If a broker or its representative "recommends" or suggests a deferred variable annuity contract to an individual (rather than to a plan fiduciary or a plan sponsor), the broker must have "a reasonable basis to believe that the [purchase] is suitable" after considering the individual's intended use of the contract and considering only the contract's "features" other than tax treatment. [Financial Industry Regulatory Authority (FINRA), Conduct Rule 2821(b)(1)(A) Members' Responsibilities Regarding Deferred Variable Annuities; *see also* FINRA Regulatory Notice 07-53 Deferred Variable Annuities–SEC Approves New NASD Rule 2821 Governing Deferred Variable Annuity Transactions (Nov. 2007)] According to the regulator's interpretation, concerning a tax-deferred retirement plan "[a broker's] representative should recommend a variable annuity [contract] *only* when its other benefits [those other than tax deferral], such as lifetime income payments [or] family protection through the death benefit . . . support the recommendation." [NASD Notice to Members 99-35, The NASD Reminds Members Of Their Responsibilities Regarding The Sales Of Variable Annuities at ¶ 11 (May 1999) (emphasis added)] Usually, this will require making a record that the individual could need at least one of the contract's insurance promises.

> **Note.** These Conduct Rules for securities brokers do not define the word "recommendation." But the regulator has interpreted it to include any oral or written communication that "reasonably would be viewed" as a suggestion that an addressee of the communication engage in a securities transaction. Almost any communication that targets a suggestion to an individual or to a class of individuals that is narrower than all investors might be a "recommendation." Likewise, a communication of unrequested information is likely to result in a "recommendation." [*See, e.g.*, NASD Notice to Members 01-23, Online Suitability–Suitability Rule and Online Communications (April 2001)]

Further, if a broker or its representative does not suggest a variable annuity contract but nonetheless handles an application for, or would be compensated on, its purchase, the broker (rather than its representative) must:

- Find that the purchase is suitable (under the standards described above), or
- Inform the individual about why the purchase is unsuitable for him or her, and then obtain the individual's reaffirmation that he or she wants to proceed with the purchase.

[FINRA Conduct Rule 2821(c) Members' Responsibilities Regarding Deferred Variable Annuities]

Note. The rule explained above requires a broker to provide some "advice" even if the individual does not want any help.

Practice Pointer. Despite the usual requirement to evaluate a contract's "suitability" on considerations other than tax treatment, a broker might find that an annuity contract is suitable for an individual—even one who has no need or desire for any insurance promise—because his or her employer's Section 403(b) plan does not permit any non-insurance investment. Such a finding would require that the broker find that it is suitable for the individual to participate under the Section 403(b) plan. [Cf FINRA Regulatory Notice 07-53 Deferred Variable Annuities–SEC Approves New NASD Rule 2821 Governing Deferred Variable Annuity Transactions at footnotes 5 and 6 (Nov. 2007)]

Note. Although not mentioned in the regulator's interpretations, a broker could find that a purchase of interests in a separate account under an annuity contract is suitable because the "all-in" expenses of the account are less than (or no more than) those of the plan's mutual funds in the same or in a similar investment category.

Caution. When the contributing author submitted this text, the FINRA had proposed that the SEC allow a delay of this Rule's effective date from May 5, 2008 until August 4, 2008. [SEC Release No. 57050, Notice of Filing of Proposed Rule Change to Delay Implementation of Certain FINRA Rule Changes Approved in SR-NASD-2004-183, 73 Fed. Reg. 531-533 (Jan. 3, 2008)] Because of the Rule's complexities (including its requirements that, without relief, would apply even to a broker that never presents any recommendation), some further delay seems possible.

Life Insurance Contracts

Q 5:22   What is a *life insurance contract?*

A *life insurance contract* is a contract in which an insurance company agrees to pay the contract owner or his, her, or its intended third-party beneficiary a sum of money when the insured (a specified human being who is the subject of the insurance) dies. Based on information about the insured's age and health, the insurance company will specify the *premium* or amount of money that it requires to accept the risk of being obligated to pay a large sum when the insured dies. Life insurance is regulated by state insurance law.

Q 5:23   How is a life insurance contract used in a Section 403(b) plan?

If an insurance contract provides only incidental life insurance protection and was issued before September 24, 2007, it can be treated as a contract held under a Section 403(b) plan. [Treas. Reg. §§ 1.403(b)-6(g), 1.403(b)-11(f)]

To qualify under the incidental-benefit rule, each insurance contract must meet certain form requirements and restrictions of Code Section 403(b). Typically, that is done by adding an endorsement to the usual form life insurance contract. Sometimes, the Section 403(b) requirements are met by having a trustee hold the life insurance contract under a trust agreement that states the provisions required by Code Section 403(b). [Ltr. Ruls. 9243031, 9324043] If an insurance contract fails to state effective restrictions, it will not be treated as part of a Section 403(b) plan. [Ltr. Rul. 9242922]

When deciding whether to maintain life insurance as part of a Section 403(b) plan, a participant should carefully consider all available disclosure information.

Retirement Income Accounts

Q 5:24   What is a retirement income account?

A retirement income account is a special kind of Section 403(b) investment established and maintained by church employers (see Q 5:25) for church employees and ministers (see Q 5:26). [I.R.C. § 403(b)(9)(B); Treas. Reg. § 1.403(b)-8(e), 1.403(b)-9(a)(2)] A church retirement income account is not restricted in what investments it may hold (see Q 5:27), but typically involves pooled investment.

A church's management and administration of a retirement income account might be governed by fiduciary duties.

Participants and other investors in retirement income accounts generally do not enjoy the protections (or bear the expenses) of securities laws. [15 U.S.C. §§ 77c(a)(13), 78c(a)(12)(A)(vi), 78c(g), 80a-3(c)(14), 80a-29(g)-(h)] A church plan's administrator must furnish written disclosure that:

> the [church] plan, or [sic] any company or account maintained to manage or hold plan assets and interests in [the church] plan, company, or account are not subject to registration, regulation, or reporting under [the Investment Company Act of 1940], the Securities Act of 1933, the Securities Exchange Act of 1934, or State securities laws; and plan participants and beneficiaries therefore will not be afforded the protection of those provisions. [15 U.S.C. § 80a-29(g)]

This disclosure must be furnished to a new participant "as soon as is practicable after joining [the] plan," and to all participants "not less frequently than annually[.]" [15 U.S.C. § 80a-29(g)]

Q 5:25   Which type of employer may use a retirement income account?

An eligible employer that is a church (or part of a convention or association of churches) may use a retirement income account as part or all of a 403(b) plan (in addition to annuity contracts and custodial accounts). [I.R.C. § 403(b)(9); *see also* I.R.C. § 414(e)(3)(A); *accord* Treas. Reg. § 1.403(b)-9(a)]

Q 5:26 Who may participate in a retirement income account?

An eligible employer's (see Q 5:25) employee or former employee, and a duly ordained, licensed, or commissioned minister of the church (even if he or she is a self-employed person) may use a retirement income account. [I.R.C. §§ 404(a)(10), 414(e)(5); Ltr. Rul. 8950086]

Q 5:27 What investments may a retirement income account hold?

A Section 403(b)(9) retirement income account may hold almost any investments, as long as the recordkeeping accurately reflects the account's interests in the assets the account invests in and each participant's interest in the account.

The assets of a retirement income account may be pooled with the assets of Section 401(a) qualified retirement plans without adversely affecting the tax qualification of any plan or the Section 403(b)(9) account. That part of the common fund that equitably belongs to each plan or account must be separately accounted for, and all assets must be held solely for the exclusive benefit of participants and their beneficiaries.

> **Note.** On a particular set of facts and circumstances, the IRS held that, with adequate separate accounting, a Section 401(a) church plan's assets and the church's general assets could be commingled without impairing either the plan's or the church's tax-exempt treatment. [Ltr. Rul. 199943039 (July 9, 1999)] It is doubtful whether the IRS would, if asked, render a similar ruling concerning a Section 403(b) church plan. The Treasury regulations under Code Section 403(b) preclude commingling retirement income accounts with "assets of the plan sponsor" but permit commingling with "a common fund with amounts devoted exclusively to church purposes[.]" [Treas. Reg. § 1.403(b)-9(a)(6)]

Q 5:28 Is a church plan or its retirement income account governed by securities laws?

No. Participants and other investors in retirement income accounts do not enjoy the protections (or bear the expenses) of securities laws. [15 U.S.C. §§ 77c(a)(13), 78c(a)(12)(A)(vi), 78c(g), 80a-3(c)(14), 80a-29(i)-(j)] A church plan's administrator must furnish written disclosure that:

> the [church] plan, or [sic] any company or account maintained to manage or hold plan assets and interests in [the church] plan, company, or account are not subject to registration, regulation, or reporting under [the Investment Company Act of 1940], the Securities Act of 1933, the Securities Exchange Act of 1934, or State securities laws; and plan participants and beneficiaries therefore will not be afforded the protection of those provisions.

This disclosure must be furnished to a new participant "as soon as is practicable after joining [the] plan," and to all participants "not less frequently than annually[.]" [Investment Company Act § 30(i), 15 U.S.C. § 80a-29(i)]

Grandfathered Investments

Q 5:29   How could a state retirement system fund be a Section 403(b) investment?

An investment under a state teachers' retirement system generally is not a permitted Section 403(b) investment. Likewise, an investment under a separately funded employee retirement reserve governed by the state insurance department's supervision generally is not a permitted Section 403(b) investment. [Rev. Rul. 82-102, 1982-1 C.B. 62, revoking Rev. Rul. 67-387, 1967-2 C.B. 153, and Rev. Rul. 67-361, 1967-2 C.B. 153]

But a contract under a plan that was established on or before May 17, 1982 in good-faith reliance on either of the revoked rulings may continue to cover those participants covered on May 17, 1982 if the plan and the investment meet all conditions required by current Treasury regulations. If either transition rule applies, the contract may continue to cover those participants covered on May 17, 1982, including "an employee who becomes covered for the first time under the plan after May 17, 1982." [Treas. Reg. § 1.403(b)-8(c)(3)]

Participant Loans

Q 5:30   Is a participant loan a permitted Section 403(b) investment?

Yes and no.

If a participant loan is provided as a provision of an annuity contract, the loan is permitted because the annuity contract is the Section 403(b) investment, and the loan made by the insurer involves a use of some of the contract's rights.

To qualify for Section 403(b) tax treatment, amounts contributed to a custodial account must be invested in SEC-registered fund shares. [I.R.C. § 403(b)(7)(A)(i)] However, the IRS has given favorable letter rulings concerning an account that permits its custodian to hold a participant loan (see chapter 11).

Q 5:31   Is a participant loan a plan investment?

Yes and no. Under a typical annuity contract, a participant loan involves a use of the contract rights and an adjustment in the contract's value. Under a typical custodial account, a participant loan is, in form, an investment of the account. In either case, a typical participant loan affects only the account of the participant, who in effect is both borrower and lender. [D.O.L. Reg. § 2550.408(b)-1(f)]

For information about the many ERISA and Code rules concerning participant loans, see chapter 11.

Q 5:32   Must a plan fiduciary collect repayments on a participant loan?

A typical participant loan affects only the account of the participant, who is in effect both borrower and lender (see Q 5:31). If a plan fiduciary has a duty to manage plan assets, a plan administrator may use discretion, usually restricted only by an arbitrary-and-capricious review standard, in collecting on a defaulted loan. [*See, e.g.,* Colaluca v. Climaco, Climaco, Seminatore, Lefkowitz & Garofolo LPA, 1997 U.S. App. LEXIS 2108 (6th Cir. 1997)] A prudent plan fiduciary might ask a borrowing participant to direct that none of the plan fiduciaries collect loan repayments. A plan fiduciary will not be liable for a loss that results from following such a direction. [ERISA § 404(c)(1)(B)]

Trusts to Hold Section 403(b) Accounts

Q 5:33   May a Section 403(b) annuity or life insurance contract be held under a trust?

Yes. The IRS has ruled that a trust that holds an annuity contract or a life insurance contract (or both) is a valid Section 403(b) plan if the trust agreement or declaration states all provisions required by Code Section 403(b) and does not state any provisions inconsistent with that section. [Ltr. Ruls. 9423031, 9324043]

Q 5:34   Can a Section 403(b)(7) custodial account invest in SEC-registered fund shares through a group trust?

Yes. Recognizing significant restrictions on both the group trust's and the custodial account's investments and operations, the IRS allowed a custodial account to use a group trust's funds-trading facility.

The IRS considered the following facts as significant to its ruling:

- The group trust, by its governing document, limited its investments to shares of SEC-registered funds.
- A fund's quoted share price must not be subject to manipulation.
- Fund shares, which typically exist only as computer-system records, are exactly fungible.
- The group trust was itself a custodianship under which the custodian had no investment discretion.

- The sole purpose of the commingling was to permit efficient execution of fund share purchases and redemptions.

The IRS required that each custodial account's interest in the group trust must "at all times be separately identifiable," and the custodian must at all times apply the provisions of the employer's plan and Code Section 403(b). Based on these restrictions, the IRS ruled that the custodial account's participation in the group trust would not cause the custodial account to fail to satisfy Code Section 403(b)(7) or cause amounts held under the account to be included in the participant's gross income. [Ltr. Rul. 9744022] It is unclear whether an applicant now could obtain such a ruling. [*See* Treas. Reg. § 1.403(b)-8(f)]

Employer Responsibility for Section 403(b) Investments

Q 5:35 How should an employer select investments for a Section 403(b) plan?

If an employer makes available (and does not endorse or maintain) a voluntary Section 403(b) plan that is not governed by ERISA (see chapter 9), the employer need not be responsible for selection of any Section 403(b) investment options. Thus, an employer might prefer to allow a broad range of investment options, while deliberately avoiding any selection decisions other than those assuring minimum contractor responsibility and efficiency to serve the employer's administrative convenience.

Caution. Some practitioners believe that it is impossible or impracticable for an employer to maintain a plan that meets the conditions for tax treatment under Code Section 403(b) while also *not* maintaining the plan for ERISA purposes. The DOL has tried to suggest that an employer can adopt a written plan without "establishing" the plan by restricting itself to merely "compiling" the terms of the annuity contracts and custodial accounts. Likewise, the DOL has tried to suggest that an employer can avoid maintaining the plan by requiring insurers and custodians to make all decisions without any supervision or discretionary coordination by or on behalf of the employer. [ERISA Coverage Of IRC § 403(b) Tax-Sheltered Annuity Programs, DOL-EBSA Field Assistance Bulletin 2007-02 (July 24, 2007)] Because the Bulletin is not a rule, regulation, or official interpretation to which a court must give any deference, and because it is unclear exactly what steps might meet EBSA's suggestion, a person who or an organization that wants to consider whether a plan might or might not be governed by ERISA should get an expert lawyer's advice.

If an employer maintains a non-ERISA plan, the employer must make its investment selections (if any) under applicable state law (see Q 5:36).

If an employer maintains an ERISA plan (see chapter 9), the employer must make any investment selection as an expert fiduciary under ERISA (see Q 5:37).

Q 5:36   What is an employer's investment responsibility for a Section 403(b) plan that is not governed by ERISA?

If a Section 403(b) plan is not governed by ERISA (see chapter 9), the employer will not have any fiduciary responsibility under ERISA for the selection of insurers and investment funds. But if ERISA does not govern the plan, ERISA does not preempt state law.

If an employer is confident that neither ERISA nor state law imposes any duty, it might be wise for an employer to take no responsibility for examining investments offered for a voluntary Section 403(b) plan, and to affirmatively warn employees that is has not evaluated any investment option. Once an employer begins to act, the law requires it to act and communicate carefully. If participants and employees are led to believe that an employer has performed some kind of investment or financial analysis, the employer could become liable—for example, under the common-law tort of negligent communication—if the analysis or communication is not as thorough and accurate as would have been done by a recognized expert in that kind of analysis or communication. [Restatement (Second) of Torts, § 552 (1977)]

Q 5:37   What is an employer's investment responsibility for an ERISA plan?

If a Section 403(b) plan is governed by ERISA (see chapter 9), the plan fiduciaries must act solely in the best interest of the plan's participants for the exclusive purpose of providing retirement benefits to participants and their beneficiaries.

ERISA requires that a fiduciary act with the care, skill, prudence, and diligence under the circumstances then prevailing that a prudent person acting as a fiduciary and familiar with retirement plan matters would use in the conduct of managing a retirement plan. [ERISA § 404(a)(1)(B); D.O.L. Reg. § 2550.404a-1(b)] Simply put, the plan fiduciary must act as an expert would. [*See, e.g.,* Katsaros v. Cody, 744 F.2d 270, 279 (2d Cir.), *cert. denied sub. nom.* Cody v. Donovan, 469 U.S. 1072 (1984); Reid v. Gruntal & Co., 763 F. Supp. 672 (D. Maine 1991); American Fed'n of Unions v. Equitable Life Assurance Soc'y, 647 F. Supp. 947 (M.D. La. 1985), *aff'd in part, rev'd in part,* 841 F.2d 658 (5th Cir. 1988); Marshall v. Glass/Metal Ass'n & Glaziers & Glassworkers Pension Plan, 507 F. Supp. 378, 384 (D. Haw. 1980); Marshall v. Snyder, 1 EBC (BNA) 1878, 1866 (E.D.N.Y. 1979); *but see* Donovan v. Cunningham, 716 F.2d 1455, 1467 n. 26 (5th Cir. 1983), *cert. denied,* 467 U.S. 1251 (1984)]

> **Note.** It is unclear whether a fiduciary can defend its conduct by arguing that a prudent expert would have done no better "under the circumstances than prevailing" if the plan's unfortunate circumstances had been caused by the fiduciary's breach.

Under ERISA's prudent-expert rule, a fiduciary must make a reasonably careful inquiry into the merits of a particular investment decision. A fiduciary's lack of familiarity with a particular form of investment is not an excuse for making an imprudent investment. If a fiduciary does not have sufficient knowledge to evaluate the merits or soundness of a proposed investment, the fiduciary must obtain expert advice in making the decision. [*See, e.g.*, Schaefer v. Arkansas Medical Soc'y, 853 F.2d 1487 (8th Cir. 1988); Katsaros v. Cody, 744 F.2d 270, 279 (2d Cir.), *cert. denied sub. nom.* Cody v. Donovan, 469 U.S. 1072 (1984); Donovan v. Cunningham, 716 F.2d 1455 (5th Cir. 1983), *cert. denied*, 467 U.S. 1251 (1984); Liss v. Smith, 991 F. Supp. 278, 297 (S.D.N.Y. 1998); Marshall v. Glass/Metal Ass'n & Glaziers & Glassworkers Pension Plan, 507 F. Supp. 378, 384 (D. Haw. 1980); *see also* Restatement (Third) of Trusts § 77 comment b & § 90 comment d (2007)]

In selecting and relying on an expert's assistance, a fiduciary must:

1. Investigate each expert's qualifications;

2. Investigate each expert's services;

3. Confirm that the expert has no conflicting interest that could interfere with the expert's ability and incentive to render advice or information solely in the plan's interest;

4. Furnish accurate and complete information to the expert to support the expert's work; and

5. Evaluate the extent to which it is prudent for the fiduciary to rely on the expert's advice or information.

[*See, e.g.*, Gregg v. Transportation Workers of America Int'l, 343 F.3d 833, 841 (6th Cir. 2003); Howard v. Shay, 100 F.3d 1484, 1489 (9th Cir. 1996); Liss v. Smith, 991 F. Supp. 278, 300 (S.D.NY 1998)] Further, if a fiduciary lacks expertise in selecting a particular kind of expert, the fiduciary might need to engage another expert to assist in selecting the expert of the kind that the fiduciary lacks expertise to select.

Even after a fiduciary has carefully selected an expert, the fiduciary must make his, her, or its own decision using the expert's advice or information. [*See, e.g.*, Howard v. Shay, 100 F.3d 1484, 1489 (9th Cir. 1996); Donovan v. Mazzola, 716 F.2d 1226 (9th Cir. 1983), *cert. denied*, 464 U.S. 1040 (1984); Whitfield v. Cohen, 682 F. Supp. 188, 194-195 (S.D.N.Y. 1988); Donovan v. Tricario, 5 EBC (BNA) 2057 (S.D. Fla. 1984) (unpublished); *see also* Restatement (Third) of Trusts § 80(2) (2007)]

A fiduciary need not make the "right" decision; rather, the fiduciary must carefully consider sufficient information. [*See, e.g.*, *In re* Unisys Savings Plan Litig, 74 F.3d 420 (3d Cir.), *cert. denied*, 519 U.S. 810 (1996); Roth v. Sawyer-Cleator Lumber Co, 16 F.3d 915 (8th Cir. 1994); Fink v. Nat'l Savings & Trust Co, 772 F.2d 951 (D.C. Cir. 1985); Donovan v. Mazzola, 716 F.2d 1226 (9th Cir. 1983), *cert. denied*, 464 U.S. 1040 (1984)] The legal standard is whether the fiduciary's procedure made a well-informed decision possible. [*See, e.g.*, GIW Industries v. Trevor, Stewart, Burton & Jacobsen, Inc, 895 F.2d 729 (11th Cir. 1990); Fink v. Nat'l Savings & Trust Co., 772 F.2d 951 (D.C. Cir. 1985); Debruyne v. Equitable Life Assurance Soc'y, 720 F. Supp. 1342 (N.D. Ill. 1989), *aff'd*, 920 F.2d 457 (7th Cir. 1990)] If a fiduciary has diligently investigated the relevant information, a court will not interfere with and will uphold the fiduciary's judgment. Following this, any review of a fiduciary's decision is based on the circumstances and the review conducted at the time the fiduciary made the decision, and not from the vantage point of "20/20 hindsight." [*See, e.g.*, Katsaros v. Cody, 744 F.2d 270, 279 (2d Cir.), *cert. denied sub nom* Cody v. Donovan, 469 U.S. 1072 (1984); Glennie v. Abitibi-Price Corp, 912 F. Supp. 993 (W.D. Mich. 1996); Lanka v O'Higgins, 810 F. Supp. 379 (N.D.N.Y. 1992); Whitfield v. Cohen, 682 F. Supp. 188 (S.D.N.Y. 1988); American Communications Ass'n v. Retirement Plan, 488 F. Supp. 479 (S.D.N.Y.), *aff'd mem*, 646 F.2d 559 (2d Cir. 1980); *see also* Restatement (Third) of Trusts § 90 comment b (2007)]

The named plan fiduciary should consider making a written investment policy statement. If the plan provides for participant-directed investment (see Qs 5:45–5:48), such an investment policy should state that the plan fiduciary's policy is to make available a broad range of no fewer than three different diversified investment options that have varying degrees of risk and return and that the selection is intended to enable the participant to achieve a balanced portfolio consistent with modern portfolio theory (see Q 5:48). Consistent with the plan fiduciary's continuing duty, the plan fiduciary should revise or reapprove the investment policy statement each year. A plan's investment policy statement is likely a document that governs the fiduciary's administration of the plan and so must be furnished to a participant, beneficiary, or alternate payee who requests it. [*See, e.g.*, Phelps v. Qwest Employees Benefit Committee, No. 04-CV-02042-LTB-OES (D. Colo. Dec. 2, 2005)]

Q 5:38   How should an ERISA plan fiduciary evaluate a provider's fees?

An ERISA plan fiduciary must discharge its duties with expert prudence solely in the interest of the plan's participants and their beneficiaries. [ERISA § 404(a)(1)] This means that a plan fiduciary that selects investment options or service providers must:

1. Establish a careful procedure for selecting investment options or service providers;

2. Select investment options and services that are appropriate for the plan;

3. Select investment and service providers that are capable of meeting the plan administrator's needs;

4. Decide that fees paid to each investment or service provider are reasonable in light of the scope and quality of services provided; and

5. Monitor investment options and service providers once selected to evaluate whether they continue to be sound choices.

A plan fiduciary is relieved from liability to the extent that a fee applies to a participant's or beneficiary's account because of his or her investment direction. For example, individual service fees may be charged to a participant for taking a participant loan, or for executing investment directions. Likewise, although some plan investment options may have benefits and charges different from other plan investment options, a plan fiduciary is not responsible for a participant's choice among plan investment options. [ERISA § 404(c); D.O.L. Reg. § 2550.404c-1(b)(2)(ii)]

Q 5:39 How do regular procedures help a fiduciary make careful decisions?

To help itself make careful decisions, a plan fiduciary should use regular procedures and collect relevant information. The use of decision-making procedures is essential in discharging fiduciary responsibility. [D.O.L. Reg. § 2550.404a-1(b)(1)(i)] Using regular procedures is important because it focuses decision-making on the relevant factors, and establishes a documented record if the fiduciary decision is challenged.

ERISA regulations provide that fiduciary review may occur "[a]t reasonable intervals," and that "[n]o single procedure will be appropriate in all cases; [rather,] the procedure adopted may vary in accordance with the nature of the plan and other facts and all circumstances relevant to the [fiduciary's] choice of the procedure." [Interpretive Bulletin 75-8, 40 Fed. Reg. 47491, FR-17 (Oct. 9, 1975), reprinted in 29 C.F.R. § 2509.75-8] In deciding the frequency and scope of fiduciary review, therefore, a plan fiduciary can and should consider the frequency with which relevant information becomes available and the time and expense involved in obtaining and reviewing that information.

Q 5:40 What should a fiduciary do when a decision involves an investment or service provider with whom he or she has a relationship?

ERISA imposes the highest duty of loyalty, including especially a fiduciary duty to avoid self-dealing. If a fiduciary is faced with the possibility of self-dealing because of his or her relationship with an investment or service provider, ERISA permits that fiduciary to remove himself or herself from that particular decision. This removal is called a *recusal.*

A fiduciary does not participate in a prohibited transaction if the fiduciary absents himself or herself from all consideration of the proposed decision and does not exercise any authority, control, or responsibility concerning the proposed decision. [D.O.L. Reg. § 2550.408b-2(f), Ex. 7; D.O.L. ERISA Adv. Ops. 99-09A (May 21, 1999), 97-23A (Sept. 26, 1997), 91-37A (Oct. 16, 1991) 86-11A (Feb. 27, 1986), 84-09A (Feb. 16, 1984), 79-72A (Oct. 10, 1979); DOL ERISA Information Letters Proskauer Rose Goetz & Mendelsohn (Sept. 26, 1996), Blitman & King (Jan. 31, 1994), Gutterman and Pollack (May 14, 1979), Rhode Island Carpenters' Pension Fund (March 13, 1979)] In addition to not voting on the proposed decision, the fiduciary should physically absent himself or herself from the meeting (or that portion of the meeting) that considers the proposed decision. [D.O.L. ERISA Adv. Op. 84-09A, n. 2 (Feb. 16, 1984)] To rely on a recusal, it is important that the recused fiduciary avoid any attempt to influence others who retain decision-making authority. [*See* D.O.L. ERISA Adv. Op. 86-11A (Feb. 27, 1986)]

Example. The Read-to-Your-Children Foundation sponsors an ERISA-governed Section 403(b) plan. Patti is one of five members of the foundation's pension committee. Her sister, Diane, is a partner of Cheswyck Investment Counsel LLP, which, along with other competitors, has proposed certain investment-advisory services for the foundation's Section 403(b) plan. When the pension committee turns to the investment adviser selection, Patti formally recuses herself, announces to the committee members that she has a potential conflict of interest (without saying what it is), instructs the committee's secretary to record her recusal in the minutes of the meeting, and then leaves the room. Patti does not talk about Cheswyck or any of the competitor investment advisers with any of the committee members. By doing all that, Patti has made a successful recusal. If Cheswyck gets the contract, Patti must also avoid involvement in reviewing Cheswyck's performance.

Recusal can be a better choice than resignation when the fiduciary has a conflict of interest only for one or a few matters and the fiduciary's consideration of other matters is valuable for the benefit of the plan.

Caution. In the DOL's view, a recused fiduciary's duties concerning a particular plan decision do not necessarily end because the fiduciary recused himself or herself. Rather, if a recused fiduciary has information that the deciding fiduciaries need to make a prudent decision, the recused fiduciary must provide that information to the deciding fiduciaries. [DOL ERISA Information Letter, William Lindsay, Local 25 Int'l Brotherhood of Elec. Workers (Feb. 23, 2005)] However, the recused fiduciary should provide the deciding fiduciaries with the information in a way that does not interfere with the recusal or otherwise reveal the recused fiduciary's conflict of interest.

Q 5:41 What should a plan fiduciary do if the other fiduciaries make a decision that is imprudent?

Under the earlier common law of trusts, any action by fewer than all the trustees, even though a majority, is void unless the trust document states that the trustees may act by a majority. But the modern trend is that if there are three or more trustees, their powers may be exercised by a majority. [Restatement (Third) of Trusts § 39 (2003); *see also* Unif Trust Code § 703(a), 7C ULA 566–570 (2006) & 2007 Supp. 49]

When a plan fiduciary is outvoted, resignation, without further action to protect the interests of participants and beneficiaries, generally is not enough to protect the outvoted fiduciary from personal liability.

According to the DOL,

> where a majority of [fiduciaries] appear ready to take action [that] would clearly be contrary to the prudence requirement of [ERISA §] 404(a)(1)(B) . . . , it is incumbent on the minority [fiduciaries] to take

all reasonable and legal steps to prevent the action. Such steps might include preparations to obtain an injunction from a Federal District court . . . , to notify the Labor Department, or to publicize the vote if the decision is to proceed as proposed. If, having taken all reasonable and legal steps to prevent the imprudent action, the minority [fiduciaries] have not succeeded, they will not incur liability for the action of the majority. Mere resignation, however, without taking steps to prevent the imprudent action, will not suffice to avoid liability for the minority [fiduciaries] once they have knowledge that the imprudent action is under consideration.

Likewise, a fiduciary's insistence that his or her "objections and the responses to such objections [if any] be included in the record of the meeting" will not be sufficient to protect the outvoted fiduciary. "[R]esignation by the [fiduciary] as a protest against [a fiduciary] breach will not generally be considered sufficient to discharge the [fiduciary's] positive duty under [ERISA §] 405(a)(3)" "to make reasonable efforts under the circumstances to remedy the breach." [DOL ERISA Interpretive Bulletin 75-5, 40 Fed. Reg. 31599 (July 28, 1975), redesignated at 41 Fed. Reg. 1906 (Jan 13, 1976), reprinted in 29 C.F.R. § 2509.75-5] Arguably, an ERISA plan fiduciary might be protected from liability if the other fiduciaries' breach was not clearly a breach. However, when considering whether any decision might be clearly a fiduciary breach, the outvoted fiduciary still must act as an expert fiduciary. [ERISA § 404(a)(1)]

For a non-ERISA plan, the common law or statutory law of trusts provides a similar or greater duty. Under either the common law or the Uniform Trust Code, a trustee must use reasonable care to prevent his or her co-trustees' breach, and, if a breach occurs, to compel his or her co-trustees to correct the breach, or to obtain the trust's restoration or other redress. [Restatement (Third) of Trusts § 39 (2003); Restatement (Third) of Trusts § 81 (2007); Unif. Trust Code § 703(g), 7C ULA 566–570 (2006) & 2007 Supp. 49] Thus, an outvoted trustee remains liable for a cotrustee's breach unless the outvoted trustee takes prudent steps to protect the trust. An outvoted trustee has a right to engage lawyers other than those who represent other trustees and (if he or she acts or acted in good faith) a right to have the trust advance or reimburse his or her expenses (including attorneys' fees). [Restatement (Third) of Trusts § 81 comment d, § 88 reporter's note to comment d (2007); F.M. English, Right of Coexecutor or Trustee to Retain Independent Legal Counsel, 66 A.L.R. 2d 1169 (1959); Lee R. Russ, Award of Attorneys' Fees Out of Trust Estate in Action by Trustee Against Cotrustee, 24 A.L.R. 4th 624 (1983); 76 Am. Jur. 2d Trusts § 738 (1992)]

For a church plan, an outvoted fiduciary who fails to take protective action might nevertheless avoid liability to the extent that the breach would not have been prevented or corrected but for requiring the fiduciary to take an action that would have interfered with his or her free exercise of religion. [U.S. Const. amend. I]

For a governmental plan, an outvoted fiduciary who fails to take protective action might be protected by sovereign immunity, governmental immunity, or public officer immunity.

Social Investment

Q 5:42   May an employer limit a Section 403(b) plan to socially-responsible investments?

Before limiting Section 403(b) investment choices, an employer should carefully consider the consequences of the choice.

First, limiting a Section 403(b) plan to less than a "reasonable choice" of investments might make the plan an ERISA plan. An employer that prefers that ERISA not govern the plan might permit (but not mandate) socially-screened investment options.

More broadly, if an employer makes any Section 403(b) investment selection, a participant or employee might argue that the employer did so as a fiduciary, whether under ERISA or state-law fiduciary standards. Whichever the fiduciary standard, "social investing" might be contrary to a fiduciary duty of prudence or loyalty, which are separate but sometimes related duties, unless the employer applied a social screen in good faith as part of the employer's expert investment analysis. [ERISA § 404(a)(1)(A); see also DOL ERISA Interpretive Bulletin 94-1, 59 Fed. Reg. 32606 (June 22, 1994), reprinted in 29 C.F.R. § 2509.94-1; IRS GCM 39870 (April 7, 1992); see generally Restatement (Third) of Trusts § 90 comment c (2007); Uniform Prudent Investor Act (1994), official comment to § 5, 7B ULA 299–300 (2000)]

Whether a fiduciary may choose socially-screened investments remains a topic of considerable debate. A fiduciary may consider social information in a fiduciary's evaluation of a fund if the fiduciary in good faith considers that information as a part of his, her, or its investment analysis and a prudent expert would not find that considering the social information impedes the proper investment analysis. A fiduciary must consider social information if a prudent expert would do so. Conversely, a fiduciary must not consider social information if the information is not truly part of the fiduciary's investment analysis.

Even if social investing results in no breach of prudence or loyalty, an employer should also consider the likelihood (and expense) of lawsuits by participants and beneficiaries.

Example. The Evangelical Lutheran Church in America and its Board of Pensions defended lawsuits concerning certain investment decisions for the Board's Section 403(b)(9) defined contribution retirement income accounts that may have at least considered the church's social investment policy. Although the Board of Pensions avoided a public trial of its fiduciary decision making, the parties incurred the unpleasantness and expense of litigation. [Basich v. Board of Pensions, Evangelical Lutheran Church in Am. & Basich Evangelical Lutheran Church in Am., 540 N.W.2d 82 (Minn. App. 1995), cert. denied, 117 S. Ct. 55 (1996) (The Board's decisions concerning social investment policy are at least related to religious doctrine or church management, and therefore "[t]he Establishment Clause of the First Amendment and the Freedom of Conscience Clause of the Minnesota Constitution deprive [a civil] court of subject matter jurisdiction," notwithstanding that the plan specified that "[a]ll controversies, disputes, and claims arising [under the plan] shall be submitted to the Minnesota Fourth Judicial District Court, Hennepin County."), reversing No. CT 93-16711 District Court for County of Hennepin, Fourth Judicial District; Basich v. Board of Pensions, Evangelical Lutheran Church in Am., 493 N.W.2d 293, 296 (Minn. App. 1992) (Retirement plan participants do not have standing to bring a derivative suit)]

A better course may be for an employer to seek out socially-responsible investment funds as Section 403(b) investment options, in addition to other prudently selected investment options, and then allow participants to choose socially-responsible investing. [*Cf.* Ltr. Rul. 9122081 (concerning a church plan)]

Q 5:43   May an ERISA plan fiduciary consider social criteria in choosing investment and service providers?

No. For an ERISA-governed plan, a fiduciary must act for the exclusive purpose of providing the plan's retirement benefits. Thus, a fiduciary must not use plan assets to express views, or furnish information on, political or social positions. Likewise, a fiduciary must choose an investment or service provider on the quality and expense of its services, and must not consider unrelated facts, such as a provider's political or social positions. [DOL-EBSA Information Letter to Jonathan P. Hiatt (May 3, 2005) ("A fiduciary may never increase a plan's expenses, sacrifice the security of promised benefits, or reduce the return on plan assets, in order to promote its views on Social Security or any other broad policy issue.")]

Q 5:44   May a plan fiduciary consider social criteria in voting plan investments?

No, unless the plan fiduciary considers social criteria only to the extent that doing so is properly part of its investment analysis. "[I]n voting proxies, the responsible fiduciary must only consider those factors that affect the value of the plan's investment[,] and may not subordinate the interests of the participants and beneficiaries in their retirement income to unrelated objectives." Further, a fiduciary must not use or "spend[] plan assets to pursue, support, or oppose a proxy proposal unless the fiduciary has a reasonable expectation that doing so will enhance the value of the plan's investment." [DOL-EBSA ERISA Adv. Op. 2007-07A (Dec. 21, 2007), *citing* Interpretive Bulletin 94-2, reprinted in 29 C.F.R. § 2509.94-2]

Making Investment Decisions

Q 5:45   What information should a plan fiduciary consider when making an investment selection?

When making a fiduciary investment selection, a plan fiduciary should obtain and carefully consider every kind of information that it could need to make a fully informed, careful, and expert choice. Of course, this includes getting complete information about every fee, charge, or expense of every investment.

Practice Pointer. A plan fiduciary should consider obtaining all of the documents that banking, insurance, securities, or other law requires to be furnished about an investment. Why? A plaintiff might argue that a failure to obtain at least the documents that the law provides for an investor's protection shows an obvious lack of prudence. While many people believe that the "official" documents usually are unhelpful and often "bury" the important information in too much text about information that a decision maker need not consider, a fiduciary's effort to read the portions of a document that are useful might alert him or her to questions that otherwise might not have occurred.

A plan fiduciary should also obtain complete information about the compensation to third persons (such as insurance agents, securities broker-dealers, trust companies, recordkeepers, and other intermediaries) that would result from buying (or continuing) an investment. Even if a fiduciary declines to accept advice from any of those persons, a plan fiduciary must know and approve the compensation of every party in interest regarding the plan. [*See* ERISA § 404(a); Glaziers and Glassworkers Local 252 Annuity Fund v. Newbridge Securities Inc, 20 EBC (BNA) 1697 (3d Cir. 1996); *In re* Unisys Savings Plan Litigation, 74 F.3d 420 (3d Cir. 1996); Morgan v. Independent Drivers Ass'n, 15 EBC (BNA) 2515 (10th Cir. 1992); Brock v. Robbins, 830 F.2d 640 (7th Cir. 1987); Donovan v. Mazola, 716 F.2d 1226 (9th Cir. 1983); McLaughlin v. Bendersky, 705 F. Supp. 417 (E.D. Ill. 1989); Benvenuto v. Schneider, 678 F. Supp. 51 (E.D.N.Y. 1988); Donovan v. Tricario, 5 EBC (BNA) 2057 (S.D. Fla. 1984) (unpublished)] Further, a plan fiduciary's duty to know and approve the compensation of every party in interest means that a plan fiduciary must receive full disclosure concerning, and as a prudent-expert fiduciary evaluate, all arrangements by which any plan investment or service provider pays or provides compensation to another investment or service provider. [*See, e.g.,* Reasonable Contract or Arrangement Under Section 408(b)(2)–Fee Disclosure, Proposed Rule, 72 Fed. Reg. 70987–71005 (Dec. 13, 2007)]

The plan fiduciary should retain all these records (see Q 5:68), and require updated information when it conducts regular reviews (see Q 5:31) of the plan's investment selection.

Q 5:46 Why should a fiduciary carefully read each prospectus?

A person who receives a prospectus is deemed to know the information stated by the prospectus. If reading a prospectus and thinking about the information stated by it would cause a person to know that he or she might have a claim against the investment's issuer (or against a broker-dealer), such presumed knowledge "starts the clock" for a statute-of-limitations period. [*See, e.g.,* Donovan v. American Skandia Life Assur. Corp., No. 02 CV 9859 MP(not reported in F. Supp. 2d), Fed. Sec. L. Rep. (CCH available through http://onlinestore.cch.com) ¶ 92,488 (S.D.N.Y. July 31, 2003), *motion for leave to amend complaint denied*, 217 F.R.D. 325, Fed. Sec. L. Rep. (CCH) ¶ 92,498 (SDNY Sept. 2, 2003). (Because the plaintiffs brought their suit more than two years after they received the prospectus, the court dismissed with prejudice all claims under the Securities Act, Securities Exchange Act, and Investment Company Act.)]

Protecting the Safety of Investments

Q 5:47   What protection is afforded fixed annuity or life insurance contracts?

An insurer's investment of its general account is regulated by state insurance law. If an insurer becomes insolvent or impaired and cannot meet its obligations, a state's life insurance guaranty association will meet those obligations, governed by state law coverage limits and assessment limits. All states and the District of Columbia have a life insurance guaranty association. The association can protect contract holders, insureds, and annuity participants against an impaired or insolvent insurer's failure to meet its contractual obligations by "reinsuring" the covered policies of the impaired or insolvent insurer, or by causing another insurer to assume the policies.

In most states, all group or individual annuity contracts and life insurance contracts are covered by the guaranty association. Some states limit or exclude coverage for "true group" contracts, but those states cover individual certificates under a group contract.

Q 5:48   How much coverage does a guaranty association typically provide?

The typical coverage limit per annuitant or insured by a guaranty association is $100,000 for cash values and $300,000 for all benefits, but some states provide greater coverage. Most states cover only residents, while some states exclude nonresidents only when they are covered by another state's guaranty law. That rarely matters, however, because every state has a guaranty association.

All states prohibit any statement regarding the guaranty association, including even reference to its existence, in the context of insurance sales. However, one state's highest court has held, on free-speech constitutional grounds, that such a ban could not be applied to a truthful and nonmisleading statement. [New Mexico Life Ins. Guaranty Assoc v. Quinn & Co., Inc., 111 N.M. 750, 809 P.2d 1278 (1991)] Some states provide for a written notice, given upon delivery of an annuity or life insurance contract that provides a basic explanation of guaranty association coverage.

Q 5:49   What protection is afforded a variable annuity?

A variable annuity contract's separate account carries no insolvency risk and thus needs no guaranty protection. The "cash value" of each variable annuity contract is supported solely by the investments of the separate accounts selected by the contract holder. An insurance company separate account is not subject to claims by anyone other than contract holders invested under that separate account. The separate account cannot be reached by other creditors—not even by the insurance company itself. [*See, e.g.,* Conn. Gen. Stat. § 38a-459; Declaratory Ruling No. IC-91-51 (Dec. 17, 1991)]

In the DOL's view, a plan fiduciary evaluating the "safety" of a variable annuity contract may consider the protection provided by an insurance company separate account. [Interpretive Bulletin 95-1, reprinted in 29 C.F.R. § 2509.95-1(c)(5)]

Q 5:50   How is an SEC-registered fund protected?

An SEC-registered fund must keep custody of its money and securities, and the form and manner of custody is regulated by federal securities law. The money and securities of an SEC-registered mutual fund typically are held by a bank custodian. Also, the officers and employees of an SEC-registered fund company must be bonded against larceny and embezzlement. [Investment Company Act of 1940 §§ 17(f), 17(g), 15 U.S.C. §§ 80a-17(f), 80a-17(g); Investment Company Act Rules 17f, 17g, 12 C.F.R. §§ 270.17f, 270.17g-1]

Q 5:51   May a plan fiduciary consider guaranty coverage when selecting an insurance company?

Yes, a plan fiduciary may consider guaranty coverage when selecting an insurance company. When making fiduciary decisions, a plan fiduciary should consider all available information that can be relevant to the decision. [*See* ERISA § 404(a)(1)] In the DOL's view, a plan fiduciary selecting an insurer "should consider . . . the availability of additional protection through state guaranty associations and the extent of their [sic] guarantees." [DOL ERISA Interpretive Bulletin 95-1, 60 Fed. Reg. 12328 (March 6, 1995), reprinted in 29 C.F.R. § 2509.95-1(c)(6)] However, because an expert fiduciary considers all relevant information, a plan fiduciary also should consider the disruption or inconvenience to the plan that might arise from the rehabilitation or liquidation of an insolvent or impaired insurer. Further, to the extent that a fiduciary considers guaranty coverage as part of his, her, or its evaluation of an insurance contract, the fiduciary also must consider the probability that the association will, at the relevant time, be able or unable to meet its guaranty obligations. [ERISA § 404(a)(1); *see* DOL ERISA Adv. Op. 2002-14A (Dec. 18, 2002)]

Protection Against Liability

Q 5:52   Can an ERISA plan exempt a plan fiduciary from liability?

No. ERISA provides that "any provision in an agreement or instrument which [sic] purports to relieve a fiduciary from responsibility or liability for any responsibility, obligation, or duty under [the fiduciary responsibility provisions of ERISA] shall be void as against public policy." [ERISA § 410(a)]

Q 5:53   Can a non-ERISA plan exempt a plan fiduciary from liability?

Under the common law of trusts and fiduciary relationships, a provision in a trust document may provide that a fiduciary does not have a duty that otherwise would be a fiduciary duty, or may relax the standard of care that applies to a duty. [Restatement (Third) of Trusts §§ 76-77 (2007)] Likewise, a non-ERISA plan document may vary a fiduciary's duties. But a trust's or other fiduciary relationship's terms must not so negate the responsibilities of a fiduciary that he, she, or it would no longer be acting as a fiduciary. [Restatement (Third) of Trusts § 77 comment d (2007); Unif Trust Code § 105, 7C ULA 428-435 (2006) & 2007 Supp. 35] Finally, a provision in a non-ERISA plan document may relieve a plan fiduciary from liability for a breach of fiduciary responsibility. [Restatement (Second) of Trusts § 222 (1959)]

Caution. A provision that might exempt a fiduciary from liability is strictly construed to limit the potential exemptions from fiduciary responsibility. [Restatement (Second) of Trusts § 222(1) and comment a (1959)] No matter how carefully written, an exemption clause cannot protect a fiduciary who acts in bad faith or with reckless indifference to the participants' or beneficiaries' interests. [Restatement (Second) of Trusts § 222(2) (1959)]

Practice Pointer. If a document "does too good of a job" in excusing an administrator, employer, or other fiduciary from liability, the Internal Revenue Service might argue that such a provision in practical effect negates a plan provision that is necessary to tax qualification as a Section 403(b) plan. The regulations require that a plan "in both form and operation" meet the requirements of Code Section 403(b). [Treas. Reg. § 1.403(b)-3(b)(3)(i) (generally effective 2009)] A person or entity knows that he, she, or it will not bear liability for failing to administer a plan provision might be tempted to neglect to apply the provision—so much so that such a provision is merely "words on paper" without any real effect.

Q 5:54   May a plan buy fiduciary liability insurance to protect the plan from a fiduciary's breach?

Yes, a plan may buy fiduciary liability insurance to protect the plan from a fiduciary's breach. If buying this insurance is the plan's expense, the contract must permit the insurer's recourse against a fiduciary for a loss that results from the fiduciary's breach of his, her, or its duty. Alternatively, an appropriate person other than the plan may pay the portion of the insurance premium that is attributable to a non-recourse provision, leaving the plan to pay no more than the portion of the insurance premium that is not attributable to a non-recourse provision. To the extent that the plan pays for fiduciary liability insurance, a fiduciary must act as a fiduciary in selecting an insurer and coverage. [ERISA § 410(b); DOL News Release 75-127 (March 4, 1975)]

Practice Pointer. Even if a fiduciary obtains his or her employer's indemnification (see Q 5:55), he or she should consider adding fiduciary liability insurance and requiring the employer to pay for a non-recourse provision. Few charitable organizations have such a large and predictable surplus that one could be confident that the employer always will be able to pay promptly a fiduciary's defense expenses and liabilities.

Q 5:55   Can an employer indemnify an ERISA plan fiduciary?

Yes. Although an ERISA plan cannot indemnify a fiduciary against his or her fiduciary breach, nothing precludes an employer (or any person other than the plan) from indemnifying a plan fiduciary, as long as the employer uses its own money rather than plan assets.

ERISA provides that "any provision in an agreement or instrument [that] purports to relieve a fiduciary from responsibility or liability for any responsibility, obligation, or duty under [the fiduciary-responsibility provisions of ERISA] shall be void as against public policy." [ERISA § 410(a)] The DOL interprets this rule to permit a plan fiduciary, usually the employer that sponsors and administers the plan, to indemnify its employees who perform the fiduciary services. But the plan may not indemnify any fiduciary. "Such an arrangement would have the same result as an exculpatory clause in that it would, in effect, relieve the fiduciary of responsibility and liability to the plan by abrogating the plan's right to recovery from the fiduciary for breaches of fiduciary obligations." Further, "[w]hile indemnification arrangements do not [necessarily] contravene the provisions of [ERISA §] 410(a), parties entering into an indemnification agreement should consider whether the agreement complies with the other [fiduciary-responsibility] provisions of [ERISA] and with other applicable laws." [DOL ERISA Interpretive Bulletin 75-4, 40 Fed. Reg. 31599 (July 28, 1975), redesignated at 41 Fed. Reg. 1906 (Jan. 13, 1976), reprinted in 29 C.F.R. § 2509.75-4] Further, a court might not enforce an indemnity provision if the court finds that the provision has the effect of setting up an incentive for a fiduciary not to perform its duty. [*See* Martin v. NationsBank of Ga., No. 1:92-cv-1474-HTW, 16 EBC (BNA) 2138 (N.D. Ga. April 6, 1993)]

Q 5:56   Can an employer indemnify a non-ERISA plan fiduciary?

Yes, usually. Nothing in the common law of trusts and fiduciary relationships precludes a third person from providing indemnification to a fiduciary, unless receiving that indemnity is a breach of the fiduciary's duty to avoid self-dealing with those whose interests might be contrary to the purposes of the trust or the interests of the participants and beneficiaries.

Whether a church will indemnify a retirement plan fiduciary may be further provided by the church's organizing documents.

Q 5:57   What limits a charitable organization's ability to indemnify its plan fiduciaries?

A charitable organization may indemnify its employees if the charity's governing body (or a duly authorized delegate) finds that providing indemnification is necessary and appropriate to the organization's ability to attract and retain officers and employees to carry out the business that furthers the organization's charitable purposes. [Treas. Reg. § 1.501(c)(3)-1] In some states, the law presumes that an employee serves as an employee-benefit plan fiduciary because his or her job duties require that work. [*See, e.g.*, NY Not-for-Profit Corp Law § 722(d)] Nevertheless, an employee who serves as a plan fiduciary would be wise to specifically request indemnification.

Notwithstanding any written agreement that purports to provide greater protection, an organization will be unable to provide indemnification unless the employee acted in good faith and reasonably believed that he or she acted in (or not opposed to) the best interests of the organization. [*See generally* Revised Model Nonprofit Corporation Act § 8.51 (ABA 1987)] Therefore, because the law requires a retirement plan fiduciary to act with the ability of a person who is expert in managing retirement plans [ERISA § 404(a)(1)], a cautious fiduciary will accept expert legal, investment, and accounting advice.

Q 5:58   Can a service provider indemnify a plan fiduciary?

No. If an insurer, custodian, insurance or securities representative, recordkeeper, or other service provider agrees to provide indemnification to an ERISA plan fiduciary, that agreement is a prohibited transaction. [ERISA § 406] Every party to the prohibited transaction must disgorge and restore to the plan all ill-gotten proceeds, and a breaching fiduciary must restore the plan to the position it would have been in had the prohibited transaction not occurred. [ERISA §§ 409, 502] A service provider may provide appropriate remedies—used solely to restore the plan's loss or expense—for its breach of its contract services. [ERISA § 408(b)(2); *see also* DOL ERISA Adv. Op. 95-26A (Oct. 17, 1995)]

Likewise, if an insurer, custodian, insurance or securities representative, record keeper, or other service provider agrees to provide indemnification to a non-ERISA plan fiduciary, accepting that agreement is a breach of the fiduciary's duty of loyalty. [Restatement (Third) of Trusts § 90 (2007)] A careful fiduciary should adopt and follow written procedures for avoiding self-dealing and conflicts of interest. [Restatement (Third) of Trusts §§ 2, 90 (2003 & 2007); *see also* 12 C.F.R. § 9.5(c)] A plan fiduciary may accept for the use of the plan a service provider's indemnification that restores the plan's loss arising from the service provider's breach of its contract services.

Q 5:59   Should a plan fiduciary keep records on the plan's investment-direction procedure and investment information?

Yes. Although ERISA does not impose a specific records-retention requirement regarding investment options, under the ERISA Section 404(c) regulations, a plan fiduciary must affirmatively prove that it is entitled to the relief from investment fiduciary responsibility permitted by ERISA Section 404(c). Because it may be a long time before all participants retire and receive all payments during retirement, a plan fiduciary might consider keeping its investment selection records (see Q 5:40), summary plan descriptions, and other investment procedure records until at least six years after the plan is terminated and fully distributed. The plan fiduciary should also consider keeping its compilations of investment information compilations until at least six years after delivery of all account statements relating to the period during which the investment could have been made. [ERISA §§ 209(a), 413]

Participant-Directed Investment

Q 5:60   What is a *participant-directed plan*?

A *participant-directed plan* is a plan under which each participant (or, after a participant's death, a beneficiary, and an alternate payee for his or her segregated subaccount) decides the investment of his or her plan account by directing investment within a broad range of options selected by the plan fiduciary.

Q 5:61   What rules apply to a participant-directed plan?

The rules that apply to a participant-directed plan turn on whether the plan is (or is not) governed by ERISA.

If a plan that provides for participant-directed investment is governed by ERISA, the plan's fiduciaries may avoid liability for participants' investment decisions by meeting the requirements of ERISA Section 404(c) (see Q 5:47).

If a plan that provides for participant-directed investment is not governed by ERISA (a church plan or a governmental plan), state law governs whether and how a plan fiduciary may avoid liability for participants' investment decisions.

Q 5:62   What does ERISA Section 404(c) provide?

If a retirement plan allows participants to choose their own investments, an employer or other fiduciary might worry about potential complaints from participants whose investments perform poorly. Following ERISA Section 404(c) gives a fiduciary a way to avoid liability for the consequences of a participant's unwise decisions. ERISA Section 404(c) provides that if a participant exercises control over the investment of his or her plan account, plan fiduciaries will not be responsible for the participant's investment decisions.

Regulations interpret and implement ERISA Section 404(c), providing guidance on what requirements a plan must meet to ensure that participants have sufficient control over the investment of their retirement plan accounts to justify shifting legal responsibility to them. [D.O.L. Reg. § 2550.404c-1]

Q 5:63   Must an employer comply with ERISA Section 404(c)?

No. Following ERISA Section 404(c) is optional. If, however, a plan meets all the requirements of ERISA Section 404(c), the employer and other plan fiduciaries are not responsible for losses that result from participants' investment decisions.

If a plan meets the ERISA Section 404(c) regulations for the most part but does not fully comply, plan fiduciaries might still be relieved from responsibility if they can show the court that their management of the plan was consistent with ERISA Section 404. [*See* Daniele and Hennessy, "Participant-Directed Retirement Plans under the Final Section 404(c) Regulations," 19 *Pension Rep.* 1992 (Oct. 19, 1992) at 1825; *but see* Brennan, "Relief at Last? DOL Final Regulations on Participant-Directed Individual Account Plans," 19 *J Pension Planning & Compliance* 1 (Spring 1993) at 50–52] Further, some employee-benefits lawyers believe that even if a plan plainly does not comply with ERISA Section 404(c), a plan fiduciary might avoid liability for the consequences of an investment direction if it can show that it properly followed the participant's or beneficiary's direction. [Eccles and Gordon, "Now That the § 404(c) Regulations Are Final, Who Cares?," 1 *ERISA Litig. Rptr.* 11, 15–23 (Aspen Publishers Dec. 1992)]

A fiduciary that overrules a participant's investment direction because it believes that the direction no longer is prudent cannot rely on the protection of ERISA Section 404(c) with respect to the overruled participant. [DOL ERISA Adv. Op. 96-02A (Feb. 9 1996)]

Q 5:64   Does complying with ERISA Section 404(c) mean an employer is absolved of liability?

Not completely. If a plan meets the conditions of ERISA Section 404(c), a plan fiduciary is relieved from liability for losses that are the direct and necessary result from participants' investment directions. However, unless the plan precludes the plan fiduciary from restricting plan investment options, a plan fiduciary is responsible for the selection (and periodic monitoring) of an appropriate menu of plan investment choices available to participants. [D.O.L. Reg. § 2550.404c-1(a)(1)] If a plan fiduciary makes any selection of the menu of plan investment options, it must act prudently in selecting and reviewing the investment options available for the plan (see Q 5:28). In addition, the plan fiduciary is responsible for providing necessary information to participants and promptly implementing their investment instructions.

A plan fiduciary that chooses to provide participant investment education might be responsible for the quality of information given. If a plan fiduciary itself provides information, it is responsible for the accuracy, completeness, and appropriateness of that information. [Interpretive Bulletin 96-1, 61 Fed. Reg. 29586 (June 11, 1996), reprinted in 29 C.F.R. § 2509.96-1(e); Restatement (Second) of Torts § 552 (1977)] If, instead, a plan fiduciary selects a service provider for participant investment education, the plan fiduciary must make a prudent selection.

Further, according to the DOL's view, a designation (or continuation) of a provider for participant investment education is itself a fiduciary act. [DOL ERISA Interpretive Bulletin 96-1, 61 Fed. Reg. 29586 (June 11, 1996), reprinted in 29 C.F.R. § 2509.96-1(e); *see also* Reich v. McManus, 883 F. Supp. 1144 (N.D. Ill. 1995); D.O.L. ERISA Adv. Op. 83-60A]

By contrast, a fiduciary might not be responsible if a participant alone selects his or her investment adviser. And a fiduciary might not be responsible if a loss results not because the fiduciary failed to act prudently in selecting an investment adviser but rather because a participant (or other directing person) chose which advice to follow or ignore:

> [I]n the context of an ERISA Section 404(c) plan, neither the designation of a person to provide education nor the designation of a fiduciary to provide investment advice to participants and beneficiaries would, in itself, give rise to fiduciary liability for loss, or with respect to any breach of [fiduciary duties], that is the direct and necessary result of a participant's or beneficiary's exercise of independent control.

[DOL ERISA Interpretive Bulletin 96-1, 61 Fed. Reg. 29586 (June 11, 1996), reprinted in 29 C.F.R. § 2509.96-1(e)]

Q 5:65   What is required to "comply" with ERISA Section 404(c)?

If a plan provides for participant-directed investment for all or some portion of plan investments and chooses to comply with the ERISA Section 404(c) regulations, the plan (or the participant-directed portion of the plan) must meet these basic requirements:

1. *Broad range of investments.* A participant must have the right to choose from a "broad range" of at least three diversified investments with varying degrees of risk and return (see Q 5:66).

2. *Investment information.* A participant must receive sufficient information to enable him or her to make informed investment decisions (see Qs 5:50–5:52). If the plan passes through voting rights of securities, the participant must receive all proxy voting materials (see Q 5:67).

3. *Investment changes.* A participant must have the right to change investments at least once each quarter or more frequently, and to receive written confirmation of account transactions (see Qs 5:67, 5:68).

Q 5:66   What constitutes a broad range of investments?

Under ERISA Section 404(c), a participant must have the right to choose from a broad range of at least three "core" diversified investments with varying degrees of risk and return.

Participant-directed investment selection must allow a participant to achieve a balanced portfolio or "a portfolio with aggregate risk and return characteristics . . . appropriate for the participant." [D.O.L. Reg. § 2550.404c-1(b)(3)] Likewise, each of the core investments must be such that when combined with investments in the other alternatives [it]tends to minimize through diversification the overall risk of a participant's . . . portfolio. [D.O.L. Reg. § 2550.404c-1(b)(3)(i)] The regulation is based on modern portfolio theory. [For a summary of the use of modern portfolio theory in trust law, see Restatement (Third) of Trusts § 90 (2007)]

Many employee-benefits practitioners suggest that, as a bare minimum, an ERISA Section 404(c) plan should have a stock fund, a bond fund, and a money-market fund. In selecting the options to be made available under a participant-directed investment plan, however, plan fiduciaries might ask themselves whether they could accept full legal responsibility for managing plan assets if that plan's investment universe were limited to the investments proposed to be made available to participants. ERISA Section 404(c) is based on the premise that, under a participant-directed plan, a participant is, in effect, his or her own investment trustee.

At least three of the core investment options must be look-through investments, such as variable annuity separate accounts or mutual funds. [D.O.L. Reg. § 2550.404c-1(b)(3)(i)(C)] A "look-through" investment must be sufficiently diversified. [D.O.L. Reg. § 2550.404c-1(b)(3)(ii)]

Q 5:67   How often must a plan allow investment changes?

A retirement plan that provides participant-directed investment may impose reasonable restrictions on the frequency of investment changes. At a minimum, however, participants must have the right to make investment changes at least once within any three-month period (for example, a calendar quarter). [D.O.L. Reg. § 2550.404c-1(b)(2)(ii)(C)(1)]

Further, a restriction on investment changes is "reasonable" only if "it permits participants . . . to give investment instructions with a frequency which [sic] is appropriate in light of the market volatility to which the investment alternative may reasonably be expected to be subject." [D.O.L. Reg. § 2550.404c-1(b)(2)(ii)(C)] Thus, for especially volatile mutual funds and variable annuity separate accounts, a right to daily instructions might be required. [D.O.L. Reg. § 2550.404c-1(b)(2)(ii)(C)]

Q 5:68   Must a participant-directed plan have procedures for accepting or conveying investment instructions?

An ERISA Section 404(c) plan must ensure that a participant has a reasonable opportunity to give investment instructions (in writing or otherwise) to an identified plan fiduciary (or other person designated by the plan fiduciary) that is obligated to comply with those instructions, except when the regulations permit refusal of the instruction (see Q 5:70). Also, a participant must have an opportunity to obtain written confirmation of his or her investment instructions.

Practice Pointer. The named plan fiduciary should make sure that the plan has a procedure for participants, beneficiaries, and alternate payees to request account corrections.

Under the ERISA Section 404(c) regulations, a plan fiduciary is relieved of fiduciary responsibility for a particular investment direction only if the participant affirmatively gives that investment direction. [ERISA § 404(c)(1)(i), 57 Fed. Reg. 46923 (Oct. 13, 1992)] However, there is an important exception for a prudently selected *qualified default investment alternative*; see Qs 5:96–5:119.

Q 5:69 May a plan administrator direct investment for a lost participant?

According to the DOL, a plan administrator may follow a uniform procedure of overriding a participant's last investment direction when the participant is missing and his or her investment direction no longer seems prudent to the plan administrator. (It is unclear how a plan administrator evaluates why an investment direction is no longer prudent for the best interests of a person it cannot locate.) Following such a procedure will not cause a plan to lose protection as an ERISA Section 404(c) plan for participants other than those whose investment directions are overridden. [DOL ERISA Adv. Op. 96-02A (Feb. 9, 1996)] However, when the plan administrator changes the investment of a missing participant's account, it does so under a full fiduciary duty to act as an expert investor in managing that participant's account according to the participant's best interests.

> **Practice Pointer.** The default-investment rule does not provide relief to a fiduciary that overrides a missing participant's last investment direction. That rule can apply only "in the absence of an investment election" and only if the individual "had the opportunity to direct the investment of the assets in his or her account but did not direct the investment of the assets[.]" [D.O.L. Reg § 2550.404c-5(a)(1), -5(c)(2)]

Alternatively, there should be no liability for following the participant's last investment direction, even if the participant cannot be located and even if that investment direction seems unwise. As long as the plan administrator has met all ERISA Section 404(c) requirements, the plan administrator may rely on the participant's last investment direction. For a plan not governed by ERISA, it is unclear whether a state's law of trusts and fiduciary relationships provides a similar absence of responsibility concerning a directed investment. [*But see generally* Uniform Trust Code § 808; Restatement (Third) of Trusts §§ 74–75 (2007)]

Q 5:70 When may a plan refuse a participant's investment instruction?

A plan may refuse to implement a participant's (or other directing person's) investment instruction if:

1. the responsible plan fiduciary knows the participant to be legally incompetent [D.O.L. Reg. § 2550.404c-1(c)(2)(iii)];
2. the instruction could result in a loss greater than the participant's account balance [D.O.L. Reg. § 2550.404c-1(d)(2)(ii)(D)]; or
3. doing so "[w]ould jeopardize the plan's tax qualified status under the Internal Revenue Code[.]" [D.O.L. Reg. § 2550.404c-1(d)(2)(ii)(C)]

Q 5:71 Must plan participants receive investments' proxy statements?

If a plan provides that a voting, tender, or similar right under an investment option is passed through to participants, the plan administrator must furnish to participants any proxy materials provided to the plan, as well as a description of the plan's provisions (if any) concerning the exercise of those rights. [D.O.L. Reg. § 2550.404c-1(b)(2)(i)(B)(1)] Further, if there is a restriction on participants' exercise of voting, tender, or similar rights regarding an investment option, the plan administrator must explain those restrictions.

Q 5:72 Must a plan fiduciary vote every proxy?

Not necessarily. In general, the right to vote a security is itself a plan investment. Therefore, the plan fiduciary generally has a fiduciary duty to vote a proxy. [DOL ERISA Interpretive Bulletin 94-2, 59 Fed. Reg. 38863 (July 2, 1994), reprinted in 29 C.F.R. § 2509.94-2] Nevertheless, a plan fiduciary need not vote a proxy if the expense of determining the appropriate vote outweighs the benefit that a favorable outcome would provide for the plan. [29 C.F.R. § 2509.94-2; DOL letters to Margaret Carroll (Investor Responsibility Research Center Inc), Howard D. Sherman (Institutional Shareholder Services Inc), J. Michael Farrell (Mar. 9–11, 1994); *see also* Restatement (Third) of Trusts § 73(b) (2007)]

Investment Communication Requirements

Q 5:73 What investment information must be furnished to a participant in a participant-directed plan?

The ERISA Section 404(c) regulations require that a participant be furnished with and have the opportunity to obtain sufficient information to become able to make informed investment decisions. [D.O.L. Reg. § 2440.404c-1(b)(2)(i)(B)] The regulations under ERISA Section 404(c) divide that information into two categories:

1. That which must routinely be furnished to every participant; and
2. That which must be furnished upon a participant's request.

If a plan fiduciary wants ERISA Section 404(c) relief from responsibility for participants' investment directions, participants must receive written information, at least for the materials required to be routinely furnished. (The regulations do not say whether foreign language materials must be furnished to a participant who cannot read English, and it is not clear what information, if any, must be provided to a participant who cannot read any language.) Furnishing the required information does not constitute giving investment advice for ERISA purposes. [ERISA § 3(21)(A); DOL ERISA Interpretive Bulletin 96-1, 61 Fed. Reg. 29586 (June 11, 1996), reprinted in 29 C.F.R. § 2509.96-1(d)(1)]

Q 5:74 What investment materials must be furnished to every participant in a participant-directed plan?

To obtain ERISA Section 404(c) relief, the following materials must be furnished to every participant in a participant-directed plan:

- A description of every investment option available under the plan, including a general description of:

—The identity of the investment manager,

—Investment objectives,

—Risk and return characteristics,

—Diversification of assets included in the portfolio, and

—Transaction fees and expenses that affect the participant's account balance (including management and investment advisors' fees, initial or deferred sales charges, and redemption or exchange fees)

- A document that meets the requirements of a profile prospectus under the federal securities laws meet these requirements of the ERISA Section 404(c) regulations [*See* 17 C.F.R. § 230.498]

- If the investment option is governed by the Securities Act of 1933, upon the participant's initial investment in that option, a copy of the most recent prospectus provided to the plan

- The name, address, and telephone number of the plan fiduciary (and, if applicable, the other person(s) designated by the plan fiduciary) responsible for providing information upon request (see Q 5:52)

- An explanation of when and how participants may give investment instructions, including an explanation of any limitations on plan investment instructions and of any restrictions on transfers to or from an investment option

- An explanation that the plan is intended to have participant-directed investment under ERISA Section 404(c), thereby relieving fiduciaries of liability for losses that are the result of the participant's investment directions

Q 5:75   What investment materials must be furnished to a participant in a participant-directed plan upon request?

The following materials must be furnished to a participant upon request; they may be requested for a particular investment option or for all investment options:

- A copy of the prospectus (including any statement of additional information) for any or all investment options

- A description of annual operating expenses (such as investment management fees or administration fees) that reduce the rate of return to the participant's account, and the aggregate amount of such expenses expressed as a percentage of average net assets of the investment option

- A copy of the financial statements and reports for any or all investment options

- Information on the value of shares or units in any or all investment options

- Information on the historical investment performance of any or all investment options, determined net of expenses, on a reasonable and consistent basis

[D.O.L. Reg. § 2550.404c-1(b)(2)(i)(B)(2)]

In fulfilling requests for the foregoing information, the plan fiduciary (or other person) may use whatever information was most recently furnished to it and need not furnish any information that it does not have. However, a plan fiduciary might have a duty to obtain the information available to it. [ERISA § 404(a)]

Q 5:76 Should an employer provide foreign-language investment materials for its non-English-speaking employees?

If an employer makes available a Section 403(b) plan that the employer intends as not a plan for ERISA purposes, it should not provide any materials because doing so might establish a plan governed by ERISA (see Q 9:2). Although an employer is permitted to summarize information furnished by the providers, the difficult choices inherent in providing a translation or even summarizing information might cause the employer to exceed the "hands-off" role required by the safe-harbor regulation. [D.O.L. Reg. § 2510.3-2(f)] But merely allowing a contractor to use its foreign-language materials as the contractor chooses should not exceed the "hands-off" role contemplated by the regulation.

A plan administrator should provide foreign-language investment materials for a plan only if it has determined, upon expert fiduciary prudence, that the expense is necessary to the administration of the plan. [ERISA § 404(a)(1)] In making such a determination, the plan fiduciary should consider whether some of those who cannot read English also cannot read any language.

It is difficult for a provider to offer foreign-language materials to describe investment options, because federal securities law prohibits the use of foreign-language materials unless the issuer also furnishes the complete prospectus in the same foreign language. [Investment Company Act Release No. 6082 (June 23, 1970); SEC No-Action Letter, American Funds Distributors Inc (publicly available Oct. 16, 1989)] Unless a fund's governing board is presented with responsible evidence that sales to those who read the foreign-language prospectuses would sufficiently benefit the fund (by increasing economies of scale) in relation to the expense, the fund's directors or trustees may have a duty to disapprove the translation expense. [*See generally* Model Business Corporation Act 2007 at §§ 8.30–8.31 (ABA 2008)]

> **Note.** If a broker-dealer or its representative allows a presentation to be translated, the broker-dealer "must take steps necessary to ensure that the translation of its presentation is accurate, regardless of whether it or its client [including a plan fiduciary] provides the translator." [NASD (now FINRA) Interpretive Letter (Nov. 26, 2001) (available at http://www.finra.org/RulesRegulation/PublicationsGuidance/InterpretiveLetters/ConductRules/P002689)]

Communications Concerning Blackouts

Q 5:77 What is a blackout?

A plan has a blackout if participants, beneficiaries, or alternate payees are restricted for at least three consecutive business days from giving an investment direction or taking a plan loan or distribution, when such a transaction ordinarily would be permitted. [D.O.L. Reg. § 2520.101-3(d)(i)] If the restriction is for fewer than three days, it is not a blackout.

Note. Although D.O.L. Regulations Section 2520.101-3(d)(i) does not define the term "business days," practitioners assume that it excludes Saturdays, Sundays, and holidays—days on which plan transactions usually would not be processed. Thus, if a plan's customary procedure is to process an instruction received on a holiday on the next business day, the holiday does not count for purposes of the blackout period.

Caution. A plan administrator should not create or recognize an unusual use of holiday as a subterfuge to avoid treating a restriction as a blackout. For example, a plan administrator in good faith might follow a recordkeeper's regular practice of implementing directions only on New York Stock Exchange days because those are the days that most SEC-registered funds set a new net asset value. But declaring a holiday when investment issuers, intermediaries, and the plan's recordkeeper are open for business could be suspect.

A blackout does not include a restriction that is or results from the following:

- Application of securities law
- A regularly scheduled restriction explained in the summary plan description
- A qualified domestic relations order (QDRO)
- The plan's procedure for determining whether a court order is a QDRO
- An act (or failure to act) on the part of a participant, a beneficiary, or alternate payee
- A third person's claim or action "involving the account of an individual participant"

Example. Plan X's procedure provides that a distribution does not become payable until 15 days after a participant initiates an address change. This procedure gives the participant and the plan administrator the opportunity to detect, by reading a confirmation, whether someone has impersonated the participant. The procedure imposes a restriction on the distribution, but it does not constitute a blackout.

Q 5:78   What is the rule regarding blackout notices?

If an individual-account retirement plan governed by ERISA will have a blackout, the plan administrator must send affected participants, beneficiaries, and alternate payees a notice explaining the blackout. [ERISA § 101(i)]

The most common reason for a blackout is a change in recordkeepers. Another reason is a change in the record keeper's computer system.

Practice Pointer. Although ERISA does not require the trustee or administrator of a church plan or governmental plan to send a blackout notice, a cautious fiduciary might want its lawyer's advice on whether sending such a notice would be prudent under other law.

Q 5:79 What must a blackout notice include?

A blackout notice must include the following information:

- The reason for the blackout
- An explanation of each investment and other plan right affected
- The expected beginning of the blackout
- The expected ending of the blackout
- An investment warning (see below)
- The name of an individual in the plan administrator's office to contact for further information

[ERISA § 101(i); D.O.L. Reg. § 2520.101-3(b)(1)(iv)–(v)]

A blackout notice may describe the beginning or end (or both) of the blackout period by referring to a calendar week rather than a particular day.

If the ability of participants, beneficiaries, or alternate payees to give investment directions is restricted during the blackout, the blackout notice must warn a recipient that he or she should evaluate the appropriateness of his or her current investment decisions because he or she will not be able to direct investments or diversify assets credited to his or her accounts during the blackout.

The notice must be written in language that can be understood by the average participant.

The blackout regulation includes a model notice. A plan that uses paragraphs 4 and 5A of the model notice in its blackout notice satisfies the requirement to inform plan participants, beneficiaries, and alternate payees that they should evaluate the appropriateness of their current investment decisions in light of their inability to direct their investments or diversify assets credited to their plan account during the blackout. Using the model notice does not provide any assurance concerning the regulation's other requirements. [D.O.L. Reg. § 2520.101-3(e)(1)]

The above requirements meet only the plan administrator's duty under ERISA Section 101(i). A plan fiduciary may have additional duties to communicate information about a blackout that participants, beneficiaries, and alternate payees need to know.

Q 5:80 To whom must a plan administrator send a blackout notice?

A plan administrator must send a blackout notice to each participant, beneficiary, or alternate payee who could be affected by an inability to give an investment direction or take a loan or distribution. [D.O.L. Reg. § 2520.101-3(a)]

Q 5:81 When must a plan administrator send a blackout notice?

A plan administrator must furnish the notice at least 30 days (but no more than 60 days) before the blackout begins. [D.O.L. Reg. § 2520.101-3] An exception may be available if the blackout period is the result of a corporate merger, an acquisition, a divestiture, or similar business transaction. In such a case, the plan administrator must furnish the notice as soon as is "reasonably practicable" [D.O.L. Reg. § 2520.101-3(b)(2)(ii)(c)]

Another exception might apply if a plan administrator "documents" its fiduciary decision that there are unforeseeable or extraordinary circumstances beyond its control or that delaying an action would constitute a breach of its fiduciary duties. Even then, a plan administrator must furnish the blackout notice "as soon as [is] reasonably possible under the circumstances." [D.O.L. Reg. § 2520.101-3(b)(2)(ii)(B)]

Q 5:82 What must a plan administrator do if a blackout does not end as scheduled?

If there is a change in either the beginning or ending of a blackout, the plan administrator must send another notice to affected participants, beneficiaries, and alternate payees "as soon as is reasonably practicable." This notice must explain any "material" change in the information furnished in the original (or most recent) blackout notice. [D.O.L. Reg. § 2520.101-3(b)(4)]

Q 5:83 What are the consequences of failing to furnish a blackout notice?

The potential consequences of failing to furnish a blackout notice include fiduciary liability for investment losses in participants' accounts, civil penalties, and criminal punishment.

Fiduciary liability. Failing to furnish a required blackout notice is a clear breach of the plan administrator's fiduciary duties. [ERISA § 404(a)(1)] ERISA provides that a fiduciary is liable to make good losses that result from the fiduciary's breach. [ERISA §§ 502, 509] Although it might be difficult to prove causation, some lawyers believe a participant, beneficiary, or alternate payee could allege that he or she would have made different investment directions had he or she received the proper notice.

Civil penalty. If a plan administrator fails to furnish a required blackout notice, the DOL may impose a penalty. The maximum penalty is $100 per affected participant, beneficiary, or alternate payee multiplied by the number of days that the plan administrator failed to furnish the notice. [D.O.L. Reg. § 2560.502e-5, 7]

Example. Wellness Healthcare Network maintains a Section 403(b) retirement plan that has 30,000 participants. Wellness, as plan administrator, changed the plan's record keeper. To do so, it imposed a blackout period starting at 4:00 p.m. on Friday, January 31, 2003. The "conversion" and reconciliation were completed in three business days, and the blackout ended at the close of business on Wednesday, February 5, 2003. Although Wellness should have sent a blackout notice no later than January 1, 2003 (30 days before the start of the blackout period), it did not send a blackout notice. In this case, the penalty is $108 million ($100 × 30,000 [$3 million] × 36 days).

Criminal punishment. A willful failure to furnish a blackout notice may be punished by a fine up to $500,000 and up to 10 years' imprisonment, in addition to punishment for related crimes. [ERISA § 501]

Market-Timing Trading

Q 5:84   What is market-timing trading?

"Market timing" refers to short-term "trading"—a purchase followed by a redemption—in fund shares. This trading tries to exploit the way a fund prices its shares in an attempt to capture short-term movements (often a day or even a few hours) in securities prices.

Some market-timing trading seeks to exploit a fund's procedure that usually values a security at the last price at which it traded on its regular securities exchange, even if that exchange closed hours before the fund values its portfolio securities. But some market-timing strategies do not necessarily depend on time-zone arbitrage or an imperfect valuation of portfolio securities. [*See, e.g.,* Borneman v. Principal Life Ins. Co., 291 F. Supp. 2d 935 (S.D. Iowa 2003)]

Q 5:85   How could "market-timing" trading harm a fund?

Because of the effects quick trading has on a fund's expenses and on whether a fund needs to buy or sell securities other than under the fund's long-term investment goal, this disruptive trading could dilute returns for long-term shareholders. Most funds discourage market timing because it interferes with managing a fund in the best interests of long-term shareholders. Some research suggests that a fund's loss or expense attributable to disruptive trading in fund shares could be significant. [*See generally* SEC Release Nos. IC-26782 (File No. S7-11-04) (Mar. 11, 2005), IC-26375A (Mar.5, 2004), IC-26288 (File No S7-27-03) (Dec. 11, 2003), IC-26287 (Dec. 11, 2003)]

Q 5:86   What are funds doing to protect a fund's investors
          from market-timing trading?

A fund's governing board must:

- approve a redemption fee, in an amount that the board finds as appropriate to restore the fund's expenses and damages that would result from market-timing redemptions (or to reduce dilution of the fund's outstanding shares), or

- must decide that such a fee is "not necessary or not appropriate."

[Investment Company Act Rule 22c-2(a)(1), 17 C.F.R. § 270.22c-2(a)(1)]

Note. This requirement applies only to a fund that allows a shareholder to redeem shares within seven calendar days after the shares were purchased. Because funds available as investment options of a Section 403(b) custodial account or variable annuity contract typically allow a redemption any business day, the requirement to adopt a redemption fee or decide that such a fee is unnecessary generally applies to most funds.

Note. This rule does not apply to a money-market fund, an exchange-traded fund, or a fund that affirmatively permits short-term trading in its shares. [17 C.F.R. § 270.22c-2(b)(1)-(3)]

Further, a fund or its underwriter must make an agreement with each "financial intermediary," including a retirement plan's recordkeeper or an insurance company that sponsors a separate account used for a variable annuity contract [17 C.F.R. § 270.22c-2(c)(1)(iii)], under which the intermediary will

- furnish, on the fund's request, information about all participants, beneficiaries, and alternate payees who indirectly bought or sold the fund's shares, including the date and amount of each indirect purchase or redemption of each participant, beneficiary, or alternate payee; and

- implement the fund's instructions "to restrict or prohibit [indirect] further purchases . . . of fund shares by a participant, beneficiary, or alternate payee who the fund identified as having engaged in plan investment directions that violate the fund's policies for protecting against frequent, short-term, or market-timing trading in fund shares."

[17 C.F.R. § 270.22c-2(a)(2)(i)–(ii)] These two requirements apply even if a fund does not have a redemption fee.

Practice Pointer. Even a fund without a redemption fee must regularly reevaluate whether it needs such a fee, and often might need information about participants' investment directions to complete that evaluation.

Practice Pointer. Under their shareholder-services agreement, a fund might engage a plan's recordkeeper to implement the fund's trading policies.

These rules are in addition to a general rule that requires a fund to adopt and implement policies and procedures reasonably designed to ensure compliance with the fund's disclosed policies regarding market timing. [Investment Company Act Rule 38a-1, 17 C.F.R. § 270.38a-1]

Providing Investment Education and Advice

Q 5:87   Must a plan fiduciary give advice to participants?

No. The ERISA Section 404(c) regulations state that a plan fiduciary need not provide advice to participants concerning their investment choices. [D.O.L. Reg.

§ 2550.404c-1(c)(4); DOL ERISA Interpretive Bulletin 96-1, 61 Fed. Reg. 29586 (June 11, 1996), reprinted in 29 C.F.R. § 2509.96-1(b)]

Nonetheless, employers might want to provide a means by which participants can get guidance about investment choices. If so, a plan fiduciary might prefer that such services be performed by a person that is appropriately regulated in that conduct, such as a registered investment adviser.

In the DOL's view, if a plan fiduciary chooses to engage a service provider for participant investment education, it must use fiduciary diligence and expertise in making or reviewing a selection. A plan fiduciary is not responsible, however, to the extent that the participant selects the education provider. [DOL ERISA Interpretive Bulletin 96-1, 61 Fed. Reg. 29586, (June 11, 1996), reprinted in 29 C.F.R. § 2509.96-1(e)]

Q 5:88 Should a plan administrator follow securities laws if it compiles plan investment information?

Yes. ERISA requires a plan fiduciary to act "with the care, skill, prudence, and diligence . . . that a prudent [person] . . . familiar with such matters [as those concerning which the fiduciary acts] would use in the conduct of an enterprise of a like character and with like aims[.]" [ERISA § 404(a)(1)(B)] In the contributing author's view, this standard suggests that a plan fiduciary communicating about investment choices must use the same expertise that someone in the business of communicating investment choices would use. Although an ERISA plan fiduciary that is not in the business of providing investment advice need not register as an investment adviser, laws and customs that apply to registered investment advisers might be evidence of what a prudent expert would do in presenting investment information.

Practice Pointer. If a plan fiduciary that is not an expert prepares any communication concerning plan investment options, it might consider asking the plan's regular employee-benefits lawyer to collaborate with a lawyer who regularly advises investment advisers about the form, content, and accompanying disclosures for such a communication.

Q 5:89 Should an employer make investment education available?

For a plan that provides participant-directed investment, the plan administrator need furnish only the "compulsory" information specified by the regulations (see Qs 5:50–5:52). [D.O.L. Reg. § 2550.404c-1(b)(2)(i)(B)]

But some practitioners believe that investment information is not meaningful for a person who has no background to evaluate that information. "While items required by the disclosure provisions, such as risk and return characteristics, historical performance, and prospectuses, are important to making investment decisions, they may be inadequate for someone who has not been given some information about general investment principles or the differences between asset classifications." [Keith R. Pyle, "Compliance under ERISA Section 404(c) with Increasing Investment Alternatives and Account Accessibility," 32 *Indiana Law Rev.* 1467 (1999)]

While the views of employee-benefits and human-resources practitioners vary widely, most employers make some form of investment education available to participants.

Q 5:90   Should a participant seek investment advice?

Although there is some evidence suggesting that American workers' investment knowledge might be improving, there also is considerable evidence that a vast majority of participants lack even the minimum knowledge and "financial literacy" needed to become capable of making informed investment decisions. Further, among those who do have enough knowledge, not all have sufficient access to investment information. Moreover, some retirement plan participants, even when capable, simply do not want to make investment decisions. [*See generally* Research papers of the Boettner Center for Pensions and Retirement Research of the Wharton School of the University of Pennsylvania (available at http://www.pensionresearchcouncil.org/boettner/publications.php)] A participant who is not already experienced in making investment decisions might want advice.

> **Note.** If a participant retains an investment adviser, the adviser's fees may be paid from the Section 403(b) contract or account. That payment is not a distribution, and has no tax consequences. [Ltr. Rul. 9316042]

Q 5:91   How should a participant evaluate an investment adviser?

Although no regulation can ensure the knowledge or competence of any person, the federal or state law that applies to a *registered* investment adviser could help an investor get the information he or she needs to evaluate an investment adviser. For example, the federal Investment Advisers Act of 1940 requires a registered investment adviser to deliver a disclosure statement that explains the adviser's methods. The information in the disclosure statement might help an investor decide whether an adviser's methods make sense.

> **Caution.** A prospective client should carefully investigate and evaluate an adviser's education, business background, reputation, and advice methods.

Q 5:92   May an investment adviser give advice about its own funds?

Yes. Notwithstanding ERISA's prohibited-transaction rule that precludes many self-dealing or other conflict-of-interest transactions, an investment adviser may give a participant, beneficiary, alternate payee, or plan advice about investing in the adviser's (or an affiliate's) funds if

1. The adviser adjusts its fee to subtract the amount of the fee received by each fund manager [PTCE 77-4, 42 Fed. Reg. 18732 (Apr. 8, 1977); *see also* D.O.L. ERISA Adv. Opinions 2005-10A (May 11, 2005), 97-15A (May 22, 1997), 93-12A and 93-13A (April 27, 1993)]; or

2. The adviser's investment advice is the work of an independent consultant, and there are significant restraints on the opportunity for the adviser to influence the work of that independent consultant or render advice other than according to the independent consultant's model. [D.O.L. ERISA Adv. Op. 2001-09A (Dec. 14, 2001)]

3. The adviser's arrangement meets the conditions of a statutory exemption.

Concerning plans not governed by ERISA, similar opportunities to manage conflicting interests in rendering investment advice might be available under a state's law of trusts and fiduciary relationships. [*See generally* Restatement (Third) of Trusts § 78(2) and comment c(8) (2007); Uniform Trust Code § 802(f)]

Of course, a participant, beneficiary, or alternate payee who considers whether to engage an investment adviser on such a basis should read carefully all disclosure information and evaluate whether the investment adviser's methods make sense. Further, a plan fiduciary that considers whether to approve the availability of an investment adviser's services should carefully evaluate whether the adviser's disclosure information is such that a participant, beneficiary, or alternate payee may independently decide to engage the investment adviser. [*See* DOL ERISA Interpretive Bulletin 96-1, 61 Fed. Reg. 29586 (June 11, 1996), reprinted in 29 C.F.R. § 2509.96-1(e)]

Eligible Investment Advice Arrangements

Q 5:93   What is the exemption for an eligible investment advice arrangement?

ERISA exempts from prohibited-transaction treatment a transaction that is:

1. providing investment advice under an eligible investment advice arrangement (see Q 5:94);

2. buying, holding, or selling a security "or other property" if doing so is "pursuant to the investment advice";

3. receiving a fee or other compensation concerning (i) or (ii).

[ERISA § 408(b)(14), added by the Pension Protection Act of 2006, Pub. L. No. 109-280, 120 Stat. 780, § 601 (Aug. 17, 2006)]

This exemption permits—with some conditions—a person licensed or registered under banking, insurance, or securities law to render advice about investments for which he, she, or it receives compensation from persons other than the plan or the person advised. The exemption attempts to protect an advised person from recommendations that could be biased or influenced by an adviser's interest in its own compensation.

Q 5:94   What is an *eligible investment advice arrangement*?

As with earlier exemptions and interpretations, the statutory exemption's conditions for an *eligible investment advice arrangement* give a *fiduciary adviser* who or that receives compensation from persons other than the plan or the person advised a choice of two ways to manage his, her, or its conflicts of interests.

Advice with level fees

A fiduciary adviser may cure self-dealing conflicts by "levelizing" fees so that total fees (including sales compensation) cannot vary based on a participant's investment choices.

> **Caution.** The DOL has released an internal interpretation concerning which persons must be counted together with a fiduciary adviser for the purposes of the level-fees condition. [DOL-EBSA Field Assistance Bulletin 2007-1 (Feb. 2, 2007)] Because this interpretation is not a regulation or rule, a court need not give any deference to it.

Advice "cleansed by an independent expert"

An adviser may avoid conflicts by rendering advice from a computer model that is decided by an independent expert, without an opportunity for the fiduciary adviser to alter or influence the advice. That independent advice must be the only advice, and a transaction is protected only if the participant alone directs it.

If the fees of the fiduciary adviser and its affiliates are not level, a computer model must:

1. Apply generally accepted investment theories that take into account the historic returns of different asset classes over defined periods of time;

2. Use relevant information about the participant, beneficiary, or alternate payee;

3. Use prescribed objective criteria to provide asset allocations comprised of plan investment options;

4. Operate in a way that's not biased in favor of any investment option offered by the fiduciary adviser or a related person; and

5. Take into account all plan investment options in advising a participant, beneficiary, or alternate payee about how he or she should direct investment of his or her plan account without inappropriate weighting of any investment option.

Although either an independent expert or the fiduciary adviser may design a computer model, an *eligible investment expert* must certify that the model meets the rules. The DOL may make requirements for these experts. A retirement plan's arrangements for an *eligible investment advice arrangement* must be approved by a plan fiduciary (usually, the employer) that is independent of the expert, the fiduciary adviser, and the issuers, managers, and distributors of the investments. An employer or other approving fiduciary is not responsible for the fiduciary adviser's particular advice, but is responsible for prudent selection and periodic review of the fiduciary adviser. Likewise, the independent plan fiduciary must decide carefully that the fiduciary adviser's and his, her, or its affiliates' compensation "all in" is no more than reasonable compensation.

The fiduciary adviser must give the participant disclosure about the investment options, the fiduciary adviser's (and his, her, or its affiliates') sales compensation, and several other subjects. Before the fiduciary adviser first gives advice, the adviser must furnish a written (which can be electronic) notice. This notice must include information about:

1. The role of any related party in developing the investment-advice service

2. The role of any related party in selecting the plan's investment options;

3. Past performance for each investment option;

4. All fees or other compensation to be received by the fiduciary adviser or an affiliate;

5. Any material affiliation or relationship of the fiduciary adviser or an affiliate concerning any investment option;

6. The manner and under what circumstances participant information will be used or disclosed;

7. The services provided by the fiduciary adviser in providing investment advice;

8. The adviser's status as a plan fiduciary concerning the advice; and

9. The participant's opportunity to make his or her own arrangements for another adviser who or that might have no material affiliation with, and receive no fees or other compensation concerning, the plan investment options.

The fiduciary adviser must keep this information up to date, and must furnish it, without charge, to the advised participant, beneficiary, or alternate payee on an annual basis, on request, or if there is a material change.

The exemption has several further disclosure requirements and other conditions that are not summarized above. Further, an arrangement can qualify for the exemption's prohibited-transactions relief only if an independent person who has appropriate experience (and certifies in writing that he or she has it) does an annual "audit" on whether the arrangement meets the requirements of the statute (including any DOL rules) and reports to the employers and other plan fiduciaries that approve the arrangement.

This exemption is available for advice rendered on or after January 1, 2007. [ERISA § 408(g), added by the Pension Protection Act of 2006, Pub. L. No. 109-280, 120 Stat. 780, § 601 (Aug. 17, 2006)]

Default Investments

Q 5:95 How may a plan fiduciary avoid liability for participants' failures to choose investments?

A plan fiduciary avoids liability for participants' failures to choose investments by following ERISA's qualified default-investment rule and prudently selecting a qualified default investment alternative (see Qs 5:96–5:119 next subchapter).

As explained in Qs 5:62–5:75, a plan fiduciary is not liable for a loss that results from a participant's, beneficiary's, or alternate payee's exercise of control in directing investment of his or her plan account. Before 2007, this relief could not apply if, despite a fair opportunity to give investment directions, an individual failed to direct investment. In the Pension Protection Act of 2006 (PPA), Congress provided relief, and directed the DOL to make a rule. [PPA, § 624] After 2007 (and perhaps after 2006 (see Q 5:101)), a retirement plan's fiduciary has some relief from responsibility for deciding how to invest a plan account of a participant, beneficiary, or alternate payee who has not directed investment. If a plan provides for investment under a *qualified default investment alternative* or QDIA (see Q 5:107) and meets several conditions, a plan fiduciary generally is not liable for what results because of investing an individual's account under a QDIA.

Qualified Default-Investment Rule

Q 5:96 What is ERISA's qualified default-investment rule?

Using a study and rule-making project that was underway before Congress enacted the PPA, the DOL on September 27, 2006 proposed and on October 24, 2007 published regulations to implement ERISA Section 404(c)(5) and other relief concerning default investments. [Default Investment Alternatives Under Participant Directed Individual Account Plans, 72 Fed. Reg. 60452–60480 (Oct. 24, 2007); codified as 29 C.F.R. § 2550.404c-5 ("Fiduciary relief for investments in qualified default investment alternatives")]

This rule provides an ERISA-governed retirement plan's fiduciary some relief from responsibility for deciding exactly how to invest a plan account of a participant, beneficiary, or alternate payee who has not directed investment. If a plan provides for investment under a *qualified default investment alternative* or QDIA and meets several conditions, a plan fiduciary is not liable for what results because of investing an individual's account under a QDIA. [D.O.L. Reg. § 2550.404c-5] The QDIA rule's relief is available not only for a default investment made under an implied-election or "automatic-contribution" arrangement but also for other default investments.

Q 5:97 Does this default-investment rule protect a fiduciary of a governmental plan or a church plan?

No, the QDIA rule interprets and implements a provision of ERISA Section 404, and so applies only to ERISA-governed plans.

Part 4 of Subtitle B of Title I of the Employee Retirement Income Security Act of 1974, as amended (ERISA) does not govern a church plan that has not elected to be governed by ERISA or a governmental plan that cannot be governed by ERISA. [ERISA § 4(b)]

Practice Pointer. A fiduciary of a governmental plan or a church plan should get his, her, or its expert lawyer's advice about relevant states' laws and what documents and procedures might help protect the fiduciary.

Q 5:98 Is the QDIA relief available only if a plan has an "automatic-contribution" arrangement?

No. Because Congress enacted the QDIA provision in the same section of the PPA that includes provisions for an automatic-contribution arrangement, an eligible automatic-contribution arrangement, and a qualified automatic-contribution arrangement, some people presumed that the relief from responsibility provided for a plan fiduciary's investment in a qualified default investment alternative is conditioned on use of one of the automatic-contribution arrangements. That is not correct. [D.O.L. Reg. § 2550.404c-5]

Q 5:99 If the QDIA rule is met, what relief does a fiduciary get?

The QDIA rule relieves a plan fiduciary from liability for a loss that is the "direct and necessary result" from investing in any *qualified default investment alternative* that met all conditions. [D.O.L. Reg. § 2550.404c-5(b)(1)]

Q 5:100 What fiduciary duties are not excused?

The QDIA rule relieves a plan fiduciary from liability for a loss only to the extent that the loss is the "direct and necessary result" from investing in any *qualified default investment alternative* that met all conditions. Every duty other than deciding the particular investment of a non-directing individual's account remains a plan fiduciary's duty.

The QDIA rule's relief does not excuse a plan fiduciary from a duty to select (and regularly monitor) a default fund or manager using expert prudence, care, skill, and diligence. [D.O.L. Reg. § 2550.404c-5(b)(2)]

Example. Once a fiduciary decides that the *category* of target-year funds is a fitting default for a plan, within that category a fiduciary must select which target-year funds are prudent for the plan's and its non-directing individuals' needs.

The QDIA rule's relief does not excuse the designating plan fiduciary (or any co-fiduciary) from a duty to satisfy itself that there is no prohibited transaction that would result from using a fund or manager. [D.O.L. Reg. § 2550.404c-5(b)(4)]

Q 5:101   What is the default-investment rule's effective date?

According to the DOL's rule, protection against liability is available for QDIA investments made on or after December 24, 2007. [Default Investment Alternatives Under Participant Directed Individual Account Plans, 72 Fed. Reg. 60452 at 60466 (Oct. 24, 2007)]

> **Note.** The PPA applies ERISA Section 404(c)(5) "to plan years beginning after December 31, 2006." [PPA, § 624] But ERISA Section 404(c)(5) provides its relief only to amounts "invested by the plan in accordance with regulations prescribed by the Secretary." Concerning amounts invested before December 24, 2007—or at least before October 24, 2007—it might be difficult to argue that amounts were invested "in accordance with" a rule that did not exist. However, even if Congress's delegation of legislative rulemaking is not unconstitutional, it is less clear whether Congress can delegate to an agency power to vary a statute's effective date, especially if the effective date is specified by Congress's Act. [U.S. Const. art. I, § 1; art. I, § 7, cl. 2; Clinton v. City of New York, 524 U.S. 417 U.S. 417 (1998); Chevron, U.S.A., Inc. v. Natural Res. Def. Council, 467 U.S. 837 (1984); Whitman v. American Trucking Ass'n, 531 457 U.S. 457, 481 (2001), *Id.* at 487 (Thomas, J. concurring)]

Rules that Apply Generally to Qualified Default Investments

Q 5:102   Must a default investment consider a participant's personal situation?

No. Whether it is targeted-retirement date or life-cycle funds (see Q 5:108) or a managed account (see Q 5:110), a default investment may ignore all of a participant's preferences and personal circumstances other than his or her age. [D.O.L. Reg. §§ 2550.404c-5(e)(4)(i), 2550.404c-5(e)(4)(iii)] A balanced fund (see Q 5:109) ignores all of a participant's preferences and personal circumstances, including his or her age. [D.O.L. Reg. § 2550.404c-5(e)(4)(ii)]

> **Example.** An asset allocation that is "optimized" under modern portfolio theory knowing only the participant's age and presuming that he or she intends to retire at the plan's normal retirement age could be a qualified default investment.

Q 5:103   Must a default investment be diversified?

Yes, the rule requires that a qualified default investment be "diversified so as to minimize the risk of large losses[.]" [D.O.L. Reg. § 2550.404c-5(e)(4)(i)-(ii)-(iii)]

Q 5:104   Must a default investment include both stocks and bonds?

Yes. Even if a fund or account is based on "generally accepted investment theories," to qualify as a QDIA it also must "provide . . . a mix of equity and fixed[-]income exposures[.]" [D.O.L. Reg. § 2550.404c-5(e)(4)(i)-(ii)-(iii)] For example, even if applying a modern-portfolio-theory model would cause a manager of a 21-year-old's account to invest entirely in stocks, a QDIA must have some investment in bonds or other fixed-income investments. Likewise, even if applying a modern-portfolio-theory model would cause a manager of a 95-year-old's account to invest entirely in bonds, a QDIA must have some investment in stock or other equity investments.

> **Note.** Would an allocation of 99 percent of an account to stock funds and 1 percent to a bond fund be a sufficient "mix" of exposures? Or would a court find that a 1 percent allocation is so small that the account lacks a meaningful fixed-income exposure? If a 1 percent allocation is not enough, how much is enough?

Q 5:105   How quickly may a participant get out of a default investment?

To be a QDIA, an investment must permit a participant, beneficiary, or alternate payee to redirect his or her plan account's assets into another plan investment option no less often than once in any three-month period and at least as often as an individual who "affirmatively" directed investment in the same fund or account. [D.O.L. Reg. § 2550.404c-5(e)(4)]

Q 5:106   What is the no-exit-charge rule for a default investment?

An individual whose account is initially invested under a QDIA might later become attentive and want to direct investment of his or her account. Recognizing this, the law removes some burdens that could interfere with an individual's opportunity to direct investment.

For the 90-day period that begins with a participant's first elective contribution, a QDIA must "not be subject to any restrictions, fees or expenses (including surrender charges, liquidation or exchange fees, redemption fees and similar expenses charged in connection with the liquidation of, or transfer from, the investment)[.]" [D.O.L. Reg. § 2550.404c-5(c)(5)(ii)(A)]

> **Note.** The DOL's rule distinguishes an "exit" fee from an "ongoing" fee that is not imposed (or does not vary) based on a participant's, beneficiary's, or alternate payee's decision that results in the plan's redemption of, or "withdrawal" from, the investment. [D.O.L. Reg. § 2550.404c-5(c)(5)(ii)(B)]

After the first 90 days, it is enough that a default investment has no restriction, fee, or expense beyond those that apply to someone who "affirmatively" directed investment in the same fund or account. [D.O.L. Reg. § 2550.404c-5(c)(5)(iii)]

> **Note.** This rule leaves a loophole. Nothing in the rule precludes an investment issuer from designing an investment offered only regarding nondirecting participants. If there is no one who "affirmatively" directed investment, even onerous restrictions or fees might nonetheless be not "otherwise

applicable to a participant or beneficiary who elected to invest in that" fund or account.

Practice Pointer. A plan fiduciary must not approve an investment that has an "exit" fee unless he or she evaluates the investment using the care, skill, and diligence that a prudent expert would use and finds that the investment is in the plan's best interests for the exclusive purpose of providing retirement benefits to participants and their beneficiaries. [ERISA § 404(a)(1)]

Different Kinds of Default Investments

Q 5:107   What kinds of investments can be a qualified default investment?

There are three kinds of investment that may be a qualified default investment:

1. a "life-cycle" or "targeted-retirement-date" fund or account (see Q 5:108);
2. a "balanced" fund or account (see Q 5:109); or
3. a "managed account" (see Q 5:112).

[D.O.L. Reg. § 2550.404c-5(e)(4)(i)-(iii)]

Although a "principal-protection" investment is not generally a qualified default investment, a plan's default-investment procedure may use it as a QDIA for up to the first 120 days of a participant's default investment (see Q 5:113).

Q 5:108   How does the default-investment rule describe a targeted-retirement-date or life-cycle fund?

The default-investment rule defines a QDIA to include (if it meets the other conditions):

> [a]n investment fund product or model portfolio that applies generally accepted investment theories, is diversified so as to minimize the risk of large losses and that is designed to provide varying degrees of long-term appreciation and capital preservation through a mix of equity and fixed income exposures based on the participant's age, target retirement date (such as normal retirement age under the plan) or life expectancy. Such products and portfolios change their asset allocations and associated risk levels over time with the objective of becoming more conservative ([that is], decreasing risk of losses) with increasing age. . . . An example of such a fund or portfolio may be a "life-cycle" or "targeted-retirement-date" fund or account.

[D.O.L. Reg. § 2550.404c-5(e)(4)(i)]

Caution. That a fund has a name that suggests that the fund is a targeted-retirement-date fund does not mean that the fund meets the QDIA conditions.

Note. A plan fiduciary who lacks enough expertise to evaluate whether a proposed investment in fact meets the conditions quoted above must get, and carefully consider, the advice of experts so that the fiduciary can make an informed, prudent, expert decision.

Q 5:109   How does the default-investment rule describe a balanced fund?

The default-investment rule defines a QDIA to include (if it meets the other conditions):

> [a]n investment fund product or model portfolio that applies generally accepted investment theories, is diversified so as to minimize the risk of large losses and that is designed to provide long-term appreciation and capital preservation through a mix of equity and fixed income exposures consistent with a target level of risk appropriate for participants of the plan as a whole. . . . An example of such a fund or portfolio may be a "balanced" fund.

The QDIA rule refers to a "balanced fund" as an example of a fund that *could* meet the quoted description. [D.O.L. Reg. § 2550.404c-5(e)(4)(ii)]

Q 5:110   What is the difference between a targeted-retirement-date fund and a balanced fund as a default-investment?

A targeted-retirement-date fund (which the contributing author calls a target-year fund) invests to meet an asset allocation that the fund considers fitting for participants of just one age cohort. (See Q 5:111.)

By contrast, a plan fiduciary that selects a balanced fund as a plan's default investment must choose such a fund based on "the characteristics of the group of employees as a whole [.]" For example, the accounts of a 70-year-old and a 20-year-old would each be invested under the same fund.

Q 5:111   How does a plan administrator use target-year funds as a default-investment?

Although other uses are possible, typically a plan administrator sets a "rules-based" default-investment procedure that it designs to invest a participant's, beneficiary's, or alternate payee's account under the target-year fund that is the nearest fit based on the individual's date of birth and assumed retirement age.

Currently, a group of target-year funds tends to be organized into five-year bands: a fund complex might offer target-year funds with the years 2000, 2005, 2010, 2015, 2020, 2025, 2030, 2035, 2040, 2045, and 2050 included in the funds' names. To use such an organization of target-year funds as a plan's qualified default investment alternative, a plan fiduciary would assume a normal retirement age (for example, 65) and invest a non-directing participant's amounts in the fund that corresponds with, or is closest to, the year that the participant would attain that age.

Example. Using the funds and assumptions described above, a plan fiduciary would "default" participants born in 1935 or earlier to the 2000 fund, and would "default" participants born in 1985 or later to the 2050 fund.

Practice Pointer. If a participant was born in 1953 (and there is no 2018 fund), does the plan invest her account in the 2020 fund, or in the 2015 fund? If a participant was born in 1959 (and there is no 2024 fund), does the plan invest his account in the 2025 fund, or in the 2020 fund? If a plan uses commercially-organized target-year funds that are available only in five-year intervals, a plan's default-investment procedure must specify "next-lower," "next-higher," "nearest," or some other ordering rule to classify every default-invested participant. These rules matter because one assumes that about 80 percent of the participants will have been born in a year that does not exactly relate to a fund's target year.

Note. Nothing in ERISA's default-investment rule precludes a plan fiduciary from designing a series of target-year accounts keyed to every year. This could be done using the same few funds that are the underlying investments of a wider-interval target-year fund.

Q 5:112   How does the default-investment rule describe a managed account?

The default-investment rule defines a QDIA to include (if it meets the other conditions):

> [a]n investment[-]management service with respect to which a fiduciary, within the meaning of paragraph (e)(3)(i) of this section, applying generally accepted investment theories, allocates the assets of a participant's individual account to achieve varying degrees of long-term appreciation and capital preservation through a mix of equity and fixed income exposures, offered through investment alternatives available under the plan, based on the participant's age, target retirement date (such as normal retirement age under the plan), or life expectancy. Such portfolios are diversified so as to minimize the risk of large losses and change their asset allocations and associated risk levels for an individual account over time with the objective of becoming more conservative ([that is], decreasing risk of losses) with increasing age. . . . An example of such a service may be a "managed account."

[D.O.L. Reg. § 2550.404c-5(e)(4)(iii)] The QDIA rule allows as a default investment an account managed by a registered investment adviser, bank, trust company, insurance company, or plan sponsor that confirms in writing that it is a plan fiduciary.

Q 5:113   Why might a plan fiduciary prefer a managed account as a default investment?

A plan fiduciary might prefer a managed account as a default investment because:

- its manager is responsible as a plan fiduciary (unlike an SEC-registered fund's manager, which is not a plan fiduciary);
- using it allows asset allocations more nearly related to a participant's age or assumed retirement age than is feasible using the five-year bands of typical target-year funds;
- a managed account's communications can educate a nondirecting participant about investing for retirement, and so might help him or her "graduate" to more involvement or better communication.

Another fiduciary to share responsibility and liability.

Recognizing that any relief from liability is never perfectly "bullet-proof," a plan fiduciary might feel comfortable obtaining an additional layer of protection by allocating a responsibility to another fiduciary. [ERISA § 405]

Allocations more nearly related to a participant's retirement age.

Even as a default investment, a managed account could give each nondirecting participant an asset allocation that is more finely tuned than the mix of a typical target-year fund, which groups participants into five-year bands.

Note. A retirement plan's investment options include one index fund for every generally recognized asset class, and a set of target-year funds, organized by five-year bands. For a nondirecting participant, the plan knows nothing about him or her beyond his or her date of birth. The plan administrator furnishes a computer file of this data to its recordkeeper. If the plan engages a managed-accounts manager, the recordkeeper shares this data with that manager.The plan's default-investment procedure states that it is grounded on an assumption that a nondirecting participant's goal is to begin his or her plan distribution in the year that he or she attains the plan's normal retirement age, that is, 65. Patsy and Potsy both were born on July 1, 1962, so the normal retirement date for each of them is July 1, 2027. Each neglects to direct his or her investment. Compare the asset allocation that results based on whether a plan's default-investment procedure uses target-year funds or managed accounts.

Target-year funds

The plan's default-investment procedure provides that the default is the target-year fund for the year of the participant's normal retirement date or, if there is none, the "next-lower" year's fund. The plan administrator invests Patsy's account under the 2025 fund.

Managed accounts

Unlike the other plan that used a 2025 fund for someone expected to retire in the middle of 2027, the investment manager simply solves its mean-variance optimization formula based on retirement on July 1, 2027. This $2\frac{1}{2}$-year difference in the math of an optimization formula might be meaningful.

Note. Some practitioners argue that small asset-allocation differences based on rounding differences in assumptions are unlikely to matter much.

However, what the DOL refers to as the "generally accepted investment theories" of modern portfolio theory includes a research finding that less than 5 percent of the variations in a retirement account's returns is attributable to selecting particular investments and more than 93 percent of the variations is attributable to strategic and tactical asset allocation among asset classes. [*See, e.g.,* Gary P. Brinson, Brian D. Singer, and Gilbert L. Beebower, "Determinants of Portfolio Performance II: An Update," *Financial Analysts Journal* (May-June 1991)] If asset allocation is so dominantly the source of returns, a prudent investor should want to optimize an asset allocation as much as it is feasible to do so.

Educating participants to become investors.

Some plan fiduciaries consider that an investment manager's communications can help a nondirecting participant "see" the relationships of how modern portfolio theory relates to investing for retirement, and "graduate" to a relationship that involves better communication and more finely considered advice. [*See* Stephen J. Lansing with Peter Gulia, The Final Frontier: Investment Advice and Professionally Managed Accounts (April 30, 2007), available at http://benefitslink.com/articles/guests/20070430_final_frontier.pdf]

Q 5:114   What is the rule for a short-term default investment?

A plan fiduciary may (but need not) specify a principal-preservation fund as a plan's default investment for a participant's first 120 days. [D.O.L. Reg. § 2550.404c-5(e)(4)(iv)] After the 120-day period, a fiduciary can continue to get QDIA relief only if it redirects the individual's account to another qualified default investment (see Q 5:106).

This ERISA rule recognizes that a plan fiduciary might prefer a short-term default that could help reduce the likelihood of a possible loss during a participant's "beginner" participation. The rule recognizes the tax law for a plan's "automatic-contribution" arrangement, which allows a plan to permit an employee to choose an "undo" distribution no later than 90 days after the first elective deferral.

Q 5:115   Why might a plan's default-investment procedure use a money-market fund for a participant's first 90 or 120 days?

Some retirement plans include an automatic-contribution arrangement under which an employee who receives a notice and does not "opt out" is deemed to have elected to make the elective contributions described by the notice. [*See* ERISA § 514(e)] Notwithstanding the general rule that a Section 403(b) plan must preclude a distribution before a participant's severance from employment (see chapter 10), a plan that includes an eligible automatic-contribution arrangement may permit, no later than 90 days after the date of the first elective deferral under the arrangement, an "undo" distribution of the participant's account attributable to the implied-election elective deferrals. [I.R.C. § 414(w)] Some plan fiduciaries worry that such a "permissible withdrawal" or "undo" distribution cannot be adjusted for an investment loss, and instead must return no less than the amount of the automatic contributions. [*See* I.R.C. § 414(w)(2)(A)(ii)] Others worry that an "undoing" participant, notwithstanding his or her inattentiveness that authorized the contributions, might be upset by an investment loss. Thus, some plan fiduciaries prefer a default investment that they assume is unlikely to result in an investment loss—for example, a money-market fund.

> **Note.** Securities law regulates what investments a fund must include or preclude if one wants to use any of the words "money market", "cash", "liquid", "money", "ready assets", or any similar term in or with any name or title of the fund. [*See* Investment Company Act Rule 2a-7(b), 17 C.F.R. § 270.2a-7(b)]

Even if a plan does not provide an "early" distribution, some plan fiduciaries consider a "principal-protection" investment as prudent for a participant's "beginner" participation; they reason that a nondirecting participant who notices an investment loss during his or her first few months as a participant might discontinue his or her contributions.

> **Practice Pointer.** For a plan fiduciary that wants the default-investment rule's relief from liability, using a short-term default investment can be effective only if the plan administrator has obtained reliable services for investing an amount in a permanent default investment as soon as the short-term period expires.

Q 5:116 Can a "stable-value" account be a qualified default investment alternative?

No. The DOL rejected requests that a "stable-value" account or stated-interest contract be included among the qualified default options.

> **Note.** The default-investment rule provides some transition relief on and after December 24, 2007 concerning amounts invested *before* December 24, 2007 under a "benefit-sensitive" investment "designed to guarantee principal and a rate of return generally consistent with that earned on intermediate investment[-]grade bonds" if "[t]here are no fees or surrender charges imposed in connection with withdrawals initiated by a participant or beneficiary" and if other conditions are met. [D.O.L. Reg. § 2550.404c-5(e)(4)(v)]

Communications About Default Investments

Q 5:117 What is a default-investment notice?

Among other conditions to get relief for a default investment, the rule requires that a participant, beneficiary, or alternate payee receive a notice "written in a manner calculated [sic] to be understood by the average plan participant" that explains at least the following information:

(1) A description of the circumstances under which assets in the individual account of a participant or beneficiary may be invested on behalf of the participant or beneficiary in a qualified default investment alternative; and, if applicable, an explanation of the circumstances under which elective contributions will be made on behalf of a participant, the percentage of such contributions, and the right of the participant to elect not to have such contributions made on the participant's behalf (or to elect to have such contributions made at a different percentage);

(2) An explanation of the right of participants and beneficiaries to direct the investment of assets in their individual accounts;

(3) A description of the qualified default investment alternative, including a description of the investment objectives, risk and return characteristics (if applicable), and fees and expenses attendant to the investment alternative;

(4) A description of the right of the participants and beneficiaries on whose behalf assets are invested in a qualified default investment alternative to direct the investment of those assets to any other investment alternative under the plan, including a description of any applicable restrictions, fees or expenses in connection with such transfer; and

(5) An explanation of where the participants and beneficiaries can obtain investment information concerning the other investment alternatives available under the plan.

[D.O.L. Reg. § 2550.404c-5(d), interpreting ERISA § 404(c)(4)(C), 404(c)(5)(B)]

Practice Pointer. The DOL chose not to provide a model notice. A plan fiduciary should check carefully that its plan's notice not only "covers all the bases" but also does a good job in using plain-language writing methods and explaining information to a class of participants who one must presume are inattentive.

Practice Pointer. Recent ERISA lawsuits assert that an ERISA section 404(c) participant-directed defense does not apply because the fiduciary did not deliver "sufficient" information. [*See, e.g.,* Peter Gulia, "Lawsuit Lessons: What must a plan fiduciary do to manage retirement plan expenses?", Pensions & Investments conferences (Feb. 2007) (available to subscribers at http://www.pionline.com)] Expect the next plaintiffs' lawyers to assert that an ERISA section 404(c)(5) qualified-default defense does not apply because the fiduciary's purported QDIA notice did not explain everything plainly enough. A smart fiduciary should use experts to write the QDIA notice, and keep evidence of how clearly it explains the information to an inattentive participant.

Q 5:118   When must a plan fiduciary deliver a default-investment notice?

To get QDIA relief, the required notice usually must be delivered at least 30 days before the first QDIA investment, and then at least 30 days before the first day of each plan year.

To get QDIA relief for a default investment under an automatic-contribution arrangement, the 30-days rule is relaxed if the participant has the right to choose an "undo" distribution during the 90 days after the date of the first elective deferral. With that provision, the notice must be delivered no later than the participant's "date of plan eligibility".

Q 5:119 What investment information must be furnished to default-invested individual?

To get QDIA relief concerning a default-invested participant, beneficiary, or alternate payee, a fiduciary must deliver to the individual the QDIA notice (see Q 5:117) and at least the information required by the ERISA Section 404(c) regulations—even if the fiduciary does not follow other aspects of the ERISA Section 404(c) regulations or does not follow the ERISA Section 404(c) regulations concerning other individuals.

"Mapping" a Change of Investment Options

Q 5:120 What is "mapping," and how does a fiduciary reduce its responsibility for a change of investment options?

Until recently, some employers had been reluctant to replace a plan investment option that might no longer be appropriate for a plan because the employer fears losing the relief from fiduciary responsibility that ERISA Section 404(c) provides for a participant-directed investment.

Beginning with 2008, a blackout and "mapping" of investment options does not cause a participant's investment to become fiduciary-directed rather than participant-directed. Instead, the law treats a participant, beneficiary, or alternate payee who had exercised control over his or her plan account before a change in investment options as still exercising control over his or her account if the conditions specified by the new law are met.

> **Practice Pointer.** Although these ERISA rules do not protect a church plan or a governmental plan, they can be a useful roadmap for what a prudent fiduciary should do.

For this rule, a *qualified change in investment options* means a change in the plan's investment options under which a participant's account is reallocated among investment options, at least one of which is new; and the "characteristics" of the new investment options, including at least those about risk and return, are, just after the change, similar to the characteristics of the replaced investment options.

> **Practice Pointer.** Even setting aside the obvious axiom that an investment's past does not predict its future, it is unclear what evidence and other diligence could make it prudent for a plan fiduciary to believe that a

mapped-into investment's "characteristics" are similar to those of the re-placed investment. Therefore, a careful fiduciary should not make these decisions without first considering the advice of an expert investment adviser.

This relief applies only if (along with the other conditions):

- The investment of the participant's account as in effect just before the change resulted from the participant's exercise of control over his or her account.

- The plan administrator furnished a written notice about the change to participants, beneficiaries, and alternate payees at least 30 but no more than 60 days before the effective date of the change of plan investment options.

- The notice included information that compares the existing and new investment options.

- The notice explained that, in the absence of a different "affirmative" investment direction, the plan will invest a participant's, beneficiary's, or alternate payee's account in new options with characteristics similar to those of the "old" investment options.

- The participant, beneficiary, or alternate payee did not give an investment direction that "overrides" (or makes inapplicable) the "mapping" that the notice describes as the default that will result in the absence of an "affirmative" direction.

Although a plan fiduciary must act prudently during a blackout period, a fiduciary meets its fiduciary duty if it acts prudently and diligently in authorizing, implementing, and managing a blackout.

Note. In the PPA, Congress directs the DOL to issue "interim final regulations" providing guidance, including safe harbors, on how plan fiduciaries can meet their fiduciary responsibilities during a blackout period. Congress directs the DOL to issue these regulations no later than mid-August 2007. As of early 2008, the DOL had not even proposed regulations.

[ERISA § 404(c)(4)]

Paying Plan Administration Expenses

Q 5:121   May the expenses of administering a Section 403(b) plan be paid from its investments?

If an employer intends a "voluntary-only" Section 403(b) plan as a plan that the employer does not establish or maintain (so that it is not a plan governed by ERISA), the employer is not involved in negotiating or paying expenses. [D.O.L. Reg. § 2510.3-2(f)] All fees and expenses are as provided by the Section 403(b) annuity contract or custodial account.

If an employer maintains an ERISA-governed Section 403(b) plan, the plan may provide that reasonable expenses of administering the plan (but not the expense of designing, creating, amending, or terminating the plan) will be charged against plan assets. [ERISA § 404(a)(1)(A)] "Reasonable" refers to a service that is "necessary" (see Q 5:122) and paying no more than reasonable compensation for such a service.

Practice Pointer. A plan fiduciary may show prudence by charging administration expenses according to a written procedure adopted by the plan administrator following the advice of expert employee benefits counsel. The plan should state a provision for restoration of any amount later found not to have been a proper expense.

Note. A plan administrator cannot obtain an ERISA advisory opinion concerning payment of expenses in a particular situation. [ERISA Proc. 76-1, § 5.04, 41 Fed. Reg. 36281 (Aug. 27, 1976)]

Caution. A penalty for late filing of Form 5500 is not a reasonable plan administration expense. [DOL ERISA Information Letter to Mark H. Sokolsky (Feb. 23, 1996)] Thus, a plan administrator must pay this penalty from its own resources, not from plan assets. Generally, an expense that results from a prohibited transaction or from a fiduciary's breach is not a proper plan expense.

Q 5:122 What makes a service "necessary" as a plan expense?

If a plan, rather than an employer, pays for a service, a decision to incur a plan expense must be made solely in the interest of participants (including eligible employees) and beneficiaries (including alternate payees) for the exclusive purpose of providing benefits to them and "defraying reasonable expenses of administering the plan[.]" [ERISA § 404(a)(1)(A)(ii)] In providing a statutory prohibited-transaction exemption for service arrangements regarding a plan, ERISA provides that a plan may pay for "services necessary for the establishment or operation of the plan". [ERISA § 408(b)(2)] Interpreting this limited exemption, the DOL's rule states that "[a] service is necessary for the establishment or operation of a plan . . . if the service is appropriate and helpful to the plan obtaining the service in carrying out the purposes for which the plan is established or maintained. [Labor Reg. § 2550.408b-2(b)] The rule-making history shows that the word necessary is not confined to its strictest sense, but instead is construed or interpreted broadly. Commenting on an earlier proposed rule, several comments advocated that a service be considered necessary only if it is essential to plan operation. The Labor and Treasury departments didn't adopt the essential expression, and instead each final rule describes a necessary service as one that's helpful in carrying out the plan's purposes. [Exemptions for the Provision of Services or Office Space to Employee Benefits Plans, the Investment of Plan Assets in Bank Deposits, the Provision of Bank Ancillary Services to Plans, and the Transitional Rule for the Provision of Services to Plans, 42 Fed. Reg. 32384 (Treasury final rule), 32389 (Labor final rule) (June 24, 1977), 41 Fed. Reg. 31838 (Treasury notice of proposed rule-making), 31874

(Labor notice of proposed rule-making) (July 30, 1976), 41 Fed. Reg. 56758 (Dec. 29, 1976) (notice of hearing on proposed rules)]

Thus, an investment-guidance service is necessary if it is *helpful* in carrying out the plan's purposes. A court ordinarily defers to a plan administrator's good-faith interpretation of the plan's purposes.

Chapter 6

Annuities

Robert J. Toth Jr., Esq.

Section 403(b) programs are, by design, funded with annuity contracts. Often referred to as tax-deferred annuities (TDAs) or tax-sheltered annuities (TSAs), these annuity contracts have evolved into hybrid contractual arrangements that defy easy classification and definition. Even the non-annuity funding arrangements for Section 403(b) plans are "deemed" to be annuity contracts for purposes of Code Section 403(b). Various state and regulatory authorities claim jurisdiction over the different functions of these contracts, which makes the understanding of the regulatory issues involved even more of a challenge. This chapter explains the fundamental rules underlying the annuity contract and outlines the various functions of these contracts in the Section 403(b) context. It attempts to weave a path through the various, and sometimes conflicting, state insurance laws, federal security laws, federal tax laws, and ERISA rules that apply when annuity contracts are used to fund a Section 403(b) program.

The Annuity Contract

Q 6:1 What is an *annuity contract?*

An *annuity contract*, under state contract law, is a type of insurance contract that is generally issued by an insurance company licensed to do business in that state. It is typically designed to provide a guaranteed income stream to the annuitant over his or her life or the joint lives of the annuitant and beneficiary. [Crouch on Insurance 2d (Rev.), § 81:1]

The annuity contract itself is generally distinct from the typical life insurance contract in that it may contain both insurance and noninsurance features. [Crouch on Insurance 2d (Rev'd), § 81:2; Nationsbank of North Carolina, NA, et al. v. The Variable Annuity Life Insurance Co., et al., 513 U.S. 251 (1995) (1995)]

The insurance features offered under such contracts include the provision of an income stream for the life of the beneficiary as well as the annuitant, guaranteed death benefits, and fixed or guaranteed minimum rates of returns on premiums deposited to the contract.

The noninsurance features that may be offered under an annuity contract include features that are similar "to a very substantial degree" to the characteristics of mutual funds. [SEC v. The Variable Annuity Life Insurance Co., 359 U.S. 65 (1959)] These include the ability to accumulate assets under the contracts in so-called separate accounts, under which the contract holder bears the investment risks.

The law governing these annuity contracts rests upon the general principles of contract law and therefore is governed by many of the same rules that apply to any other type of contract. [Law and the Life Insurance Contract, Muriel L. Crawford and William T. Beadles, 1989, Richard D. Irwin, Inc., page 55] The major differences between general contract law and annuity contract law lie in the special laws that states have passed to deal with specific insurance contracts issues. These include such items as exemptions from gambling statutes, accounting and investment practices, special agency law rules, and rules that govern the handling of premiums. Further, to the extent that the contract contains noninsurance features, the contract principles may be generally displaced by federal regulation.

The terms of an annuity contract are subject to review and approval by state insurance authorities (Q 6:4). The amount and type of review will often vary with the type of contract being submitted, but no annuity contract can be issued in a state without prior approval (or *deemed* approval) of the state. Unlike normal contracts, which can be amended with the agreement between the parties, amendments to an annuity contract generally must be submitted to the state for approval, unless the state has granted prior approval making a particular term *amendable* without its prior consent. Amendments to insurance contracts will often take the form of a separate state filing, and are sometimes referred to as *riders.*

Q 6:2 Is there a difference between an annuity policy and an annuity contract?

No. Those terms are used interchangeably. A policy is a contract of insurance.

Q 6:3 What are an *annuitant,* a *contract holder,* and a *beneficiary* under an annuity contract?

An *annuitant* is the person who is entitled to the benefit of the annuity policy, the insured person. The *contract holder,* or owner of the contract, is the person who applies for and purchases the annuity policy. The owner may or may not be the annuitant. But if there is an insurance feature in the contract, the owner of the contract must have an insurable interest in the person being insured. [Crouch on Insurance 3d, § 8:4]

In an individual contract arrangement, the annuitant is also typically (but not necessarily) the owner. In a group arrangement, the sponsor of a Section 403(b) arrangement is often the owner, who will then name its employees as annuitants. The *beneficiary* under the annuity contract is the person who is entitled to the death benefit payable under the policy. Typically, the annuitant has the right to name the beneficiary under the policy, although Section 403(b) plans governed by ERISA may restrict this ability under certain circumstances.

The rights of the annuitant, owner, and beneficiary are typically described in the annuity contract.

Q 6:4 Are there different kinds of annuity contracts?

There are many kinds of annuity contracts and the large variety and combination of features that can be offered under such contracts defy simple classification. Annuities are flexible financial instruments that can be designed by an insurance company, by use of its financial wherewithal, to accommodate the insurance and investment needs of a variety of policyholders and distribution networks. There are a number of terms that attempt to classify such contracts either by type of owner, deposit, period of payout, or by features within the contract. Examples of such terms include single premium, periodic premium, variable premium, variable annuity, fixed annuity, group annuity, individual annuity, and others. However, few of these labels accurately describe the nature of the contracts; they are most relevant for purposes of state filing requirements. These terms are also often used differently by different insurance companies. Given the ability of an insurance company to customize any of these contracts, an understanding of any particular annuity contract can only come from the reading of the terms of the contract itself rather than reliance upon its label.

The simplest type of annuity contract will offer a guaranteed stream of payment over a person's lifetime in return for a single, lump-sum premium payment. This type of benefit forms the basis of all annuity contracts. However, there are variations as vast as the marketplace's needs.

Annuities sold under Section 403(b) plans are among the most complex annuities. They can be issued as group contracts or on an individual basis. They can be single premium or accept ongoing periodic premiums. The contracts can be designed to offer a variety of investment options from investment managers unrelated to the insurance company, or they can simply offer a guaranteed return on a guaranteed principal over a set period of time. These Section 403(b) annuity contracts may offer any number of insurance features such as enhanced death benefits, guarantees on investments in variable accounts, flexible and variable payouts, and long-term care. The annuities may be specially designed by insurance companies for the needs of a particular segment of the Section 403(b) market, such as state optional retirement programs or health care systems, and may (or may not) provide for a varying level of administrative services. They can be sold as stand-alone products or integrated into a comprehensive plan of an employer which provides for other kinds of plans or investment products. They can be designed to be distributed through certain sales channels such as individual agents, consulting firms, or broker/dealers. In addition to these varied and complex designs, each Section 403(b) annuity contract is required to comply with the rules governing Section 403(b) and, where applicable, ERISA.

The IRS issued new Code Section 403(b) regulations on July 26, 2007 which greatly complicates the relationship between the terms of the annuity contracts, the rules governing 403(b) and the newly required plan document.

Q 6:5   What types of annuities can be held under a Section 403(b) program?

Any type of annuity contract that meets the requirements outlined in Q 6:6 can be used to fund a Section 403(b) arrangement. This includes deferred contracts designed to make lifetime payouts, contracts designed for asset accumulation (including variable contracts or fixed contracts), or a combination of these. However, under the Code Section 403(b) regulations, life insurance policies may no longer be purchased under a Section 403(b) arrangement.

Though any annuity contract meeting the requirements outlined in Q 6:6 (typically by use of adding a Section 403(b) *rider* to a contract) can be purchased for a Section 403(b) plan, the Code Section 403(b) regulations have made it very difficult for employers to use annuities which are not specifically designed to be used as a TDA. This is because the regulations require insurance companies to coordinate the administration of their contracts with the administration of the contracts of other insurance companies, a task which is logistically challenging using annuities that were not specifically designed for the Section 403(b) market.

Q 6:6   What are a tax-deferred annuity (TDA), a Section 403(b) annuity, and a tax-sheltered annuity (TSA)?

All three are different names for the same kind of contract issued by an insurance company and purchased by, or on behalf of, employees of 501(c)(3) organizations, churches, or public educational organizations described in Code Section 170(b)(1)(A)(ii). [I.R.C. § 403(b)(1)] Contributions to these contracts are considered, in insurance parlance, *premiums,* and must all come through the employer. These premiums may be paid by an employee's before-tax deferrals or employer contributions, although employers may also permit after-tax contributions to these policies. An annuity contract must be purchased from an insurance company in order to qualify as a TDA [Rev. Rul. 82-102, 1982-1 C.B. 62], and the terms of the contract must provide for the annuitization of the benefit. [Rev. Rul. 68-487, 1968-2 C.B. 187] (though the Code Section 403(b) regulations contemplate that this Revenue Ruling will be superseded). However, as noted elsewhere in this book, a TDA is not the only funding vehicle by which favorable tax treatment under Code Section 403(b) can be obtained.

Code Section 401(g) defines an annuity for Section 403(b) purposes as including a nontransferable face-amount certificate as defined in Section 2(a)(15) of the Investment Company Act of 1940. [15 U.S.C. § 80-2]

In addition to the above-mentioned basic annuity requirements, a TDA program must also meet a host of requirements in order to qualify for favorable tax treatment as discussed elsewhere in this book. Although state law generally governs the terms of the annuity contract, the Internal Revenue Code will not grant favorable treatment to deposits made to an annuity contract unless it contains certain terms. Not all of the terms of a qualified TDA program need to be contained in the contract, but the annuity contract (or an employer's written plan, if it is controlling) purchased as part of a properly operated TDA program should provide for the following:

1. The nonassignability and nonforfeitability of employees' rights under the contract and the contract itself [I.R.C. §§ 401(g), 403(b)(1)(C)];

2. The dollar limitation on salary reduction contributions under Code Section 403(b)(1)(E);

3. The minimum and incidental benefit distribution rules similar to those under Code Section 401(a)(9);

4. Limitations on the withdrawals of salary reduction contributions under Code Section 403(b)(11); and

5. Allowance for the direct rollover of eligible rollover contributions under Code Sections 403(b)(10) and 401(a)(31).

It is important to recognize, however, that there are a host of other written requirements associated with maintaining a TDA in addition to the written terms of the annuity contract itself. The Code Section 403(b) regulations now impose a written document requirement which requires that all material elements of the arrangement (including which contracts are available, eligibility, limitations, and the time and form of distributions) and an allocation of authority under the plan are outlined. Security laws will also impose their own documentation requirements, including the delivery of prospectuses and compliance with the trading restrictions and redemption fee rules under SEC Rule 22(c)(2). (*See* http://sec.gov/rules/final/ic-26782.pdf.)

Q 6:7   What is an *individual TDA?*

An *individual TDA* is a contract typically designed to be sold directly to an individual through payroll reduction. The insurance contract is a contract between the insurance company and the Section 403(b) participant and all duties under the law flow between those two parties. Even though the employer may have made the arrangements for the employee to make contributions to such contracts, the employer typically has no contractual rights under those annuities unless the employer is also the owner.

All deposits into the individual contract are allocated exclusively to the individual owner. Although an employer has the ability to discontinue making deposits to any particular insurance company's contracts, the employer has no ability to force the owner of an individual contract to transfer the funds under that contract to the contract of a different carrier, custodial account, or retirement income account without the consent of the policyholder, nor has the ability to control the investment decisions under the contract, unless specifically provided for in the contract.

An employer is permitted to own an individual annuity contract for the benefit of the individual plan participant. This may happen under several circumstances. For example, when the employer adopts an automatic enrollment program and doesn't have the employee approval required by security laws for purchase of the registered annuity contract, the employer may buy the contract in its own name. Employers seeking to administer a vesting program may place non-vested dollars into an employer owned individual contract (which are then treated as *403(c)* contracts) until they are vested, and then transfer those sums to the individual's Section 403(b) contract.

In spite of the contractual rules imposed by state law, the Code Section 403(b) regulations attempt to overlay a series of restrictions which may not be consistent with the terms of an individual TDA contract. Often the employer, which will be held responsible for complying with the new restrictions, will have little ability to effectively impose these new restrictions on an individual contract.

Q 6:8   What is a *group TDA?*

A *group TDA* is a contract that covers "a number of individual persons by one comprehensive policy, with certificates issued to participants as evidences of such coverage, usually for the primary purpose of protecting and providing for employees." [Appleman, Insurance Law and Practice, § 41] Although the persons insured from time to time may vary as the group changes, "the employee and his dependants are third-party beneficiaries . . . and are all bound by the terms of the contract." [Appleman, Insurance Law and Practice, § 41]

The group contract itself must meet all of the Section 403(b) features outlined in Q 6:6.

The owner of a group TDA contract is usually the employer, although it may be an association of employers or other such group. The employer owner of an annuity policy does not have omnipotent authority with regard to the policy; those rights are defined by the terms of the policy and may be severely restricted. Thus, for example, the terms of a group contract may grant the right to name the beneficiary to the annuitant/employee or limit the ability to transfer funds to another contract only to the employee/annuitant.

There are two important types of group annuity contracts, *allocated* and *unallocated* contracts. An *unallocated* group annuity contract is one under which no individual records are kept by the insurance company, and the only records kept are account balances at the plan level. It is the responsibility of the contract owner (or its third-party administrator) to accurately allocate that account balance to individual plan participants. The insurance company's obligations run only to the group contract owner, not to individual plan participants. The *allocated* group annuity contract is of the type where the account records of individual Section 403(b) participants are kept within the contract itself at the participant level and the insurer has certain obligations to individual plan participants.

Q 6:9   Do annuity contracts provide plan administration?

Insurance companies typically provide some measure of plan administrative services as part of their TDAs, as annuity contracts can provide for both insurance and noninsurance services. For example, loan administration, tax reporting, distribution processing, asset allocation and other services are often provided with the typical TDA. It is highly unlikely, however, for any annuity contract to provide for the full range of administrative services now called for by the Code Section 403(b) regulations. Many of these services will need to be arranged by virtue of a separate services agreement with the insurer or third-party administrator. It will be critical to review the terms of any annuity contract to determine the extent to which it will fulfill the requirements of the Code Section 403(b) regulations.

Q 6:10   Who controls the annuity contract?

Knowing which party has authority over the assets in the contract, loans, distribution and other terms of an annuity contract has become a critical issue under the Code Section 403(b) regulations and with the SEC's activity to control trading within a contract. Every annuity policy is a contract, whose operation is controlled by its terms. To determine whether any party has the ability to exercise any control over any particular feature, one must look to the contract terms themselves.

The ramifications on Section 403(b) compliance can be significant. As a striking example of the impact, consider the employer who is responsible for tracking deposits to the contract to ensure that those contributions do not exceed allowable limits. The terms of the annuity policy, however, may not permit the employer to force a corrective distribution. The result, should the employee not elect to correct, is that the *non-corrected* portion of the contract will be considered to be part of a *403(c)* plan, not a Section 403(b) plan. The vendor will be required to track and account separately for those amounts and the employer's plan documents likely will need to accommodate such an arrangement.

Q 6:11   How is a TDA terminated?

A TDA is a contract between the policyholder and the insurance company, whereby the insurance company is obligated to perform under the terms of the contract, while the annuitant or owner is not obliged under the contract to make contributions. The TDA itself is not actually *terminated* until it is completely *surrendered* to the insurance company, ceasing the insurer's contractual obligation. The contractual termination occurs upon surrender whether or not the plan is terminated or not. Thus, the surrender of a contract to roll those amounts into another contract is a termination of the TDA.

This is not to be confused with the termination of a Section 403(b) plan. The Code Section 403(b) regulations now permit the termination of a Section 403(b) plan and the subsequent distribution of its assets. A distribution of the assets includes the delivery to the plan participant of a *fully paid* annuity contract. The contract which is distributed, however, still remains a Section 403(b) contract, even though it is not subject to a plan document or an information services agreement. [Treas. Reg. § 1.403(b)-10(a)(1)] The amounts under the terminated plan that are distributed as part of a Section 403(b) contract will not be taxed until distributions are actually made from the contract itself. [Treas. Reg. § 1.403(b)-7(a)]

Insurers

Q 6:12   Can only insurance companies issue annuity contracts?

Prior to the passage of the Financial Services Modernization Act of 1999, also called the Gramm-Leach-Bliley Act of 1999 (GLB Act), there was substantial litigation and regulatory activity attempting to determine whether, or to what extent, financial institutions other than insurance companies could issue annuity contracts and to determine the nature and tax treatment of such financial instruments. The Comptroller of the Currency attempted to permit national banks the authority to issue annuity contracts. The IRS issued a final regulation [63 Fed Reg 1054 (Jan 8, 1998)] under which it refused to give Code Section 72 annuity tax treatment to annuities issued by entities other than insurance companies, treating such noninsurance company annuities as debt instruments, effectively rendering them unavailable for TDAs.

The GLB Act answered both of those questions. Effective January 1, 1999, the writing of annuity contracts is subject to regulation by state insurance laws, effectively prohibiting any institution other than a licensed insurer from issuing annuities. Second, all annuity contracts that are subject to Code Section 72 are considered insurance and can only be issued by a licensed insurer.

Q 6:13   What kind of insurance guarantees are available under annuity contracts?

TDAs have historically been known for two types of insurance guarantees: the guaranteed lifetime payout and the guarantees of principal (Qs 6:15–6:17). Straight annuitization, however, has not had wide acceptance in the market-place because of its severe limitations. Annuities have changed dramatically over the past decade in response to consumers' concerns. Insurance companies have developed sophisticated hedging strategies that have enabled them to bring to the market innovative products that are designed to address a number of concerns that have made simple annuitization relatively unpopular. In addition to providing asset accumulation, the new generation of annuities can provide a number of other insurance features. Examples include, but are not limited to, features like variable annuitization that provide lifetime income while giving the policyholder equity participation; guaranteed minimum account values that lock in investment gains over a period of time; guaranteed withdrawal benefits that guarantee the ability to withdraw at least a certain amount over a set period of time regardless of what happens to the market; guaranteed minimum income benefits that ensure the purchase of a minimum income stream beginning at a certain time regardless of what happens in the market; enhanced death benefits that permit some level of death benefit even while receiving an annuitized benefit. Though these types of arrangements are typically offered outside of employer sponsored plans, they are becoming available as part of Section 403(b) arrangements as well.

Insurance guarantees can only be offered as part of an insurance contract and cannot currently be made available under a Section 403(b) custodial account. Any of these guarantees should be reviewed to ensure compliance with Section 403(b) rules, including the minimum distribution and incidental benefit rules.

Q 6:14   What kinds of investment accounts can insurers maintain under a TDA?

Not all TDAs are required to have investment accounts. A TDA can merely offer the purchase of a lifetime stream of income. However, where the TDA also serves as an investment vehicle (which is typically the case for TDAs), there are generally two types of investment accounts that can be maintained under the typical *asset accumulation* TDA. The first type of investment account is the *fixed, guaranteed,* or *stable value* account. Under this type, the insurance company will guarantee both the principal and a minimum return on the principal. The investment risk under a fixed account remains with the insurer.

The second type of investment account is the variable separate account. Under this type, the insurance company guarantees neither interest nor principal. The investment risk under the variable separate account remains with either the annuitant or owner, depending on the specific account terms.

Insurance companies are creating a new generation of annuity contracts in response to market demands, which combine features of fixed accounts, variable separate accounts, and income guarantees in unusual ways, ways which often defy traditional classification. It is critical, then, to closely review the terms of the contracts being purchased.

Q 6:15 What is the *general account* of an insurer?

The general account of an insurer is the account out of which insurance companies run their businesses. It holds the "general assets" of an insurer, which are those assets to which the insurance company holds complete title and interest and which are subject to the claims of its creditors. It is the fund from which its operating expenses and general corporate obligations—including those of an insured nature—are paid. The investment, disposition, and financial reporting of these assets are highly regulated by the state that licenses the insurer. Among other things, the state may require that the insurer file specific information concerning its business transactions, its current financial condition, and its annual financial reports in a format mandated by the state; allow its records to be regularly audited by the states; maintain certain levels of assets, reserves, and surplus; and restrict the amount and types of different investments made from an insurance company's general assets. [*See* Crouch on Insurance 3d ed, §§ 2:24–2:30]

Payments of principal and earnings to a TDA contract holder from the guaranteed account under an annuity contract, or payment of periodic payments from the annuitization of the benefit under a TDA, are made from the insurer's general account. No contract holder has any claim against any specific asset of the insurer's general account, except as may be otherwise dictated by state law governing the insolvency of insurance carriers.

Q 6:16 How does a guaranteed, or fixed, account function?

The exact nature of any fixed or guaranteed fund is defined by the terms of the annuity policy. Generally, however, such funds are based on the same premise.

The insurance company, in its role as a state-licensed insurer, has the ability to insure the investment risks of its policyholders. This is done by guaranteeing the principal of any amounts deposited in the guaranteed fund against any market loss, along with the guarantee of a minimum rate of return on the guaranteed principal. This guaranteed rate must meet, at a minimum, the rate required to be credited by the Standard Nonforfeiture Law of the state of issue.

A contract may also provide that, in either the insurer's discretion or in accordance with a certain rate schedule contained in the contract, additional interest above the guaranteed minimum may be credited. The amounts and terms of these additional interest accruals will vary by insurance contract.

The principal and interest due under the contract are contractual obligations of the insurance company and are paid out of its general assets. No policyholder is secured by, or has a claim to, any specific asset of the insurer. Further, the guarantees are not related to any specific investments of the insurer.

The insurer's ability to obligate itself to pay any particular interest rate depends in large part on its ability to successfully invest its general assets at favorable terms (and in accordance with the state insurance laws governing the investments of the insurer's general assets). Thus, the guaranteed account can provide an enhanced interest rate only if it also imposes limitations on the liquidity of the guaranteed account. Restricted liquidity on movement of money from the account gives the insurer the ability to commit to longer range, higher return investments.

The liquidity restrictions often will limit the amount of money that may be transferred out of a guaranteed account over a certain period of time, although some contracts may also permit free, unlimited transfer upon the payment of a market value adjustment. A market value adjustment typically is designed to reflect the rates that would be available had the funds been invested in short-term, highly liquid vehicles. This may result in some loss of earnings (though typically not principal) to the contract holder under some circumstances, so the policyholder should consider the economic impact of any decision to withdraw funds under a market value adjustment before moving forward. The guarantee against loss of principal will not extend to market value adjustments applied against early withdrawals from the guaranteed account.

Likewise, insurers may also offer free liquidity from their general account assets. Typically, however, these types of arrangements result in lower rates of returns to the policyholder as the insurance company must invest in shorter term investments in order to fulfill such obligations.

Payments for bona fide benefits are often an exception to the application of market value adjustments. TDAs tend to be benefit responsive, allowing unlimited transfer of funds from the guaranteed account to a participant upon the occurrence of a distributable event under Code Section 403(b)(11). However, some TDAs may not be benefit responsive, an important element to consider when purchasing these contracts.

Q 6:17   What is an annuity's *stable value* fund?

There is no standard definition of *stable value* fund for purposes of insurance contracts. Such a term is often a reference to a fixed or guaranteed account described in Q 6:16, which is a guarantee based upon an insurance company's general account. Often, however, *stable value* is a reference to a particular type of guarantee, where the crediting rate (and changes to it) is computed using the performance of an external index that is specifically identified in the contract, combined with a mathematical formula which *smooths* changes in that index over a stated time period.

Q 6:18   What are the *separate accounts* of an insurer?

Insurance company *separate accounts* are often referred to as *pooled separate accounts* or *variable separate accounts.* They are the vehicles by which insurance companies can offer equity markets investments to their policyholders. They are called *separate accounts* because they are held *separately* from an insurance company's general account (*see* Qs 6:15–6:17).

The variable separate account under a TDA is an account under which the entire risk of the underlying investments rests with the contract holder, not the insurance company. The assets of the separate accounts are held and accounted separately from the general account of the insurance company and are generally subject to less stringent investment restrictions than the general account. The variable accounts' funds are typically invested primarily in stocks and other equities, although there may be a wide range of assets underlying such accounts (such as real estate investments). The earnings from these accounts vary with the success of the insurance company's investment experience. Holders of variable accounts are not able to depend on the insurance company's paying a fixed return, as are insureds in a guaranteed account. [Beverly Otto v. The Variable Annuity Life Insurance Co., 814 F.2d 1127 (7th Cir. 1987)]

Although the insurance company holds title to the assets of a separate account, the assets in the separate, variable accounts are held on behalf of the policyholders. As such, under state law, the assets of the separate accounts are not subject to the claims of the creditors of the insurance company.

A variable separate account for a TDA is required by securities laws to register as a security, as these accounts do not have the same exemptions from registration as do separate accounts used in insurance contracts for Section 401(k) plans. Insurance companies serve as the underwriters for these accounts, and typically hire independent investment managers who operate under a sub-advisor agreement with the insurance company. Mutual fund companies have created a special class of mutual funds which are designed to be offered only under insurance company variable separate accounts, and which are generally not available to be purchased by consumers outside of annuity contracts.

Q 6:19 Can a TDA offer publicly traded mutual funds through its separate accounts?

Yes. Beginning November 16, 1999 and effective for all years, a TDA can offer publicly traded mutual funds through its separate accounts. The IRS issued Revenue Procedure 99-44 [1999-48 I.R.B. 598] by which Revenue Ruling 81-225 [1981-2 C.B. 12] was modified to the extent it applies to contracts issued to Section 403(a), Section 403(b), and Section 401(a) plans. This is important because a variable annuity, other than those for the before-noted retirement plans, cannot otherwise offer publicly traded mutual funds as investments under those contracts.

However, you will still see few publicly traded mutual funds in a Section 403(b) annuity. Historically, Revenue Ruling 81-225 was issued to outline the *diversification* requirements for annuity contracts under Code Section 817(h). The purpose was to deny annuity treatment for investments that are publicly available to investors and investments that are made, in effect, at the direction of the investor, where the insurance company's separate account was not adequately diversified so as to have a broad general investment strategy.

To deal with this restriction, insurance companies offered (and continue to offer) so-called clone funds, or insurance series mutual funds, within their annuity contract separate accounts. These are separate accounts that are managed under a sub advisor agreement between an insurance company and an investment manager, where the investment manager manages the separate account assets in the same manner as it manages the publicly traded mutual fund assets. Thus, the performance of the mutual fund and similarly managed separate accounts will not mirror each other, though they will often track each other.

Expenses

Q 6:20 What expenses are contained within a TDA?

It is inaccurate to cast an annuity contract as merely an investment contract in the manner of a mutual fund. Annuity contracts are best viewed as a contract providing a package of investment (Qs 6:14–6:19), insurance (Q 6:13), and administrative services (Q 6:8), for which a variety of fees are paid. These fees include the *mortality and expense,* or M&E charge; contingent deferred sales charges or CDSC; investment management fees; market value adjustments or MVAs; service charges; 12b-1 fees; and transfer agent fees. TDAs with variable separate accounts are required to be registered securities, and any such charge will be disclosed in its prospectus.

Q 6:21 What is the mortality and expense charge under a TDA?

The mortality and expense, or M&E, charge is typically the most significant charge within a variable TDA. It takes its name from securities laws, which require the terms use in prospectuses. The amount of the charge will vary with the type of TDA purchased and the type of mortality risk undertaken by the insurer. Several other risks may also be included in this charge, such as the investment risks related to the guarantee of principal, the guarantee of a minimum rate of return, the guarantee of minimum annuitization rates, and the guarantee of a set level of administrative charges over the lifetime of the contract. The administrative cost portion of the M&E charge should not be underestimated. Unlike mutual funds, annuity contracts often combine insurance and investment features into a single arrangement. They often allow daily trading between separate accounts managed by unrelated managers without extra fees and often provide for a significant level of administrative services without additional fees. In addition, they are required to maintain certain investment standards as regulated by the various state insurance departments.

The M&E charge is stated as a percentage of assets and is typically a deduction in the computation of the funds daily net asset value (NAV).

Q 6:22   What are surrender charges, or contingent deferred sales charge, under a TDA?

A surrender charge, or a contingent deferred sales charge (CDSC), is the fee that an insurance company is entitled to assess against all of the assets in the contract, in accordance with the schedule set forth in the policy, upon early termination of the contract. The charges are generally stated as percentages of assets under the contract. These charges generally do not apply to a bona fide benefit distribution following a distributable event under Code Section 403(b)(11), but generally do apply in a transfer to a TDA of another carrier under Treasury Regulations Section 1.403(b)-10(b). They generally are reduced annually over a period of time and usually will not apply after the completion of the contractual period. These charges are designed to reimburse the insurance company for the contract sales and setup expenses it incurs when establishing the contract. Treasury Regulations Section 1.403(b)-11(b)(2)(B) raises the issue of whether or not surrender charges may be assessed upon the transfers within a plan, as the regulation requires that the accumulated benefit be the same after the transfer as before.

Q 6:23   What is the market value adjustment under a TDA?

A market value adjustment (MVA) may be found in certain contracts that contain a stable value fund or a guaranteed fund (Qs 6:15–6:17). An MVA is an adjustment to a withdrawal or transfer from the annuity's general account benefit, and is assessed when the withdrawal occurs under certain market conditions; when the withdrawal exceeds a stated percentage; where a competing fund is adopted by a plan; or a combination of the three. The purpose of the charge is to protect the interest rates that are being provided to the pool of policyholders supported by the general account.

Unlike money market funds or bank certificates of deposits, the assets used to fund an insurance company's general account benefits are invested over long investment horizons stretching over several years. Insurers plan these investments based upon, in part, the expectation that a certain percentage of the funds will have certain longevity. Early withdrawal of these funds could cause early liquidation of these long-term assets, or cause the incurring of certain other expenses to protect those assets. The effect of these withdrawals can be exacerbated if made during unfavorable market conditions.

The MVA is typically computed using some sort of interest sensitive index. It may be a one-way MVA, that is, it will only be made when the insurance company may be in a loss position; or it may be *two-way*, that is, a positive adjustment will be made if the insurance company is in a gain position.

Q 6:24   What are investment management charges under a TDA?

Variable separate accounts are a form of registered investment companies that are structured, managed, and governed in ways that are similar to mutual funds. The assets within these accounts may be actively managed by sub-advisors retained by the insurance company whose investment management fees are charged directly against the separate account, which results in adjustment against the funds' daily net asset value. The separate accounts may also purchase shares of special classes of mutual funds which are designed for insurance company separate accounts. The investment management charges related to these shares are also counted against the funds' NAV.

Q 6:25 What are 12b-1 fees under a TDA?

12b-1 fees are fees for marketing and distribution expenses that can be charged against the NAV of mutual funds and insurance company registered separate accounts. They must be made in accordance with a *12b-1 plan* that is formally adopted by the funds' Board of Directors. The funds can only be used for marketing and distribution purposes. A more detailed explanation of these fees can be found at the SEC's Web site at http://www.sec.gov/answers/mffees.htm#distribution.

Q 6:26 What are service charges under a TDA?

The terms of the TDA may provide for separate charges for a variety of services under the contract. It is not unusual to find account maintenance charges, loan charges, asset allocation charges, and an array of other services charges. The charges are typically stated as a flat dollar amount. All such charges are required to be expressly in writing in the contracts.

Q 6:27 What role do ERISA fee disclosures and Form 5500 play in a TDA?

If the TDA is part of a Section 403(b) program that is governed by ERISA, the fees described in Qs 6:20–6:26 may have to be collected and disclosed for certain employers. The DOL has promulgated regulations under ERISA Section 408(b)(2) under which the reasonableness of the fees charged under these programs will rely, in part, on their disclosure. These disclosure rules are coordinated with a new set of reporting rules which, beginning for plan years beginning 2009, will require many Section 403(b) plans to report on the Form 5500 annual report the fees described above.

Regulations and Restrictions

Q 6:28 Who regulates the terms of an annuity contract?

The states and the federal government have concurrent jurisdiction over the various pieces of the annuity contract. To determine whether state or federal rules apply in any particular circumstance, the nature of the contract term at issue needs to be determined first.

Q 6:29 When do state regulations apply?

Generally, under the McCarran-Ferguson Act [15 U.S.C. §§ 1011–1015], the exclusive regulation of the *business of insurance* is reserved to the states. Thus, each of the 50 states regulates both the insurance terms under annuity contracts issued in their states and the insurance companies issuing those contracts. The contract language, and any amendments to the contract language, must be filed with the various state insurance departments, which often require the prior approval of that department. Annuity contracts may not be sold in any state, nor may any contract amendment be made effective in that state, without first meeting that state's statutory or regulatory requirements. Because of the sometimes different requirements of each state, the terms of the same kind of annuity contract from the same insurance company can vary slightly from state to state.

The states sometimes attempt to regulate the noninsurance features of an annuity contract and will reserve to themselves the ability to approve or disapprove *all* of the terms of an annuity contract. This will sometimes cause a conflict in areas where the state does not have exclusive jurisdiction. Thus, for example, the Securities and Exchange Commission and the U.S. Department of Labor may exercise authority over noninsurance terms [*see*, for example, Rule 151, under the Securities Act of 1933, 17 C.F.R. § 230.151; and ERISA § 514, 29 U.S.C. § 1144], yet the state may require approval of any language that may be mandated by federal regulation. (This means that, for example, even though Code Section 403(b) requires that certain terms be written in an annuity contract, those terms cannot amend a state-approved policy without the approval of the appropriate state authority.)

The typical insurance practices that are exclusively regulated by the states include the insurance marketing and selling practices within the state; the marketing materials used to sell insurance within the state; the licensing and monitoring of insurance company activities; the licensing and monitoring of insurance agent activities; the issuance of insurance contracts; the language used in the insurance contract; the insurance terms offered under an insurance contract; the reserving of assets supporting an insurance contract; the manner in which the general assets of an insurer are invested; the manner in which separate accounts of the insurer are structured; the types of benefits offered under an insurance policy; the payment of benefits under an insurance policy; policyholder rights against an insurance company; the handling of public or customer complaints against an insurance company; and communications between the insurance company and its contract holders. By no measure is this list exhaustive.

The Gramm-Leach-Blilely (GLB) Act substantially changed the manner in which states regulate the sale of insurance. Although certain state regulatory activities have been grandfathered, the rules regarding the sale, marketing, and cross-selling of insurance may be set by the federal government.

Q 6:30 What types of annuity contract terms are regulated by federal law?

The purpose of the McCarran-Ferguson Act was not to insulate state insurance regulation from the reach of all federal law, but to protect state regulation against inadvertent federal intrusion—for example, through the enactment of a federal statute that describes an affected activity in broad, general terms of which the insurance business happens to be one part. [American Deposit Corporation and Blackfeet National Bank v. James, Schacht, 84 F.3d 834 (7th Cir. 1996)]

Thus, typical annuity contract activity regulated by the federal government includes the offering and selling of investment contract features under an annuity contract, the handling of an employee benefit plan's *plan assets* under an insurance contract, and the provision of non-risk shifting of employee benefits and services under employee benefit plans.

This means that certain annuity contracts may be subject to regulation under the Investment Company Act, the Securities Act of 1933, and the Securities Exchange Act of 1934. It also means that insurance brokers may be required to be registered with the Financial Industry Regulatory Authority (FINRA, formerly the National Association of Security Dealers (NASD)), contract terms may be subject to the rules under ERISA, and the benefits provided under an annuity product may be governed by a variety of federal labor laws.

Q 6:31 What is the *business of insurance* for the purposes of determining whether state or federal rules apply?

The courts have generally adopted a three-part test to determine whether a particular contract term is part of the business of insurance:

1. Does the practice shift risk to the insurer?
2. Is the practice an integral part of the policy relationship between the insurer and the insured?
3. Is the practice limited to companies engaged in the insurance industry?

[Group Life & Health Ins. Co. v. Royal Drug Co., 440 U.S. 205 (1979)]

The transference of risk is essential, although each part of the test is not necessarily weighted equally, nor do all three tests necessarily have to apply. [*See* Kentucky Ass'n of Health Plans v. Miller, 538 U.S. 328 (2003), for a discussion of the application of the McCarran-Ferguson definition of *business of insurance* as it applies in the ERISA context, outlining the differences in applying it under an ERISA preemption analysis and other federal laws that apply to insurance.]

Q 6:32 What is the McCarran-Ferguson Act?

The McCarran-Ferguson Act [15 U.S.C. §§ 1011–1015] is the 1945 federal law that granted nearly exclusive jurisdiction over the regulation of the business of insurance to the states. [*See* The McCarran-Ferguson Act of 1945: Reconceiving the Federal Role in Insurance Regulation, Jonathan R. Macey and Geoffery P. Miller, 68 New York University Law Review 13-88 (1993) for a discussion of the Act] It imposed a rule "that state laws enacted for the purpose of regulating the business of insurance do not yield to conflicting federal statutes unless the federal statute specifically provides otherwise." [U.S. Dep't of Treasury v. Fabe, 508 U.S. 491 (1993)]

Among other things, this Act has allowed insurance companies to work cooperatively together without fear of violating federal antitrust statutes and to help develop a series of model laws, known as the NAIC Model Acts, that have been used by most states as a guide to establish relatively uniform insurance laws. It has generally prevented the development of a body of federal insurance law by reserving that function to the various states.

Q 6:33   What are the NAIC Model Acts?

The NAIC is the National Association of Insurance Commissioners. With the support of the insurance industry, the NAIC has promulgated a series of model laws that attempt to set standards among the several states for the laws that govern insurance practices. No state is required to adopt the model acts, and state legislatures often modify them when enacting them into law. When dealing with the model act adopted by any state, it is necessary to review that particular state's version of the model act before reaching any decision on its applicability.

However, even with the model acts, there can still be significant differences in the substance and form of regulation of annuity contracts from state to state.

Q 6:34   What privacy rules apply to annuity contracts?

As insurance contracts, state privacy laws generally also apply to annuity contracts. The NAIC model privacy act establishes "standards for the collection, use and disclosure of information gathered in connection with insurance institutions, agents or insurance support organizations." [*See* Law and the Life Insurance Contract, Muriel L. Crawford and William T. Beadles, 1989, Richard D. Irwin, Inc. p. 55] The act stresses the importance of balancing the insurer's need for information and the public's need for fairness in insurance information practices. With certain exceptions, disclosure of personal information to third parties by an insurer, agent, or insurance support organization can be made only with the written authorization of the person covered by the policy.

Under individually owned TDAs, the employer may not have the right to certain information under those contracts. Under a group policy, the employer/contract holder may have more expansive rights to information. These rules will vary from state to state, and it is important to check each state's rules for particulars.

If the plan is subject to Title I of ERISA, the state privacy law may be preempted by ERISA Section 514 and, instead, disclosure would be subject to ERISA's fiduciary rules.

The GLB Act is an essential element of the scheme of privacy rules. All financial institutions, not only financial holding companies, are required to comply with fairly strict rules governing the sharing of nonpublic personal financial data of their customers. As of the effective date of the statute, the insurance company will be required to offer to each of its policyholders the right to opt out of the transfer of personal data to nonaffiliated third parties; to disclose this opt-out policy; to publish its privacy guidelines for its contract holders; and to comply with certain rules governing the transfer of data between affiliates. The regulations governing those rules were promulgated through the joint efforts of the National Credit Union Administration, the federal banking agencies, the Secretary of the Treasury, the Securities and Exchange Commission, and the Federal Trade Commission. The GLB Act does not supersede state privacy laws. To the extent that the state privacy requirements are more stringent, the state law applies.

These privacy rules conflict in many respect with the Code Section 403(b) regulations for certain employers. The Code Section 403(b) regulations require that an employer enter into information sharing agreements with Section 403(b) vendors by which personal data related to the TDAs are shared and reported. To the extent that ERISA does not apply, and to the extent that the terms of the TDA do not specifically allow for the sharing of private data, employers will be unable to meet the information sharing requirements of the regulations.

Q 6:35   Federal security law: What kinds of TDAs need to be registered with the Securities and Exchange Commission under the Securities Act of 1933?

Under Section 3(a)(8) of the Securities Act of 1933, annuity contracts or optional annuity contracts are generally exempt from registration. [*See* 51 Fed. Reg. 20,254 for the preamble and comments to the adoption of Rule 151, which describes the safe harbor by which an annuity contract will be considered as being exempt from registration] Essentially, if the issuer is bearing a mortality or meaningful investment risk, registration of the contract will not be required.

If the contract contains insurance company separate accounts that permit the investment of premiums in separate accounts through which the investment risks are transferred to the policyholder, registration of the separate account is required. [Rule 151, Securities Act of 1933, 17 C.F.R. § 230.151] Note that the contract itself is typically not registered, but the separate accounts within the contract are.

It is not unusual for a contract to be a hybrid, by which a policyholder may elect to direct the assets under the contract into either a variable separate account or a guaranteed account. Under this circumstance, the separate accounts are required to be registered, but the guaranteed fund is not—even if the two funds are in the same contract.

Q 6:36 Internal Revenue Code: Can the Internal Revenue Service regulate the terms of an annuity contract?

The Internal Revenue Code does not, strictly speaking, regulate the terms of an annuity contract. The federal tax rules governing these contracts are, instead, more persuasive and indirect in nature: The Code dictates the manner in which a contract containing certain terms will be taxed. Thus, for example, if an annuity contract does not meet the federal tax definition of an annuity, it cannot be used as part of a Section 403(b) annuity program. This means that insurance companies strive to write annuity products that will have the intended tax effect—although no federal tax law directly requires them to do so.

This has been complicated by the issuance of regulations by the IRS that attempt to transform Section 403(b) annuity programs into employer-based retirement plans with similar requirements to Section 401(k) plans. The terms of the Section 403(b) contracts will be required to closely reflect the terms of the employer's plan document or risk disqualification of all of the TDAs under the plan.

Q 6:37 ERISA: Does ERISA's savings clause prevent Title I of ERISA from governing the TDAs because they are insurance contracts?

No. ERISA Section 514 outlines the manner in which ERISA relates to state laws. It generally preempts state laws from applying to ERISA plans, except that state laws relating to insurance, banking, and securities are saved from this broad preemption. [ERISA § 514(b)(2)(A)]

The courts have generally held, however, that this savings clause for insurance contracts applies only to those terms of the contract that relate to the business of insurance, but in a way that is generally different in the ERISA context from the general application of that rule. [*See* Kentucky Ass'n of Health Plans v. Miller, 538 U.S. 328 (2003) for a discussion of the application of the McCarran-Ferguson definition of *business of insurance* as it applies in the ERISA context, outlining the differences in applying it under an ERISA preemption analysis and other federal laws that apply to insurance]

This means that ERISA can govern the noninsurance activities of an employer, where the plan would otherwise be governed by ERISA.

Q 6:38 ERISA: Will the purchase of individual contracts avoid coverage of the plan by Title I of ERISA?

The purchase of individual contracts or group contracts will not, by themselves, affect the determination of whether a TDA arrangement will be subject to Title I of ERISA. [D.O.L. Reg. § 2510.3-2(f)] The key elements that will determine ERISA coverage will be the type of entity (governments and churches, generally, are exempt from coverage) and the amount of employer involvement. Purchasing a group policy for a Section 403(b) plan, where the employer is the owner of the policy, is not sufficient in and of itself to trigger ERISA status.

The Code Section 403(b) regulations have given rise to the issue of whether compliance with the Section 403(b) rules will trigger Title I coverage for private tax-exempt employers. The DOL has addressed this issue, by effectively stating that mere compliance with the tax regulations will not, by itself, trigger Title I duties. However, such a determination must be made on a case by case basis. The DOL issued Field Assistance Bulletin 2007-02, describing its position. [*See* Appendix E and https://www.dol.gov/ebsa/pdf/fab2007-2.pdf]

Q 6:39   What fiduciary rules apply to a TDA?

If the plan is subject to ERISA, then the plan and annuity contract are also subject to the fiduciary rules under Part 4 of Title I of ERISA. The more pressing question is whether state common law fiduciary rules will affect Section 403(b) plan sponsors who are not otherwise governed by ERISA. There has been little, if any, litigation to date on this issue. However, with the Code Section 403(b) regulations requiring increased involvement in the operation of the plan by plan sponsors, state fiduciary rules will increasingly come to apply.

Q 6:40   Does the participant have the right to choose any TDA carrier to which he or she wishes to make ongoing contributions?

No. The employer has the right to choose the insurance carriers to which the employees are able to make elective deferrals. As long as the employer does not unreasonably restrict the number of carriers, this decision alone will not cause the TDA to be subject to Title I of ERISA. [D.O.L. Reg. § 2510.3-2(f)]

An employee may (unless the plan otherwise prohibits it) transfer previously deferred amounts to a Section 403(b) contract of his or her choosing under Revenue Ruling 90-24. [1990-1 C.B. 97]

Q 6:41   Can an annuity contract be held by a trustee or a custodian?

Yes. In Private Letter Ruling 9423031, the IRS concluded that an annuity contract, otherwise meeting the requirements of Sections 403(b) and 401(g), can be held by a trust, as long as the trust is obligated to forward all contributions contributed to it on behalf of the annuitant to the annuity contract. This is true even where there is no contractual obligation between the employer and the trust.

Q 6:42   What is the *free look* period, and why doesn't it violate the withdrawal provisions under Code Section 403(b)(11)?

Most states grant to policyholders a period of time in which to reconsider their purchase of an annuity contract. This is referred to as a *free look* period, which is typically ten days long—but may vary from state to state. An insurer is required to return any payments made by a contract holder after any timely rescission of the annuity application.

There is little guidance on whether the free look violates Code Section 403(b)(11). One valid argument is that the initial deferral is not yet technically a Section 403(b) deferral because, under state law, it is not yet irrevocable with regard to amounts already earned. [Treas. Reg. § 1.403(b)-1(b)(3)] Upon the passage of the statutorily mandated free-look period, that initial deferral then becomes irrevocable.

Q 6:43   What happens if a contract fails to be a TDA?

A contract that fails to meet the requirements of a TDA contract may cause all of the contributions to that contract to be considered taxable in the year in which those contributions were made. In a group contract, this could cause all the contributions under that contract that were made while it was a faulty contract to be considered taxable to the employees.

However, taxation on earnings on the contributions to an annuity contract held by or on behalf of a natural person are deferred until they are distributed from the contract—even if the contract fails to meet the TDA rules (as long as the contract still qualifies as an annuity contract). [I.R.C. § 72] This position is supported under the Code Section 403(b) regulations, which treat failed Section 403(b) contracts (or the portion of the Section 403(b) contract that fails to meet the Section 403(b) rules) as a *nonqualified* contract under Code Section 403(c). [Treas. Reg. § 1.403b-3(d)(1)(iii)]

Chapter 7

Section 403(b)(7) Custodial Accounts

Regina M. Watson, Esq.
T. Rowe Price Associates, Inc.

With the enactment of the Employee Retirement Income Security Act of 1974 (ERISA), Congress significantly increased the flexibility of investments permissible for Section 403(b) arrangements. Under ERISA, Section 403(b) arrangements are allowed to invest in qualified custodial accounts holding only shares of regulated investment companies. A regulated investment company is a domestic corporation that is registered under the Investment Company Act of 1940, either as a management company or as a unit investment trust, or that is a common trust fund under the Internal Revenue Code. Employer contributions made to a qualified custodial account are treated as contributions for tax-sheltered annuities and thus are tax-qualified under Code Section 403(b). The custodian must be a bank or, under certain circumstances, a nonbank custodian approved by the IRS. Payments may not be made under the custodial account before the employee dies, reaches age 59½, separates from service, becomes disabled, or, in the case of certain contributions under a salary reduction agreement, encounters financial hardship. Contributions to a Section 403(b) custodial account are excludable from an employee's gross income as if they were made to a Section 403(b) annuity contract.

Requirements

Q 7:1   When did custodial accounts holding mutual fund shares become permissible investments for Section 403(b) arrangements?

In 1974, Congress passed the Employee Retirement Income Security Act of 1974 (ERISA), amending Code Section 403(b) to permit the funding of Section 403(b) arrangements with custodial accounts. Prior to 1974, the only permissible investment for Section 403(b) arrangements was annuity contracts (and retirement income accounts for churches). [ERISA § 1022(e)]

Q 7:2   What are the structural requirements for a custodial account under a Section 403(b)(7) arrangement?

Detailed structural requirements for a custodial account were proposed via regulation by the IRS under Code Section 403(b) in 1978; however, amid industry controversy, these requirements have never been finalized by the IRS. These IRS proposed regulations provide as follows:

1. The custodial agreement must be in writing and must be made between the employer and the custodian;
2. The employer must make at least one contribution to the custodial account that is excludable from an eligible employee's compensation;
3. The custodian must be a bank or other eligible entity meeting certain requirements (see Q 7:5);
4. The custodial account assets must be administered for the exclusive benefit of participating employees and their beneficiaries;
5. The primary purpose of the account must be to provide retirement benefits. The custodian must begin to make payments to an employee within a reasonable time after the employee retires;
6. The custodial agreement must specify that no benefits will be paid or made available to any recipient before an employee dies, attains age 59½, separates from service, becomes disabled, or encounters financial hardship;
7. The custodial account must be invested solely in shares of one or more regulated investment companies, as defined under Code Section 851 (see Q 7:8);
8. A distribution from the custodial account may be used to purchase an annuity contract but must not be used to purchase an annuity contract that provides a life insurance benefit;

9. Separate accounts must be established and maintained for each participating employee;

10. The custodian must have no discretionary authority over the investments held in the custodial account;

11. The custodial agreement may permit participants to select the mutual funds and move investments from one mutual fund to another;

12. The employer sponsoring the Section 403(b) arrangement must be the beneficial owner of the shares in the account maintained for the employee by the custodian;

13. The custodian or its nominee must be the shareholder of record for the mutual fund shares;

14. If the custodian is not a bank, the custodial agreement must provide for the removal of the nonbank custodian upon notice that it has failed to comply with necessary requirements and that the employer must substitute another custodian.

[Prop. Treas. Reg. § 1.403(b)(1)-(h)]

In subsequent private letter rulings, the IRS has permitted alternative custodial structures. For example, in Private Letter Ruling 9234027, the IRS permitted an employer creating a Section 403(b) plan to establish individual accounts for each participant or to establish a commingled or master custodial arrangement with each participant maintaining an undivided interest in the master custodial account. [Ltr. Rul. 9234027]

Q 7:3 Can a trustee be used in lieu of a custodian under Code Section 403(b)(7)?

Yes. A trust arrangement may be used in lieu of a custodial agreement for a Section 403(b) arrangement. For the most part, trust and custodial arrangements are used interchangeably with respect to the custodial account requirement. [See, e.g., Treas. Reg. § 1.401(f)-1]

Q 7:4 Who can be a custodian of a Section 403(b)(7) custodial account?

A custodian for a Section 403(b)(7) arrangement must be either:

1. A bank (see Q 7:5); or

2. Another entity that demonstrates to the satisfaction of the IRS that it is capable of administering a custodial account in accordance with IRS requirements.

[I.R.C. §§ 403(b)(7), 401(f)(2)]

Q 7:5   What requirements must a bank satisfy to be the custodian of a Section 403(b)(7) custodial account?

For purposes of a Section 403(b)(7) arrangement, the term *bank* means the following:

1. A federal or state bank or trust company, a substantial part of whose business consists of receiving deposits and making loans or of exercising fiduciary powers similar to those permitted to national banks under the authority of the Comptroller of the Currency; [I.R.C. §§ 401(f)(2), 408(n)(1), 581]

2. An insured credit union (within the meaning of Section 101(6) of the Federal Credit Union Act; [I.R.C. §§ 401(f)(2), 408(n)(2)] and

3. A corporation that, under the laws of the state of its incorporation, is subject to supervision and examination by the Commissioner of Banking or other officer of the state in charge of the administration of the banking laws of the state.

[I.R.C. §§ 401(f)(2), 408(n)(3); Treas. Reg. § 1.408-2(b)(2)(i)]

Q 7:6   What must a firm (other than a bank) demonstrate to the IRS in order to be approved as a custodian or trustee for Section 403(b)(7) accounts?

Under Code Section 401(f)(2), a firm other than a bank (see Q 7:5) may apply for IRS written approval as a custodian. The IRS provides a specific procedure for receiving approval as a nonbank custodian or trustee under Revenue Procedure 95-4. [1995-1 I.R.B. 187] Under IRS requirements, the nonbank custodian or trustee must demonstrate in detail its ability to act within the acceptable rules of fiduciary conduct. Such a demonstration must include the following elements:

1. Sufficient diversity of ownership to ensure the uninterrupted performance of its fiduciary duties notwithstanding the death or change of its owners;

2. An established place of business in the United States;

3. Fiduciary experience or expertise sufficient to ensure that it will be able to perform all its fiduciary obligations;

4. A high degree of solvency commensurate with its obligations;

5. Experience and competence for accounting for interests of a large number of individuals;

6. Experience and competence with respect to other activities associated with handling of retirement funds, such as safely handling, buying and selling securities, and collecting income;

7. Compliance with the rules of fiduciary conduct and the proper administration of fiduciary powers;

8. Maintenance of records of certain fiduciary-related functions, separate from other records;

9. Adequate bonding of all employees performing fiduciary duties;

10. Retaining of legal counsel to advise on fiduciary matters;

11. Maintenance of a separate trust division under the immediate supervision of a specially designated individual;

12. For applications received by the IRS after January 5, 1995, satisfaction of an initial net worth requirement; and

13. Arrangement for an annual audit of fiduciary books by an independent public accountant.

[I.R.C. § 401(f); Treas. Reg. §§ 1.408-2(e)(1) *et seq.*]

Q 7:7   Can an individual be the custodian of a Section 403(b)(7) custodial account?

No. Given the requirements of a trustee or custodian, most notably the requirement of diversity of ownership (see Q 7:6), an individual *person* cannot qualify as a trustee or custodian. [Treas. Reg. § 1.408-2(e)(2)(i)(A)]

Regulated Investment Companies

Q 7:8   What is a *regulated investment company*?

Assets held in a Section 403(b)(7) custodial account must be invested exclusively in a domestic corporation that is a regulated investment company satisfying the requirements described below. [I.R.C. § 403(b)(7)(C)] A *regulated investment company* means any domestic corporation that, at all times during the taxable year,

1. Is registered with the Securities and Exchange Commission under the Investment Company Act of 1940, as amended, as either a closed-end or open-end management company or as a unit investment trust;

2. Is treated under the Investment Company Act of 1940 as a business development company; or

3. Is a common trust fund or similar fund excluded under the Investment Company Act of 1940 from the definition of *investment company* and satisfying certain requirements under the Code. [I.R.C. § 851(a)]

Tax Treatment

Q 7:9   What is the tax treatment of contributions to a Section 403(b)(7) custodial account?

Contributions to a Section 403(b)(7) custodial account are excludable from an eligible employee's gross income as if they were made to a Section 403(b) annuity contract. Unless otherwise specified within Code Section 403(b), Section 403(b)(7) custodial accounts must comply with the Section 403(b) rules. [I.R.C. § 403(b)(7)]

Q 7:10   What is the tax treatment of earnings on investments held in a Section 403(b)(7) custodial account?

Regulated investment companies bear no tax liability for investment earnings (e.g., capital gains and dividends). Investment earnings are generally passed through to each shareholder. Shareholders then include the taxable share of the investment earnings in their adjusted gross income for the taxable year in which the earnings were received. However, contributions and investment income credited to a Section 403(b)(7) custodial account are exempt from federal income tax until they are distributed. [I.R.C. § 403(b)(7)(B)] Thus, any investment earnings credited to an employee's custodial account are reinvested in investment company shares.

Account Transfers and Exchanges

Q 7:11   May a participant transfer Section 403(b) plan benefits from one custodian to another without incurring a taxable event?

Yes. The IRS recognizes transfers of funds between Section 403(b)(7) custodial accounts and Section 403(b)(1) annuity contracts as nontaxable events if certain conditions are satisfied.

In Revenue Ruling 90-24, the IRS approved a method of transferring an individual's interest from one Section 403(b) arrangement to another Section 403(b) arrangement. If funds are transferred from one 403(b) investment to another investment, there is no actual or constructive distribution of funds (as described by Code Section 403(b)(4)) if the transferred funds continue after the transfer to be subject to the same or more stringent distribution restrictions. [Rev. Rul. 90-24, 1990-1 C.B. 97].

The informal method of a Revenue Ruling 90-24 transfer was eliminated by the final Code Section 403(b) regulations published on July 26, 2007 and generally effective for taxable years beginning after December 31, 2008. [Treas. Reg. § 1.403(b)-11(a)] The final Code Section 403(b) regulations essentially split transfers into two transaction types, exchanges and transfers, each with separate rules. An *exchange* is a transaction that occurs within the same Section 403(b) plan and a *transfer* is essentially a rollover to another 403(b) plan. [See Q 10:57 for additional details on transfers and exchanges under the final Code Section 403(b) regulations]

Q 7:12   What are the requirements for an exchange under final Code Section 403(b) regulations?

An exchange under the final Code Section 403(b) regulations must occur within the same Section 403(b) plan and is only allowed if:

1. The written plan document allows for such exchanges;
2. The value of the account after the exchange equals the value of the account before the exchange;
3. The distribution restrictions are maintained; and
4. The employer and custodian enter into a written information sharing agreement.

[Treas. Reg. § 1.403(b)-10(b)(2)]

Although the final Code Section 403(b) regulations are generally effective on January 1, 2009, the new exchange rules apply to exchanges occurring after September 24, 2007. See Q 10:59 for additional details regarding exchanges.

Q 7:13   What is an *information sharing agreement*?

Under the final Code Section 403(b) regulations, the plan sponsor and the 403(b) account custodian must enter into an *information sharing agreement* (ISA) which provides for the exchange of information sufficient to satisfy applicable tax requirements, such as loan limits and hardship distribution requirements. Specifically, the information must include:

1. The participant's employment and information that takes into account other Section 403(b) contracts or qualified employer plans, such as whether a severance from employment has occurred for purposes of the distribution restrictions and whether the hardship withdrawal rules in the regulations are satisfied; and
2. Contributions that have been made by the employer necessary to satisfy other tax requirements, such as whether a plan loan constitutes a deemed distribution.

[Treas. Reg. § 1.403(b)-10(b)(2)(c)(1)-(2)]

The IRS guidance assumes if a custodian is eligible to receive ongoing Section 403(b) plan contributions, the plan sponsor and that custodian are already coordinating such information, and thus an ISA is not required. (See Q 10:60 for additional details regarding the requirements of an information sharing agreement.)

Q 7:14   What are the requirements for a plan-to-plan transfer under the final Code Section 403(b) regulations?

The final Code Section 403(b) regulations allow a transfer of Section 403(b) assets to a new Section 403(b) plan if:

1. The participant is an employee or former employee of the receiving plan;

2. Both the transferor and receiving plans permit such transfers;

3. The value of the account after the exchange equals the value of the account before the exchange; and

4. Distribution restrictions are maintained.

[Treas. Reg. § 1.403(b)-10(b)(3)]

Transfers made on or before September 24, 2007 and which were compliant with Revenue Ruling 90-24 are grandfathered and thus exempt from the requirements of the final Code Section 403(b) regulations. (See Q 10:62 for additional details on the plan-to-plan transfer rules.)

Q 7:15   How do the grandfather rules apply to Revenue Ruling 90-24 transfers?

Custodial accounts established pursuant to a Revenue Ruling 90-24 transfer through September 24, 2007 are grandfathered and thus exempt from the requirements of the final Code Section 403(b) regulations. Such accounts do not need to be included under a written plan document. The custodian can interact directly with the plan participant and an ISA with the plan sponsor is not required. [See Qs 10:63, 10: 64 for additional details regarding the application of the grandfather rules to Revenue Ruling 90-24 transfers]

Q 7:16   How are Section 403(b) accounts treated if the custodian is not an approved vendor of the employer or the employer is out of business?

Prior to the final Code Section 403(b) regulations, custodians would interact directly with the plan participant; no employer involvement was necessarily required to execute a transaction. Under the new regulations, however, a custodian may have accounts from a Section 403(b) plan where the custodian is not an approved vendor of the employer or where the employer is out of business (Orphan Accounts). Under such circumstances, no exchange of information can occur and thus, the final Code Section 403(b) regulations cannot be satisfied.

To accommodate these and other situations, on November 27, 2007, the IRS released Revenue Procedure 2007-71. Under this procedure, orphan accounts established before January 1, 2005 are grandfathered under the final Code Section 403(b) regulations if no contributions were made to the account after December 31, 2004. These orphan accounts do not need to be included under the written plan document and an ISA is not required. The plan participant would interact directly with the custodian to execute a transaction.

Transitional relief is available under Revenue Procedure 2007-71 for orphan accounts established with a custodian between January 1, 2005 and December 31, 2008. This relief applies to orphan accounts established or receiving contributions from January 1, 2005 through December 31, 2008 and to Revenue Ruling 90-24 exchanges after September 24, 2007, which received contributions under the plan in the year after the custodial account was established. (See Q 10:61 for additional details regarding the transitional relief.)

Distributions

Q 7:17   When may participants take a distribution from their Section 403(b)(7) custodial accounts?

Code Section 403(b)(7) provides that under the custodial account, a distribution comprised of employer nonelective and salary reduction contributions may not be paid or made available to the employee before age $59\frac{1}{2}$, except in the case of:

1. Death;
2. Disability (as defined for purposes of premature Section 401(a) qualified plan distributions under Code Section 72(m)(7));
3. Severance from employment;
4. Financial hardship; or
5. Has a qualified reservist distribution (see Q 10:44).

[I.R.C. § 403(b)(7)(A)(ii)]

Effective January 1, 1989, distributions on account of financial hardship are limited to an employee's contributions that are made pursuant to a salary reduction agreement. [I.R.C. § 403(b)(7)(A)(ii)] Investment earnings on salary reduction contributions are not eligible for hardship withdrawal after 1988; however, pre-1989 earnings on pre-1989 contributions are still available for hardship withdrawal. [TAMRA, Pub. L. No. 100-647 § 1101A(c)(11)]

(See Q 10:55 for additional details on what qualifies as a financial hardship for Section 403(b) purposes.)

Chapter 8

Application of Federal Securities Laws to Section 403(b) Arrangements

David S. Goldstein, Esq.
Sutherland Asbill & Brennan LLP

Of the several federal laws that pertain to securities, three have particular relevance for Section 403(b) arrangements: the Securities Act of 1933, the Securities Exchange Act of 1934, and the Investment Company Act of 1940. This chapter briefly discusses the general relevance of these laws to Section 403(b) arrangements.

Q 8:1 What federal securities laws may apply to Section 403(b) programs?

Three federal securities laws may apply to Section 403(b) programs, as follows:

1. The Securities Act of 1933 (the 1933 Act), which requires that every offer and/or sale of a security by U.S. mail or through interstate commerce be registered with the Securities and Exchange Commission (SEC) unless an exemption from this requirement is available for the security or the transaction. [1933 Act §5] The 1933 Act also prohibits the use of the U.S. mail or interstate commerce to employ a scheme to defraud or obtain money or property by means of material misstatements or omissions in the offer or sale of a security (an *antifraud provision*). [1933 Act §17] Because, as explained below, securities could be deemed to be issued in connection with most Section 403(b) programs in most circumstances, the 1933 Act and rules thereunder could apply to Section 403(b) programs or to funding vehicles (or persons operating funding vehicles) that support such programs;

2. The Securities Exchange Act of 1934 (the 1934 Act) also has an antifraud provision that would cover the offer or sale of a security deemed to be issued in connection with a Section 403(b) program; [1934 Act §10]

3. The Investment Company Act of 1940 (the 1940 Act) imposes numerous requirements on collective or pooled investment vehicles that come within its definition of an investment company unless an exclusion from this definition is available.

Q 8:2 Are all applicable federal securities laws and rules thereunder addressed in this chapter?

No. A discussion of all of the possibly applicable federal securities laws and related rules and regulations would require a considerably longer and more detailed chapter than is appropriate for this publication. This chapter highlights the major federal securities law issues that arise in connection with most Section 403(b) programs and therefore could affect their sponsors or administrators, or collective or pooled investment vehicles (or other funding vehicles) supporting such programs (or sponsors of such vehicles).

Q 8:3 When might the 1933, 1934, or 1940 Acts apply to a Section 403(b) program?

The registration requirements of the 1933 Act and rules thereunder could apply whenever a Section 403(b) program, an insurance company issuing an annuity contract used to support a Section 403(b) program, or a pooled or collective investment vehicle used to support a Section 403(b) program is deemed to have issued a security in connection with the program. The antifraud provisions of both the 1933 Act and the 1934 Act could apply whenever a security issued in connection with a Section 403(b) program is offered or sold. The 1940 Act could apply to any collective or pooled investment vehicle used to support a Section 403(b) program. In certain circumstances, however, exemptions or exclusions are available under each of these statutes (or under SEC staff interpretations of them) for Section 403(b) programs and certain investment vehicles supporting such programs.

Q 8:4 What type of security might be issued in connection with a Section 403(b) program?

Generally, three types of securities might be issued in connection with any employee benefit plan, including a Section 403(b) program. They are:

1. A security issued by the employer and held as an asset of the plan (or directly by an employee or plan participant pursuant to the plan);

2. A security representing a participant's interest in the plan (or a related trust or investment vehicle supporting the plan); and

3. A security representing the plan's interest in a collective or pooled investment vehicle in which the plan invests.

The most common type of security issued in connection with employee benefit plans of ordinary industrial corporations is, of course, shares of the corporation's stock. Obviously, eligible employers do not issue this type of security. Indeed, they generally do not issue securities of any kind in connection with Section 403(b) programs (see Q 8:7).

Most other types of securities issued in connection with employee benefit plans generally, and Section 403(b) programs in particular, arise from the existence of an investment contract (see Q 8:5). The definition of a security under the 1933 Act contains a list of instruments that are securities, including an investment contract. [1933 Act §2(1)] An investment contract exists when an investment is made in a common venture with a reasonable expectation that profits will be made from the entrepreneurial or managerial efforts of others. [SEC v. WJ Howey Co., 328 U.S. 293 (1946)]

Although no clear legal authority exists on this point, it is conceivable that a security in the form of an investment contract could be deemed to exist in connection with a Section 403(b) program where the program is maintained by the employer (i.e., subject to the Employee Retirement Income Security Act of 1974 (ERISA)). Otherwise, an investment contract security does not appear to exist in connection with an employee's interest in a Section 403(b) program or with an employer issuing a security to such an employee. In contrast, a security in the form of an investment contract is more likely to exist in connection with an employee's interest in a pooled or collective investment vehicle or other security supporting a Section 403(b) program.

A security representing an interest in a pooled or collective investment vehicle also may be deemed to be held by a Section 403(b) program that it supports, as might an annuity contract that is a security.

Q 8:5 What is the traditional SEC staff analysis of investment contracts in connection with employee benefit plans generally?

The SEC staff has historically relied on the investment contract test to reach the conclusion that participants' interests in employee benefit plans, particularly qualified plans, are often securities. After the Supreme Court concluded in 1980 that participant interests in involuntary, noncontributory pension plans are not securities under the 1933 Act or the 1934 Act, the SEC staff issued two releases in which it expressed the view, based on the investment contract analysis, that participant interests in plans that are both voluntary and contributory generally come within the definition of a security under the 1933 Act. [Rel. 33-6188 (Feb. 1, 1980); Rel. 33-6281 (Jan. 15, 1981)] The SEC staff also indicated in these releases that participant interests in plans that are involuntary, and participant interests in plans that are voluntary but not contributory, are generally not securities under the 1933 Act.

Federal courts have not always agreed with the SEC staff that participant interests in voluntary contributory plans are securities. Since 1981, several lower federal courts have concluded that participant interests in a variety of different types of qualified plans (including voluntary contributory plans) are not securities. Generally, these federal courts gave considerable weight to two factors that the SEC staff did not consider significant: (1) that contributions to retirement plans are not a traditional investment decision, and (2) that ERISA provides comprehensive regulation of qualified plans.

The SEC staff also relied on the investment contract analysis to conclude that a qualified plan's interest in a collective or pooled investment vehicle is a security under the 1933 Act. [Rel. 33-6188] Although registration under the 1933 Act would generally be required of securities arising from participant interests in qualified plans and from such plans' interests in collective or pooled investment vehicles, exemptions are usually available from this requirement (see Q 8:12).

Q 8:6   How does traditional SEC staff analysis of investment contracts in connection with employee benefit plans apply to Section 403(b) programs?

Section 403(b) programs differ from qualified plans in that there usually is not a separate trust or other plan asset in which employees can have an interest that could be considered a security. Nevertheless, the investment contract theory can be applied to an eligible employee's interest in an insurance company separate account supporting a Section 403(b) variable annuity contract or a Section 403(b)(7) custody account holding mutual fund shares to find a security. Therefore, even though a Section 403(b) program does not generally take the form of a separate legal entity and cannot easily be deemed to hold a security in the form of an interest in a separate account or custody account, interests in such pooled or collective investment vehicles can be considered to be issued directly to the eligible employee in connection with a Section 403(b) program. Likewise, interests in certain types of fixed Section 403(b) annuity contracts can be deemed to be securities of an insurance company issued directly to the eligible employee.

Whether, in fact, an interest in a pooled or collective investment vehicle should be considered issued directly to the eligible employee depends on the facts and circumstances. In most cases, such as where individual variable annuity contracts are issued to each eligible employee in a pure salary reduction program, an interest in a separate account (in the form of a variable annuity) is being issued directly to the employee. In such a case, the interest almost always must be registered as a security with the SEC under the 1933 Act and the separate account as an investment company under the 1940 Act. Such registrations, in turn, trigger other federal securities law requirements, such as the issuing insurance company's obligation to deliver prospectuses to eligible employees and the selling broker-dealer's responsibility to provide eligible employees with confirmation statements. In other cases (such as group variable annuity contracts issued in circumstances where the employer or other program fiduciary plays a significant intermediary role in making investment options available), an argument can be made that the interest in a separate account should be treated as being issued to the employer or other group contract owner. However, even in these circumstances, the SEC staff has generally treated Section 403(b) program participants as the primary investors because they make important investment decisions for themselves generally without oversight from group contract owners. [American Council of Life Insurance (Nov. 28, 1988);

Principal Mutual Life Insurance Company (July 22, 1992)] As a result, interests in separate accounts issued through group variable annuity issuers almost always must be registered as securities under the 1933 Act and the separate accounts as investment companies under the 1940 Act.

Q 8:7   How does traditional SEC staff analysis of investment contracts in connection with qualified plans and Section 403(b) programs relate to Section 457 plans?

The federal courts have not decided and the SEC and its staff have not published any position as to whether a Section 457 plan participant's interest in a Section 457 plan is a security or whether such a plan's interest in a collective or pooled investment vehicle is a security. Nevertheless, it is probable that, based on an investment contract analysis, the SEC staff would conclude that a Section 457 plan's investment in a collective or pooled investment vehicle is a security and, where participant interests in a Section 457 plan are not securities issued by the employer, interests in the plan may be securities (see Qs 8:5, 8:6).

In general, from a federal securities law standpoint, Code Section 457(g) now makes eligible Section 457 plans of public employers [I.R.C. § 457(e)(1)(A)] significantly different from eligible Section 457 plans of tax-exempt employers [I.R.C. § 457(e)(1)(B)] and noneligible Section 457 plans [I.R.C. § 457(f)] It is likely that the SEC staff would conclude that eligible Section 457 plans of public employers should be treated in the same manner as qualified plans because of the existence of dedicated plan *assets* (see Qs 8:4, 8:5). Indeed, without opining as to whether a participant's interest in a Section 457(e)(1)(A) plan, or such a plan's interest in a collective or pooled investment vehicle, is a security, the SEC staff confirmed to a private sponsor of collective or pooled investment vehicles that such vehicles and eligible Section 457 plans of public employers that invest in them may generally rely on the exemption from the registration requirements of the 1933 Act found in Section 3(a)(2) thereof and on the exclusion from the definition of an investment company found in Section 3(c)(11) of the 1940 Act. [Massachusetts Mutual Life Ins. Co (Aug. 10, 1998)]

In contrast, it is likely that the SEC staff would treat other Section 457 plans in the same manner that they treat nonqualified deferred compensation plans of ordinary for-profit corporations. Although the SEC staff has not specifically addressed Section 457 plans in this context, it has informally taken the position in recent years that nonqualified deferred compensation plans generally give rise to a security issued by the employer called a deferred compensation obligation. Although this position appears to have been taken in connection with top-hat plans and excess benefit plans rather than Section 457 plans, informal discussions between private practitioners and SEC staff members suggest the use of a two-step analysis by the SEC staff that is equally applicable to Section 457 plans other than Section 457(e)(1)(A) plans:

1. Due to the unfunded nature of nonqualified deferred compensation plans, participants in such plans rely on the employer's promise to pay and

therefore, if an investment contract exists, it is a contract issued by the employer.

2. Absent an appropriate exemption, deferred compensation obligations generally are subject to the registration requirements of the 1933 Act where such plans have an investment as well as a tax-planning goal that might be viewed as an investment contract (see Q 8:4). During the last several years, a number of companies have registered deferred compensation obligations under the 1933 Act (on Form S-8) in connection with top-hat and excess benefit plans.

The SEC staff's position regarding deferred compensation obligations is based on the idea that the plan is not a separate issuer. Under this analysis, a nonqualified deferred compensation plan would generally not be a separate issuer unless it limited participants' rights against the employer (e.g., limited the participants' rights to a specific pool of assets). For example, use of a rabbi trust to *fund* plan obligations should not make the plan a separate issuer, but use of a secular trust for this purpose probably would make the trust or the plan a separate issuer. [The Goldman Sachs Group, Inc., SEC No-Action Letter (March 8, 2005)]

For a more comprehensive discussion of the applicability of federal securities laws to Section 457 plans, see chapter 10 of *457 Answer Book* (Aspen Publishers, 2008).

Q 8:8 What is the definition of offer and sale under the 1933 Act?

Generally, the SEC staff considers participation in a voluntary contributory employee benefit plan to be the result of an offer and sale to the participant of any security issued by the plan or the employer. Although the SEC staff has never addressed this question specifically in the context of a Section 403(b) program, it seems obvious that salary reduction amounts under a Section 403(b) program are voluntary and contributory and that any security issued in connection with a Section 403(b) program does not escape the registration requirements of the 1933 Act on the grounds that there is no offer or sale.

Q 8:9 Are definitions under the 1934 Act different from those under the 1933 Act?

As it might relate to a Section 403(b) program, the term *security* has the same definition under the 1934 Act as it would under the 1933 Act, and the antifraud provisions of the 1934 Act would apply where an offer or sale occurs as defined in the 1933 Act.

Q 8:10 When must the issuer of a registered security deliver a prospectus to eligible employees?

Unless an exemption is available (see Q 8:12), where a security in the form of an interest in a separate account or bank custody account can be considered to be issued directly to an eligible employee in a Section 403(b) program, it must be registered with the SEC under the 1933 Act (see Q 8:6). The same is true for interests in certain fixed annuity contracts issued to eligible employees (see Q 8:6). Once it registers the security, the issuer (and any person who sells the security) becomes subject to the prospectus delivery requirements of the 1933 Act, as described below. Though a separate account is the issuer of an interest in itself (through a variable annuity contract), the sponsoring insurance company acts in place of the separate account and shoulders the prospectus delivery responsibilities. In the case of a fixed annuity contract registered as a security, the issuing insurance company has the prospectus delivery obligations. In the case of a custody account, though the account would technically be the issuer, the SEC permits the mutual fund whose shares are held in the account to act as the issuer and be responsible for prospectus delivery (see Q 8:15).

The prospectus delivery requirements of the 1933 Act can generally be summarized as follows. Section 2(10) of the 1933 Act broadly defines the term *prospectus* to include any prospectus, notice, circular, advertisement, letter, or communication, written or by radio or television, which offers any security for sale or confirms the sale of any security. Thus, virtually any communication other than an oral communication relating to a security is a prospectus. However, Section 2(10) contains two important exclusions from its definition of a prospectus.

1. A communication about a security given after the effective date of a registration statement for that security which is preceded or accompanied by a statutory prospectus is not a prospectus (often referred to as "supplemental" sales literature);

2. A communication that does no more than identify the security, state its price, and state by whom orders for the security will be executed is not a prospectus (a so-called "tombstone" advertisement).

Section 10 of the 1933 Act outlines the requirements as to what information must be included in various types of prospectuses. Section 10(a) defines a traditional or full prospectus that must be included in any registration statement (a *statutory prospectus*). A prospectus meets the requirements of Section 10(a) if it contains all the information required by the form for the registration statement of which it is a part. Section 10(b) refers to a *summary* or *omitting* prospectus which only contains limited information. Rules 482 and 498 under the 1933 Act each define a type of omitting prospectus and the types of information that each must or may contain. Rule 482 defines the criteria for permissible advertisements for separate accounts and mutual funds, while Rule 498 defines those for *profile* prospectuses.

Section 5(b)(1) of the 1933 Act, in effect, prohibits the distribution of a prospectus relating to a security unless the prospectus meets the requirements of Sections 10(a) or 10(b) of the 1933 Act. Because virtually any communication other than an oral communication (or *supplemental* sales literature or a tombstone advertisement) relating to a security is a prospectus, it must meet the requirements of Section 10 of the 1933 Act. In contrast, oral communications, such as offers by an issuer or broker-dealer over the telephone to sell a security, are not prospectuses and do not have to meet the requirements of Section 10.

Therefore, a broker-dealer may offer a security for sale, or even sell a security, over the telephone without delivering a statutory or omitting prospectus, but as soon as any written communication is delivered in connection with the sale (such as a confirmation statement or an application), Section 5(b)(1) of the 1933 Act triggers the requirements of Section 10 unless the communication is a tombstone advertisement or is preceded or accompanied by a statutory prospectus.

Section 5(b)(2) of the 1933 Act, in effect, prohibits the distribution of securities for sale or delivery after sale unless accompanied or preceded by a statutory prospectus. Therefore, the delivery of registered annuity contracts or mutual fund shares must be preceded or accompanied by the delivery of a statutory prospectus for the contracts or funds. Taken together, Sections 5(b)(1) and 5(b)(2) require delivery of a statutory prospectus no later than the delivery of the security or the confirmation of the sale, whichever occurs first.

The primary prospectus delivery requirements of Section 5 of the 1933 Act apply to any person using the mails or other means of interstate commerce to sell or deliver, or to offer to purchase or sell a security. Broker-dealers and their registered representatives are therefore subject to Section 5 in connection with registered annuity contracts and mutual fund shares that they offer or make available. Similarly, Section 15(c) of the Securities Exchange Act of 1934 and Rule 15c2-8 thereunder impose additional prospectus delivery requirements on broker-dealers in certain circumstances. Therefore, generally speaking, responsibility for meeting the prospectus delivery requirements applicable to issuers of securities is shared by broker-dealers selling the securities.

Q 8:11   What entities might be investment companies subject to the 1940 Act in connection with a Section 403(b) program?

Any collective or pooled investment vehicle that is deemed under the investment contract analysis to issue a security to a Section 403(b) program (or, for that matter, a qualified plan) would likely come within the definition of an investment company under the 1940 Act. This would include insurance company separate accounts and bank custody accounts holding mutual fund shares. It also clearly includes mutual funds whose shares are held by insurance company separate accounts (thereby indirectly supporting a variable annuity contract funding a Section 403(b) program) or bank custody accounts.

Q 8:12   What exemptions are available from the registration requirements of the 1933 Act?

Except for church plans, no specific exemption is generally available from the registration requirements of the 1933 Act for securities issued in connection with Section 403(b) programs. (Even if an exemption is available, the offer and sale of such securities is still subject to the antifraud provisions of the 1933 Act and the 1934 Act.) In fact, the exemption available for qualified plans and certain other employee benefit plans specifically excludes Section 403(b) programs from its coverage.

Section 3(a)(2) of the 1933 Act exempts both participant interests in most employee benefit plans and interests of such plans in collective or pooled investment vehicles. Specifically, Section 3(a)(2) exempts from the registration provisions of the 1933 Act any interest or participation in a single or collective trust maintained by a bank, or any security arising out of a contract issued by an insurance company, which interest, participation, or security is issued in connection with:

1. A plan that qualifies under Code Section 401;
2. An annuity plan that meets the requirements for the deduction of the employer's contributions under Code Section 404(a)(2); or
3. A governmental plan as defined in Code Section 414(d).

Section 3(a)(2), however, also carves out from these exempt securities:

1. Interests in single trust funds and separate accounts maintained by an insurance company for a single employer that invest more than the amount of the employer's contribution in securities issued by the employer or its affiliates;
2. Plans covering individuals who are employees within the meaning of Code Section 401(c); and
3. Plans funded by Section 403(b) annuity contracts.

Unfortunately, this demonstrates Congress's clear intent to make securities issued in connection with Section 403(b) programs subject to the registration requirements of the 1933 Act unless another exemption is available.

Other possibly applicable exemptions include the following:

Government and municipal securities. Section 3(a)(2) exempts from the registration requirements of the 1933 Act any security issued by the United States or any territory thereof, or by the District of Columbia, or by any state of the United States, or by any political subdivision of a state or territory, or by any public instrumentality of one or more states or territories, or by any person controlled or supervised by and acting as an instrumentality of the government of the United States pursuant to authority granted by Congress. In other words, government and most municipal securities are exempt from the registration requirements of the 1933 Act. Arguably, to the extent that a state or municipal government is an eligible employer that is deemed to have issued a security in the form of an investment contract with an employee, Section 3(a)(2) could exempt such a security from the registration requirements of the 1933 Act.

Nonprofit organizations. Section 3(a)(4) of the 1933 Act exempts from the Act's registration requirements any security issued by a person organized and operated exclusively for religious, educational, benevolent, fraternal, charitable, or reformatory purposes and not for pecuniary profit, and no part of the net earnings of which inures to the benefit of any person, private stockholder, or individual. Section 3(a)(4) also exempts any security issued by a collective or pooled investment vehicle that is excluded from the definition of an investment company by Section 3(c)(10) of the 1940 Act. Arguably, to the extent that one of the foregoing types of nonprofit organizations is an eligible employer that is deemed to have issued a security in the form of an investment contract with an employee, Section 3(a)(4) could exempt such a security from the registration requirements of the 1933 Act.

Intrastate transactions. Section 3(a)(11) of the 1933 Act exempts from the Act's registration requirements any security that is part of an issue offered and sold only to persons resident within a single state or territory, where the issuer of such security is a person resident and doing business within, or, if a corporation, incorporated by and doing business within, such state or territory.

Church plans. Section 3(a)(13) of the 1933 Act exempts from the Act's registration requirements any security issued by or any interest or participation in any church plan excluded from the definition of an investment company under Section 3(c)(14) of the 1940 Act (see Q 8:13). Section 3(a)(13) also exempts any security issued by or any participation in a pooled or collective investment vehicle if substantially all of the activities of the vehicle relate to such a church plan or its administration.

Private offerings. Section 4(2) of the 1933 Act exempts from the Act's registration requirements any transaction not involving a public offering. Commonly known as the private offering exemption, Section 4(2) covers offerings made to a limited number of investors who are sophisticated in business matters and have access to the types of information about an issuer that otherwise would be obtained through a registration statement under the 1933 Act. Legal authority regarding the scope of a private offering versus a public offering is generally limited and is extremely limited in the context of any security issued in connection with a Section 403(b) program. To the author's knowledge, no such authority exists regarding a Section 403(b) program. Regulation D under the 1933 Act [1933 Act rules 501-508] does provide safe harbors for several specific types of private offerings, but these would likely be impractical for most Section 403(b) plans. Because of the complexity of the private offering exemption, competent securities counsel should be consulted before reliance is placed on this exemption.

Q 8:13 What exemptions are available from the registration and other requirements of the 1940 Act?

Other than for church plans, no specific exemption or exclusion exists from the definition of an investment company for pooled or collective investment vehicles deemed under the investment contract analysis to be issuing a security in connection with a Section 403(b) program.

Section 3(c)(11) of the 1940 Act excludes from the definition of an investment company under that Act the following:

1. Any employees' stock bonus, pension, or profit-sharing trust that qualifies under Code Section 401;

2. Any governmental plan described in Section 3(a)(2)(C) of the 1933 Act;

3. Any collective trust fund maintained by a bank consisting solely of assets of such trusts or governmental plans, or both; and

4. Any insurance company separate account containing assets derived solely from: (a) contributions under plans qualifying under Code Section 401 and/or contributions meeting the requirements for deduction of an employer's contribution under Code Section 402(a)(2), (b) contributions under governmental plans in connection with which interests, participations, or securities are exempted from the registration requirements of the 1933 Act by Section 3(a)(2)(C) of the 1933 Act, and (c) advances made by an insurance company in connection with the operation of such a separate account.

None of these exclusions, however, would exclude insurance company separate accounts supporting variable Section 403(b) annuity contracts, Section 403(b)(7) bank custody accounts holding mutual fund shares, or the mutual funds themselves from the definition of an investment company.

Section 3(c)(14) of the 1933 Act excludes from the definition of an investment company any church plan described in Code Section 414(e), if no part of the plan's assets may be used for, or diverted to, purposes other than the exclusive benefit of plan participants and beneficiaries. Section 3(c)(14) also excludes from the definition of an investment company any pooled or collective investment vehicle that (1) is established by a person eligible to establish and maintain a church plan under Code Section 414(e) and (2) substantially all of the activities of which consist of (a) managing or holding assets contributed to such church plan(s) or other assets that are permitted under the Code to be commingled with church plan assets or (b) administering or providing benefits pursuant to church plans.

Exclusions from the definition of an investment company result in a plan, or a pooled or collective investment vehicle supporting a plan, not being subject to the 1940 Act. In contrast, where, as in the case of qualified plans and church plans, securities issued by (or interests or participations in) such plans or vehicles are exempted from the registration requirements of the 1933 Act, the antifraud provisions of the 1933 Act still apply to the offer and sale of such securities and interests.

Q 8:14   What exemptions are available from the requirements of the 1934 Act?

Section 3(a)(12) of the 1934 Act includes in its list of exempted securities only those securities exempted by Section 3(a)(2)(A)–(C) of the 1933 Act (see Q 8:12).

Q 8:15   What is the status of bank custody accounts holding mutual fund shares pursuant to Code Section 403(b)(7)?

In response to a no-action letter request from the Investment Company Institute, the SEC staff took a position many years ago that it would not recommend enforcement action to the Commission if bank custody accounts holding mutual fund shares did not register as investment companies under the 1940 Act and if interests in such accounts were not registered under the 1933 Act. [Investment Company Institute (Oct. 21, 1974)] The SEC staff position was predicated on several conditions, including (1) that the custodian or trustee has no investment discretion with regard to the account and does not otherwise manage the account in any way, (2) that the prospectus and various reports from the mutual fund be provided to the eligible employee, and (3) that the prospectus contain appropriate disclosure about Section 403(b) programs and custody accounts. A similar position was taken by the SEC staff several years later in response to a no-action letter request from an employer sponsoring a Section 403(b) program that included 403(b)(7) custody accounts. [Cleveland Clinic Foundation (Aug. 12, 1979)]

A recent request to reduce the obligation to provide eligible employees with prospectuses and other reports was denied by the SEC staff. [Lincoln National Life Insurance Company (Jan. 30, 2003)]

Q 8:16   What is a no-action letter?

In a no-action letter, a party writes to the SEC staff and requests that the staff take a position that it would not recommend enforcement action to the SEC under specific statutory provisions and related rules if the writer proceeds in the manner described. The writer almost always provides a legal analysis supporting its assertion that the requested position is consistent with (or at least not inconsistent with) the statutory provisions and related rules as well as any SEC or SEC staff interpretations thereof (e.g., prior no-action positions). The SEC staff usually takes no-action positions without agreeing or disagreeing with the writer's legal analysis; therefore, readers often must draw inferences about the staff's views about this analysis from the request letter and the staff's response. Often no-action positions are subject to various conditions, and one can usually infer a fair amount about the SEC staff's thinking from the conditions. Although a court may give weight to a no-action position, such positions are not, strictly speaking, interpretations of the law by the SEC or its staff and are not binding on anyone but the staff (e.g., they would not be binding on a private litigant).

Q 8:17   Do the withdrawal restrictions applicable to elective deferrals under Code Section 403(b)(11) conflict with certain provisions of the 1940 Act?

Yes, in certain circumstances. Subject to certain grandfathering exceptions, the Tax Reform Act of 1986 (TRA '86) added subsection (11) to Code Section 403(b) thereby making certain withdrawal restrictions applicable to amounts attributable to elective deferrals under Section 403(b) annuity contracts. Such amounts may only be withdrawn when an employee (the contract owner or group contract participant) attains age $59\frac{1}{2}$, separates from service, dies or becomes disabled, or in the case of hardship (see Q 10:50). Section 27(i) of the

1940 Act, however, requires that any variable annuity contract issued in connection with an insurance company separate account registered under the 1940 Act as an investment company be fully redeemable (i.e., permit full surrender without restrictions). Section 22(e) of the Act requires, in effect, any insurance company issuing such a contract to redeem it within seven days of a surrender request by its owner (or, where appropriate, by a group contract participant).

Shortly before the applicable provisions of TRA '86 took effect, in response to a no-action letter request from the American Council of Life Insurance, the SEC staff took a position that it would not recommend enforcement action to the Commission if registered separate accounts issuing variable annuity contracts in connection with 403(b) programs restricted the redeemability of amounts attributable to elective deferrals. [American Council of Life Insurance (Nov. 28, 1988)] This position, however, was subject to a number of conditions. They are that the insurance company, on behalf of the separate account, must do the following:

1. Include appropriate disclosure regarding the redemption restrictions imposed by Code Section 403(b)(11) in each 1933 Act registration statement, including the prospectus, used in connection with the offer of the contract;

2. Include appropriate disclosure regarding the redemption restrictions imposed by Code Section 403(b)(11) in any sales literature used in connection with the offer of the contract;

3. Instruct sales representatives who solicit prospective contract owners (or group contract participants) to purchase the contract specifically to bring the redemption restrictions imposed by Code Section 403(b)(11) to the attention of the prospective owners (or participants);

4. Obtain from each owner (or participant) who purchases a Section 403(b) variable annuity contract, prior to or at the time of such purchase, a signed statement acknowledging the owner's (or participant's) understanding of: (a) the redemption restrictions imposed by Code Section 403(b)(11) and (b) the investment alternatives available under the employer's Section 403(b) program, to which the owner (or participant) may elect to transfer contract value; and

5. Include in any registration statement filed in connection with the contract, a representation that this no-action position is being relied upon and that conditions in (1) through (4) above have been complied with.

In addition to the foregoing, the SEC staff also imposed a condition relating to the transfer of contract values among and between investment options under Section 403(b) contracts. The SEC staff position indicates that a registered separate account or its insurance company sponsor may not limit or deny transfer requests from contract owners (or participants) unless the limitation or denial is necessary in order for the contracts to meet the requirements of Code Section 403(b). Moreover, a separate account or insurance company may only establish that the limitation or denial is necessary if it has an IRS ruling or written opinion of counsel to that effect.

New Treasury Regulations promulgated in July 2007 [Treas. Reg. § 1.403(b)-6(b)] apply to employer contributions to Section 403(b) programs, with withdrawal restrictions similar to those found in Code Section 403(b)(11). The 1988 SEC staff position discussed above does not cover the new withdrawal restrictions. Therefore, unless the American Council of Life Insurance or other industry participants obtain an extension of the 1988 position from the SEC staff before the January 2009 effective date of the new withdrawal restrictions, the restrictions will conflict with Sections 27(i) and 22(e) of the 1940 Act.

Chapter 9

ERISA Requirements

Michael S. Sirkin, Esq.
Proskauer Rose LLP

Gary E. Herzlich, Esq.
Teachers Insurance and Annuity Association—College
Retirement Equities Fund

The Employee Retirement Income Security Act of 1974, commonly referred to as ERISA, affects a broad range of plans, funds, and programs. It applies to any such arrangement established or maintained by an employer to provide retirement income or deferral of income to employees. ERISA provides participants—and their spouses and beneficiaries—with extensive rights and imposes stringent duties on fiduciaries. Depending upon its structure, a Section 403(b) arrangement may be subject to the reach of ERISA. Great care must be taken to structure and administer the arrangement properly and, where applicable, ensure compliance with the requirements of ERISA. This chapter explains the circumstances under which a Section 403(b) arrangement is subject to ERISA and discusses the relevant requirements and issues with regard to vesting schedules, joint and survivor annuities, beneficiary designations, amendments to the plan, disclosures and reporting, and fiduciary matters.

Circumstances Under Which a Section 403(b) Arrangement Is Subject to ERISA

Q 9:1 What types of Section 403(b) arrangements are subject to ERISA?

Any Section 403(b) arrangement, other than one maintained by a church or governmental entity (see Q 9:14), in which the employer's involvement extends beyond the narrow limitations set forth in Department of Labor (DOL) Regulations Section 2510.3-2(f) (see Q 9:2) will be subject to ERISA. Essentially, the DOL regulation on this issue exempts from ERISA those Section 403(b) arrangements in which the employer's involvement is limited to making information available as to insurance company and/or mutual fund products, withholding salary reduction contributions, and forwarding the contributions to the applicable funding agent.

Q 9:2 What types of Section 403(b) arrangements are exempt from ERISA?

ERISA applies to all Section 403(b) arrangements except those that are specifically exempted. ERISA does not apply to arrangements maintained by a church or government entity. The DOL regulation exempts from the Title I definitions of "employee pension benefit plan" and "pension plan" those Section 403(b) arrangements in which contributions are made only pursuant to a salary reduction agreement and in which employer involvement is minimal. Section 403(b) arrangements that are exempted from the Title I definitions of "employee pension benefit plan" and "pension plan" are not subject to the requirements of ERISA.

A Section 403(b) arrangement falls within the DOL regulation requirements for exemption if it is maintained in accordance with the following narrowly drawn limitations:

1. Participation is completely voluntary for employees;

2. All rights under the annuity contract or custodial account are enforceable solely by the employee, by a beneficiary of such employee, or by any authorized representative of such employee or beneficiary;

3. The sole involvement of the employer is limited to any of the following:

 a. Permitting annuity contractors (which include agents and brokers) to publicize their products to employees;

 b. Requesting information concerning proposed funding media, products, or annuity contractors;

    c. Summarizing or otherwise compiling the information provided with respect to the proposed funding media or products that are made-available, or the annuity contractors whose services are provided, in order to facilitate review and analysis by the employees;

    d. Collecting and remitting annuity or custodial account payments as required by salary reduction agreements or by agreements to forgo salary increases, and maintaining records of such payments;

    e. Holding in the employer's name one or more group annuity contracts covering its employees; or

    f. Limiting the funding media or products available to employees, or the annuity contractors who may approach employees, to a number and selection designed to afford employees a reasonable choice in light of all relevant circumstances; and

4. The employer receives no direct or indirect consideration or compensation in cash or otherwise other than reasonable compensation to cover expenses properly and actually incurred in the performance of the employer's duties pursuant to the salary reduction agreements.

[D.O.L. Reg. § 2510.3-2(f)]

Q 9:3 What is the impact of compliance with the written plan requirement under final Code Section 403(b) regulations on the exemption of a Section 403(b) arrangement under DOL Regulations Section 2510.3-2(f)?

The DOL issued Field Assistance Bulletin (FAB) 2007-02 in conjunction with the issuance of the final Code Section 403(b) regulations to address the impact that compliance with the written plan requirement (see Q 9:12) under the final regulations could have on the DOL exemption under DOL Regulations Section 2510.3-2(f). FAB 2007-02 provides that compliance with the final Code Section 403(b) regulations, including adoption of a written plan, will not necessarily cause a Section 403(b) arrangement to become covered by Title I of ERISA. The Field Assistance Bulletin explains that compiling the benefit terms of the contracts and the responsibilities of the employer, annuity providers and participants is a function similar to the information collection and compilation activities expressly permitted under the ERISA exemption. Nevertheless, a caveat is in order. An employer desiring to comply with the ERISA exemption should carefully navigate compliance with the Section 403(b) written plan requirement, as inherent tensions exist between the labor regulation and the tax regulation. The Field Assistance Bulletin noted that the new Code Section 403(b) regulations offer employers considerable flexibility in shaping the extent and nature of their involvement under a tax-sheltered annuity program. A written plan that gives the employer discretionary responsibility or results in discretionary decisions regarding plan administration would cause the plan to fail to satisfy the exemption. Thus the manner in which an employer complies with the Section 403(b) regulations would need to be analyzed on a case-by-case basis to determine whether or not the arrangement would be exempt from ERISA.

Q 9:4 Is a Section 403(b) arrangement that limits the number of insurance carriers and/or mutual fund companies available to employees for investment of their salary reduction contributions subject to ERISA?

An employer may limit the investment choices available to its employees only when doing so would not preclude affording employees a reasonable choice of both products and funding companies in light of all relevant circumstances. If an employer limits access of funding alternatives to the extent that its employees would not have a reasonable choice of investment alternatives from among those that have indicated a desire to service its employees, the employer would be deemed to have violated the criteria set forth in DOL Regulations Section 2510.3-2(f) and would be deemed to have established or maintained a pension plan. The arrangement would thereby become subject to ERISA.

The preamble to the regulation states that the provision is designed to prevent an employer who does not wish to be deemed to be maintaining a pension plan from restricting investment products available to employees or limiting the available funding companies to one selected by the employer when several seek to make their services or products available to employees, unless even in the presence of any such limitations the employees are still afforded a reasonable choice in light of relevant circumstances. The preamble explains that there is no requirement that the employer seek out funding companies.

Q 9:5 What factors would be relevant to a decision as to whether employees are afforded a reasonable choice?

The factors relevant to whether an employer's employees are afforded a reasonable choice vary with each case, based on the relevant circumstances. The preamble to the regulation provides the following examples of types of factors that might be relevant in determining whether a reasonable choice has been afforded:

1. The number of employees affected;
2. The number of contractors that have indicated interest in approaching employees;
3. The variety of available products;
4. The terms of the available arrangements;
5. The administrative burdens and costs to the employer; and
6. The possible interference with employee performance resulting from direct solicitation by funding companies.

Q 9:6 Is a Section 403(b) arrangement that provides employer contributions subject to ERISA?

Yes. DOL Regulations Section 2510.3-2(f) (see Q 9:2), which sets forth narrow criteria exempting a Section 403(b) arrangement from ERISA, permits an employer to collect salary reduction contributions and forward them to the funding agent. An arrangement that provides any contributions other than salary reduction contributions creates employer involvement beyond what is permitted by the exemption. Such an arrangement would be subject to ERISA.

Q 9:7   Is a Section 403(b) arrangement that mandates employee contributions subject to ERISA?

Yes. Any arrangement in which participation is other than completely voluntary would subject the arrangement to ERISA. [D.O.L. Reg. § 2510.3-2(f)]

Q 9:8   Are there circumstances under which a Section 403(b) arrangement that is not intended to be an ERISA Section 403(b) plan can inadvertently become one?

Yes. An employer's intent to be exempt from ERISA is irrelevant for purposes of determining whether the arrangement will be subject to ERISA. The controlling factor is the extent of employer involvement. This situation can ultimately result in potential liabilities because the arrangement will not have been administered in accordance with the ERISA requirements, such as joint and survivor annuities and spousal consents.

Q 9:9   Does employer certification of "hardship" to permit withdrawals or permitting repayment of loans through payroll deduction cause a Section 403(b) arrangement to become subject to ERISA?

Employer determination of eligibility for "hardship" runs the risk of requiring employer involvement in excess of that contemplated by DOL Regulations Section 2510.3-2(f). The DOL has issued an advisory opinion setting forth formal guidance relating to this issue. It states that to the extent an employer must evaluate circumstances and exercise judgment, those actions are an exercise of control that exceeds the limited involvement contemplated by the regulation. Thus, any independent review, investigation, or discretionary evaluation would cause the Section 403(b) arrangement to be deemed an ERISA 403(b) plan. In contrast, to the extent an employer merely certifies to the funding agent facts within the employer's knowledge as employer (for example, an employee's attendance record or compensation level) or transmits to the funding agent another party's certification of facts (for example, a doctor's certification of an employee's physical condition), the advisory opinion states that such actions would be ministerial in nature and would not exceed the limited involvement contemplated by the regulation. [D.O.L. Adv. Op. 94-30 A (Aug. 19, 1994)]

While this scenario is not addressed by the advisory opinion, special care should be taken if the hardship "safe harbor" is used by the funding agent because the act of preventing employees from making other employee contributions to enforce the safe harbor may in itself cause a problem. If this methodology is used, it may be best merely to follow an irrevocable direction of the employee, to the extent permitted under the regulations, and limit the employer's involvement in attempting to administer compliance.

In proposed loan regulations released in January 1998, the IRS noted in a footnote that the DOL had advised that permitting employees to make repayments of loans made in connection with the tax-sheltered annuity program through payroll deductions as part of the employer's payroll deduction system would not necessarily cause the program to fail to satisfy the requirement of the exemption from ERISA if the program operates within limitations set by the exemption regulation. [Preamble to Reg. 209476-82, Fed. Reg., vol. 63, no. 1, Jan. 2, 1998]

Q 9:10 Would implementation of an automatic enrollment policy cause a Section 403(b) arrangement to be subject to ERISA?

It would appear that this would be the case. An arrangement that provides for an automatic enrollment, whereby absent an affirmative election, a specified percentage of salary would be withheld and contributed to a 403(b) plan on behalf of participants and allocated to a default funding vehicle in a predetermined manner, would appear to be subject to ERISA to the extent the arrangement otherwise relies on DOL Regulations Section 2510.3-2(f) for exemption. Automatic enrollment would appear to mandate more employer involvement than the regulation appears to permit.

State wage law concerns and fiduciary responsibility concerns had stood in the way of broad utilization of automatic enrollment provisions. The Pension Protection Act of 2006 (PPA) addressed both of these concerns. Widespread use had been discouraged by the application of those state wage laws which prohibit deduction from an employee's wages without affirmative employee election. Uncertainty surrounded whether ERISA preempted these state wage laws. The PPA amended ERISA to provide that ERISA will in fact preempt state wage laws that prohibit or have the effect of restricting an automatic contribution arrangement. Preemption is, of course, limited to ERISA covered plans. Use of automatic enrollment provisions had also been discouraged by heightened fiduciary responsibility concerns in connection with the suitability of a designated default investment. Pursuant to the PPA, compliance with the qualified default investment alternative (QDIA) requirements can help to limit those fiduciary concerns. (See Q 9:86.) As a result, interest in automatic enrollment policies has started to rise and implementation of automatic enrollment policies is likely to continue to become more prevalent.

Q 9:11 Does an employer's vote in an insurance company demutualization cause the arrangement to become subject to ERISA?

No. In PWBA Opinion Letter 2001-03A, the DOL dealt with the issue of whether the exemption from ERISA is effected if an employer, as contract holder, votes on the approval of the demutualization and selects an allocation method for distributing the proceeds among employees covered by the group contract. The Opinion Letter was specifically addressed to the demutualization of the Prudential Insurance Company of America.

In reaching the conclusion that such action does not result in the arrangement becoming subject to ERISA, the DOL recognized that:

1. The actions of Prudential, independent of the employer, gave rise to the employer's need, as the titled group contract holder, to take action on behalf of the covered employees with regard to the demutualization;

2. The employer would be acting in accordance with specific provisions in New Jersey law governing the demutualization and pursuant to the requirements of Prudential's Plan of Reorganization that is being approved and supervised by the New Jersey Commissioner of Insurance; and

3. The vote on the demutualization and the decision on the method of allocation of proceeds thereunder are unique, one-time acts that do not involve the employer retaining any discretion regarding the ongoing administration or operation of the Section 403(b) arrangements.

Note. The Pension and Welfare Benefits Administration (PWBA) has been renamed the Employee Benefits Security Administration (EBSA). The name change became effective February 3, 2003.

Q 9:12   Is a Section 403(b) arrangement or plan required to be maintained as a written plan?

Yes. An ERISA Section 403(b) plan has historically been required to be established and maintained pursuant to a written document. This means that an ERISA Section 403(b) plan has had to be evidenced by a written document and administered in accordance with the terms of the written document. [ERISA § 402(a)(1)] The ERISA written plan document did not apply to non-ERISA plans, and the Code did not mandate a written plan document. The final Code Section 403(b) regulations, like the proposed regulations, promulgated by the IRS, introduce a written plan requirement effective January 1, 2009. [Treas. Reg. §§ 1.403(b)-3(b)(3), 1.403(b)-3(d)(1)(i), 1.403(b)-3(d)(1)(ii)] The written plan must contain material plan terms and conditions, including eligibility, contributions, applicable limitations, the contracts and accounts available under the plan, and the time and form under which benefits are distributable.

Failure to operate a plan in accordance with its terms could adversely affect all of the contracts issued by the employer to the employee or employees with respect to whom the operational failure occurred. The Code Section 403(b) plan requirement applies to both ERISA plans and non-ERISA plans, including governmental plans, church plans, and plans that are exempt from ERISA under DOL Regulation Section 2510.3-2(f).

Q 9:13   Do the Section 403(b) regulations mandate use of a single plan document?

No. The regulations do not require a single written plan document. The IRS has made it clear that the written plan requirement does not mandate use of a single plan document. The requirement can be satisfied by bundling more than one document. The written plan can be comprised of separate documents and separate contracts, and may incorporate other documents by reference, such as an annuity contract and custodial agreement. However, the employer is obligated to ensure that there are no conflicts among the documents.

Use of multiple documents can pose challenges. In particular, reliance on multiple documents generally may pose operational compliance challenges, and reliance on multiple contracts from multiple funding vehicles may pose challenges of ensuring consistency between and among the documents. It is imperative that the terms of the written plan and the terms of underlying annuity contracts used as funding vehicles under the plan align. In the event of a conflict, the terms of the plan will control. But, an annuity contract provides legally binding rights and obligations. A conflict could thereby cause a plan to fail to comply with operational compliance requirements and could carry taxable consequences with regard to funds held under the contact.

Q 9:14   Is either a governmental plan or a church plan subject to ERISA?

As a general rule, neither a governmental plan, as defined in ERISA Section 3(32), nor a church plan, as defined in ERISA Section 3(33), is subject to Title I of ERISA.

A governmental plan is a plan established or maintained for its employees by the government of the United States, by the government of any state or political subdivision thereof, or by any agency or instrumentality of any of the foregoing. It also includes certain plans to which the Railroad Retirement Act of 1935 or 1937 applies. [ERISA §§ 3(32), 4(b)(1)]

A church plan is a plan established or maintained for its employees by a church or by a convention or association of churches that is exempt from tax under Code Section 501. The definition of a church plan includes specific requirements for identifying employees of the church and employees who are employed in connection with an unrelated trade or business. In certain instances, church-controlled organizations might also qualify for the church exemption. [ERISA §§ 3(33), 4(b)(2)]

If a church or convention or association of churches that maintains any church plan makes an election under Code Section 410(d), then various Code requirements, including participation, vesting, and funding requirements, would apply. Such an election, if made, is irrevocable.

Vesting

Q 9:15   What vesting schedules are available to a Section 403(b) arrangement with regard to employee contributions?

An employee's rights in his or her accrued benefits derived from salary reduction contributions must be nonforfeitable at all times. [ERISA § 203(a)(1)]

Q 9:16   What vesting schedules are available to an ERISA 403(b) plan with regard to employer contributions?

An employee's rights to his or her accrued benefits derived from all employer contributions must be subject to one of the following accelerated vesting schedules:

1. *Three-year vesting.* An employee who completes three years of service has a non-forfeitable right to 100 percent of the employee's accrued benefits derived from employer contributions.

2. *Two- to six-year vesting.* An employee has a nonforfeitable right to 20 percent of the employee's accrued benefits derived from employer contributions for each year of service beginning with the participant's second year of service and ending with 100 percent after six years of service.

3. *Alternative vesting.* An employee has a nonforfeitable right to a percentage of the employee's accrued benefits derived from employer contributions in accordance with a schedule that is at least as generous as one of the foregoing schedules.

EGTRRA had previously changed the law to apply the above vesting schedules to employer matching contributions. The Pension Protection Act of 2006 (PPA) subsequently subjected all employer contributions to the vesting schedule requirements referenced above for contributions for plan years beginning on or after January 1, 2007. The slower five-year vesting schedule or three-to-seven-year vesting schedule that had been permitted under prior law may continue to be applied to employer non-matching contributions made for plan years beginning before January 1, 2007. However, a plan that continues to apply the slower vesting schedules for those employer non-matching contributions made for plan years beginning before January 1, 2007 would face the potentially burdensome administrative practice of maintaining dual vesting schedules for a period of years.

Special rules apply to governmental and church plans.

Q 9:17   Are there special vesting issues that apply to a Section 403(b) plan?

After many years of debate, the IRS determined in 1995 that a contribution made under Code Section 403(b) is deemed "made" for Code Section 415 purposes at the time the contribution is initially made, rather than in the year the contribution vests. [*See* IRS Ann. 95-33 (Apr. 17, 1995)]

The final Code Section 403(b) regulations clarify that if employer contributions to a Section 403(b) plan are not vested at the time of contribution, the annuity contract to which those contributions are made will be treated as a contract to which Code Section 403(c) applies. Nonetheless, the contract would not be taxable under Code Section 403(c) principles, provided that at all times the contract otherwise satisfies the requirements of Code Section 403(b). Pursuant to the regulations, the contract would become treated as a Section 403(b) contract at the time that the employee's interest becomes nonforfeitable.

If the interests of a particular employee are partially vested, then the contract would be treated as bifurcated such that the vested portion would be deemed a Section 403(b) contract and the non-vested portion would be treated as a contract to which Code Section 403(c) applies.

Joint and Survivor Annuity Requirements

Q 9:18   Is a Section 403(b) plan subject to the joint and survivor annuity requirements of ERISA?

If a Section 403(b) plan is subject to ERISA, the joint and survivor annuity rules of ERISA Section 205 will apply. A Section 403(b) plan not subject to ERISA would not be subject to these rules, because the Code requirements on joint and survivor annuities do not apply to Section 403(b) plans. A Section 403(b) plan that is structured as a money purchase plan clearly would be subject to the joint and survivor annuity requirements. Even a Section 403(b) plan that is structured like a profit-sharing plan with a discretionary contribution is likely to be subject to the joint and survivor annuity requirements, due to the structure of the annuity contracts. There is a stronger argument that discretionary contribution plans using only a custodial agreement may not be subject to the joint and survivor annuity requirements. The law is unclear, however.

Q 9:19   What spousal rights are afforded by ERISA Section 205?

A Section 403(b) plan that is subject to ERISA is required to provide (1) accrued benefits payable to a vested, married participant who does not die before the annuity starting date in the form of a qualified joint and survivor annuity (in the case of a single participant, these benefits must be payable in the form of a single-life annuity), and (2) accrued benefits payable to a vested, married participant who dies before the annuity starting date in the form of a qualified preretirement survivor annuity to the surviving spouse.

Generally, spousal consent is required for a married participant to receive benefits in any form other than a joint and survivor annuity. Spousal consent is not required in the case of an automatic cash-out of an account whose value is equal to or less than $5,000. Final regulations, effective in 2000, eliminated the look-back rule for most distributions and allow a mandatory distribution of an account value of $5,000 or less, even though that participant's account value may have exceeded $5,000 at an earlier distribution date. However, the look-back rule is not eliminated if the participant is receiving a distribution of an optional form of benefit under which at least one scheduled payment is still payable. Spousal consent is also not required if it is established to the satisfaction of a plan representative that there is no spouse, the spouse cannot be located, or the plan participant is legally separated or the participant has been abandoned (within the meaning of local law) and the participant has a court order to such effect.

A plan may also provide that a qualified joint and survivor annuity and a qualified preretirement survivor annuity will not be provided if the participant and the spouse have not been married throughout the one-year period ending on the earlier of (1) the participant's annuity starting date or (2) the date of the participant's death. [ERISA § 205(g); Treas. Reg. § 1.401(a)-20]

Participation Requirements

Q 9:20   Is a Section 403(b) plan subject to participation requirements for employer contributions?

Section 403(b) plans subject to ERISA are required to provide for minimum participation standards under ERISA Section 202(a). These provisions are similar to those that apply under Code Section 410(a). While Section 403(b) plans are not subject to Code Section 410(a), similar provisions apply under ERISA Section 202. The impact of ERISA Section 202 may not be readily apparent in the case of a plan that excludes employees who normally work less than 20 hours per week. Frequently an excluded employee who normally works less than 20 hours per week will work less than 1,000 hours in the applicable 12-month computation period. But in the case of an employee who normally works less than 20 hours per week yet exceeds the 1,000 hour threshold, exclusion of the employee could inadvertently cause the plan to violate the ERISA minimum participation requirements.

Q 9:21   What are the minimum participation requirements that apply to employer contributions under ERISA?

A pension plan may not require, as a condition of participation, that an employee complete a period of service with the employer maintaining the plan extending beyond the later of (1) the date on which the employee attains the age of 21 or (2) the date on which he or she completes one year of service.

There is an exception in the case of any plan that provides that after no more than two years of service each participant has a right to 100 percent of his or her accrued benefit under the plan. In that case, the waiting period can be two years of service instead of one year of service. In addition, where a plan is maintained exclusively for employees of an educational organization (as defined in Code Section 170(p)(1)(A)(ii)) and has 100 percent vesting after one year of service, the age may be 26 instead of 21. However, this exception may not be used if the two-year exception is used.

Q 9:22   May a Section 403(b) plan exclude participation of an employee based on his or her age when hired?

No. ERISA Section 202(a)(1)(A)(2) prohibits this.

Q 9:23   When the participation requirement refers to years of service, what is meant by years of service?

A year of service refers to a 12-month period during which the employee has not less than 1,000 hours of service. Such a period is measured with reference to the date on which the employee's employment commenced, except that the measurement period may shift thereafter to the first day of the plan year and the measurement to a plan-year basis if the employee does not complete 1,000 hours of service during the initial 12-month period.

Q 9:24   Once the employee has met the minimum age and service requirements, when must he or she be entitled to participate in the Section 403(b) plan with regard to employer contributions?

An employee who satisfies the minimum age and service requirements must be entitled to commence participation in the plan no later than the earlier of (1) the first day of the first plan year beginning after the date on which the employee satisfied such requirements or (2) the date six months after the date on which he or she satisfied such requirements.

Death Benefit Beneficiary Designations

Q 9:25   May a participant in a Section 403(b) plan that is subject to ERISA designate a death benefit beneficiary other than his or her spouse?

A married participant may designate a death benefit beneficiary other than his or her spouse, with proper spousal consent, subject to particular limitations in the case of a participant who has not yet attained age 35 (see Q 9:26). The spouse of a married participant is entitled to be named the beneficiary with regard to the actuarial equivalent value of the qualified joint and survivor annuity interest. A married participant can, of course, designate his or her spouse as the beneficiary with regard to an amount greater than the actuarial equivalent value of the qualified joint and survivor annuity interest. If a married participant decides to designate a nonspousal beneficiary with regard to any amount greater than 50 percent of such vested value, the result of which would be to provide the spouse with an amount less than the actuarial equivalent value of the qualified joint and survivor annuity interest, the designation of the nonspousal beneficiary of the portion in excess of 50 percent will be effective only with proper spousal consent.

Q 9:26   What is the effect of a participant's age on his or her ability to make an effective beneficiary designation for his or her death benefits?

A married participant generally may designate a nonspousal beneficiary, with spousal consent, only on or after the first day of the plan year in which the participant attains age 35. A plan may, however, provide for an earlier nonspousal designation, provided that such waiver becomes null and void at the beginning of the plan year in which the participant's 35th birthday occurs. In order to provide for a continued nonspousal designation, a participant who attains his or her 35th birthday would have to make a new designation, with spousal consent, after the date the prior designation becomes null and void. Notwithstanding the age 35 limitation, any participant who incurs a termination of employment may make an effective nonspousal designation without regard to age. [Treas. Reg. § 1.401-(a)(20)]

Amendments

Q 9:27   Must a prospective cutback of benefits under a Section 403(b) plan be preceded by an ERISA Section 204(h) notice?

ERISA Section 204(h) requires a plan administrator to provide advance written notice, commonly referred to as a 204(h) notice, in the event of an amendment to an applicable pension plan that provides for a significant reduction in the rate of future benefit accrual. The Economic Growth and Tax Relief Reconciliation Act of 2001 (EGTRRA) revised ERISA Section 204(h) and added Section 4980F to the Internal Revenue Code. Code Section 4980F imposes a tax on the failure of an applicable pension plan to provide advance written notice in the event of an amendment to the plan that provides for a significant reduction in the rate of future benefit accrual. It appears that these rules do not apply to a Section 403(b) plan because the revised rules, including those under the proposed regulation, apply only to a defined benefit plan and to an individual account plan that is subject to the minimum funding standards of Code Section 412. Final regulations issued by the DOL in April 2003 clarify that ERISA Section 204(h), as revised, no longer applies to an individual account plan that is subject to the minimum funding standards of ERISA Section 302 but is not subject to the minimum funding standards of Code Section 412. This is the case with Section 403(b) plans. Indeed, the final regulations specify that the requirement does not apply to Section 403(b) plans.

Q 9:28   What is the significance of the ERISA Section 204(g) anticutback rule?

ERISA Section 204(g) prohibits an ERISA 403(b) plan from eliminating an optional form of benefit with regard to those benefits attributable to service performed prior to adoption of the amendment. A plan may be amended, however, to eliminate an optional form of benefit on a prospective basis.

While the language of ERISA Section 204(g) appears to be clear, in two scenarios its impact may not be readily apparent. First, in the case of a plan that in the past has changed funding vehicles or in the future intends to do so, ERISA Section 204(g) requires the plan to preserve the optional forms of benefits offered by the prior funding vehicle or funding vehicles with regard to those benefits that accrued during the time those forms of benefit had been offered. The second, and perhaps less apparent, scenario involves the case where a Section 403(b) plan permits participants to move assets into the plan from a prior plan. In such a case, the receiving Section 403(b) plan may permit the participant's assets to move into the plan either by means of a transfer or by means of a rollover. Where the plan permits transfers into the plan, ERISA Section 204(g) would apply, and the receiving plan would have to preserve the optional forms of benefits with regard to transferred assets. Where the plan permits movements of assets into the plan by means of rollover, however, ERISA Section 204(g) would not apply. Thus, from an administrative standpoint of dealing with ERISA Section 204(g), frequently it has been more desirable to limit asset movement to rollovers and to bar the availability of transfers between plans.

Congress, the Department of the Treasury, and the IRS recognized the practical problems employers faced complying with ERISA Section 204(g). After concluding that payment forms could be replicated in a meaningful way through alternative means, they determined that the cost of compliance and the administrative burdens placed on employers outweighed the benefits individuals gained from a plan preserving the optional forms of benefit.

EGTRRA codified recent regulatory relaxation of the anticutback rule. Pursuant to the modifications, a defined contribution plan to which benefits are transferred will not be treated as violating the anticutback rule of Code Section 411(d)(6), or the parallel Section 204(g) of ERISA, merely because the transferee plan does not provide some or all of the forms of distribution previously available under the transferor plan if:

1. The plan receives a direct transfer of the participant's or beneficiary's accrued benefits, or the plan results from a merger or other transaction that has the effect of a direct transfer (including consolidations of benefits attributable to different employers within a multiple employer plan);

2. The terms of both the transferor plan and the transferee plan authorize the transfer;

3. The transfer occurs pursuant to a voluntary election by the participant or beneficiary that is made after the participant or beneficiary received a notice describing the consequences of making the election; and

4. The transferee plan allows the participant or beneficiary to receive any distribution to which the participant or beneficiary is entitled under the transferee plan in the form of a single-sum distribution.

Except to the extent provided by regulations, a defined contribution plan similarly will not be treated as violating Code Section 411(d)(6), or the parallel Section 204(g) of ERISA, merely because the plan is amended to eliminate a form of distribution previously available under the plan if:

1. A single-sum distribution is available to the participant at the same time or times as the form of distribution being eliminated; and

2. The single-sum distribution is based on the same or greater portion of the participant's accrued benefit as the form of distribution being eliminated by the amendment.

Final regulations released in 2005 specify the requirements that a plan sponsor must follow in order to eliminate an optional form of benefit without violating the anticutback rules under the Internal Revenue Code. As expected, the final regulations removed an advance notice requirement, thereby allowing a plan sponsor to more easily eliminate optional distribution forms. Plans subject to ERISA will still need to continue to communicate any such plan amendment by means of a timely distributed summary of material modifications or an updated summary plan description.

Q 9:29   Is the enforceability of a Section 403(b) plan amendment subject to compliance with ERISA Section 402(b)(3)?

An ERISA 403(b) plan document should contain a specific amendment procedure that not only reserves the right to amend and terminate the plan, but also identifies the person or entity with authority to do so and the procedure for doing so. The U.S. Supreme Court reversed a decision by the Third Circuit that effectively would have required that a reservation of authority to amend specifically identify the committee or individual(s) with authority to amend rather than simply refer to the employer or "the Company." [Schoonejongen v. Curtiss-Wright Corp., 18 F.3d 1034 (3d Cir. 1994), *rev'd and remanded*, 131 L. Ed. 2d 625 (1995)] Although the Supreme Court reversed the Third Circuit decision and held that a reservation to the "Company" sufficed, it is nevertheless advisable to be specific in the plan documents. In addition, the summary plan description should ideally provide sufficient information so that the names of the individuals serving in the relevant capacities can be ascertained.

In *Schoonejongen v. Curtiss-Wright Corp.*, the Third Circuit had refused to recognize the validity of a plan amendment that would have terminated retiree health benefits, pointing to the failure of the plan document to set forth a specific amendment procedure. The Third Circuit had held that in order to implement a reserved right to amend the plan, the plan document was first required, in accordance with ERISA Section 402(b)(3), to contain an amendment procedure identifying the individual or entity having authority to amend the plan and the procedure for doing so.

The Supreme Court ruled that it sufficed if the plan documents broadly reserved to the "Company" the right to amend. The Supreme Court's opinion is in accord with most lower court decisions before the Third Circuit decision in

Curtiss-Wright. These prior cases held that where a plan document unambiguously reserves the right of a plan sponsor to amend or terminate a plan, the right to do so may be implemented. [*See, e.g.,* Alday v. Container Corp., 906 F.2d 660 (11th Cir. 1990), *cert. denied,* 498 US 1026 (1991); Moore v. Metropolitan Life Ins. Co., 856 F.2d 488 (2d Cir. 1988); Musto v. American Gen. Corp., 861 F.2d 897 (6th Cir. 1988), *cert. denied,* 490 U.S. 1020 (1989)]

Although the Supreme Court's holding in *Curtiss-Wright* has largely removed the risks from not being specific in a reservation of rights, plan sponsors should consider implementing the following measures:

- The plan document for every employee benefit plan should contain a specific amendment procedure. This can be accomplished by identifying the person or entity with amendment authority and the manner in which an amendment must be made. As a precautionary measure, the entity with amendment authority should not be identified merely as the "Company" or the "Employer," but as a specific body or committee (for example, the board of directors, the pension committee, or the plan administrator). Participants should also be furnished with (or, at a minimum, have access to) sufficient information to ascertain the names of the individuals serving in these capacities. This information should be contained in the plan document and communicated in the plan's summary plan description. Even though the Supreme Court has acknowledged that less specificity will suffice, it is better to be specific.

- The procedure for implementing an amendment should be specifically indicated in the plan document and the SPD. Even according to the Third Circuit in *Curtiss-Wright,* a plan that does not at present have an amendment procedure can be amended to include such a procedure by "formal action of those who possess the sponsor's final management authority. . . ."

Bonding and Plan Assets

Q 9:30   What bonding requirements apply to an ERISA 403(b) plan?

As a general rule, every fiduciary of an employee benefit plan and every person who handles funds or other property of such a plan must be bonded. It is unlawful for any person who must be bonded to receive, handle, disburse, or otherwise exercise custody or control of any plan funds or other property without being properly bonded. [ERISA § 412]

Nevertheless, the DOL may exempt a plan from the bonding requirements where it finds that either other bonding arrangements or the overall financial condition of the plan would be adequate to protect the interests of the beneficiaries and participants.

Q 9:31   When do contributions to a Section 403(b) plan become plan assets for purposes of the bonding requirements?

In 1985, the DOL published temporary regulations addressing the point at which any given item becomes "funds or other property" of the plan for purposes of the bonding requirements. The regulations provide that contributions to a plan normally become funds or other property of the plan if and when they are taken out of the general assets of the employer and segregated in some manner, paid over to a corporate trustee, or used to purchase benefits from an insurance carrier or service or other organization. If no such segregation from the general assets is made of monies to be turned over to a corporate trustee or insurance company prior to actual transmittal of such monies, the contributions become funds or other property of the plan at the time of transmittal. In such a case, the funds or other property of the plan would not normally be subject to handling, and bonding would not be required for any person with respect to the purchase of such benefits. However, if the particular arrangement was such that monies derived from, or by virtue of, the contract did subsequently flow back to the plan, bonding may be required if such monies returning to the plan are handled by plan administrators or other individuals. [D.O.L. Temp. Reg. § 2580.412-5]

Q 9:32   Is a bond required of a fiduciary that is a trust company or of an insurance company?

Generally, no bond is required of a fiduciary that is a trust company or an insurance company that is subject to supervision or examination by federal or state authority and has combined capital and surplus of $1 million (or such higher amount as prescribed by the Secretary of Labor). Bonding may be required, however, with regard to other fiduciaries. [ERISA § 412(a)(2)]

Q 9:33   Do the plan asset rules apply to an ERISA 403(b) plan?

Yes. Any Section 403(b) plan that is an ERISA plan is subject to the plan asset rules.

Under the plan asset rules, amounts that a participant has withheld from his or her wages for contributions to a plan become assets of the plan as of the date on which these amounts can reasonably be separated from the employer's general assets, but in no event later than the 15th business day of the month following the month in which these amounts would otherwise have been payable to the participant in cash. The determination of what constitutes a reasonable period is based on the facts and circumstances, including the employer's current practices. [D.O.L. Reg. § 2510.3-102(a)] The maximum time period may be extended for 10 days if the following conditions are met:

1. A true and accurate written notice is given to all plan participants within five business days after the end of such extension period stating that the employer has elected to take the extension, that the affected contributions have been transmitted to the plan, and particularly, the reason that the

employer cannot reasonably timely segregate the salary reduction contribution within the prescribed time period;

2. Prior to such extension period, a performance bond or an irrevocable letter of credit in favor of the plan must be obtained; and

3. Within five business days after the end of the extension period, a copy of the notice must be provided to the Secretary of Labor, together with a certification as to distributions and the obtaining of the bond or letter of credit.

The extension may not be used more than twice in any plan year unless interest is paid on the contributions that were subject to the extensions.

The final Code Section 403(b) regulations impose a less rigid requirement than the ERISA requirement, and should therefore not have a meaningful impact on ERISA plans. The Treasury regulations mandate that contributions to the plan must become plan assets within a period that is no longer than is reasonable for proper administration of the plan. Only by way of example do the regulations provide that 15 business days following the month in which these amounts would otherwise have been paid to the participant would be a reasonable period.

Disclosure and Reporting

Q 9:34 What is a *summary plan description*?

A *summary plan description* (SPD) is an understandable and detailed summary description of an employee benefit plan's provisions that must be provided to plan participants and beneficiaries. The importance of SPDs cannot be overstated. As a practical matter, the SPD is often the only document provided to participants summarizing the salient features of a plan. For this reason, SPDs are usually at the center of benefit and plan communication disputes.

ERISA and the various DOL regulations impose numerous requirements as to the information that must be included in an SPD. [ERISA §§ 102(a)(1), 102(b); D.O.L. Reg. §§ 2520.102-2, 2520.102-3]

The regulations contain a laundry list of items and information that must be included in the SPD:

- The plan's eligibility requirements for participation and benefits
- A description of provisions regarding nonforfeitable benefits
- A statement identifying the circumstances that may result in disqualification or ineligibility for benefits, or in denial, loss, forfeiture, or suspension of benefits that a participant or beneficiary might otherwise reasonably expect the plan to provide
- A foreign-language notice offering foreign-language assistance and explaining the procedures for obtaining such assistance if (1) the plan has fewer than 100 participants and 25 percent or more of such participants are

literate only in the same foreign language, or (2) the plan has more than 100 participants and the lesser of 500 (or more) or 10 percent of the participants are literate only in the same foreign language [D.O.L. Reg. § 2520.102-2(c)]

- The name of the plan and, if different, the name by which the plan is commonly known by its participants and beneficiaries
- The type of plan and the type of plan administration
- The name and address of the entity that maintains the plan
- The name and address of the plan's agent for service of legal process, as well as a statement that service may be made upon the plan administrator
- The name, business address, and telephone number of the plan administrator
- The names, titles, and addresses of the principal place of business of each funding agent
- The plan's vesting provisions, age and service requirements, and normal retirement age [D.O.L. Adv. Op. No. 85-05A (Feb. 5, 1985)]
- A description of procedures governing qualified domestic relations orders or, alternatively, a statement regarding how to obtain a copy of such procedures
- If applicable, a statement that the plan is maintained pursuant to one or more collective bargaining agreements and that the agreements may be obtained by participants and beneficiaries upon written request or are available for inspection
- The source of contributions to the plan
- The identity of any funding medium or organization through which benefits are provided
- The date of the end of the plan year
- The basis on which plan records are maintained (e.g., calendar or fiscal year)
- The employer identification number assigned to the plan by the IRS and the plan number
- The plan's claims review and appeals procedures
- The plan's requirements concerning eligibility for participation and benefits
- A statement of ERISA rights (the DOL has provided a model statement)
- A statement concerning termination insurance coverage
- A description of how and when the plan may be terminated and of benefits, rights, and obligations of participants and beneficiaries on termination (including a summary of the disposition of plan assets on termination) [DOL ERISA Tech. Rel. 84-1 (May 4, 1984)]
- A description of any joint and survivor benefits and requirements concerning election

[D.O.L. Reg. § 2520.102-3]

In general, SPDs must contain information that is "sufficiently accurate and comprehensive to reasonably apprise such participants and beneficiaries of their rights and obligations under the plan." [ERISA § 102(a)(1)]

The law does not require that SPDs contain information specifically tailored to each participant's individual situation. Rather, an SPD should focus on describing general rules in a comprehensible and understandable manner. [Maxa v. John Alden Life Ins. Co., 972 F.2d 980, 985 (8th Cir. 1992), *cert. denied*, 113 S. Ct. 1048 (1993); *see also* Bowerman v. Wal-Mart Stores, Inc., 226 F.3d 574, 590 (7th Cir. 2000), and Watson v. Deaconess Waltham Hosp., 298 F.3d 102, 115 (1st Cir. 2002)]

Q 9:35   Is a plan administrator required to distribute an SPD?

The plan administrator of an ERISA 403(b) plan is required to distribute an SPD. A non-ERISA 403(b) arrangement is not required to have an SPD.

Title I of ERISA requires the plan administrator to furnish each participant in the plan and each beneficiary who is receiving benefits under the plan with an SPD. The SPD must be furnished within 90 days after an individual becomes a participant or first receives benefits as a beneficiary or, generally in the case of a new plan, within 120 days of the earlier date the plan is established or becomes subject to ERISA. Amendments to a plan must be followed by a summary of material modifications within 210 days after the end of the plan year in which the change was adopted. The plan administrator must also furnish an updated SPD every five years which reflects all plan amendments adopted during the interim period. If there have been no amendments, the five-year period is extended to ten years.

Plan administrators are required to use measures "reasonably calculated to ensure actual receipt" of the SPD by plan participants and beneficiaries. Where the plan's method of distribution is reasonable, the plan administrator is not required to prove actual receipt of the SPD by participants.

Prior to enactment of the Taxpayer Relief Act of 1997 (TRA '97), ERISA required administrators of plans that were subject to the reporting and disclosure requirements of ERISA to automatically file SPDs and summaries of material modifications with the DOL in a timely manner. TRA '97 eliminated this requirement. Instead, plan administrators are required to file these (and related) documents with the DOL only upon the request of the DOL. Failure to comply within 30 days of the request can result in civil penalties of up to $110 per day. [ERISA §§ 101, 102, 104, 502(c)(1), 502(c)(6); D.O.L. Reg. §§ 2520.102-2, 2520.104A-3, 2520.104A-4, 2520.104B-1, 2520.104B-2, 2575.502C-1]

Q 9:36   How must an SPD communicate the required information?

As an additional requirement, SPDs must be "written in a manner calculated to be understood by the average plan participant." [ERISA § 102(a)(1); D.O.L. Reg.

§ 2520.102-2(a)] This means plain English, wherever possible, except where a foreign language is required. One problem area is the issue of boilerplate provisions. The DOL has prescribed standard language for the "ERISA rights statements," which should be included without substantial changes in every SPD. [D.O.L. Reg. § 2520.102-2(t)] Moreover, the claims procedure must be described in the SPD. Whenever standard language is added to communications, it should be reviewed by people familiar with the audience, as well as by legal counsel.

Q 9:37 Does a disclaimer in an SPD, stating that the plan documents govern, negate inaccuracies in the SPD?

Considering the comprehensive nature of the information that is required to be provided in SPDs, there should not be, in theory, any inconsistencies between the SPD and the plan document. However, SPDs often contain disclaimer provisions to the effect that, in the event of any inconsistency between the plan and the SPD, the plan will govern.

Even though this type of disclaimer is frequently found in SPDs and the law is not fully settled, a significant line of case law holds that "[w]here . . . the terms of a plan and those of a plan summary conflict, it is the plan summary that controls." [Burstein v. Ret. Plan for Employees of Allegheny Health Educ. and Research, 334 F.3d 365, 379 (3d Cir. 2003) (SPD stating how benefits would vest controlled); Washington v. Murphy Oil USA, Inc., 497 F.3d 453, 458–459 (5th Cir. 2007) (SPD providing that vesting occurred upon completion of five years controlled); Burke v. Kodak Ret. Plan, 336 F.3d 103, 110 (2d Cir. 2003); Heidgerd v. Olin Corp., 906 F.2d 903, 908 (2d Cir. 1990) (severance pay plan document referred to restriction not described in SPD); *see also* Feifer v. Prudential Ins. Co., 306 F.3d 1202 (2d Cir. 2002) (plan summary providing for long-term disability payments without offsets, controlled for duration plan summary was in circulation); Bergt v. Retirement Plan for Pilots Employed by Mark Air, Inc., 293 F.3d 1139 (9th Cir. 2002) (where plan document and SPD conflict, term favorable to employee will prevail; contract term construed against the drafter)]

Although a limited number of cases have upheld the power of disclaimers, the trend appears to be toward their invalidation. [Helwig v. Kelsey-Hayes Co., 93 F.3d 243, 249 (6th Cir. 1996) (disclaimer ineffective against SPD's promise of lifetime health coverage); Manginaro v. Welfare Fund of Local 771, 21 F. Supp. 2d 284, 296 (S.D.N.Y. 1998) (plan shortened limitation on actions omitted from SPD held not enforceable despite disclaimer)] Therefore, it is important that all plan communications, including SPDs, be reviewed periodically for consistency with plan documents.

As an added measure, a plan fiduciary may wish to distribute plan documents to plan participants. In reviewing inaccurate SPD language, several courts have found that the plan document controlled where it was distributed to the plan participants because the participants seeking relief could not be said to have relied upon the SPD. [Chiles v. Ceridian Corp., 95 F.3d 1505 (10th Cir. 1996); Aiken v. Policy Management Systems Corp., 13 F.3d 138, 141–142 (4th Cir. 1993)]

Q 9:38   Should an SPD expressly reserve the right to interpret the terms of the plan?

Yes. In drafting an SPD, plan fiduciaries should ensure that the SPD contains language reserving to a specified fiduciary (for example, the plan administrator) the sole and absolute discretionary authority to interpret the terms of the plan, determine benefit eligibility, and resolve ambiguities or inconsistencies in the plan. Inclusion of such language will protect fiduciary decisions from judicial scrutiny under a *de novo* standard of review and ensure that courts will apply the more lenient arbitrary and capricious standard of review. [Firestone Tire & Rubber Co v. Bruch, 489 U.S. 101 (1989)]

Q 9:39   Should an SPD expressly reserve the right to amend or terminate the plan?

Yes. The SPD should also contain sufficient language granting to a specified entity, board, committee, or individual (such as the board of directors or an authorized committee) the sole and absolute discretionary authority to amend or terminate the plan (in whole or in part) and to change or discontinue the type and amount of benefits offered by the plan and the rules for benefit eligibility, at any time and for any reason. This is a settlor function (see Qs 9:61–9:63).

Q 9:40   What methods of distribution does ERISA require to satisfy its reporting and disclosure requirements?

Where certain material is required to be furnished by operation of law, or upon request, the plan administrator must use measures reasonably calculated to ensure actual receipt of the material by participants and beneficiaries. [D.O.L. Reg. § 2520.104b-1] The plan administrator, as defined in ERISA Section 3(16)(A), is responsible for providing the required communications. [ERISA §§ 101(a), 104(b)]

Material that is required to be furnished upon written request to the administrator should be mailed to the address provided by the requesting individual or personally delivered. [D.O.L. Reg. § 2520.104b-1(b)(2)]

Material that is required to be furnished to all participants (and all beneficiaries receiving benefits under a plan) "must be sent by a method or methods of delivery likely to result in full distribution." In-hand delivery to employees at their worksites is an acceptable method of distribution. It is also acceptable to insert the information in a periodical or publication (for example, a union newsletter or employer publication), provided that the plan's distribution list is comprehensive and up to date and that there is a prominent notice on the front of the publication as to the inclusion of the information. However, "stacking" the material at a specified location (such as a plan office, union hall or office, or worksite) is not an acceptable method of distribution.

Material may be mailed by first-, second-, or third-class mail. However, distribution by third-class mail is acceptable only if return and forwarding postage is guaranteed and address correction is requested. Moreover, any letter that is returned with an address correction must be re-sent by first-class mail or personally delivered. [D.O.L. Reg. § 2520.104b-1(b)(1)]

The DOL issued final regulations in April 2002 addressing standards for the disclosure of employee benefit information, including SPDs and summaries of material modifications (SMMs), by means of electronic media. This information may be distributed to participants who have effective access to electronic documents at their workplace. The regulations also require that a plan participant affirmatively consent to receive the specified documents in this manner.

Q 9:41 Must the plan administrator provide benefit statements to participants and beneficiaries?

The PPA amended ERISA Section 105(a)(1)(A) to require pension benefits statements to be furnished at least once each calendar quarter if the participant or beneficiary has the right to direct the investment of assets or otherwise has his or her own account under the plan. In other situations, such as a defined benefit plan, the requirement only applies upon written request.

The statement must indicate the total benefits accrued, which portion is nonforfeitable, if any, and the earliest date on which the benefits will vest. It must also include the value of each investment. If the participant or beneficiary has the right to direct the investment, the notice must include an explanation of the limitations or restrictions or the right to direct and the importance of a well balanced and diversified investment portfolio, including a statement of the risk that holding more than 20 percent of a portfolio in the security of one entity may not be adequately diversified. The notice must also refer the participant or beneficiary to the DOL Web site for sources of information on individual investing and diversification.

All explanations must be written in a manner to be understood by the average plan participant.

The EBSA has issued Field Guidance 2006-3 and 2007-3 permitting good-faith compliance with the law until regulations are issued. The DOL acknowledges that use of multiple statements from different sources can satisfy the statement requirement. It also notes that in addition to the electronic delivery requirements of DOL Regulations Section 2520.104b-1, statements can be delivered in accordance with Treasury Regulations Section 1.401(a)-21.

The plan administrator may also deliver statements through secure Web sites if there is continuous access to such statements provided that the participants and beneficiaries receive notification that explain such availability and that they can request and obtain, free of charge, a paper version. Field Bulletin 2006-3 also contains a model notice as to the investment cautions and prescribes the DOL Web site, http://www.dol.gov/ebsa/investing.html.

Q 9:42   Is a Form 5500 annual return required to be filed on behalf of a Section 403(b) plan?

An ERISA 403(b) plan is required to have a Form 5500 annual return filed. Responsibility for filing lies with either the employer or the plan administrator. A non-ERISA 403(b) plan is not subject to this requirement.

The Form 5500 annual return is a report filed pursuant to both ERISA and the Code. The Form 5500 instructions indicate that a 403(b) plan maintained pursuant to either Code Section 403(b)(1) or Code Section 403(b)(7) is required to comply. The source of authority has differed depending upon the funding vehicles used by the plan. Treasury Regulations Section 301.6058-1(a)(2) provides that custodial accounts under Code Section 403(b)(7) are subject to the requirements and does not even address Code Section 403(b)(1). A Section 403(b)(1) plan, as well as a plan using Section 403(b)(7) custodial account funding, however, would be required to file under ERISA's filing requirements if such a plan is subject to Title I of ERISA. [Treas. Reg. § 301.6058-1(a)(2); ERISA §§ 104, 4065]

Q 9:43   What parts of Form 5500 must be completed on behalf of an ERISA 403(b) plan?

Beginning with the 2009 plan year, ERISA 403(b) plans will be subject to full Form 5500 disclosure requirements. On November 16, 2007, the DOL, the IRS, and the Pension Benefit Guaranty Corporation issued Form 5500 regulations that make numerous revisions to Form 5500 filing requirements, including subjecting ERISA 403(b) plans to the same annual reporting rules that apply to other ERISA covered pension plans.

Historically, Section 403(b) plans were generally subject to only limited Form 5500 reporting. A Section 403(b) plan was viewed less in the nature of a plan than an arrangement under which only an annuity would be purchased on behalf of an employee, or pursuant to which a mutual fund custodial account would be established on behalf of the employee. Amendments to Code Section 403(b) have gradually diminished the extent to which the rules governing Section 403(b) plans differ from the rules governing other employer based plans, most notably Section 401(k) plans. These and other contributing factors prompted the shift to expanded reporting requirements. The limited Form 5500 filing responsibilities with which ERISA 403(b) plans generally complied will no longer be sufficient beginning with the 2009 plan year.

Q 9:44   Is an ERISA 403(b) plan required to have an audit conducted?

Yes, beginning with the 2009 plan year, a large ERISA 403(b) plan, which is generally a plan with 100 or more participants as of the beginning of the plan year, will be required to have an independent audit conducted as part of its Form 5500 filing.

Q 9:45   Can a failure to timely file a Form 5500 be cured?

Yes, with limitations. The EBSA established the Delinquent Filer Voluntary Compliance Program (DFVC) to encourage, through the assessment of reduced civil penalties, delinquent plan administrators to comply with their annual reporting obligations under Title I of ERISA.

Under Section 502(c) of ERISA, the Secretary of Labor has the authority to assess civil penalties of up to $1,100 per day against plan administrators who fail or refuse to file complete and timely annual reports (Form 5500 Series Annual Return/Reports) as required under ERISA Section 101(b)(4). The program established by the EBSA provided that civil penalties for noncompliance with the annual reporting requirements may be assessed at $50 for each day that an annual report is filed after the date that it was required to be filed, without regard to any extensions. Plan administrators who fail to file an annual report may be assessed a penalty of $300 per day, up to $30,000 per year, until a complete annual report is filed. The DOL may waive all or part of a civil penalty assessed on an administrator's showing that there was reasonable cause for the failure to file a complete and timely annual report.

Plan administrators who fail to file timely annual reports for plan years beginning after 1987 may take advantage of the DFVC program by complying with filing requirements and paying the specified civil penalties. However, the DFVC program is not available to plan administrators who either: (1) have been notified in writing of the DOL's intention to assess a civil penalty under ERISA Section 502(c) for failure to file a timely annual report or (2) otherwise have been notified in writing by the DOL of a failure to file a timely annual report under Title I of ERISA.

Q 9:46   Does the Sarbanes-Oxley Act of 2002 apply to an ERISA 403(b) plan?

The Sarbanes-Oxley Act of 2002 [Pub. L. No. 107-204] amended ERISA to require plan administrators of individual account plans to provide written notice to affected participants and beneficiaries of any blackout period during which their rights to direct or diversify investments or obtain a loan or a distribution under a plan may be temporarily suspended, limited, or modified. The DOL has provided a model notice under Section 101(i) of ERISA as part of a final rule issued on January 24, 2003. The final rule also implements a civil penalty under Section 502 of ERISA, establishing a civil penalty applicable to a plan administrator's failure or refusal to provide notice of a blackout period. These provisions could apply to an ERISA 403(b) plan in a scenario whereby a change in the plan's funding vehicles or a change in the plan's recordkeeper results in the imposition of a temporary investment allocation limitation, or a loan or distribution restriction, on participants and beneficiaries.

The Sarbanes-Oxley Act also prohibits a director or officer from purchasing or selling during any blackout period any equity security of the company acquired in connection with his or her employment. Although these insider trading restrictions of the Sarbanes-Oxley Act appear to apply to an ERISA 403(b) plan, application of these restrictions seems to have no practical meaning in the context of a Section 403(b) plan because an employer maintaining a Section 403(b) plan does not issue public stock.

Compliance with Claims Procedures

Q 9:47 What is a benefits claim?

A benefits claim is a request made by or on behalf of a participant or beneficiary for plan benefits. [D.O.L. Reg. § 2560.503-1(e)]

Q 9:48 When is a benefits claim deemed filed?

Under regulations effective for claims filed beginning in 2002, every employee benefit plan is required to establish and follow reasonable procedures governing the filing of benefit claims, notification of benefit determinations, and appeal of adverse benefit determinations. [D.O.L. Reg. § 2560.503-1(b)] If a plan fails to establish or follow claims procedures consistent with the requirements of DOL Regulations Section 2560.503-1, a claimant shall be deemed to have exhausted the administrative remedies available under the plan and shall be entitled to pursue any remedy under ERISA Section 502(a) on the basis that the plan failed to provide a reasonable claims procedure that would yield a decision on the merits of the claim. [D.O.L. Reg. § 2560.503-1(1)] The time period for a determination begins when a claim is filed in accordance with the plan's reasonable procedures, without regard to whether all the necessary information accompanies the filing.

Q 9:49 Does an ERISA plan need explicit, written procedures for processing claims for benefits and reviewing the denial of claims?

ERISA generally requires a plan to provide adequate notice in writing of the denial of a claim for benefits and to give a reasonable opportunity for full and fair review of the decision denying the claim. [ERISA §§ 503(1), 503(2)]. The procedures for accomplishing these goals are commonly called claims procedures. DOL regulations provide the following guidelines for determining when claims procedures are reasonable:

- The procedures must be described in the SPD.
- The procedures must not contain any provision, or be administered in such a way, that unduly inhibits or hampers filing or processing a claim.
- The procedures must comply with the rules for claim procedures set forth in the DOL regulations.
- The procedures must specifically provide for certain written notices to participants and beneficiaries.

The DOL had issued proposed regulations in 1998 that broadly addressed claims procedures, notice requirements, and information that must be included in an SPD. The DOL subsequently issued final regulations, effective with respect to claims filed on or after January 1, 2002. Although they apply to all ERISA covered plans, the final regulations limit the scope of the aforementioned earlier modifications principally to group health plans and disability plans.

Q 9:50 When must a claimant be informed that a benefits claim has been denied?

A claimant whose claim is denied in whole or in part must be notified in writing within a reasonable time after the plan receives the claim, not to exceed 90 days. If an extension is required, the claimant must receive written notice of the extension before the end of the initial 90-day period. The notice must specify the circumstances requiring the extension and the date by which the plan expects to render the final decision. The extension cannot exceed 90 days from the end of the initial 90-day period.

If a plan fails to establish or follow claims procedures consistent with the requirements of Labor Regulations Section 2560.503-1, a claimant shall be deemed to have exhausted the administrative remedies available under the plan and shall be entitled to pursue any remedy under ERISA Section 502(a) on the basis that the plan failed to provide a reasonable claims procedure that would yield a decision on the merits of the claim.

Q 9:51 What information must a claim denial contain?

A written notice of claim denial issued by the plan administrator or insurer must give the following information in a manner calculated to be understood by the claimant:

1. The specific reason(s) the claim was denied;
2. Specific reference to the pertinent plan provisions on which the denial was based;
3. An explanation of what additional material or information is necessary, and why, for the claimant to perfect the claim; and
4. An explanation of the appeals procedure by which the claimant can submit the claim for review and the time limits applicable to such procedures, including a statement of the claimant's right to bring a civil action under ERISA Section 502(a).

[D.O.L. Reg. § 2560.503-1(g)]

Q 9:52 What are a claimant's procedural rights on an appeal of a claim denial?

The claimant must have at least 60 days after receipt of written notice of a claim denial to file a request for review of the denied claim. The claimant or an authorized representative must be permitted to make a written application to the plan requesting a review of the claim and must be permitted to review pertinent documents and submit issues and comments in writing. Plan procedures need not allow the claimant or a representative to appear in person; review of denied claims can be required to be made solely upon written submissions. Plan procedures must provide for a review that takes into account all comments, documents, and records submitted by the claimant relating to the claim, without regard to whether the information was submitted or considered in the initial review. [D.O.L. Reg. § 2560.503-1(h)]

Q 9:53   When must an appeal be decided?

Generally, a decision on appeal must be made within 60 days after the plan receives the request for review. If an extension is required, the claimant must receive written notice of the extension before the end of the initial 60-day period. The notice must specify the circumstances requiring the extension and the date by which the plan expects to render the final decision. The extension cannot exceed 60 days from the end of the initial 60-day period.

If the named fiduciary that has responsibility for reviewing claims is a committee or board that holds meetings at least quarterly and a claim is received at least 30 days in advance of the next meeting, the claim must be heard at the next meeting. If an extension is required, the decision must be made by the third meeting after initial receipt of the request for appeal. [D.O.L. Reg. § 2560.503-1(i)]

Q 9:54   What information must a decision on appeal contain?

A written notice of appeal denial issued by the named fiduciary for hearing appeals must give the following information in a manner calculated to be understood by the claimant:

1. The specific reason(s) the appeal was denied;
2. Specific reference to the pertinent plan provisions on which the denial was based;
3. A statement that the claimant is entitled to receive upon request and free of charge access to copies of information relevant to claimant's claim for benefits; and
4. A statement of the claimant's right to bring an action under ERISA Section 502(a).

[D.O.L. Reg. § 2560.503-1(j)]

Q 9:55   Can a fiduciary's compliance with claims procedures reduce the risk of fiduciary liability?

Yes. Ordinarily, if the plan documents contain reasonable claims procedures (including appeals procedures) and the plan fiduciary has complied with them, a claimant must first exhaust the administrative remedies provided under the claims procedures before suing for benefits. Absent unusual circumstances, a trial court should enter summary judgment against a plan participant or beneficiary who has failed to exhaust administrative remedies. [Summers v. UNUM Life Ins. Co. of America, 35 Fed. Appx. 489, 491 (9th Cir. 2002); Kross v. Western Elec. Co., 701 F.2d 1238 (7th Cir. 1983)] By contrast, a fiduciary's failure to comply with reasonable claims procedures (for example, by failing to communicate the reasons for a benefit denial) may result in the granting of a claimant's benefits by a court if the claimant has effectively been denied the opportunity for a full and fair review of the claim. [Halpin v. WW Grainger Inc., 962 F.2d 685 (7th Cir. 1992)]

Assignment or Alienation

Q 9:56   Can benefits under a Section 403(b) plan be assigned or alienated?

ERISA's anti-alienation rules generally prohibit the assignment or alienation of plan benefits. Exceptions exist under ERISA in the case of a qualified domestic relations order and plan loans. [ERISA §§ 206(d)(2), 206(d)(3)] TRA '97 modified the prohibition against assignment and alienation by carving out an additional exception. Pursuant to the modification, the prohibition against assignment or alienation will not apply to offset any offset of a participant's benefits provided under an employee pension plan against an amount the participant is required to pay to the plan pursuant to a court order arising from:

1. A judgment of conviction for a crime involving the plan;
2. A civil judgment (or consent order or decree) entered by a court in an action brought in connection with a breach (or alleged breach) of fiduciary duty under ERISA; or
3. A settlement agreement entered into by the participant and either the Secretary of Labor or the Pension Benefit Guaranty Corporation in connection with a breach (or alleged breach) of fiduciary duty under ERISA by a fiduciary or any other person.

The modification continues to maintain some protection for spouses of participants who are not involved in the crime or breach (or alleged breach) of fiduciary duty. [Pub. L. No. 105-34, § 1502(a), adding ERISA §§ 206(d)(4), 206(d)(5); Pub. L. No. 105-34, § 1502(b), adding I.R.C. §§ 401(a)(13)(C), 401(a)(13)(D)]

Fiduciary Matters

Q 9:57   Is a Section 403(b) plan subject to ERISA's fiduciary rules?

Yes. Any Section 403(b) plan that is subject to ERISA (see Qs 9:1–9:8) will be subject to the fiduciary rules under ERISA. A non-403(b) arrangement will not be subject to the ERISA fiduciary rules, but will be subject to those existing at common law or applicable state statutes.

Q 9:58   What standards govern the conduct of a fiduciary?

ERISA sets forth a standard of conduct to which a plan fiduciary must conform in the discharge of his or her duties to a plan. In a fiduciary capacity, the fiduciary is obligated to:

1. Act solely in the interest of plan participants and their beneficiaries;

2. Act for the exclusive purpose of providing benefits to plan participants and their beneficiaries and defraying reasonable expenses of administering the plan;

3. Exercise the care, skill, prudence, and diligence under the circumstances then prevailing that a prudent person acting in a like capacity and familiar with such matters would exercise in the conduct of an enterprise of a like character and with like aims;

4. If the plan is not intended to comply with Code Section 404(c), diversify the investment of plan assets to minimize the risk of large losses, unless under the circumstances it is clearly prudent not to do so; and

5. Act in accordance with the documents and instruments governing the plan insofar as the documents and instruments are consistent with ERISA.

[ERISA § 404(a)]

Although ERISA is the primary statute that governs the conduct of fiduciaries, a fiduciary must also be familiar with relevant provisions of other laws that may apply to his or her conduct. These include, for example, the Code, various labor laws (for example, the Age Discrimination in Employment Act (ADEA), the Americans with Disabilities Act of 1990 (ADA), the Family and Medical Leave Act (FMLA), and the Labor-Management Relations Act of 1947 (LMRA or Taft-Hartley Act)); certain securities laws (such as the Securities Act of 1933, the Securities and Exchange Act of 1934, the Investment Advisors Act of 1940, and the Investment Company Act of 1940); state laws that are not preempted by ERISA; banking laws (for example, FDIC regulations); state insurance requirements; and certain federal criminal statutes. If a fiduciary is not familiar with the requirements of the relevant laws, he or she is obligated to consult with others who are knowledgeable in such laws.

Q 9:59   Do the ERISA fiduciary rules differ from the common-law fiduciary rules?

Yes, to a certain extent. While Congress acknowledged that the fiduciary responsibility provisions of ERISA incorporated various principles of the fiduciary rules under the common law of trusts, it also modified the common law of trusts in a manner that was appropriate for employee benefit plans. [S. Rep. No. 127, 93d Cong., 1st Sess. 30 (1973); H.R. Rep. No. 533, 93d Cong., 1st Sess. 11 (1973); H.R. Rep. No. 1280, 93d Cong., 2d Sess. 301 (1974)] Under ERISA preemption, the ERISA fiduciary duty requirements generally supersede the common law of trusts and exclusively set forth the standard of conduct for fiduciaries. [ERISA § 514(a)]

For example, the standard of care imposed on fiduciaries under ERISA is generally stricter than the usual "prudent person" rule embodied in the common law of trusts. In general, the common law of trusts requires trustees to meet the standard of care, skill, and caution of a prudent person, without regard to a specialized level of expertise, while ERISA requires trustees (as well as other fiduciaries) to meet the standard of a "prudent expert"—that is, someone familiar with matters relating to employee benefit plans. Under the common law of trusts, if a trustee is more skillful than the "average" prudent person, he or she must exercise the skill that he or she has. [III Scott, Law of Trusts §§ 227.1, 227.2, 227.3]

Another distinction may be found with respect to the diversification requirement. Although ERISA expressly requires diversification of plan assets, the common law of trusts has historically not imposed upon trustees the duty to diversify (although there is a growing consensus under the common law that the duty of prudence includes the duty to diversify). [III Scott, Law of Trusts §§ 227, 228]

Q 9:60   Who is a fiduciary under ERISA in connection with an ERISA 403(b) plan?

A person is a fiduciary under ERISA with regard to an ERISA 403(b) plan to the extent that the person:

1. Exercises any discretionary authority or discretionary control with regard to management of the plan;
2. Exercises any authority or control with regard to management or disposition of the assets of the plan;
3. Renders investment advice for a fee or other compensation, direct or indirect, with respect to monies or other property of the plan, or has any authority or responsibility to do so; or
4. Has any discretionary authority or discretionary responsibility in the administration of the plan.

[ERISA § 3(21)(A)]

Q 9:61   What types of activities will typically render a person a fiduciary of a plan under ERISA?

Any activity performed by a person that is within the scope of the functions described in Q 9:58 will render that person a fiduciary with respect to the plan. Any person becomes a fiduciary if he or she performs or has the authority or responsibility to perform any activity relating to the management, investment, or administration of a plan. Examples of activities that would render a person a fiduciary include:

1. Appointing other plan fiduciaries;
2. Delegating responsibility to or allocating duties among other plan fiduciaries;
3. Selecting and monitoring plan investment vehicles;
4. Acquiring or disposing of plan assets;
5. Interpreting plan provisions; and
6. Making decisions under the plan.

A person who performs activities of only a purely ministerial nature (such as calculating benefits, processing claims, and maintaining records) generally is not a fiduciary of a plan under ERISA.

DOL regulations list the following functions as ministerial and therefore nonfiduciary in nature:

1. Applying rules to determine eligibility for participation in benefits;
2. Calculating service and compensation for benefit purposes;
3. Preparing employee communications material;
4. Maintaining participants' service and employment records;
5. Preparing reports required by government agencies;
6. Calculating benefits;
7. Explaining the plan to new participants and advising participants of their rights and options under the plan;
8. Collecting contributions and applying them as specified in the plan;
9. Preparing reports covering participants' benefits;
10. Processing claims; and
11. Making recommendations to others for decisions with respect to plan administration.

An individual who performs only these ministerial duties and who does not have or exercise any fiduciary powers may still have to be bonded, as required under ERISA Section 412, if he or she handles funds of the plan. [D.O.L. Reg. § 2509.75-8, D-2]

Q 9:62   Is fiduciary status governed by a person's title or function?

Based on ERISA's definition of a fiduciary (see Q 9:58), an individual's status as a fiduciary is determined based upon the person's function rather than title. Under the approach mandated by ERISA, an individual's characterization as a fiduciary will be determined by whether a person actually exercises sufficient and appropriate authority or control.

The term *fiduciary* is defined broadly enough to include plan sponsors, members of boards of trustees or boards of directors of the entities sponsoring plans, members of plan committees (such as administrative committees, benefit committees, and investment committees), trustees, investment managers (which include insurance companies and mutual fund companies), administrative service providers, consultants, attorneys, accountants, and plan professionals.

Notwithstanding the general focus on function, some offices or positions of a plan by their very nature can cause an individual to be automatically classified as a fiduciary. This would come about in the case of an office or position that by its nature requires that a person who holds it perform one or more of the fiduciary functions set forth by ERISA Section 3(21)(A) and listed in Q 9:58. For example, a plan administrator, by the very nature of the position, will have "discretionary authority or discretionary responsibility" in the administration of the plan. As a result, any individual holding such a position would immediately be deemed a fiduciary.

Other offices and positions should be examined, on a case-by-case basis, to determine whether they involve the performance of any of the functions described in Q 9:58. For example, a plan might designate as a "benefit supervisor" a plan employee whose sole function is to calculate the amount of benefits to which each plan participant is entitled in accordance with a mathematical formula contained in the written instrument pursuant to which the plan is maintained. The benefit supervisor, after calculating the benefits, would then inform the plan administrator of the results of his or her calculations, and the plan administrator would authorize the payment of benefits to a particular plan participant. Since the benefit supervisor does not exercise any discretionary authority in performing the benefit computation, or any of the other functions described in Q 9:58, the benefit supervisor would not be a plan fiduciary.

However, the plan might designate as a benefit supervisor a plan employee who has the final authority to authorize or disallow benefit payments in cases where a dispute exists as to the interpretation of plan provisions relating to eligibility for benefits. Under these circumstances, the benefit supervisor would be a plan fiduciary, since the benefit supervisor exercises discretionary authority in the administration of the plan and exercises control over the disposition of plan assets. [D.O.L. Reg. § 2509.75-8]

Q 9:63 What is a *settlor function*?

A *settlor function* is an action or decision made by the sponsoring employer (or, in the case of a collectively bargained plan, the employers and the employee representatives) rather than by a fiduciary exercising discretion. ERISA only imposes fiduciary obligations on the trustees and fiduciaries of a plan; nonfiduciaries are not bound by these provisions. In this regard, the DOL, the courts, and (in recent legislative history) Congress have recognized a distinction between settlor (or "grantor") functions, which are not subject to the fiduciary provisions of ERISA, and fiduciary activities, which must conform to ERISA. This distinction is based on the common law of trusts. Just as a settlor (grantor) of a trust is not performing a fiduciary role in deciding to create the trust, so the sponsoring employer of an ERISA plan is not performing a fiduciary role in designing an ERISA plan.

The Supreme Court has recognized that individuals can simultaneously serve as ERISA plan fiduciaries and officers of the sponsoring employer. [Pegram v. Herdrich, 530 U.S. 211, 225–226 (2003)] Such individuals, especially when performing settlor functions such as design of the plan, and not as fiduciaries, are permitted to take actions that benefit the employer. [*Pegram*, 530 U.S. at 225 (noting that an employer can be an ERISA fiduciary for some purposes, but may still permissibly act in its nonfiduciary capacity that is to the disadvantage of plan beneficiaries); *see also* Caltagirone v. NY Community Bancorp, Inc., 2007 U.S. App. LEXIS 29516 (2d Cir. Dec. 20, 2007); Siskind v. Sperry Retirement Program, 47 F.3d 498, 506–507 (2d Cir. 1995), *rev'g* 795 F. Supp. 614 (S.D.N.Y. 1992)]

Q 9:64   What are the most common settlor functions?

The most common settlor functions are design decisions concerning the establishment of the plan, the benefits to be provided, the classes of employees to be included or excluded, and the amendment and termination of the plan.

Where an employer decided to implement an early retirement program at selected facilities only as part of (and as an amendment to) an existing retirement benefits plan that applied to all of the employer's facilities, neither the employer nor the retirement board that administered its retirement programs violated any of ERISA's fiduciary duties. The determination of who would be eligible for the early retirement program was "purely a corporate management decision," and such design decisions may be made by the employer without reference to ERISA's fiduciary obligations. [Trenton v. Scott Paper Co., 832 F.2d 806 (3d Cir. 1987), *cert. denied*, 485 U.S. 1022 (1988); *see also* Hughes Aircraft v. Jacobson, 523 U.S. 432, 443–444 (1999)] In a leading case, the Ninth Circuit ruled that where an employer offered early retirement benefits to be paid out of plan assets in exchange for the employee's execution of a waiver encompassing ADEA rights and other employment-related claims against the employer, the employer engaged in a prohibited transaction. [Spink v. Lockheed Corp., 60 F.3d 616 (9th Cir. 1995)] The Supreme Court, however, reversed the Ninth Circuit and held that ERISA does not prevent an employer from conditioning the receipt of early retirement benefits upon plan participants' waivers of employment claims and that when an employer adopts, modifies, or terminates a pension plan, it does not act as a fiduciary but as a settlor. [Lockheed Corp. v. Spink, 517 U.S. 882 (1996)]

To the extent implementation of a settlor function requires the exercise of discretion, such implementation, if properly documented and exercised, should ordinarily not be transformed into a fiduciary function. In one recent case, a pension committee appointed by the employer was a named fiduciary and was also the entity expressly authorized to adopt amendments to the pension plan. The plan document provided that "discretionary actions" taken by the committee "with respect to classification" must be uniform and applicable to all persons similarly situated. The committee effectively delegated to the employer a decision to add an early retirement program of limited scope to the plan and to determine which classes of employees at which locations would be eligible for the program. The district court held that the delegation of the power to amend the plan to add an early retirement program whose scope was determined by the employer was a discretionary (fiduciary) action taken by the committee. The Second Circuit reversed the district court, holding that the addition of an early retirement program was an amendment of the plan and as such constituted a settlor function exempt from rules of fiduciary responsibility. [Siskind v. Sperry Retirement Program, 47 F.3d 498 (2d Cir. 1995), *rev'g* 795 F. Supp. 614 (S.D.N.Y. 1992)] The Second Circuit in *Sperry* distinguished the amendment of a single-employer plan from the amendment of a multiemployer plan, jointly administered by trustees representing employers and trustees appointed by and representing the union. Trustees of a jointly administered plan under certain circumstances can have a fiduciary duty not to amend the plan documents in the employers' interest and against the interest of participants and beneficiaries. This distinction, however, may not be as relevant in light of the Supreme Court's decision in *Spink* and *Hughes Aircraft*. [Hartline v. Sheet Metal Workers Pension Fund, 286 F.3d 598, 599 (D.C. Cir. 2002) (affirming district court's determination that trustees engaged in nonfiduciary plan design function when they set contribution rates and benefit structure)]

Q 9:65   When can a fiduciary perform a settlor function?

Any person may simultaneously act in a fiduciary capacity and in a nonfiduciary capacity as an agent of the sponsoring employer.

Example. An employer's pension committee is the named fiduciary and plan administrator of its overfunded defined benefit pension plan and acts on behalf of the board of directors in making design decisions. The pension committee decides to terminate the pension plan, to purchase and distribute annuity contracts, and to establish a successor money purchase (defined contribution) plan. The pension committee is a fiduciary and is subject to fiduciary standards in allocating surplus assets and in choosing an insurer to issue annuity contracts. [*See* D.O.L. Interp. Bulletin 95-1, 60 Fed. Reg. 12328 (Mar. 6, 1995) (selecting an annuity provider is a fiduciary function)] By contrast, senior functions include the decision to establish a successor plan and the design of such a plan after a valid termination of the prior plan. The pension committee is not subject to fiduciary standards in performing these settlor functions. [Letter from Dennis M. Kass of the PWBA to John M. Erlenborn of the ERISA Advisory Council (Mar. 13, 1986)] Based on the foregoing, while establishment of a Section 403(b) plan and the contribution level are settlor functions, it is likely that selection of the annuity provider or other funding vehicle for a Section 403(b) plan is a fiduciary function.

Even if the sponsoring employer makes a design decision that constitutes a settlor function, plan fiduciaries, such as trustees or plan administrators, may be called upon to implement the decision. Such implementation may remain a fiduciary function. [101st Cong., 2d Sess., Statement of the Managers, Revenue Reconciliation Act of 1990, at 170, 172 (Oct. 26, 1990)]

Q 9:66   How broad is the scope of the fiduciary's duty in selecting an annuity provider?

DOL Advisory Opinion 2002-14A expands on Labor Regulations Section 2509.95-1(c) and DOL Interpretative Bulletin 95-1. The Advisory Opinion clarifies that the fiduciary should ascertain, among other factors, the amount and extent to which the annuity provider is covered by state guarantees. It stresses that the fiduciary has a duty to engage a qualified independent expert to evaluate such factors if the fiduciary did not have the necessary level of expertise to evaluate the creditworthiness of an annuity provider.

The PPA directed the Secretary of Labor to issue final regulations clarifying that the selection of an annuity contract as an optional form of distribution from an individual account plan is not subject to the safest available annuity standard but is subject to all otherwise applicable fiduciary standards.

In response, the EBSA promulgated Labor Regulations Section 2550.404A-4. It provides that:

1. Upon the purchase of an annuity from an insurer as a distribution of benefits from an individual account plan, the plan's liability for those benefits is transferred to the annuity provider. Accordingly, the selection of an annuity provider is a fiduciary responsibility.

2. The fiduciary requirements of selection are satisfied if the fiduciary:

    (a) Engages in an objective, thorough, and analytical search for the purpose of identifying and selecting providers from which to purchase annuities;

    (b) Appropriately determines either that the fiduciary had, at the time of the selection, appropriate expertise to evaluate the selection or that the advice of a qualified, independent expert was necessary;

    (c) Gives appropriate consideration to information sufficient to assess the ability of the annuity provider to make all future payments under the annuity contract;

    (d) Appropriately considers the cost of the annuity contract in relation to the benefits and administrative services to be provided under such contract;

    (e) Appropriately concludes that, at the time of selection, the annuity provider is financially able to make all future payments under the annuity contract and the cost of the annuity contract is reasonable in relation to the benefits and services to be provided under the contract; and

    (f) If the annuity provider is to provide multiple contracts over time, periodically review the continuing appropriateness of the foregoing conclusions.

A fiduciary is not required to review the appropriateness of an annuity provider for an individual participant or beneficiary.

Q 9:67 What is the DOL's position on payment of expenses out of plan assets?

The determination as to whether to pay a particular expense out of plan assets is a fiduciary act governed by ERISA's fiduciary responsibility provisions.

Expenses of administering a plan include direct expenses properly and actually incurred in the performance of a fiduciary's duties to the plan. The DOL has long taken the position that there is a class of discretionary activities which related to the formation, rather than the management, of plans. These are settlor functions (see Q 9:63).

Expenses incurred in connection with the performance of settlor functions are not reasonable expenses of a plan as they are incurred for the benefit of the employer and should be paid by the employer. However, reasonable expenses incurred in connection with the implementation of a settlor decisions are generally payable by the plan.

In Advisory Opinion 2001-01A, the DOL "clarified" the views it expressed in Advisory Opinion 97-03A. It dealt with the issue of whether the tax-qualified status of plans confers benefits upon both the plan sponsor and the plan. In 97-03A, the DOL stated that in the case of a plan that is intended to be tax qualified, a portion of the expenses attendant to tax qualification activities may be reasonable plan expenses.

In 2001-01A the DOL clarified that 97-03A does not require an apportionment of all tax qualification related expenses. Instead it noted that, while fiduciaries must determine whether the activities are settlor in nature, they need not take into account the benefit a plan's tax-qualified status confers on the employer. The Advisory Opinion notes that any such benefit should be viewed as an integral component of the incidental benefits that flow to plan sponsors generally by virtue of offering a plan.

It must be stressed that favorable tax treatment of a Section 403(b) plan under Code Section 403(b), which is the equivalent of tax-qualified status for a Section 401 plan, has no tax benefit for the employer since by statute it is either a tax-exempt entity or a governmental entity.

Advisory Opinion 2000-01A also sets forth a number of hypothetical situations examining sponsor expenses versus plan administrative expenses. Among the plan administrative expenses are the following:

- Benefit calculations, including those with regard to retirement windows
- Communication costs of providing information to participants and beneficiaries
- Plan amendments to comply with tax law changes
- Routine nondiscrimination testing
- Plan amendments to comply with ERISA
- Production and distribution of individual benefit statements

- The portion relating to plan matters of the costs associated with the preparation and distribution of benefits booklets
- Outsourcing costs attributable to plan administration

A plan fiduciary must also determine whether the plan document permits payment of the expense and whether the expense is reasonable.

Q 9:68 What is a *named fiduciary*?

A *named fiduciary* is a fiduciary who is either designated in the plan document and SPD as the named fiduciary or designated as such by an employer pursuant to a procedure specified in the plan. Common examples of named fiduciaries are the sponsoring employer, the employer's board of directors, and independent entities such as a bank or insurance company. Unlike other individuals or entities who must perform fiduciary functions described in ERISA Section 3(21)(A) to be deemed a fiduciary, a named fiduciary is automatically classified as a fiduciary.

A plan governed by ERISA must provide for one or more named fiduciaries. [ERISA § 402(a)] The plan document and SPD should explicitly designate the plan's named fiduciaries. [D.O.L. Reg. § 2509.75-5, FR-1] While the better practice is for the plan to explicitly identify the named fiduciary, the named fiduciary requirement can also be satisfied without making specific reference to the term "named fiduciary." This would be the case if the plan document clearly identifies one or more persons by name or title, combined with a statement that such person or persons have authority to control and manage the operation and administration of the plan. For example, the requirement would be satisfied if a plan document provides that the plan committee (identified by name or title) will control and manage the operation and administration of the plan. [D.O.L. Reg. § 2509.75-5, FR-1]

A named fiduciary may be an individual, employee organization, corporation, unincorporated organization, association, partnership, joint venture, mutual fund company, joint stock company, trust, or estate. If a plan document designates a corporation or other entity that is not an individual as a named fiduciary, it should provide for the designation of specified individuals or other persons to carry out specified fiduciary responsibilities under the plan. [ERISA §§ 3(9), 3(21)(A); D.O.L. Reg. § 2509.75-5, FR-3]

Q 9:69 What is the purpose of designating, and what are the duties of, a named fiduciary?

The purpose of designating a named fiduciary is to enable employees and other interested persons to ascertain who is responsible for operating the plan. [D.O.L. Reg. § 2509.75-5, FR-3] The advantage of designating a named fiduciary is to focus liability for mismanagement with a measure of certainty by limiting the exposure of liability to that named person or entity. In the absence of conduct that falls within the rules governing cofiduciary liability, the liability of a fiduciary who is not a named fiduciary is generally limited to the functions the fiduciary performs with respect to the plan, and the fiduciary will not be personally liable for all phases of the management and administration of the plan.

A named fiduciary, however, is jointly and severally responsible with cofiduciaries for controlling and managing the operation and administration of a plan. A named fiduciary also has the responsibility to hear benefit and claims appeals of participants and beneficiaries under the plan's claim procedures. [ERISA § 503(2)]

Plan documents may provide for the allocation of responsibilities (other than responsibilities relating to the management or control of plan assets, unless such authority is delegated to an investment manager) among named fiduciaries, and may authorize named fiduciaries to delegate limited fiduciary responsibilities to others. [ERISA § 405(c)(1)]

Q 9:70 What are the primary fiduciary duties under ERISA?

The primary fiduciary duties under ERISA are to act solely in the interest of the plan participants and beneficiaries and to:

1. Act for the exclusive purpose of providing benefits to participants and beneficiaries (and defraying reasonable administrative expenses);
2. Act with the care, skill, prudence, and diligence under the circumstances of a prudent person;
3. Diversify the investment of plan assets to minimize the risk of large losses; and
4. Act in accordance with the plan documents and Titles I and IV of ERISA.

[ERISA § 404(a)(1)]

Q 9:71 What is the fiduciary duty to monitor?

A fiduciary's duties with regard to the delegation of certain fiduciary responsibilities do not end once the fiduciary has prudently selected and delegated its duties to another person. A fiduciary's duty to monitor the actions of those individuals to whom fiduciary responsibilities have been delegated generally requires the appointing fiduciary to review and evaluate, at reasonable intervals, the performance of other fiduciaries to whom fiduciary responsibilities are delegated. Such review should be accomplished in a manner that may be reasonably expected to ensure that the performance of the delegatee fiduciary complies with the terms of the plan and all statutory standards, including ERISA's exclusive benefit, prudence, diversification, and prohibited transaction rules. [D.O.L. Reg. § 2509.75-8, FR-17]

There is no single procedure that will be appropriate in all cases. The procedure adopted may vary with the nature of the plan and other facts and circumstances relevant to the choice of the procedure. [D.O.L. Reg. § 2509.75-8, FR-17; Whitfield v. Cohen, 682 F. Supp. 188, 196 (S.D.N.Y. 1988) (a "fiduciary must ascertain within a reasonable time whether an agent to whom he has delegated a trust power is properly carrying out his responsibilities"); *see also In re* AEP ERISA Litig., 327 F. Supp. 2d 812, 832–833 (S.D. Ohio 2004); Electronic Data Sys. Corp. ERISA Litig., 305 F. Supp. 2d 658, 670 (E.D. Tex. 2004); Kling v. Fidelity Mgmt. Trust Co., 323 F. Supp. 2d 132, 142–143 (D. Mass. 2004)]

Failure to investigate an investment manager (thereby imprudently selecting an investment manager) alone may not be sufficient to hold the fiduciary liable for an imprudent investment. A plaintiff alleging an imprudent investment may also need to establish that an adequate and thorough investigation would have revealed that the investment was objectively imprudent. [E.g., Fink v. Nat'l Savings & Trust Co., 772 F.2d 951, 962 (D.C. Cir. 1985) (Scalia, J., *concurring in part and dissenting in part*) (noting that a fiduciary's breach of the duty to investigate and evaluate investments does not necessarily constitute breach of the duty to invest prudently: "[There] are two related but distinct duties imposed upon a trustee: to investigate and evaluate investments, and to invest prudently. Neither does the faithful discharge of the first satisfy the second, nor does the breach of the first constitute breach of the second." For example, a trustee who fails to investigate may nevertheless make a lucky investment that turns out to be a prudent investment; in such a case, an action for damages arising from an imprudent investment would not be sustained); Whitfield v. Cohen, 682 F. Supp. 188, 195 (S.D.N.Y. 1988) (discussing whether "an adequate and thorough investigation would have revealed evidence that the [investment] was totally unsound"); Landgraff v. Columbia/HCA Healthcare Corp. of Am., 2000 U.S. LEXIS 21831 (M.D. Tenn. May 24, 2000); Keach v. U.S. Trust Co., N.A., 313 F. Supp. 2d 818, 867 (C.D. Ill. 2004)]

Q 9:72   Can a delegating fiduciary be relieved of its duty to monitor the performance of those individuals to whom fiduciary responsibilities have been delegated?

No. The delegation of fiduciary responsibilities does not relieve the delegating fiduciary of the duty to monitor periodically the performance of the individuals to whom such responsibilities have been delegated. [D.O.L. Reg. § 2509.75-8, FR-17; Whitfield v. Cohen, 682 F. Supp. 188, 196–197 (S.D.N.Y. 1988) (trustees had the duty to monitor investment manager's performance with reasonable diligence and to withdraw the investment if it became clear or should have become clear that the investment was no longer proper for the plan)]

In a recent Information Letter [Feb. 23, 2005, to Mr. William Lindsay of Local 25 IBEW] the Department of Labor indicated that, while recusing oneself from a fiduciary decision may avoid a prohibited transaction, it does not relieve the fiduciary from his or her fiduciary duties, including providing any material information he or she may have that could impact another fiduciary making an appropriate and prudent decision.

Q 9:73   Can a fiduciary be liable for an unwitting violation of ERISA's fiduciary duties?

Yes. Even if a fiduciary is unaware that he or she is violating ERISA's fiduciary duties, the fiduciary may still be liable for the violation. The ERISA standard of conduct is an objective one: good faith is not sufficient. [*See, e.g.*, Katsaros v. Cody, 744 F.2d 270, 279 (2d Cir.), *cert. denied*, 469 U.S. 1072 (1984) (A fiduciary's lack of familiarity with investments is no excuse; under an objective standard, a fiduciary must be judged according to the standards of others acting in a like capacity and familiar with such matters. If the fiduciary cannot adequately and objectively judge the merits of a particular course of action, the fiduciary is not off the hook simply because it did not know that it breached ERISA duties. In this instance, the fiduciary had an obligation to seek outside assistance.)]

Similarly, a fiduciary will be liable, under ERISA, for engaging in a prohibited transaction if he or she "knows or should have known" that the transaction is prohibited. [ERISA § 406(a)(1)] Excise taxes under the Code will be imposed on a fiduciary for engaging in certain transactions as a disqualified person, even if he or she does not satisfy the "knows or should have known" standard. [I.R.C. §§ 4975(c)(1)(E), 4975(c)(1)(F)]

However, in certain cases of cofiduciary liability, the fiduciary must be aware that it is involved in a breach of fiduciary duty before liability attaches. For instance, cofiduciary liability will be imposed if the fiduciary knowingly participates in, knowingly undertakes to conceal, or has knowledge of an act or omission of another fiduciary that is a breach of fiduciary duty, unless he or she makes reasonable efforts under the circumstances to remedy the breach. [ERISA §§ 405(a)(1), 405(a)(3)]

Q 9:74   What is the liability of a named fiduciary?

If a named fiduciary prudently allocates responsibilities in accordance with procedures set forth in the plan document, a named fiduciary will not be liable for acts and omissions of other named fiduciaries in carrying out fiduciary responsibilities that have been allocated to them, except as provided by ERISA's general rules of cofiduciary responsibility and ERISA's standards for establishment and implementation of allocation procedures. [D.O.L. Reg. § 2509.75-8, FR-13] Similarly, if a named fiduciary prudently designates persons who are not named fiduciaries to carry out fiduciary responsibilities, a named fiduciary will not be liable for acts and omissions of such designated fiduciaries, except as provided by ERISA's general rules of cofiduciary responsibility and subject to ERISA's standards for prudently designating fiduciaries. [D.O.L. Reg. § 2509. 75-8, FR-14]

Q 9:75   What is the legal standard for determining whether a fiduciary's acts are prudent?

The standard for prudence depends on the circumstances. "The scope of the fiduciary's duty of prudence is . . . limited to those factors and circumstances that a prudent person having similar duties and familiar with such matters would consider relevant, whether the context is one of plan investments or otherwise." [44 Fed. Reg. 37,222–37,223 (July 20, 1979) (DOL release accompanying D.O.L. Reg. § 2550.404a-1(b))]

Q 9:76 Are a fiduciary's actions judged by the standard of an ordinary person or that of an expert?

Particularly in the context of investing plan assets, a fiduciary charged with an investment decision must act as a prudent expert would under similar circumstances, taking into account all relevant substantive factors as they appeared at the time of the investment decision, not in hindsight. This standard under ERISA "is not that of a prudent lay person, but rather of a prudent fiduciary with experiences dealing with similar enterprises." [Whitfield v. Cogen, 682 F. Supp. 188, 194 (S.D.N.Y. 1988), *quoting* Marshall v. Snyder, 1 Employee Benefits Cas. (BNA) 1878, 1886 (F.D.N.Y. 1979); *see also* Difelice v. US Airways, Inc., 397 F. Supp. 2d 758, 772 (E.D. Va. 2005)]

The fiduciary's conduct is to be judged against generally accepted conduct in the investment industry. "The prudence standard charges fiduciaries with a high degree of knowledge. The standard measures the decisions of plan fiduciaries against the decisions that would be made by experienced investment advisers." [Joint Comm. on Tax'n, Overview of the Enforcement and Administration of the Employee Retirement Income Security Act of 1974, at 12 (JCX-16-90) (June 6, 1990)]

Q 9:77 Does a fiduciary have an obligation to seek the assistance of an expert to satisfy the prudence requirement?

Fiduciaries have an affirmative duty to seek the advice and counsel of independent experts when their own ability is insufficient under the circumstances. Not all plan fiduciaries can be expert in all phases of employee benefit plan investments and administration, nor can they have knowledge of the entire range of activities integral to the operation of a plan. A fiduciary who lacks the expertise needed to address an issue prudently should promptly seek and retain a professional who has the expertise to assist the fiduciary in the decision. For example, plan trustees breached the prudence standard in connection with a $2 million loan to a bank when they considered only the information presented by the interested parties who sought the loan and failed to conduct an independent investigation. [Katsaros v. Cody, 744 F.2d 270, 279 (2d Cir.), *cert. denied*, 469 U.S. 1072 (1984); *see also* Bussian v. R.J.R. Nabisco, Inc., 223 F.3d 286, 300–301 (5th Cir. 2000)] Merely seeking independent advice is not enough. A fiduciary who consults and relies on an independent expert is required to provide the expert with complete and accurate information, investigate the expert's qualifications, and justify reliance on the expert. [Chao v. Hall Holding Co., 285 F.3d 415 (6th Cir. 2002)]

Q 9:78 What is the difference between "substantive prudence" and "procedural prudence"?

The DOL, the courts, and commentators have distinguished between two types of prudence: substantive and procedural. The former refers to the merits of the decision made by the fiduciary; the latter addresses the process through which the fiduciary reaches his or her decision.

As long as there is no conflict of interest that would impair the fiduciary's exercise of independent judgment, a fiduciary who considers the appropriate substantive factors ("substantive prudence") and does so using proper procedures ("procedural prudence") will satisfy the prudence requirement. [Katsaros v. Cody, 744 F.2d 270, 279 (2d Cir.), *cert. denied,* 469 U.S. 1072 (1984)]

Q 9:79   What substantive factors must a fiduciary consider in connection with plan investments?

To satisfy the statutory obligation of prudence in connection with plan investments, a fiduciary must give "appropriate consideration" to the following substantive factors:

1. The investment must be evaluated as part of the plan's overall portfolio;
2. The design of the portfolio, including the investment, must be reasonable for the purposes of the plan;
3. The risk of loss and opportunity for gain (or other return) must be favorable, relative to alternative investments;
4. The investment must take into consideration the diversification of the portfolio;
5. The investment must take into consideration the liquidity and current return of the entire portfolio relative to anticipated cash-flow requirements of the plan; and
6. The investment must take into consideration the projected return of the portfolio relative to the funding objectives of the plan.

[D.O.L. Reg. § 2550.404a-1(b)]

Q 9:80   What is procedural prudence in the context of investing plan assets?

To satisfy procedural prudence in the context of investing plan assets, the fiduciary must:

1. Employ proper methods to investigate, evaluate, and structure the investment, including the retention of professional advisors if the fiduciary lacks the expertise himself or herself;
2. Act in a manner in which others who act in a like capacity and are familiar with such matters would act; and
3. Exercise independent judgment when making investment decisions.

[Lanka v. O'Higgins, 810 F. Supp. 379 (N.D.N.Y. 1992) (A "contrarian" investment advisor satisfied these requirements.)]

Q 9:81   Does ERISA require that a Section 403(b) plan have an investment policy statement?

The choice of investment vehicles made available under a plan and the ongoing monitoring of those investment vehicles are fiduciary functions. ERISA requires that a fiduciary exercise these responsibilities in a prudent manner. ERISA does not explicitly require that a plan's investment policy be documented in writing.

An investment policy statement is a formal document that delineates the plan's investment policy, objectives and guidelines. A written document intended to guide plan fiduciaries can certainly serve a very useful function in the discharge of fiduciary duties. In the last several years, defined contribution plans seem to have moved with increasing frequency toward providing an investment policy statement. As more plans decide to make investment advice available to plan participants, the trend of offering investment policy statements is likely to continue. The practice may yet rise to the level of a best practice, but does not appear to be mandated by ERISA.

Q 9:82   Is a Section 403(b) plan subject to the prohibited transaction rules?

ERISA's prohibited transaction rules apply to all plans that are subject to ERISA. Therefore, if a Section 403(b) plan is subject to ERISA, it will be subject to the prohibited transaction rules under ERISA. [*See* ERISA § 406]

The Code's prohibited transaction rules, however, apply only to tax-qualified plans (that is, plans that are granted tax-favored status by meeting the requirements under Code Section 401), qualified annuities (that is, annuity contracts purchased by an employer for an employee under a plan that meets the requirements of Code Section 404(a)(2) and is granted tax-favored status under the Code), IRAs, and individual retirement annuities. Since Section 403(b) plans are not qualified plans under the Code, they are not subject to the Code's prohibited transaction rules.

Q 9:83   Could a plan fiduciary continue to meet its fiduciary obligations under an ERISA 403(b) plan while offering investment advice under the plan pursuant to an arrangement whereby an investment adviser advises on its own or affiliated products?

Yes. A plan fiduciary can continue to meet its fiduciary obligations while offering investment advice under the plan, provided that the advice is offered pursuant to an eligible investment advice arrangement whereby (1) the advice is offered pursuant to a prohibited transaction exemption, (2) the fiduciary adviser is required to comply with the terms of the applicable prohibited transaction exemption, and (3) the advisory arrangement includes a written acknowledgement by the fiduciary investment adviser that the adviser is a plan fiduciary for the purpose of giving advice.

In order to foster broader access to advice programs, the PPA added two new statutory exemptions to ERISA. The new exemptions are a computer model exemption and a compensation based exemption. The computer model exemption must (1) apply generally accepted investment theories that take into account the historic returns of different asset classes over defined periods of time, (2) utilize relevant information about the participant (which may include age, life expectancy, retirement age, and risk tolerance), (3) utilize prescribed objective criteria to provide asset allocation portfolios comprised of investment options under the plan, (4) operate in a manner that is not biased in favor of any investment options offered by the fiduciary adviser or a related person, and (5) take into account all investment options under the plan in specifying how a participant's account balance should be invested without inappropriate weighting of any investment option. Under the compensation based exemption, any fees (including any commission or other compensation) received by a fiduciary adviser for investment advice or with respect to the sale, holding, or acquisition of any security or other property must not vary depending on the basis of the investment option selected. Provided that the fees received in the recommended funding option are the same, and other applicable requirements are met, the exemption may apply. Numerous additional requirements apply, regardless of the exemption selected. In addition, the plan fiduciary remains responsible for prudently selecting an investment adviser and for prudently monitoring the performance of the adviser. The plan fiduciary need not, however, monitor specific investment advice given to any particular plan participant.

In 2007, the DOL issued Field Assistance Bulletin 2007-01, which clarifies that the statutory exemptions added by the PPA did not invalidate or otherwise affect prior guidance issued by the DOL concerning investment advice. Specifically, the Field Assistance Bulletin clarifies that: (1) Interpretive Bulletin 96-1, in which the DOL identified categories of investment-related information and materials that do not constitute investment advice, and (2) DOL Advisory Opinion 2001-09A, in which the DOL concluded that a financial services company may provide investment advice in a fiduciary capacity in connection with methodologies developed and overseen by an independent third-party expert, without violating the prohibited transaction rules, were neither invalidated nor otherwise affected by the PPA.

Q 9:84   What are the duties of fiduciaries if mutual fund activities are under investigation?

On February 17, 2004, a senior official of the DOL issued a statement as to the duties of fiduciaries in light of the then ongoing mutual fund investigations. These investigations included those involving late trading and market-timing abuses. The official's statement noted that ERISA requires that fiduciaries discharge their duties prudently. This requires a deliberative process with fiduciaries becoming as well informed as possible under the circumstances.

The statement goes on to note that, where specific funds have been identified as under investigation, fiduciaries must consider the nature of the alleged abuses, the potential economic impact of the abuses on the plan's investments, the steps taken by the fund to limit the potential for such abuses in the future, and any remedial action taken or contemplated to make investors whole. The statement also points out that these issues may extend to mutual funds and pooled investment funds beyond those currently identified, and that fiduciaries must make sure that they have sufficient information to conclude that such funds have procedures and safeguards in place to limit their vulnerability to abuse.

The statement also noted that the guiding principle for fiduciaries should be to ensure that appropriate efforts are being made to act reasonably, prudently, and solely in the interests of participants and beneficiaries. The statement went on to note that the appropriate course of action will depend on the particular facts and circumstances relating to a plan's investment in a fund and that plan fiduciaries should follow prudent plan procedures relating to investment decisions and document their decisions.

Q 9:85   Are fiduciaries relieved of fiduciary responsibility if participants or beneficiaries have control over plan assets?

ERISA Section 404(c) relieves the fiduciary from liability for diversification of plan assets (but not other fiduciary responsibilities) if individual accounts are involved, the participant or beneficiary exercises "control" over the assets in his account, and the participant or beneficiary has an opportunity to choose from a broad range of investment alternatives. To satisfy the requirements a plan must:

1. Give the participant or beneficiary a reasonable opportunity to give investment instructions to an identified plan fiduciary who is obligated to comply with such instructions;

2. Give the participant or beneficiary the opportunity to obtain sufficient information to make informed decisions with regard to investment alternatives available under the plan, and incidents of ownership appurtenant to such investments. This would require the participant or beneficiary being provided with:

   • An explanation that the plan is intended to constitute a plan described in ERISA Section 404(c) and that the fiduciaries of the plan may be relieved of liability for any losses that are the direct and necessary result of investment instructions given by such participant or beneficiary

   • A description of the investment alternatives available under the plan and, with respect to each designated investment alternative, a general description of the investment objectives and risk and return characteristics of each such alternative, including information relating to the type and diversification of assets comprising the portfolio of the designated investment alternative

   • Identification of any designated investment managers

   • An explanation of the circumstances under which participants and beneficiaries may give investment instructions and an explanation of any specified limitations on such instructions under the terms of the plan, including any restrictions on transfers to or from a designated investment alternative, and any restrictions on the exercise of voting, tender, and similar rights appurtenant to a participant's or beneficiary's investment in an investment alternative

- A description of any transaction fees and expenses that affect the participant's or beneficiary's account balance in connection with purchases or sales of interests in investment alternatives (e.g., commissions, sales loads, deferred sales charges, redemption, or exchange fees)

- The name, address, and phone number of the plan fiduciary (and, if applicable, the person or persons designated by the plan fiduciary to act on his behalf) responsible for providing the information to be provided upon request of a participant or beneficiary and a description of the information which may be obtained on request

- In the case of plans that offer an investment alternative designed to permit a participant or beneficiary to directly or indirectly acquire or sell any employer security (employer security alternative), a description of the procedures established to provide for the confidentiality of information relating to the purchase, holding, and sale of employer securities, and the exercise of voting, tender, and similar rights by participants and beneficiaries, as well the name, address, and phone number of the plan fiduciary responsible for monitoring compliance with the procedures

- In the case of an investment alternative that is subject to the Securities Act of 1933, and in which the participant or beneficiary has no assets invested, immediately following the participant's or beneficiary's initial investment, a copy of the most recent prospectus provided to the plan. This condition will be deemed satisfied if the participant or beneficiary has been provided with a copy of the most recent prospectus immediately prior to the participant's or beneficiary's initial investment in such alternative, and

- Subsequent to an investment in an investment alternative, any materials provided to the plan relating to the exercise of voting, tender, or similar rights that are incidental to the holding in the account of the participant or beneficiary of an ownership interest in such alternative to the extent that such rights are passed through to participants and beneficiaries under the terms of the plan, as well as a description of or reference to plan provisions relating to the exercise of voting, tender or similar rights

3. The participant or beneficiary must be provided by the identified plan fiduciary (or a person or persons designated by the plan fiduciary to act on his behalf), either directly or upon request, the following information, which shall be based on the latest information available to the plan:

- A description of the annual operating expenses of each designated investment alternative (e.g., investment management fees, administrative fees, transaction costs) that reduce the rate of return to participants and beneficiaries, and the aggregate amount of such expenses expressed as a percentage of average net assets of the designated investment alternative

- Copies of any prospectuses, financial statements and reports, and any other materials relating to the investment alternatives available under the plan, to the extent such information is provided to the plan

- A list of the assets comprising the portfolio of each designated investment alternative that constitute plan assets, the value of each such asset (or the proportion of the investment alternative that it comprises), and, with respect to each such asset that is a fixed-rate investment contract issued by a bank, savings and loan association, or insurance company, the name of the issuer of the contract, the term of the contract, and the rate of return on the contract

- Information concerning the value of shares or units in designated investment alternatives available to participants and beneficiaries under the plan, as well as the past and current investment performance of such alternatives, determined, net of expenses, on a reasonable and consistent basis, and

- Information concerning the value of shares or units in designated investment alternatives held in the account of the participant or beneficiary

4. A plan does not fail to provide opportunity for a participant or beneficiary to exercise control over his or her individual account merely because it:

   - Imposes charges for reasonable expenses. A plan may charge participants' and beneficiaries' accounts for the reasonable expenses of carrying out investment instructions, provided that procedures are established under the plan to periodically inform such participants and beneficiaries of actual expenses incurred with respect to their respective individual accounts

   - Permits a fiduciary to decline to implement investment instructions by participants and beneficiaries. A fiduciary may decline to implement participant and beneficiary instructions:

     —Which would result in a prohibited transaction and

     —Which would generate income that would be taxable to the plan

5. A plan may impose reasonable restrictions on the frequency with which participants and beneficiaries may give investment instructions. In no event, however, is such a restriction reasonable unless, with respect to each investment alternative made available by the plan, it permits participants and beneficiaries to give investment instructions with a frequency that is appropriate in light of the market volatility to which the investment alternative may reasonably be expected to be subject, provided that:

   - At least three of the investment alternatives made available, which constitute a broad range of investment alternatives, permit participants and beneficiaries to give investment instructions no less frequently than once within any three-month period, and either:

     —At least one of the investment alternatives permits participants and beneficiaries to give investment instructions with regard to transfers into the investment alternative as frequently as participants and beneficiaries are permitted to give investment instructions with respect to any investment alternative made available by the plan that permits participants and beneficiaries to give investment instructions more frequently than once within any three-month period, or

—With respect to each investment alternative that permits participants and beneficiaries to give investment instructions more frequently than once within any three-month period, participants and beneficiaries are permitted to direct their investments from such alternative into an income-producing, low-risk, liquid fund, subfund, or account as frequently as they are permitted to give investment instructions with respect to each such alternative and, with respect to such fund, subfund, or account, participants and beneficiaries are permitted to direct investments from the fund, subfund, or account to an investment alternative meeting the necessary requirements as frequently as they are permitted to give investment instructions with respect to that investment alternative, and

- With respect to transfers from an investment alternative that is designed to permit a participant or beneficiary to directly or indirectly acquire or sell any employer security (employer security alternative) either:

  —All the investment alternatives meeting the necessary requirements of this section permit participants and beneficiaries to give investment instructions with regard to transfers into each of the investment alternatives as frequently as participants and beneficiaries are permitted to give investment instructions with respect to the employer security alternative, or

  —Participants and beneficiaries are permitted to direct their investments from each employer security alternative into an income-producing, low-risk, liquid fund, subfund, or account as frequently as they are permitted to give investment instructions with respect to such employer security alternative and, with respect to such fund, subfund, or account, participants and beneficiaries are permitted to direct investments from the fund, subfund, or account to each investment alternative meeting the necessary requirements of as frequently as they are permitted to give investment instructions with respect to each such investment alternative.

In the statement from a senior DOL official, discussed in Q 9:84, it was noted that 404(c) protection is not lost by imposition of reasonable redemption fees or the placing on the sale of shares reasonable limits on the number of times a participant can move in and out of a particular investment within a particular period so long as such rules comply with the volatility requirements, are allowed by the plan, and are clearly disclosed. If not contemplated under the terms of a plan, they would affect 404(c) protection as well as the "blackout period" notice requirements.

6. A plan offers a broad range of investment alternatives only if the available investment alternatives are sufficient to provide the participant or beneficiary with a reasonable opportunity to:

- Materially affect the potential return on amounts in his or her individual account with respect to which he or she is permitted to exercise control and the degree of risk to which such amounts are subject

- Choose from at least three investment alternatives:

    —Each of which is diversified

    —Each of which has materially different risk and return characteristics

    —Which in the aggregate enable the participant or beneficiary to choose among them to achieve a portfolio with aggregate risk and return characteristics at any point within the range normally appropriate for the participant or beneficiary; and

    —Each of which, when combined with investments in the other alternatives, tends to minimize through diversification the overall risk of a participant's or beneficiary's portfolio.

In determining whether a plan provides the participant or beneficiary with a reasonable opportunity to diversify investments, the nature of the investment alternatives offered by the plan and the size of the portion of the individual's account over which the individual is permitted to exercise control must be considered. Where such portion of the account of any participant or beneficiary is so limited in size that the opportunity to invest in look-through investment vehicles is the only prudent means to assure an opportunity to achieve appropriate diversification, a plan may satisfy the requirements of this paragraph only by offering look-through investment vehicles.

Where look-through investment vehicles are available as investment alternatives to participants and beneficiaries, the underlying investments of the look-through investment vehicles must be considered in determining whether the plan satisfies the necessary requirements.

A fiduciary has no obligation under part 4 of Title 1 of the Act to provide investment advice to a participant or beneficiary under an ERISA Section 404(c) plan.

If a participant or beneficiary of an ERISA Section 404(c) plan exercises independent control over assets in his or her individual account, then such participant or beneficiary is not a fiduciary of the plan by reason of such exercise of control.

If a participant or beneficiary of an ERISA Section 404(c) plan exercises independent control over assets in his or her individual account, then no other person who is a fiduciary with respect to such plan shall be liable for any loss, or with respect to any breach of part 4 of title I of the Act, that is the direct and necessary result of that participant's or beneficiary's exercise of control.

The PPA amended ERISA Section 404(c) to provide that fiduciary relief under ERISA Section 404(c) will not apply during any blackout period during which the ability of such participant or beneficiary to direct the investment of assets is suspended. If, however, a change is to cause an investment to be reallocated among one or more remaining or new options offered in lieu of the terminated options and the characteristics of the options are similar to the eliminated ones (a "mapping") and at least 30 days and no more than 60 days prior to the effective date of such a change written notice is given to the participants or beneficiaries (including information comparing the existing and new investment options and the mapping if other instructions are not given), the participant or beneficiary has not provided other investment instructions and the prior investment alternatives were selected by the participant or beneficiary, then ERISA Section 404(c) protection continues.

Q 9:86 Are fiduciaries liable for the results from default investments if the participant does not elect a form of investment?

Generally, unless a participant exercises actual control over plan investments, the plan fiduciaries will be responsible for the prudence and diversification of the default investments in the participant's account. The PPA addressed this issue and created safe-harbor relief for plan fiduciaries as to diversification, but not prudence. In October 2007, the EBSA issued final rules to implement the safe-harbor provisions [D.O.L. Reg. § 2550.404c-5]

Fiduciaries are relieved of any fiduciary liability for the investment of plan funds in qualified default investment alternatives (QDIAs) and the results thereof (but not for the prudence selection of the QDIA funds) if they satisfy the requirements of the rule.

Generally, a QDIA for a Section 403(b) plan must be:

1. An investment fund product or model portfolio that applies generally accepted investment theories, is diversified so to minimize the risk of large losses and that is designed to provide varying degrees of long-term appreciation and capital presentation through a mix of equity and fixed income exposures based on the participant's age, target retirement date (such as normal retirement age under the plan) or life expectancy. Such products and portfolios change their asset allocations and associated risk levels over time with the objective of becoming more conservative (i.e. decreasing risk of losses) with increasing age. Asset allocation decisions for such products and portfolios are not required to take into account risk tolerances, investments or other preferences of an individual participant. An example of such a fund or portfolio may be a "life-cycle" or "targeted retirement date" fund or account; or

2. An investment fund product or model portfolio that applies generally accepted investment theories, is diversified so as to minimize the risk of large losses and that is designed to provide long-term appreciation and capital preservation through a mix of equity and fixed income exposures consistent with a target level of risk appropriate for participants of the plan as a whole. Asset allocation decisions for such products and portfolios are not required to take into account the age, risk tolerances, investments or

other preferences of an individual participant. An example of such fund or portfolio may be a balanced fund; or

3. An investment management service with respect to which a fiduciary, applying generally accepted investment theories, allocates the assets of a participant's individual account to achieve varying degrees of long-term appreciation and capital preservation through a mix of equity and fixed income exposure, offered through investment alternatives available under the plan, based on the participant's age, target retirement date (such as normal retirement age under the plan) or life expectancy. Such portfolios are diversified so as to minimize the risk of large losses and change their asset allocation and associated risk levels for an individual account over time with the objective of becoming more conservative (i.e., decreasing risk of losses) with increasing age. Asset allocation decisions are not required to take into account risk tolerances, investments or other preferences of an individual participant. An example of such service may be a "managed account."

In order for the relief of investment in QDIA by the fiduciaries where the participant does not make an election to apply, the participant must have had the opportunity to direct the investments of the assets. In addition, notice must be given to participants at least 30 days in advance of the date of plan eligibility or at least 30 days in advance of the first investment in the QDIA and at least 30 days in advance of each subsequent plan year. In addition, it can be given on or before the first date of plan investment if the employee has a right of withdrawal within 90 days under the automatic enrollment rules. The preamble to the regulations makes clear that even if not given before the first investment, the QDIA rules will apply as to any investments made after the 30-day notice is given.

The notice must be in writing and calculated to be understood by the average plan participant and must contain the following:

1. Description and conditions in which funds may be invested in QDIA;
2. Explanation of the right to direct investments;
3. Description of the QDIA and the fees and expenses attendant to it;
4. Description of the right to direct the investment to other investment alternatives, including a description of any applicable restrictions, fees or expenses in connection with the transfer; and
5. Description of where investment information on the other investments is available.

The EBSA has promulgated a form of notice that can be used to satisfy the notice requirements. Such notice must be provided as a separate notice and cannot be combined with other notices other than that for automatic enrollment. The notice, however, may be distributed with other notices.

Participants on whose behalf assets are invested in a QDIA must be able to transfer such assets to all of the other available funds under the Plan with foregoing consistent to that afforded to other participants and beneficiaries (but not less frequently than once within any three-month period). Such transferred amounts, or those withdrawn pursuant to the automatic enrollment regulations, cannot be subject to any restriction fees or expenses (including surrender charges, liquidation or exchange fees or redemptions), but are subject to the ongoing fees charged for the operation of the investment itself (such as investment management fees, distribution and/or service fees, 12b-1 fees, or legal, accounting, transfer agent, and similar administrative expenses). After 90 days, QDIA transfer or withdrawal fees cannot be greater than those for participants who elected to invest in such fund. While the plan fiduciary need not decide which of the qualified default investment alternatives is most appropriate for participants, they still must prudently select and monitor the investment fund, model portfolio or investment management service utilized within a category.

The participants in QDIAs are entitled to the same materials required to be provided to participant under ERISA Section 404(c) (see Q 9:85).

Q 9:87 Can a Section 403(b) plan provide for automatic contribution arrangements?

The PPA amended ERISA Section 514 to add new Section (e). It permits the plan sponsor to make automatic contributions to a Section 403(b) plan based on a uniform percentage of compensation until the participant elects otherwise and to invest them in QDIAs (see Q 9:86). The plan administrator is required to give participants annual written notice of the automatic contribution and the participant's right to terminate or change it.

Q 9:88 Are there penalties for not timely giving notices?

The PPA amended ERISA Section 514 to add Subsection (e)(3), under which the plan administrator of a plan with an automatic contribution arrangement is required to provide each participant to whom the arrangement applies, notice of the participant's rights and obligations under such arrangement. If the provision is violated, the DOL may access a civil penalty of not more than $1,000 per day for each violation.

EBSA has also determined that use of the sample IRS notice on qualified automatic contribution arrangements and eligible automatic contribution arrangements will satisfy the requirements of ERISA Section 514(e)(3).

Q 9:89 Can a Section 403(b) arrangement charge former employees a pro rata share of the arrangement's reasonable administrative expenses, but not charge current employees?

Yes, it can. In Revenue Ruling 2004-10 the IRS interprets Code Section 411(a)(11). This interpretation would also apply to the similar provision in

ERISA Section 203(d), which applies to Section 403(b) arrangements subject to ERISA.

The IRS acknowledged that former employees can be charged reasonable administrative charges and current employees not charged without violating the rule on not allowing significant detriment to former employees leaving their money in the plan after termination of employment.

The IRS recognized that not every allocation of plan expenses is reasonable and that, if the method is not reasonable, it could result in a significant detriment. For example, the Revenue Ruling noted that allocating the expenses of active employees pro rata to all accounts, including former employees, while allocating the expenses of former employees only to their accounts would not be reasonable, since former employees would then bear more than an equitable portion of the plan's expenses.

Q 9:90   When is a fiduciary liable for engaging in a prohibited transaction under ERISA?

A fiduciary is liable under ERISA for engaging in a prohibited transaction involving any ERISA plan, including a Section 403(b) plan, if the fiduciary knew or should have known that he or she caused the plan to engage in a prohibited transaction. A fiduciary is liable for losses to the plan arising from a prohibited transaction in which the plan engaged if the fiduciary would have known that the transaction involving the particular party in interest was prohibited had the fiduciary acted as a prudent person. Prudence is determined based on the particular facts and circumstances of the case. In general, for a fiduciary to be prudent in the case of a significant transaction, the fiduciary must make a thorough investigation of the other party's relationship to the plan to determine whether the party is a party in interest. In the case of a normal and insubstantial day-to-day transaction, it may be sufficient to check the identity of the other party against a roster of parties in interest that is periodically updated. [ERISA Conf. Comm. Rep.]

Q 9:91   What are the penalties for engaging in a prohibited transaction?

ERISA imposes traditional trust law remedies, such as damages and either criminal or civil penalties, for the fiduciary's breach of his or her duties under ERISA. [ERISA §§ 501, 502]

In contrast to the Code, which imposes a mandatory excise tax on a disqualified person or party in interest who participates in a prohibited transaction involving a qualified plan [I.R.C. § 4975], ERISA provides for the imposition of a civil penalty on a party in interest who participates in a prohibited transaction involving an ERISA plan that is a nonqualified plan, such as a Section 403(b) plan. [ERISA § 502(i)]

Although fiduciaries are parties in interest, they are subject to the penalty only if they act in a prohibited transaction in a capacity other than that of a fiduciary. Pursuant to ERISA Section 502(i), the penalty may be in an amount up to 5 percent of the "amount involved" in each such transaction, as defined in Code Section 4975(f)(4), for each year (or part thereof) during which the prohibited transaction continues. The "amount involved" is the greater of the fair market value of the property (and money) given or the fair market value of the property (and money) received. The valuation date for purposes of calculating the 5 percent penalty is the date on which the prohibited transaction occurred. [I.R.C. § 4975(f)(4)] Generally, if the transaction is not corrected within 90 days of notice, the penalty may be increased to an amount up to 100 percent of the amount involved. To avoid a 100 percent penalty, the prohibited transaction must be corrected in the period beginning with the date on which the prohibited transaction occurs and ending 90 days after the mailing of the notice of deficiency with respect to the 100 percent penalty. The DOL may grant an extension if it determines that the extension is "reasonable and necessary" to correct the prohibited transaction. It should be noted that the penalty is under ERISA Section 502(i), which applies to ERISA 403(b) plans, and not under Code Section 4975.

Q 9:92   Can a prohibited transaction be corrected?

Yes. A prohibited transaction can be corrected by undoing the transaction to the extent possible, but in any case placing the plan in a financial position no worse than the position it would have been in had the party in interest acted under the highest fiduciary standards. [ERISA § 502(i)] This requirement may be even more severe than the imposition of the penalty, as the "undoing" of a transaction may be far costlier than the amount of penalty involved. The party in interest, however, cannot choose between paying the penalty and "undoing" the transaction, as the penalty is continuously imposed for each year the prohibited transaction occurs, until it is corrected.

Effective April 14, 2000, the DOL established a Voluntary Fiduciary Correction (VFC) program, which is designed to encourage the voluntary and timely correction of certain transactions and the restoration of losses to employee benefit plans resulting from fiduciary breaches. Transactions may be corrected without a determination that there is an actual breach; there need only be a possible breach.

If an applicant is in full compliance with all of the terms and procedures set forth under the VFC program, the EBSA will issue a "no-action letter" with respect to the transaction identified. Pursuant to the no-action letter, the EBSA will not initiate a civil investigation under Title I of ERISA regarding the applicant's responsibility for any transaction described, or assess a civil penalty under ERISA Section 502(l) on the correction amount paid to the plan or its participants. Relief is limited to the transactions identified in the application and the persons who are correcting those transactions. Correction under the VFC program does not preclude any other governmental agency, including the IRS, from exercising any rights it may have with respect to the transactions that are the subject of the application.

The DOL implemented the final version of the VFC program effective April 29, 2002. The final version covers 15 prohibited transactions, expanding the interim program, which covered 13. In November 2002, the DOL finalized class exemption PTE 2002-51, which exempts plans participating in the VFC Program from Code Section 4975 excise taxes for four prohibited transactions:

1. Failure to transmit participant contributions to a plan within prescribed time limits;

2. The plan's making a loan at fair market interest to a party in interest with respect to the plan;

3. Purchase or sale of an asset between a plan and a party in interest at fair market value; and

4. The sale of real property to a plan by the employer and the leaseback of the property to the employer, at fair market value and fair market rental rate.

In addition, the IRS stated it would not seek to impose excise taxes for *any* of the VFC program prohibited transactions so long as the requirements for the class exemption were met. [Ann. 2002-31, 2002-19 I.R.B. 908]

Q 9:93 May a plan purchase insurance to cover any liability or losses resulting from a prohibited transaction?

Yes. A plan may purchase insurance for its fiduciaries or for itself to cover liability or losses occurring by reason of the act or omission of a fiduciary, provided that the insurance policy permits recourse by the insurer against the fiduciary for the breach of fiduciary obligation. [ERISA § 410]

Q 9:94 May an employer that sponsors a plan, or an employee organization whose members are covered by the plan, indemnify a fiduciary?

Yes. Although ERISA prohibits the indemnification and exculpation of the fiduciary by the plan, ERISA permits the indemnification of the fiduciary by an employer that sponsors the plan or by an employee organization whose members are covered by the plan. This indemnification does not relieve the fiduciary of responsibility or liability for fiduciary breaches; rather, it leaves the fiduciary fully responsible and liable but permits another party to satisfy any liability incurred by the fiduciary. Therefore, this indemnification is not void as against public policy under ERISA Section 410. [D.O.L. Reg. § 2509.75-4]

Q 9:95 May an employer that sponsors a plan limit the liability of, or indemnify, service providers?

In Advisory Opinion 2002-08A [Aug. 20, 2002], the DOL said that clauses limiting liability and indemnifying service providers were not "per se" violations of ERISA Section 401(a)(1)(B) or Section 408(b)(2), but it noted that any agreement that protects the service provider against fraud or willful misconduct is void against public policy. At a minimum, the fiduciary is obliged to assess comparable services at comparable prices from other service providers who may give a plan greater protection. [D.O.L. Adv. Op. 2002-08A]

Q 9:96   May a fiduciary purchase insurance to cover any liability or losses resulting from a prohibited transaction?

Yes. A fiduciary may purchase insurance to cover such liability from and for his or her own account. [ERISA § 410]

Q 9:97   Can a nonfiduciary be subject to liability for a prohibited transaction?

Yes. If the nonfiduciary is a party in interest, he or she is subject to the penalty imposed by the DOL for participating in a prohibited transaction violation. [ERISA § 502(i)] Further, ERISA imposes a 20 percent civil penalty upon any person who knowingly participates in fiduciary breaches or other violations by a fiduciary of Part 4 of Title I of ERISA (including prohibited transactions). [ERISA § 502(l)] The scope of this 20 percent civil penalty provision will be discussed below. Also, as will be discussed below, the Supreme Court has held that monetary damages cannot be recovered from nonfiduciaries who knowingly participate in a breach of fiduciary duty under ERISA where the nonfiduciary did not have any monetary gain from the breach. [Mertens v. Hewitt Assocs., 124 L. Ed 2d 161 (1993)]

At one time, there was a split in authority as to whether a nonfiduciary could be subject to monetary damages under ERISA for engaging in a prohibited transaction. For example, in *McDougall v. Donovan* [539 F. Supp. 596 (N.D. Ill. 1982)], the court held that, since ERISA grants the Secretary of Labor broad authority to bring actions under ERISA, equitable enforcement authority is not limited solely to actions against fiduciaries for their participation in prohibited transactions. Therefore, the Secretary also has the authority to seek restitution to recover ill-gotten gains from nonfiduciary parties in interest. Several circuit courts have agreed with this position. [*See also* Thorton v. Evans, 692 F.2d 1064 (7th Cir. 1982) (district court erred in dismissing a complaint alleging conspiracy to defraud a pension fund on the ground that defendants were not fiduciaries, since nonfiduciaries who aided fiduciaries in breaching their fiduciary duty may be sued and may be liable to the extent they have profited from the breach)] In *Harris Trust & Savings Bank v. Salomon Smith Barney, Inc.* [530 U.S. 238 (2000)], the Supreme Court did not resolve the issue of whether restitution is available. The Court found that equitable relief was available in action against a nonfiduciary, and this relief included restitution of the property, disgorgement, and disgorgement of profits. [*Harris Trust*, 530 U.S. at 249–250; *see also* Great-West & Annuity Ins. Co. v. Knudson, 534 U.S. 204 (2002)]Courts have gone even further and held that monetary damages may be recovered from a nonfiduciary even in situations where the nonfiduciary did not profit from his or her participation in the breach. Thus, in *Foltz v. US News & World Report, Inc.* [627 F. Supp. 1143, 1167–1168 (D. D.C. 1986)], the court permitted recovery of damages by former employees against an appraiser retained by the plan where the employees were harmed by the appraiser's undervaluation of employer stock held by the plan. [*See also dicta* in Thorton v. Evans, 692 F.2d 1064, 1078 (7th Cir. 1982) (the court stated that it is the participation in the breach—not profit—by the nonfiduciary that is the predicate for liability)] However, in *Nieto v. Ecker* [845 F.2d 868 (9th Cir. 1988)], the court rejected the reasoning of *Foltz* and held that a nonfiduciary cannot be liable for a breach of fiduciary duty under ERISA where the third party did not profit from the breach. This issue was resolved by the Supreme Court.

In *Mertens v. Hewitt Associates* [124 L. Ed. 161 (1993)], the Supreme Court held that a nonfiduciary who does not profit from a breach is not liable for monetary damages resulting from his or her actions. In *Mertens*, an actuarial firm failed to change the plan's actuarial assumptions to reflect the plan's additional costs attributable to an employer's early retirement incentive program. As a result of Hewitt's failure, the plan became underfunded and it was ultimately terminated by the PBGC. Following the termination, participants received only the benefits guaranteed by ERISA, which were lower than their full benefits due under the plan. The Court held that only remedies that are traditionally viewed as equitable can be recovered from a nonfiduciary. Therefore, compensatory damages resulting from the undervaluation of plan costs could not be recovered from the actuarial firm.

> **Note.** The Court expressed uncertainty as to whether ERISA affords a cause of action of any sort against nonfiduciaries who participate in a fiduciary breach. Thus, it was unclear to the Court whether restitution of ill-gotten gains can be recovered from a nonfiduciary under ERISA. The Court expressed the view that the ERISA Section 502(l) provision that imposes a 20 percent civil penalty on any person who knowingly participates in a fiduciary breach can be interpreted as referring to cofiduciaries, who are expressly liable for their knowing participation under ERISA Section 405(a).

Q 9:98   Is an insurance company a fiduciary under ERISA with regard to Section 403(b) assets that are under its authority or control?

The answer depends on the nature of the investment vehicles under which the Section 403(b) assets are maintained.

The Supreme Court, in *John Hancock Mutual Life Insurance Co. v. Harris Trust & Savings Bank* [114 S. Ct. 517 (1993)], examined this issue by looking at the definition of *plan assets*. It decided that resolution of this issue depends upon whether, with regard to such assets, the investment risk is to be borne by the insurance company itself or by the plan participants. In affirming the decision of the Second Circuit, the Court narrowly construed the "guaranteed benefit policy" exclusion. The Court wrote that where an insurance company allocates investment risk to itself, the exclusion applies. Thus, the insurance company would be beyond the reach of the fiduciary rules with regard to those assets in connection with which it provides guaranteed benefit payments or a fixed rate of return. On the other hand, the Court held that with respect to those assets in connection with which the insurance company provides no guaranteed benefit payments or fixed rates of return, the insurance company is a fiduciary under ERISA. Therefore, certain assets held in an insurance company's general account could be considered plan assets, and the insurance company would, with respect to such assets, be an ERISA fiduciary. Such assets would also be subject to ERISA's prohibited transaction rules.

The DOL published PTE 95-60 in response to *Harris Trust*, so as to permit insurance companies to go forward with arm's-length transactions that involve general account assets arising from contracts issued to ERISA covered plans. The Small Business Job Protection Act of 1996 subsequently amended ERISA Section 401, adding a new Section 401(c), requiring the Secretary of Labor to issue regulations to clarify the status of plan assets held in an insurance company's general account. Section 401(c) directs the Secretary of Labor to issue regulations applicable to policies issued on or before December 31, 1998, to provide guidance for the purpose of determining, in cases where an insurance company issues one or more policies to or for the benefit of an employee benefit plan (and such policies are supported by assets of the insurance company's general account), which assets of the insurance company (other than plan assets held in its separate accounts) constitute plan assets for purposes of ERISA and the Code.

The DOL published a proposed regulation late in 1997 and a final regulation in January 2000. The final regulation provides conditions, which include extensive disclosure requirements, under which an insurance company would not be deemed a fiduciary with regard to general account policies (other than guaranteed benefit policies, the assets of which are not considered plan assets in any event) issued on or before December 31, 1998. Pursuant to Congress's amendment to Section 401 of ERISA, the relief provided in the regulation applies only to nonguaranteed benefit policies issued on or before December 31, 1998. All general account contracts issued on or after January 1, 1999, that are not guaranteed benefit policies will be subject to ERISA's fiduciary provisions.

In its decision on remand in *Harris Trust & Savings Bank v. John Hancock Mutual Life Insurance Co* [302 F.3d 18 (2d Cir. 2002)], the Second Circuit held that where an insurance company is subject to ERISA's general fiduciary duty, this duty did not extend to releasing funds in a manner other than that specified by the contract. ERISA, the court stated, does not explicitly resolve tension that may exist between plan documents and fiduciary obligations imposed on plan administrators, but where parties negotiate the terms of a contract governing a plan, then the administrators, by following the terms of the contract, cannot be in breach of fiduciary duty.

Q 9:99 Does providing an investment-related educational program for plan participants and beneficiaries constitute fiduciary investment advice under ERISA?

No. The recent rise in the number of participant-directed individual account plans, which can be found in either qualified plans or Section 403(b) plans, has led to the recognition of the importance of providing participants and beneficiaries with sufficient information with regard to investment principles and strategies to assist them in making informed investment decisions. In turn, this recognition has led to concerns that providing any such information or materials may be deemed investment advice that causes the provider of such advice to rise to the level of a fiduciary and may cause potential liability.

In 1996, the DOL issued long-awaited guidance that clarifies its interpretation of ERISA's fiduciary provisions as they apply to investment-related educational programs for plan participants and beneficiaries. The guidance is set forth in DOL Interpretive Bulletin 96-1. The bulletin identifies categories of information and materials that may be provided to plan participants and beneficiaries that the DOL has determined will not constitute investment advice under ERISA's definition of a fiduciary. The bulletin essentially establishes safe harbors under ERISA for plan sponsors and service providers. The permitted categories are as follows:

1. *Plan information.*

    a. Information about the plan, including the benefits of plan participation, the benefits of increasing plan contributions, the impact of preretirement withdrawals on anticipated retirement income, and the terms of operation of the plan; and

    b. Information on investment alternatives under the plan (e.g., descriptions of investment objectives and philosophies, risk and return characteristics, and historical return information or related prospectuses), without referencing the appropriateness of any particular investment option for a particular participant or beneficiary.

2. *General financial and investment information.*

    a. General financial and investment concepts such as risk and return, diversification, dollar cost averaging, compounded return, and tax-deferred investment;

    b. Historical performances of different asset classes (e.g., equities, bonds, or cash) based on standard market indices;

    c. Effects of inflation;

    d. Estimating future retirement income needs;

    e. Determining investment time horizons; and

    f. Assessing risk tolerance.

3. *Asset allocation models.* Information and materials (e.g., pie charts, graphs, or case studies) that provide participants and beneficiaries with models of asset allocation portfolios of hypothetical individuals with different time horizons and risk profiles.

4. *Interactive investment materials.* Questionnaires, worksheets, software, and similar materials that provide participants and beneficiaries a means to estimate future retirement needs and to assess the impact of different asset allocations on retirement income.

The categories and information described above are not intended by the DOL to be exclusive. They are intended as examples of information and materials that may be furnished without constituting investment advice under ERISA's definition of a fiduciary. [*See* DOL Interpretive Bulletin 96-1 in Appendix A]

Q 9:100   What was the "Year 2000" problem, and to what extent were plan fiduciaries obligated to address this problem?

Commonly referred to as the "Year 2000" or "Y2K" problem, this issue arises when a computer performing a date-dependent function produces erroneous results because the system recognizes years only by the last two digits, causing a "00" entry to be read as the year 1900 rather than the year 2000. Computer systems with this limitation were generally expected to experience malfunctions on or after January 1, 2000. Most did not.

Like most business operations, employee benefit plans could have been disrupted by the Year 2000 problem because they rely on computers to perform critical operations such as benefit calculations and payments. In addition, employee benefit plan investments would have been affected where the underlying businesses of plan investments experience financial loss from the Year 2000 problem.

The DOL had indicated that, in accordance with ERISA fiduciary responsibility provisions, plan fiduciaries must have established and implemented prudent procedures for ensuring Year 2000 compliance with respect to a plan. [*See* PWBA release, July 23, 1998] Such procedures were expected to include, to the extent appropriate, the evaluation of (1) the plan's own computer system; (2) the plan sponsor's computer system; (3) the plan's service provider's computer system; and (4) the computer systems relating to the plan's investments. [PWBA release, Dec. 12, 1998] In investment decision making, plan fiduciaries had to take prudent measures to protect the plan from the potential adverse effect of the Year 2000 problem on plan asset investments. Finally, it was expected that a plan fiduciary would establish and implement a contingency plan designed to protect the interests of the plan and its participants and beneficiaries in the event a Year 2000 problem arose in any of these areas. While Year 2000 problems are hopefully no longer a concern, the DOL position generally serves as excellent guidance for plan fiduciaries in fulfilling their fiduciary duties in implementing computer systems and in assuring the capabilities of service providers.

Q 9:101   Is the custodian responsible for the directions of the named fiduciary with regard to plan investments?

While the DOL has not addressed the issue of custodians, in Field Assistance Bulletin No. 2004-03 it did address the issue of directed trustees with regard to public securities. By analogy, much of the guidance would seem to apply to custodians of Section 403(b) plans. In that bulletin, the DOL noted that the directed trustee must ensure that the direction is proper within the scope of the plan documents. It also stressed that a direction that is proper under the plan documents could still be improper under ERISA if the directed trustee knows or should know it is a prohibited transaction under ERISA Section 406 or violates the prudence requirements of ERISA Section 404(a)(1). The directed trustee may rely on representations unless it knows it to be false and need not second guess or duplicate the work of the plan fiduciaries. It must, however, disclose nonpublic information that may be in the possession of the involved portion of the named fiduciary organizations.

Q 9:102 Can a financial institution that holds assets of an abandoned plan distribute benefits to plan participants and beneficiaries?

The DOL issued regulations that would allow a financial institution to distribute benefits of an abandoned plan to plan participants and beneficiaries. [D.O.L. Reg. §§ 2520.103-13, 2550.404a-3, 2578.1] Abandoned plans, sometimes referred to as orphan plans, historically have been handled by the DOL on a case-by-case basis, with the involvement of the courts. The regulations establish standards for determining when a plan may be considered abandoned and deemed terminated, create procedures for winding up the affairs of the plan and distributing benefits to plan participants and beneficiaries, and provide guidance on who is entitled to carry out the winding up process.

The regulations specify that all determinations of plan abandonment, as well as related activities necessary to the termination and winding up of a plan, may be performed only by a qualified termination administrator (QTA). A person or entity can qualify as a QTA only if first, it is eligible to serve as a trustee or an issuer of an individual retirement plan that is within the meaning of Code Section 7701(a)(37), and second, the individual or entity actually holds the assets of the plan on whose behalf it will serve as the QTA. As such, a bank, trust company, mutual fund family, or insurance company could serve as a QTA. The guidance provides that a plan may be considered to be abandoned if (1) no contributions have been made to (or no distributions have been made from) the plan for a period of 12 months, or where circumstances known to the QTA suggest that the plan is or may be abandoned, such as in the case of the bankruptcy of the plan sponsor, and (2) following reasonable efforts to locate or communicate with the known plan sponsor, the QTA determines that the plan sponsor no longer exists, cannot be located, or is unable to maintain the plan. The regulations describe specific steps that would constitute "reasonable efforts."

Following a QTA's determination that a plan has been abandoned, the plan will generally be deemed terminated on the 90th day following the date the QTA provides notice of its determination and its election to serve as QTA with the DOL.

To help to clarify and limit the scope of responsibilities and liability of QTAs, and to thereby encourage participation in a formal process, the regulations establish specific guidelines on how to wind up such plans. For example, the regulations provide guidance on gathering plan records, calculating benefits that are payable to participants and beneficiaries, notifying them of the termination and their rights, and distributing their benefits. They also provide specific guidance on payment of plan expenses.

Q 9:103   Would a plan provision that directs an automatic rollover to an IRA cause a plan fiduciary to breach its fiduciary duty?

Pursuant to EGTRRA, unless a participant affirmatively elects otherwise, a mandatory distribution that exceeds $1,000 and is an eligible rollover distribution must be rolled over directly to a designated default IRA. The DOL has issued a final regulation that establishes a safe harbor under which a fiduciary will be deemed to have satisfied his or her fiduciary responsibilities in connection with an automatic rollover. [D.O.L. Reg. § 2550.404a-2]

The regulation is designed to address fiduciary liability concerns with regard to selection of the IRA provider and monitoring of the IRA investment allocation. It is noteworthy that compliance with the safe harbor is not intended to represent the exclusive means by which a fiduciary can satisfy its fiduciary duties.

A fiduciary will qualify for the safe harbor if it meets all of the following six conditions:

1. The present value of the benefit cannot exceed the maximum amount under Code Section 401(a)(31)(B).
2. The rollover must be made to an individual retirement account or to an individual retirement annuity.
3. The fiduciary must enter into a written agreement with the IRA provider that provides the rolled over funds will be invested in an investment product designed to preserve capital and to provide a reasonable rate of return.
4. The fees and expenses charged to the designated default IRA cannot exceed the fees and expenses charged by the funding company for comparable IRAs.
5. Participants and beneficiaries must be furnished with a summary plan description or a summary of material modifications that describes the plan's automatic rollover provisions.
6. The plan fiduciary may not engage in a prohibited transaction in the selection of the IRA provider or investment funds.

The regulation indicates that to the extent the agreement between the plan fiduciary and the IRA provider complies with the safe harbor, the plan fiduciary is entitled to rely on the representations of the provider and need not monitor the provider's compliance with the terms of the agreement after the rollover. Subject to complying with the terms of the agreement and the safe harbor, the plan fiduciary's responsibilities with respect to the mandatory distribution could end at the time the assets are placed with the IRA provider. Moreover, the DOL expressed the view that the rollover of the entire plan benefit to which a participant is entitled ends the participant's status as a plan participant and the distributed assets cease to be plan assets.

Chapter 10

Distributions

Evan Giller, Esq.
Teachers Insurance and Annuity Association—College
Retirement Equities Fund

Barbara N. Seymon-Hirsch, Esq.
Davis & Harman LLP

Bryan W. Keene, Esq.
Davis & Harman LLP

The Section 403(b) tax-sheltered annuity contract, mutual fund separate account, or church plan retirement account is a tax-deferred vehicle.* While deferral continues, the Section 403(b) owner enjoys the benefit of tax-free accumulation. A point is reached, however, when this benefit may not continue for 100 percent of the account. Then, minimum distributions are required to commence, or else severe penalties may be imposed. In the case of Section 403(b) plans, the commencement date may be delayed until as late as age 75 with respect to amounts that were contributed and earned before 1987. When this apportionment is not successfully implemented, distributions of Section 403(b) accounts must commence under the rule that otherwise applies to post-1986 accumulations: no later than the April 1 of the calendar year following the later of (1) the calendar year in which the Section 403(b) participant attains age 70½ or (2) the calendar year in which the participant retires. In the event of earlier death, distributions may be required to start even sooner. Participants not subject to the age 70½-based required beginning date may

---

* Unless otherwise noted, references to a "403(b) contract" will include a 403(b) tax-sheltered annuity, mutual fund separate account, and church plan retirement account.

continue to apply the somewhat different distribution rules that formerly applied.

Although distributions sometimes may be accelerated and begin sooner than required, a 10 percent penalty may result if the Section 403(b) participant makes withdrawals before age 59½. Furthermore, distributions are taxable when made, so an earlier distribution date results in an earlier tax liability than would have resulted from a later distribution date.

On July 26, 2007, the IRS issued final Code Section 403(b) regulations that significantly changed many of the rules previously applicable to Section 403(b) arrangements, in particular tax-free transfer rules other than rollovers. Accordingly, this chapter incorporates and reflects the new rules applicable to Section 403(b) contracts under the final regulations.

Requirements Governing Timing and Amount of Benefit Distributions

Q 10:1   Are Section 403(b) plans subject to the minimum distribution requirements?

Yes. Because the purpose of a Section 403(b) plan is to provide an employee with retirement benefits, employees cannot defer the receipt of income indefinitely. All Section 403(b) plans (annuity contracts under Code Section 403(b)(1), custodial accounts under Code Section 403(b)(7), and retirement income accounts under Code Section 403(b)(9)) must comply generally with the minimum distribution requirements under Code Section 401(a)(9). By regulation, the distribution rules that are applicable to individual retirement annuities and individual retirement accounts apply to Section 403(b) contracts with two major exceptions: (1) the definition of the required beginning date is different (see Q 10:3), and (2) the special rule in Treasury Regulations Section 1.408-8, A-5 (allowing the surviving spouse of an IRA holder to treat the IRA as the spouse's own account) does not apply (see Q 10:31). [I.R.C. § 403(b)(10); Treas. Reg. § 1.403(b)-6(e)(2)-(4)] However, the Code Section 401(a)(9) requirements apply only to the portion of the accumulation that has accrued after December 31, 1986 (i.e., contributions made and all earnings credited after that date). Thus, if records are properly maintained, the pre-1987 account balance (the "grandfathered balance," i.e., the value of the account on December 31, 1986) is not subject to the minimum distribution rules, and the required distribution amount is calculated using only the post-1986 accumulation. This rule applies equally to annuity contracts, custodial accounts, and retirement income accounts. The grandfathered balance is subject to adjustments and to other distribution rules (see Q 10:17). [Treas. Reg. § 1.403(b)-6(a)(6)]

Q 10:2 What regulations must be followed to meet the required minimum distribution rules established in Code Sections 403(b)(10) and 401(a)(9)?

On July 27, 2007, the IRS issued final Code Section 403(b) regulations which included regulations under Code Section 403(b)(10), setting out the requirement that a Section 403(b) contract or custodial account meet requirements similar to the requirements of Code Section 401(a)(9). Treasury Regulations Section 1.403(b)-6(e) provides that a Section 403(b) contract must meet the requirements of Code Section 401(a)(9) in both form and operation.

On April 17, 2002, the IRS released final, temporary, and proposed regulations providing guidance on the minimum distribution rules. These regulations replaced the prior proposed regulations that were issued on July 27, 1987 [52 Fed. Reg. 29070] and on January 17, 2001 [66 Fed. Reg. 3928]. These regulations apply for determining required minimum distributions (RMDs) for calendar years beginning on or after January 1, 2003. On June 15, 2004, the IRS finalized the temporary and proposed regulations that had been issued as part of the April 17, 2002, release. [T.D. 9130, 69 Fed. Reg. 33,288 (June 15, 2004), corrected T.D. 9130, 69 Fed. Reg. 68,077 (Nov. 23, 2004)] Although the final regulations are effective for calendar years beginning on or after January 1, 2003, a distribution in calendar year 2003, 2004, or 2005 that does not satisfy the new rules was still deemed to be in compliance with Code Section 401(a)(9) if it was based on a reasonable and good faith interpretation of the statute. A reasonable and good faith interpretation included compliance with the previous sets of regulations. For governmental plans, the reasonable and good faith standard applied until the end of the calendar year that contained the 90th day after the opening of the first legislative session of the legislative body with the authority to amend the plan that began on or after June 15, 2004, if such 90th day was after December 31, 2005.

Q 10:3 When are benefit distributions to a participant required to begin under the minimum distribution requirements?

Benefit distributions from the portion of the account balance that accrues after December 31, 1986, that is, contributions made and all earnings credited after that date, must begin no later than the required beginning date. The required beginning date is the later of April 1 of the calendar year following the calendar year in which the employee attains age 70½ or April 1 of the calendar year following the calendar year in which the employee retires. [I.R.C. § 401(a)(9)(C), as amended by § 1404 of Small Business Job Protection Act of 1996 (SBJPA)] Prior to January 1, 1997, the required beginning date for non-governmental plans was generally April 1 of the calendar year following the calendar year in which the employee attained age 70½ even if the employee was still employed.

Q 10:4 What is a distribution calendar year?

A distribution calendar year is a calendar year for which a minimum distribution is required. If an employee's required beginning date is April 1 of the calendar year following the calendar year in which the employee attains age 70½, the first distribution calendar year is the year in which the employee attains 70½. If the required beginning date is April 1 after the calendar year in which the employee retires, the calendar year in which the employee retires is the first distribution calendar year.

Distributions for an employee's first distribution calendar year must be made on or before the required beginning date, the April 1 following the distribution calendar year. Distributions for subsequent distribution calendar years must be made on or before the end of that year.

Q 10:5 Can a Section 403(b) plan be amended to eliminate the right of a current participant to receive a distribution at age 70½ while still employed, without violating the anticutback rules of ERISA?

By regulation effective June 5, 1998, it was not a violation of the anticutback rules for a plan to have eliminated preretirement distributions commencing at age 70½, in order to conform with the definition of *required beginning date* as amended by SBJPA. The regulation provides that such an amendment

1. Applies only to employees who attain age 70½ in or after a calendar year that begins after the later of December 31, 1998, or the date that the amendment is adopted;
2. Does not preclude an employee who retires after age 70½ from receiving benefits in a form that would have been available had the employee retired in the year he or she attained age 70½ (except as otherwise required by Code Section 401(a)(9); and
3. Was adopted no later than the end of the remedial amendment period for adopting amendments to comply with SBJPA or December 31, 1998.

[Treas. Reg. § 1.411(d)-4, A-10]

Q 10:6   Will a plan satisfy the minimum distribution requirements if it provides that the required beginning date is the date as defined prior to the SBJPA amendments (i.e., April 1 of the calendar year following the calendar year in which the employee attained age 70½)?

Yes. A plan can provide for minimum distributions to commence no later than an employee's pre-SBJPA required beginning date (see Q 10:3) of April 1 of the calendar year following the calendar year in which the employee attained age 70½. However, for purposes of the excise tax in Code Section 4974 (see Q 10:32)and the eligible rollover rules in Code Section 402(c), the required beginning date is that date as defined by the SBJPA amendments (i.e., April 1 of the calendar year following the later of the calendar year in which the employee attains age 70½ or retires). Thus, no excise tax will apply to the employee under Code Section 4974 prior to the calendar year in which the employee retires.

Q 10:7   When does a participant attain age 70½?

A participant attains age 70½ as of the date six months after the 70th anniversary of his or her birth. As an example, an employee whose date of birth is June 30, 1930, attained age 70 on June 30, 2000, and age 70½ on December 30, 2000. If the employee is not still employed, the required beginning date is April 1, 2001. If the employee's date of birth is July 30, 1930, the employee attained age 70½ on January 30, 2001, and the required beginning date is April 1, 2001. [Treas. Reg. § 1.401(a)(9)-2, A-3]

Q 10:8   Must distributions made before the required beginning date meet the minimum distribution requirements?

Generally, distributions made before the employee's required beginning date for calendar years before the employee's first distribution calendar year (see Q 10:3) do not need to comply with the minimum distribution requirements. However, if distributions begin under a lifetime option, such as an annuity, before the required beginning date for the first distribution calendar year, the option will fail to satisfy the distribution rules at the time payments begin if distributions to be made under the option for any of the employee's distribution calendar years will not meet the distribution requirements. [Treas. Reg. § 1.401(a)(9)-2, A-4]

Q 10:9   How must benefits be distributed to the participant as of the required beginning date if they commence before his or her death?

Either the post-1986 accumulation must be distributed to the participant in full not later than the required beginning date, or the participant's interest must be distributed in periodic payments, beginning not later than the required beginning date, over the life of the participant or over the joint lives of the participant and a designated beneficiary. Alternatively, this payment period must be a period not extending beyond the life expectancy of the participant or the joint life expectancy of the participant and a designated beneficiary. The payments must be made not less frequently than annually. [Treas. Reg. §§ 1.401(a)(9)-2, 1.401(a)(9)-5] Benefits may be in the form of annual distributions from an individual account or in the form of an annuity.

Q 10:10   What is the applicable account balance when distributions are being made from an individual account?

The applicable accumulation is the accumulation as of the last valuation date in the calendar year preceding the distribution calendar year reduced (where available) by the grandfathered accumulation (see Q 10:16). Thus, if the distribution calendar year (see Q 10:4) is 2007, and the plan provides for daily valuation, the applicable accumulation is the accumulation value (as reduced by the grandfathered amount) on December 31, 2006.

In addition, in accordance with Treasury Regulations Section 1.401(a)(9)-6, A-12, prior to the date that an annuity contract is "annuitized," the entire interest under the contract equals the dollar amount credited to the employee or beneficiary under the contract plus the actuarial present value of any additional benefits (such as survivor benefits in excess of the dollar amount credited to the employee or beneficiary) that will be provided under the contract. However, these additional benefits may be disregarded if:

1. the only additional benefit provided under the contract is the right to receive a final payment upon death that does not exceed the excess of the premiums paid less the amount of prior distributions, or
2. the sum of the dollar amount credited to the employee or beneficiary under the contract and the actuarial present value of the additional benefits is no more than 120 percent of the dollar amount credited to the employee or beneficiary under the contract and the contract provides only for the following types of additional benefits:
   - additional benefits that, in the case of a distribution, are reduced by an amount sufficient to ensure that the ratio of such sum to the dollar amount credited does not increase as a result of the distribution, and
   - an additional benefit described in (1) above.

Q 10:11   When distributions are being made from an individual account plan to the participant not in the form of an annuity, how is the required minimum distribution amount calculated?

Under the regulations, the required minimum distribution is equal to the quotient obtained by dividing the applicable account balance by the applicable distribution period. In general, the applicable distribution period for distribution calendar years up to and including the employee's date of death is determined by reference to a table found in Treasury Regulations Section 1.401(a)(9)-9, which is provided in Appendix C of this book. This table is utilized whether or not the participant has named a beneficiary and, with one major exception, regardless of the age of that beneficiary (see Q 10:12). The age used to calculate the required amount for purposes of this table is the employee's age as of the employee's birthday in the relevant distribution calendar year. The distribution period under the table is the joint life expectancy of the employee plus a hypothetical joint annuitant who is 10 years younger, all determined as of the employee's age in the year of the distribution. Thus, under these regulations, the life expectancy is "recalculated" each year for all participants and all beneficiaries.

Q 10:12   When is the applicable distribution period for distributions during an employee's lifetime determined without reference to the table set out in Treasury Regulations Section 1.401(a)(9)-5?

If the employee's sole designated beneficiary is the employee's spouse, the applicable distribution period is the longer of the period set forth in the table or the joint life expectancy of the employee and spouse using their attained ages as of their birthdays in the distribution calendar year. [Treas. Reg. § 1.401(a)(9)-5, A-4(b)] The joint life expectancy is computed using the table in A-3 of Treasury Regulations Section 1.401(a)(9)-9.

Q 10:13   When is the spouse considered to be the sole designated beneficiary?

The spouse is the sole designated beneficiary for the purpose of determining the applicable distribution period during the employee's lifetime if the employee and the employee's spouse are married on January 1 of a distribution calendar year, even if they do not remain married throughout the year. [Treas. Reg. § 1.401(a)(9)-5, A-4(b)(2)]

Q 10:14   If the participant meets the distribution requirements by receiving periodic payments from an annuity contract, what amount must be paid out each year?

Distributions will satisfy the requirements of these rules if they are in the form of periodic annuity payments for the employee's life or for the joint lives of the employee and the beneficiary, or over a period certain. The life annuity may also provide for a period certain. The period certain generally is not permitted to exceed the applicable distribution period (see Q 10:12) for the employee. However, if the employee's sole beneficiary is the employee's spouse and the annuity provides only a period certain and no life annuity, the period certain may be the longer of the applicable distribution period or the joint life and survivor expectancy of the employee and the spouse. Annuity payments must commence on or before the employee's required beginning date.

Annuity payments must be made at uniform intervals not to exceed one year. The payments must not increase, or they must increase only as follows:

- In accordance with a cost-of-living index issued by the Bureau of Labor Statistics. The increases can be on an annual basis, or less frequently and cumulative since the most recent increase as long as there is no actuarial increase to reflect having not provided increases in the interim years
- Under certain survivor benefit arrangements where the designated beneficiary dies or is no longer the beneficiary pursuant to a qualified domestic relations order
- To provide cash refunds of employee contributions upon an employee's death
- To pay for increased benefits under the plan
- When an account balance is being annuitized under an insurance company contract, if the total future expected payments exceed the account value being annuitized, the payments may be increased
    —by a constant percentage, applied at least annually
    —to provide a payment upon the death of the employee equal to the excess of the account value being annuitized over the total of payments before the death of the employee
    —as a result of certain dividend payments or other payments that result from certain actuarial gains
    —an acceleration of payments under the annuity, defined as a shortening of the payment period with respect to an annuity or a full or partial commutation of the future annuity benefits. An increase in the payment amount will meet this rule only if the total future expected payments under the annuity is decreased.

[Treas. Reg. § 1.401(a)(9)-6, A-14].

The minimum distribution requirement will be satisfied if the entire account balance is annuitized in accordance with these rules. If a portion of the account balance is annuitized, the remaining amount in the account must be distributed in accordance with the individual account rules.

If distributions are in the form of a joint and survivor annuity with a nonspouse beneficiary, the payment to the beneficiary is subject to the minimum distribution incidental (MDIB) benefit rules (see Q 10:27).

Q 10:15 How is the minimum distribution amount determined when a participant holds more than one contract?

The amount that must be distributed in each distribution calendar year must be determined separately for each Section 403(b) contract. However, if an employee holds more than one contract, the amounts that must be distributed from each contract may be totaled and the distribution taken from one or more of the contracts. An employee may only aggregate contracts he or she holds as an employee. If contracts are held as a beneficiary, they may only be aggregated with other contracts held as a beneficiary of the same decedent. Distributions from Section 403(b) contracts cannot be aggregated with IRAs for this purpose. [Treas. Reg. § 1.403(b)-6(e)(7)]

Calculation and Distribution of Grandfathered Amounts

Q 10:16   How does the application of the grandfathered amount reduce the applicable accumulation?

The grandfathered amount is, generally, the account balance as of December 31, 1986. The value of the grandfathered amount can be deducted from the accumulation on the valuation date in order to obtain the applicable accumulation. However, in order to determine the grandfathered amount that may be deducted, the December 31, 1986, accumulation must be adjusted. Any amount distributed, in any calendar year, that is in excess of the amount needed to satisfy a required distribution amount in that calendar year will be treated as having been distributed from the pre-1987 account balance and will be subtracted from the grandfathered balance. [Treas. Reg. § 1.403(b)-6(e)(6)] Thus, the grandfathered amount is not subject to the general minimum distribution rules. Grandfathered amounts must be distributed in a manner that satisfies the incidental benefit requirements (see Q 10:17).

To subtract the grandfathered amount from the applicable accumulation, the annuity issuer or the custodian must maintain records of the grandfathered balance, keep track of the necessary adjustments, and make this information available to the participant or beneficiary. If proper records are not kept, the entire account balance will be treated as subject to the required distribution rules. [Treas. Reg. § 1.403(b)-6(e)(6)]

Q 10:17   What distribution rules apply to the grandfathered amount?

The final Code Section 403(b) regulations published on July 26, 2007 provide that the pre-1987 account balance may be distributed in accordance with the minimum distribution incidental benefit (MDIB) rules set forth in the regulations, or in accordance with the incidental benefit rules under Treasury Regulations Section 1.401-1(b)(1)(i). [Treas. Reg. § 1.403(b)-(6)(e)(6)] The IRS has interpreted the incidental benefit rules under Treasury Regulations Section 1.401-1(b)(1)(i) as mandating that the commencement of payments from Section 403(b) contracts begin no later than when the participant attains age 75. [Ltr. Rul. 9345044] In one private letter ruling, the IRS has also said that it is irrelevant whether the individual to whom this rule applies is a retired or an active participant. [Ltr. Rul. 9345044] According to this private letter ruling, this means that employees who work until age 75 must begin distributions of their grandfathered amount, even though distributions from the nongrandfathered amount need not be taken until the April of the year following the year of retirement. In light of the change in the required beginning date effected by

SBJPA (see Q 10:3), it is likely that Private Letter Ruling 9345044 does not reflect the current position of the IRS.

In addition, the IRS has ruled that the incidental benefit rules under Treasury Regulations Section 1.401-(b)(1)(i) provided that benefits payable to the participant must equal at least 50 percent of the present value of the total payments to be made to the participant and beneficiaries other than spousal beneficiaries. [Rev. Rul. 72-241, 1972-1 C.B. 108] Thus, the joint payout options otherwise available to participants and nonspousal beneficiaries under the contract may be limited to meet this rule to the extent that it is applicable.

If an employee chooses to apply the MDIB rules in the final Code Section 403(b) regulations, rather than the rules under Treasury Regulations Section 1.401-1(b)(1)(i), distribution of the grandfathered amount would have to begin in accordance with those rules by the required beginning date (see Q 10:3).

Distributions After Death of Participant

Q 10:18   How must distributions be made after the death of a participant if distributions began before the participant's death?

If the participant has begun distributions and dies before the entire interest has been distributed, the remaining portion of the participant's interest must be distributed at least as rapidly as under the distribution method that was being used as of the date of death. [I.R.C. § 401(a)(9)(B)(i)] If distributions are being made from an individual account, the amount that must be distributed in each distribution calendar year is equal to the quotient obtained by dividing the applicable accumulation (see Q 10:10) by the applicable distribution period. The length of the applicable distribution period is determined as follows:

1. If the employee has a designated beneficiary as of the applicable date after his or her death (see Q 10:23), the applicable distribution period is the remaining life expectancy of the designated beneficiary. For nonspouse beneficiaries, the remaining life expectancy is determined by using the beneficiary's age in the year following the year of the participant's death, and reducing that number by one in each subsequent year. If the spouse is the employee's sole beneficiary, the remaining life expectancy is determined each year by reference to the surviving spouse's birthday in the distribution calendar year following the employee's death. After the surviving spouse's death, the applicable distribution period is the spouse's remaining life expectancy as of the spouse's birthday in the calendar year of his or her death, reduced by one in each succeeding year. [Treas. Reg. § 1.401(a)(9)-5, A-5]

2. If there is no designated beneficiary as of the applicable date, the applicable distribution period is the life expectancy of the employee using the age of the employee as of his or her birthday in the calendar year of his or her death, reduced by one in each succeeding year.

In each case, the life expectancies are computed using the tables in Treasury Regulations Section 1.401(a)(9)-9.

Under the prior proposed regulations, the applicable distribution period depended upon whether the participant was recalculating his or her life expectancy and whether the designated beneficiary, if any, was a spouse who was recalculating life expectancy. [1987 Prop. Treas. Reg. § 1.401(a)(9)-1, B-5]

Q 10:19   If required distributions are being made to an employee under an annuity contract, how long may a period certain extend payments to a beneficiary?

If the employee's sole beneficiary is his or her spouse as of the annuity starting date, the period certain under the annuity being paid to the employee cannot exceed the joint life expectancy of the employee and the spouse using their ages as of their birthdays in the calendar year that contains the annuity starting date.

If an employee's sole beneficiary is not the employee's surviving spouse, the period certain may not exceed the shorter of the applicable distribution period for the employee (see Q 10:11) for the calendar year that contains the annuity starting date, or the joint life expectancy of the employee and the employee's designated beneficiary, using the beneficiary as of the annuity starting date and their ages as of their birthdays in the calendar year that contains the annuity starting date.

Under some circumstances, a distribution in the form of a period certain can be changed. A period certain-only annuity can be changed to another form at any time, as long as the future payments under the modification satisfy Code Section 401(a)(9) and the end point of the new period certain, if any, is not later than the end point available at the original annuity starting date. [Treas. Reg. § 1.401(a)(9)-6, A-13]

Q 10:20   How must distributions be made after the death of a participant if distributions are not treated as having already begun?

If a participant dies before distributions have begun, there are two basic methods for distributing the participant's accumulation:

1. *The five-year rule.* The entire interest of the participant must be distributed by December 31 of the calendar year that contains the fifth anniversary of the participant's death. This distribution can be made to any individual or entity that is a beneficiary under the contract. [I.R.C. § 401(a)(9)(ii)]

2. *The life expectancy rule.* Any portion of a participant's interest that is payable to a designated beneficiary (see Q 10:23) must be distributed, beginning by December 31 of the calendar year following the year of the participant's death, over the life of the beneficiary or over a period not extending beyond the life expectancy of the beneficiary. If the designated

beneficiary is the participant's spouse, the distributions must begin on or before the later of (a) December 31 of the calendar year following the year of the participant's death or (b) December 31 of the calendar year in which the participant would have turned 70½. [I.R.C. § 401(a)(9)(iii) and (iv)] If there is a nonspouse beneficiary designated along with the spousal beneficiary, the spousal rule cannot be used. [Treas. Reg. § 1.401(a)(9)-3] However, if the contract is divided into separate accounts and one account has a spousal beneficiary and the other has a nonspousal beneficiary, each account may be treated separately for the purpose of applying this rule. [Treas. Reg. § 1.401(a)(9)-8]

If distributions are being made from an individual account, the amount distributed in each distribution calendar year is equal to the quotient obtained by dividing the applicable accumulation by the applicable distribution period. The applicable distribution period is determined as follows:

If the employee has a designated beneficiary as of the applicable date after his or her death (see Q 10:23), the applicable distribution period is the remaining life expectancy of the designated beneficiary.

1. For nonspouse beneficiaries, the remaining life expectancy is determined by using the beneficiary's age in the year following the year of the participant's death, and reducing that number by one in each subsequent year.

2. If the spouse is the employee's sole beneficiary, the remaining life expectancy is determined each year by reference to the surviving spouse's birthday in the distribution calendar year following the employee's death. After the surviving spouse's death, the applicable distribution period is the spouse's remaining life expectancy as of the spouse's birthday in the calendar year of his or her death, reduced by one in each succeeding year. [Treas. Reg. § 1.401(a)(9)-5, A-5]

If distributions are being made in the form of an annuity, the period certain for any distributions commencing after death cannot exceed the applicable distribution period used when calculating distributions to beneficiaries from an individual account.

Q 10:21   When are distributions considered to have begun to the participant in order to determine which distribution rule to apply after the participant's death?

If distributions are begun before the participant's required beginning date, but not paid as an annuity, the payments are not considered to have begun until the required beginning date. Therefore, if the participant dies before the required beginning date and had received nonannuity distributions, the participant is deemed to have not begun distributions for the purpose of applying the rules for distributions after death.

Example 1. Karen retires in 2002 at age 65½ and begins to take withdrawals from her contract. Benefits are not considered to have begun until her required beginning date, or April 1, 2008. If she dies after beginning benefits but before the required beginning date, her beneficiary must follow the distribution rules that apply when a participant has died before benefits have begun. [Treas Reg § 1.401(a)(9)-2, A-6]

If the plan provides that the required beginning date is April 1 of the calendar year following the calendar year in which the employee turns 70½, an employee who dies after that date but prior to retirement is treated as having died after the required beginning date.

However, if distributions have irrevocably commenced as an annuity that conforms with the minimum distribution rules, distributions will be considered to have begun on the date the annuity commenced regardless of the employee's required beginning date.

> **Example 2.** In Example 1, if Karen had received her benefits in the form of an annuity and died before her required beginning date, her beneficiary must follow the distribution rules that apply when a participant has died after benefits have begun. [Treas. Reg. § 1.401(a)(9)-6, A-10]

Q 10:22   How is it determined whether the five-year rule or the life expectancy rule applies to a distribution?

When an employee dies before his or her required beginning date, distribution of the employee's entire interest must be made in accordance with either the five-year rule or the life expectancy rule (see Q 10:20). The regulations provide that if a Section 403(b) contract does not specify the method of distribution, the distribution must be made in accordance with the following rules:

1. If the employee has a designated beneficiary as of the applicable date, distributions are to be made in accordance with the life expectancy rule.

2. If the employee has no designated beneficiary, distributions are to be made in accordance with the five-year rule.

The contract or plan may adopt a provision specifying either method, or a provision that allows employees or beneficiaries to elect which method will apply. [Treas. Reg. § 1.401(a)(9)-3] The contract or the underlying plan may contain a provision specifying which of the two methods to use, or it may allow employees and beneficiaries to elect the method to be used. In the event that an election is permitted, it must be made no later than the earlier of (1) December 31 of the calendar year in which distributions would be required to commence in order to satisfy the requirements of the exception to the five-year rule or (2) December 31 of the calendar year that contains the fifth anniversary of the date of the death of the participant. As of that date, the election is irrevocable and applies to all future years. [Treas. Reg. § 1.401(a)(9)-3, A-4]

The regulations contain a transition rule that allows a beneficiary who is receiving payments under the five-year rule to switch to the life expectancy rule under certain circumstances. [Treas. Reg. §§ 1.401(a)(9)-1, A-2(b)(2), 1.401(a)(9)-3, A-4]

Designated Beneficiaries

Q 10:23 Who is the designated beneficiary?

A beneficiary is a designated individual who is entitled to a portion of a participant's benefits, contingent on the participant's death or other specified event. The designated beneficiary is determined by the terms of the contract or plan. The contract or plan can designate an individual as a beneficiary or can allow the participant to elect a beneficiary. As long as the individual is identifiable under the contract or plan as of the required beginning date or as of the date of the participant's death, the individual need not be specified by name. The designated beneficiary may be a class of individuals even if the class is capable of expansion or contraction (e.g., the participant's children) as long as it is possible at the date the beneficiary is determined to identify the member of the class with the shortest life expectancy. [Treas. Reg. § 1.401(a)(9)-4]

Q 10:24 When is the designated beneficiary determined?

In general, the employee's designated beneficiary is determined based on the beneficiaries designated as of the September 30 following the calendar year of the employee's death. Thus, if a beneficiary named as of the date of the employee's death disclaims in favor of another beneficiary or receives his or her full distribution under the plan by the September 30 following the year of the employee's death, that person is not taken into account in determining the employee's designated beneficiary for purposes of the required distribution rules. However, if the distributions are in the form of an irrevocable annuity, the designated beneficiary will be determined as of the annuity starting date. [Treas. Reg. § 1.401(a)(9)-6, A-10]

Q 10:25 Under what circumstances may a person other than an individual be considered to be a designated beneficiary?

In general, only individuals may be designated beneficiaries for purposes of the minimum distribution rules. If an entity other than an individual is designated under the plan as a beneficiary, the participant is treated as having no designated beneficiary. In such a case, upon the death of the participant before the required beginning date, all distributions must be made in accordance with the five-year rule (see Q 10:20). Upon the death of the participant after the required beginning date, the distribution period is limited to the remaining life expectancy of the employee (see Q 10:18).

However, if a trust is named as beneficiary, special rules apply. All beneficiaries of the trust with respect to the trust's interest in the contract are treated as designated beneficiaries if, as of the later of the date on which the trust is named the beneficiary or the required beginning date, the trust meets the following requirements:

1. The trust is a valid trust under state law or would be but for the fact that there is no corpus.

2. The trust is irrevocable or will, by its terms, become irrevocable upon the death of the employee.

3. The beneficiaries of the trust are identifiable from the trust instrument.

4. Certain documentation has been provided to the plan administrator. In general, prior to the death of the employee, he or she must either

   a. provide to the plan administrator a copy of the trust instrument and agree to provide the administrator with any amendments, or

   b. provide the plan administrator with a list of all beneficiaries and certify the completeness of the list and provide a copy of the trust if requested.

After the death of the employee, the trustee must provide the plan administrator with a final list of all beneficiaries or a copy of the trust document by October 31 of the calendar year following the calendar year in which the employee died.

If the above requirements are met, the beneficiaries of the trust will be treated as the employee's beneficiaries for purposes of the required distribution rules. If the above requirements are not met, a trust that is named the beneficiary of a contract will not be considered a designated beneficiary. [Treas. Reg. § 1.401(a)(9)-4, A-5, 6]

Q 10:26   If the participant has more than one designated beneficiary, which designated beneficiary's life expectancy will be used to determine the distribution period?

If more than one individual is designated as a beneficiary by a participant, the designated beneficiary with the shortest life expectancy will be the designated beneficiary for purposes of determining the distribution period. Except in the case of a qualifying trust (see Q 10:25), if an entity other than an individual is designated as a beneficiary, the participant will be treated as having no designated beneficiaries even if there are also individuals designated as beneficiaries. [Treas. Reg. § 1.401(a)(9)-4, A-3]

Minimum Distribution Incidental Benefit Requirements

Q 10:27   How do the incidental benefit requirements apply to Section 403(b) contracts?

The incidental benefit requirements stipulate that any benefit provided by a contract that is other than a retirement benefit must be incidental to the payment of retirement benefits to the participants. Prior to the Tax Reform Act of 1986 (TRA '86), the incidental benefit requirement mandated that the form of distribution chosen must provide that the present value of the payments to be made to the participant would be more than 50 percent of the present value of the total value of payments to the participant and his or her beneficiaries. [Rev. Rul. 72-241, 1972-1 C.B. 108] The IRS has also interpreted this rule prior to TRA '86 as requiring that distributions from Section 403(b) contracts commence when the participant attains age 75 (see Q 10:17). [Ltr. Rul. 9345044]

This incidental benefit rule was codified for Section 403(b) contracts in TRA '86 as the MDIB requirements. The final Code Section 403(b) regulations published on July 26, 2007, provide that the entire account balance, including the grandfathered amount (see Q 10:16), must satisfy the MDIB rules. However, the grandfathered amounts will satisfy the MDIB rules by meeting either the rules that are under Treasury Regulations Section 1.401-1(b)(1)(i) [*see* Rev. Rul. 72-241, 1972-1 C.B. 108] or the rules that apply to the accumulation amounts that are not grandfathered (i.e., the post-1986 accruals). [Treas. Reg. § 1.403(b)-6(e)(6)]

Q 10:28   What are the minimum distribution incidental benefit (MDIB) requirements?

For a distribution to satisfy the minimum distribution requirements, the amount or form of the distribution must meet the MDIB requirements as well as the general distribution requirements described previously. In general, the regulations under Code Section 401(a)(9) greatly simplified the application of these rules from the prior proposed regulations. A distribution to an employee from an individual account will satisfy the MDIB rules if they follow the requirements described in Q 10:11, if distributions are being made in the form of a single life annuity to the employee, or if distributions are made in the form of a joint and survivor annuity where the spouse is the employee's sole beneficiary.

If the participant's benefit is in the form of a joint and survivor annuity for the lives of the participant and a beneficiary other than the participant's spouse, the MDIB requirements are satisfied only if, after the participant's required beginning date, the periodic amount payable to the beneficiary after the participant's death does not exceed the "applicable percentage" of the periodic amount paid to the participant. The applicable percentage is set out in a table in the regulations, and is based on the differential between the ages of the participant and the nonspouse beneficiary. However, if the participant's annuity starting date is at an age younger than age 70, an adjustment is made to the age differential. The adjusted age differential is determined by decreasing the age difference by the number of years the employee is younger than age 70 at the annuity starting date. This effectively allows for a higher applicable percentage after a participant's death for employees who commence benefits at earlier ages. [Treas. Reg. § 1.401(a)(9)-6, A-2] It is based on the excess of the age of the participant over the age of the beneficiary as of their attained ages as of their birthdays in a calendar year. For example, if the participant is 20 years older than a nonspouse beneficiary, the periodic payment to the beneficiary on the death of the participant can be no greater than 73 percent of the periodic payment that had been made to the participant. If the employee has more than one beneficiary, the applicable percentage will be the percentage using the age of the youngest beneficiary.

For the special MDIB rules that apply to grandfathered amounts in a Section 403(b) contract, see Q 10:17.

Q 10:29   How do exchanges or transfers between Section 403(b) contracts affect the minimum distribution requirements?

A contract exchange between Section 403(b) contracts is not treated as a distribution. If a transfer is made prior to the participant's first distribution calendar year, the accumulations in both the transferor and transferee contracts are adjusted accordingly. The grandfathered amount transferred retains its character as a pre-1987 balance. [Treas. Reg. § 1.403(b)-6(e)(6)(iv),] Although there is no specific authority in the regulations, it appears that if the transfer is partial, the grandfathered amount should be transferred pro rata. However, in the case of a transfer from an insolvent insurer, the IRS held that, for purposes of determining the minimum distribution required, a partial transfer to a new contract would be treated as consisting first of the unrecovered pre-1987 account balance from the original contract. [Ltr. Rul. 9442030]

If a portion of the accumulation is transferred in a distribution calendar year, the regulations require that the transferor plan determine the amount of the required distribution for that year. The transferor plan may satisfy the minimum distribution requirements by segregating the distribution amount and not transferring it. The regulations provide that the amount may be retained by the plan and distributed on the date required. [Treas. Reg. § 1.401(a)(9)-7, A-3]

Q 10:30   Can an amount that must be distributed as a required distribution be rolled over?

No. A required distribution is not an eligible rollover distribution. [I.R.C. § 402(c)(4)] An amount that is distributed by one plan and rolled over to another plan is still treated as a distribution by the distributing plan for purposes of determining required minimum distributions. For purposes of determining the required minimum distributions in the receiving plan, the employee's benefit is increased by the amount rolled over for the calendar year following the year of the distribution. If the amount rolled over is received in a different calendar year from the year distributed, the amount rolled over is deemed to have been received in the year it was distributed. [Treas. Reg. § 1.401(a)(9)-7]

Q 10:31   Can the surviving spouse of an employee who is the sole beneficiary of a Section 403(b) contract treat the contract as his or her own after the death of the employee?

No. The rule that a surviving spouse who is the sole beneficiary of an IRA owner can treat the IRA as his or her own after the owner's death does not apply to Section 403(b) contracts.

Q 10:32   What is the penalty for failure to make a required minimum distribution?

There is an excise tax imposed on the payee (employee or beneficiary) equal to 50 percent of the amount by which the required distribution exceeds the actual distribution during the calendar year. The IRS may waive the excise tax if the payee establishes that the shortfall was due to reasonable error and reasonable steps are being taken to remedy it. The tax will be automatically waived if the payee is the sole beneficiary whose distribution is being determined under the life expectancy rule (see 10:20) and the entire benefit is distributed by the end of the fifth calendar year that contains the employee's date of death [I.R.C. § 4974; Treas. Reg. § 54.4974-2, A-7]

Special rules apply to a contract issued by an insurance company that is in state insurer delinquency proceedings. A participant will not be considered to be in violation of the minimum distribution requirements if payments under the contract have been reduced or suspended, as long as any other unaffected account or portion of the contract is utilized (and exhausted, if necessary) to make distributions. If the reduction or suspension of payments ceases, the amount of any shortfall in a prior distribution must be made up to the extent that additional payments are made available. The shortfall must be made up by no later than December 31 of the calendar year following the year in which the additional payments are received. [Rev. Proc. 92-10, 1992-1 C.B. 661]

Q 10:33   What specific minimum distribution requirements must be set out in a Section 403(b) plan?

Under the final Code Section 403(b) regulations published on July 26, 2007, a Section 403(b) contract must be maintained pursuant to a written plan that must contain all of its material terms and conditions, including the time and form of benefit distributions. [Treas. Reg. § 1.403(b)-3(b)(3)] A plan may incorporate other documents by reference, including an insurance contract or custodial account. Thus, a plan document or underlying contract or custodial account should generally set forth the statutory rules of the minimum distribution requirements including the MDIB rules. The plan or underlying funding vehicle should provide that distributions will be made in accordance with applicable regulations or rulings.

Q 10:34   If an employee has an outstanding loan at the required beginning date, how is the required distribution amount determined?

In the case of an individual account, the accumulation used to determine the required distribution is, generally, the accumulation as of the last valuation date in the calendar year preceding the distribution calendar year. There is no provision for decreasing this accumulation by the amount of an outstanding loan. Therefore, the accumulation used for determining the required distribution cannot be reduced by any outstanding loan amount.

Taxation and Investment in the Contract

Q 10:35 How are distributions from Section 403(b) contracts taxed?

Distributions from both annuities and custodial accounts are taxed in accordance with the rules of Code Section 72. All payments are taxed as ordinary income except for the amounts that were previously taxed. These previously taxed amounts constitute investment in the contract (IVC) and will not be taxed again on withdrawal. IVC is allocated to each withdrawal on a pro rata basis.

For distributions made in the form of an annuity, an exclusion ratio is used to determine the amount of each payment attributable to IVC. The exclusion ratio is a fraction, the numerator of which is IVC and the denominator of which is the expected return under the contract calculated as of the annuity starting date. A similar ratio is used to determine the taxable amount of distributions not in the form of an annuity. In these cases, the numerator is IVC and the denominator is the account balance. [I.R.C. § 72(e)(8)]

Q 10:36 How is the expected return under the contract calculated?

The expected return will vary depending on the type of annuity. Factors that affect the calculation are whether the annuity is variable or fixed, whether it provides payment for life or for a fixed period of years, whether it uses a single life expectancy or has a joint and survivor feature, and whether it has a guarantee period.

For annuity starting dates beginning on or before November 18, 1996, the expected return of all life annuities is determined according to the rules of Treasury Regulations Section 1.72-6 with reference to the annuity tables of Section 1.72-9. Gender-neutral tables, which were issued in 1986, must be used if contributions were made after June 30, 1986.

For annuity starting dates after November 18, 1996, basis recovery for annuity payments from Section 403(b) annuities will be determined in accordance with the rules set out in Code Section 72(d). In accordance with these rules, the portion of each annuity payment that represents a return of basis will equal the participant's total basis at the annuity starting date divided by the number of anticipated payments. In turn, the number of anticipated payments will be determined based on age, from a statutory table. This method does not apply for participants who are over age 75 at the annuity starting date unless there are fewer than five years of guaranteed payments under the annuity. A separate table is provided for annuities payable on the lives of more than one individual, for distributions with annuity starting dates after December 31, 1997. [I.R.C. § 72(d)(1)(B)(iii) and (iv)]

Q 10:37 What amounts comprise IVC?

Generally, any amount contributed to the contract that was taxable to the employee constitutes IVC. This includes after-tax employee contributions,

contributions that exceeded the exclusion allowance or the Code Section 415 limit, the amount of any policy loans to the extent repaid into the contract after being included in income as taxable distributions, and the taxable portion of any life insurance premium where the policy was used as part of the Section 403(b) contract. This general rule does not apply to contributions that exceeded the elective deferral limit of Code Section 402(g) and were not withdrawn by April 15 of the subsequent year. The employee will not receive IVC for these amounts even though the contributions were taxable. In accordance with the final Code Section 403(b) regulations published on July 26, 2007, life insurance contracts issued after September 24, 2007 cannot be used to fund Section 403(b) plans. [Treas. Reg. § 1.403(b)-8(c)(2)]

Under Code Section 72(f), a contribution paid by an employer can also result in IVC if it would not have been includible in the gross income of the employee under the law applicable at the time of contribution had it been paid directly to the employee. An exception is made for employer contributions on behalf of employees working abroad. Employer contributions to an annuity contract attributable to foreign services do not constitute IVC, even if such amounts would not have been includible in the gross income of the employee by reason of Code Section 911 ($80,000 exclusion for foreign earned income) if paid directly to the employee at the time of contribution. There is some grandfathering of contributions made for foreign services prior to 1963.

Q 10:38   Does the pro rata rule apply to all nonannuity distributions?

No. Prior to TRA '86, nonannuity distributions were allocated first to the recovery of IVC and the excess, if any, was allocated to income. This cost-recovery method was repealed effective July 1, 1986. A grandfathering rule was provided for IVC accumulated by December 31, 1986, that is withdrawn in a preannuity starting date distribution for (1) private (nongovernment) plans that permitted in-service withdrawals on May 5, 1986, and (2) government plans regardless of whether they permitted in-service withdrawals (although the plans must have permitted preannuity starting-date distributions on May 5, 1986). Under this special rule, distributions are allocated on the basis of the cost-recovery rule until IVC accumulated at December 31, 1986, is recovered. Remaining IVC is allocated under the pro rata rule. [TRA '86 § 1122, as amended by the Technical and Miscellaneous Revenue Act of 1988 (TAMRA) § 1011A(b)(11)]

Q 10:39   What happens if the participant dies before all IVC is recovered?

For annuities with a starting date after July 1, 1986, a deduction for unrecovered IVC is permitted to be taken on the return filed for the annuitant's last taxable year. If the contract had a guarantee period and the beneficiary does not recover IVC, the beneficiary may deduct unrecovered IVC. [I.R.C. § 72(b)(3)]

Q 10:40   How is IVC allocated when partial transfers are made from one Section 403(b) contract to another Section 403(b) contract?

IVC is allocated on a pro rata basis when contract exchanges or plan-to-plan transfers are made. For example, assume contract A was purchased partially with after-tax employee contributions. The value of contract A is $10,000, of which $4,000 is after-tax contributions. The employee transfers $5,000 to contract B. The IVC in contract B would be $2,000. [*See* Treas. Reg. § 1.403(b)-10(b)(3)(i)(G)]

If an interest in an annuity contract is transferred to a spouse or former spouse pursuant to a qualified domestic relations order (QDRO), IVC will be allocated on a pro rata basis. [I.R.C. § 72(m)]

Q 10:41   May employee contributions and earnings thereon be treated as a separate contract?

Yes, if the contributions were made under a defined contribution Section 403(b) plan and the employee contributions and earnings are accounted for separately under the contract. [I.R.C. § 72(d)]

Q 10:42   Are all Section 403(b) contracts owned by the participant aggregated when the taxable portion of a distribution is being determined?

No. The exclusion ratio is determined on a contract-by-contract basis for Section 403(b) contracts.

Q 10:43   Does the penalty tax on early distributions apply to Section 403(b) distributions?

Yes. Under Code Section 72(t), an additional tax of 10 percent of the amount includible in gross income applies to early distributions from qualified retirement plans as defined in Code Section 4974(c). A Section 403(b) contract is a qualified retirement plan for these purposes.

Q 10:44   What distributions are exempt from the penalty tax?

The penalty tax does not apply to distributions that are made:

- After attainment of age 59½;
- After the death of the participant;
- On account of disability;
- As part of a series of substantially equal periodic payments for the life or life expectancy of the participant or the joint lives or joint life expectancies of the participant and the designated beneficiary where the series of payments begins after separation from service;

- After separation from service after attainment of age 55;
- To an alternate payee pursuant to a qualified domestic relations order;
- To the extent the payment does not exceed the amount allowable as a medical care deduction under Code Section 213;
- Distributions after 1999 made on account of an IRS levy on the Section 403(b) arrangement under Code Section 6331; or
- As a "qualified reservist distribution," which generally means a distribution attributable to elective deferrals under a 403(b) annuity that is (1) made to a reservist or national guardsman (as defined in 37 U.S.C. § 101(24)) who was called to active duty between September 11, 2001, and December 31, 2007, for a period in excess of 179 days or for an indefinite period of time, and (2) made during the period beginning on the date of the order or call to duty and ending at the close of the active duty period. (An individual who receives such a distribution can repay the distribution to an individual retirement plan at any time during the two-year period after the end of the active duty period.)

[I.R.C. § 72(t)(2)]

Q 10:45 When can the exception for "substantially equal periodic payments" be used?

The exception for substantially equal periodic payments is available only if the participant terminated employment before beginning the periodic payments. [I.R.C. § 72(t)(3)(B)] A second requirement is that the payments cannot be substantially modified (other than by reason of death or disability) within a five-year period beginning on the date of the first payment or, if later, at age 59½. [I.R.C. § 72(t)(4)]

IRS Notice 89-25 [1989-1 C.B. 662] describes three methods for determining whether payments constitute a series of "substantially equal periodic payments." The first method provides that the annual payment may be calculated in the same way minimum distribution payments under Code Section 401(a)(9) are calculated. The second method provides for the calculation of an annual payment by amortizing the account balance and using a reasonable interest rate, over the life or joint life expectancies of the participant and a designated beneficiary, if any. The third method provides for the calculation of an annual payment by dividing the account balance by an annuity factor derived using reasonable mortality factors and interest rates.

In October 2002, the IRS released Revenue Ruling 2002-62 [2002-42 I.R.B. 710], which modifies Notice 89-25, effective for any series of payments commencing on or after January 1, 2003. The rules of Revenue Ruling 2002-62 also may be used for distributions commencing in 2002. Revenue Ruling 2002-62 describes three methods (similar to the three methods described in Notice 89-25) for determining whether payments constitute a series of substantially equal periodic payments.

The first method, referred to as the "required minimum distribution method," provides that the annual payment is determined by dividing the account balance for each year by the number from the "chosen life expectancy table" for that year. Under this method, the account balance, the number from the chosen life expectancy table, and the resulting annual payments are redetermined each year.

The second method, referred to as the "fixed amortization method," provides that the annual payment is determined by amortizing in level amounts the account balance over a specified number of years determined using the chosen life expectancy table and the "chosen interest rate." Under this method, the account balance, the number from the chosen life expectancy table, and the resulting annual payment are determined once for the first distribution year and the annual payment is the same amount in each succeeding year. The IRS also has ruled privately that a method of calculating annual payments that is based on the fixed amortization method but under which the account balance is redetermined each year (thus resulting in payments that vary in amount from year to year, rather than being level) will result in substantially equal periodic payments for purposes of Code Section 72(t). [*See* Ltr. Ruls. 200432024, 200432021]

The third method, referred to as the "fixed annuitization method," provides that the annual payment is determined by dividing the account balance by an annuity factor that is the present value of an annuity of $1 per year beginning at the participant's age and continuing for the life of the participant (or the joint lives of the participant and the beneficiary). The annuity factor is derived using a mortality table set forth in Revenue Ruling 2002-62 and the chosen interest rate. Under this method, the account balance, the annuity factor, the chosen interest rate, and the resulting annual payment are determined once for the first distribution year and the annual payment is the same amount in each succeeding year. As with the fixed amortization method, the IRS also has ruled privately that a method of calculating annual payments that is based on the fixed annuitization method but under which the account balance is redetermined each year (thus resulting in payments that vary in amount from year to year, rather than being level) will result in substantially equal periodic payments for purposes of Code Section 72(t). [*See* Ltr. Rul. 200432023]

For purposes of Revenue Ruling 2002-62, the "chosen life expectancy table" is one of the following:

- The uniform lifetime table set forth in Revenue Ruling 2002-62;
- The single life expectancy table in Treasury Regulations Section 1.401(a)(9)-9, A-1; or
- The joint and last survivor table in Treasury Regulations Section 1.401(a)(9)-9, A-3.

Special rules apply with respect to which table may be chosen. The "chosen interest rate" may be any interest rate that is not more than 120 percent of the federal mid-term rate (determined in accordance with Code Section 1274(d) for either of the two months immediately preceding the month in which the distribution begins). The "account balance" that is used to determine payments must be determined in a reasonable manner based on the facts and circumstances.

Revenue Ruling 2002-62 provides special rules regarding modifications to a series of substantially equal periodic payments. In general, if such a modification occurs, the penalty tax of Code Section 4974(c), plus interest for the deferral period, is recaptured. [I.R.C. § 72(t)(4)] Under all three methods described in Revenue Ruling 2002-62, such a modification will occur if, following the date the account balance is determined under the applicable method, there is (1) any addition to the account balance (other than gains or losses), (2) any nontaxable transfer of a portion of the account balance to another arrangement, or (3) a rollover by the taxpayer of the amount received resulting in such amount not being taxable. However, Revenue Ruling 2002-62 [2002-42 I.R.B. 710] permits a one-time change to the required minimum distribution method that will not be treated as a "modification" to a series of periodic payments. Under this special rule, an individual who begins distributions in a year using the fixed amortization method, the fixed annuitization method, or a method of calculating substantially equal periodic payments commencing before 2003 may in any subsequent year switch to the required minimum distribution method to determine the payment for the year of the switch and all subsequent payments. If a switch to the required minimum distribution method is made, that method must be used in all subsequent years.

Q 10:46   Must the employee have attained age 55 prior to separation from service in order to take advantage of the exception for payments made after separation from service?

Under IRS Notice 87-13, the exception is available if (1) it is made after the employee has separated from service for the employer maintaining the plan and (2) such separation from service occurred during or after the calendar year in which the employee attained age 55. This is a slight expansion of the statutory language, which requires that the separation occur after attainment of age 55.

Q 10:47   What constitutes disability?

Individuals are considered disabled if they are unable to engage in any substantial gainful activity by reason of any medically determinable physical or mental impairment that can be expected to result in death or to be of long-continued and indefinite duration. [See I.R.C. § 72(m); Treas. Reg. § 1.72-17A(f)]

Q 10:48   Does the penalty tax apply to hardship distributions?

Yes. The provisions of Code Section 72(t) will apply to hardship distributions unless the participant can meet one of the exceptions to the tax (see Q 10:44).

Withdrawal Restrictions

Q 10:49   Which withdrawal restrictions apply to Section 403(b) annuity contracts?

There are various restrictions depending on the type of contribution. Amounts attributable to elective deferrals can be withdrawn only when the employee attains age 59½, has a severance from employment (for distributions prior to 2002, "separates from service"), dies, or becomes disabled, in the case of hardship, or a qualified reservist distribution (see Q 10:44). Hardship withdrawals are limited to the withdrawal of elective deferral contributions; income on such amounts cannot be withdrawn. [I.R.C. § 403(b)(11)] Amounts in an annuity contract as of December 31, 1988, are grandfathered, and withdrawal restrictions do not apply.

Mandatory employee salary reduction contributions, contributions made pursuant to a one-time irrevocable election by the employee at the time of his or her initial eligibility to participate in the plan, after-tax contributions, and employer contributions are not subject to withdrawal restrictions under Section 403(b) annuity contracts because they are not elective deferrals, if the annuity contract was issued prior to January 1, 2009. [*See, e.g.,* I.R.C. § 402(g)(3)] However, withdrawals of these contributions may be limited under the terms of the employer's plan.

Under the final Code Section 403(b) regulations that were published on July 26, 2007, for contracts issued on or after January 1, 2009, a contract is permitted to distribute benefits attributable to employer contributions to the participant no earlier than upon the earlier of the participant's severance from employment or upon the prior occurrence of some event, such as after a fixed number of years, the attainment of a stated age, or disability. [Treas. Reg. § 1.403(b)-6(b)] Prior to the final Code Section 403(b) regulations, the only amounts that were subject to withdrawal restrictions under Section 403(b) annuity contracts (as opposed to custodial accounts) were amounts attributable to elective deferrals. The final Code Section 403(b) regulations changed this, making all types of contributions and earnings under any Section 403(b) annuity contract issued on or after January 1, 2009, subject to some form of withdrawal restriction. The final regulations do not address how transfers or exchanges of Section 403(b) annuity contracts that occur after December 31, 2008, will be affected. However, the IRS may treat all amounts under any "new" contract that results from such a transaction as being subject to the stricter withdrawal restrictions of the final regulations, even if those amounts were not subject to the stricter rules before the transfer or exchange.

Q 10:50   Which withdrawal restrictions apply to Section 403(b)(7) custodial accounts?

All amounts in custodial accounts are subject to withdrawal restrictions. No amounts can be paid prior to the time the employee dies, attains age 59½, has a severance from employment (for distributions prior to 2002, "separates from service"), becomes disabled, or, in the case of contributions made under salary reduction agreements, encounters financial hardship. [I.R.C. § 403(b)(7)(A)(ii)] Amounts in an account as of December 31, 1988, are grandfathered only with respect to hardship withdrawals. Hardship withdrawals of both contributions and earnings can be made from these amounts. Amounts attributable to elective deferrals may also be withdrawn if the withdrawal is a qualified reservist distribution (see Q 10:44).

Q 10:51   For purposes of the changes to Sections 403(b)(11) and 403(b)(7)(A)(ii) made by the Economic Growth and Tax Relief Reconciliation Act of 2001 (EGTRRA), what is the difference between separation from service and severance from employment?

A separation from service occurs only upon a participant's death, retirement, resignation, or discharge, and not when the employee continues the same job for a different employer as a result of the liquidation, merger, consolidation, or other similar corporate transaction. In general, this interpretation of the phrase separation from service has been referred to as the same desk rule. [Rev. Rul. 79-336, 1979-2 C.B. 187]

A severance from employment occurs when a participant ceases to be employed by the employer that maintains the Section 403(b) plan in connection with the contract or custodial account. Thus, the same desk rule does not apply under the severance from employment standard. Pursuant to the change in the law enacted by EGTRRA, the severance from employment standard applies with respect to distributions after December 31, 2001.

[H.R. Conf. Rep. No. 107-84, at 256–257 (2001)]

Q 10:52   How do the withdrawal restrictions apply when a participant has a severance from employment with one employer and continues to contribute to the same Section 403(b) contract under a subsequent employer's plan?

There is no guidance directly on this point, but, apparently, once a triggering event has occurred with respect to an accumulation, the withdrawal restrictions should no longer apply with regard to such amount, although withdrawal restrictions may apply to future contributions. However, the IRS has issued Revenue Ruling 2004-12 in which it ruled that the distribution restrictions of Code Sections 403(b)(7) and 403(b)(11) do not apply to amounts attributable to rollovers that are maintained in separate accounts. As a result, unless a restriction is imposed by the issuer or the employer, participants generally may withdraw amounts attributable to rollover contributions at any time, even though distribution of other amounts under the Section 403(b) program may be restricted.

Q 10:53   How do the withdrawal restrictions apply when funds are subject to a contract exchange or plan-to-plan transfer between annuity contracts and custodial accounts?

Once funds are subject to the withdrawal restrictions imposed on custodial accounts, they remain subject to these restrictions after transfer to an annuity contract. [Treas. Reg. §§ 1.403(b)-10(b)(2)(i)(C), 1.403(b)-10(b)(i)(G)] Funds transferred from annuity contracts to custodial accounts become subject to the more restrictive custodial account rules. If funds covered by the grandfather rule (described in Q 10:49) are transferred to a custodial account, it appears the benefit of grandfathering is lost even if the funds are subsequently transferred back to an annuity.

Q 10:54   Is payment of investment expenses or investment advisor fees from a Section 403(b) contract considered a withdrawal?

No. The IRS has taken the position in private letter rulings that where the annuity contract is solely liable for the payment of investment expenses or investment advisory fees, the direct payment is an expense of the contract and not a taxable distribution. [*See* Ltr. Ruls. 9332040, 9316042, 9047073]

Hardship Distributions

Q 10:55   What are the rules for determining hardship with respect to elective deferrals under Section 403(b) annuities and all contributions under Section 403(b)(7) custodial accounts?

Pursuant to the final Code Section 403(b) regulations, which the Treasury Department published on July 26, 2007, a hardship distribution has the same meaning as a distribution under the regulations governing Section 401(k) plans and is subject to the same rules and restrictions. In general, a hardship distribution is limited to the accumulation in the contract attributable to elective deferral contributions, but not the income on those contributions (see Qs 10:49–10:50). [Treas. Reg. § 403(b)-6(d)(2)] Under these rules, two tests must be met before a hardship distribution may be made. The participant must have an immediate and heavy financial need, and the distribution must be necessary to satisfy the financial need.

Test 1. The hardship distribution must result from an immediate and heavy financial need of the participant. The specific needs that are deemed to satisfy the requirement are:

- Medical expenses incurred by the participant, the participant's spouse, or dependents;
- Purchase of the participant's principal residence;

- Payment of the next 12 months of postsecondary tuition and related educational fees for the participant, the participant's spouse, or dependents; or

- Prevention of eviction from the participant's principal residence or foreclosure of a mortgage on the principal residence.

[Treas. Reg. § 1.401(k)-1(d)(2)(iv)(A)]

The IRS has reserved the right to add to this safe-harbor list. An employer can make its own determination of financial need but should be prepared to justify the decision. Whether a need is an immediate and heavy financial need is to be determined based on all relevant facts and circumstances. The regulations give an example, noting that funeral expenses would usually qualify, while purchase of a boat would not. [Treas. Reg. § 1.401(k)-1(d)(2)(iii)(A)]

Test 2. The distribution must be necessary to satisfy the financial need. This requires a showing that (1) the amount of the distribution does not exceed the amount required to relieve the participant's financial need and (2) such need may not be satisfied from other resources reasonably available to the participant. [Treas. Reg. § 1.401(k)-1(d)(2)(iii)(B)] This test can be met in one of two ways at the employer's option.

Employee's Representation. The employee represents that the need cannot be satisfied from certain resources. Unless the employer has actual knowledge to the contrary, the employer can rely on an employee's written representation that the need cannot be relieved by:

- Insurance;

- Reasonable liquidation of the employee's assets;

- Cessation of elective deferrals to the plan; or

- Other distributions or loans from the employer's plan(s) or a commercial loan.

[Treas. Reg. § 1.401(k)-1(d)(2)(iii)(B)]

The representation would usually take the form of a certification, with the employee attesting to the above facts. For purposes of this test, the employee's resources are deemed to include those assets of his or her spouse and minor children that are reasonably available to the employee. For example, a vacation home owned by the employee and his or her spouse would be deemed a resource of the employee. However, property held for the employee's child under the Uniform Gifts to Minors Act would not be treated as a resource of the employee. Under the employee's representation approach, it is not necessary to stop contributions to the plan.

Safe Harbor. The employer relies on the safe harbor for distributions deemed necessary to satisfy financial need. The elements of the safe harbor are the following:

- The distribution is not in excess of the need;

- All other distributions and loans have been taken from all employer plans;

- All employer plans provide that employee elective deferrals and employee contributions be suspended for at least 6 months (12 months for hardship distributions received before 2002); and

- For hardship distributions received prior to 2001, all employer plans reduce the employee's elective deferral limit for the next calendar year by the employee's elective deferrals in the calendar year of the hardship distribution. This limitation does not apply for calendar years beginning after December 31, 2001, for hardship distributions received after 2000.

[Treas. Reg. § 1.401(k)-1(d)(2)(iv)(B); IRS Notice 2002-4, 2002-2 I.R.B. 298]

> **Note.** Although the final Code Section 403(b) regulations published on July 26, 2007 generally prohibit procedures that rely on employee certification (*see* Treas. Reg. § 1.403(b)(3)(2)(ii) and T.D. 9340), the final regulations also state that the hardship distribution rules that apply to Section 401(k) plans apply to Section 403(b) plans. [Treas. Reg. § 1.403(b)-6(d)(2)] The hardship distribution rules that apply to Section 401(k) plans allow reliance on employee representations in some circumstances. [Treas. Reg. § 1.401(k)-1(d)(3)(iv)(C)]

The employer may wish not to become involved in certifying hardship if the Section 403(b) arrangement is exempt from coverage under ERISA in accordance with 29 C.F.R. Section 2510.3-2. In Advisory Opinion 94-30A, the Department of Labor has taken the position that an employer's involvement in verifying hardship can cause an arrangement to lose its exemption from ERISA coverage.

The PPA requires the Treasury Department to modify regulations for determining whether a participant in a Section 403(b) plan has had a hardship for purposes of Code Section 403(b)(11)(B), such that an event that would be viewed as a hardship if it occurred with respect to the participant will be considered a hardship if it occurs with respect to the participant's beneficiary under the plan. Thus, the regulations should permit distributions if a hardship occurs to a beneficiary under the plan to the same extent that they would permit distributions if the same event had occurred to the participant. The IRS has issued a notice stating that Section 403(b) plans may begin allowing such hardship distributions beginning August 17, 2006. [IRS Notice 2007-7, 2007-5 I.R.B. 395, Q&A-5]

Death Benefits

Q 10:56 How are death benefits under a Section 403(b) annuity contract taxed?

Generally, the value of the annuity is includible in the participant's gross estate in the same manner as other retirement plan payments. [I.R.C. § 2039]

Payments to the beneficiary are subject to income tax as income in respect of a decedent. If estate tax was paid on the value of the annuity, an income tax deduction is available to the person receiving the annuity payments. [*See* I.R.C. § 691]

Rollovers, Exchanges, and Transfers

Q 10:57   Can amounts be moved from one Section 403(b) contract to another tax-free?

Yes, if certain conditions are met.

Amounts can be moved tax-free from one Section 403(b) contract to another as a rollover under Code Section 403(b)(8). [*See* Treas. Reg. §§ 1.403(b)-7(b), 1.403(b)-10(d)] Amounts also can be rolled over tax-free from a Section 403(b) contract to an IRA or other eligible retirement plan. (See Q 10:79.)

In addition, amounts can be moved from one Section 403(b) contract to another Section 403(b) contract tax-free using an intra-plan exchange or a plan-to-plan transfer pursuant to the final Code Section 403(b) regulations, which the Treasury Department published on July 26, 2007. [T.D. 9340] The final Code Section 403(b) regulations generally are effective for taxable years beginning after 2008, but certain transition rules apply. (See Q 10:61 for a discussion of the applicable transition rules.) Under the final Code Section 403(b) regulations, an exchange involves moving moneys between Section 403(b) contracts that are part of the same employer's Section 403(b) plan. [Treas. Reg. § 1.403(b)-10(b)(1)(i) and (2)] In contrast, a transfer under the final Code Section 403(b) regulations involves moving moneys from one employer's Section 403(b) plan to another employer's Section 403(b) plan. [Treas. Reg. § 1.403(b)-10(b)(1)(i) and (3)] Specific requirements apply to exchanges and transfers under the final Code Section 403(b) regulations. (See Qs 10:59 and 10:62 for a discussion of those requirements.)

The final Code Section 403(b) regulations effectively eliminated the ability to transfer amounts between Section 403(b) contracts pursuant to Revenue Ruling 90-24 [1990-1 C.B. 97] after 2008, subject to certain transition rules.

Q 10:58   May a Section 403(b) annuity be transferred, tax free, to another Section 403(b) funding vehicle as a Code Section 1035 tax-free exchange?

No. Unlike nonqualified deferred annuity contracts, Section 403(b) annuities may not be assigned. The IRS has issued only one revenue ruling [Rev. Rul. 73-124, 1973-1 C.B. 200] in which it outlined the procedures a participant must follow in order to effect a Code Section 1035 exchange of nonassignable Section 403(b) annuities. However, the IRS revoked Revenue Ruling 73-124 prospectively when it issued Revenue Ruling 90-24. [*But see* Greene v. Comm'r, 85 T.C. 1024 (1986), in which the IRS acquiesced in result only (AOD CC-1986-044)] In addition, other than rollovers, the final Code Section 403(b) regulations published on July 26, 2007, provide for only two methods of moving moneys between Section 403(b) contracts on a tax-free basis: an intra-plan exchange or a plan-to-plan transfer. Those regulations provide specific requirements for effectuating an exchange, which differ from the requirements that might otherwise apply under Code Section 1035. [*See* Treas. Reg. § 1.403(b)-10(b)]

Q 10:59 What is an exchange under the final Code Section 403(b) regulations published in 2007?

An exchange of Section 403(b) contracts, within the meaning of the final Code Section 403(b) regulations published on July 26, 2007, occurs when a participant or beneficiary exchanges a Section 403(b) contract that was issued in connection with a particular employer's Section 403(b) plan for another Section 403(b) contract that is issued in connection with that same employer's plan. Such an exchange is not treated as a distribution for purposes of the distribution restrictions applicable to Section 403(b) contracts. Therefore, such an exchange may occur pursuant to the final Code Section 403(b) regulations before a severance from employment or other distribution event. An exchange is allowed under the final Code Section 403(b) regulations only if the following conditions are met:

- The plan under which the contract is issued must provide for the exchange.
- The participant or beneficiary must have an accumulated benefit immediately after the exchange that is at least equal to his or her accumulated benefit immediately before the exchange (taking into account the accumulated benefit under both Section 403(b) contracts immediately before the exchange). This condition is satisfied if the exchange would satisfy Code Section 414(l)(1) if the exchange were a transfer of assets.
- The new contract must be subject to distribution restrictions with respect to the participant that are at least as stringent as those imposed under the contract being exchanged.
- The employer must enter into an information sharing agreement with the issuer of the new contract under which those parties agree to provide each other with certain information from time to time. This requirement generally is intended to ensure that the new contract remains part of the employer's Section 403(b) plan. (See Q 10:60 for further discussion on information sharing agreements.)

[Treas. Reg. § 1.403(b)-10(b)(2)]

Although the final Code Section 403(b) regulations generally are effective for taxable years beginning after 2008, the new exchange rules apply to exchanges occurring after September 24, 2007. Exchanges that occurred prior to that date are subject to the rules in existence at that time (i.e., Revenue Ruling 90-24). [Treas. Reg. § 1.403(b)-11(g)] (See Q 10:61 for a discussion of applicable transition rules.)

Q 10:60   What is an *information sharing agreement?*

An *information sharing agreement* is a written agreement between the sponsor of a Section 403(b) plan and a life insurance company or custodian that provides Section 403(b) contracts in connection with that plan (i.e., a vendor). An information sharing agreement is required to effectuate an exchange of Section 403(b) contracts within the meaning of the final Code Section 403(b) regulations that were published on July 26, 2007. (See Q 10:59.)

Under an information sharing agreement, the parties must agree to provide each other with the following information from time to time:

- Information necessary for the contract issued in the exchange and any other contract that was issued in connection with the employer's Section 403(b) plan to satisfy Code Section 403(b). This includes, for example, information about the participant's employment status and information that takes into account qualified plans maintained by the employer and other Section 403(b) contracts held by the participant in connection with the employer's Section 403(b) plan (such as whether a severance from employment has occurred for purposes of the distribution restrictions in Treasury Regulations Section 1.403(b)-6 and whether the hardship withdrawal rules of Treasury Regulations Section 1.403(b)-6(d)(2) are satisfied).

- Information necessary for the resulting contract, or any other contract that was issued in connection with the employer's Section 403(b) plan, to satisfy other tax requirements (such as whether a plan loan satisfies the requirements of Code Section 72(p)).

The requirement for an information sharing agreement relates generally to the requirement under the final Code Section 403(b) regulations that Section 403(b) contracts be maintained pursuant to a written defined contribution plan. The written plan must include, inter alia, the contracts available under the plan (i.e., the choice of vendors to whom contributions can be remitted). [Treas. Reg. § 1.403(b)-3(b)(3)] Model Section 403(b) plan language that the IRS has provided for use by public schools indicates that the information sharing agreement requirement does not apply with respect to a Section 403(b) contract that is identified under the written plan as a contract to which contributions may be made under the plan. [Rev. Proc. 2007-71, 2007-51 I.R.B. 1184] As a result, the final Code Section 403(b) regulations treat a Section 403(b) contract issued in an exchange as being maintained pursuant to a written plan (and identified as a contract available under the plan) if (1) the contract is issued by a vendor that is identified in the written plan as being a vendor to whom contributions can be remitted under the plan, or (2) an information sharing agreement is in place between the plan sponsor and the vendor. Thus, a separate information sharing agreement is not needed if the vendor that will issue the new contract to be received in the exchange is a vendor already identified in the written plan as a vendor to which contributions can be made under the plan, because that contract will already be subject to information sharing requirements pursuant to the written plan. In that regard, notwithstanding the specific application of the requirement for a separate information sharing agreement to a vendor that does not receive contributions from the plan, the IRS has stated that the same information must be shared by vendors that do receive contributions from the employer and those that do not.

As a result of the foregoing, the final Code Section 403(b) regulations allow participants and beneficiaries to exchange their Section 403(b) contracts for other Section 403(b) contracts that the employer has not specifically identified as being available under the plan, as long as the information sharing agreement and other applicable requirements are met. Compared to prior law (i.e., Revenue Ruling 90-24), this regime under the final Code Section 403(b) regulations imposes significant restrictions on the ability to transfer amounts among Section 403(b) contracts, but retains some of the flexibility that the prior regime provided by facilitating contract exchanges in circumstances where an information sharing agreement (or its equivalent) is in effect.

Q 10:61 What transition rules apply to the exchange provisions of the final Code Section 403(b) regulations published in 2007?

The final Code Section 403(b) regulations published on July 26, 2007, generally impose new requirements on exchanges of Section 403(b) contracts under the same employer's Section 403(b) plan. (See Qs 10:59 and 10:60.) However, such transactions that occurred prior to September 25, 2007, are not subject to the new requirements that the final Code Section 403(b) regulations impose on Section 403(b) contract exchanges. Such pre-September 25, 2007, transactions are governed by Revenue Ruling 90-24, and they are not subject to the written plan or information sharing agreement requirements otherwise imposed by the final Code Section 403(b) regulations. [Treas. Reg. § 1.403(b)-11(g)]

Generally, the final Code Section 403(b) regulations are not effective until 2009. Until then, Revenue Ruling 90-24 still technically governs transactions that would be characterized as exchanges under the final Code Section 403(b) regulations. However, any such transaction occurring after September 24, 2007, will be subject to the exchange provisions of the final Code Section 403(b) regulations as of January 1, 2009. Thus, for example, if a direct transfer is made pursuant to Revenue Ruling 90-24 after September 24, 2007, an information sharing agreement must be in place between the plan sponsor and the issuer of the new Section 403(b) contract no later than December 31, 2008. In other words, Revenue Ruling 90-24 transfers can occur between September 24, 2007, and January 1, 2009, without an information sharing agreement being in place at the time of the transfer. In addition, a special transition rule applies if the plan sponsor and the vendor are unable to enter into an information sharing agreement by 2009 that covers the interim contract issued between September 24, 2007, and January 1, 2009. Specifically, if the interim contract is exchanged before July 1, 2009, in an exchange permitted under Revenue Ruling 90-24 for a contract issued by an issuer that is either receiving contributions as part of the employer's Section 403(b) plan or has an information sharing agreement as set forth in the final Code Section 403(b) regulations, then the information sharing agreement requirement does not apply to the interim contract.

Another special transition rule is generally available for Section 403(b) contracts issued in an exchange (within the meaning of the final Code Section 403(b) regulations) after September 24, 2007, and before January 1, 2009. If the issuer of such a contract does not receive contributions under the Section 403(b) plan in a year after the contract was issued, the contract will not fail to satisfy Code Section 403(b) for the year merely because the contract is not part of a written plan under the final Code Section 403(b) regulations (including being subject to an information sharing agreement), as long as the employer makes a reasonable, good faith effort to include the contract as part of the employer's plan. (This transition rule also applies to contracts issued in the specified date range if the reason for the issuer not receiving contributions is unrelated to a prior exchange, such as where the issuer was discontinued as a vendor under the plan.) This transition rule is not available if the vendor receives any contributions for any participant under the employer's Section 403(b) plan (whether for the participant whose contract is being exchanged or for any other participant). In such cases, the contract that is issued in the exchange must be part of the written plan or be subject to an information sharing agreement between the vendor and the plan sponsor.

Two alternative methods can be used to satisfy the reasonable, good faith standard of the foregoing transition rule:

- The employer can collect available information concerning the relevant issuers (other than issuers that ceased to receive contributions before January 1, 2005) and notify them of the name and contact information for the person in charge of administering the employer's plan for the purpose of coordinating information necessary to satisfy Code Section 403(b).

- Alternatively, a reasonable, good faith effort also includes the issuer taking action before making any distribution or loan to the participant or beneficiary that constitutes a reasonable, good faith effort to contact the employer and exchange any information that may be needed in order to satisfy Code Section 403(b) with the person in charge of administering the employer's plan.

Finally, a fourth transition rule applies in certain cases involving a Section 403(b) contract held by a former employee or a beneficiary. Any such contract that ceases to receive contributions before 2009 continues to be subject to the requirements of Code Section 403(b) and the final Code Section 403(b) regulations. However, a plan will not be treated as failing to satisfy the written plan requirement of the final Code Section 403(b) regulations if the plan does not include terms relating to those contracts. If the participant or beneficiary requests a loan from the contract, the relief in the prior sentence is available only if the issuer makes reasonable efforts to determine whether the loan is permitted under Code Section 72(p). Generally, reasonable efforts do not include merely relying on information from the participant or beneficiary. [Rev. Proc. 2007-71] (See Q 1:32 for further discussion of transition rules applicable to the final Code Section 403(b) regulations.)

Q 10:62   What is a plan-to-plan transfer under the final Code Section 403(b) regulations?

A plan-to-plan transfer, within the meaning of the final Code Section 403(b) regulations published on July 26, 2007, occurs when a Section 403(b) plan of a particular employer transfers some or all of its assets (including actual Section 403(b) contracts or any assets held in custodial accounts or retirement income accounts that are treated as Section 403(b) contracts) to a Section 403(b) plan of a different employer. A plan-to-plan transfer made pursuant to the final Code Section 403(b) regulations is not treated as a distribution for purposes of the distribution restrictions applicable to Section 403(b) contracts. Therefore, a plan-to-plan transfer may occur pursuant to the final Code Section 403(b) regulations before a severance from employment or other distribution event. A plan-to-plan transfer is allowed under the final Code Section 403(b) regulations only if the following conditions are met:

- In the case of a participant, the participant must be a current or former employee of the employer for the receiving plan, and in the case of a beneficiary of a deceased participant, the participant must have been a current or former employee of the employer for the receiving plan.

- Both the transferor plan and the receiving plan must provide for transfers.

- The participant or beneficiary whose assets are being transferred must have an accumulated benefit immediately after the transfer that is at least equal to his or her accumulated benefit before the transfer. This condition is satisfied if the transfer would satisfy Code Section 414(l)(1).

- The receiving plan must impose restrictions on distributions that are at least as stringent as those imposed under the transferor plan.

- If a plan-to-plan transfer does not involve all of the participant's or beneficiary's interest in the plan, the transferee plan must treat the amount transferred as a continuation of a pro rata portion of his or her interest in the transferor plan (e.g., a pro rata portion of the interest in any after-tax employee contributions).

If certain conditions relating to permissive service credits and repayments under Code Section 415 are met, a Section 403(b) plan is permitted to provide for plan-to-plan transfers of its assets to a qualified plan under Code Section 401(a). Otherwise, the final Code Section 403(b) regulations limit plan-to-plan transfers to those occurring between Section 403(b) plans. [Treas. Reg. § 1.403(b)-10(b)(1) and (4)]

The plan-to-plan transfer rules of the final Code Section 403(b) regulations generally are effective for taxable years beginning after 2008. See Q 10:82 for a discussion of the differences between a plan-to-plan transfer and a direct rollover.

**Q 10:63   What is a direct transfer between Section 403(b)
            funding vehicles pursuant to Revenue Ruling 90-24?**

A direct transfer between Section 403(b) funding vehicles pursuant to
Revenue Ruling 90-24 is a tax-free transfer made directly between contract
issuers or account custodians that is not a distribution under Code Section 72 or
a deemed distribution. Generally, transfers can be made pursuant to Revenue
Ruling 90-24 through 2008, when the final Code Section 403(b) regulations that
were published on July 26, 2007, take effect. However, the final Code Section
403(b) regulations impose certain requirements on such transactions that occur
after September 24, 2007, subject to certain transition rules. (See Qs 10:57,
10:59, 10:60, and 10:61.)

**Q 10:64   What are the differences between an exchange of
            Section 403(b) contracts under the final Code Section
            403(b) regulations published in 2007 and a direct transfer
            between Section 403(b) contracts pursuant to Revenue
            Ruling 90-24?**

Exchanges of Section 403(b) contracts made pursuant to the final Code
Section 403(b) regulations that were published on July 26, 2007, are subject to
a number of requirements that were not imposed on direct transfers made
pursuant to Revenue Ruling 90-24, including the requirement that the plan
sponsor and the contract issuer enter into an information sharing agreement.
(See Q 10:59.) Other than these additional requirements, an exchange under the
final Code Section 403(b) regulations and a direct transfer pursuant to Revenue
Ruling 90-24 are similar. For example, neither transaction is treated as a
distribution for purposes of the withdrawal restrictions that apply to Section
403(b) contracts, and both transactions require that any new contract issued in
the transaction continues to apply the same or more stringent withdrawal
restrictions as those that applied under the old contract.

**Q 10:65   Must a Section 403(b) plan or a Section 403(b)
            contract include a provision allowing for exchanges
            or plan-to-plan transfers in order to satisfy the final
            Code Section 403(b) regulations published in 2007?**

A Section 403(b) plan does not need to provide for exchanges or plan-to-plan
transfers in order to satisfy Code Section 403(b) or the final Code Section 403(b)
regulations that were published on July 26, 2007. However, if a Section 403(b)
plan does not include such provisions, then exchanges and plan-to-plan transfers are not permitted under the plan. (See Qs 10:59 and 10:62.) Thus, in order
for any exchange or plan-to-plan transfer to occur under the final Code Section
403(b) regulations, the plan must provide for the exchange or plan-to-plan
transfer. In the case of plan-to-plan transfers, both the transferor plan and the
receiving plan must provide for the transfer. [Treas. Reg. § 1.403(b)-10(b)]

Similarly, the final Code Section 403(b) regulations do not require a Section
403(b) contract to include an exchange provision. However, to the extent that

exchanges are permitted under the Section 403(b) plan in connection with which the contract was issued, it may be advisable to include an exchange provision in the contract that the payee may exercise in order to ensure compliance with the requirements applicable to exchanges under the final Code Section 403(b) regulations, such as the requirement that any distribution restrictions remain at least as stringent under the contract received in the exchange.

Q 10:66 Must a Section 403(b) plan or a Section 403(b) contract contain a direct transfer option in order to satisfy Revenue Ruling 90-24?

Revenue Ruling 90-24 is silent on this point. However, any such option provided by a Section 403(b) plan or a Section 403(b) contract could cause confusion after 2008, which is the effective date of the final Code Section 403(b) regulations that were published on July 26, 2007. The final Code Section 403(b) regulations effectively eliminate the ability to transfer amounts between Section 403(b) contracts pursuant to Revenue Ruling 90-24 [1990-1 C.B. 97] after 2008, subject to certain transition rules. In addition, any transfers made pursuant to Revenue Ruling 90-24 between September 24, 2007, and January 1, 2009, are subject to certain requirements under the final Code Section 403(b) regulations, including a requirement that the plan sponsor and the issuer of the new contract enter into an information sharing agreement. (See Qs 10:57, 10:59, 10:60, and 10:61.)

Q 10:67 May the participant receive the check and personally transfer the funds under the final Code Section 403(b) regulations published in 2007 or under Revenue Ruling 90-24?

No.

Q 10:68 Who may make an exchange under the final Code Section 403(b) regulations published in 2007 or a direct transfer under Revenue Ruling 90-24?

A current employee, a former employee, or a beneficiary of a former employee are all eligible to effect a direct transfer between Section 403(b) contracts pursuant to the final Code Section 403(b) regulations that were published in 2007 or pursuant to Revenue Ruling 90-24.

Q 10:69 May exchanges or direct transfers occur between Section 403(b) annuity contracts and custodial accounts?

Yes. However, if the funds to be exchanged or transferred are subject to the early distribution restrictions set forth in Code Section 403(b)(11) or Code Section 403(b)(7)(A)(ii) at the time of exchange or transfer, then the funds must continue to be subject to the same or more stringent distribution restrictions after the transfer occurs. [*See* Treas. Reg. § 1.403(b)-10(b); Rev. Rul. 90-24]

Q 10:70   If a participant has made after-tax contributions, how is his or her basis transferred in an exchange, plan-to-plan transfer, or direct transfer?

The final Code Section 403(b) regulations that were published on July 26, 2007, state that any interest in after-tax contributions is carried over in a plan-to-plan transfer, including any such transfer of only a portion of the participant's interest in the plan (in which case a pro rata interest in any after-tax contributions is carried over). [Treas. Reg. § 1.403(b)-10(10(b)(3)(i)(G)] Although not expressly addressed by the final Code Section 403(b) regulations, it appears that similar treatment would apply to any after-tax contributions involved in an exchange of Section 403(b) contracts governed by the final Code Section 403(b) regulations.

Similarly, Revenue Ruling 90-24 provides that where a Section 403(b) contract contains after-tax employee contributions and part of the account balance is directly transferred to another Section 403(b) contract, a pro rata portion of the after-tax amounts will also be treated as having been directly transferred to the new carrier.

Presumably, the foregoing treatment also applies in the case of designated Roth contributions under Code Section 402A, which are made on an after-tax basis. Any designated Roth contributions held in a Section 403(b) contract must be accounted for separately from non-Roth contributions. [Treas. Reg. § 1.403(b)-3(c)]

Q 10:71   In an exchange or transfer between Section 403(b) contracts, will the employee lose any grandfathering that may have applied to such exchanged or transferred funds under the transferor Section 403(b) contract?

No. Unlike a tax-free rollover, an exchange or transfer is not treated as a distribution from a Section 403(b) plan. This treatment applies to an intra-plan exchange or a plan-to-plan transfer made pursuant to the final Code Section 403(b) regulations that were published on July 26, 2007, as well as to a direct transfer made pursuant to Revenue Ruling 90-24. Thus, the exchange or transfer of Section 403(b) amounts between annuity contracts that are attributable to the employee's December 31, 1986, or December 31, 1988, account balance will retain any grandfathered status to which the funds were entitled prior to the exchange or transfer, as long as the transferor provides the required information to the transferee, such amounts are accounted for separately, and such amounts continue to be clearly identified under the new contract. However, pursuant to the final Code Section 403(b) regulations and Revenue Ruling 90-24, an exchange or transfer from a Section 403(b)(7) custodial account to a Section

403(b) annuity contract will subject the transferred amounts to the more restrictive Section 403(b)(7) withdrawal restrictions.

Q 10:72 Must the entire account balance under a Section 403(b) contract be exchanged or transferred in order to comply with the final Code Section 403(b) regulations published in 2007 or with the requirements of Revenue Ruling 90-24?

Under Revenue Ruling 90-24, participants may directly transfer, tax free, all or any portion of the balance in their Section 403(b) contract to another Section 403(b) contract. However, the transferor and transferee Section 403(b) contracts may have their own restrictions for transferring and accepting, respectively, a direct transfer pursuant to Revenue Ruling 90-24. Furthermore, Section 403(b) plan restrictions, if any, may also apply to direct transfers made pursuant to Revenue Ruling 90-24.

Similarly, the final Code Section 403(b) regulations that were published on July 26, 2007, state that, if a plan-to-plan transfer (i.e., moving amounts from one plan to another plan) involves less than a complete transfer of the participant's or beneficiary's entire interest in the plan, then the transferee plan must treat the transferred amounts as a continuation of a pro rata portion of the participant's or beneficiary's interest in the transferor plan. Thus, for example, the transferee plan must treat the amount transferred as a pro rata continuation of the participant's or beneficiary's interest in any after-tax contributions. [Treas. Reg. § 1.403(b)-10(b)(3)(G)]

The final Code Section 403(b) regulations are silent on whether partial exchanges of Section 403(b) contracts are permitted. However, the exchange provisions of the final Code Section 403(b) regulations are generally intended to replace the direct transfer rules of Revenue Ruling 90-24, which, as described above, allow for direct transfers of a portion of a participant's or beneficiary's account balance. In addition, the final Code Section 403(b) regulations clearly allow for plan-to-plan transfers of less than a participant's full interest in the plan. As a result, it appears that partial exchanges of Section 403(b) contracts would be allowed under the final Code Section 403(b) regulations.

Q 10:73 May amounts that are subject to the Section 403(b)(11) or Section 403(b)(7)(A)(ii) withdrawal restrictions be exchanged or transferred?

Yes. However, the final Code Section 403(b) regulations that were published on July 26, 2007, require that any amounts involved in an intra-plan exchange or plan-to-plan transfer must continue to be subject to the same or more stringent withdrawal restrictions. Similarly, Revenue Ruling 90-24 requires that the transferred funds must continue, after the transfer, to be subject to the same or more stringent distribution restrictions as were imposed on them prior to the transfer by Code Section 403(b)(11) or Section 403(b)(7)(A)(ii).

Q 10:74 Is employer consent required to effect an exchange of Section 403(b) contracts under the final Code Section 403(b) regulations published in 2007?

The final Code Section 403(b) regulations that were published on July 26, 2007, permit an exchange of Section 403(b) contracts under the same employer's Section 403(b) plan only if the written plan provides for exchanges (and certain other requirements are met). In addition, in certain cases the employer must enter into an information sharing agreement with the issuer of the contract received in the exchange. To this extent, the final Code Section 403(b) regulations require the employer's consent to an exchange of Section 403(b) contracts under the employer's Section 403(b) plan.

Q 10:75 Is employer consent required to effect a plan-to-plan transfer under the final Code Section 403(b) regulations published in 2007?

Yes.

Q 10:76 Is employer consent required to effect a Section 403(b) direct transfer pursuant to Revenue Ruling 90-24?

Revenue Ruling 90-24 is silent on this point. Where the Section 403(b) contract from which the transfer is being made contains elective deferral contributions only (and the earnings on such amounts) and was not purchased under a written plan, employer consent should not be required. However, if the Section 403(b) contract from which the transfer is being made was purchased under a written plan, employer consent may be required depending on the terms of the Section 403(b) funding vehicle and Section 403(b) plan. In addition, the final Code Section 403(b) regulations that were published on July 26, 2007, impose certain requirements on direct transfers made pursuant to Revenue Ruling 90-24 after September 24, 2007. (See Qs 10:57, 10:59, 10:60, and 10:61.)

Q 10:77 Is a Section 403(b) plan or a Section 403(b) contract required to permit exchanges or transfers?

No. The final Code Section 403(b) regulations that were published on July 26, 2007, do not require a Section 403(b) plan or a Section 403(b) contract to permit exchanges or plan-to-plan transfers within the meaning of those regulations. In addition, Revenue Ruling 90-24 does not require that a Section 403(b) contract permit direct transfers from or into such contract.

Q 10:78 What is a *rollover?*

A *rollover* is a tax-free transfer of all or any portion of an eligible rollover distribution amount from a Section 403(b) annuity contract or custodial account into an eligible retirement plan that accepts rollover contributions.

Q 10:79   What is an *eligible retirement plan*?

In the case of eligible rollover distributions received prior to 2002 from Section 403(b) contracts or accounts, an *eligible retirement plan* was limited to:

- An IRA under Code Section 408(a) or (b); and
- Another Code Section 403(b) contract or custodial account.

Pursuant to a change in law enacted by EGTRRA, for eligible rollover distributions received after 2001, an eligible retirement plan includes, in addition to those listed above, the following types of plans:

- A qualified plan under Code Section 401(a);
- A qualified annuity under Code Section 403(a); and
- A governmental Code Section 457(b) plan that agrees to separately account for amounts rolled over from other types of arrangements.

[I.R.C. §§ 402(c)(8)(B), 402(c)(10)]

Q 10:80   What is the difference between a direct rollover and an indirect rollover?

A direct rollover is a direct payment of an eligible rollover distribution to an eligible retirement plan that will accept the rollover. The employee is not taxed on any taxable portion of the distribution directly rolled over, and no portion of the eligible rollover distribution amount is withheld in income taxes.

An indirect rollover is any amount of an eligible rollover distribution that is not directly rolled over to an eligible retirement plan (e.g., an amount paid directly to the employee). Federal income tax withholding of 20 percent applies to the taxable portion of such amount, and the remaining 80 percent is subject to tax if not rolled over to an eligible retirement plan within 60 days of the distribution (see Q 10:107).

Q 10:81   What is an eligible rollover distribution from a Section 403(b) annuity contract or custodial account?

Pursuant to Code Section 402(c)(4), and the regulations issued thereunder, an eligible rollover distribution from a Section 403(b) annuity contract or custodial account generally is any distribution from the Section 403(b) annuity contract or account, other than the following:

1. A required minimum distribution. A plan administrator is permitted to assume there is no designated beneficiary for purposes of determining the balance of the minimum distribution.

2. Any distribution upon hardship of the employee.

3. A distribution that is one of a series of substantially equal periodic payments made at least annually (1) for the life or life expectancy of the employee or the joint lives or joint life expectancies of the employee and

the employee's designated beneficiary, or (2) for a specified period of ten years or more.

Therefore, where a participant elects, for example, a five-year period certain annuity payout of pension benefits and such amounts are not required minimum distributions, the taxable portion of each such annuity payment will be treated as an eligible rollover distribution. Additionally, the IRS has the authority, and has exercised such authority in issuing final regulations, to exclude certain items of income, other than those noted above, from the definition of eligible rollover distribution. [I.R.C. § 402(c)(4)]

4. Elective deferrals (under Code Section 402(g)(3)), employee contributions, and earnings on each returned because of the Code Section 415 limits.

5. Corrective distributions of excess deferrals (under Code Section 402(g)) and earnings.

6. Loans treated as deemed distributions (under Code Section 72(p)). But plan loan offset amounts may be eligible rollover distributions. [*See* Treas. Reg. § 1.402(c)-2, Q&A-9]

7. Distributions to a payee other than the employee, the employee's surviving spouse, or a spouse or former spouse who is an alternate payee under a QDRO.

Q 10:82   What are some of the differences between a direct rollover and other methods of moving moneys between Section 403(b) contracts or Section 403(b) plans tax-free?

An eligible rollover distribution that is directly rolled over to an eligible retirement plan is considered to be a distribution followed by an immediate rollover. Therefore, amounts subject to Code Section 403(b)(11) or 403(b)(7) withdrawal restrictions are not eligible for rollover. [*See* Frank v. Aaronson, 95 Civ. 1518 (S.D.N.Y. Oct. 16, 1996)] Additionally, because a direct rollover is considered a distribution option, the spousal consent and other similar participant and beneficiary protection rules that would otherwise apply to a distribution from the Section 403(b) funding vehicle will apply to an eligible rollover distribution that is directly rolled over to an eligible retirement plan. Furthermore, because a direct rollover generally is considered a distribution from the transferor plan, any rights and options available under the transferor plan are not required to be preserved under the transferee/receiving plan or Section 403(b) annuity contract or custodial account. [Treas. Reg. § 1.401(a)(31)-1, Q&A 14] In addition, amounts that are rolled over to another Section 403(b) plan are freely distributable, and do not remain subject to the withdrawal restrictions of Code Sections 403(b)(11) or 403(b)(7), unless the plan to which the amounts were rolled over provides otherwise.

In contrast, a plan-to-plan transfer within the meaning of the final Code Section 403(b) regulations that were published on July 26, 2007, is not treated as a distribution from the plan, and instead is treated as a continuation of the transferor plan. Thus, amounts subject to withdrawal restrictions under Code Section 403(b)(11) or 403(b)(7) may be included in a plan-to-plan transfer, provided that the requirements applicable to such transfers under the final Code Section 403(b) regulations are met. (See Q 10:62 for a discussion of those requirements.) Because the transferred amounts are treated as a continuation of the original plan, it also is possible that any defects suffered by the transferor plan that affected its status under Code Section 403(b) could carry over to the transferee plan. This result generally would not occur in the case of a direct rollover because a rollover is treated as a distribution from the old plan, which potentially makes a direct rollover a more attractive alternative for moving moneys between Section 403(b) plans (assuming that applicable withdrawal restrictions do not prohibit the rollover). Unlike a rollover, a plan-to-plan transfer is not limited to plan assets allocable to the participant or spouse beneficiary, and can involve any beneficiary with an interest in the plan. Finally, unlike a direct rollover, a plan-to-plan transfer from a 403(b) plan generally can be made only to another 403(b) plan. However, if certain conditions relating to permissive service credits and repayments under Code Section 415 are met, a Section 403(b) plan is permitted to provide for plan-to-plan transfers of its assets to a qualified plan under Code Section 401(a). [Treas. Reg. §§ 1.403(b)-10(b)(1), 1.403(b)-10(b)(4)]

Similar to a plan-to-plan transfer, an exchange of Section 403(b) contracts within the meaning of the final Code Section 403(b) regulations is not treated as a distribution from the plan. Rather, it is treated as a nontaxable transaction occurring within the same Section 403(b) plan. Thus, amounts subject to withdrawal restrictions under Code Section 403(b)(11) or 403(b)(7) may be included in an exchange, provided that the requirements applicable to exchanges under the final Code Section 403(b) regulations are met (including the requirement for an information sharing agreement). (See Qs 10:59 and 10:60 for a discussion of those requirements.) Likewise, because an exchange is a transaction involving two Section 403(b) contracts that are part of the same Section 403(b) plan, the transaction and the resulting contracts remain subject to all provisions of the Section 403(b) plan. Unlike a rollover, a Section 403(b) contract cannot be exchanged for anything other than another Section 403(b) contract.

Finally, a direct transfer between Section 403(b) contracts pursuant to Revenue Ruling 90-24 is generally not treated as a plan distribution. Therefore, amounts subject to Section 403(b)(11) or 403(b)(7) withdrawal restrictions may be transferred to another 403(b) contract, provided that the transferee 403(b) contract imposes withdrawal restrictions on the transferred amounts at least as stringent as those the transferor 403(b) contract imposed prior to the transfer. Additionally, where amounts are directly transferred from a Section 403(b) contract or account issued under a plan subject to ERISA to another Section 403(b) contract or account, it is arguable that the transferred benefits may be a transfer of benefits for purposes of Code Section 411(d)(6). Finally, unlike a rollover, a direct transfer of Section 403(b) amounts made pursuant to Revenue Ruling 90-24 may not be made to an IRA and is not limited to the participant or spouse beneficiary—any beneficiary under a Section 403(b) annuity is generally eligible to effect a direct transfer between Section 403(b) funding vehicles under Revenue Ruling 90-24.

Q 10:83   Do amounts rolled over from a Section 403(b) contract or custodial account to an eligible retirement plan retain any grandfathering treatment (i.e., required distribution amounts and withdrawal restrictions) to which such amounts may have been subject prior to the rollover?

Although the IRS has not ruled on this issue, the answer for rollovers from a Section 403(b) contract or custodial account to an eligible retirement plan other than another Section 403(b) contract or custodial account is definitely no, and the answer is probably no for rollovers from a Section 403(b) funding vehicle to another Section 403(b) contract or custodial account. Any amount rolled over to an eligible retirement plan from a Section 403(b) annuity, either as a direct rollover or a rollover made within the 60-day period, is treated as a distribution from the Section 403(b) annuity followed by a rollover contribution. Therefore, because a rollover presupposes that a distribution must first occur and is not a transfer of assets, Section 403(b) amounts that are transferred to an eligible retirement plan other than another Section 403(b) contract or custodial account as a rollover will lose any Section 403(b) grandfathering treatment to which such funds may have been entitled prior to the rollover. It is likely that similar treatment will result for rollovers to another Section 403(b) vehicle. However, because a rollover of Section 403(b) amounts must first be distributable, any loss of grandfathering with respect to the Section 403(b)(11) withdrawal restrictions should not adversely affect the participant.

Q 10:84   Is a Section 403(b) contract or custodial account required by its terms to allow for eligible rollover distributions?

Yes. A Section 403(b) contract or custodial account, by its terms, must permit direct rollovers of eligible rollover distributions. However, the IRS has provided no guidance concerning what, if any, language a Section 403(b) contract or custodial account should include.

Q 10:85   When is the determination made of whether payments are substantially equal for a specified period for purposes of the eligible rollover distribution rules?

The determination of whether payments are substantially equal for a specified period is made at the time the distributions commence. If a change occurs that causes subsequent payments to fail to be substantially equal to prior payments, a new determination must be made as to whether the subsequent payments are eligible rollover distributions, without regard to any payments made prior to the modification. [Treas. Reg. § 1.402(c)-2, Q&A 5]

Q 10:86   What are the procedures for making a direct rollover?

A direct rollover may be accomplished by "any reasonable means of direct payment to an eligible retirement plan." [Treas. Reg. § 1.401(a)(31)-1, Q&A 3] Reasonable means include delivery of a check to the eligible retirement plan by the participant, provided that the check is made payable in such a manner that it may be negotiated only by the new Section 403(b) or IRA contract or account issuer. However, even if the eligible rollover distribution is paid to the distributee, rather than being directly rolled over, the distributee may contribute the eligible rollover distribution (or any portion thereof) to an eligible retirement plan as a rollover within 60 days from the date on which the distributee received the distribution. The amount rolled over will be excluded from gross income. In such case 20 percent tax would have been withheld from the amount distributed to the payee and, in order to effect a rollover of the entire eligible rollover distribution, the payee must, within this 60-day period, come up with out-of-pocket funds to cover the amount of tax withheld. [IRS Notice 2002-3, 2002-2 I.R.B. 289]

Q 10:87   What portion of the eligible rollover distribution rules is applicable to Section 403(b) annuities?

The rules applicable to direct rollovers and income tax withholding with respect to eligible rollover distributions from a qualified plan apply to a Section 403(b) contract or account as though it were a qualified plan, and the payer of the Section 403(b) eligible rollover distribution is treated as the plan administrator. [I.R.C. § 403(b)(8)(B); Treas. Reg. § 1.403(b)-7]

Q 10:88   Is a Section 403(b) plan required to permit a participant to roll over all or any portion of an eligible rollover distribution?

Yes. A Section 403(b) plan must be amended to include a provision to permit participants to elect to have any distribution that is an eligible rollover distribution directly transferred to an eligible retirement plan that accepts direct rollovers. [Treas. Reg. § 1.403(b)-7]

A participant is permitted to elect a direct rollover of any portion of an eligible rollover distribution. Therefore, subject to certain *de minimis* rules, a plan or payer may not require a payee to directly roll over "all or nothing" of an eligible rollover distribution. [Treas. Reg. § 1.401(a)(31)-1, Q&A 9]

Q 10:89   Is a Section 403(b) annuity contract or custodial account required to permit direct rollovers of eligible rollover distributions?

Yes.

Q 10:90   May a payee divide an eligible rollover distribution?

A payer is permitted (but not required) to allow a payee to divide an eligible rollover distribution into separate distributions for direct rollover to two or more eligible retirement plans. However, the plan administrator or payer is permitted to limit the distributee to a single direct rollover for each eligible rollover distribution. For example, assume John Doe wants to effect a direct rollover of an eligible rollover distribution of $100,000. However, John Doe wishes to instruct the payer to directly roll over $50,000 of the $100,000 eligible rollover distribution to an IRA issued by Insurance Company X and the remaining portion of the distributable amount, $50,000, to an IRA issued by Bank Y. The payer may limit John Doe to a single direct rollover with respect to each eligible rollover distribution, which in this example is $100,000. However, the payer should apply such rules uniformly with respect to all distributees under the plan. [Treas. Reg. § 1.401(a)(31)-1, Q&A 10]

Q 10:91   May a participant roll over after-tax amounts?

Yes. Changes in the law made by EGTRRA allow a participant to roll over after-tax amounts from a Section 403(b) contract or account to an IRA either as a direct rollover or as a 60-day "indirect" rollover. After-tax amounts may not be rolled over from an IRA to a Section 403(b) contract or account. [*See* I.R.C. §§ 403(b)(8)(B), 402(c)(2); IRS Notice 2002-3, 2002-2 I.R.B. 289]

In addition, after-tax amounts may be rolled over from a Section 403(b) contract or account to another such contract or account, but only if (1) the other contract or account provides separate accounting for the after-tax amounts, and (2) the rollover is made via a direct rollover. [*See* IRS Notice 2002-3]

The Code and the legislative history of EGTRRA would appear to allow after-tax amounts to be rolled over from a Section 403(b) contract or account to a qualified trust which is part of a defined contribution plan, but only if (1) the plan agrees to separately account for amounts transferred, including separately accounting for after-tax amounts, and (2) the "rollover" is made via a direct rollover. [I.R.C. §§ 403(b)(8)(B), 402(c)(2); H.R. Conf. Rep. No. 107-84, at 251 (2001)] However, recent IRS guidance addressing rollovers of after-tax amounts from Section 403(b) contracts and accounts does not address this issue, and therefore it is unclear whether such rollovers are permissible. [*See* IRS Notice 2002-3] Future IRS guidance may clarify this point.

Q 10:92   Do any *de minimis* rules apply to the direct rollover and tax-withholding requirements applicable to eligible rollover distributions?

Yes. The plan administrator or payer is permitted to require that, if the participant/payee elects to have only part of an eligible rollover distribution directly rolled over to an eligible retirement plan, that part be equal to at least $500. Also, if the entire amount of an eligible rollover distribution is $500 or less, the plan administrator or payer is not required to allow the participant/payee to divide the distribution. In this instance, the payer may require the participant/payee to choose either to make or not make a direct rollover of the entire eligible rollover distribution. [Treas. Reg. § 1.401(a)(31)-1, Q&A 9]

A Section 403(b) annuity contract or custodial account may also limit a participant/payee's right to elect a direct rollover with respect to eligible rollover distributions that are reasonably expected to total less than $200 during a year (or any lower minimum amount specified by the plan administrator/payer), although these amounts may still be eligible for rollover by the employee within 60 days from receipt of the distribution. However, all eligible rollover distributions made within the same calendar year to the participant/payee under the same plan must be aggregated in determining whether the $200 floor is reached. In the event that the payer or plan administrator does not know at the time of the first distribution (which is less than $200) whether additional eligible rollover distributions will be made during the year for which aggregation is required, the payer is not required to withhold tax from the first distribution. [Treas. Reg. § 1.401(a)(31)-1, Q&A 11]

Q 10:93 Is a Section 403(b) plan or annuity required to accept direct rollover contributions from another Section 403(b) plan or annuity?

No. [Treas. Reg. § 1.401(a)(31)-1, Q&A 13]

Q 10:94 Is a payee required to directly roll over the entire portion of an eligible rollover distribution?

No. (However, see discussion of *de minimis* rules at Q 10:92.) Additionally, a plan administrator or payer is not required (but is permitted) to allow the participant/payee to divide an eligible rollover distribution into separate distributions to be directly rolled over to two or more eligible retirement plans. However, the plan administrator or payer is permitted to limit the participant/payee to a single direct rollover for each eligible rollover distribution (see Q 10:90). [Treas. Reg. § 1.401(a)(31)-1, Q&A 10]

Q 10:95 What is a required minimum distribution for purposes of determining what is an eligible rollover distribution?

If a minimum distribution is required in any year, all amounts distributed during that calendar year are treated as required minimum distributions and, therefore, not eligible rollover distributions, as long as the total required minimum distribution for that year has not yet been made. If the total required minimum distribution for any year is not made in that calendar year, "the amount that was required but not distributed is added to the amount required to be distributed for the next calendar year in determining the portion of any distribution in the next calendar year that is a required minimum distribution." [Treas. Reg. § 1.402(c)-2, Q&A 7]

Q 10:96   In determining what is a required minimum distribution, do any special rules apply to periodic annuity payments from Section 403(b) annuity contracts?

Yes. For purposes of determining what is or is not an eligible rollover distribution, the entire amount of any periodic annuity payment from a Section 403(b) annuity made on or after January 1 of the year in which the employee attains (or would have attained) age 70½ will be treated as a required minimum distribution for purposes of being treated as not eligible for rollover. Any amount distributed before January 1 of the year in which the employee attains or would have attained age 70½ will not be treated as a required minimum distribution for purposes of the eligible rollover distribution rules and therefore may be an eligible rollover distribution, if it otherwise qualifies. [Treas. Reg. § 1.402(c)-2, Q&A 7]

Q 10:97   Is the payer permitted to require the payee to furnish it with certain information prior to effecting a direct rollover?

The plan administrator/payer may require a payee who elects a direct rollover option to provide adequate information in a timely manner regarding the eligible retirement plan to which the direct rollover is to be made. However, the payer may neither prescribe unreasonable procedures for effecting a direct rollover nor require information "that effectively eliminates or substantially impairs the distributee's ability to elect a direct rollover. [Treas. Reg. § 1. 401(a)(31)-1, Q&A 6]

Q 10:98   What information may a payer rely on in giving effect to an employee's request for a direct rollover?

A payer may rely on the following employee-provided information: the name of the recipient plan, a representation from the designated recipient plan that the plan is an eligible retirement plan, and any other information necessary to accomplish the direct rollover by the means selected for delivery. [Treas. Reg. §§ 1.401(a)(31)-1, Q&A 6, 31.3405(c)-1, Q&A 7]

Q 10:99   Do the eligible rollover distribution rules apply to spouse beneficiaries?

Yes. A distribution to a surviving spouse (or to an alternate payee pursuant to a QDRO) is an eligible rollover distribution if it otherwise meets the requirements of an eligible rollover distribution. Effective for eligible rollover distributions received after 2001, the surviving spouse may roll over such an eligible rollover distribution to an eligible retirement plan as if the surviving spouse were the deceased employee. [I.R.C. § 402(c)(9)]

Q 10:100   May distributions to a nonspouse beneficiary qualify as eligible rollover distributions?

Yes. Under prior law, a distributee other than the employee or the employee's surviving spouse (or former spouse who is an alternate payee under a QDRO) was not permitted to roll over distributions from a qualified plan or Section 403(b) annuity. Therefore, such distributions were not eligible rollover distributions and were not subject to the 20 percent withholding requirements. For distributions after December 31, 2006, the PPA changed this rule to allow for "direct trustee-to-trustee transfers" by a nonspouse beneficiary of amounts under a Section 403(b) annuity contract to an IRA that has been established to receive the distribution on behalf of the beneficiary. Such a transfer is treated as a direct rollover of an eligible rollover distribution for purposes of Code Section 402(c). The IRA is treated as an "inherited IRA" within the meaning of Code Section 408(d)(3)(C), and the required minimum distribution rules of Code Section 401(a)(9)(B) apply to the IRA (other than the special rule for surviving spouses under Code Section 401(a)(9)(B)(iv)). [I.R.C. § 402(c)(11); IRS Notice 2007-7]

Q 10:101   If the participant effects a rollover into an IRA and intends to later roll over the proceeds back into a Section 403(b) annuity or account, should a separate IRA be established as a conduit to accept the IRA rollover?

Yes. [I.R.C. § 408(d)(3); H.R. Conf. Rep. No. 107-84, at 250 (2001)]

Q 10:102   How much time does a participant have to complete a rollover?

To the extent a participant does not accomplish a direct rollover, a participant may roll over an eligible rollover distribution within 60 days from the date the distribution is received. For distributions made after 2001, the Secretary of the Treasury may waive this 60-day requirement where the failure to waive the requirement would be against equity or good conscience, including casualty, disaster, or other events beyond the reasonable control of the participant. [I.R.C. § 402(c)(3)(B). *See, e.g.,* Ltr. Ruls. 200401020, 200401023, 200401024, and 200401025 for situations in which the IRS waived the 60-day time limit for rollovers.]

Effective January 27, 2003, for distributions occurring after December 31, 2001, such a waiver is granted automatically if the failure to complete a rollover within the required 60 days is due solely to an error on the part of a financial institution, if the following conditions are satisfied:

1. The financial institution receives funds on behalf of a taxpayer before the expiration of the 60-day rollover period;
2. The taxpayer follows all procedures required by the financial institution for depositing the funds into an eligible retirement plan within the required 60 days;

3. Had the financial institution deposited the funds as instructed by the taxpayer, it would have been a valid rollover; and

4. The funds are deposited into an eligible retirement plan within one year from the beginning of the 60-day rollover period.

[Rev. Proc. 2003-16, 2003-4 I.R.B. 1]

In other situations, a taxpayer may apply for a hardship exception to the 60-day rollover requirement under normal IRS procedures for requesting a Private Letter Ruling. In determining whether to grant a waiver, the IRS will consider all relevant facts and circumstances, including the following:

1. Errors committed by a financial institution (other than those resulting in an automatic waiver, as described above);

2. The taxpayer's inability to complete a rollover due to death, disability, hospitalization, incarceration, restrictions imposed by a foreign country, or postal error;

3. The taxpayer's use of the amount distributed (e.g., in the case of payment by check, whether the check was cashed); and

4. The time elapsed since the distribution occurred.

[Rev. Proc. 2003-16, 2003-4 I.R.B. 1]

The time for making a rollover also may be postponed in the event of service in a combat zone or in the case of a presidentially declared disaster or a terrorist or military action. [I.R.C. §§ 7508, 7508A; Treas. Reg. § 301.7508-1; Rev. Proc. 2002-71, 2002-46 I.R.B. 850]

Under prior law, the 60-day period could not be extended even if the failure to meet the deadline was through no fault of the participant. [Ltr. Ruls. 9145036, 8548073; Treas. Reg. § 1.402(c)-2, Q&A 11]

Q 10:103   How do the eligible rollover distribution rules apply to a series of periodic payments that began prior to 1993, which was the effective date of the eligible rollover distribution rules?

The regulations clarify that a distribution after 1992 is not an eligible rollover distribution if, after taking into account distributions prior to 1993, it would not be an eligible rollover distribution. For example, assume that in 1980 a participant in a Section 403(b) arrangement elected a 15-year term certain payout. Although as of January 1, 1993, the remaining payments would be made for three years, distributions made after 1992 will not constitute eligible rollover distributions because the term certain payout was elected for 15 years, notwithstanding that the payments began prior to 1993. [Treas. Reg. § 1.402(c)-2, Q&A 5(e)]

Q 10:104 Are hardship withdrawals of amounts attributable to Section 403(b) elective deferrals eligible rollover distributions?

No. Effective for distributions after 2001, Code Section 402(c)(4) was amended to exclude "any distribution which is made upon hardship of the employee." Prior to 2002, Code Section 402(c)(4) excluded from the definition of eligible rollover distribution "any distribution described in section 401(k)(2)(B)(i)(IV)." Special rules applied to hardship distributions made in 1999. [*See* IRS Notice 99-5, 1999-3 I.R.B. 10]

Q 10:105 Do the eligible rollover distribution requirements apply to periodic annuity payments from a Section 403(b) annuity for a term certain of less than ten years?

Yes. Provided a payment does not constitute a required minimum distribution, the taxable portion of each payment in the series made under a term certain annuity payout option of less than ten years would be an eligible rollover distribution. Any eligible rollover distribution that is not directly rolled over would be subject to withholding at a rate of 20 percent with no ability to elect out. [I.R.C. §§ 402(c)(4), 403(b)(8)]

Q 10:106 When a participant effects a direct rollover from a Section 403(b) annuity to an IRA, is that participant eligible, under tax laws, to make a custodian-to-custodian transfer from that IRA to another IRA within the same calendar year as the direct rollover?

Yes, provided the direct rollover IRA permits custodian-to-custodian transfers and provided the new IRA permits the acceptance of custodian-to-custodian transfers. (Custodian-to-custodian transfers between IRAs are not treated as distributions for federal income tax purposes.) The direct rollover requirements were not intended to affect the treatment of direct transfers under other provisions of the Code. Furthermore, a direct rollover from a Section 403(b) annuity would not be taken into account for purposes of the rule limiting rollovers from one IRA to another IRA to no more than one per year under Code Section 408(d)(3)(B) because a direct rollover is not a rollover from one IRA to another. [Treas. Reg. § 1.402(c)-2, Q&A 16]

Q 10:107 What are the effects if a participant chooses not to directly roll over an eligible rollover distribution?

The effects are as follows:

- The payee will receive only 80 percent of the eligible rollover distribution because the payer would have been required to withhold 20 percent in federal taxes from the taxable portion of the eligible rollover distribution. In some states, state income tax withholding may also be required.

- The distribution will be taxed in the current year to the extent it is not rolled over to an eligible retirement plan within 60 days from the date the payee received it. If the payee receives the payment before age 59½, the 10 percent additional tax under Code Section 72(t) may also apply.

Q 10:108   May a participant who receives an eligible rollover distribution elect to roll over such amount other than as a direct rollover?

Yes. If a payee has an eligible rollover distribution paid to him or her, all or part of such a distribution may still be rolled over to an eligible retirement plan that accepts rollover contributions as long as the rollover is completed within 60 days from the date the payee received the distribution. However, after-tax amounts paid directly to the participant in an eligible rollover distribution may be rolled over within this 60-day period only to an IRA and not to any other type of plan or arrangement. (See Q 10:91.)

In connection with a 60-day or "indirect" rollover, the payer is still required to withhold 20 percent in federal taxes (and any applicable state income tax withholding) of the taxable portion of the eligible rollover distribution to the extent it is paid to the payee, even if the distribution is subsequently rolled over. The portion of the payment that is rolled over will not be taxed until it is received as a distribution.

The payee may roll over up to 100 percent of the eligible rollover distribution, including an amount equal to the 20 percent that was withheld. However, if the payee chooses to roll over 100 percent of the eligible rollover distribution amount, the payee must find other money within the 60-day period to contribute to the eligible retirement plan to replace the 20 percent tax that was withheld. On the other hand, if the payee rolls over only the 80 percent that was received, the payee will be taxed on the 20 percent portion of the distribution that was withheld in taxes. [See IRS Notice 2002-3, 2002-2 I.R.B. 289; Treas. Reg. § 1.402(c)-2, Q&A 11]

Q 10:109   May a participant roll over amounts from a Section 403(b) arrangement to a Roth IRA?

Yes. Under prior law, taxpayers who wished to roll over amounts from their Section 403(b) annuity contracts to Roth IRAs were required to follow a two-step process by first rolling over amounts from the contract to a traditional IRA, then converting the traditional IRA to a Roth IRA. For distributions after December 31, 2007, the PPA changes this rule to permit distributions from Section 403(b) annuity contracts to be rolled over directly to a Roth IRA, but only if the rollover meets the requirements of Code Section 403(b)(8). The rules that apply to rollovers from a traditional IRA to a Roth IRA would also apply, including, prior to 2010, a limitation on individuals with adjusted gross income in excess of $100,000. The Tax Increase Prevention and Reconciliation Act of 2006 modified this rule such that the $100,000 income eligibility rule does not apply after 2010.

Q 10:110 What are the effects of electing or not electing a direct rollover of an eligible rollover distribution?

These effects can be illustrated by the following examples:

Example 1. *Direct Rollover—100 Percent.* Gerald, age 57, has decided to terminate employment and is entitled to a distribution of $100,000 from his Section 403(b) annuity. This distribution is an eligible rollover distribution. Gerald has not made any after-tax contributions to the annuity. He requests a distribution of $100,000 and completes an authorization form that instructs the Section 403(b) issuer to directly roll over his pension money to an IRA with the financial institution of his choice. Gerald has already contacted the financial institution that issues the IRA to complete the proper paperwork so that it may accept the IRA direct rollover and provide the necessary information to the Section 403(b) issuer. By electing a direct rollover, Gerald has accomplished the following:

- He has avoided the 20 percent income tax withholding (and any state tax withholding) otherwise required;
- He has not incurred any current federal or state income tax liability on the eligible rollover distribution; and
- The 10 percent additional tax penalty for certain distributions received prior to age 59½ did not apply because he qualified for the age 55 exception to the 10 percent penalty.

Example 2. *No Direct Rollover.* Assume the same facts as in Example 1. Gerald is entitled to a distribution of $100,000, which is an eligible rollover distribution. However, Gerald does not elect a direct rollover of any portion of the eligible rollover distribution; therefore, the payer will withhold 20 percent in federal income tax ($20,000) from the eligible rollover distribution amount. Gerald will receive a check in the amount of $80,000, assuming no state income tax is also required to be withheld. If he wishes to roll over any portion of the $100,000 pension distribution, he must do so within 60 days from the date he receives the $80,000 distribution. Gerald will get a credit of $20,000 on his income tax return for the 20 percent in taxes withheld. Assume that Gerald decides to roll over the $80,000 in cash he received but is not able to come up with an additional $20,000 out-of-pocket to enable him to roll over the entire $100,000. Therefore, because Gerald cannot roll over the $20,000 withheld, it is includible as ordinary income on his income tax return. Gerald received the distribution after terminating employment after age 55 and, therefore, he is not subject to a 10 percent additional penalty tax on the $20,000 he did not roll over.

Tax Withholding and Reporting

Q 10:111 Which federal income tax-withholding rules apply to distributions from Section 403(b) annuity contracts or accounts?

The federal income tax-withholding requirements, including the rate at which withholding applies, depend on whether a distribution is or is not an eligible rollover distribution (see Table 10-1 at the end of this chapter for illustrations). However, special rules apply for hardship withdrawals in 1999. [See IRS Notice 99-5, 1999-3 I.R.B. 10]

Q 10:112 Which tax-withholding requirements apply for amounts that are not eligible rollover distributions?

Federal income tax withholding from the taxable portion of distributions that are not eligible rollover distributions from Section 403(b) annuities is required unless the payee is eligible to and does in fact elect not to have income tax withheld by filing an election with the payer. Where the payee does not elect out of withholding, the rate of income tax to be withheld depends on whether the distribution is nonperiodic or periodic. [I.R.C. §§ 3405(a), 3405(b)]

Q 10:113 What is a periodic distribution for tax-withholding purposes?

A periodic distribution includes an annuity payment, which means a series of payments payable for a period of more than a year and taxable under Code Section 72 as an amount received as an annuity. [Temp. Treas. Reg. § 35.3405-1, Q&A 9]

Q 10:114 What rate of withholding applies to periodic distributions?

For periodic payments, federal income tax will be withheld from the taxable portion of the distribution by treating the payment as wages under IRS wage withholding tables, using the marital status and number of withholding allowances elected by the payee on an IRS Form W-4P, or acceptable substitute, filed with the payer. Where the payee has not filed a Form W-4P, or acceptable substitute, with the payer, the payee will be treated as married claiming three withholding allowances. [I.R.C. § 3405(a)] Special rules apply where the payee has not provided the payer with a proper taxpayer identification number or where the payments are sent outside the United States or U.S. possessions. [I.R.C. §§ 3405(e)(12), 3405(e)(13)]

Q 10:115 What rate of withholding applies to nonperiodic distributions?

For nonperiodic distributions that are not eligible rollover distributions, where a payee has not elected out of withholding, income tax will be withheld at a rate of 10 percent from the taxable portion of the distribution. [I.R.C. § 3405(b)]

Q 10:116   Which special tax-withholding rules apply to distributions where the payee has not furnished a correct taxpayer identification number?

Where a payee has not furnished the payer with the correct taxpayer identification number (for individuals, this is generally the payee's Social Security number) for distributions that are not eligible rollover distributions, any election out of withholding will be ineffective, 10 percent tax will be withheld with respect to nonperiodic payments, and, for periodic payments, withholding will be calculated by treating the payee as single claiming zero withholding allowances. [I.R.C. § 3405(e)(12)]

Q 10:117   What federal income tax-withholding requirements apply to eligible rollover distributions?

Federal income tax withholding is required at a rate of 20 percent from the taxable portion of any distribution that is an eligible rollover distribution to the extent it is not directly rolled over to an eligible recipient plan. Payees cannot elect out of income tax withholding with respect to such distributions. [I.R.C. § 3405(c)]

A distributee of an eligible rollover distribution and the plan administrator or payer are permitted to enter into an agreement to provide for withholding in excess of 20 percent from an eligible rollover distribution. Special rules apply to such agreements. [Treas. Reg. § 31.3405(c)-1, Q&A 3]

Q 10:118   What is the rate of withholding on eligible rollover distributions?

That portion of an eligible rollover distribution that is not directly rolled over to an eligible recipient plan is subject to 20 percent federal income tax withholding.

Q 10:119   May a payee elect not to have federal income tax withheld from a Section 403(b) distribution?

It depends. A payee may not elect out of the 20 percent withholding required from an eligible rollover distribution. However, with respect to distributions that are not eligible rollover distributions, a payee may generally elect not to have taxes withheld by filing a written election with the payer.

[I.R.C. §§ 3405(a)(2), 3405(b)(2)]

Q 10:120   Is the payer required to notify payees of the tax-withholding requirements applicable to distributions from Section 403(b) annuities?

Yes. The nature of the notice, as well as when it must be provided to payees, depends on whether the notice relates to a distribution that is or is not an eligible rollover distribution.

Q 10:121   What notice requirements apply to eligible rollover distributions?

With respect to Section 403(b) annuities, the payer is required, within a "reasonable period of time" before making an eligible rollover distribution from an eligible retirement plan, to provide the recipient with a written explanation of the following:

1. The provisions allowing the direct rollover of the distribution to an eligible retirement plan;

2. The provisions requiring the withholding of federal income tax from the eligible rollover distribution at a rate of 20 percent to the extent it is not directly rolled over to an eligible retirement plan;

3. The provisions under which the eligible rollover distribution will not be subject to income tax to the extent it is rolled over, other than as a direct rollover, by the participant to an eligible retirement plan within 60 days from the date it is received by the participant (however, in such case, the 20 percent mandatory income tax withholding would already have been deducted from the taxable portion of the eligible rollover distribution that was paid directly to the participant); and

4. The fact that an election to make or not make a direct rollover of one payment in a series of periodic payments will apply to all subsequent payments in the series unless the distributee subsequently changes the election (if the payer chooses to provide for this treatment).

[I.R.C. § 402(f); Treas. Reg. §§ 1.401(a)(31)-1, Q&A 12, 1.402(f)-1, Q&A 3, 1.403(b)-7]

Q 10:122   May a contract issuer provide the notice and election required under Code Section 402(f) in connection with a distribution that is an eligible rollover distribution through a medium other than a written paper document?

The IRS has finalized certain amendments to various income tax regulations which would permit, and set forth standards for, the transmission of certain federal tax-withholding notices, including the notice required under Code Section 402(f), through an electronic medium reasonably accessible to the participant to whom the notice is given, in lieu of providing notice via the traditional method of a written paper document. The electronic notice system must be "reasonably designed to give the notice in a manner no less understand-able to the [payee] than a written paper document." [Treas. Reg. § 1.402(f)-1, Q&A-2, Q&A-5, Q&A-6]

Q 10:123   Is there a sample notice that may be provided to payees of eligible rollover distributions?

Yes. The IRS issued Notice 2002-3, in which it provided a safe-harbor explanation that plan administrators and payers may provide to recipients of eligible rollover distributions from qualified plans, Section 403(b) annuities, and Section 457(b) "governmental plans" concerning the direct rollover, 20 percent tax withholding, and certain other tax provisions affecting such distributions. Use of this safe-harbor explanation by plan administrators and payers will satisfy the eligible rollover distribution notification requirements if it is provided to the recipient of an eligible rollover distribution within a reasonable period of time before the eligible rollover distribution is made. [Treas. Reg. § 1.402(f)-1, Q&A 1] Notice 2002-3 replaces and makes obsolete Notice 2000-11. [2000-6 I.R.B. 572] [*See also* IRS Announcement 2002-46 (providing a safe-harbor explanation in Spanish)]

Q 10:124   May a payer customize the IRS safe-harbor explanation?

Yes. The payer may customize the safe-harbor explanation by omitting any portions that do not apply to the plan, custodial account, or annuity. For example, because Section 403(b) funding vehicles do not provide for distribu-tions of employer stock or other employer securities, such a section contained in the safe-harbor explanation could, but is not required to, be eliminated. Additionally, a payer may include information with the safe-harbor explanation, provided this additional information is not inconsistent with the safe-harbor explanation.

Alternatively, plan administrators or payers may choose to design their own written explanation of eligible rollover distributions for recipients. However, any explanation must contain the information required to be provided under Code Section 402(f) and must be written in a manner designed to be easily understood by recipients. [IRS Notice 2002-3]

Q 10:125   When must the payer of an eligible rollover distribution provide the payee with notice of the direct rollover requirements?

The payer of an eligible rollover distribution must furnish a participant with notice of the direct rollover requirements within a "reasonable" time period prior to making an "eligible rollover distribution" (see the discussion at Q 10:121 for the content requirements of the notice). For distributions from qualified plans, this reasonable time period is generally the same as the time period required under Code Section 411(a)(11) for obtaining consent to a distribution (i.e., generally no more than 90 days and no less than 30 days prior to the distribution). However, the final regulations clarify that a participant may waive the 30-day notification period by affirmatively electing to make or not make a direct rollover. [Treas. Reg. § 1.402(f)-1, Q&A 2] Participants are allowed to waive the 30-day notification period (but not the 90-day period) by affirmatively electing to make or not make a direct rollover with respect to any distribution after written notice has been received.

In order to use this waiver approach, the participant must be informed by the plan administrator or, where applicable, the payer, that the participant has at least 30 days to consider the direct rollover option after notice is provided. This information must be provided "using any method reasonably designed to attract the attention of the participant." Therefore, such information may be provided in the Code Section 402(f) direct rollover notice or in a separate document (e.g., attached to or incorporated into the distribution request form).

Q 10:126   Do any special rules exist concerning the timing required for providing the eligible rollover distribution notice for Section 403(b) funding vehicles?

Treasury Regulations Section 1.403(b)-7(b)(3), confirms that in the case of Section 403(b) funding vehicles, for purposes of satisfying the reasonable period of time rule, the plan timing rules contained in Treasury Regulations Section 1.402(f)-1 will apply.

Q 10:127   How do the notice and direct rollover election requirements apply to periodic payments that are eligible rollover distributions?

In the case of a series of periodic payments where each such payment is generally an eligible rollover distribution (e.g., a term certain of less than ten years), the requirement that a written explanation be provided to recipients prior to an eligible rollover distribution is satisfied if notice is provided within a reasonable period of time before the first payment of such series of payments and annually thereafter. A Section 403(b) plan or funding vehicle is permitted to treat a participant's election to make or not make a direct rollover with respect to one payment in a series of periodic payments as applying to all subsequent payments in the series after the election is made and before it is revoked. However, in such case, the employee must have the right to change a previous election to make or not make a direct rollover with respect to subsequent payments in the series and be given written notice that the election to make or not make a direct rollover will apply to all future payments in the series until the employee subsequently changes the election. [Treas. Reg. § 1.401(a)(31)-1, Q&A 12] Special rules may apply in the case of notices provided to payees via electronic means.

Q 10:128   **Is the payer required to notify payees of their right to elect out of withholding for distributions that are not eligible rollover distributions?**

Yes. The time and manner of such notification depends on whether the distribution is periodic or nonperiodic.

Q 10:129   **What information must be provided in the withholding notice for distributions that are not eligible rollover distributions?**

A payer will satisfy the notice requirements if it provides the payee with a copy of IRS Form W-4P. In lieu of providing the payee with IRS Form W-4P, the payer must satisfy the requirements contained in IRS News Release IR-83-3, January 7, 1983, or Temporary Regulations Section 35.3405-1 Section D, Notice and Election Procedures.

Q 10:130   **May a contract issuer provide the notice and election required under Code Section 3405(e)(10)(B) to a payee through a medium other than a written paper document?**

The IRS has finalized certain amendments to various income tax regulations that would permit, and set forth standards for, the transmission of certain federal tax-withholding notices through an electronic medium reasonably accessible to the participant to whom the notice is given, in lieu of providing notice via the traditional method of a written paper document. The electronic notice system must be "reasonably designed to give the notice in a manner no less understandable to the [payee] than a written paper document." [Ann. 99-6, 1999-4 I.R.B. 24; Treas. Reg. § 35.3405-1, D-35]

Q 10:131   **When must tax-withholding notice be given for periodic distributions that are not eligible rollover distributions?**

Notice of the election procedures concerning withholding must be provided not earlier than six months before the first payment and not later than when making the first payment. However, notice must always be given when making the first payment. An abbreviated notice must be provided at least once each calendar year, at the same time each year, of the right to make and revoke the election. [I.R.C. § 3405(e)(10)(B)(i)] Special rules may apply in the case of notices provided to payees via electronic means.

Q 10:132   **When must notice be given for nonperiodic distributions that are not eligible rollover distributions?**

Notice should be given not earlier than six months prior to the distribution and not later than the time that will give the payee reasonable time to respond to the payer concerning withholding. [Temp. Treas. Reg. § 35.3405-1, Q&A D9]

Q 10:133   When must a payer give effect to a withholding election by the payee for distributions that are not eligible rollover distributions?

For nonperiodic distributions, the payee has the right to make or revoke an election at any time prior to the distribution. For periodic payments, the withholding election is generally given effect as provided in Code Section 3402(f)(3) for a Form W-4 certificate filed to replace an existing certificate. [Temp. Treas. Reg. § 35.3405-1T, Q&As D11, D12]

Q 10:134   Which withholding requirements apply to payees with foreign addresses?

Generally, where a periodic or nonperiodic payment is delivered outside the United States or its possessions, the payee may not elect out of withholding. [I.R.C. § 3405(e)(13)]

Q 10:135   What are the general tax reporting requirements applicable to distributions from Section 403(b) annuities?

Code Section 6047(d) authorizes the Secretary of the Treasury to prescribe by forms or regulations the reporting requirements for any plan from which, or any contract under which, any designated distribution may be made. However, no information return is required to be filed for distributions to any individual during any year unless such distributions aggregate $10 or more.

Code Section 3405(e)(1)(A) defines the term designated distribution as including any payment or distribution from or under a commercial annuity. Code Section 3405(e)(1)(B) excludes from the definition of designated distribution "the portion of a distribution or payment which it is reasonable to believe is not includible in gross income." The term commercial annuity is defined in Code Section 3405(e)(6) as including a Section 403(b) annuity contract or custodial account. Therefore, a life insurance company issuing Section 403(b) annuity contracts or accounts is required to file the appropriate returns and reports regarding the contracts or accounts it issues as prescribed in IRS forms or regulations.

Temporary Treasury Regulations Section 35.3405-1T, Q&A E8 provides the general rule that information reporting under Code Section 6047(d) is required any time there is a designated distribution to which Code Section 3405 applies. Therefore, absent IRS forms or regulations to the contrary, information reporting under Code Section 6047(d) applies only when there is a designated distribution to which Code Section 3405 applies.

Q 10:136   Are direct rollovers reportable on Form 1099-R?

Yes. Distributions from Section 403(b) annuity contracts or accounts are currently reportable under Code Section 6047. Because a direct rollover is treated as a distribution to the payee followed by an immediate rollover to an eligible retirement plan, the IRS requires that such rollovers be reported on Form 1099-R. [Treas. Reg. § 31.3405(c)-1, Q&A 16]

Q 10:137   Are exchanges or direct transfers between Section 403(b) funding vehicles reportable?

No. Because exchanges of Section 403(b) contracts or direct transfers between Section 403(b) contracts are not distributions or deemed distributions, such transfers are not currently reportable on Form 1099-R.

The tax-free exchange or direct transfer between Section 403(b) contracts involves transfers under which no amounts are distributed or made available to the participants. [*See* Treas. Reg. § 1.403(b)-10(b)(1)(i); Rev. Rul. 90-24, and the instructions to Form 1099-R] In no case is there an actual distribution to the participant. Furthermore, applying the rationale of Letter Ruling 9045068, the transfers would not be considered designated distributions and therefore would not require information reporting, absent IRS rules to the contrary.

Q 10:138   How is a rollover reported by a payer?

The manner in which a rollover is reported depends on whether it was a direct rollover or made within the 60-day rollover period. An eligible rollover distribution amount that is distributed to the employee and subsequently rolled over within 60 days from receipt is reportable by the payer on IRS Form 1099-R like any distribution. However, a direct rollover of an eligible rollover distribution is reportable by the payer using a special code in box 7 on IRS Form 1099-R to designate a direct rollover.

Q 10:139   How is the 10 percent penalty on certain distributions before age 59½ reported?

The 10 percent additional tax on certain distributions before age 59½ cannot be withheld. The payer will, when issuing Form 1099-R to report the distribution, enter a code to indicate that the additional tax may or may not apply. The participant may be required to complete IRS Form 5329 to claim an exception to the additional tax or to calculate the amount of additional tax owed. [See instructions to IRS Form 5329]

Q 10:140   What are the state tax-withholding requirements applicable to Section 403(b) distributions?

Most states that have individual income tax provisions also permit state income tax to be withheld from Section 403(b) payments if the payee requests and the payer so agrees. Other states provide that, subject to certain *de minimis* rules, a payer is required to withhold state income tax from Section 403(b) pension payments if requested to do so in writing by the payee. However, some states require that state income tax be withheld, in a manner similar to the federal tax-withholding requirements. The manner and rate of such withholding will vary, depending upon the state involved. (For example, California, Oregon, Massachusetts, Virginia, Maine, and Vermont are states that have laws requiring that state income tax be withheld.)

Current federal tax law prohibits a state from taxing the pension income of individuals who neither reside nor are domiciled in such state despite the fact that the pension income may be attributable to services that had been performed in such state by the individual.

Q 10:141   Do the reporting requirements applicable to IRAs in connection with required minimum distributions apply to Section 403(b) contracts?

The final required minimum distribution regulations issued by the IRS in April 2002 retain the basic rule in the 1987 and 2001 proposed regulations that a Section 403(b) contract is treated as an IRA for purposes of satisfying the required minimum distribution rules. The final regulations included a provision that delegates to the IRS authority to require tax reporting with respect to required minimum distribution amounts from IRAs. The preamble to the final regulations specified that this delegation of authority also applies to Section 403(b) contracts by virtue of Section 403(b) contracts generally being treated as IRAs for purposes of the final required minimum distribution rules. However, contemporaneously with the issuance of the final required minimum distribution regulations, the IRS released Notice 2002-27, which provided that no tax reporting is required at this time with respect to required minimum distributions from Section 403(b) contracts. Nevertheless, the IRS is authorized to impose such requirements in the future.

Table 10-1. Federal Income Tax-Withholding Requirements Applicable to Section 403(b) Distributions (Chart does not address distributions to nonspouse beneficiaries, including ERDs to nonspouse beneficiaries that may only be rolled over to an IRA.)

Illustrations	Is this an "eligible[*] rollover distribution" to which 20% of withholding will apply to the extent not directly rolled over to an "eligible retirement plan"?	Do the TEFRA[**] withholding rules apply?
(1) Death benefit (not a minimum required distribution)		
(a) Preretirement[***] nonperiodic death benefit payment to spouse beneficiary	Yes. I.R.C. § 402(c)(4)	No.

Table 10-1. (*cont'd*)

Illustrations	Is this an "eligible* rollover distribution" to which 20% of withholding will apply to the extent not directly rolled over to an "eligible retirement plan"?	Do the TEFRA** withholding rules apply?
(b) Preretirement periodic death benefit payments to spouse beneficiary		
(i) payments for term certain of less than 10 years	Yes.	No.
(ii) payments for term certain of 10 years or more or where a life contingency is involved	No.	Yes.
(c) Postretirement lump-sum death benefit to spouse beneficiary	Yes. Treas. Reg. § 1.402(c)-2, Q&As 5 & 6	No.
(d) Postretirement death benefit to spouse beneficiary—continuation of periodic payments that were not eligible rollover distributions to decedent	No. Treas. Reg. § 1.402(c)-2, Q&A 5	Yes.
(e) Same as (d) above except continuation of periodic payments that were eligible rollover distributions to decedent	Yes. I.R.C. § 402(c)(4)	No.
(2) Joint and survivor annuity—payments for life with continued payments to survivor for life		
(a) Periodic life payments to participant	No (payments for life). I.R.C. § 402(c)(4)	Yes.
(b) Periodic (life continuation) payments to spouse or nonspouse joint annuitant	No (payments for life). I.R.C. § 402(c)(4)	Yes.

Table 10-1. (*cont'd*)

Illustrations	Is this an "eligible* rollover distribution" to which 20% of withholding will apply to the extent not directly rolled over to an "eligible retirement plan"?	Do the TEFRA** withholding rules apply?
(3) Amounts payable for life with a term certain guaranteed (e.g., 5, 10, 15, or 20 years)		
(a) Periodic life payments to participant	No (payments for life). I.R.C. § 402(c)(4)	Yes.
(b) Continuation of periodic payments to spouse beneficiary for remainder of guaranteed period	No. I.R.C. § 402(c)(4)	Yes.
(c) Lump-sum payment to spouse beneficiary representing	Yes. Treas. Reg. § 1.402(c)-2, Q&As 5 & 6	No.
(4) Periodic payments to participant or spouse beneficiary for a term certain that are not minimum required distributions—no life contingency involved		
(a) Periodic payments for term certain of less than 10 years	Yes. I.R.C. § 402(c)(4)	No.
(b) Periodic payments for term certain of 10 years or more	No.	Yes.
(5) Periodic payments made to employee before year in which employee attains or would have attained age 70½	Maybe (depends on term of payments). Treas. Reg. § 1.402(c)-2, Q&A 7	Maybe.
(6) Nonperiodic distribution to employee participant beginning at age 70½	No, to the extent it is a minimum required distribution. I.R.C. § 402(c)(4)	Yes (for minimum required distribution portion).
(7) Variable annuity payments		
Treated same as fixed annuity payments	Treas. Reg. § 1.402(c)-2, Q&A 5	

Table 10-1. (*cont'd*)

Illustrations	Is this an "eligible* rollover distribution" to which 20% of withholding will apply to the extent not directly rolled over to an "eligible retirement plan"?	Do the TEFRA** withholding rules apply?
(8) **In-service withdrawals to employee participants (not including hardship)**	Yes. Treas. Reg. § 1.402(c)-2, Q&As 3 & 4	No.
(9) **Loans—deemed distributions**	No. Treas. Reg. § 1.402(c)-2, Q&A 4	Yes (special TEFRA withholding provisions apply).
(10) **Loans—loan offset amounts**	Yes, to the extent it otherwise qualifies. Treas. Reg. § 1.402(c)-2,Q&A 9	No (special withholding rules apply).
(11) **Hardship withdrawals**	No. I.R.C. § 402(c)(4)	Yes.

---

*Pertains to taxable portion of distribution only.

**As used in this chart, the term TEFRA is used to indicate that the federal income tax-withholding provisions applicable to distributions that are ERDs do not apply, and the payer must instead apply the tax-withholding rules applicable under IRC § 3405 to distributions that are not eligible rollover distributions.

***As used in this chart, the term *preretirement* is intended to mean "before benefits commence."

Q 10:142   Is any relief from the rules governing distributions from Section 403(b) contracts available to victims of Hurricanes Katrina, Rita, and Wilma?

Yes. In 2005, Congress passed the Katrina Emergency Tax Relief Act of 2005, which provides relief from certain rules that otherwise apply to distributions from Section 403(b) contracts and other qualified retirement plans. The relief is available to any "qualified Hurricane Katrina distribution," which is defined to include a distribution from a Section 403(b) contract made on or after August 25, 2005, and before January 1, 2007, to an individual whose principal place of abode on August 28, 2005, was located in Louisiana, Mississippi, Alabama, or Florida and who sustained an economic loss by reason of Hurricane Katrina. [Notice 2005-92, 2005-51 I.R.B. 1] If a distribution is a qualified Hurricane Katrina distribution, the following relief is available:

- *Penalty tax on early distributions.* The 10 percent additional tax of Code Section 72(t) does not apply. (See Q 10:43 and Q 10:44.) Also, in the case of an individual who is receiving a series of substantially equal periodic payments within the meaning of Code Section 72(t)(2)(A)(iv), the receipt of the distribution will not be treated as a change in such payment stream for purposes of Code Section 72(t)(4) (see Q 10:45).

- *Income inclusion.* The distribution can be included in income ratably over three years.

- *Recontribution.* The distribution will be treated as though it were paid in a direct rollover to an eligible retirement plan if the distribution is eligible for tax-free rollover treatment and is recontributed to an eligible retirement plan within three years of the date of the distribution. Individuals must use Form 8915, "Qualified Hurricane Katrina Retirement Plan Distributions and Repayments," to report any recontribution made during the taxable year and to determine the amount of the distribution includible in income for the taxable year. In addition, distributions made from a Section 403(b) contract after February 28, 2005 and before August 29, 2005, that were intended to be used for the purchase or construction of a principal residence in an area affected by Hurricane Katrina may be recontributed to an eligible retirement plan if done so by February 28, 2006.

- *Eligible rollover distribution rules.* The rules for eligible rollover distributions in Code Sections 401(a)(31), 402(f), and 3405 are not applicable to the distribution. Thus, the individual need not be offered a direct rollover option, the notice otherwise required by Code Section 402(f) need not be provided, and the otherwise mandatory 20 percent withholding rules of Code Section 3405(c)(1) do not apply (although the voluntary withholding requirements of Code Section 3405(b) continue to do so) (see Qs 10:80, 10:90, 10:121).

- *Withdrawal restrictions.* The distribution is treated as meeting the withdrawal restrictions of Code Section 403(b)(11) or Section 403(b)(7)(A)(ii), as applicable.

- *Loans.* For loans made on or after September 24, 2005, and before January 1, 2007, the $50,000 aggregate limit in Code Section 72(p)(2)(A)(i) is increased to $100,000 and the rule in Code Section 72(p)(2)(A)(ii) limiting the aggregate amount of loans to one-half of the employee's vested accrued benefit is increased to 100 percent of the employee's vested accrued benefit. In addition, for loans that are outstanding on or after August 25, 2005, if the due date for any repayment occurs during the period beginning on August 25, 2005 and ending on December 31, 2006, such due date is delayed for one year. Subsequent repayments for the loan must be appropriately adjusted to reflect the delay and any interest accruing for such delay, and the period of delay must be disregarded in determining the five-year period and the term of the loan under Code Sections 72(p)(2)(B) and (C).

[Notice 2005-92, 2005-51 I.R.B. 1]

The amount of qualified Hurricane Katrina distributions cannot exceed $100,000 for any individual. In addition, the definition of qualified Hurricane Katrina distribution is not limited to amounts withdrawn solely to meet a need arising from Hurricane Katrina. In determining whether the rules summarized above apply, plan sponsors can rely on reasonable representations from a distributee with respect to his or her principal place of abode on August 28, 2005, and whether the distributee suffered an economic loss by reason of Hurricane Katrina (absent the plan sponsor's actual knowledge to the contrary).

Qualified Hurricane Katrina distributions must be reported on Form 1099-R. If the payor is treating the payment as a qualified Hurricane Katrina distribution and no other appropriate code applies, the payor may use distribution code 2 (early distribution, exception applies) in box 7 of Form 1099-R. The payor also may use distribution code 1 (early distribution, no known exception).

Prior to the enactment of the Katrina Emergency Tax Relief Act of 2005, the IRS issued administrative relief that is similar to the relief provided in the legislation. [Ann. 2005-70, 2005-40 I.R.B. 682] The Gulf Opportunity Zone Act of 2005 extended to victims of Hurricanes Rita and Wilma the same relief with respect to distributions that the Katrina Emergency Tax Relief Act of 2005 extended to victims of Hurricane Katrina.

Chapter 11

Loans, Life Insurance, and Plan Termination

Richard A. Turner, Esq.
AIG Retirement

Loans are an important feature in many Section 403(b) programs. Historically, loans have often been permitted unless the plan prohibited or restricted their availability. In many cases there was no written plan governing the program that might impose such prohibitions or restrictions. However, under final Code Section 403(b) regulations, which are generally effective January 1, 2009, most contracts and accounts are required to be maintained under a written plan, and loans will only be available from those contracts and accounts if they are permitted under the plan. Certain contracts outside the plan may still allow loans; however, there may be additional obligations to confirm information regarding loan balances under other contracts or accounts before processing such loans. In general, the regulations also impose new requirements regarding the extent to which information may be provided solely by the participant, such as information about loans under other contracts and accounts in the plan or in other plans of the employer.

When permitted, loans in effect give participants an opportunity to borrow from, and then repay, themselves. However, loans should not be permitted to adversely affect the participant's primary goal of retirement savings. As a result, loans are subject to very specific limits on amounts, as well as requirements for repayment.

Until September 24, 2007, a Section 403(b) plan or program was permitted to offer new life insurance contracts, provided that the life insurance protection was incidental to the primary purpose of retirement savings. Effective September 24, 2007, no new life insurance contracts may be established; however, a plan may permit contracts already in effect to continue to receive new contributions, transfers, and rollovers provided that the new requirements of the final Code Section 403(b) regulations are satisfied. This new rule does not affect the availability of annuity contracts in these same plans. For permitted contributions, in determining whether the life insurance protection is incidental, the same rules that apply to qualified plans generally apply to Section 403(b) programs. The cost of life insurance protection is taxable to the participant each year. The IRS released guidance in 2001 and 2002 that revised the method for quantifying that cost. Death benefits from the life insurance policies are generally taxable to the beneficiary to the extent of the policy's cash value on the date of death, less the previously reported cost of insurance and any other unrecovered investment in the contract. The amount of the death benefit that exceeds the cash value will be excluded from income as proceeds from life insurance.

The subject of plan terminations has historically presented some unique questions in the context of Section 403(b) plans, because the tax rules contained no exception from the general distribution restrictions in the event of plan termination. The extent of those questions often depended upon whether the plan was subject to Title I of the Employee Retirement Income Security Act of 1974 (ERISA). If ERISA did not apply, it may have been easy simply to freeze the plan, ceasing all contributions and lifting any additional distribution restrictions imposed by the plan. If Title I of ERISA did apply, there had been questions about how to satisfy ERISA termination rules without violating the applicable tax restrictions. Final Code Section 403(b) regulations have added a new distribution event to allow distributions upon plan termination, provided that specific requirements are satisfied.

Loans

Q 11:1   May loans be offered in Section 403(b) programs?

Yes. Loans may be offered from an annuity, life insurance contract, or custodial account that qualifies under Code Section 403(b) and will be treated as being made from the employer's Section 403(b) plan. [I.R.C. § 72(p)(5); Treas. Reg. § 1.72(p)-1, Q&A 2; Treas. Reg. § 1.403(b)-6(f)] If the contract or account is held under a written plan, however, this loan feature is only available if the plan so permits. One way the plan might permit loans is to incorporate by reference the features of the contracts and accounts, including any loan features. In addition, the plan need not require that all such contracts and accounts permit loans, nor must it require the loan features to be identical in the underlying contracts and accounts. The plan may permit different loan provisions under different contracts or accounts, as long as the loan terms of all of the contracts and accounts satisfy applicable tax requirements. If a contract or account is not under such a plan, loans may still be available; however, in some cases the ability to rely solely upon participant representations for information regarding other outstanding loans, for purposes of applying loan limitations to multiple contracts, accounts, and plans related to the same employer, has been reduced. [Rev. Proc. 2007-71, 2007-51 I.R.B. 1184] Loans are frequently made directly between the insurer (or the custodian) and the participant.

A number of requirements must be satisfied, however, in order to prevent a loan from being a taxable distribution to the participant—either as an actual distribution or as a "deemed distribution"—at the time it is made. (These requirements apply also to contracts that met the requirements of Code Section 403(b), but that have since failed to satisfy those requirements.) [Treas. Reg. § 1.72(p)-1, Q&A 2(e)]

Note. Reference will be made throughout this chapter to Treasury Regulations Section 1.72(p)-1. Reference will also be made to amendments to that regulation, which are effective for assignments, pledges, and loans made on or after January 1, 2004, but do not apply to loans made under an insurance contract that is in effect on December 31, 2003, if the insurance carrier is required to offer loans to contract holders that are not secured (other than by the participant's or beneficiary's benefit under the contract).

If the Section 403(b) program is subject to the requirements under Title I of the Employee Retirement Income Security Act of 1974 (ERISA), a loan from the plan (including a loan under the terms of an annuity contract held under the plan) will be treated as a prohibited transaction, subjecting the fiduciary(ies) to potential liability, unless the loan program has at least been authorized by a written provision in the plan. In addition, either the plan or a loan program authorized by the plan must satisfy specific ERISA requirements, including the following:

- Making loans available to all participants and beneficiaries on a reasonably equivalent basis;
- Not making loans available to highly compensated employees, officers, and directors in greater amounts than for other employees;
- Charging a reasonable rate of interest that provides the plan with a return commensurate with the interest rates charged by persons in the business of lending money for loans that would be made under similar circumstances; and
- Adequately securing the loan so that it may be reasonably anticipated that loss of principal or interest will not result from the loan.

[ERISA §§ 406(a)(1)(B), 408(b)(1); 29 C.F.R. 2550.408b-1]

Also, if the ERISA 403(b) plan is subject to qualified joint and survivor annuity and qualified preretirement survivor annuity rules, married participants must obtain spousal consent for loans over $5,000 if the total accrued benefit subject to security is greater than $5,000. [ERISA § 205(c)(4)] (However, see Q 11:38 regarding special rules available for victims of Hurricanes Katrina, Rita, and Wilma in fall 2005.) Loans from ERISA 403(b) plans, contracts, or accounts will often be approved by a plan fiduciary before they are processed by the investment provider, unless the plan provider is a fiduciary or unless the plan fiduciary has given sufficiently specific direction to the investment provider so that processing the loan without specific plan fiduciary direction may nevertheless be considered a nondiscretionary activity.

Many Section 403(b) programs are exempt from Title I of ERISA and are thus exempt from these additional ERISA requirements. For example, Section 403(b) programs sponsored by public schools and public colleges, universities, and hospitals, as well as many church Section 403(b) plans, are exempt from ERISA Title I. In addition, Section 403(b) programs sponsored by private tax-exempt employers, which consist solely of voluntary employee contributions and sufficiently limited employer involvement, will also be exempt from Title I of ERISA. See chapter 9 for more detailed discussion of how Title I of ERISA applies to Section 403(b) programs, including the impact of Department of Labor guidance released in July 2007. [D.O.L. Field Assistance Bulletin 2007-02 (July 24, 2007)]

Loans as Distributions

Q 11:2   Under what circumstances will a loan be treated as an actual distribution from the plan or contract at the time it is made?

A loan will be treated as an actual distribution unless the transaction creates an actual debtor-creditor relationship. Thus, the loan will be treated as an actual distribution from the plan if there is either an express or tacit understanding that the loan will not be repaid. [Treas. Reg. § 1.72(p)-1, Q&A 17]

If a loan is considered to be an actual distribution, and if the participant is eligible for such a distribution, then it would appear to be an eligible rollover distribution, subject to mandatory 20 percent withholding, as well as the notice requirements applicable to such distributions. If a loan is considered to be an actual distribution, and if the participant is not eligible for a distribution of the amount of the loan, then the loan will cause the contract or account to fail to satisfy the requirements of Code Section 403(b). [I.R.C. §§ 403(b)(11), 403(b)(7)(A)(ii)]

Q 11:3 If a loan is not treated as an actual distribution, under what circumstances can the loan still be taxable as a deemed distribution when it is issued?

If a loan is not considered an actual distribution when it is made, it will still be taxable if it is a deemed distribution. A loan (or a portion thereof) will be a deemed distribution to the participant unless it satisfies certain requirements:

1. The loan must be evidenced by a legally enforceable agreement. [Treas. Reg. § 1.72(p)-1, Q&A 3] The agreement must be in writing, unless it is in an electronic medium that satisfies specific requirements or in another form approved by the IRS. The agreement only needs to be signed if a signature is required for the agreement to be enforceable under applicable law; and

2. The agreement must clearly identify an amount borrowed, a loan term, and a repayment schedule, each of which satisfies applicable requirements. [Treas. Reg. § 1.72(p)-1, Q&A 3] An agreement maintained in an electronic medium will not qualify as a legally enforceable agreement, under (1) above, unless the electronic medium:

   a. Is reasonably accessible to the participant or beneficiary;

   b. Is reasonably designed to preclude any individual other than the participant or beneficiary from requesting a loan; and

   c. Provides the participant or beneficiary with a reasonable opportunity to review and to confirm, modify, or rescind the terms of the loan before the loan is made.

It is generally expected that the IRS and the Department of the Treasury will issue proposed regulations regarding electronic signatures and related issues in the near future.

If the loan exceeds applicable dollar or percentage limits (see Q 11:7), only the excess portion of the loan will be a deemed distribution, provided that all other requirements are satisfied.

A deemed distribution is taxable to the participant but is not treated as an actual distribution for the purposes of Code Section 403(b)(11), which identifies the withdrawal restrictions for Section 403(b) annuities. [Treas. Reg. § 1.72(p)-1, Q&A 12] Even if the participant was otherwise ineligible for an actual distribution, the deemed distribution does not by itself result in adverse tax consequences beyond the taxation of the deemed distribution to the participant.

Note. Presumably, a deemed distribution is also not an actual distribution for the purposes of Code Section 403(b)(7). However, with respect to Section 403(b) investments, this provision of the regulation refers only to Code Section 403(b)(11). Whether any particular meaning, either favorable or unfavorable for loans from 403(b)(7) custodial accounts, is intended is unclear.

If part or all of a loan is a deemed distribution when the loan is issued, that amount will be reportable on Form 1099-R. It may not be rolled over to an eligible retirement plan. Withholding will apply unless it is waived. [Treas. Reg. § 1.72(p)-1, Q&A 12; I.R.C. § 3405(b)] A portion of the deemed distribution may be nontaxable if the contract contained after-tax amounts. [Treas. Reg. § 1.72(p)-1, Q&A 11; I.R.C. § 72(e)(8)]

See Q 11:24 for the treatment of loans that are not repaid according to their terms.

Q 11:4 Are these actual or deemed distributions subject to the 10 percent premature distribution penalty?

Both actual and deemed distributions arising from plan loans will be subject to a 10 percent premature distribution penalty if they occur prior to the participant's attaining age 59½, unless an exception to the penalty applies. [Treas. Reg. § 1.72(p)-1, Q&A 11; I.R.C. § 72(t); see also Plotkin v. Comm'r, T.C. Memo 2001-71]

Loan Availability

Q 11:5 Who may borrow from a Section 403(b) plan?

Loans may be made available to almost anyone who has a Section 403(b) annuity or other qualifying Section 403(b) investment. That includes current employees, both part-time and full-time. It also includes former employees — terminated vested employees and retirees—if they retained their Section 403(b) contracts. As a practical matter, this distinguishes Section 403(b) plans from many Section 401(k) plans, which often distribute the participant's account upon the employee's separation from service, ending plan features such as loans. Loans may also be made available to beneficiaries after the participant's death (to the extent that the beneficiary has contract or account rights). [I.R.C. § 72(p)] Whether loans are available under a particular plan or investment will depend upon the terms of the plan or investment.

Q 11:6 Must a Section 403(b) program allow loans?

Neither the Internal Revenue Code nor ERISA requires that loans be offered from the plan or from the Section 403(b) investment. Whether loans are offered, and the manner in which they are offered, is determined by the terms of the plan and the investment.

State insurance laws generally do not require annuity contracts to include a loan feature; however, those laws often restrain the insurance company's ability to limit loans if they are offered. Whether a particular investment product or vehicle offers loans will be determined by the surrounding documents, such as the governing annuity or life insurance contract or custodial agreement.

Many Section 403(b) programs consist solely of an employee's salary reduction agreement with the employer and the investment vehicle the employee has selected (generally, either an annuity contract or a custodial account). However, if an employer has elected to impose additional requirements on participant accounts under its Section 403(b) program, through a written plan document, that plan document may include limitations on the availability of loans. For example, the plan might allow loans only to current employees or in the event of financial hardship.

> **Note.** If a Section 403(b) plan sponsor is a private not-for-profit organization, and if the employer's plan is presently exempt from the requirements of Title I of ERISA, the employer and the employer's counsel should carefully consider any such change. Section 403(b) plans of private not-for-profit organizations are generally exempt from ERISA, as long as the employer's involvement is limited, essentially, to making investment alternatives available to employees who wish to participate (see chapter 9 for a detailed discussion of the application of ERISA to Section 403(b) plans). To avoid inadvertently establishing an ERISA plan, contractual rights under the program's Section 403(b) annuities must be exercised only by the participant. If the employer imposes material restrictions upon a participant's exercise of contractual loan rights, such as limiting loan availability to cases of financial hardship, or exercises other substantive rights under the contract, then the plan is subject to ERISA unless either the church plan or government plan exemption is met. [D.O.L. Reg. § 2510.3-2(f); D.O.L. Field Assistance Bulletin No. 2007-02 (July 24, 2007)]

Limitations on Amounts

Q 11:7 Are there limits on the amount of nontaxable loans that may be made to a participant in a Section 403(b) program?

Loans are subject to the stated limits, if any, in the plan and in the underlying investment. Apart from the plan and the investment, however, loans from Section 403(b) plans are limited by a 50/50 rule—they generally cannot exceed the lesser of:

1. $50,000; or

2. 50 percent of the present value of the participant's nonforfeitable accrued benefit under the plan.

[I.R.C. § 72(p)]

In a large number of Section 403(b) programs, all contributions are 100 percent vested (i.e., nonforfeitable), so the second limit is typically 50 percent of the participant's account balance. See Q 11:8 and Q 11:9 for rules where a participant owns more than one contract or participates in more than one plan.

If a portion of the participant's contract or account is pledged as collateral for a loan, these limits will be applied only to the actual amount loaned. This is true regardless of whether the loan is made directly from the account or from the annuity issuer with a security interest in a portion of the account. Therefore, if the collateral exceeds the amount loaned, the excess collateral is not counted against these limits. [Treas. Reg. § 1.72(p)-1, Q&A 1]

$50,000 limit. The $50,000 limit was one of the first limits on plan loans. It restricted the amount that could be borrowed at any time. However, before Congress further refined this limit, nothing prevented a participant from repaying a loan in full and then reborrowing the same money. Participants were thus able to maintain continuous tax-free access to a significant portion of their pre-tax retirement savings.

To curb this perceived abuse, as part of the Tax Reform Act of 1986 (TRA '86) Congress added a one-year lookback rule, which remains in effect today. [Tax Reform Act of 1986, Pub. L. No. 99-514 § 1133 (1986)] The lookback in effect reduces the $50,000 limit by the largest outstanding loan balance during the past 365 days, to determine the maximum new loan. Since the lookback is a moving window, the old potential for gaming is effectively gone.

50 percent limit. A participant may not borrow more than 50 percent of the nonforfeitable account balance in his or her 403(b) plan. The 50 percent limit will not be violated if the loan does not exceed the lesser of (1) $10,000 or (2) 100 percent of his or her vested account balance. [I.R.C. § 72(p)(2)(A)(i)] Thus, under the Code requirements, a participant with a vested account value of $10,000 may borrow his or her entire account balance.

However, care should be taken when applying this special rule to smaller accounts in 403(b) plans that are subject to the requirements of Title I of ERISA. Loans from ERISA 403(b) plans must be adequately secured if they are to avoid being considered prohibited transactions. [D.O.L. Reg. § 2550.408b-1(f)] The adequate security rule will not allow more than 50 percent of the participant's vested account balance to be used as collateral for the loan. To comply with this rule, loans made or renewed after October 18, 1989, are not permitted to exceed the 50 percent limit, even with smaller account values where the $10,000 floor would apply, unless outside collateral is obtained to secure the excess over 50 percent. Unlike the Code, ERISA takes into account any collateral in excess of the amount loaned for purposes of applying the 50 percent limit.

Loans secured by employee deductible contributions (made in years before 1987) are treated as taxable without regard to IRS loan limitations.

These limits apply at the time a loan is taken. Events that occur after a loan is taken and cause the loan to exceed 50 percent of the participant's vested account balance do not disqualify an existing loan (although they will affect the employee's ability to take additional loans). [I.R.C. § 72(p)(2)(A); D.O.L. Reg.

§ 2550.408b-1(f)(2)] For example, a participant's account may be partially invested in variable annuities or mutual funds, which can fluctuate in value. In addition, a participant might take a permitted withdrawal while the loan is outstanding. Neither of these subsequent events should disqualify a previously issued loan even if, following the event, the loan exceeds 50 percent of the employee's vested account balance.

> **Example.** Rebecca Smith is a participant in an ERISA 403(b) plan that has both employer contributions and employee deferrals, all of which are 100 percent vested. Her annuity account balance is $18,000. Her maximum nontaxable loan is $10,000 (the greater of 50 percent of her account balance or $10,000). However, if she borrows the entire $10,000, the loan will not be "adequately secured" under the ERISA rules, and thus she will need to provide at least $1,000 of additional collateral for the loan. She will want to check her plan and her Section 403(b) annuity to see whether the use of outside collateral is permitted because in most Section 403(b) arrangements, it is not.

Certain individuals affected by Hurricane Katrina in August 2005 are permitted to take larger loans than are permitted under the basic rules, for a specified period of time. Those rules are described in Q 11:38.

Beginning January 1, 2006, employers may permit employees to direct some or all of their elective deferrals into after-tax Roth 403(b) contracts or accounts. [I.R.C. § 402A] The same loan limitations apply regardless of whether the participant's contributions are made to a traditional pre-tax Section 403(b) annuity contract or account, to an after-tax Roth 403(b) contract or account, or to both.

Q 11:8 How do these limits apply if the participant has more than one Section 403(b) annuity?

To apply the IRS loan limits, all of an employee's contracts and accounts in an employer's Section 403(b) plan or program (including both traditional and Roth 403(b) contracts and accounts) are treated as one annuity. [I.R.C. § 72(p)(2)(D)] If an employee had a separate Section 403(b) annuity from a previous employer and if that annuity was not transferred into the current employer's plan, then the other annuity should qualify for a separate set of loan limitations.

If an employee has multiple Section 403(b) annuities within an employer's plan, he or she may total the value of the annuities and borrow 50 percent of the total, up to $50,000 (as adjusted), in any combination from the annuities. [Treas. Reg. § 1.403(b)-1(b)(4); Ltr. Rul. 8742008] This may be important if one or more of the participant's Section 403(b) investments do not allow loans. Of course, the ability of the participant to borrow larger amounts from any one contract also depends on the terms of the plan and of the contracts. It should also be noted, however, that aggregating two, small plan accounts may reduce the amount the participant can borrow from either of the plan accounts, because the $10,000 floor may no longer apply.

> **Note.** In the past, plan sponsors, administrators, or product issuers who requested information from a participant regarding loans from other plans

generally were permitted to rely on the information that the participant provided, unless they knew that information was not correct. This has been the position articulated in the preamble to Treasury Regulations Section 1.72(p)-1 (as amended by T.D. 9021, Dec. 3, 2002). However, the final Code Section 403(b) regulations and subsequent guidance have imposed limitations on the ability of the plan sponsor and plan investment and service providers to rely solely upon information provided by the participant, either:

- generally,
- in model plan language (which is not mandatory), or
- as a condition of establishing good-faith reliance (i.e., with respect to accounts of former employees that are maintained with previously discontinued providers).

Example. ABC Corporation, a charitable organization, has established an ERISA 403(b) plan that consists solely of employer discretionary contributions and also allows employees to defer a portion of their salary to annuities in a separate non-ERISA 403(b) program. Both the ERISA plan and the non-ERISA program allow nontaxable loans, and neither accepts outside collateral.

Josh, a relatively new ABC employee, has vested account balances in the ERISA plan and the non-ERISA program of $9,000 and $11,000, respectively. Josh took a loan of $8,500 from his salary deferral Section 403(b) annuity contract under the non-ERISA program. Then he applied to the ERISA 403(b) plan for a loan. When the administrator of the ERISA 403(b) plan saw on Josh's loan application that he already had an $8,500 loan from his non-ERISA annuity, the plan loan was limited to $1,500.

Why? Josh's ERISA plan vested balance, by itself, would seem to justify a loan of up to $4,500 (the ERISA 50 percent limit without outside collateral; the IRS limit, if this were a non-ERISA 403(b) annuity, would be $9,000). However, aggregation of the two Section 403(b) annuities results in a maximum nontaxable loan total of $10,000, and Josh has already borrowed $8,500.

The Code's aggregation rule will not override the ERISA adequate security requirement. Thus, a participant's vested balance in a non-ERISA 403(b) annuity should not be counted to satisfy the ERISA 50 percent limit.

The reverse situation holds more promise. Using the Code's aggregation rule, one could count a participant's nonforfeitable account balance in an employer's ERISA 403(b) plan to determine the maximum nontaxable loan from the participant's non-ERISA 403(b) annuity under the Code's 50 percent limit. However, if the non-ERISA 403(b) plan was relying upon the IRS model plan language applying these limits, it appears that this option would not be available.

Q 11:9   How do the loan limits apply if the employer sponsors additional plans?

The Code's limits for nontaxable loans apply to all of the employer's plans as if they were a single plan. [I.R.C. §72(p)(2)(D)] The plans to which the aggregation rule applies include qualified plans (pension; profit-sharing, including both traditional and Roth 401(k); money purchase), government plans (state retirement systems, optional retirement plans), church plans, and 403(b) plans of the employer.

In aggregating with qualified plans, the participant can count the value of a nontransferable annuity distributed from a qualified plan because such contracts may also permit loans. [Prop. Treas. Reg. § 1.72(p)-1, Q&A 1] This aggregation should include only the present value of nonforfeitable benefits accrued during the period of service with the employer whose plans are being aggregated. Thus, if an employee has accrued benefit service within a state defined benefit plan through employment with two or more employers within the state, the employee should count only the benefits under the state defined benefit plan that were accrued during the period of service with the employer sponsoring the Section 403(b) arrangement.

The "employer" includes partnerships and proprietorships under common control, controlled groups, and affiliated service groups. [I.R.C. § 72(p)(2)(c)]

Aggregation of these plans to apply the loan limits can be quite beneficial to the participant. Many plans (including many state retirement plans for employees of public educational institutions) do not allow loans. Aggregation allows the employee's vested account value in these plans (or, for defined benefit plans, the present value of the employee's nonforfeitable accrued benefit allocable to service with the current employer) to be added to the employee's vested Section 403(b) balance to determine the permissible loan. (As noted in Q 11:8, if the Section 403(b) plan is relying upon the IRS model plan language in applying these limits, it appears that this option would not be available.) However, this aggregation can also be limiting because such aggregation can result in the loss of the $10,000 floor, which might apply to the Section 403(b) plan if viewed separately, and can trigger the application of a single $50,000 ceiling.

Q 11:10   Should a participant's vested interest in a public employer's eligible Section 457 deferred compensation plan be counted in applying the loan limits to plans of that employer?

Eligible governmental deferred compensation plans are considered "government plans" for purposes of Code Section 72(p). [Treas. Reg. § 1.457-7(b)(3)] They are thus subject to the requirements of Code Section 72(p), including the aggregation of accounts under plans sponsored by the same employer in determining a participant's loan eligibility and loan limitations.

Q 11:11   How do the loan limits apply when a new loan is used to repay or refinance an existing loan?

Whenever a loan is replaced with another loan, that replacement is considered a refinancing. [Treas. Reg. § 1.72(p)-1, Q&A 20, as revised in the corrections to final regulations published in 68 Fed. Reg. 9532 (Feb. 28, 2002)] A refinancing can include a loan transfer (see Q 11:30) when any terms of the original loan are being changed. Whether a transfer involves the continued maintenance of the original loan by the new investment or service provider or the replacement of the original loan by a new loan will likely depend on the circumstances. In the event of a refinancing, the loans (old and new) must satisfy the amount limitations in the Code, based on the account value at the time of the refinancing. How those limits apply, however, depends on whether the repayment period has been lengthened beyond the maximum allowable period for the original loan (which may be greater than the actual remaining loan term).

If the repayment period has not been lengthened beyond the original loan's maximum allowable repayment period, the refinanced loan is tested as a single loan for purposes of applying the loan limitations. If the repayment period has been lengthened beyond the original loan's maximum allowable repayment period, the original loan must be counted twice in applying the loan limitations—once as part of the new loan and again as the original loan—*unless* the new loan payments are sufficient to repay the original loan over the maximum allowable repayment period for the original loan. [Treas. Reg. § 1.72(p), Q&A 20]

Note. It is acceptable to reamortize a loan at a new interest rate when, for example, a participant takes advantage of falling interest rates to reduce the required loan payment. In addition, if the remaining loan term is shortened, the original loan is counted only once.

Example 1. Denise Sanchez received a loan of $19,000 from her Section 403(b) annuity nine months ago. Her quarterly payments are $1,161.98. The current loan balance is $16,607. Her nonforfeitable account balance is $122,000. She wants to take a new loan of $35,000, repayable in quarterly installments over five years, and use a portion of the loan to repay her existing outstanding loan.

To pay off the additional loan amount over 60 months would require quarterly repayments of $1,124.86, based on the interest rate under her loan agreement. If her quarterly payments for the remaining portion of the original loan term (51 months) are at least $2,286.84 ($1,161.98 for the original loan, plus an additional $1,124.86 for the additional loan amount), then the new loan will be treated as two separate loans, and the maximum new loan is $47,607 ($50,000 – $2,393, where $2,393 represents the difference between her maximum loan in the last 12 months and her current loan balance). If her quarterly payments for the first 51 months of the new loan are less than $2,286.84, then both the old loan and the total new loan will be considered to be outstanding at the time the new loan is taken, and the loan limit will be $31,000 ($50,000 – $2,393 – $16,607), resulting in $4,000 of the new $35,000 loan being treated as a deemed distribution.

Example 2. Donald Burns received a 15-year principal residence loan under the terms of his ERISA 403(b) annuity contract nine years ago. The current loan balance is $30,000, and Donald's account balance is $90,000. Donald's largest outstanding loan balance in the past 12 months is $34,000. He wants to take advantage of lower interest rates provided on new loans and borrow an additional $15,000. He replaces his original loan with a single $45,000 loan, repayable in level quarterly installments over five years. Donald's new loan term does not exceed the maximum allowable loan term for the original loan. As a result, the original loan is only counted once, as part of the new loan, in applying the loan limitations, and his new loan satisfies the loan limits.

Q 11:12   May a participant take more than one loan?

Yes, subject to any limits imposed by the plan or the underlying investment. The 2002 amendments to Treasury Regulations Section 1.72(p)-1, when they were in proposed form, would have limited a participant to two loans from a Section 403(b) plan in any year. The limitation on the number of loans was removed when the amendments were published in final form. [See 67 Fed. Reg. 71823] However, there are limitations on a participant's ability to obtain additional loans if the participant has an existing loan that is in default and has not been repaid or treated as a distribution (see Q 11:29).

Q 11:13   May loans from Section 403(b) plans or programs be extended using a credit card?

The preamble to the 2002 amendments to Treasury Regulations Section 1.72(p)-1 indicates that because no limit is imposed on the number of loans a participant may take, there is "no Section 72(p) barrier to credit card loans that otherwise meet the requirements of that section." [See 67 Fed. Reg. 71823] The preamble does not (and could not), however, attempt to address any plan or ERISA issues that might arise, or any issues that might arise under state insurance law with respect to such loans under an annuity contract issued under the plan.

Q 11:14   What happens if an employee exceeds Code or ERISA loan limits?

If the loan otherwise satisfies applicable Code requirements but exceeds the Code limits, the excess portion of the loan will be a deemed distribution (see Q 11:3).

If the 50 percent limit is exceeded in an ERISA 403(b) plan, the loan will constitute a prohibited transaction (see chapter 9 for further discussion of the effect of prohibited transactions on ERISA plans).

Interest Rates

Q 11:15   How is the loan interest rate determined?

In non-ERISA 403(b) contracts, the interest rate is typically determined by the investment provider, under the terms of the contract or account. For those plans, there are no statutory minimum interest rates. States that regulate insurance and annuity contracts often establish maximum interest rates for those contracts, or methods for determining the maximum rate. Typically, some or all the interest charged on the loan is credited to the employee's account, either on an ongoing basis under the terms of the contract or when the loan payments are actually made.

ERISA 403(b) plans that seek to comply with the ERISA "reasonable rate of interest" requirement will seek to ensure that the plan does not forgo a reasonable rate of return to offer the loan. In setting the interest rate, the plan will look to interest rates charged by persons in the business of lending money for loans that would be made under similar circumstances. [D.O.L. Reg. § 2550.408b-1(e)] In determining the "similar circumstances," the plan might consider the following questions:

1. Are loan payments being made by payroll deduction or preauthorized withdrawal from the employee's checking account? If so, to the extent that the lender reasonably believes that the borrower's employment will continue or that the checking account is likely to have sufficient funds, the plan may look to rates that other lenders offer their preferred customers, who have a lower probability of default.

2. Does the participant have any funds that might be available for immediate withdrawal to satisfy the loan in the event of default? If not, then the plan may want to factor possible delays in foreclosure into the determination of "similar circumstances" in the event of default. Annuity balances as of December 31, 1988, plus employer contributions to an annuity and earnings on those contributions, could be eligible for withdrawal upon a loan default, if the plan permits the withdrawal. [I.R.C. § 403(b)(11)] If the lender is an insurance company offering a policy loan, state law will restrict or eliminate the insurer's discretion in evaluating credit risks for this purpose.

A plan or contract may be required to limit the interest charged on a loan to 6 percent for individuals who enter military service after the loan is taken. [50 U.S.C. App. § 526 (2002)] This requirement generally will apply only during the period of military service.

Q 11:16   Is loan interest deductible?

Interest on loans secured only by a participant's elective deferrals is not deductible. [I.R.C. §§ 163, 72(p)(3)] Nor is interest on loans to a key employee. Except where a loan is secured by elective deferrals or made to a key employee, interest on loans secured by a qualified residence of the participant (principal residence, plus one other property used as a residence and designated by the participant) may be deductible, subject to limits. [I.R.C. § 163] Because many Section 403(b) investment vehicles do not permit the use of outside collateral, the qualified residence interest deduction may have limited applicability to Section 403(b) plans. Investment interest or business-related interest may also be deductible, subject to the above limitations.

Repayment Requirements

Q 11:17   How must the loan be repaid?

The loan must be repaid according to its terms. A new loan issued today must require substantially level payments that are made at least quarterly. [I.R.C. § 72(p)(2)(C)]

Q 11:18   May repayment be suspended during a leave of absence?

In some cases, this level amortization can be suspended for up to a year, if permitted by the plan or the contract, in the event of a leave of absence. However, the suspension is allowed only if the participant's pay during the leave (after reduction for income and employment tax withholding) is insufficient to make the scheduled loan payments. [Treas. Reg. § 1.72(p)-1, Q&A 9] It appears that this exception applies only if the loan agreement so provides. Otherwise, a missed payment would trigger taxation of the entire loan (see Q 11:26). If this "leave of absence" exception is used, the loan must still be repaid within not more than five years (or longer, for a principal-residence loan). Repayment after the leave of absence can be accomplished by either:

1. Making larger payments after the leave, to repay the loan within the period previously established; or

2. Making payments not less than the regularly scheduled payments, and repaying the entire remaining loan balance within the maximum period allowed for loans of that type.

Suspension of repayment may also be permitted during a period when the participant is performing services in the uniformed military services. [I.R.C. § 414(u)] The suspension applies only if the plan so provides. Upon suspension, the loan repayment period may be extended up to the loan's maximum repayment period at the time the loan was issued, plus the length of the suspension period.

Example. When Janet Hirsch entered the uniformed military service, she had an outstanding loan under her Section 403(b) annuity contract. She had taken the loan a year earlier, for a two-year repayment period. Janet returned from military service two years later. Upon her return, the maximum permissible repayment period for her annuity contract loan (assuming no additional plan limitations) was four years. The maximum repayment period initially was five years, three years longer than the original repayment period. Two of the five years remained when Janet returned from uniformed military service. Including the two years of military service, Janet has a maximum repayment period of four years.

In the wake of the terrorist attacks of September 11, 2001, the IRS issued a list of deadlines for time-sensitive acts that may be postponed in future guidance under Code Sections 7508 and 7508A, relating to acts required of individuals serving in the armed forces, in support of such armed forces in combat, and taxpayers affected by a presidentially declared disaster. [Rev. Proc. 2001-53, 2001-47 I.R.B. 506; updated in January 2004 by Rev. Proc. 2004-13, 2004-4 I.R.B. 335] Among those deadlines listed are the repayment requirements under Code Section 72(p). The Revenue Procedure does not by itself extend a repayment deadline; however, it does indicate that the IRS may extend such a deadline in the future. Thus, for example, after the events of September 11, 2001, the IRS provided relief under Code Section 7508A, including relief for certain affected participants with loans. If the last day to perform an act, including the making of a loan payment, fell within the period from September 11, 2001, to November 30, 2001, then the deadline for performing that act was extended by 120 days. [Notice 2001-68; 2001-47 I.R.B. 504] (See also Q 11:38 for additional relief for victims of Hurricanes Katrina, Rita, and Wilma in Fall 2005.)

Q 11:19 What is the maximum term of a loan from a Section 403(b) plan or arrangement?

The loan agreement must require repayment within five years unless the loan proceeds are used to acquire a dwelling unit that will, within a reasonable time, be used as the participant's principal residence. [I.R.C. § 72(p)(2)(B)]

Principal-residence loans need not be secured by the principal residence. However, see Q 11:16 regarding the deductibility of interest on a principal-residence loan.

No specific repayment period is required for principal-residence loans; however, the loan repayment period must be a reasonable term, which may be at least 15 years. [See Example, Treas. Reg. § 1.72(p)-1, Q&A 8]

Loan term limitations have been modified, for a specified window of time, for many individuals affected by Hurricanes Katrina, Rita, and Wilma in fall 2005 (see Q 11:38).

Principal-Residence Loans

Q 11:20 What is a *principal-residence loan*?

The determination of what is a principal residence follows the rules in Code Section 121. [Treas. Reg. § 1.72(p)-1, Q&A 5] If an individual has multiple residences, the determination of which one is the principal residence is a facts and circumstances test. Whether loan proceeds are used to acquire a principal residence can depend on whether the proceeds are disbursed directly to a third party for the purchase of the residence or paid to the participant. If the loan proceeds are disbursed directly to a third party for the purchase of the residence, they are considered to have been used to acquire that residence. [Temp. Treas. Reg. § 1.163-8T(c)(3)] If the loan proceeds are distributed to the participant in cash or deposited into the participant's account, then the loan is treated as incurred to acquire the residence if expenditures to acquire the residence are made within 90 days before or after the date the loan proceeds are disbursed. [IRS Notice 88-74, 1988-2 C.B. 385] The refinancing of a principal-residence loan can sometimes be treated as a principal-residence loan if certain tracing requirements are met. Also, debt incurred to acquire the interest of a spouse or former spouse in a residence, when incident to divorce or legal separation, can be treated as debt for the acquisition of the principal residence.

Q 11:21 What happens if the terms of the loan agreement fall outside of these repayment requirements?

If a loan does not require substantially level payments at least quarterly, or repayment within five years for non-principal-residence loans, the entire loan will be treated as a deemed distribution from the plan at the time the loan is made (see Q 11:3).

Q 11:22 Are some loans grandfathered from these repayment requirements?

Some existing loans may not be subject to one or more of the current requirements. Principal-residence loans made before January 1, 1987, were not subject to the $50,000 limit. For these pre-1987 loans, any amount that was not paid at the end of the loan term was to be treated as a distribution at that time. [Sen. Comm. Notes, TEFRA] These loans could have provided for a balloon payment at the end of the term, perhaps with interest-only payments during the term of the loan. Few, if any, of these loans are still in existence.

Generally, if one of these grandfathered loans is renewed, renegotiated, extended, or revised, it will be treated as a new loan on the date of the renewal, renegotiation, extension, or revision and be subject to the rules currently in effect.

Correction of Defects Under IRS Correction Programs

Q 11:23 Can loan defects be corrected under any of the self-correction or IRS-approved correction programs available to sponsors of Section 403(b) programs?

Certain loan defects may be corrected using these programs. Specifically, loan defects that violate the withdrawal restrictions of Code Section 403(b)(11) or Code Section 403(b)(7) (see Q 11:2) can be corrected using these programs, provided that the other requirements of the specific program to be used are met. [Rev. Proc. 2003-44, 2003-1 C.B. 1051] Loan defects that violate applicable withdrawal restrictions may result in the taxation of some or all of the participant's account(s) under the plan, as well as the application of federal payroll taxes to affected nonelective contributions on which such payroll taxes would not otherwise have been paid.

A Section 403(b) loan that is treated as a deemed distribution (see Qs 11:3, 11:24) and not as an actual distribution is still taxable to the participant but does not produce the other adverse consequences that result from a defect that violates applicable withdrawal restrictions. As a result, such a defect is generally ineligible for, and not relevant to, any self-correction or IRS-approved correction program, with the exception of a new specific reporting rule applicable to certain correction submissions to the IRS under the Voluntary Correction Program (VCP). [Rev. Proc. 2003-44, § 6.07]

Consequences of Failure to Repay

Q 11:24   What happens if the participant fails to make a payment?

The plan and the participant may face two sets of consequences if a payment is not made when due—consequences under the loan agreement and tax (and tax reporting) consequences.

Many Section 403(b) loan agreements provide that if a payment is not made when due and if the participant is eligible for a withdrawal equal to the missed payment, an automatic withdrawal will be processed—and tax reported—to make up the missed payment.

If the participant is not eligible for a withdrawal, the loan agreement will often allow a grace period to make up the missed payment, during which interest may continue to accrue. However, many plans will stop the interest accruals during the grace period if the payment is ultimately made during this period.

Special rules may apply to individuals affected by such events as presidentially declared disasters (see Q 11:18). Additional special rules apply to certain victims of Hurricanes Katrina, Rita, and Wilma (see Q 11:38).

Q 11:25   What constitutes a default?

While ERISA generally leaves the definition of default to the plan, fiduciary considerations may require that the loan be declared due and payable in full when a default has occurred. It is not clear, however, whether such an acceleration would be necessary or proper if the participant is not eligible for a distribution at the time of the default. To avoid making the loan a prohibited transaction, the loan program must clearly identify the events that will constitute default and the steps that will be taken to preserve plan assets in such a case, and the loan must generally be consistent with practices of an entity in the business of making similar types of loans. [D.O.L. Reg. § 2550.408b-1(e)]

In cases where ERISA does not impose a requirement that the loan agreement accelerate upon default (including plans that are not subject to ERISA), the terms of loan agreements can vary widely. Some agreements will accelerate the loan, while others may not. In either case, a foreclosure cannot take place until the participant is eligible for a distribution of the defaulted loan amount. [I.R.C. §§ 403(b)(11), 403(b)(7)(A)(ii); Treas. Reg. § 1.72(p)-1, Q&A 13]

Q 11:26   What tax reporting obligations apply to the plan or to the investment provider if the participant misses a payment?

If a participant is eligible for a distribution in the amount of the missed payment, it seems clear that the loan agreement may permit a withdrawal from the annuity contract to make the payment, provided that such a provision in the loan agreement is not equivalent to an "express or tacit understanding that the loan will not be repaid" (see Q 11:2). While this withdrawal may be an eligible rollover distribution, it will not be subject to mandatory 20 percent withholding, unless there is a distribution of cash to the participant at the same time. It would appear necessary, however, to provide a rollover notice before the distribution. [Treas. Reg. §§ 31.3405(c)-1, Q&A 9; 1.403(b)-2, Q&A 3; 1.402(f)-1, Q&A 1]

With respect to defaults for which no distribution can be made immediately, the entire outstanding loan balance must be reported as a deemed distribution regardless of whether the loan agreement provides for acceleration. [Treas. Reg. § 1.72(p)-1, Q&A 10] Thus, if the participant misses a payment, the entire loan becomes taxable. A deemed distribution does not affect the ability to have excludable contributions made to the participant's Section 403(b) contract or account during the year of the default. [Treas. Reg. § 1.72(p)-1, Q&A 12] However, either a single default or multiple defaults resulting from an "express or tacit understanding that the loan will not be repaid" would be considered an actual distribution, rather than a deemed distribution, and would result in the loss of this exclusion.

A loan agreement can allow a grace period, referred to in the regulation as a "cure period," which will delay the taxation of the outstanding loan balance for up to (but not more than) one calendar quarter beyond the calendar quarter in which the missed payment occurred.

Example. Participant A's next loan payment is due March 25, and Participant B's next loan payment is due January 2. For both loans, the maximum grace period for the next payment will end on June 30.

In all cases, however, if the terms of the loan agreement are more restrictive, those terms will govern. For example, if the loan agreement provides no grace period (or cure period), the outstanding loan balance becomes taxable immediately after a payment is missed. [Treas. Reg. § 1.72(p)-1, Q&A 10]

Q 11:27 Should interest that accrues on the loan after a default be treated as an additional deemed distribution, and reported, every year?

No. [Treas. Reg. § 1.72(p)-1, Q&A 19] However, the post-default interest will still be relevant for certain purposes, such as determining eligibility for a subsequent loan.

Q 11:28 What are the tax consequences of a subsequent foreclosure on a previously defaulted loan?

The loan foreclosure is not a separate taxable event. [Treas. Reg. § 1.72(p)-1, Q&A 19] Loan repayments made after the loan has been treated as a deemed distribution will be treated as after-tax contributions to the plan; however, such amounts will not be subjected to contribution limitations or nondiscrimination rules. A defaulted loan that has been neither foreclosed nor repaid will continue to be counted, along with post-default interest accruals, in determining eligibility for a subsequent loan. [Treas. Reg. § 1.72(p)-1, Q&A 19]

Q 11:29   If a participant's account includes a loan that has been defaulted but not foreclosed, offset, or repaid, can the participant take an additional nontaxable loan?

Yes, but only if there is an agreement between the employer, the participant, and the plan providing for repayment of the loan by way of payroll deduction. [Treas. Reg. § 1.72(p)-1, Q&A 19, as revised by corrections under 68 Fed. Reg. 9532] The payroll-deduction requirement would be waived if the loan were secured by additional collateral held outside the plan. Termination of the mandatory payroll deduction before the new loan is repaid would result in taxation of the entire outstanding balance of that loan. For purposes of this requirement, it would not seem to matter whether the prior defaulted loan had been foreclosed, offset, or repaid before the termination of the payroll deduction.

Transfers

Q 11:30   May a participant transfer a loan between Section 403(b) investments?

Yes. Under both the final Code Section 403(b) regulations and prior law, transfers of an individual's interest in one Section 403(b) investment to another Section 403(b) investment are permitted, provided that applicable requirements are satisfied. [Treas. Reg. § 1.403(b)-10(b); Rev. Rul. 90-24, 1990-1 C.B. 97] Under the final Code Section 403(b) regulations, the transfer may take the form of a plan-to-plan transfer ("transfer") or of a transfer within the same plan ("exchange"). Neither set of rules imposes restrictions on the type of interest that may be transferred. Thus, interests in the Section 403(b) investment that have already been taxed, or that are encumbered by a loan, may be transferred.

This conclusion is consistent with prior IRS treatment of a similar qualified plan issue. In a private ruling, the IRS approved the transfer of a plan interest encumbered by a loan as part of a qualified plan trustee-to-trustee transfer. [Ltr. Rul. 8950008]

It appears that transfers are not permitted between traditional Section 403(b) contracts or accounts and Roth 403(b) contracts or accounts. In the event of such a prohibition, transfers of loans between traditional and Roth 403(b) arrangements would not likely be permitted, though there is no specific authority on this point.

Q 11:31   May a participant loan be transferred to a Section 403(b) annuity as part of a rollover from another Section 403(b) annuity or from a non-Section 403(b) plan (such as a Section 401(a), 403(a), 401(k), or governmental 457(b) plan)?

Yes. [Treas. Reg. §§ 1.401(a)(31)-1, Q&A 16; § 1.403(b)-2, Q&A 2] The IRS has recognized such a transfer between two employer-sponsored 401(k) plans in one private ruling that suggests the IRS may be willing to consider a transfer of a promissory note as part of an otherwise valid rollover. In Letter Ruling 9729042, the IRS concluded that a transfer of a promissory note to a new obligee, along with a change in repayment frequency (from weekly to semimonthly) would not be taxable to the participant and would not cause the loan to be treated as a new loan for testing purposes (see Q 11:33). The ruling addressed a rollover between two 401(k) plans. Assuming exactly the same circumstances, it would be reasonable to expect any IRS position favoring such a rollover to be applied in the same fashion to a rollover between Section 403(b) annuities.

There is a possible exception, however, for Roth 403(b) accounts. Rollovers from such accounts may only be made to another Roth account (Roth 403(b), Roth 401(k), or Roth IRA). [I.R.C. § 402A]

Q 11:32   Must a Section 403(b) arrangement allow transfers or rollovers to another Section 403(b) arrangement?

Neither the final Code Section 403(b) regulations nor Revenue Ruling 90-24 [Treas. Reg. § 1.403(b)-10(b); 1990-1 C.B. 97] requires either Section 403(b) plans or Section 403(b) investments to make or accept trustee transfers. Such transfers (or exchanges) are subject to the terms of the plan and the underlying investment product(s). However, a refusal to permit the transfer must be consistent with other applicable laws as well as with the terms of the contract (in the case of an annuity contract). There is no legal requirement that an obligee agree to distribute and transfer a loan in a rollover distribution. Thus, it is always important to review the plan as well as the applicable loan agreement and, where applicable, the underlying contract or custodial agreement, before attempting such a transfer or rollover.

Q 11:33   If the participant transfers a loan, will it be treated as a new loan?

Generally, the loan should not be treated as a new loan unless a substantive term is changed in the transfer that would cause the transfer to be a renegotiation, extension, renewal, or revision of the original loan. If such a substantive term is changed, then it will be treated as a new loan as of the date of the transfer. [TRA '86 § 1134(e); Ltr. Rul. 8950008]

In the course of a loan transfer, it can be important to be aware of the precise terms of the existing loan in order to avoid potential problems with qualifying the transferred loan as a new loan. Several factors may be different between the existing and the proposed new loan structure, including the charging and crediting of interest, as well as the repayment frequency and repayment methodology.

If the terms of the original promissory note are transferred intact, so that the transfer consists solely of a change of obligee (the party to which the payments are to be paid), then there would not appear to be a basis for considering the loan to be a new loan for purposes of applicable Code limitations and requirements. That would be consistent with the approach taken under TRA '86, for determining whether an existing loan would become subject to new TRA '86 requirements. However, if a substantive term is changed in the transfer, such as the interest rate or the repayment term, for example, the loan may be subject to retesting under applicable requirements. Whether it also becomes a new loan for determining whether the refinancing rules in the proposed regulation would apply appears to be an open question. See Q 11:11 for a discussion of the rules applicable to refinanced loans.

If a transferred loan is treated as a new loan because a substantive term is changed, the loan still might not be taxable upon transfer. Whether it is taxable will depend on whether the new loan, and the associated account, can satisfy the current loan limitations. See Q 11:11 for a discussion of the rules set out in the regulations. In addition, if a previously valid loan term (e.g., five years) is shortened in the transferred loan, this change, while making it a new loan, should not alone cause the loan to be taxable.

If the loan being transferred was a principal-residence loan, it could continue to be a principal-residence loan only if:

1. The loan was considered a transferred loan; or
2. The loan was considered a new loan for testing purposes, but still satisfied the tracing rules applicable to principal-residence loans (see Q 11:20).

Q 11:34   What is a *substantive term*?

It is unclear which terms are substantive and cannot be changed without causing the loan to be treated as a new loan. Three items that are usually central to any loan are principal, interest, and term. While the fixed term (e.g., five years) cannot be lengthened without triggering taxation of the entire loan balance, it can presumably be shortened. Also, the schedule of repayments may be changed from, for example, monthly to quarterly. While the amount of remaining principal on the initial loan is fixed by the existing loan, the participant may decide to take an additional loan at the time of the transfer or exchange. If this is taken as part of the loan issued under the transfer or exchange, this will be a change in a substantive term. Finally, a change in the loan interest rate is probably also a change in a substantive term.

Note. In a private letter ruling by the IRS regarding a rollover of a loan, a change in repayment frequency was not treated as triggering testing requirements for the transferred loan (see Q 11:31).

When a Loan Is Treated as a Distribution

Q 11:35   Is a participant required to transfer a loan in a transfer or exchange?

No. The participant may either leave the loan in the original contract or pay it off. If he or she is eligible, the participant may elect to have the loan treated as a distribution and then transfer the remaining account value.

If the loan is distributed to the participant with no cash, no withholding will be required. [Treas. Reg. § 31.3405(c)-1, Q&A 9] However, if cash is also distributed to the participant (rather than being rolled over directly to an IRA or to another Section 403(b) annuity), the payer should withhold 20 percent of the taxable portion of the distribution—including the amount needed to extinguish the loan—up to a maximum of the cash that was distributed.

> **Example.** A participant receives a distribution from a traditional (non-Roth) Section 403(b) account of a $6,000 loan and $1,000 in cash, for a total of $7,000. There are no pre-tax amounts in the account, so 100 percent of the distribution is taxable. Twenty percent of the total distribution is $1,400. However, the plan is not required to withhold more than is actually distributed. Therefore, only $1,000, the amount of cash distributed, is actually withheld. The total distribution of $7,000 is reported to the IRS on Form 1099-R.

Q 11:36   May a plan distribute a loan before the employee is eligible for a distribution?

No. If a plan loan is offset as part of a transfer or exchange, or as a result of a loan default, at a time when the participant is not eligible for a distribution of the offset amount, the offset would clearly violate the withdrawal restrictions applicable to Section 403(b) annuities and custodial accounts. [I.R.C. §§ 403(b)(11), 403(b)(7)(A)(ii)] Such a violation of the withdrawal restrictions would cause the transferor annuity to fail to qualify under Code Section 403(b), causing the subsequent transfer to fail to satisfy the requirements under both current and prior law [Treas. Reg. § 1.403(b)-10(b); Rev. Rul. 90-24, 1990-1 C.B. 97]

Q 11:37   May a Section 403(b) arrangement distribute a loan as a required distribution after the employee attains age 70½?

Some Section 403(b) arrangements allow loans to continue after an employee is required to begin taking distributions. There is no apparent reason the employee could not instruct that a distribution be processed and applied to the loan. If the loan repayment distribution did not exceed the amount of the required distribution, 20 percent withholding would not be required. [I.R.C. § 402(a)(4)(B)]

Q 11:38   How have rules regarding loans from Section 403(b) contracts and accounts been affected by recent guidance following Hurricane Katrina and similar natural disasters?

In response to the massive devastation of Hurricane Katrina in August 2005, as well as damages from additional hurricanes not long thereafter, the IRS and Congress sought to meet the needs of affected plan participants. That guidance included the liberalization of some of the loan rules and repayment deadlines.

Under the Katrina Emergency Tax Relief Act of 2005 [KETRA, H.R. 3768, Pub. L. No. 109-73, 119 Stat. 2016 (2005)] and the Gulf Opportunity Zone Act [GOZA, H.R. 4440, Pub. L. No. 109-135, 119 Stat. 2577 (2005)], individuals whose principal place of residence:

- on August 28, 2005, was within the Hurricane Katrina disaster area and who sustained an economic loss on account of Hurricane Katrina;
- as of September 23, 2005, was within the Hurricane Rita disaster area and who sustained an economic loss due to Hurricane Rita; and
- as of October 23, 2005, was within the Hurricane Wilma disaster area and who sustained an economic loss due to Hurricane Wilma

are permitted to increase the 50 percent IRS loan limitation, applied to the aggregate of their plans, to 100 percent, up to a maximum of $100,000. The DOL confirmed that plans subject to ERISA may increase the security for plan loans to 100 percent, in compliance with the provisions of KETRA, to participants and beneficiaries affected by the hurricanes. [IRS Notice 2005-92, Fn. 3; D.O.L. Release 05-2188-NAT] In addition, KETRA and GOZA also permit those affected individuals to delay any loan payment due:

- between August 25, 2005, and December 31, 2006 (Hurricane Katrina);
- between September 23, 2005, and December 31, 2006 (Hurricane Rita); and
- between October 23, 2005, and December 31, 2006 (Hurricane Wilma)

for up to one year, and to ignore that delay for purposes of determining compliance with the maximum five-year period and the level amortization requirements. Interest could continue to accrue during the period of the delay. Upon resumption of payments, the payment amount can be adjusted to amortize the loan over the remaining loan period. If plan amendments are necessary to permit an employer to extend these benefits to individuals affected by Hurricanes Katrina, Rita, or Wilma, such amendments may be made retroactively, but must be made on or before the last day of the first plan year beginning on or after January 1, 2007 (2009 for governmental plans), or such later date as the Secretary may prescribe. A plan is permitted to rely on a participant's reasonable representations that the participant qualifies for the special treatment for loans unless the plan administrator or other responsible person has actual knowledge to the contrary. [IRS Notice 2005-92 (Dec. 19, 2005)]

The IRS provided safe-harbor guidance for satisfying KETRA/GOZA loan provisions. In order to qualify under the safe harbor, the loan suspension period may end no later than December 31, 2006. The loan repayments must resume upon the end of the suspension period and the term of the loan may be extended by the duration of the suspension period. Thus, under the safe harbor, payments on a loan taken out after December 31, 2005, may not be suspended the full year allowed by the acts. [IRS Notice 2005-92 (Dec. 19, 2005)]

IRS guidance also permits plan administrators and service providers to lift or relax certain procedural requirements, such as obtaining certain documentation, if they make a good-faith effort under the circumstances to comply with the requirements. In addition, the administrator or service provider must make a reasonable attempt to obtain the foregone documentation as soon as practical. [IRS Ann. 2005-70 (Oct. 3, 2005)] For example, a loan might require the consent of a living spouse. If the participant was unable because of the disaster following Hurricane Katrina to provide a death certificate for the deceased spouse, and if the plan made a good-faith effort to comply with the requirements before issuing the loan but did not receive the death certificate, the plan would be required to obtain the death certificate as soon as practical.

Life Insurance

Q 11:39   May life insurance be purchased under a Section 403(b) arrangement?

Life insurance may no longer be offered as an additional benefit within Section 403(b) arrangements, effective September 24, 2007. [Treas. Reg. § 1.403(b)-8(c)(2)] Life insurance was permitted to be offered prior to that date, and life insurance contracts in effect prior to September 24, 2007 may continue to receive contributions and transfers (or exchanges). However, contributions to Section 403(b) life insurance are limited, and a portion of that contribution is taxable to the participant each year. A large portion of the death benefit of Section 403(b) life insurance will usually be nontaxable to the beneficiary. The life insurance protection cannot extend beyond retirement, under the Section 403(b) program.

Underwriting

Q 11:40   Are there specific underwriting rules for Section 403(b) life insurance contracts?

Some Section 403(b) life insurance is offered on a guaranteed issue (no underwriting) or simplified issue (limited underwriting) basis. However, there are no apparent barriers to full underwriting, provided that it is not done in a manner that would involve the employer in questions of impermissible discrimination. Of course, in the case of Section 403(b) programs sponsored by public employers, there are no Code restrictions that would limit an employer's ability to discriminate in the offering of life insurance in the Section 403(b) plan.

Rates for the Section 403(b) life insurance contract must be gender neutral. [Arizona Governing Committee for Tax Deferred Annuity & Deferred Compensation Plans v. Norris, 463 U.S. 1073 (1983)]

Insurance on Family Members

Q 11:41   May a Section 403(b) life insurance policy include insurance on family members?

Benefits for persons other than the employee—even family members—may not be included. A policy with a family rider, insuring the employee's spouse and children, will not qualify as a Section 403(b) life insurance policy. [Rev. Rul. 69-146, 1969-1 C.B. 132]

Limitations on Amount of Premiums

Q 11:42   What are the limits on life insurance in Section 403(b) plans?

The benefits of life insurance protection in a Section 403(b) plan must be incidental to the central purpose of retirement savings. The rules for determining whether life insurance is incidental in a Section 403(b) plan are the same as the rules that apply to qualified plans. [Rev. Rul. 74-115, 1974-1 C.B. 100] Generally, to satisfy the incidental benefit requirement, the contributions to the employer's plan used to purchase a permanent policy (whole life insurance with nonincreasing premiums and nondecreasing death benefits) must always be less than 50 percent of total contributions to the plan for that participant. [Rev. Rul. 66-143, 1966-1 C.B. 79] The limit for temporary (term life and universal life) insurance is 25 percent. The distinction between permanent and temporary insurance is that in the permanent insurance policy, only part of the premiums will be used to provide life insurance benefits, and the balance will accumulate in the same manner as in a Section 403(b) annuity or Section 403(b)(7) custodial account.

If the Section 403(b) plan is set up as a defined benefit plan (mostly in older plans), the life insurance policy death benefit may not be more than 100 times the participant's accrued benefit.

Q 11:43   May life insurance premiums be paid with accumulated earnings from a Section 403(b) annuity or from dividends from a Section 403(b) life insurance policy, rather than from new plan contributions?

Yes. However, the premiums paid in this manner still count in applying the 50 percent/25 percent test, as applicable, to the employee's historical Section 403(b) contributions to the employer's Section 403(b) arrangement. [Rev. Rul. 57-213, 1957-1 C.B. 157] In addition, any transfers from another Section 403(b) contract or account, or rollovers, must be consistent with the terms of the plan and satisfy applicable rules governing transfers, exchanges, and rollovers.

Q 11:44   May contributions from a previous employer's plan be counted in applying the 50 percent/25 percent test?

Yes, in some cases. The limit applies to all contributions allocated to the employee under the arrangement, including rollover contributions. Since an employer may also pay the premiums on an employee's contract established with a previous employer, it would not appear that the result should be different with contributions already in the account.

Q 11:45   May contributions and earnings in a Section 403(b)(7) custodial account be transferred to a Section 403(b) life insurance policy to pay premiums?

Amounts held in a Section 403(b)(7) custodial account may be transferred or exchanged to a Section 403(b) life insurance contract as long as other requirements applicable to the transfer or exchange are satisfied. However, the life insurance contract would be required to include withdrawal limitations at least as restrictive as those in the custodial account. [Treas. Reg. § 1.403(b)-10(b)] However, it appears that only account values from traditional Section 403(b) accounts may be transferred to a life insurance policy that is (or that is part of) a traditional Section 403(b) contract. To be consistent with such a rule, only account values from Roth 403(b) account values may be transferred to Roth 403(b) contracts.

Q 11:46   May a participant's multiple Section 403(b) annuities be aggregated to apply the 50 percent/25 percent test?

Yes. The limit applies to the total of contributions to all of the employee's Section 403(b) annuities (both traditional pre-tax Section 403(b) accounts and Roth 403(b) accounts) in the employer's plan or arrangement.

Note. In the past, there may have been an argument for combining all of the employee's Section 403(b) account balances regardless of whether they have been transferred into the current plan. Purchasing life insurance under each separate account is not prohibited. Such purchases under each separate account would not seem to be materially different from aggregating all of the accounts at the outset. However, under new plan-based requirements in the final Code Section 403(b) regulations, it would appear that such aggregation, if it was previously permitted, may not be permitted under the new rules.

Q 11:47   May a participant's Section 403(b) plan account be aggregated with another plan type to apply the 50 percent/25 percent limit?

No. Unlike the loan limits, the limit on life insurance applies to the Section 403(b) plan separately. [Treas. Reg. § 1.403(b)-1(c)(3)]

Correction of Defects Under the IRS Voluntary Correction Program

Q 11:48   If a plan fails to satisfy the incidental benefit requirement, may this defect be corrected in one of the self-correction or IRS-approved correction alternatives now available to Section 403(b) programs?

Yes, it may, provided that the other requirements of the selected program are met. If for any participant the premiums for life insurance exceed the limits and violate the incidental benefit requirements, this can cause that participant's annuities to cease to qualify under Code Section 403(b). Such a defect might be self-corrected, or it might be included in a submission under the IRS Voluntary Correction Program (VCP). [Rev. Proc. 2006-27, 2006-1 C.B. 945]

Transfer of Assets to a Section 403(b) Annuity

Q 11:49   May the cash value in a Section 403(b) life insurance policy be transferred into another Section 403(b) annuity?

Yes. The insurance policy is treated as an annuity under Code Section 403(b). However, it appears that if the life insurance policy is funded with traditional pre-tax contributions, such a transfer could be made only to another traditional pre-tax Section 403(b) contract.

Taxation of Estimated Insurance Cost

Q 11:50   Are life insurance premiums within a Section 403(b) arrangement tax deferred?

Not entirely. The estimated cost of the term insurance (COI) is taxable to the employee in the year that it is incurred under the policy and tax reported to the participant at the end of the year. However, the amount reported is not included in the participant's income to determine his or her maximum excludable contribution for the year. [Rev. Rul. 68-304, 1968-1 C.B. 179]

Q 11:51   How is the COI determined?

The COI that is reported is determined by dividing the net amount at risk by 1,000, and then multiplying the result by a term insurance rate. The net amount at risk is the difference between the death benefit and the contract's surrender value on the last day of the year.

The term insurance rate is the smaller of:

1. The insurance company's yearly renewable term (YRT) cost, per $1,000 of the amount at risk, for standard risks; or
2. The term cost from an IRS table of rates, based on the insured's age.

[Notice 2002-8, 2002-4 I.R.B. 398]

In the case of arrangements entered into after January 28, 2002, for periods after December 31, 2003, the insurance company's YRT rates may be used only if:

- Those rates are made known to anyone who applies to the insurer for term coverage; and
- The insurer regularly sells term insurance at those rates to individuals who apply for term insurance coverage through the insurer's normal distribution channels. [Notice 2002-8, 2002-1 C.B. 398]

The term costs from the IRS table of rates, reproduced in the Notice, represent a material increase in the rates from rates used prior to the Notice, referred to as "PS-58" rates.

Example. Aaron Nezda is 52 years old. His Section 403(b) account includes a life insurance policy with a face amount of $50,000 and a cash value of $8,600. The net amount at risk is $41,400. The issuing company does not have a yearly renewable term policy from which to determine an annual term cost. Under the new table, the standard one-year term rate for Aaron's age is $2.81 per thousand. The taxable amount that will be reported to him on a Form 1099-R will be $2.81 ($41,400 ÷ 1,000), or $115.21. This amount is not subject to 20 percent withholding and is not eligible for rollover to an IRA or other Section 403(b) plan. [Treas. Reg. § 1.402(c)-2, Q&A 4]

Life Insurance Loans

Q 11:52 May an employee take a loan from a life insurance policy in a Section 403(b) arrangement?

Yes, subject to the limits on loans in Section 403(b) plans. The loan, however, must be a bona fide loan that meets IRS requirements. The participant must intend to repay, and the loan must require repayment in substantially level installments not less frequently than quarterly (see Q 11:17). The repayment requirement is somewhat foreign to life insurance loans, which, under state insurance laws, are generally netted out of the policy's death proceeds if they are not repaid before the insured's death.

An automatic premium loan (APL) used to make a premium payment will count both as a loan, reducing the participant's eligibility for additional loans, and as a life insurance premium, for applying the 50 percent/25 percent limit. As a premium, the portion representing the annual cost of insurance will also be taxable.

Regular loans may also be taken, within the 50 percent/$50,000 limit. State insurance laws may limit the ability to restrict loans in the life insurance policy; however, if the loan limits are applied to an aggregated Section 403(b) arrangement, a maximum loan from the life insurance policy will often be well within the loan limits for the arrangement as a whole. This limitation alone may be insufficient, however, for larger contracts, where the $50,000 limit—not the 50 percent limit—is controlling.

Beneficiaries

Q 11:53 Who can be the beneficiary of a Section 403(b) life insurance policy?

If the arrangement is not subject to ERISA, the beneficiary designation is subject to any applicable state insurance law limitations, but can generally be anyone the participant wishes to name. Distributions upon the death of the participant need to satisfy applicable IRS distribution requirements (see chapter 10). If the policy is owned by a trust and the Section 403(b) requirements are satisfied in the trust rather than the policy, the trust might require that the trustee be the beneficiary of any life insurance contracts so that the trustees can pay trust beneficiaries designated by the employee. In the case of an ERISA 403(b) plan, beneficiary designations must satisfy the spousal consent rules described in chapter 12 as well as any applicable qualified joint and survivor annuity (QJSA) and qualified preretirement survivor annuity (QPSA) requirements. For more information regarding beneficiary designations generally, refer to chapter 12.

Taxation of Death Benefits

Q 11:54   How are death benefits from a Section 403(b) life insurance policy taxed?

The cash surrender value of the policy immediately before the employee's death will be taxable to the beneficiary to the extent that it exceeds the sum of:

1. The term cost previously taxed to the participant; and

2. Any other unrecovered investment in the policy, including previously reported policy loans.

Note. In years prior to 1997, up to $5,000 of the cash surrender value may have been excluded as an employer-paid death benefit. This exclusion was eliminated by SBJPA, for participants dying after August 20, 1996.

The remainder of the death benefit is excludable from the beneficiary's gross income as proceeds from life insurance. [I.R.C. § 101(a)(1)]

Distribution of Life Insurance Contracts

Q 11:55   Are there any limitations on the manner of distributing contracts to participants, such as upon retirement?

In contrast to qualified plans, in which such policies are often owned by the trust established to hold plan assets, in many cases the participant will be the owner of the life insurance contract in the Section 403(b) arrangement. Nevertheless, if a life insurance contract is distributed from a Section 403(b) program to the participant, such a distribution would be subject to rules regarding such distributions.

IRS guidance with respect to life insurance in defined benefit plans described in Code Section 412(i), and to qualified plans generally, also would be applicable to Section 403(b) plans offering life insurance.

Under this guidance, if the plan is subject to Code Section 401(a)(4) (generally, Section 403(b) plans that are not governmental or church plans and include nonelective employer or employee contributions):

1. The right to purchase the contract from the plan may not be made available to highly compensated employees before retirement; and

2. The rights of nonhighly compensated employees to purchase the life insurance contracts from the plan must be of equal or greater value than the purchase rights of highly compensated employees.

[Rev. Rul. 2004-21]

In addition, if the life insurance contract is distributed to the participant from the plan, the valuation of the policy, for purposes of determining the taxable income to the participant, must be based upon the fair market value of the contract, taking into account the value of all features of the contract that provide an economic benefit to the employee. [Treas. Reg. § 1.402(a)-1] This represents a new rule over and above the rule articulated in Notice 89-25, under which the total policy reserves might be used rather than the cash surrender value to determine the amount of the taxable distribution. [Notice 89-25, 1989-1 C.B. 662, Q&A 10] The IRS has created two safe harbors for determining the fair market value of a life insurance contract, depending on whether the contract is a "variable contract" or a "non-variable contract." [Rev. Proc. 2005-25, 2005-17 I.R.B. 962]

Plan Termination

Q 11:56   May a Section 403(b) plan be frozen or terminated?

Yes, a Section 403(b) plan can be frozen or terminated. [Treas. Reg. § 1.403(b)-10(a)]

Q 11:57   Must the employer wait until the January 1, 2009 general effective date of the final Code Section 403(b) regulations to terminate the plan?

No. An employer is permitted to adopt the regulations in advance of the general effective date, provided that such adoption is consistent and complete. A written plan will not be required in order to terminate prior to January 1, 2009. [Treas. Reg. § 1.403(b)-11(a)]

Q 11:58   What are the requirements for freezing a Section 403(b) plan?

Freezing a Section 403(b) plan in many cases might require little more than ceasing contributions. If the plan is governed by a written plan (and all plans will be so governed when they become subject to the final Code Section 403(b) regulations, generally January 1, 2009), freezing the plan would likely require a plan amendment to formalize the cessation of contributions. For purposes of the Code and, if applicable, Title I of ERISA, the frozen plan must continue to satisfy applicable requirements. A written plan that is frozen would likely require an amendment to cease future contributions and, if subject to Title I of ERISA, would also require corresponding notifications to plan participants.

Q 11:59   What are the requirements for terminating a Section 403(b) plan?

Any Section 403(b) plan may have provisions permitting termination of the plan. [Treas. Reg. § 1.403(b)-10(a)] However, if amounts in the plan are subject to distribution restrictions under Code Section 403(b), including elective deferrals, amounts held in a custodial account, and employer contributions to an annuity established after 2008, a distribution upon termination is only permitted if certain conditions are satisfied, including:

- All accounts under the plan must be distributed as soon as administratively practicable following the termination. If any accounts are not distributed, the termination may fail, not only requiring continued maintenance of the plan, but also potentially characterizing any distributions taken as part of the termination as violations of applicable withdrawal restrictions. For purposes of this requirement, a distribution can consist of a distribution of an annuity contract.

Note. While the regulations are silent on this point, it would seem reasonable that the relinquishment of plan restrictions on, and control over, an existing annuity contract could be viewed as a distribution of that contract. Similar analysis could also be applied to individual certificates under a group annuity contract, since for purposes of Code Section 403(b) such certificates are treated as the contract. [Treas. Reg. § 1.401-9]

- If any amounts distributed in the termination otherwise would have been subject to withdrawal restrictions under the Code, then no Section 403(b) contributions of any type (elective, nonelective) may be made for any employee of the employer for 12 months following the last termination distribution. For this purpose, a subsequent Section 403(b) plan covering less than 2 percent of the employees previously eligible for the terminated plan will be disregarded.

Because all accounts must be distributed, either in cash or through distribution of an annuity contract, one of the first requirements is identification of all accounts under the plan, and determining whether they can be distributed.

Q 11:60   What are some possible challenges in identifying the accounts under the plan?

Accounts can fall into a number of categories:

- All accounts with current providers are under the plan unless they are grandfathered 90-24 contracts or accounts. [Treas. Reg. § 1.403(b)-10(b)]
- Accounts with former plan providers generally fall outside the plan if the provider was deselected prior to 2005; and, accounts maintained with

former providers deselected after 2004 but before 2009, for former employees also fall outside the plan.

- Accounts of current employees maintained with providers deselected after 2004 but before 2009 are required to be included in the plan; however, IRS guidance recognizes that not all of those accounts will be incorporated into the plan, and provides a reasonable good-faith effort exception in the event that they are not so included.

- All accounts with plan providers deselected after 2008 remain in the plan as long as the account remains in existence unless it is transferred into another plan.

[Rev. Proc. 2007-71, 2007-51 I.R.B. 1184]

Unless all accounts required to be included in the plan are included in the termination, the termination generally cannot occur, and the distribution restrictions are not waived.

Q 11:61   If all affected accounts are identified, are there any possible concerns that could still prevent the termination distribution?

In some situations, the employer will not have authority to require a distribution out of the participant's account. This could occur, for example, if the Section 403(b) program has only recently become subject to the terms of a written plan. This detail can take on even more importance if the employer is a private tax-exempt employer that has relied upon an exclusion for the plan from Title I of ERISA because the employer possessed no contract rights under the plan. (See Q 11:1.) A current exercise of such contract rights could raise significant questions about the validity of the employer's prior position, including the appropriateness of not filing Form 5500 as well as various potential violations of ERISA restrictions, including loan limitations and spousal consent requirements.

An alternative for accomplishing the plan termination without a distribution of the accounts is to distribute annuity contracts. However, if the plan includes any Section 403(b)(7) custodial accounts, this would appear to require that such accounts be transferred (or exchanged) to an annuity contract.

Q 11:62   Are there additional special issues for plans that may have been terminated prior to publication of the final Code Section 403(b) regulations?

Prior to the final Code Section 403(b) regulations, in the absence of clear guidance, plan sponsors seeking to terminate an ERISA 403(b) plan may have concluded that a formal termination for purposes of Title I of ERISA, including the filing of a final Form 5500, could be accomplished if:

- it was coupled with a full relinquishment of employer rights or controls over the contracts and accounts in the plan, and

- it did not involve any distributions in violation of applicable distribution restrictions.

In such a circumstance, where an employer treated the plan as terminated for ERISA purposes, it is unclear whether under the final Code Section 403(b) regulations that employer should take additional action. If all accounts were annuity contracts, such additional action might be nothing more than documenting the elimination of distribution restrictions. (However, if this were viewed as a current termination for federal tax purposes, it could also require a 12-month cessation of contributions under other existing Section 403(b) plans of the employer, if any.) If the accounts include any custodial accounts, and if a termination distribution cannot be accomplished, there could be additional complications, such as:

- it might be necessary to treat all of the accounts as being under a plan, for which a plan document is now required; and,
- if the accounts do not include nonelective employee or employer contributions, it might be necessary to determine whether that plan qualifies for the general exemption under Title I of ERISA.

Chapter 12

Beneficiary Designations

Peter Gulia, Esq.
Fiduciary Guidance Counsel

Making a beneficiary designation is an important part of retirement and estate planning. While a Section 403(b) benefit will not pass by a will, a participant's beneficiary designation affects his or her overall estate plan. This chapter focuses on a participant's use of his or her valuable right to name a beneficiary, and explains some opportunities and restrictions in making a beneficiary designation, including marriage and family rights that restrain a beneficiary designation.

Many participants assume (often incorrectly) that they lack sufficient wealth for estate and inheritance tax issues to be of concern. Because a taxable estate can include nonprobate assets, such as retirement benefits, life insurance, and the decedent's homes, this chapter includes some basic information concerning estate and inheritance taxes.

Last but not least, this chapter ends with a "top-ten" list of common mistakes that people make with beneficiary designations, and how one might avoid those mistakes.

Author's Usage Note

For convenience, this chapter uses several words in a specially defined context.

This chapter sometimes distinguishes between an ERISA plan, a governmental plan, and a church plan. In this context, an ERISA plan refers to a plan that is governed by Title I of ERISA, a governmental plan refers to a plan described in ERISA § 3(32), and a church plan refers to a plan described in ERISA § 3(33) that has not elected to be governed by ERISA. Furthermore, this chapter uses the expression "non-ERISA" to refer to a governmental plan, a church plan, or to a plan that an employer intends as a plan that meets the conditions for tax treatment under Code Section 403(b) but not a plan that would be governed by ERISA.

This chapter uses the word "contract" to refer to an annuity contract, a custodial account, or another form of investment that Code Section 403(b) permits as an eligible investment (see chapter 5).

In this chapter, "payer" refers to any custodian, insurer, plan administrator, or other person responsible for deciding or paying a claim under a governmental plan.

This chapter uses the word "state" in its popular meaning to refer to the District of Columbia or any state, commonwealth, territory, possession, or similar jurisdiction within the United States. Because this chapter has many references to state law, this chapter makes parallel references to a "state" (rather than to the lawyers' word "jurisdiction") for reading ease. For example, although the District of Columbia is not a state, law that applies to a person because he or she resides in the District of Columbia is state law, as distinguished from U.S. law or federal law, which applies throughout the United States.

Author's Citations Note

This chapter includes many general explanations of state laws. To support each such statement with citations to more than 50 state laws would be unwieldy in this chapter's summary. Moreover, an employee-benefits practitioner usually is interested first in a general sense of the state laws. To these ends, the chapter frequently cites the Uniform Probate Code, Uniform Trust Code, and other uniform acts recommended by the National Conference of Commissioners on Uniform State Laws [www.nccusl.org]. A reader who wants to find whether a particular state enacted a statute based on a uniform law might begin with this chapter's citations to Uniform Laws Annotated [ULA], which includes citations for states' adoptions of, and variations from, the recommended uniform laws.

Because most employee-benefits practitioners do not use printed volumes to read federal or state statutes or regulations, this chapter's citations to statutes and regulations omit publisher and year references. A reader may find statutes efficiently and inexpensively by using Aspen Publishers' Loislaw service (for more information, visit www.loislaw.com or call 1-877-471-5632).

Specialty citations are in the forms and with the abbreviations customary to employee-benefits or tax practitioners, including the abbreviations shown in the book's front matter.

About Beneficiary Designations

Q 12:1 Is a Section 403(b) benefit disposed by a participant's will?

No. A Section 403(b) annuity contract or custodial account will include a provision by which a participant may designate his or her beneficiary or beneficiaries. The beneficiary designation applies even if the participant's will attempts to state a contrary disposition or to revoke a beneficiary designation. [See generally Restatement (Third) of Property: Wills and Other Donative Transfers § 7.1 comment d (2003)] Indeed, if a beneficiary change could be effected by a will, a responsible insurer or custodian would be unwilling to make any payment until a court had determined the correct distribution of a participant's estate. [See, e.g., Stone v. Stephens, 155 Ohio 595, 600–601, 99 N.E.2d 766 (Ohio 1951)] Understanding that a will does not change a Section 403(b) beneficiary results simply from applying the terms of the Section 403(b) plan or contract, which typically includes provisions for an intended third-party beneficiary. Yet some states for convenience include in the probate statutes provisions that explicitly recognize non-testamentary transfers. [See generally Unif. Probate Code §§ 1-201(4), 8 pt. I ULA 38 (1998) & Supp. 11 (2006), 6–101, 8 pt. II ULA 430-432 (1998) & Supp 173–174 (2006), 6-104, 8 pt. II ULA 467–474 (1998), 6-201, 8 pt. II ULA 480–482 (1998)] Even without a statute, courts have held that a will cannot override a beneficiary designation. [See generally, Restatement (Third) of Property: Wills and Other Donative Transfers § 7.1 comment d (2003)]

Note. A beneficiary's right under a non-ERISA Section 403(b) contract arguably might be subject to the State of Washington's Testamentary Disposition of Nonprobate Assets Act. [*See* Wash Rev. Code §§ 11.11.003–11.11. 903] But even concerning a participant who is a resident or domiciliary of Washington, that statute might not apply because a typical Section 403(b) custodial account agreement includes a governing law clause and few (if any) of these choose Washington law.

Concerning a non-ERISA plan, state law may supplement a contract's or account's provisions concerning the manner of making a beneficiary designation. For instance, New York law requires that a beneficiary designation be signed. [New York Estates, Powers and Trusts Law § 13-3.2]

For an ERISA plan, only the plan's provisions govern a beneficiary designation. [ERISA § 514; Egelhoff v. Egelhoff, 532 U.S. 141 (2001)]

Additional Reasons for Naming a Beneficiary

Q 12:2   Are there other reasons, beyond providing a death benefit, why a participant would want to name a beneficiary?

Yes. There are at least two kinds of benefits—other than the death benefit itself—that might be obtained by naming a beneficiary. They are described below.

A beneficiary, even if he or she is not a surviving spouse, may direct a rollover. If a Section 403(b) plan so provides, a designated beneficiary, even if he or she is not the participant's surviving spouse, may instruct a direct rollover into his or her IRA. [I.R.C. § 402(c)(11), added by PPA, § 829]

Caution. A state might have an income tax law that does not follow the Internal Revenue Code. Before a beneficiary directs a rollover (or even decides to take a distribution), he or she should get expert advice about whether each state of which he or she is a resident or a domiciliary [*see* 4 U.S.C. § 114] would recognize the rollover, or would tax the distribution, even if rolled over for federal income tax purposes.

A hardship distribution can be based on the need of a beneficiary who is not a spouse or dependent. Without waiting for a participant to meet a plan's severance or other conditions that may permit a distribution, a Section 403(b) plan may permit a payment to meet a participant's hardship. A hardship must be based on the participant's need, which can include some needs concerning a participant's spouse or dependent. Further, a plan may provide that an event (including a medical expense) that would meet the plan's hardship conditions if it happened concerning a participant's spouse or dependent is a hardship if it happens concerning "a person who is a beneficiary under the plan with respect to the participant." [PPA, § 826] In the IRS's view, such a rule applies only concerning a primary beneficiary—that is, one who "has an unconditional right to all or a portion of the participant's account balance under the plan upon the death of the participant." [IRS Notice 2007-7, 2007-5 I.R.B. 395 (Jan. 29, 2007) at Q&A-5(a)]

Practice Pointer. Nothing in the Code requires a plan sponsor, insurer, or custodian to make this change, but many will want to.

Note. In California, Connecticut, Massachusetts, New Hampshire, New Jersey, Oregon, and Vermont, state law might require a public schools employer's plan that allows a direct rollover by an opposite-sex spouse to include this beneficiary-rollover provision to the extent that the provision is needed so that the governmental plan (which itself is state law) does not discriminate against an opposite-sex marriage, civil union, or domestic partnership that has legal rights and burdens equal to another marriage. Further, the provision seems likely in Hawaii, Maine, and Washington.

Persons Who Can Be a Beneficiary

Q 12:3   Who can be a beneficiary?

Unless a plan or contract otherwise provides, any person can be a beneficiary.

Note. For the purposes of rules concerning whether a plan or contract has the tax treatment of Section 403(b), regulations under Section 403(b) define a beneficiary to include a person who becomes entitled to a benefit as an alternate payee under a domestic-relations order. [*See* Treas. Reg. § 1.403(b)-2(a)(3)] This chapter does not follow that usage. For an explanation of qualified domestic relations orders, see chapter 13.

Q 12:4   May a participant designate his or her dog or cat as a beneficiary?

No. A beneficiary must be a person, whether a natural person or a non-natural person (such as a corporation), that can indorse a negotiable instrument, such as the check that pays the plan distribution.

Nonetheless, a participant may name as his or her beneficiary under a Section 403(b) plan a trustee of a trust for a pet animal's care, or a person selected to care for a pet animal.

Note. If a Section 403(b) distribution is paid to a pet's caretaker who does not serve as a trustee, the distribution is that person's income. If a Section 403(b) distribution is paid to a trustee who serves under a valid trust (even if the trust is legally unenforceable), the distribution is the trust's income. A pet trust is subject to federal income tax at the rates that apply to a married person who files a separate return. Although a trust normally has a deduction in the amount of trust distributions, "since the amounts of income required to be distributed . . . and amounts properly paid, credited, or required to be distributed under [the relevant Internal Revenue Code sections] are limited to distributions intended for beneficiaries, a deduction under those sections is not available for distributions for the benefit of a pet animal. Similarly, such distributions are not taxed to anyone." [Rev. Rul. 76-476, 1976-2 C.B. 192] These rules are consistent with the idea that trust income generally should not be taxed more than once, but should be taxed.

Q 12:5 May a participant designate a charity as his or her beneficiary?

Yes. A participant may designate a charity as a beneficiary. Although some states previously had statutes that would have voided some charitable gifts made soon before a donor's death or for more than a specified portion of his or her estate, those statutes were declared unconstitutional. [*See, e.g.,* Estate of Cavill, 329 A.2d 503 (Pa. 1974)] States repealed all of these statutes.

For a participant who already has fairly provided for his or her spouse and children, a charitable gift might be worthwhile. Many people who have worked for a charity or in education are inclined to continue that work by making a gift to a charitable organization.

> **Caution.** A charitable-organization employer should avoid inappropriately inducing its employees to name the charity as a beneficiary. In addition to consequences under other laws, doing so could interfere with rights under an ERISA plan or might cause a Section 403(b) plan to become an ERISA plan. [*See* ERISA § 510; D.O.L. Reg. § 2510.3-2(f)]

> **Practice Pointer.** For a person who already has decided to make charitable gifts on death and expects his or her estate to be subject to a significant federal estate tax, some financial planners suggest that using a retirement plan benefit might be an efficient way to provide the gift. They suggest this because a retirement plan benefit provided to a noncharitable beneficiary is subject to both federal income tax and federal estate tax (except for deaths in 2010), while a capital asset enjoys a "stepped-up" basis and is not subject to income tax until the beneficiary sells the asset. Other planners point out that the federal income tax deduction for federal estate tax attributable to property that is income in respect of a decedent partially mitigates the "double tax." [*See* I.R.C. § 691(c)] Along with this, they argue that a retirement plan might permit longer income tax deferral while post-death income on capital assets will subject the beneficiary to income tax. Considering which course might be "right" turns on the donor's and the planner's assumptions. Further, nontax factors might favor one approach over another.

Although a Section 403(b) benefit will be included in the participant's taxable estate for federal estate tax purposes, an estate has a deduction for the amount that properly passes to charity. [I.R.C. § 2055] Further, although Section 403(b) distributions would otherwise be included in income for federal income tax purposes, a charitable organization is exempt from federal income tax on its receipts from charitable gifts. [I.R.C. § 501(a)]

Making a Beneficiary Designation

Q 12:6   Who may make a beneficiary designation?

Ordinarily, only the participant may make a beneficiary designation. However, a Section 403(b) contract may permit a beneficiary to name a further contingent beneficiary if the Section 403(b) participant had not designated all of the Section 403(b) benefit. [*See* Ltr. Rul. 199936052 (June 16, 1999) (concerning an IRA)]

Such a provision can cause the Section 403(b) benefit that remains undistributed at each beneficiary's death to be subject to federal estate tax and state inheritance tax, notwithstanding that the same benefit was previously taxed upon the participant's death. [I.R.C. §§ 2041(a)(2); Treas. Reg. §§ 20.2041-1(b)] A federal estate tax may be postponed if the beneficiary names his or her spouse as the succeeding beneficiary and that spouse has power to take the entire remaining benefit. [I.R.C. §§ 2056; Ltr. Rul. 199936052 (June 16, 1999)]

A more typical Section 403(b) contract provision for a situation in which there is no other designated beneficiary provides any undistributed benefit to the personal representative of the participant's estate.

Note. Although a participant's estate might have been closed, an estate may be reopened for subsequent administration upon the discovery of property that was not disposed by the previous administration. [*See generally,* Unif. Probate Code § 3-1008, 8 pt. I ULA 300–302 (1998) & Supp. 83 (2006)]

Practice Pointer. A careful participant would make a complete beneficiary designation that contemplates all possibilities. A participant who does not want to specify his or her alternate takers could create a trust, which could include a power of appointment for a beneficiary to name a further beneficiary.

Q 12:7   Why should a participant read a beneficiary designation form?

Plan administrators, custodians, and insurers design beneficiary-designation forms anticipating the possibility that a participant might give incomplete or ambiguous instructions. For example, many forms provide that if a participant has not specified how to divide a benefit, it will be divided among all beneficiaries in equal shares.

A beneficiary-designation form might include other "gap-fillers" or "default" provisions, some of which might be surprising to a participant. For example, a beneficiary-designation form might provide that a beneficiary change for *any* Section 403(b) account with the custodian will change the beneficiary for *every* Section 403(b) account with the custodian. Some Section 403(b) plans provide that the beneficiary designated under a pension or life insurance plan is the "default" beneficiary. Because provisions of this kind might frustrate one's intent, a participant should read each beneficiary-designation form.

Q 12:8 Must a beneficiary designation be witnessed?

Usually, no. For a church plan, governmental plan, or other non-ERISA plan, most states' laws do not require that a beneficiary designation be signed in the presence of a notary or otherwise witnessed. Even if a plan's administrator adopts a form that calls for witnesses, the plan administrator usually has discretion to excuse an absence of witnesses. [*See, e.g.,* Lowing v. Public School Employees' Retirement Board, 766 A.2d 306 (Pa. Commw. 2001)]

For an ERISA plan, a beneficiary designation by a participant who has a spouse that would provide a benefit to any person other than the spouse usually must be witnessed, or it will be entirely or partially ineffective.

Q 12:9 Will a beneficiary designation made under a power of attorney be accepted?

A plan administrator, insurer, custodian, or trustee may, but is not required to, accept a beneficiary designation made by an agent under a power of attorney. Typically, a plan administrator will decline to act unless the power of attorney document expressly states a power to change beneficiary designations. [*See, e.g.,* Pension Committee Heileman-Baltimore Local 1010 IBT Pension Plan v. Bullinger, 1992 U.S. Dist. LEXIS 17325 (D. Md. Oct. 29, 1992); Clouse v. Philadelphia, Bethlehem & New England Railroad Co., 787 F. Supp. 93 (E.D. Pa. 1992); *see also* Restatement (Second) of Agency § 37 (1957)]

For a Section 403(b) contract that is not held under a plan, state law governs whether an insurer or custodian may or must permit the actions of an agent under a power of attorney.

Practice Pointer. If (because a contract is not held under a plan) state law might apply, a practitioner should consider which state's law might apply, and should consider drafting a power-of-attorney document to meet the state laws of all states that might be involved.

Example. Melite is a public school teacher who resides in Pennsylvania. She holds an individual variable annuity contract that was issued when she lived in Ohio, and that contract provides that it is governed by Ohio laws. She also has a custodial account, and that account's agreement provides that it is governed by Delaware's internal laws, "without regard to conflict-of-laws principles." Rather than assume that a power of attorney that meets the requirements of Pennsylvania's statute would be sufficient, Melite's lawyer drafts a document that conforms not only to Pennsylvania laws but also to Delaware and Ohio laws. Doing so is less expensive than researching which law would apply under either contract. And following all states' laws gives Melite a better likelihood that her document will be relied on.

Substantial Compliance Doctrine

Q 12:10   What is the doctrine of substantial compliance?

When recognized, the doctrine of substantial compliance excuses a contract holder's failure to effect a change of beneficiary according to the contract's terms if he or she intended to change his or her beneficiary and did everything reasonably in his or her power to effect the change. [*See, e.g.,* Prudential Ins. Co. v. Withers, 127 F.3d 1106 (9th Cir. 1997); Phoenix Mutual Life Ins. Co. v. Adams, 30 F.3d 554 (4th Cir. 1994); Cipriani v. Sun Life Ins. Co., 757 F.2d 78 (3d Cir. 1985); Provident Mutual Life Ins. Co. of Phila. V. Ehrlich, 508 F..2d 129 (3d Cir. 1975); Dennis v. Aetna Life Ins. & Annuity Co., 873 F. Supp. 1000 (E.D. Va. 1995); Prudential Ins. Co. v. Bannister, 448 F. Supp. 807 (W.D. Pa 1978); Pimentel v. Conselho Supreme de Union Portuguese ad Estrada ad California, 6 Cal. 2d 182 (Cal. 1936); Saunders v. Severs, 221 Cal. App. 2d 539 (Cal. Dist. Ct. App. 1963); IDS Life Ins. Co. v. Estate of Groton, 112 Idaho 847 (Idaho 1987); State Employees' Retirement System of Illinois, 131 Ill. App. 3d 997 (Ill. 1985); Haynes v. Metropolitan Life Ins. Co., 166 N.J. Super. 308 (N.J. App. Div. 1979); Riley v. Wirth, 313 Pa. 362 (Pa. 1933); Sprout v. Travelers Ins. Co., 289 Pa. 351 (Pa. 1927); Caruthers v. $21,000, 290 Pa. Super. 54 (Pa. Super. 1981); Dale v. Phila. Board of Pensions & Retirement, 702 A.2d 1160 (Pa. Commw. 1997)] Courts find that this equitable doctrine of substantial compliance circumvents "a formalistic, overly technical adherence to the exact words of the change of beneficiary provision in a given [contract]." [Phoenix Mutual Life Ins. Co. v. Adams, 30 F.3d 554, 563 (4th Cir. 1994)]

> **Note.** The doctrine of substantial compliance, which is one manifestation of the doctrine of substantial performance of a contract, has been criticized as defeating freedom of contract. [*See, e.g.,* Grant Gilmore, The Death of Contract 74 (1974)]

A payer's interpleader or other circumstances that make a payer a mere stakeholder do not lessen the need for a claimant to show the participant's substantial compliance with a plan's or contract's procedure for making a beneficiary designation. [*See, e.g.,* McCarthy v. Aetna Life Ins. Co., 681 N.Y.S.2d 790 (N.Y. 1998)]

Q 12:11   Does the doctrine of substantial compliance apply to Section 403(b) contracts under a non-ERISA plan?

Yes, in most states. If ERISA does not preempt state law, a state court likely would apply a relevant state's doctrine of substantial compliance (see Q 12:10).

Q 12:12   Does the doctrine of substantial compliance apply to an ERISA plan?

If a plan is governed by ERISA, the doctrine of substantial compliance should apply only if the plan administrator in its discretion decides to use such a concept to aid its own interpretation or administration of the plan.

To determine the beneficiary under an ERISA plan, a court should hold that any state's doctrine of substantial compliance is preempted. [ERISA § 514; *see* Egelhoff v. Egelhoff, 532 U.S. 141 (2001); *see, e.g.,* Phoenix Mutual Life Ins. Co. v. Adams, 30 F.3d 554 (4th Cir. 1994); Continental Assurance Co. v. Davis, 24 EBC (BNA) 2273 (N.D. Ill. Aug. 11, 2000); Metropolitan Life Ins. Co. v. Hall, 9 F. Supp. 2d 560 (D. Md. 1998); Fortis Benefits Ins. Co. v. Johnson, 966 F. Supp. 987 (D. Nev. 1997); First Capital Life Ins. Co. v. AAA Communications Inc., 906 F. Supp. 1546 (N.D. Ga. 1995)] However, two federal courts have held that a state's common-law doctrine of substantial compliance supplements an ERISA plan's provisions. [Bank America Pension Plan v. McMath, 206 F.3d 821 (1999), *cert. denied* 121 S. Ct. 358 (2000); Peckham v. Gem State Mutual of Utah, 964 F.2d 1043 (10th Cir. 1992)]. In the absence of findings by the plan administrator, the Fourth Circuit found that a state's doctrine of substantial compliance may be replaced by a federal common-law doctrine of substantial compliance. [Phoenix Mutual Life Ins. Co. v. Adams, 30 F.3d 554 (4th Cir. 1994)] Although two of three federal circuits considering the question have held that ERISA does not necessarily preempt a state's doctrine of substantial compliance, the contributing author's view is that ERISA preempts any such law relating to an ERISA plan. [ERISA § 514]

> **Practice Pointer.** Unless a plan provision is contrary to ERISA, an ERISA plan administrator must administer a plan according to the plan's documents. [ERISA § 404(a)] Therefore, if a plan states that any doctrine of substantial compliance will not apply, the plan administrator must interpret and administer the plan without using such a doctrine.

Further, if a plan grants the plan administrator discretion in interpreting or administering the plan, a court will not interfere with the plan administrator's decision unless it was an abuse of discretion. [*See* Firestone Tire & Rubber Co. v. Bruch, 489 U.S. 101 (1989)]

Lost Beneficiary Designation

Q 12:13   What should a plan administrator or payer do if it cannot locate a beneficiary designation because records were destroyed?

Even with prudent efforts to safeguard records, circumstances beyond a plan administrator's, insurer's, or custodian's control might result in the destruction of plan or contract records. If so, a payer should try to "reconstruct" a beneficiary designation using the best evidence available to it.

That records are lost or destroyed does not discharge a payer from its obligation to administer a plan or contract. When deciding whether to pay any benefit to a potential beneficiary, a payer must act in good faith and must use reasonable procedures, especially when deciding who is a participant's beneficiary. When a record is lost or destroyed, a payer may use the most reliable evidence available to it. For example, a claimant might furnish a copy of a beneficiary designation. A payer might use its discretion to rely on a document that appears to be a copy of a participant's beneficiary designation. A payer should do so, however, only if it has adopted and uses reasonable procedures designed to detect a forgery. Further, when a claimant submits evidence that he or she is the participant's beneficiary, a payer must take reasonable steps to consider whether the evidence is credible.

[*See generally* DOL PWBA, FAQs for Plan Sponsors, Fiduciaries and Service Providers Related to the Events of September 11th, http://www.dol.gov/ebsa/faqs/faq_911_3.html (visited Feb. 3, 2008)]

Default Beneficiary Designation

Q 12:14   What happens when a participant did not make a beneficiary designation?

A retirement plan may state a "default" beneficiary designation that applies when the participant did not make a valid beneficiary designation. A typical default provision pays the nondesignated benefit to the personal representative of the participant's estate. (This is not the provision recommended by the contributing author.) An ERISA plan might provide the death benefit to the participant's surviving spouse and then to the participant's personal representative only if there is no surviving spouse.

If, under community-property law (see Qs 12:51–12:55), a portion of the participant's retirement plan benefit belongs or belonged to the participant's spouse, the spouse (or the spouse's beneficiaries or heirs) might have a claim against the participant's personal representative for payment of the spouse's community property. In Alaska, Arkansas, Colorado, Connecticut, Florida, Hawaii, Kentucky, Michigan, Montana, New York, North Carolina, Oregon, Virginia, and Wyoming, the Uniform Disposition of Community Property Rights at Death Act might apply. [*See generally* Unif. Disp. Comm. Prop. Rights at Death Act, 8A U.L.A. 213–227 (2003)]

Laws and External Documents That Might Affect a Beneficiary Designation

Q 12:15   Does a divorce revoke a beneficiary designation?

Whether a divorce revokes a beneficiary designation turns on:

1. whether ERISA or state law governs the retirement plan,

2. which state's law (if any) applies, and

3. what that state's law (when applicable) provides.

Concerning a church plan, a governmental plan, or another non-ERISA plan, state law may apply. In many states, a divorce will not revoke a beneficiary designation that names the ex-spouse. [In Matter of Declaration of Death of Dominick Santos Jr., 282 N.J. Super. 509, 660 A.2d 1206 (1995); Hughes v. Scholl, 900 S.W.2d 606 (KY 1995); Stiles v. Stiles, 21 Mass. App. Ct. 514 (1986);

O'Toole v. Central Laborers' Pension & Welfare Funds, 12 Ill. App. 3d 995 (1973); Gerhard v. Travelers Ins. Co., 107 N.J. Super. 414 (Chancery Div. 1969)] Some states have statutory provisions that attempt to provide that a divorce or annulment has the effect of making the former spouse not a beneficiary except as otherwise specified by a court order. [*See generally* Unif. Probate Code § 2-804(b), 8 pt. I ULA 217 (1998)] Even when the relevant state has such a statute, it might not apply if a contract or account has contrary provisions. Many contracts include a provision that a divorce or anything other than a beneficiary change form accepted by the insurer or custodian has no effect on the beneficiary designation. In any case, state law will protect a payer that pays the beneficiary of record unless the payer has received a court order restraining payment or at least a written notice that states a dispute about who is the lawful beneficiary. [*See generally* Unif. Probate Code §§ 2-804(g), 2-804(h), 8 pt. I ULA 218–219 (1998)]

For an ERISA plan, ERISA preempts all state laws. [ERISA § 514] Therefore, only the plan's terms will govern whether a divorce or other circumstance has any effect on the plan beneficiary designation. [ERISA §§ 404(a), 514; Egelhoff v. Egelhoff, 532 U.S. 141 (2001); Boggs v. Boggs, 520 U.S. 833 (1997), *reh'g denied*, 521 U.S. 1138 (1997)]

Practice Pointer. A plan sponsor should consider whether it might be helpful for a plan to state expressly that any annulment, divorce, marital separation, or other event or circumstance has no effect under the plan.

Practice Pointer. After a divorce, a participant should remember to change or confirm his or her beneficiary designation.

Q 12:16   What happens when a beneficiary designation is contrary to an external agreement?

A payer pays according to the plan's or contract's provisions and applicable law, and need not consider external documents. However, once a payer has paid a beneficiary, a person who has rights under an external agreement may pursue remedies under state law. [*See, e.g.,* Kinkel v. Kinkel, 699 N.E.2d 41 (Ohio 1998) (A custodian correctly paid a participant's named beneficiary, but the participant's children later recovered from the participant's surviving spouse)]

Q 12:17   May an executor participate in a court proceeding concerning a disputed benefit?

Often, no. A personal representative of a participant's estate may participate in a court proceeding concerning a disputed benefit only if the personal representative is a bona fide claimant. If a personal representative does not make any claim of right to the benefit, however, such a personal representative has no justiciable claim or standing to participate in a court proceeding. [*See, e.g.,* Deaton v. Cross, 184 F. Supp. 2d 441 (D. Md. 2002)]

Q 12:18 Why would a divorced participant not want to name his or her young child as a beneficiary?

A divorced participant might not want to name his or her young child as a beneficiary if doing so might have the effect of putting money in the hands of the child's other parent—the participant's former spouse.

A payer wants to be sure that a payment is a satisfaction of the plan or contract. Ordinarily, a beneficiary's deposit or negotiation of a check that pays a retirement plan distribution is the beneficiary's acceptance of the payer's satisfaction of the beneficiary's claim under the plan or contract.

A *minor* is a person still young enough that he or she cannot make a binding contract. At common law, the age of majority was 21. Now, all but three states' laws generally end a person's minor status at age 18.

Before a child reaches age 18 (or the other age of competence to make binding contracts), his or her conservator may disaffirm an agreement or promise the child made. After a child reaches age 18 (or the other "full age"), he or she may disaffirm an agreement or promise he or she made before he or she reached the age of competence to make contracts. [*See generally*, Restatement (Third) of Property: Wills and Other Donative Transfers § 8.2 (2003); Restatement (Second) of Contracts §§ 12–15 (1981)] A payer will not take the risk that paying a distribution is not a satisfaction of plan or contract obligations. Thus, payers usually are unwilling to pay a Section 403(b) plan's or contract's benefit to a minor.

To facilitate payment in these circumstances, most plans permit payment to a minor's conservator, natural guardian, or Uniform Transfers to Minors Act custodian. [*See generally*, Susan N. Gary and Nancy E. Shurtz, Nontax Considerations in Testamentary Transfers to Minors, in Carmine Y. D'Aversa, ed., *Tax, Estate, and Lifetime Planning for Minors* ch. 10 pp. 295–336 (ABA 2006)] If a participant named his or her child as a beneficiary (rather than naming as beneficiary a trustee or custodian), a payer is likely to honor a claim made by the child's conservator. If a child's other parent is living, most courts would maintain or appoint the parent as the child's guardian. In some states, the law presumes that a court should consider a child's parent or natural guardian to serve also as the child's conservator. [*Cf.* Manley v Detroit Auto Inter-Insurance Exchange, 127 Mich. App. 444, (Mich. App. 1983), *motion denied*, 357 N.W.2d 644 (Mich. App. 1983), *remanded on other grounds* 425 Mich. 140 (Mich. 1986) with *In re* Estate of Fisher, 503 So.2d 962 (Fla. App. 1987) (child's "natural guardian" was not the guardian of his property); *see generally* Unif. Probate Code § 5-413(6)-(7), 8 pt. II U.L.A. 390–391 (1998) & Supp. 137--138 (2006)]

Using Trusts

Q 12:19 What is a *living trust*?

A trust refers to a person's right to the beneficial enjoyment of property to which another person holds the legal title. A *living trust* is a trust that is created and takes effect during the settlor's life. [*See generally,* Bryan A. Garner, *Black's Law Dictionary*, 999 (8th ed. 2004)] A typical living trust is revocable. If a living trust is irrevocable, it necessarily involves at least one beneficiary other than the trust's creator. [*See generally,* Restatement (Third) of Trusts, § 2 (2003)]

Q 12:20   Can a participant own his or her Section 403(b) contract in a living trust?

No. If a trust can be revoked or amended, as is customarily permitted with the kind of trust that many people call a living trust (see Q 12:19), the trust declaration or agreement could not ensure that during the participant's lifetime the Section 403(b) benefit will be used only for the participant's benefit. The rights under a Section 403(b) contract must be nonforfeitable for the participant. [I.R.C. § 403(b)(1)(C)]

> **Practice Pointer.** There is no particularly good reason to put a Section 403(b) contract into a living trust. A Section 403(b) contract already is nonprobate property that will pass according to its beneficiary designation.

Q 12:21   Can a trust be a beneficiary of a Section 403(b) contract?

Yes. A participant may name a trust as beneficiary of a Section 403(b) contract or account. The trust must be legally in existence (or completed such that it would be legally in existence upon the trustee's receipt of money or property) before the participant makes the beneficiary designation.

To make a correct beneficiary designation, a participant should designate the trustee, as trustee of the trust, as beneficiary. Even if that is not done, an insurer or custodian might treat a designation of a trust as though it were a designation of the duly appointed and then-currently serving trustee of the trust.

A beneficiary of a trust will not be a designated beneficiary for the purposes of minimum distribution rules (see chapter 10) unless the trust meets specified requirements, which include that the beneficiaries are identifiable under the trust instrument, and certain information is certified to the plan administrator (if any) (see chapter 10). [Treas. Reg. § 1.401(a)(9)-4, Q&A 5]

Q 12:22   What is a *subtrust*?

A *subtrust* is a portion of a trust that is administered according to provisions different from those that apply to other subtrusts or other portions of the whole trust.

In the context of using life insurance to fund retirement plans, the word *subtrust* is used by some lawyers to refer to an estate-planning concept in which a life insurance contract and a subtrust are administered according to trust provisions intended to ensure that the life insurance contract will not be treated as part of the participant/insured's estate for federal estate tax purposes.

Family Rights That Restrain a Beneficiary Designation

Failing to Provide for a Spouse

Q 12:23   May a participant make a beneficiary designation that does not provide for his or her spouse?

The validity of a beneficiary designation that does not provide for a participant's spouse turns on whether:

- The plan is governed by ERISA or by state law;
- The plan is a governmental plan, a church plan, or neither of those; or
- The plan states any provisions beyond those required by other applicable law.

Q 12:24   May an ERISA plan participant make a beneficiary designation that does not provide for his or her spouse?

No, unless his or her spouse consents. To the extent that a Section 403(b) contract is held under an ERISA plan, a participant's beneficiary designation that fails to provide for his or her spouse will be invalid, either for 100 percent of the death benefit or the value of the plan's qualified preretirement survivor annuity (QPSA), whichever is provided by the plan, unless the participant made a qualified election that was supported by the spouse's notarized consent (see chapter 9). [ERISA § 205]

Just as a person who is not yet a spouse cannot give a spouse's consent (see Q 12:34), a participant who is not yet divorced or separated cannot change his or her beneficiary without his or her spouse's consent. [ERISA § 205; see Davis v. College Suppliers Co., 813 F. Supp. 1234 (S.D. Miss. 1993); Merchant v. Corder, 1999 U.S. App. LEXIS 15689 (4th Cir. July 12, 1999)]

If an ERISA plan was not amended to state a QPSA or other spouse's death benefit as required by the Retirement Equity Act of 1984, a surviving spouse (who has not consented otherwise) is nonetheless entitled to a QPSA or, if the plan does not provide any benefit as an annuity, the entire account balance. [See, e.g., Lefkowitz v. Arcadia Trading Co., 996 F.2d 600 (2d Cir. 1993)]

The rule that a spouse's consent must be witnessed by a notary or plan representative is strict. Even when a spouse admitted that she signed the spouse's consent, it was not valid without a notary's certificate. [Lasche v. George W Lasche Basic Profit Sharing Plan, 111 F.3d 863 (11th Cir. 1997)]

Q 12:25   May a governmental plan participant make a beneficiary designation that does not provide for his or her spouse?

Many governmental *pension* plans have a survivor annuity or spouse's consent provision; but this kind of provision is less common for a public schools employer's Section 403(b) plan.

If Louisiana's law applies, a distributee who receives benefits under a retirement plan of a governmental employer is not subject to the claims of forced heirs. [La. Civ. Code Ann. art. 1505]

Q 12:26   May a church plan participant make a beneficiary designation that does not provide for his or her spouse?

Many church plans have a survivor annuity or spouse's consent provision.

Example. The ELCA Retirement Plan of the Evangelical Lutheran Church in America does not recognize a participant's designation of a beneficiary other than his or her spouse unless there is no spouse or the spouse consented, in the presence of a notary, on the form required by the ELCA Board of Pensions. [*See* ELCA Retirement Plan, Summary Plan Description at pages 16–19 (effective Jan. 1, 2008) (available at http://www.elcabop.org)]

Q 12:27   May a Section 403(b) participant under a non-ERISA plan make a beneficiary designation that does not provide for his or her spouse?

Usually, yes. To the extent that a Section 403(b) contract is not held under an ERISA-governed plan and the plan does not state a survivor annuity or spouse's consent provision, an insurer or custodian will, in the absence of any court order or written notice of a dispute, give effect to a participant's beneficiary designation.

If the participant's spouse did not receive his or her share provided by state law, a distributee might be liable to the participant's personal representative or surviving spouse to the extent that state law provides for a spouse's elective share to be payable from nonprobate property. [*See generally* Unif. Probate Code § 2-204, 8 pt. I ULA 104–105 (1998)]

In Louisiana, a payer may follow a participant's beneficiary designation. [La. Rev. Stat. §§ 23:638, 23:652] Nonetheless, a distributee who receives benefits under a church plan or another nongovernmental Section 403(b) plan (including a plan that is not a plan within the meaning of ERISA) must account for and pay over benefits to the participant's surviving spouse to the extent that payment is necessary to satisfy the spouse's community-property rights and usufruct. [TL James & Co. v. Montgomery, 332 So. 2d 834 (La. 1976)]

Different law may apply for members of a native American tribe. [Jones v. Meehan, 175 U.S. 1 (1899); *see also* Davis v. Shanks, 15 Minn. 369 (1870); Hasting v. Farmer, 4 N.Y. 293 (1850); Dole v. Irish, 2 Barb. 639 (1848)] However, a native American tribe's law usually applies between or among members of the tribe and often cannot be enforced against persons outside the tribe.

Q 12:28   Must a payer tell an ex-spouse when a participant changes his or her beneficiary designation contrary to a court order?

No, in the absence of a court order that commands the payer to furnish specified information, a payer has no duty to furnish information about a particular beneficiary designation change:

> Absent a promise or misrepresentation, the courts have almost uniformly rejected claims by plan participants or beneficiaries that an ERISA administrator has to volunteer individualized information taking account of their peculiar circumstances. This view reflects ERISA's focus on limited and general reporting and disclosure requirements [citations omitted], and also reflects the enormous burdens an obligation to proffer individualized advice would inflict on plan administrators.

[Barrs v. Lockheed Martin Corp., 287 F.2d 202 (1st Cir. 2002)] Even when a plan administrator is governed by ERISA Section 404's greatest fiduciary duties, courts have not required a plan administrator to furnish an alternate payee information beyond that required by an express statutory or plan provision. For a non-ERISA plan, it seems unlikely that a court would impose a duty greater than federal courts have applied concerning ERISA plans.

Failing to Provide for a Child

Q 12:29   Can a participant make a beneficiary designation that does not provide for his or her child?

In the United States, only Louisiana and Puerto Rico provide a forced share for a decedent's children. In Louisiana, a person generally cannot entirely disinherit his or her child who is under age 23 or under a permanent disability. [*See* La. Rev. Civil Code, art. 1493–1495] Puerto Rico has similar provisions to protect children. [P.R. Laws title 31 § 2362, §§ 2411–2463] In other states, a participant usually may disinherit his or her children. In some states, a modest family allowance sometimes is required for the surviving spouse or, if there is no surviving spouse, the decedent's children. [*See generally,* Unif. Probate Code §§ 2-403, 2-204, 8 pt. I ULA 141–142 (1998) & Supp. 34–35 (2006)]

In Louisiana, a plan administrator may follow the participant's beneficiary designation. [La. Rev. Stat. §§ 23:638, 23:652] A distributee who receives benefits under a church plan or another nongovernmental plan must account for and pay over benefits to the participant's surviving spouse to the extent that payment is necessary to satisfy the spouse's community property rights and usufruct and to the participant's children or forced heirs to the extent that payment is necessary to satisfy their légitime. [TL James & Co v. Montgomery, 332 So. 2d 834 (La. 1976)] A distributee who receives benefits under a governmental plan is not subject to the claims of forced heirs. [La. Civ. Code Ann. Art. 1505]

Different law may apply for members of a native American tribe. [Jones v. Meehan, 175 U.S. 1 (1899); *see also* Davis v. Shanks, 15 Minn. 369 (1870); Hasting v. Farmer, 4 N.Y. 293 (1850); Dole v. Irish, 2 Barb. 639 (1848)]

Whether it is called légitime, legitimate portions, or compulsory portions in civil-law nations, family provision or family maintenance in nations following English law, or ahl al-fara'id under the Koran, in most nations other than the United States, a person is limited in his or her right or privilege to "disinherit" his or her children. [*See, e.g.,* Egypt, Law of Testamentary Dispositions of 1946, Law of Inheritance of 1943; England and Wales, Inheritance (Provision for Family and Dependants) Act 1975; India-Pakistan, Muslim Family Laws Ordinance of 1961]

Practice Pointer. A participant who resides in a nation other than the United States should consult an expert lawyer before he or she makes a beneficiary designation that does not provide for his or her spouse and children.

Spouse's Rights

Q 12:30   What are the ways a participant's surviving spouse might have rights to a participant's Section 403(b) benefit?

A participant's surviving spouse might have the following rights to a participant's Section 403(b) benefit:

1. Survivor-annuity or spouse's consent rights provided by the plan;
2. Elective-share rights under state law; or
3. Community property rights under state law.

ERISA Survivor Benefits

Q 12:31   What benefits must an ERISA plan provide to a participant's spouse?

For a distribution that begins before a participant's death, a plan must, unless an exception applies, provide a qualified joint and survivor annuity (QJSA) (see Q 12:32). [ERISA §§ 205(a)(1), 205(b)]

Ordinarily, a defined contribution plan that is not governed by ERISA funding standards need not provide a QJSA as long as a participant does not elect that his or her retirement benefit be paid as a life annuity. [ERISA § 205(b)(1)(C)(ii)]

Practice Pointer. Previously, the IRS had an informal view that merely providing an annuity as a plan's default distribution option was in effect a participant's election of that annuity for the purposes of the survivor annuity rule. The IRS no longer takes that position. Nonetheless, if a plan provides a life annuity as a normal form of benefit, a plan sponsor may amend the plan to provide that every annuity is an optional form of benefit or to eliminate every annuity option. Such an amendment is not a cutback of accrued benefits. [ERISA § 204(g)(2)(B); Treas. Reg. § 1.411(d)-4, Q&A-2(e)] Once the amendment is effective, the plan need not provide a QJSA unless (if the plan permits) a participant affirmatively chooses it or chooses a different life annuity and fails to deliver a qualified election.

Caution. Some practitioners suggest designing or amending a plan to preclude annuity options. Moreover, some suggest that a plan not provide any form of benefit beyond a single sum. Although nothing in ERISA restrains a plan sponsor from making such a provision or amendment, a plan sponsor might consider whether an absence of some options would make it difficult or impossible for a distribution to obtain favorable treatment as a "pension" under state income tax laws. [See, e.g., N.Y. Tax Law §§ 612, 617-a; 72 PS § 7303; 61 Pa. Code § 101.6(c); Bickford v. Commonwealth, 533 A.2d 822 (Pa. 1987)]

For a distribution that begins after a participant's death, a plan must provide a qualified preretirement survivor annuity (see Q 12:33) or an alternate survivor benefit (see Q 12:34). [ERISA §§ 205(a)(2), 205(b)]

Q 12:32 What is a qualified joint and survivor annuity?

A qualified joint and survivor annuity (QJSA) is an annuity for the participant's life with a survivor annuity for his or her surviving spouse's life. The periodic payment of the survivor annuity must be no less than 50 percent (and no more than 100 percent) of the payment during the joint lives of the participant and his or her spouse. A QJSA is the actuarial equivalent of an annuity only on the participant's life. [ERISA § 205(d)]

Note. If an ERISA-governed plan provides a QJSA, the plan must permit a participant to elect that his or her benefit be paid as a qualified optional survivor annuity. A qualified optional survivor annuity (QOSA) means a joint-and-survivor annuity that includes a recurring payment in its survivor phase that's equal to the applicable percentage of the payment during the participant's life. If a plan's normal QJSA provides a survivor-phase payment that is less than 75 percent of the payment during the participant's life, the applicable percentage is 75. If a plan's normal QJSA provides a survivor-phase payment that is at least 75 percent of the payment during the participant's life, the applicable percentage is 50. As with other survivor annuity forms, a qualified optional survivor annuity must be at least the actuarial equivalent of a single-life annuity for the participant's life. A plan that is required to provide a survivor annuity must provide at least two different QJSAs, in addition to a QPSA. A plan administrator's written explanations of a plan's survivor annuity options must explain all of the options, including the new QOSA. The minimum election period for survivor annuity choices is 180 days. A plan amendment made solely to meet the QOSA requirement generally does not violate the anti-cutback rule. However, this anti-cutback relief does not protect taking away a subsidized QJSA unless an equivalent or greater subsidy remains in at least one of the amended plan's other payout forms of that kind. The new law requiring these

QOSA provisions applies to plan years that begin on or after January 1, 2008. A later date could apply to a plan maintained under a collective bargaining agreement. [ERISA § 205(c)-(d), as amended by PPA § 1004]

Q 12:33   What is a qualified preretirement survivor annuity?

For a defined-contribution plan, a qualified preretirement survivor annuity (QPSA) is the annuity that results from using no less than half the participant's vested account balance to buy an annuity for the surviving spouse's life. [ERISA § 205(e)(2)]

Q 12:34   What is an alternative survivor benefit?

A defined contribution plan that is not governed by ERISA funding standards may omit both a QJSA and a QPSA if the plan (in addition to meeting other conditions) provides that, absent a qualified election, the benefit that remains after a participant's death belongs to the participant's surviving spouse. [ERISA § 205(b)(1)(C)]

Q 12:35   What is a qualified election?

A Section 403(b) plan governed by ERISA may include a provision that assures a participant's surviving spouse some retirement income after the participant's death and must include a provision that assures a survivor benefit if the participant dies before plan distributions begin. [ERISA § 205] A plan must permit a participant to "waive" one or more of these benefits. [ERISA § 205(c)(1)(A)] To do so, the participant must deliver to the plan administrator a qualified election. [ERISA § 205(c)(2)] Ordinarily, such an election has no effect unless the participant's spouse consents to the election. [ERISA § 205(c)(2)(A)] In addition, a participant's qualified election must meet several form, content, and procedure requirements.

Q 12:36   Who is a spouse?

In some circumstances, it can be unclear, for the purposes of ERISA Section 205, whether a person is or is not a spouse, and which of two or more persons is a participant's spouse or surviving spouse.

ERISA states no definition for its use of the word spouse. Further, ERISA states no provision concerning whether a putative spouse is or is not a spouse for any purpose of ERISA Section 205.

Q 12:37   When a participant is survived by a spouse and a putative spouse, which one is treated as the participant's surviving spouse?

There is no rule; whether a putative spouse, a real spouse, both, or neither is treated as a participant's spouse depends on a plan administrator's, arbitrator's, or judge's thoughts about what might be desirable in the particular circumstances.

The following two cases had opposite results. In the contributing author's view, neither court explained the real reason for its decision.

Example 1. In 1965, John and Susie married in Louisiana. In 1970, a Louisiana court ordered a judgment of separation, but not any divorce or dissolution of their marriage. In 1973, Susie, while still married to John, "married" Milton. In 2000, John, while still married to Susie, "married" Gwendolyn in Texas. In 2001, John died (while still married to Susie and "married" to Gwendolyn). He was domiciled in Texas when he died. After John's death, each of Susie and Gwendolyn submitted a claim to his pension plan for a survivor annuity; each claimed that she was John's surviving spouse. The pension plan included the following provision: "All questions pertaining to the validity of construction of this Pension Plan shall be determined in accordance with the laws of the State of Illinois and, to the extent of preemption[,] with the laws and regulations of the United States." (As cited below, these are the relevant facts of a real case.) In resolving the plan administrator's interpleader, the court considered whether to apply Louisiana law, Texas law, Illinois law, or some combination of them in deciding which claimant (if either) was John's surviving spouse. Notwithstanding that neither of the claimants had argued for it, the court chose Texas law. Further, the court used Texas *property* law to resolve the *status* question needed to apply an ERISA plan's provision that preempts state law. Following this, the court found that Susie's acceptance of the benefits of her fraudulent "marriage" to Milton precluded her from asserting that she was John's surviving spouse, and recognized Gwendolyn as an innocent putative spouse to be treated as if she had been a spouse. [Central States, S.E. & S.W. Areas Pension Fund v. Gray, 2003 U.S. Dist. LEXIS 18282 (N.D. Ill. Oct. 10, 2003)]

Example 2. In 1966, Douglas married Ann in Ohio. They lived together in Ohio from 1966 to 1982. In 1972, Douglas began a relationship with Rita. In 1982, Ann left Douglas and moved to Tennessee. In 1985, Douglas and Rita "married" in Nevada. Each of Ann and Rita submitted claims for several benefits to be provided to Douglas' surviving spouse. The pension plan provided that it "shall be construed, governed[,] and administered in accordance with the laws of the State of Michigan[,] except where [sic] otherwise required by Federal law." In resolving the plan administrator's interpleader, the court considered whether to apply federal law, Michigan law, or Ohio law, or some combination of them in deciding which claimant (if either) was John's surviving spouse.

Note. In both of these cases, the court did not apply the contractual choice of law and, even further, ignored the plan's provision that the plan be construed using the plan-specified state law.

Note. Courts' procedures for an interpleader, which focus on the arguments of the competing claimants and often do not require a stakeholder to assert a position, increase the likelihood that a court will render a decision that is unhelpful for future plan administration. [*See, e.g.*, Croskey v. Ford Motor Company-UAW, 28 Employee Benefits Cas. (BNA) 1438, (S.D.N.Y. May 6, 2002)]

Practice Pointer. Before deciding to interplead competing claims, a fiduciary should consider which person or persons will pay the attorneys' fees and other expenses of the interpleader. If the plan might bear the expenses, a fiduciary should consider whether paying the expenses is a prudent or necessary use of plan assets. Instead, a plan administrator might use claims procedures and the deference afforded to a discretionary decision-maker to protect the plan against "double" liability, while setting up some opportunity for lower expenses (or at least delaying an expense), or even no incremental expense.

Q 12:38 What must a spouse do to consent to a participant's qualified election?

In addition to meeting other form, content, and procedure requirements, a spouse's consent to a participant's election (see Q 12:35) must:

1. Be in writing;
2. Name a beneficiary that cannot be changed without the spouse's consent or expressly consent to the participant's beneficiary designations (without further consent); and
3. Acknowledge the effect of the participant's election.

[ERISA § 205(c)(2)(A)(i)]

Further, a consent has no effect unless "the spouse's consent . . . is witnessed by a plan representative or a notary public[.]" [ERISA § 205(c)(2)(A)(iii)] A premarital agreement cannot serve as a spouse's consent.

Courts have held that a plan administrator must comply with these requirements, even if there is no doubt that a spouse's consent was informed, voluntary, and genuine. [*See, e.g.*, McMillan v. Parrott, 913 F.2d 310 (6th Cir. 1990); Lasche v. George W. Lasche Basic Retirement Plan, 870 F. Supp. 336, 338, (S.D. Fla. 1994); *see also* Alfieri v. Guild Times Pension Plan, 446 F. Supp. 2d 99 (E.D.N.Y. 2006)] A spouse's sworn statement in his or her spouse's consent that the spouse consents to the participant's beneficiary designation is ineffective if in fact the beneficiary-designation part of the documents had not been completed when the spouse signed. [ERISA § 205(c)(2)(A); Davis v. Adelphia Communications Corp., 475 F. Supp. 2d 600 (W.D. Va. 2007); *but see* Vilas v. Lyons, 702 F. Supp. 555 (D. Md. 1988) (a plan administrator may rely on a spouse's sworn statement that he or she received and read the required explanation of the spouse's rights)]

Q 12:39 May a spouse's guardian sign the spouse's consent?

Yes. Even if the electing participant is the spouse's guardian, he or she may give the spouse's consent. [Treas. Reg. § 1.401(a)-20, Q&A-27] However, a guardian must act in the best interests of his or her ward. A guardian serves under a court's supervision and must account for his or her actions in court. Further, some guardianship decisions require a court's approval before the guardian implements the decision. [*See generally*, Unif. Probate Code § 2-206, 8 pt. I ULA 115–118 (1998)] It may be difficult to persuade a court that turning away money is in a surviving spouse's best interest. Although a participant may suggest making an irrevocable designation naming a trust for his or her spouse's benefit as the plan beneficiary, most retirement plans do not permit an irrevocable beneficiary designation.

Q 12:40   May proof of a spouse's consent be given in an electronic notarization?

Yes, but not really.

A Treasury regulation allows a notary's or plan representative's certificate to be furnished by electronic means, but requires that the spouse's consent have been signed in the physical presence of the notary or plan representative. [Treas. Reg. § 1.401(a)-21(d)(6)(i)&(ii)]

Note. An electronic notarization is useful if each relying person has arranged in advance to receive and inspect an electronic apostille concerning a particular notary's electronic credentials. A capacity to accept electronic notarizations can be useful to those businesses and government agencies that process a large volume of transactions that depend on authenticated signatures. But a typical retirement plan, even if it has many claims and distributions, does not have enough claims that require a spouse's consent to motivate the plan's administrator to put effort and resources into arrangements for receiving electronic notarizations.

Q 12:41   Who is a plan representative?

ERISA does not define its use of the term *plan representative*. [ERISA §§ 3, 205] Nor does the legislative history of the Retirement Equity Act of 1984 explain what Congress meant by a plan representative. [S. Rep. No. 98-575 to accompany H.R. 4280, 98th Cong., 2d Sess. (1984), *reprinted in* 1984 USCCAN 2547, 2560]

Many practitioners assume that a person is a plan representative for the limited purpose of administering a plan's provisions required or permitted by ERISA Section 205 if the plan administrator has authorized the person to witness a spouse's consent.

In a case that involved facts and forms typical of a retirement plan's service arrangements, a federal court found that the litigants who asserted that a spouse's consent had been witnessed did not offer enough evidence even to allege that a securities broker-dealer's employee was a plan representative. [Lasche v. George W Lasche Basic Retirement Plan, 870 F. Supp. 336, 339 (S.D. Fla. 1994)]

Q 12:42 Who is a notary?

ERISA does not define its use of the term *notary public*. [ERISA §§ 3, 205] Nor does the legislative history of the Retirement Equity Act of 1984 explain what Congress meant by a notary public. [S. Rep. No. 98-575 to accompany H.R. 4280, 98th Cong., 2d Sess. (1984), *reprinted in* 1984 USCCAN 2547, 2560]

Many practitioners assume that Congress intended to describe a person state law recognizes as one whose certificate that he or she witnessed an acknowledgment will be recognized as conclusive evidence that the acknowledgment was made. Usually, a recognized official's certificate that he or she witnessed an acknowledgment is conclusive evidence that the acknowledgment was made. [*See generally* Unif. Acknowledgment Act §§ 9–10, 12 ULA 16–19 (1996) & Supp. 2 (2003)] In most states, an acknowledgment may be made before a judge, court clerk, recorder of deeds, or notary. [*See generally* Unif. Acknowledgment Act §§ 2–3, 12 ULA 8–10 (1996)] In New Jersey, a lawyer, if he or she is a licensed attorney, may certify an acknowledgment or affidavit. [NJSA § 41:2-1]

When a person is not present in the United States, his or her acknowledgment may be made before a U.S. ambassador, consul, consular officer, or consular agent. [22 U.S.C. §§ 4215, 4221]

Q 12:43 How may a person in military service make an acknowledgment?

A person who is:

1. A member of the armed forces;
2. A former member of the armed forces entitled to retired or retainer pay and legal assistance, or the dependent of an active or former member if the dependent is entitled to legal assistance;
3. A person serving with, employed by, or accompanying the armed forces outside the United States; or
4. A person governed by the Uniform Code of Military Justice outside the United States

may make his or her acknowledgment, affidavit, deposition, or other statement that calls for a notarial act before a military officer described below. [10 U.S.C. §§ 1044, 1044a(a)(1)–(4)]

The following persons may officiate and certify a notarial act:

1. A judge advocate or reserve judge advocate;
2. A civilian attorney who serves as a legal assistance attorney;
3. An adjutant, assistant adjutant, or personnel adjutant, whether on active or reserve duty; or
4. A person designated by another statute or by a regulation of any of the armed forces.

[10 U.S.C. § 1044a(b)(1)–(4)]

Q 12:44   Must a notary be independent of the participant?

Yes. Although nothing in ERISA Section 205 requires that a witness to a spouse's consent be independent of the electing participant, at least two courts have interpreted the statute to include such a requirement:

> [T]he district court focused on the fact that the notary public before whom Mr. Jensen had purportedly signed the document was Mrs. Jensen herself—a circumstance that the court concluded would render the document ineffective as a spousal waiver. The court explained its thinking thus: Generally, it is considered contrary to public policy for a notary to take an acknowledgement of an instrument to which he or she is a party. [citation omitted] [C]ongress, through the [Retirement Equity Act], wanted a spouse to carefully consider a decision to waive retirement benefits without pressure from the other spouse and so imposed the requirement that the waiver be witnessed by a plan representative or a notary. To permit a spouse to act as notary to an instrument concerning their own benefits would appear to undermine this congressional intent.

[Howard v. Branham & Baker Coal Co., No. 91-5913, 968 F.2d 1214 (Table) (6th Cir. 1992) (unpublished disposition), *quoting and affirming* No. 90-00115 (E.D. Ky.) (unpublished order); *accord* Lasche v. George W. Lasche Basic Retirement Plan, 870 F. Supp. 336, 339 (S.D. Fla. 1994)]

The federal courts' view is consistent with state laws concerning when a notary properly may officiate and the legal effect of a notary's certificate that he or she witnessed an acknowledgment. [1 Am. Jur. 2d Acknowledgments § 16]

Q 12:45   Must a plan representative be independent of the participant?

Yes. Although nothing in ERISA Section 205 requires that a witness to a spouse's consent be independent of the electing participant, at least one federal court has interpreted the statute to include such a requirement. A plan administrator who was the same person as the electing participant could not, even though he was a plan representative (or even if he was the only plan representative), witness his spouse's consent. [Lasche v. George W. Lasche Basic Retirement Plan, 870 F. Supp. 336, 339 (S.D. Fla. 1994)]

Practice Pointer. If a lawyer or financial planner who advises a participant about making a beneficiary designation that would provide for anyone other than the participant's spouse knows that the participant also is a plan administrator, trustee, or other fiduciary, the lawyer or planner should advise the participant to ask his or her spouse to sign the consent in the presence of an independent notary. Failing to give that advice might be malpractice.

Because ERISA permits a plan administrator to rely on a spouse's consent witnessed by a notary, it seems unlikely that a federal court would find that it could be prudent for a plan administrator to rely on a spouse's consent witnessed only by the interested participant or someone who is subordinate to the interested participant. [ERISA §§ 205(c)(6), 404(a)(1)]

Q 12:46   What should a plan administrator do if it relied on a notary's false or incorrect certificate?

If a plan administrator acted according to ERISA's fiduciary duties when it decided to accept a spouse's consent, the consent (or purported consent), even if not properly witnessed, nonetheless discharges the plan from liability to the extent of the payments made before the plan administrator knew that the consent did not meet the requirements of ERISA Section 205 and of the plan. [ERISA § 205(c)(6)] If the plan administrator acted according to ERISA's fiduciary duties, it is not liable to the spouse. [ERISA § 404(a)(1)] Of course, the plan administrator must promptly correct or stop payments once it knows that a spouse's consent was not properly witnessed.

If a plan incurs an expense because the plan administrator relied on a notary's certificate, the plan's fiduciary may be under a duty to evaluate whether it is in the plan's best interest to pursue a claim or lawsuit against the notary. [ERISA § 404(a)(1)] A notary is responsible for damages caused by his or her negligent performance of his or her duties. [John D. Perovich, Annotation, Liability of Notary Public or His Bond for Negligence in Performance of Duties, 44 ALR 3d 555 (1972); Kenneth W. Biedzynski, 58 Am. Jur. 2d Notaries Public (Liability for Notarial Acts—Negligent Acknowledgment) § 60 (2002)]

Q 12:47   Is a plan administrator protected from liability if it relied on a participant's statement about why his or her spouse's consent was not needed?

Maybe. ERISA includes the following protection from liability: "If a plan fiduciary acts in accordance with part 4 of this subtitle [ERISA's fiduciary-responsibility provisions] in . . . making a determination under paragraph (2) [concerning whether the participant's spouse consented to the participant's election, or whether such a consent was excused], then such . . . determination shall be treated as valid for purposes of discharging *the plan* from liability *to the extent of* payments made pursuant to such Act [sic]." [ERISA § 205(c)(6) (emphasis added)] Some statements in the Retirement Equity Act's legislative history suggest total relief: "If the plan administrator acts in accordance with the fiduciary standards of ERISA . . . in accepting the representations of the participant that the spouse's consent cannot be obtained, then the plan will not be liable for payments to the surviving spouse." [Senate Rep. No. 575, 98th Cong., 2d Sess. 14 (1984), *reprinted in* 1984 U.S.C.C.A.N. 2547, 2560] But one court construed the "to the extent" phrase to mean that a plan must pay the surviving spouse an amount or amounts based on what remains of the benefit that would have been provided in the absence of the participant's false election after subtracting the amounts the plan paid. [Hearn v. Western Conference of Teamsters Pension Trust Fund, 68 F.3d 301 (9th Cir. 1995)]

Caution. Under the Ninth Circuit's precedent, a plan might be liable to pay some benefit to a participant's surviving spouse despite the fact that, because the plan administrator did not breach any fiduciary duty, the plan has no claim by which the plan can obtain extra money to pay the surviving spouse. Thus, the expense of paying a benefit to the surviving spouse is an expense that the plan administrator must allocate to other plan accounts and, unless the plan provides otherwise, may allocate to other participants' and beneficiaries' accounts.

Elective-Share Rights

Q 12:48   What is an elective-share right?

In almost all states that do not provide community property (see Qs 12:51–12:55), a decedent's surviving spouse may elect to take a share of the decedent's property, even if the decedent's will and other transfers had not provided for his or her spouse. [*See generally*, Restatement (Third) of Property: Wills and Other Donative Transfers § 9.1(a) (2003)]

Q 12:49   How much is a surviving spouse's elective share?

In many states, a surviving spouse's elective share is one-third of the decedent's estate. In a few, it is one-half. [*See generally*, Restatement (Third) of Property: Wills and Other Donative Transfers § 9.1(a) (2003)]

In some states, the elective-share percentage increases under a schedule based on the duration of the marriage. A typical schedule has an elective-share percentage that ranges from 3 percent for a marriage that lasted one year to 50 percent for a marriage of 15 years or more.

Q 12:50   Is an elective share computed on all property?

Some states compute an elective share only on probate property. But many states now provide that an elective share is computed on an augmented estate that includes several items of nonprobate property. [*See generally*, Restatement (Third) of Property: Wills and Other Donative Transfers § 9.1(b)-(c) (2003)] Further, some states have detailed rules for counting this augmented estate. [*See generally* Unif. Probate Code §§ 2-203–2-210, 8 pt. I U.L.A. 103-125 (1998) & Supp. 31–33 (2006)]

Community Property

Q 12:51   What is *community property*?

Community property is a term of art that lawyers use to refer to a regime that treats each item of property acquired by either spouse of a married couple during the marriage and while the couple are domiciled in a community property state (see Q 12:52) as owned equally by each spouse. Each spouse's ownership exists presently, notwithstanding that the other spouse currently may hold title to or have control over the property. Generally, a right under a Section 403(b) plan or contract is community property to the extent earned during the marriage and while the participant was domiciled in a community-property state. Although it is sometimes difficult to evaluate when a retirement plan interest was "earned," a typical community-property regime will treat an individual-account retirement plan right as earned during the marriage to the extent that contributions were made while the participant was married and domiciled in a community-property jurisdiction. In Wisconsin, the nonparticipant's community-property right in a retirement plan or deferred compensation plan (including a Section 403(b) contract) terminates on the nonparticipant's death if the nonparticipant's death occurs before the participant's death. [Wis. Stat. Ann. §§ 766.31(3), 766.62(5)]

> **Note.** A typical community-property statute refers to a community of *spouses*, and often provides no useful definition concerning what the word "spouse" means. Even if a state does not recognize same-sex marriages made in the state, it is less clear whether a state would recognize a same-sex couple's marriage or quasi-marriage made in another state. Further, a court might apply community-property law to protect the expectations of a non-spouse in a relationship that, in a judge's view, resembled marriage.

In a separate-property system (which applies in 41 states and all U.S. territories and possessions other than Puerto Rico), an item of property normally belongs to the person who has title to it, paid for it, earned it, or otherwise acquired it. Although any property owned by a married person may become subject to equitable distribution upon a divorce or other marital dissolution, the property belongs completely to the person who owns it until a court makes an order. (For more information on domestic relations orders, see chapter 13.)

Q 12:52   Which states are community property states?

Arizona, California, Idaho, Louisiana, Nevada, New Mexico, Puerto Rico, Texas, Washington, and Wisconsin are community property jurisdictions.

Community property law varies considerably from state to state. For example, if all Section 403(b) contributions under a plan or contract were made before the participant was married but investment earnings accrued after the marriage, some states would classify the entire plan or contract (including investment earnings) as separate property, while others might classify those investment earnings that accrued after the marriage as community property.

Wisconsin is the only state to have adopted as its community property law the Uniform Marital Property Act recommended by the National Conference of Commissioners on Uniform State Laws. [Wis. Stat. §§ 766.001–766.97; *see generally*, Unif. Marital Property Act, 9A pt. I U.L.A. 103-158 (1998) & Supp. 24–27 (2004)]

Alaska gives its married residents a choice of whether to use a separate property regime or a community property regime. The separate property regime applies unless the married couple agree to use a community property regime.

If the couple choose community property, they may use a written community property agreement or a community property trust to vary some of the state law provisions that otherwise would govern their community property. [Alaska Stat. § 34.77.020 et seq.]

Q 12:53 May community property law be applied to nonspouses?

Maybe. In a state that applies community-property law to determine the property rights of married persons but does not recognize common-law marriage, a court might apply community-property law to protect the expectations of a nonspouse in a relationship that, in a judge's view, resembled marriage. Arizona, California, and Louisiana provide community-property rights to a putative spouse, but not to a meretricious nonspouse. [Stevens v. Anderson, 75 Ariz. 331 (Ariz. 1953); Calif. Civil Code § 4452; La. Civil Code Ann. Arts. 117–118] Even for a couple in which neither person believed that he or she was married or had a spouse, Washington applies community-property law to a couple who have or had a "committed intimate relationship" (whether opposite-sex or same-sex), and may do so even after a relationship's end that results from either person's death. [Olver v. Fowler, 168 P.3d 348 (2007); Vasquez v. Hawthorne, 145 Wash. 2d 103 (Wash. 2001); Connell v. Francisco, 127 Wash. 2d 339 (Wash. 1995); Warden v. Warden, 36 Wash. App. 693 (1984); *In re* Marriage of Lindsey, 101 Wash. 2d 299 (Wash. 1984); *In re* Brenchley's Estate, 96 Wash. 223 (Wash. 1917)]

Other legal theories for adjusting the property rights of putative spouses or meretricious spouses include express or implied contract, partnership, and unjust enrichment.

Q 12:54 How does community property law affect payment of benefits under a Section 403(b) plan that is governed by ERISA?

Not at all. ERISA preempts state laws that relate to an ERISA 403(b) plan. [ERISA § 514]

Instead, ERISA provides its own rules designed to protect a spouse [ERISA § 205] (see chapter 9 on survivor annuity requirements) or surviving spouse [ERISA § 205] (see chapter 9 on death benefit beneficiary designations) or to accept a court order that divides a participant's benefit to provide a benefit for the participant's spouse or former spouse. [ERISA § 206(d)(3)] (See chapter 13 on qualified domestic relations orders.)

Q 12:55 How does community property law affect death benefits under a Section 403(b) contract that is not held under an ERISA plan?

If a participant in a Section 403(b) contract that is not subject to ERISA designates a beneficiary other than his or her spouse for more than half of (or, more precisely, the participant's separate property plus community property rights in) his or her account balance or annuity value, the spouse may have a right under state law to obtain a court order invalidating the beneficiary designation, or at least as much of it as would leave the spouse with less than half of, or the spouse's community property right in, the benefit.

Nevertheless, an insurer, custodian, or other payer may pay based on the beneficiary designation it has on record until it receives a court order restraining payment or written notice that the spouse asserts his or her rights.

Tenancy by the Entirety

Q 12:56   What is *tenancy by the entirety*?

A *tenancy by the entirety* is a form of concurrent property ownership that recognizes the special unity of a married couple. A tenancy by the entirety can be created only if required unities of title, interest, possession, time, and person (a valid marriage) all exist. [Restatement (First) of Property § 67] Along with other requirements, two persons can become cotenants in a tenancy by the entirety only if they are legally married. Unlike other kinds of joint tenancy, each of the two spouses owns all of the property. However, neither spouse acting alone can dispose of the property. A tenancy by the entirety ends on the death of either spouse, or on the divorce or other dissolution of the marriage. Of those states that recognize tenancy by the entirety as an available form of property ownership, some allow it only for *real property* (such as a couple's home), and some allow it for both real property and personal property (see Q 12:58). [*See generally*, Restatement (Third) of Property: Wills and Other Donative Transfers § 6.2, reporter's note 13 to comment f (2003)]

Q 12:57   Why might a person want to own property in a tenancy by the entirety?

Because neither spouse alone can dispose of the property (see Q 12:56), a tenancy by the entirety may provide useful protection against the claims of creditors. For example, if only one of the two spouses is bankrupt, the bankruptcy trustee generally cannot reach property held in a tenancy by the entirety.

Practice Pointer. For a detailed explanation of protections from creditor that may result from a tenancy by the entirety, see Lewis D. Solomon and Lewis J. Saret, Asset Protection Strategies (Aspen Publishers, 2007).

However, a Section 403(b) participant might not need the protection that a tenancy by the entirety, when available, could provide. A benefit under an ERISA plan is not subject to the claims of the participant's creditors (other than the plan itself). [ERISA §§ 206(d)(1), 514] Likewise, a Section 403(b) benefit is excluded from a participant's bankruptcy estate. [11 U.S.C. § 522]

For either ERISA or non-ERISA Section 403(b) benefits, a federal tax lien supersedes any ERISA, plan, or contract restraints. [I.R.C. §§ 6321, 6331; Treas. Reg. § 1.401(a)-13(b)(2)] A federal tax lien may attach to a taxpayer's property rights in a tenancy by the entirety, even if the taxpayer's spouse is not a debtor. [United States v. Craft, 535 U.S. 274 (2002)]

Finally, a married person might prefer a tenancy by the entirety simply because it reflects his or her beliefs about the nature of marriage.

Q 12:58 Can a participant transfer a Section 403(b) benefit into a tenancy by the entirety?

No. A Section 403(b) participant will be unable to transfer his or her rights under a Section 403(b) contract into a tenancy by the entirety for one or more of the following reasons:

1. State law does not recognize tenancy by the entirety.
2. The Section 403(b) contract rights are personal property that cannot be the subject of a tenancy by the entirety.
3. State law precludes a conveyance of property into a tenancy by the entirety.
4. ERISA requires that the Section 403(b) benefit cannot be assigned or alienated.
5. The Section 403(b) contract, in a provision required by the Internal Revenue Code, precludes any transfer.

At common law, a married couple cannot hold *personal property* (property other than land and the buildings fixed onto the land) in a tenancy by the entirety. This is still the rule in some states. At common law, one spouse who solely owns property cannot convey that property into a tenancy by the entirety. While some states now allow such a transfer, those provisions are of no use to a Section 403(b) participant because the participant lacks the power to transfer his or her rights under the Section 403(b) contract. [I.R.C. §§ 403(b)(1), 403(b)(7)(A)]

If a Section 403(b) benefit is governed by an ERISA plan, the benefit cannot be assigned or alienated. [ERISA § 206(d)(1)] Besides, even a non-ERISA 403(b) contract, to obtain tax treatment as a Section 403(b) contract, will provide that benefits cannot be assigned, alienated, or transferred. An annuity or life insurance contract must be nontransferable. [I.R.C. §§ 401(g), 403(b)(1)] A custodial account must provide that the benefits cannot be assigned or alienated. [I.R.C. §§ 401(f), 403(b)(7)(A)]

Thus, even in those states that recognize tenancy by the entirety as an available form of property ownership, it cannot apply to a Section 403(b) contract because the participant cannot transfer ownership.

Using Agreements to Change a Spouse's Rights

Premarital Agreements

Q 12:59   What is a *premarital agreement*?

A *premarital agreement* is an agreement made between two persons who are about to marry concerning property rights that arise from marriage. Typically, a premarital agreement provides that one or both of the soon-to-be spouses waive one or more of the property rights that a spouse would otherwise have. A premarital agreement can waive a spouse's right to a share of the other's estate. Within limits required by public policy, a premarital agreement can specify what property division will apply if the marriage ends in divorce.

In a state with a law based on the Uniform Premarital Agreement Act (1983), the parties to a premarital agreement may contract concerning property rights, the support of a spouse or former spouse, making a will or trust, and "[t]he ownership rights in and disposition of the death benefit from a life insurance policy." [Unif. Premarital Agreement Act § 3(a)(6), 9C ULA 43–46 (2001) & Supp. 2–3 (2003)] A court will not enforce an agreement to the extent that it would cause a spouse or former spouse to become eligible for public assistance. [Unif. Premarital Agreement Act § 6(b), 9C ULA 48–55 (2001) & Supp. 4–5 (2003)] A party to a premarital agreement may not waive child support, and a premarital agreement cannot adversely affect child support. [Unif. Premarital Agreement Act § 3(a)(7), 3(b), 9C ULA 43–46 (2001) & Supp. 2–3 (2003)]

Generally, a premarital agreement must be written. In New York, a premarital agreement must be in writing signed by the parties, and must be acknowledged by the parties in the presence of a notary public or similar officer. [*See, e.g.,* N.Y. Domestic Relations Law § 236B(3)]

Many state statutes or court decisions add further requirements. Typically, each party should fully disclose his or her financial circumstances to the other. In particular, a waiver of a spouse's right to take a portion of the other spouse's estate might be enforced only if preceded by adequate disclosure of the other's net worth. [*See, e.g.,* Thies v. Lowe, 903 P.2d 186 (Mont. Sup. 1995)] In some states, a person need not disclose an asset that was not subject to his or her control. [*See, e.g.,* Perelman's Estate, 438 Pa. 112 (1970)] Further, the better practice is for each party to get the advice of a lawyer of his or her choosing. [Slaughter Estate, 14 Fiduc. Rep. 2d (Bisel) 349] Even when the proponent's lawyer warns the other party to seek independent legal advice, an agreement might be invalid if the proponent's lawyer fails to explain to the unrepresented party that person's disadvantages under the agreement and why he or she needs legal advice. [Bonds v. Bonds, 99 Cal. Rptr. 2d 252 (Cal. 2000); Matter of Estate of Lutz, 563 N.W.2d 90 (N.D. 1997); *In re* Marriage of Foran, 834 P.2d 1081 (Wash. App. 1992)]

Note. Courts are especially reluctant to enforce an agreement that was presented just before the wedding ceremony. Although some suspect that judges are sympathetic to the "pressure" to sign that might come from an understandable desire to avoid the embarrassment of canceling a wedding, the formal reason for not enforcing a "last-minute" agreement is that a lack of time interfered with the offeree's opportunity to obtain legal advice. [*See, e.g.*, Hoag v. Dick, 799 A.2d 391 (Maine 2002)]

Practice Pointer. A guidebook organizes the authors' explanations of relevant law and drafting suggestions based on whether the couple are both young, both old, or of different ages, and whether the spouses or soon-to-be spouses are similar or different in wealth. [Gary N. Skoloff, Richard H. Singer, Jr., and Ronald L. Brown, *Drafting Prenuptial Agreements* (Aspen Publishers 2007)]

In states that do not regulate premarital agreements by statute, courts apply ordinary contract law principles, but with extra scrutiny recognizing the confidential relationship of those engaged to marry. [*See generally*, Restatement (Third) of Property: Wills and Other Donative Transfers § 9.4(b)-(c) (2003)]

A premarital agreement that makes reasonable provision for the surviving spouse might be enforced even in the absence of full and fair disclosure. [*See, e.g.*, Groff's Estate, 341 Pa. 105 (1941)] An unreasonable agreement will be enforced only if there was full and fair disclosure. [*See, e.g.*, Vallish Estate, 431 Pa. 88 (1968); *see generally* Unif. Premarital Agreement Act § 6(a)(2), 9C ULA 48–55 (2001) & Supp. 4–5 (2003)] An agreement that was reasonable when made may become unreasonable through changed circumstances. [*See, e.g.*, Rider v. Rider, 22 Fam. Law. Rep. 1454 (Ind. Sup. 1996)]

Q 12:60   Can a premarital agreement waive a right to a non-ERISA Section 403(b) benefit?

Yes. Even if a surviving spouse is entitled to an elective share, community property, or other protective rights under state law, an expertly prepared premarital or marital agreement (see Qs 12:62–12:64) should be sufficient to eliminate or waive those rights. [Unif. Probate Code § 2-207, 8 pt. I ULA 118–121 (1998)] Along with other requirements, a typical premarital agreement must be in writing and signed by the parties and usually is acknowledged by the parties in the presence of a notary public or similar officer.

In some circumstances, it might be difficult to enforce the terms of a premarital agreement. At least one court has held that an offset against contract rights in recognition of a surviving spouse's receipt of retirement benefits (that were not provided by the premarital agreement) could be an ERISA violation, notwithstanding that the person applying the offset had no connection to any ERISA plan. This was so because the offset had the effect of "discriminating" against the spouse because she exercised her right to a benefit under an ERISA plan. [*See, e.g.*, Mattei v. Mattei, 126 F.3d 794 (1997) (construing ERISA § 510)]

Q 12:61   Can a premarital agreement waive a spouse's right to a Section 403(b) benefit under an ERISA plan?

No. First, a premarital agreement rarely includes all of the form requirements necessary to state a valid spouse's consent to waive rights under ERISA. [ERISA

§ 205] Second, the Treasury department has stated its interpretation (which has legal effect not only concerning the Code but also concerning ERISA Section 205) that a premarital agreement cannot constitute a waiver of survivor annuity rights. [Treas. Reg. § 1.401(a)-20, Q&A 28] Most important, the spouse's consent to a participant's qualified election must be signed by the spouse, and a person making a premarital agreement is not yet a spouse.

All federal court decisions on this question have held that a premarital agreement cannot be used to waive a spouse's ERISA Section 205 rights. [*See, e.g.,* Hurwitz v. Sher, 982 F.2d 778 (2d Cir. 1992), *cert. denied,* 113 S. Ct. 2345 (1993); Hagwood v. Newton, 282 F.3d 285 (4th Cir. 2002); Howard v. Branham & Baker Coal Co., 968 F.2d 1214 (6th Cir. 1992); Pedro Enterprises Inc. v. Perdue, 998 F.2d 491 (7th Cir. 1993); National Auto Dealers & Assoc. Retirement Trust v. Arbeitman, 89 F.3d 496 (8th Cir. 1996); Ford Motor Co. v. Ross, 129 F. Supp. 2d 1070, 1073–1074 (E.D. Mich. 2001); Callahan v. Hutsell, Callahan & Buchino, 813 F. Supp. 541 (W.D. Ky. 1992); Nellis v. Boeing, (not officially reported), 15 EBC (BNA) 1651, 18 Fam. Law Rep. 1374 (D. Kan. 1992); Zinn v. Donaldson Co., 799 F. Supp. 69 (D. Minn. 1992)]

At least one court decision has held that a premarital agreement (or, presumably, a marital agreement) cannot waive a qualified joint and survivor annuity if the spouse could not know what he or she would waive because the plan had not yet been created. [Pedro Enterprises v. Perdue, 998 F.2d 491 (7th Cir. 1993)]

Marital Agreements

Q 12:62   What is a *marital agreement*?

A *marital agreement* is an agreement made between two persons who already are spouses concerning property rights that arise from their marriage. Typically, a marital agreement provides that one or both of the spouses waive one or more of the property rights that a spouse otherwise would have. A marital agreement can waive a spouse's right to a share of the other's estate. [*See generally,* Restatement (Third) of Property: Wills and Other Donative Transfers § 9.4(a) (2003)] Within limits required by public policy and basic fairness, a marital agreement can specify what property division will apply if the marriage ends in divorce.

Generally, a marital agreement must be written. In New York, a marital agreement must be in writing signed by the parties and must be acknowledged by the parties in the presence of a notary public or similar officer. [*See, e.g.,* N.Y. Domestic Relations Law § 236B(3)]

Many state statutes or court decisions add additional requirements meant to ensure basic fairness. Even if no statute applies specified conditions, courts use heightened scrutiny, recognizing the confidential relationship of spouses. [*See generally,* Restatement (Third) of Property: Wills and Other Donative Transfers § 9.4(b)–(c) (2003)] Typically, each party should fully disclose his or her financial circumstances to the other. Further, the better practice is for each party to get the advice of a lawyer of his or her choosing. Some states require that a marital agreement be fair and equitable. [*See, e.g.,* Pacelli v. Pacelli, 319 N.J. Super. 185 (N.J. Super. Ct. 1999)]

A marital agreement is void if it was signed under the threat of a divorce. [*See, e.g.,* Sharp Estate, 1979 Pa. Dist. & Cnty. Dec. LEXIS 267 (Pa. C.P. 1979)]

Q 12:63   Can a marital agreement waive a spouse's right to a non-ERISA Section 403(b) benefit?

Yes. Even if a surviving spouse is entitled to an elective share, community property, or other protective rights under state law, an expertly prepared postmarriage agreement should be sufficient to eliminate or waive those rights. [Unif. Probate Code § 2-207, 8 pt. I ULA 118–121 (1998)]

Q 12:64   Can a marital agreement waive a spouse's right to an ERISA 403(b) benefit?

Yes, a marital agreement can waive a spouse's right to an ERISA § 403(b) benefit if the postmarriage agreement states all of the form requirements necessary to state a valid spouse's consent. [ERISA § 205] To accomplish this, a family lawyer should consult an expert employee-benefits lawyer and each plan administrator.

Simultaneous Deaths

Q 12:65   What should a payer do if there is doubt concerning the order of deaths?

For many retirement plans, the order of deaths between a participant and a beneficiary is irrelevant. A carefully drafted plan should state that a person cannot be a beneficiary if he or she is not living at the time a benefit is to be paid or becomes payable. Even in the absence of such language, a plan administrator's procedure may adopt the same rule.

If an ERISA plan administrator must decide the order of deaths between a participant and a beneficiary (or among potential beneficiaries) and the plan does not provide a presumption concerning the order of deaths, the plan administrator need not follow any state's simultaneous-death statute. [ERISA § 514(b); *cf.* Apostal v. Laborer's Welfare & Pension Fund, 195 F. Supp. 2d 1052 (N.D. Ill. 2002)] If the plan does not provide a specific rule, a plan administrator might choose to follow a relevant state's law (see Qs 12:66–12:67), treating such an invented rule as the plan administrator's interpretation.

Q 12:66   What is the typical simultaneous-death rule?

The "old" Uniform Simultaneous Death Act, adopted by many states, provides that if "there is no sufficient evidence that the persons have died otherwise than simultaneously, the property of each person shall be disposed of as if he [or she] had survived [the other person]." [Unif. Simultaneous Death Act § 1 (1940)] The Uniform Probate Code provides that a person cannot qualify as an heir unless he or she survives the first decedent for 120 hours. Further, the person who would claim through the heir has the burden of proving the duration that the heir survived the first decedent. [Unif. Probate Code §§ 2-104, 2-702 (1998)] The 1991 version of the Uniform Simultaneous Death Act has a substantially identical rule.

> **Practice Pointer.** For tax-planning purposes, a wealthy participant may prefer to vary these "default" rules by express language in his or her beneficiary designation. [*See, e.g.,* Treas. Reg. § 20.2056(e)-2(e)] Even if state law applies to the plan, state law will permit a different provision if it is stated by the plan or the participant's beneficiary designation. [*See, e.g.,* N.Y. Est. Powers & Trusts Law § 2-1.6(e)]

Alternatively, a common-disaster clause or a delay clause of up to six months does not disqualify property for the federal estate tax marital deduction. [I.R.C. § 2056(b)(3); Treas. Reg. § 20.2056(b)-3(b)]

If it becomes necessary for an ERISA plan administrator to determine the order of deaths between or among potential beneficiaries and the retirement plan does not provide a presumption concerning the order of deaths, it might be prudent for the plan administrator to indulge a presumption that all persons who died within a few days of one another died at the same time and survived to the relevant time.

If a plan administrator decides claims under a non-ERISA plan, the plan administrator might be required to follow state law.

Q 12:67 Is there a federal common law of ERISA concerning simultaneous deaths?

No. At common law, when two or more persons died in a common disaster, there was no presumption for or against any person surviving another. [*See, e.g.,* People v. Eulo, 482 N.Y.S.2d 436 (N.Y. 1984)] Moreover, there is no clear consensus in states' statutes. [*See generally,* Restatement (Third) of Property: Wills and Other Donative Transfers § 1.2, statutory note (2003)]

Absentees

Q 12:68 What should a payer do when someone says a participant or beneficiary is absent and presumed dead?

Under ordinary circumstances, a plan administrator, insurer, custodian, or other payer should not presume a participant's or beneficiary's death. Instead, a plan administrator or payer should require the claimant (usually the next beneficiary) to prove the absentee's death by an appropriate court order.

Under the common law, a person was presumed dead if he or she had been absent for a continuous period of seven years. [*See, e.g.,* 20 Pa. Cons. Stat. Ann.

§ 5701(b) & comment] Likewise, an absentee's exposure to a specific peril was a sufficient ground for presuming death. [*See, e.g.,* 20 Pa. Cons. Stat. Ann. § 5701(c) and comment] Further, death may be inferred if survival of the absentee would be beyond human expectation or experience. [*See, e.g., In re* Katz's Estate, 135 Misc. 861 (Sup. Ct. 1930)] Courts sometimes required considerable evidence of an unexplained absence. For example, a person's absence from the places where his relatives resided together with his failure to communicate with his relatives was not enough to show that he was absent from his residence without explanation. [Estate of Morrison v. Roswell, 92 Ill. 2d 207 (1982)]

In 1939, the Uniform Absence as Evidence of Death and Absentees Property Act reversed the common-law rules: the fact that a person had been absent for seven years (or any duration) or had been exposed to a specific peril did not set up a presumption of death; instead, these facts were merely evidence for a court or jury to consider in making its own finding of whether the absentee's death had occurred. [*See* National Conference of Commissioners on Uniform State Laws, Uniform Absence as Evidence of Death and Absentees Property Act § 1 (1939); Armstrong v. Pilot Life Insurance Co., 656 S.W.2d 18 (Tenn. Ct. App. 1983)]

The Uniform Probate Code, portions of which have been adopted in many states, returns to a presumption. A person is presumed dead after he or she has been absent for a continuous period, such as three, four, five, or seven years. [*Cf.* Minn. Stat. § 576.141; N.J. Stat. Ann. § 3B:27-1; N.Y. Est. Powers & Trusts Law § 2-1.7; 20 Pa. Cons. Stat. Ann. § 5701(c)] However, a person who seeks a declaration of the absentee's death must demonstrate to a court's satisfaction that the absentee has not been heard from after diligent search or inquiry and that his or her absence is not satisfactorily explained. [*See, e.g.,* 20 Pa. Cons. Stat. Ann. §§ 5702–5705]

Unless sufficient evidence proves that death occurred sooner, the end of the waiting period is deemed the date of death. [*See, e.g.,* Hubbard v. Equitable Life Assurance Society of the United States, 248 Wis. 340 (1946); Hogaboam v. Metropolitan Life Ins. Co., 248 Wis. 146 (1946)]

The presumption of an absentee's death does not necessarily apply to all property in the same way. For example, some states do not use the presumption to provide a life insurance death benefit. [*See, e.g.,* Armstrong v. Pilot Life Ins. Co., 656 S.W.2d 18 (Tenn. Ct. App. 1983)]

Usually, the person who would benefit from the absentee's death bears the burden of proof.

Note. The terrorist attacks of September 11, 2001, focused renewed attention on laws that permit a finding of death based on exposure to a specific peril. [*See* N.J. Stat. Ann. §§ 3B:27-1, -6; N.Y. Est. Powers & Trusts Law § 2.17(b); 20 Pa. Cons. Stat. Ann. § 5701(c); *see also* Chiaramonte v. Chiaramonte, 435 N.Y.S.2d 523 (Sup. Ct. 1981); Zucker's Will, 219 N.Y.S.2d 72 (Sup. Ct. 1961); Bobrow's Estate, 179 N.Y.S.2d 742 (Sup. Ct. 1958); Brevoort's Will, 73 N.Y.S.2d 216 (Sup. Ct. 1947)]

An ERISA plan's administrator need not follow state law and instead may make its own rules and use discretion in deciding whether or when a person's death occurred. [*See* Apostal v. Laborer's Welfare & Pension Fund, 195 F. Supp. 2d 1052 (N.D. Ill. 2002)]

Disclaimers

Q 12:69   What is a *disclaimer*?

A *disclaimer* (also called a *renunciation* in some states) is a written instrument in which a beneficiary states that he or she does not want to receive a benefit. To be valid and to achieve tax purposes, the disclaimer document must carefully state certain requirements (see Q 12:75).

Q 12:70   Is a disclaimer permitted under a Section 403(b) plan or contract?

Yes, for a disclaimer made by a beneficiary. While there is no tax ruling that is specific to a Section 403(b) plan or contract, other rulings provide some guidance. Although there was some doubt as to whether a Section 401(a) qualified plan administrator's action based on a disclaimer might violate the anti-alienation provisions required by ERISA Section 206(d) and Code Section 401(a)(13), the IRS has found that a disclaimer does not violate the anti-alienation requirement. [GCM 39858, 1991 WL 776304 (Sept. 9, 1991)] Because an individual retirement account or annuity (IRA) is not subject to the anti-alienation requirement, the IRS more easily recognized disclaimers for IRAs. [Ltr. Ruls. 9226058, 9037048, 8922036] On similar reasoning, disclaimers should be permitted for a Section 403(b) plan or contract.

A plan administrator, insurer, custodian, or trustee may, but is not necessarily required to, accept a disclaimer.

Q 12:71   What is the effect of a disclaimer?

If a beneficiary makes a valid disclaimer that the plan administrator, insurer, or custodian accepts, the benefit will be distributed as though the beneficiary/disclaimant had died before the participant's death or before the creation of the benefit disclaimed. [*See generally,* Unif. Disclaimer of Property Interests Act (1999), 8A ULA 159–189 (2003), Unif. Disclaimer of Property Interests Act (1978), 8A ULA 191–208 (2003)]

Q 12:72   What is the tax effect of a disclaimer?

If a beneficiary makes a valid disclaimer that also meets all requirements of Code Section 2518, the disclaimed benefit will not be in the disclaimant's estate for federal estate tax purposes, and will not be the disclaimant's income for federal income tax purposes. [I.R.C. § 402, 2518; Treas. Reg. § 25.2518-1] Most states have a similar rule for state death tax purposes.

Q 12:73   Why would someone want to make a disclaimer?

Although most people do not lightly turn away money, sometimes there may be a good reason to make a disclaimer. A typical reason is to complete tax-oriented estate planning. For example, a beneficiary might prefer to make a disclaimer to help accomplish one or more of the following estate-planning goals:

- Changing a restricted transfer in favor of a beneficiary into an unrestricted transfer to the same beneficiary
- Changing an unrestricted transfer to a beneficiary into a restricted transfer in favor of the same beneficiary
- Limiting a transfer to a child or other nonspouse to permit the participant's spouse to delay the required beginning date
- Limiting a transfer to a child or other nonspouse to permit the participant's spouse to make a rollover
- Limiting a transfer to a child or other nonspouse to increase the marital deduction
- Limiting a transfer to a spouse as needed to "equalize" the effective transfer tax rate of each spouse
- Limiting a transfer to a spouse as needed to fully use the generation-skipping tax exemption of the first spouse to die
- Limiting a transfer to a spouse as needed to avoid an estate transfer surtax [I.R.C. § 2001(c)(2)]
- Providing a designated beneficiary to lengthen the Section 403(b) benefit's tax deferral
- Providing or increasing a gift to charity.

If a beneficiary makes a valid disclaimer that also meets all requirements of Code Section 2518, the disclaimed benefit will not be in the disclaimant's estate for federal estate tax purposes and will not be the disclaimant's income for federal income tax purposes. Most states have a similar rule for state death tax purposes.

Another frequent use is to correct a "wrong" beneficiary designation.

Example. Matthew, a hospital technician, saved for retirement using a Section 403(b) annuity. When he applied for this Section 403(b) contract, he was single and designated his father and mother as beneficiaries. Subsequently, Matthew married Laura. Shortly after returning from their honeymoon, Matthew was killed in an accident at the hospital's emergency room. His parents believed that if Matthew had thought about it, he would have wanted his wife to be his beneficiary. Therefore, each of them filed a disclaimer with the insurance company. Although the parents could not directly control who would get the benefit, their lawyer advised them that the annuity contract's default provision (see Q 12:7), together with their state's intestacy law, would result in Laura's receiving the benefit. All family members felt that that was a morally sound result and what Matthew would have wanted. The use of disclaimers thus allowed the family to achieve a desired outcome.

Another reason to make a disclaimer is to not receive a benefit that would be taken by the disclaimant's creditors. Some courts find that a disclaimer is a fraudulent transfer and thus is void. [*See, e.g.,* Pennington v. Bigham, 512 So. 2d 1344 (Ala. 1987); Stein v. Brown, 480 N.E.2d 1121 (Ohio 1985)] And some states by statute bar a disclaimer by an insolvent beneficiary. [*See, e.g.,* Fla. Stat. Ann. § 732.801(6); Mass. Gen. Laws Ann. Ch. 191A § 8; Minn. Stat. Ann. § 525. 532(c)(6)] Federal law or state law is most likely to bar a disclaimer that could interfere with a government's opportunity to collect on a debt to the government. [*See, e.g.,* State v. Murtha, 427 A.2d 807 (Conn. 1980); *accord* Dep't of Income Maint. v. Watts, 558 A.2d 998 (Conn. 1989); *but see In re* Estate of Kirk, 591 N.W.2d 630 (Iowa 1999)] If these rules do not apply, a disclaimer is not a fraudulent transfer. [*See, e.g.,* Cal. Probate Code § 283; Essen v. Gilmore, 607 N.W.2d 829 (Neb. 2000)] Even a valid disclaimer does not avoid a federal tax lien. [Drye v. United States, 528 U.S. 49 (1999)]

Caution. A beneficiary should not make a disclaimer unless he or she first gets his or her lawyer's advice that doing so will not be a federal health care crime. [42 U.S.C. § 1320a-7b(a)(6)]

Q 12:74 Can a beneficiary's executor or agent disclaim?

If a plan permits a beneficiary to disclaim a plan benefit, whether that power can be exercised only by the beneficiary personally or by the beneficiary's executor, personal representative, guardian, or attorney-in-fact as a fiduciary depends on the plan's language. Unless the plan document states that a power to disclaim can be exercised by an executor, personal representative, guardian, or attorney-in-fact, only the beneficiary personally may exercise the power to disclaim. [R. Scott Nickel, as Plan Benefit Administrator of the Thrift Plan of Phillips Petroleum Co. v. Estate of Lurline Estes, 122 F.3d 294 (5th Cir. 1997)]

For a Section 403(b) contract not held under any plan, it is unclear whether a similar result would apply under state law. In some states, a personal representative may disclaim an interest and the disclaimer relates back to the disclaimant's death or even to the death of the person making the disclaimant a beneficiary. [*See, e.g.,* Texas Probate Code § 37A; Rolin v. IRS, 588 F.2d 368 (2d Cir. 1978) (applying New York law)]

Even if a fiduciary has power under applicable law to make a disclaimer [*see generally,* Unit Disclaimer of Property Interests Act (1999) § 11, 8A ULA 180 (2003)], such a disclaimer might not be a qualified disclaimer for federal tax purposes. [*Cf.* Ltr. Ruls. 200013041, 9615043, 9609052 (disclaimer recognized) with Ltr. Rul. 9437042 (disclaimer not recognized); *see also* Rev. Rul. 90-110, 1990-2 C.B. 209 (disclaimer by trustee not a qualified disclaimer)]

Q 12:75   **What are the requirements for a valid disclaimer?**

To be effective for federal tax purposes, a disclaimer must meet all of the following requirements:

- The disclaimer must be made before the beneficiary accepts or uses any benefit.
- The disclaimant must not have received any consideration for the disclaimer.
- The benefit must pass without any direction by the disclaimant.
- The disclaimer must be in writing and must be signed by the disclaimant.
- The writing must state an irrevocable and unqualified refusal to accept the benefit.
- The writing must be delivered to the plan administrator or insurer or custodian.
- The writing must be so delivered no later than nine months after the date of the participant's death or the date the beneficiary attains age 21 (whichever is later).
- The disclaimer must meet all requirements of applicable state law.

[I.R.C. § 2518; Treas. Reg. § 25.2518-2; GCM 39858, 1991 WL 776304 (Sept. 9, 1991)]

Note. The Fifth Circuit has interpreted the tax regulations' no-consideration condition as limited to bargained-for consideration. In the view of that court, leading a disclaimant to understand that he or she would otherwise be provided for or that his or her needs would be considered does not necessarily vitiate the tax-qualified treatment of a disclaimer if the disclaimer is valid under non-tax law. [Estate of Monroe v. Comm'r, 124 F.3d 699 (5th Cir. 1997); *see also* Estate of Lute v. United States, 19 F. Supp. 2d 1047 (D. Neb. 1998)]

State law will provide additional requirements for a valid disclaimer. For example, in some states, a disclaimer must state the disclaimant's belief that he or she has no creditor that could be disadvantaged by the disclaimer. In some situations, especially when the beneficiary is a minor child or an incapacitated person, a disclaimer may require court approval. Even when court approval is not required, state law may require that a disclaimer is not valid unless filed in the appropriate probate court. [*See generally*, Unif Probate Code § 2-801, 8 pt. I ULA 206–210 (1998)]

In addition to state law and tax law requirements, the Section 403(b) contract and the plan (if any) may impose further requirements on a disclaimer.

Practice Pointer. If a surviving spouse wants to make a tax-qualified disclaimer of a portion of what otherwise would be his or her rights under a QTIP trust, the estate's executor and the QTIP trust's trustee might first divide the QTIP trust into separate trusts. An assignment of any portion of a spouse's interest in a QTIP trust is a taxable gift of that trust's principal. [Treas. Reg. § 25.2519-1(a)] But a disclaimer is not an assignment. [*Cf.* Ltr.

Ruls. 200122036, 200044034; *see generally,* Unif. Disclaimer of Property Interests Act (amended 2002) § 5(f), 8A ULA 166–170 (2003)]

Who Can Give Advice

Q 12:76   May a financial services representative give advice about a beneficiary designation?

A financial services representative may give practical information about how to fill in the beneficiary form of an annuity or life insurance contract or a custodial account agreement that he or she solicits or solicited, but he or she must not give advice about the legal effect of a beneficiary designation. Further, a nonlawyer must warn a person about the risks of acting without advice. [*See, e.g., In re* Opinion No. 26 of the Committee on Unauthorized Practice, 654 A.2d 1344 (N.J. 1995); *see generally,* Restatement (Second) of Torts § 552 (1977)]

Except when done by a properly admitted lawyer, giving legal advice, even for free, is a crime or offense in most states of the United States. Even if the nonlawyer explicitly states that he or she is not a lawyer, it is still a crime to give legal advice.

Note. The contributing author asks readers to understand that this chapter's description of the law does not reflect his view about what the law ought to be. Rather, he believes that any person should be free to give legal advice (and to bear responsibility for his, her, or its advice).

Of course, any criminal punishment is in addition to the nonlawyer's liability to his or her "client" for any inappropriate advice. Courts have not hesitated to impose liability on a nonlawyer for giving incorrect or even incomplete advice. [Buscemi v. Intachai, 730 So. 2d 329 (Fla. App. 1999) (nonlawyer financial planner who gave legal advice could be held liable for failure to do so properly), review denied, 744 So. 2d 452 (Fla. 1999); Banks v. District of Columbia Dep't of Consumer & Regulatory Affairs, 634 A.2d 433 (D.C. 1993); Cultum v. Heritage House Realtors, Inc., 694 P.2d 630 (Wash. 1985); Bowers v. Transamerica Title Ins. Co., 675 P.2d 193 (Wash. 1983); Webb v. Pomeroy, 655 P.2d 465 (Kan. Ct. App. 1982); Biakanja v. Irving, 49 Cal. 2d 647 (Cal. 1958)] A nonlawyer will be held to the same standard of care and expertise as a lawyer. [Williams v. Jackson Co, 359 So. 2d 798 (Ala. Civ. App. 1978), *writ denied,* 359 So. 2d 801 (1978); Wright v. Langdon, 274 Ark. 258 (Ark. 1981); Biakanja v. Irving, 49 Cal. 2d 647 (Cal. 1958); Ford v. Guarantee Abstract & Title Co., 553 P.2d 254 (Kan. 1976); Torres v. Fiol, 110 Ill. App. 3d 9 (1982); Latson v. Eaton, 341 P.2d 247 (Okla. 1959); Bowers v. Transamerica Title Ins. Co., 675 P.2d 193 (Wash. 1983); Mattieligh v. Poe, 57 Wn.2d 203 (1960); *see also* Correll v. Goodfellow, 125 N.W.2d 745 (Iowa 1964); Brown v. Shyne, 242 N.Y. 176 (N.Y. 1926)] This duty, even for a nonlawyer, includes the duty to have and use specialist expertise, or to refer one's "client" to an appropriate specialist.

A nonlawyer plan administrator also will be liable for incorrect or incomplete advice. Although a lawsuit against an ERISA plan's administrator or other fiduciary grounded on state-law claims, such as negligent misrepresentation or negligent communication, is preempted [Griggs v. E. I. DuPont de Nemours & Co., 237 F.3d 371 (4th Cir. 2001); Farr v. U.S. West, Inc., 151 F.3d 908 (9th Cir. 1998)], a plan administrator's incorrect statement might be a breach of its fiduciary duty to furnish accurate and non-misleading information. [*See* Griggs v. E. I. DuPont de Nemours & Co., 237 F.3d 371 (4th Cir. 2001)]

Many Section 403(b) plan participants believe they cannot afford legal advice. Although a financial services representative should urge a participant to obtain expert legal advice, it may be impractical to avoid participants' questions asked in the course of filling out a Section 403(b) application. Perhaps it is not the unauthorized practice of law to furnish widely known general information that does not involve applying the law to a specific factual situation.

> **Practice Pointer.** If a participant expresses a desire to make a beneficiary designation that would provide anything less than 100 percent of his or her death benefit for his or her spouse, a nonlawyer financial planner should urge the participant to seek the advice of an expert lawyer.

Q 12:77   Can written materials give guidance about beneficiary designations?

Maybe. In Texas, any restriction against the unauthorized practice of law does not preclude "written materials, books, forms, computer software, or similar products if the products clearly and conspicuously state that the products are not a substitute for the advice of an attorney." [Texas Government Code § 81.101(c); Unauthorized Practice of Law Comm. v. Parsons Tech., Inc., 1999 U.S. Dist. LEXIS 813 (N.D. Tex. Jan. 22, 1999)]

In other states, it is unclear whether such publications would be so protected. Notwithstanding America's constitutional protections for free speech, at least one court found that mere written publications, without oral communication, was the crime of unauthorized practice of law. [*See, e.g.,* Unauthorized Practice of Law Comm. v. Parsons Tech., Inc., 1999 U.S. LEXIS 813, (N.D. Tex. Jan. 22, 1999) (before enactment of Texas Government Code § 81.101(c)), *vacated* 179 F.3d 956 (5th Cir. 1999)] In the contributing author's view, the court's decision, had it not been vacated, would have been reversed on review or appeal.

Although some ERISA plan administrators might guess that ERISA preempts state laws, ERISA does not preempt criminal laws, which might include some laws that restrain the unauthorized practice of law. [ERISA § 514(b)(7)]

Q 12:78   Does the lawyer who drafts a person's will need to know about his or her beneficiary designation under a Section 403(b) contract?

Yes. Professor John Langbein observed that many Americans die with several wills—maybe one that was written in a lawyer's office and a dozen others that were filled out on standard forms. For most people, those forms—beneficiary designations—dispose of far more money and property than the will does. [John H Langbein, The Nonprobate Revolution and the Future of the Law of Succession, 97 Harvard L. Rev. 1108 (Mar. 1984)]

Making a beneficiary designation under a 403(b) contract is an important part of estate planning. Although a Section 403(b) benefit will not pass by a will (see Q 12:1), the Section 403(b) beneficiary designation does affect a person's overall estate plan. A participant should make sure his or her lawyer knows the beneficiary designation the participant made under each Section 403(b) contract and should ask for the lawyer's advice about whether to consider changing any beneficiary designation.

Q 12:79   May a lawyer give advice about a beneficiary designation?

Yes. A lawyer may render advice about law as long as he or she writes or speaks his or her advice while present in a state in which he or she is admitted to practice law. [*See, e.g.*, Estate of Condon, 64 Cal. Rptr. 2d 789 (Cal. Ct. App. 1997)] Also, a lawyer may render advice while in a state in which he or she is not admitted if the advice is reasonably related to the lawyer's proper activity in a state in which he or she is admitted. [*See generally*, Restatement (Third) Law Governing Lawyers § 3(3) (2001)]

Common Mistakes

Q 12:80   What are some of the common mistakes people make with beneficiary designations?

Because people enroll in retirement plans or Section 403(b) contracts quickly, they sometimes make beneficiary designations that are less than carefully considered. Here is an explanation of some common mistakes.

1. *Failing to coordinate a beneficiary designation's provisions with those made in other nonprobate designations, trusts, and a will.* Although a beneficiary designation's provisions need not be the same as those of a participant's will or other dispositions, if they are different, the participant should understand why he or she has made different provisions and whether they are likely to add up to a combined result that he or she wants.

2. *Failing to consider whether a beneficiary designation is consistent with tax-oriented planning.* A participant might have had a lawyer's advice about how to leave his or her estate, including both probate and nonprobate property, to achieve a desired tax outcome. Making a beneficiary designation without considering its effect on the participant's tax-oriented plan could result in an unanticipated tax.

3. *Making a beneficiary designation that a plan administrator, insurer, or custodian will refuse to implement.* For example, a participant might try to make a beneficiary designation that refers to terms that may be

used in a will or trust but are precluded by his or her Section 403(b) plan or contract. A plan administrator's interpretation of the beneficiary designation without the offending terms might result in a disposition quite different from what the participant intended.

4. *Not naming specific beneficiaries—for example, writing "all my children, equally" or describing a class.* When a beneficiary designation refers to information that is not in a retirement plan's or Section 403(b) contract's records, a plan administrator, insurer, or custodian may decide that the participant did not make a beneficiary designation, or it may allow a claimant an opportunity to name every person in the class and prove that there are no others. Since it is difficult to prove the nonexistence of an unidentified person, even the opportunity to correct the participant's beneficiary designation would result in significant frustration and delay.

5. *Neglecting to use a beneficiary's Social Security number (or individual taxpayer identification number), especially for a daughter.*

Example 1. Harold Smith had three children—John, Catherine, and Alice. He named them his beneficiaries using only their given names. By the time of Harold's death many years later, John and Alice had married. John had no special difficulty claiming his benefit. But Alice, who had changed her surname to Carpenter, was required to submit proof that she is the same person as Alice Smith. Because an identifying number assigned by the Social Security Administration or the IRS is unique, this difficulty could have been avoided had Harold put Alice's Social Security number on the beneficiary designation form.

Caution. Some participants will want to balance this use of a clear identifier against concerns about a potential for identity theft.

6. *Naming a minor as a beneficiary without considering who the minor's guardian would be.* For example, a divorced participant might not want to name his or her young child as a beneficiary if doing so might have the effect of putting money in the hands of the child's other parent, the participant's former spouse. Instead, the participant might name a suitable trustee or custodian.

7. *Naming a son or daughter as a beneficiary without considering his or her prudence.*

Example 2. Philip names his daughter, Britney, as beneficiary of his custodial account. When Philip dies, Britney is age 19, and no longer a minor under applicable law. Although Britney should use the money to pay her $25,000 sophomore year college tuition, she buys a new car and then neglects to pay the second car insurance premium. When the uninsured car is stolen, Britney has nothing left from her father's gift. A participant who wants to benefit his or her child should consider the child's maturity and decide whether to appoint a suitable trustee to manage the child's benefit.

8. *Forgetting to give a copy of the beneficiary designation to the beneficiary.* A plan administrator, insurer, or custodian has no duty or

obligation to contact a participant's beneficiaries to invite them to submit a claim. Indeed, many service providers specifically avoid doing so because such a communication might invite fraudulent claims. A beneficiary might not claim a benefit if he or she is unaware that he or she is a beneficiary. Likewise, the beneficiary might have difficulty claiming the benefit if he or she does not know the name of the plan administrator, insurer, or custodian.

9. ***Naming one's estate as the beneficiary.*** Some participants think that naming one's estate as beneficiary is a way to avoid inconsistency in their estate plan. Although such a beneficiary designation might serve to avoid inconsistency, it has disadvantages. For example, amounts paid or payable to an executor or personal representative for the estate are available to a decedent's creditors. Further, a benefit's "run" through an estate might, because of accounting and timing differences, result in a larger income tax than the tax that would have resulted if the recipient had received the benefit directly. [I.R.C. §§ 1, 72, 641–691]

10. ***Failing to make a beneficiary designation at all.*** A participant who has difficulty making up his or her mind about a beneficiary designation is unlikely to have read a plan's summary plan description or a Section 403(b) contract's terms carefully enough to understand the effect of the plan's or contract's default provision (see Q 12:7).

Practice Pointer. A planner might suggest that the risks of failing to make a beneficiary designation outweigh the risks of a less than perfectly considered beneficiary designation. In those circumstances, a planner might remind the participant that a typical plan or contract allows a participant to change his or her beneficiary designation at any time.

11. ***Forgetting to review one's beneficiary designation.*** A participant should review his or her beneficiary designations on a periodic basis and whenever there is a significant change in his or her family or financial status.

Example 3. Martha names her husband, John, as her beneficiary under an ERISA plan. Although Martha wants to make sure that their children, Peter and Maria, will be provided for, she trusts her husband to take care of the whole family. When Martha and John divorce some years later, Martha neglects to change her beneficiary designation. After Martha's death, John submits his claim to the plan administrator. The plan administrator follows the plan's terms, which do not revoke a beneficiary designation because of a participant's divorce (see Q 12:5). The plan pays John, and he spends the money without considering the needs of Peter and Maria.

The common mistakes described above are only some of the many errors participants may make. Although a Section 403(b) benefit is meant to be consumed mostly during a participant's retirement years, a participant's death may occur before retirement. Therefore, a participant should exercise his or her valuable right to name a beneficiary and exercise that right wisely.

Chapter 13

Qualified Domestic Relations Orders

Peter Gulia, Esq.
Fiduciary Guidance Counsel

Although a Section 403(b) plan or contract is intended to provide retirement benefits primarily for a participant, domestic-relations laws in all states recognize interests in retirement plans as property subject to division on the dissolution of a marriage. The Employee Retirement Income Security Act of 1974, as amended (ERISA) and the Internal Revenue Code include provisions designed to create a workable regime to permit retirement plans and Section 403(b) contracts to meet those marital-property expectations. ERISA requires a plan governed by ERISA to permit a qualified domestic relations order (QDRO). The Internal Revenue Code provides that a payment to an alternate payee does not "tax-disqualify" a Section 403(b) plan or contract if the payment was made under a QDRO. The federal law tries to balance a nonparticipant alternate payee's right to receive a retirement benefit with a plan administrator's need for administrative efficiency and certainty.

Author's Usage Note

For convenience, this chapter uses several words in a specially defined context.

This chapter sometimes distinguishes between an ERISA plan, a governmental plan, and a church plan. In this context, an ERISA plan refers to a plan that is governed by Title I of ERISA, a governmental plan refers to a plan described in ERISA Section 3(32), and a church plan refers to a plan described in ERISA Section 3(33) that has not elected to be governed by ERISA. This chapter uses the expression "non-ERISA" to refer to a governmental plan, a church plan, or a plan that an employer intends as a plan that meets the conditions for tax treatment under Code Section 403(b) but not as a plan that would be governed by ERISA.

This chapter uses the word "contract" to refer to an annuity contract, a custodial account, or another form of investment that Code Section 403(b) permits as an eligible investment. (See chapter 5)

In this chapter, "payer" refers to any custodian, insurer, plan administrator, or other person responsible for deciding or paying a claim under a plan or contract.

This chapter uses the word "state" in its popular meaning to refer to the District of Columbia or any state, commonwealth, territory, possession, or similar jurisdiction within the United States. Because this chapter has many references to state law, this chapter makes parallel references to a "state" (rather than to the lawyers' word "jurisdiction") for reading ease. For example, although the District of Columbia is not a state, law that applies to a person because he or she resides in the District of Columbia is state law, as distinguished from U.S. law or federal law, which applies throughout the United States.

Author's Citations Note

This chapter includes many general explanations of state laws. To support each such statement with citations to more than 50 state laws would be unwieldy in this chapter's summary. Moreover, a pension practitioner usually is interested first in a general sense of the state laws. To these ends, the chapter frequently cites uniform acts recommended by the National Conference of Commissioners on Uniform State Laws [www.nccusl.org]. A reader who wants to find whether a particular state enacted a statute based on a uniform law might begin with this chapter's citations to Uniform Laws Annotated [ULA], which includes citations for states' adoptions of, and variations from, the recommended uniform laws.

Because most employee-benefits practitioners do not use printed volumes to read federal or state statutes or regulations, this chapter's citations to statutes and regulations omit publisher and year references. A reader may find statutes efficiently and inexpensively by using Aspen Publishers' Loislaw service (for more information, visit www.loislaw.com or call 1-877-471-5632).

Specialty citations are in the forms and with the abbreviations customary to employee benefits or tax practitioners.

Overview

Q 13:1   Why did Congress create the qualified domestic relations order?

Before 1984, many plan administrators (and some Section 403(b) insurers and custodians) refused to honor state court orders that purported to assign a participant's benefit to the participant's spouse or former spouse. They believed that the provisions of the Employee Retirement Income Security Act of 1974 (ERISA) and the Internal Revenue Code (Code) that prohibited alienation of a participant's benefit precluded a plan from permitting payment to a person other than the participant. And many plan administrators believed that a state court order was preempted by ERISA.

To provide a workable solution, the Retirement Equity Act of 1984 (REA) [Pub. L. No. 98-397, 98 Stat. 1426] enacted an ERISA provision requiring every ERISA plan to provide for payment following a qualified domestic relations order (QDRO). Also, REA amended ERISA to provide that payment pursuant to a QDRO is an exception to ERISA's anti-alienation requirement. [ERISA § 206(d)(3)(A)]

Q 13:2   What kind of Section 403(b) plan must accept a QDRO?

If a Section 403(b) plan is governed by Title I of ERISA, it must "provide for the payment of benefits in accordance with" a QDRO. [ERISA § 206(d)(3)(A)]

A church plan that has not elected to be governed by ERISA or a governmental plan (which cannot be governed by ERISA) is not required by ERISA to accept a QDRO. If, however, ERISA does not govern a plan, state law is not preempted, and a domestic-relations court may use its contempt powers to compel a plan administrator to accept a QDRO.

Note. For some governmental plans, the plan administrator might have sovereign, governmental, or public officer immunity that protects against monetary liability from his, her, or its decision to refuse a court order. However, some courts (often a different court than the domestic-relations court) have power to order a government official to do, or refrain from doing, a particular act.

Note. A church plan might have constitutional grounds to refuse a court order that would interfere with the free exercise of its religious doctrine or church management. [*Cf.* Basich v. Board of Pensions, Evangelical Lutheran Church in Am. and Basich v. Evangelical Lutheran Church in Am., 540

N.W.2d 82 (Minn. Ct. App. 1995), *rev. denied*, (unpublished order), Minn. Sup. Ct. (Jan. 25, 1996) *cert. denied*, 117 S. Ct. 55 (1996)]

Concerning a Section 403(b) contract under a plan that is not an ERISA-governed plan, an insurer or custodian usually will accept an order (if it is a QDRO). Also, an insurer or custodian might accept a court order that is not a QDRO to the extent required by applicable state law.

Note. Most Section 403(b) plans are individual-account or defined-contribution plans. Further, for tax years that begin on or after January 1, 2009 (or the effective date that applies concerning a plan maintained under a collective-bargaining agreement) regulations provide (with one pre-TEFRA exception for a church's defined-benefit plan that was in effect on September 3, 1982) that a plan has the tax treatment provided by Code Section 403(b) only if the plan is a defined contribution plan. [*See* Treas. Reg. §§ 1.403(b)-3(b)(3)(i), 1.403(b)-10(f)(2)] Therefore, this chapter assumes that Section 403(b) plans and contracts provide benefits on a defined-contribution basis.

Federal law has two sets of QDRO rules concerning Section 403(b) plans and contracts: (1) ERISA Section 206(d)(3) provides that an ERISA-governed plan must pay benefits as directed by a QDRO, and (2) Code Section 414(p) describes the types of domestic relations orders that will be recognized for federal income tax purposes to permit a pre-retirement distribution and to shift income to an alternate payee who is or was the participant's spouse (see Qs 13:47–13:50).

Q 13:3 What happens if a nonparticipant spouse or former spouse fails to obtain a QDRO?

In the absence of a QDRO, a nonparticipant spouse or former spouse might have little or no ability to protect his or her marital property rights.

Example. Debbie and Chet were married for several years. After they separated, they signed a separation agreement. The agreement provided that Debbie "shall receive half of Chet's 403(b) account." Eventually, Debbie was granted a final divorce decree. Debbie did not know, however, that she needed to ask the court to incorporate or merge the separation agreement into the divorce decree.

Debbie sent a copy of the separation agreement and the divorce decree to the plan administrator of Chet's 403(b) account, asking that the plan pay her half of Chet's account. The plan administrator responded with a formal claim denial letter stating that the separation agreement was not a QDRO because it was not part of a court order. Soon after, Chet left his job, and took a distribution of his entire 403(b) account. Chet did not pay Debbie any portion of the proceeds; indeed, he spent the entire amount of the distribution.

Debbie sued the plan administrator. After removing the lawsuit to federal court, the plan administrator argued that there had been no QDRO delivered to it before it determined to pay Chet's plan benefit. The plan administrator had no duty or authority to put a stop on paying Chet's benefit once it had decided that the document furnished to it was not a QDRO. Moreover, the separation agreement was not even a domestic relations order. Debbie did not have any rights as a spouse, because she was not Chet's spouse at the time he claimed a distribution. The court dismissed Debbie's lawsuit and ordered her to reimburse the plan administrator's attorneys' fees.

A plan administrator has no duty or authority to restrain distribution of a participant's benefit except during the time that the plan administrator is making a determination on whether a domestic relations order is a QDRO. [ERISA § 206(d)(3)(H)] Therefore, a potential alternate payee should act diligently to make sure that the court makes an order, and to deliver the court order to the plan administrator.

Q 13:4   What is *bifurcation*?

Bifurcation refers to the discretionary power of a court to enter a divorce decree before resolution of financial claims, such as equitable distribution. Before proceeding to bifurcate status and property issues, a court must find that bifurcation is fair to both divorcing parties. When a court considers one party's bifurcation request, the other party's mere assertion that bifurcation would harm him or her is not enough; an objector must prove that harm would result from granting a divorce before property issues are resolved. [*See, e.g.,* Leese v. Leese, 369 Pa. Super. 104, 534 A.2d 1101 (1987); Taylor v. Taylor, 349 Pa. Super. 423, 503 A.2d 439 (Pa. Super. 1986); Wolk v. Wolk, 318 Pa. Super. 311, 464 A.2d 1359 (Pa. Super. 1983)]

Bifurcation of a divorce proceeding might be disadvantageous to a prospective alternate payee because a retirement benefit might be paid before a QDRO provides any rights. If a divorce is granted, a distribution no longer requires the consent of a person who is no longer the participant's spouse. [ERISA § 205]

Bifurcation disadvantages a less-wealthy spouse in several ways, including the following:

- If the wealthier spouse dies, a former spouse is not entitled to an elective share of the estate.
- If the wealthier spouse dies, the former spouse must litigate his or her equitable-distribution claim against the estate. Doing so might be impeded by evidence rules. [*See, e.g.,* Pastuszek v. Pastuszek, 346 Pa. Super. 416, 499 A.2d 1069 (Pa. Super. 1985)]
- A former spouse might become no longer covered as a regular beneficiary under a health plan. Even if COBRA continuation coverage is available, it is more expensive and less valuable.
- A person who is no longer a spouse has no power to decline to consent to a distribution that is other than a qualified preretirement survivor annuity (QPSA) or provided to a person other than the prospective alternate payee. [ERISA § 205]

If any of these disadvantages applies, a person who otherwise would become a former spouse should consider objecting to bifurcation of a divorce proceeding.

Q 13:5 May a QDRO provide for a putative spouse from a void marriage?

No, but practically yes.

To be a QDRO an order first must be a DRO. A DRO must provide alimony payments, child support, or marital property rights to a spouse or former spouse. [ERISA § 206(d)(3)(B)(ii)(I); I.R.C. § 414(p)(1)(B)(i)] Because a void marriage means that the purported marriage never existed, the putative spouse (i.e., a person who participates, in good faith, in a void marriage) never was a spouse. If an order provides for a person other than a participant's spouse, child, or other dependent, such an order is not a DRO.

Although some might argue that "[a]n individual . . . who . . . has as his [or her] principal place of abode the home of the [participant] and is a member of the [participant's] household" is a dependent, "[a]n individual is not a member of the [participant's] household if . . . the relationship between such individual and the [participant] is [or was] in violation of local law." [See I.R.C. § 152(a)(9)] Thus, even if the participant provided more than half the putative spouse's support, it is unclear whether a putative spouse in a void marriage could be a participant's dependent. [See Untermann v. Comm'r, 38 T.C. 93 (Tax Court 1962) (taxpayer's second "marriage" was invalid and therefore his "wife" could not be his dependent because he lived with her in violation of local law); Estate of Buckley v. Comm'r, 37 T.C. 664 (Tax Court 1962); Turnipseed v. Comm'r, 27 T.C. 758 (Tax Court 1957); see also Ensminger v. Comm'r, 610 F.2d 189 (4th Cir. 1979), cert. denied 446 U.S. 941, 100 S. Ct. 2166 (disallowing dependent exemption claimed for taxpayer's support of a 21-year-old woman as "lewd" cohabitation); but see Borax Estate v. Comm'r, 349 F.2d 666 (2d Cir. 1965), cert. denied 383 U.S. 935; In re Shackelford, 3 B.R. 42 (W.D. Mo. Bkrtcy 1980); see generally, 5 U.S.C. § 7342, 33 U.S.C. § 909, 43 U.S.C. § 390bb].

A marriage might be void if any of the following applies:

- One of the parties was married to someone else when the purported marriage took place
- The parties are too closely related to one another
- Either of the parties was unable to consent to a marriage because he or she was insane or under a mental disability
- Either of the parties was unable to consent because he or she had not attained a sufficient age
- A party did not truly consent because he or she was fraudulently induced to enter into the purported marriage
- Either of the parties failed to satisfy a necessary health condition
- The ceremony or agreement failed to meet necessary formalities

Even when a court annuls a marriage or otherwise finds that a purported marriage was a nonmarriage, a putative spouse who acted in good faith usually is entitled to alimony and child support. [See, e.g., Steadman v. Turner, 357 Pa. Super. 361, 516 A.2d 21 (Pa. Super. 1986); see also 20 C.F.R. §§ 440.345, 440.346]

In some states, finding a nonmarriage means that equitable distribution does not apply. In other states, equitable distribution applies equally to a divorce or an annulment. [*See, e.g.,* 23 Pa. Cons. Stat. Ann. § 3502(a)]

Although an order that provides for a putative spouse is not a DRO, some lawyers suggest that a plan administrator may rely on the court order's description of the alternate payee. In the view of the DOL, a plan administrator need not evaluate the correctness of a state court's determination that a person is or was a spouse under state domestic-relations law. [D.O.L. Adv. Op. 92-17A (Aug. 21, 1992)] In practice, a domestic-relations court that enters an order directing a retirement plan to provide for a putative spouse often inaccurately describes, inadvertently or deliberately, that person as a spouse.

> **Note.** A putative spouse is not entitled to a QPSA or similar death benefit that turns on being a participant's surviving spouse. [ERISA § 205; *see also* Boyd v. Waterfront Employers ILA Pension Fund, 182 F.3d 907 (4th Cir. 1999) (a woman who had not divorced her first husband was therefore not married to her second "husband" and so was not entitled to a survivor annuity)] Even a putative spouse who is blameless and was a victim of fraud is not entitled to a QPSA or death benefit as a surviving spouse. [Grabois v. Jones, 89 F.3d 97 (2d Cir. 1996); *but see, e.g.,* Central States, Southeast and Southwest Areas Pension Fund v. Gray, 2003 WL 22339272 (N.D. Ill. Oct. 10, 2003); Croskey v. Ford Motor Company-UAW, Civil Action No 01-1094, 28 Employee Benefits Cases (BNA) 1438, 2002 WL 974827 (S.D.N.Y. May 6, 2002)]

Q 13:6 May a QDRO be used to pay claims based on marital torts?

No. To be a QDRO an order first must be a DRO. A DRO must provide alimony payments, child support, or marital property rights to a spouse or former spouse. [ERISA § 206(d)(3)(B)(ii)(I); I.R.C. § 414(p)(1)(B)(i)] Although the dignitary torts of alienation of affections, conversation, enticement, and seduction could occur only in the context of a marriage, it is doubtful that a claim to damages from such a tort is a marital property right. A spouse's right against interference with his or her marriage is a right based on his or her personal dignity. The fact that recovery is provided only to the wronged spouse reveals that such a right is not marital property.

Q 13:7 May a QDRO be used to pay child support?

Yes. A QDRO is a domestic relations order (DRO) that provides for an alternate payee and meets form requirements. [ERISA § 206(d)(3); I.R.C. § 414(p)(1)(A)] A DRO includes an order that "relates to the provision of child support." [ERISA § 206(d)(3)(B)(ii)(I); I.R.C. § 414(p)(1)(B)(i)] Several court decisions have recognized the use of a QDRO to pay child support. [*See, e.g., In re* Marriage of LeBlanc, 944 P.2d 686 (Colo. App. 1997); Rohrbeck v. Rohrbeck, 318 Md. 28, 566 A.2d 767 (Md. 1989); Baird v. Baird, 843 S.W.2d 388 (Mo. 1992); Arnold v. Arnold, 154 Misc.2d 715, 586 N.Y.S.2d 449 (N.Y. 1992); Stinner v. Stinner & Bethlehem Steel Corp., 523 A.2d 1161 (Pa. 1987)]

If a child's custodial parent is the participant's spouse or former spouse, receiving child support payments from an insurer or custodian following a QDRO might be disadvantageous to the custodial parent if he or she (rather than the child) is the alternate payee. Child-support payments received are not income. [I.R.C. §§ 71, 215; Blair v. Commissioner, T.C. Memo 1988-581 (Tax Court 1988)] However, an alternate payee who is the participant's spouse or former spouse is, for federal income tax purposes, the distributee of a QDRO distribution. [I.R.C. § 402(e)(1)(A)]

> **Practice Pointer:** If a custodial parent uses a QDRO to collect child support payments, his or her lawyer should make sure that the court order specifies that the child (rather than the custodial parent) is the payee. The custodial parent also should seek a court appointment to obtain authority to collect these payments, and use the proceeds, as the child's conservator, trustee, Uniform Transfers to Minors Act custodian, or agent.

In the Department of Labor's (DOL's) view, "[I]f an alternate payee is a minor or is legally incompetent, [a QDRO] can require payment to someone with legal responsibility for the alternate payee (such as a guardian or a [person] acting in loco parentis in the case of a child, or a trustee [sic] acting as an agent for the alternate payee)." [DOL Pension and Welfare Benefits Administration, *QDROs, The Division of Pensions Through Qualified Domestic Relations Orders*, Q 1-9 (1997); *see* ERISA Adv. Op. 2002-03A (June 7, 2002) (child support enforcement agency treated as child's "agent")]

> **Caution.** Unlike a regulation adopted after notice in the Federal Register, an opportunity for comments, and other aids to reliability provided by the Administrative Procedure Act and other federal laws, the DOL's view (explained in its QDRO booklet and a later ERISA Advisory Opinion) is not an interpretation to which a court must give any deference. Further, the DOL lacks authority concerning the application of any federal tax.

Q 13:8   Should a divorce lawyer engage an actuary?

Yes, a divorce lawyer should engage an actuary because negotiating a division of a Section 403(b) benefit might involve considering other benefits. [*See generally*, Gary A. Shulman and David I. Kelley, *Dividing Pensions in Divorce* (Aspen Publishers 2nd ed. 2007)]

All but a few Section 403(b) plans are in the form of an account balance or defined contribution plan, as distinguished from a defined benefit or "pension" plan. Many divorce lawyers assume that it is a relatively simple matter to divide an account balance, especially if the plan permits a distribution to the alternate payee before the participant's earliest retirement age. But a couple might have other pension rights that cannot be divided so easily.

Some pension rights cannot be divided at all. For example, a domestic relations court cannot alter Social Security benefits. [42 U.S.C. §§ 4051–407; Boulter v. Boulter, 930 F.2d 112 (D. Nev. 1997)] Further, Social Security benefits might not be community property or marital property. [*See generally* McCarty v.

McCarty, 453 U.S. 210 (1981)(military pension); Hisquierdo v. Hisquierdo, 439 U.S. 572 (1979)(railroad pension); Free v. Bland, 369 U.S. 663 (1962); Wissner v. Wissner, 338 U.S. 655 (1950)]

On the other hand, nothing precludes divorcing parties from negotiating a settlement agreement that provides an "unequal" division of a Section 403(b) plan or contract, or other property, to reflect an impairment that arises from pension rights that are difficult or impossible to divide. For instance, a divorce can substantially reduce or even eliminate a nonworker spouse's Social Security benefits. [42 U.S.C. §§ 402–416; 20 C.F.R. §§ 404.310–404.346] A divorce lawyer might need an actuary's evaluation of such an impairment to support a negotiating position.

Concerning other pension plans, a divorce lawyer should be aware that there are several ways to value the portion of the unknown future benefits that can be assumed to have accrued during the marriage. Likewise, there are different ways to value the effect that unknown subsequent events may have on the benefits that may be provided. [*See generally*, Marvin Snyder, *Value of Pensions in Divorce* (Aspen Publishers 3d ed. & 2007 Supp.)]

Requirements of a Qualified Domestic Relations Order

Q 13:9 What is a domestic relations order?

For QDRO purposes, a domestic relations order must be an order "made pursuant to a State domestic relations law . . . ." [ERISA § 206(d)(3)(B)(ii)(II); I.R.C. § 414(p)(1)(B)(ii)] The DRO that underlies a QDRO must be a court order; that is, a private agreement between spouses is not a domestic relations order. [Stinner v. Stinner & Bethlehem Steel Corp., 523 A.2d 1161 (Pa. 1987)]

In the DOL's view, a state domestic relations law includes community property law only insofar as such law ordinarily is applied to determine alimony, child support, and property division in domestic relations proceedings. [D.O.L. Adv. Op. 90-46A (Dec. 4, 1990)]

Q 13:10 What makes a court order a QDRO?

A QDRO is a DRO (see Q 13:9) that:

1. Is made under a state's domestic relations law or community property law (see below);
2. Relates to the provision of marital property rights, alimony, or child support to a spouse (or former spouse), child, or other dependent of the participant;
3. Specifies each plan to which the order applies;
4. Specifies the name and last known mailing address of the participant;
5. Specifies the name and last known mailing address of the alternate payee;

6. Recognizes, creates, or assigns to an alternate payee a right to receive all or a portion of the participant's benefit under a Section 403(b) plan or contract;

7. Specifies the fixed or determinable amount payable to each alternate payee;

8. Specifies the number of payments, or the period to which the order applies;

9. Does not require any Section 403(b) plan or contract to provide additional vesting;

10. Does not require any Section 403(b) plan or contract to provide additional benefits;

11. Does not require any Section 403(b) plan or contract to provide any form of benefit not otherwise provided under the plan (if any) and Section 403(b) contract; and

12. Does not require any Section 403(b) plan or contract to pay to an alternate payee benefits that are required to be paid to another alternate payee under a previously determined QDRO.

[ERISA §§ 206(d)(3)(B), 206(d)(3)(C), 206(d)(3)(D); I.R.C. § 414(p)(1)–(3); Treas. Reg. § 1.401(a)-13(g)(iii)(A)]

Practice Pointer. A QDRO must be a court order. A private agreement between spouses is not a DRO. A court judgment, decree, or order is required. [*See* Stinner v. Stinner & Bethlehem Steel Corp., 523 A.2d 1161 (Pa. 1987)]

A QDRO cannot require a plan to pay a joint and survivor annuity for the life of the alternate payee and his or her subsequent spouse or beneficiary. [I.R.C. § 414(p)(4)(A)(iii)]

When directed to a governmental plan, a DRO is treated as a QDRO for federal income tax purposes, even if the DRO does not meet many of the QDRO requirements. [I.R.C. § 414(p)(11)]

Q 13:11 Must a QDRO state the participant's or alternate payee's Social Security number?

No. Stating a participant's or alternate payee's Social Security number (SSN) or Individual Taxpayer Identification Number (ITIN) is not one of the enumerated conditions required for a DRO to be a QDRO. [ERISA § 206(d)(3)(C)(i)]

Before concerns about identity theft and related frauds became widely known, many plans' sample orders (see Q 13:38) suggested including the Taxpayer Identification Number (SSN or ITIN) in the same clause that stated a party's name and last known mailing address. Knowing a participant's number helps a plan administrator and its record-keeper find the participant record, and knowing a potential alternate payee's number facilitates setting up a record-keeping subaccount for that person and, if the alternate payee is or was the participant's spouse, tax-reporting a distribution.

Following increasing awareness of public access to court records, divorce practitioners and the divorcing parties themselves often insist on omitting these identifying numbers from the court order itself. A plan administrator, insurer, custodian, or other payer should not object if the participant or alternate payee furnishes and certifies the number that the payer needs for tax-reporting purposes.

Practice Pointer. One common solution is for each party to submit with the DRO a one-page form that includes a penalties-of-perjury statement consistent with IRS Forms W-4P and W-9 and that includes a description of the order to which this certification relates.

Q 13:12   Must a QDRO state the alternate payee's residence address?

No. An order qualifies as a QDRO if the order, along with meeting other conditions, "clearly specifies . . . the name and *mailing address* of each alternate payee[.]" [ERISA § 206(d)(3)(C)(i) (emphasis added)] The address recited in an order need not be the address of a place where the alternate payee resides. Further, the address need not be the alternate payee's only mailing address; it is enough that the address is a mailing address at which the alternate payee could receive mail. [Mattingly v. Hoge, Civil Action No. 07-5253 (6th Cir. Jan. 8, 2008)]

Q 13:13   Must a QDRO state all the required information?

Yes, to be a QDRO a court order must state every fact and every provision that the statute—whether ERISA or the Code—requires to qualify an order as a QDRO.

However, some courts have presumed to "cure" an order and treat it as though it were a QDRO. [*See, e.g.,* Metropolitan Life Ins. Co. v. Bigelow, 283 F.3d 436 (2d Cir. 2002); Trustees of the Directors Guild of America v. Tise, 234 F.3d 415 (9th Cir. 2000); Stewart v. Thorpe Holding Co. Profit Sharing Plan, 207 F.3d 1143 (9th Cir. 2000); *In re* Williams, 50 F. Supp. 2d 951, 959–960 (C.D. Cal. 1999); Metropolitan Life Ins. Co. v. Marsh, 119 F.3d 415 (6th Cir. 1997); Metropolitan Life Ins. Co. v. Wheaton, 42 F.3d 1080 (7th Cir. 1994); Carland v. Metropolitan Life Ins. Co., 935 F.2d 1114 (10th Cir. 1991), *cert. denied,* 502 U.S. 1020 (1991); *see also* Hawkins v. Comm'r, 86 F.3d 982, 65 U.S.L.W. 2044, 78 AFTR.2d 96-5114, 96-1 U.S.T.C. ¶ 50,316, 20 EBC (BNA) 1513, Pension Plan Guide (CCH) ¶ 23920R (10th Cir. 1996) (appeals court reversed Tax Court and treated order as QDRO for tax purposes)]

Although state court decisions cannot be precedent concerning the construction or interpretation of ERISA, the Code, or an ERISA plan, practitioners understand that some state courts might be hostile to the statute's requirement that a QDRO specify the alternate payee's mailing address. [Tolstad v. Tolstad, 527 N.W.2d 668, 673 (N.D. 1995); Stinner v. Stinner, 520 Pa. 374, 554 A.2d 45, 49, *cert. denied,* 492 U.S. 919(1989)] Other courts recognize that a QDRO requires literal compliance.

In the contributing author's view, the court decisions that treat QDRO requirements as mere formalities that can be excused are wrongly decided. First, customary statutory construction precludes a construction that makes a legislature's chosen words meaningless. Further, the QDRO statute's information requirements also have public policy purposes. "The purpose [of the specificity requirements] is to reduce the expense of ERISA plans by sparing plan administrators the grief they experience when because of uncertainty concerning the identity of the beneficiary they pay the wrong person, or arguably the wrong person, and are sued by a rival claimant." [Metropolitan Life Ins. Co. v. Wheaton, 42 F.3d 1080, 1084 (7th Cir. 1994)] In addition, the QDRO rules are designed to promote efficiency and avoid unnecessary expense in plan administration. [*In re* Gendreau, 122 F.3d 815, 817–818 (9th Cir. 1997)]

Q 13:14   Is a court order to refrain from changing a beneficiary a QDRO?

Usually not. In a divorce proceeding, a domestic relations court sometimes makes (or is deemed to have made) an order that restrains one or both of the divorcing parties from taking actions that could frustrate the court's ability to divide property between the parties. For example, a court might order a participant to refrain from changing his or her beneficiary designation under any retirement plan.

Unless such an order specifies a payment to an alternate payee and meets the other requirements of the QDRO rule (see Q 13:10), it is not a QDRO. If an order is not a QDRO, the Section 403(b) plan administrator, insurer, or custodian might have no obligation to act following the order.

Example. Ken is a participant in his employer's ERISA-governed Section 403(b) plan. In a divorce proceeding, a domestic relations court ordered Ken and his wife, JoAnn, not to dispose of, or transfer, any marital assets while the proceeding was pending. In violation of this order, Ken changed his beneficiary designation under the plan from JoAnn to his children by a previous marriage. After Ken's death, the plan benefit was properly payable to the designated beneficiaries. Because the domestic relations court's order was not a QDRO, ERISA preempted it.

[*See, e.g.,* Central SE & SW Areas Pension Fund v. Howell, 227 F.3d 672 (6th Cir. 2000)]

Even if a court order relates to a non-ERISA 403(b) plan or contract (and thus is not preempted), a plan administrator, insurer, or custodian usually need not follow an order if it was not named in the court proceeding, served with legal process, and afforded a court hearing. Further, to comply with a Section 403(b) contract's anti-alienation provision, an insurer or custodian must make a reasonable effort to resist a court order that is not a QDRO.

Q 13:15   Is a court order to refrain from taking a distribution a QDRO?

Usually not. In a divorce proceeding, a domestic relations court sometimes makes an order that restrains one or both of the divorcing parties from taking actions that could frustrate the court's ability to divide property between the parties. For example, a court might order a participant to refrain from taking a distribution under any retirement plan or account, including a Section 403(b) contract.

Unless such an order specifies a payment to an alternate payee and meets the other requirements of the QDRO rule (see Q 13:10), it is not a QDRO. If an order is not a QDRO, the Section 403(b) plan administrator, insurer, or custodian might have no duty to act on the order.

> **Example.** In their divorce proceeding, a domestic relations court ordered Jack and Jill not to dispose of, or transfer, any marital assets while the proceeding was pending (but didn't yet provide a payment to either of them). In violation of this order, Jack took a full distribution from his 403(b) contract. Soon after receiving this payment, he spent all the money. When Jill tried to sue the custodian for paying Jack when it knew that he was restricted by a court order, the court dismissed Jill's lawsuit and ordered her to pay the custodian's attorneys' fees because she should have known that her lawsuit was frivolous.

> **Caution.** A person who receives money that was paid based on a divorcing person's act in violation of a court order might be subject to a constructive trust in favor of the eventual rightful owners of the property. A divorce lawyer should not accept a fee payment from his or her client if the lawyer knows (or should know) based on the surrounding circumstances that the client became able to pay the fee because of a violation of a court order.

Q 13:16   Can a foreign nation's court order be a QDRO?

No. A court order can be a QDRO only if, along with other requirements, the order is a domestic relations order. ERISA provides that a DRO is an order "made pursuant to a State domestic relations law. . . ." [ERISA § 206(d)(3)(B)(ii)(II); I.R.C. § 414(p)(1)(B)(ii)] (See Q 13:9.)

ERISA defines the term *state* to include any State of the United States, the District of Columbia, Puerto Rico, the Virgin Islands, American Samoa, Guam, Wake Island, and the Canal Zone. [ERISA § 3(10)] The Code provides only that the term *state* includes the District of Columbia. [I.R.C. § 7701(a)(10)]

If a state court recognizes a foreign nation's judgment in a domestic relations matter and makes its own order, that state court order might be a DRO that can be determined to be a QDRO. For example, the Uniform Interstate Family Support Act sometimes provides for a state court's enforcement of a registered child-support order made by a foreign nation's court. Under that Act, a state court will enforce such an order under specified conditions that include an appropriate basis for personal jurisdiction. Most states exercise personal jurisdiction over a nonresident defendant to the extent permitted by the U.S. Constitution's protection of due process of law. Thus, if the defendant was not personally present before the foreign nation's court, he or she must have had some contact with the foreign nation such that a legal proceeding against him or her there does not offend traditional notions of fair play and substantial justice." [*See* International Shoe Co. v. State of Washington, 326 U.S. 310 (1946)] If the Uniform Interstate Family Support Act does not apply, a state court will not enforce an order of a foreign nation's court unless the foreign court had both jurisdiction over the subject matter and a procedure that does not offend the current forum state's public policy. [Uniform Enforcement of Foreign Judgments Act of 1964]

Q 13:17   Must a plan administrator reject an order that is missing identifying information?

Yes. Because an order that does not specify the required identifying information (see Q 13:10) is not a QDRO, a plan administrator that implements such an order violates the plan's and the Section 403(b) contract's anti-alienation provisions. [ERISA §§ 206(d), 514(b)(7); I.R.C. § 403(b)(1)(C)] Yet the DOL has stated its unofficial view that when an otherwise qualifying order misstates or omits identifying information, the plan administrator may, from its records or reasonable inquiry, "supplement the order with the appropriate identifying information." [QDROs: The Division of Pensions Through Qualified Domestic Relations Orders (DOL PWBA 1997)] This view is plainly contrary to the unambiguous text of the statute. [ERISA § 206(d)(3); I.R.C. § 414(p)]

Q 13:18   What should a plan administrator do when a court order is ambiguous?

If an order is ambiguous, the order is not a QDRO. To be a QDRO, an order must "clearly specify" all of the required elements (see Q 13:10). [I.R.C. § 414(p)(2); ERISA § 206(d)(3)(C)]

If a plan administrator is in doubt about how to give effect to a court order, it is very likely that the order is not a QDRO.

Because many divorce lawyers submit defective orders, a plan administrator often is tempted to treat a defective order as a QDRO. Because a plan administrator's effort to correct or resolve a defect might adversely affect one of the parties, yielding to this temptation can lead to further litigation.

In *Hullett,* the federal courts upheld a plan administrator's decision that a defective order was a QDRO. [Hullett v. Towers Perrin Forster & Crosby Inc., 38 F.3d 107 (1994)] In the contributing author's opinion, the court erred in this decision by applying Pennsylvania law rather than ERISA, by finding in dicta that the district court could review *de novo* the plan administrator's decision that the order was a QDRO, and by remanding to the district court rather than to the plan administrator for "fact finding" to resolve the ambiguous provisions of the order incorrectly determined to be a QDRO. Perhaps this expensive litigation could have been avoided had the plan administrator properly decided that the order was not a QDRO.

Q 13:19   May a QDRO direct payment to the alternate payee's lawyer?

No. A QDRO cannot create or recognize a right for a person other than an alternate payee. [ERISA § 206(d)(3)(B)(i); I.R.C. § 414(p)(1)(A)] An alternate payee cannot be anyone other than a spouse, former spouse, child, or other dependent of the participant. [ERISA § 206(d)(3)(k); I.R.C. § 414(p)(8)] Therefore, a QDRO may not direct payment to the alternate payee's lawyer. [*See* Johnson v. Johnson, Pension Plan Guide (CCH) ¶ 23,957T (N.J. Super. Ct. 1999)] However, a QDRO may direct payment to an alternate payee in an amount that reflects attorneys' fees within the child support ordered. [*See* Trustees of Directors Guild of Am. V. Tise, 234 F.3d 415 (9th Cir. 2000)]

A court order other than a QDRO has no effect regarding an ERISA plan. [ERISA § 514(b)(7)] Although for a non-ERISA 403(b) contract it is possible to use a court order other than a QDRO, it is unlikely that the participant's lawyer will allow the alternate payee's lawyer to do so—a payment following a court order other than a QDRO results in tax on the participant (see Q 13:49).

Q 13:20   Can a QDRO provide for a spouse in a same-sex couple?

Maybe. Even when recognized under applicable state law, a marriage of a same-sex couple might not be recognized in applying either ERISA or the Code. "In determining the meaning of any Act of Congress . . . , the word 'marriage' means only a legal union between one man and one woman as husband and wife, and the word 'spouse' refers only to a person of the opposite sex who is a husband or a wife." [1 U.S.C. § 7]

Another approach may accomplish the desired effect, however. That is, a QDRO may provide for a dependent of the participant. [ERISA § 206(d)(3)(B) (ii)(I); I.R.C. § 414(p)(1)(B)(i)] If the participant provides sufficient support for his or her spouse in a same-sex couple, the nonparticipant may be a dependent. [I.R.C. § 152]

Even if a QDRO is effective to permit a distribution to a participant's same-sex spouse, it might not shift income tax to the alternate payee. Only an alternate payee who is the participant's spouse or former spouse as the United States Code defines that term is treated as a distributee. Any other distribution, even if paid under a valid QDRO, is treated as a distribution to the participant. Further, a QDRO distribution paid to an alternate payee who is not the participant's spouse or former spouse (as the United States Code defines that term) cannot be rolled over. [I.R.C. §§ 402(c), 402(d)(4)(J), 402(e)(1)(A); Notice 89-25, 1989-1 C.B. 662, Q&A 4]

If an alternate payee is a nonspouse for federal income tax purposes, the plan administrator or payer must withh[o]ld from the [QDRO] distribution as if the . . . participant were the payee. [Notice 89-25, 1989-1 C.B. 662, Q&A 3] The participant may make his or her withholding certificate on IRS Form W-4P.

Q 13:21   What is the importance of earliest retirement age?

A QDRO cannot require a plan to pay an alternate payee until the participant's earliest retirement age. [I.R.C. §§ 414(p)(3)(A), 414(p)(4)(A)] For this purpose, *earliest retirement age* means the earlier of:

1. The first date that the participant is entitled to a distribution; or
2. The later of:
   (a) The date the participant attains age 50; or
   (b) The earliest date the participant could receive a distribution if the participant separated from service.

[I.R.C. § 414(p)(4)(B); ERISA § 206(d)(3)(E)(ii)]

Example. Susan has a 403(b) annuity contract that imposes no distribution restrictions other than those required by Code Section 403(b)(11). Susan divorces Tom when both of them are in their early 30s. If Susan continues to work for her employer, a QDRO cannot order a payment to Tom until Susan reaches age 50. If, however, Susan quits her job or is fired, a QDRO could require that Tom be paid immediately.

The rule that precludes a distribution to the alternate payee until the participant's earliest retirement age (unless the plan expressly specifies otherwise) is strictly construed. [Dickerson v. Dickerson, 803 F. Supp. 127 (E.D. Tenn. 1992); Stott v. Bunge Corp., 800 F. Supp. 567 (E.D. Tenn. 1992)] Whether a defined contribution plan should permit a QDRO distribution before the participant's earliest retirement age is a plan design choice.

Note. If finding an earliest retirement age for QDRO purposes turns on considering a hypothetical separation from service, it is unclear how a plan administrator should interpret a term that—although it previously had significance concerning whether a participant might be entitled to a distribution or how he or she might be taxed on a distribution—now ordinarily has no independent significance.

Q 13:22   May a plan or contract permit payment to an alternate payee before the participant's earliest retirement age?

Yes. A plan (or a contract) may permit payment to an alternate payee before the participant's earliest retirement age. [Treas. Reg. § 1.401(a)-13(g)(3); H.R. Conf. Comm. Rep. on Pub. L. No. 99-514 (Tax Reform Act of 1986), 99th Cong., 2d Sess. at II-858 (1986); Ltr. Rul. 8837013; *accord* Treas. Reg. § 1.403(b)-10(c)]

Practice Pointer: Some plan sponsors choose to permit an immediate distribution to an alternate payee, believing that to do so is simpler than keeping a court order open for many years while waiting for the participant to reach retirement. Other plan sponsors decide that it is inappropriate to pay an alternate payee before the participant becomes entitled to receive a distribution. Further, such a provision might lead to fraud (see Q 13:44).

Q 13:23   Can an order made after the participant's death be a QDRO?

Maybe. A DRO does not fail to be a QDRO "solely because of the time at which it is issued." [29 C.F.R. § 2530.206(c); Pension Protection Act of 2006, Pub. L. No. 109-280, 120 Stat. 780, § 1001(1)(B) (2006)] However, a DRO may fail to be a QDRO because it would require the plan to provide a "type" or "form" of benefit that the plan does not otherwise provide. [29 C.F.R. § 2530.206(d); Pension Protection Act of 2006, Pub. L. No. 109-280, 120 Stat. 780, § 1001(2) (2006)] For a defined benefit plan, an order made after the participant's death, even if the order "relates back" to the time of an earlier court order for state law purposes (see Q 13:24), might not be a QDRO if such an order would require the plan to provide a death benefit that the plan does not provide (which might be because the benefit had lapsed), or otherwise would "require the plan to provide increased benefits (determined on the basis of actuarial value)." [ERISA § 206(d)(3)(D)(i)–(ii); Samaroo (Robichaud) v. Samaroo, 193 F.3d 185 (3d Cir. 1999); *but see* Files v. Exxon Mobil Pension Plan, 428 F.3d 478 (3d Cir. 2005) (the court assumed that a separate interest did not require increased benefits); Patton v. Denver Post Corp., 326 F.3d 1148 (10th Cir. 2003), *affirming*, 179 F. Supp. 2d 1232 (D. Colo. 2002); Payne v. GM/UAW Pension Plan, 1996 WL 943424 (E.D. Mich. 1996)]

However, the same benefit-soundness concerns typically are not involved with a plan that defines its benefits in terms of a participant's individual account, has no funding duties or obligations that could be affected by recognizing an order as a QDRO, and permits a participant to designate any beneficiary to receive his or her undistributed account. As long as the participant's account has not been distributed and the order does not interfere with the rights of a surviving spouse, an order made after the participant's death might nonetheless be a QDRO. [*See, e.g.,* Hogan v. Raytheon Co., 302 F.3d 854 (8th Cir. 2002); Trustees of Directors Guild of Am. V. Tise, 234 F.3d 415 (9th Cir. 2000), *amended by,* 255 F.3d 661 (9th Cir. 2000); Patton v. Denver Post Corp., 326 F.3d 1148 (10th Cir. 2003); IBM Savings Plan v. Price, No. 2:04-CV-187 (D. Vt. 2004); *but see* Rivers v. Central & SW Corp., 186 F.3d 681 (5th Cir. 1999)] Of course, to be a QDRO a DRO must meet all of the QDRO requirements, including that the order must not require the plan to provide a "type" or "form" of benefit that the plan does not otherwise provide (see Q 13:10).

Practice Pointer. The unpleasantness and expense of needless litigation usually can be avoided if the alternate payee's lawyer obtains an appropriate order before the participant's death, and prepares that order to state that the former spouse is deemed the participant's surviving spouse to the extent of any distribution or benefit required under the order.

Q 13:24   What is a *nunc pro tunc* order?

Translated from Latin, *nunc pro tunc* means "now for then."

In theory, a court issues a *nunc pro tunc* order only to correct a clerical error or omission in the records of its proceedings. Some courts make an order to "clarify" an "ambiguity" in an earlier order. In practice, many judges use the legal fiction of a *nunc pro tunc* order to do what had been entirely omitted. Notwithstanding an order that ostensibly was final, often a *nunc pro tunc* order is a "do-over."

> **Practice Pointer.** A plan administrator need not (and should not) consider whether a court order violates state law, as long as it is an order. That an order violates state law does not cause the order to fail to qualify as a QDRO. [Blue v. UAL Corp., 160 F.3d 383 (7th Cir. 1998)]

A *nunc pro tunc* order does not fail to be a QDRO "solely because the order is issued after, or revises, another domestic relations order or qualified domestic relations order" or "solely because of the time at which it is issued." [29 C.F.R. § 2530.206(b)-(c); PPAof2006 § 1001(1)(A)-(B)] However, a DRO may fail to be a QDRO because it would require the plan to provide a "type" or "form" of benefit that the plan does not otherwise provide. [29 C.F.R. § 2530.206(d); Pension Protection Act of 2006, Pub. L. No. 109-280, 120 Stat. 780, § 1001(2) (2006)]

Special Provisions

Q 13:25   Can a QDRO provide survivor benefits to an alternate payee?

Yes, if the alternate payee is the participant's former spouse. A QDRO may provide that an alternate payee who is a former spouse of the participant be treated as the participant's surviving spouse for all or some purposes of the ERISA survivor annuity rules. [ERISA § 206(d)(3)(F); I.R.C. § 414(p)(5); Treas. Reg. § 1.401(a)-13(g)(4)] If used, such a provision could wholly or partly deprive the participant's current spouse of survivor benefits to which he or she otherwise might become entitled. [ERISA § 206(d)(3)(F)(i); I.R.C. § 414(p)(5)(A); Treas. Reg. §§ 1.401(a)-13(g)(4)(iii)(B), 1.401(a)-13(g)(4)(iii)(C)] If the former spouse who is treated as a current spouse dies before the participant's annuity starting date, the participant's actual current spouse is treated as the current spouse, except as otherwise provided by another QDRO. [Treas. Reg. § 1.401(a)-13(g)(4)(iii)(C)]

> **Note.** A QDRO cannot provide surviving-spouse treatment to an alternate payee who is not the participant's former spouse. [Hamilton v. Plumbers and Pipefitters National Pension Fund, 433 F.3d 1091 (9th Cir. 2006), *cert. denied sub nom* Hamilton v. Wash. State Plumbing & Pipefitting Ind. Pension Plan, 2006 U.S. LEXIS 5808 (2006)]

In the absence of an express statement in a QDRO that the former spouse will be treated as the participant's surviving spouse, a preretirement survivor annuity is payable to the participant's current spouse, even if that means that the former spouse receives no payment (because the participant died before becoming entitled to receive retirement benefits). [*E.g.* Dugan v. Clinton, No. 86-C-8492, 1987 WL 24805 (N.D. Ill. 1987)]

Practice Pointer. If a divorce practitioner is not certain that a QDRO distribution will be paid immediately, he or she should make sure that the court order states that the alternate payee is the surviving spouse, at least to the extent of the amount owing to the alternate payee.

Q 13:26   What happens if a participant's Section 403(b) account is loaned out and there is no money to pay the alternate payee?

Because a QDRO cannot require a Section 403(b) plan or contract to provide additional benefits (see Q 13:10), a QDRO cannot order a payment to an alternate payee that the Section 403(b) issuer would not be obligated to pay the participant.

Example. Larry, who is age 61 and retired, is a participant under a Section 403(b)(7) custodial account. The account, currently valued at $9,000, comprises $2,000 worth of fund shares and a $7,000 plan loan receivable over five years. If a court enters a domestic relations order directing an immediate payment of $4,500 (50 percent of $9,000) to Fiona, Larry's former spouse, the order is not a QDRO, because the custodian could raise only about $2,000 by selling fund shares, and the loan agreement provides for level repayments quarterly over five years. Instead, the court could order an immediate payment of $2,000 and a $2,500 interest in the custodial account with distributions payable only after the custodian receives loan repayments.

If a Section 403(b) account is "loaned out," an alternate payee might consider seeking a court order directing the participant to inform the alternate payee if the participant fails to meet any scheduled loan repayment. An order directing the plan administrator or the custodian to inform the alternate payee that the participant has failed to meet a loan repayment is not a QDRO (see Q 13:10), and concerning an ERISA-governed plan is preempted. [ERISA § 206(d)(3); I.R.C. § 414(p)]

Q 13:27   Can an alternate payee designate a beneficiary?

Maybe. If a QDRO does not provide for immediate distribution to the alternate payee, and therefore the alternate payee is treated as having an interest in the participant's account, the QDRO may provide for the alternate payee to designate, according to the provisions of the plan, a beneficiary for the alternate payee's portion of the participant's account. An alternate payee's right to designate a beneficiary for his or her portion cannot be any greater than the participant's right to designate a beneficiary, however. [Treas. Reg. § 1.401(a)-13(g)(4)(iii)(B)]

Q 13:28   Can a QDRO be used to waive spouse's consent and survivor annuity rules?

Yes. A QDRO may provide that a current spouse shall not be treated as a current spouse of the participant for all or some purposes of the survivor annuity rules. Likewise, a QDRO may provide that a spouse waives all future rights to a qualified preretirement survivor annuity (QPSA) or qualified joint and survivor annuity (QJSA). [Treas. Reg. § 1.401(a)-13(g)(4)(ii)]

> **Practice Pointer.** Although, to the dismay of many estate-planning lawyers, a premarital agreement is not effective as a spouse's consent to a qualified election (see Qs 12:38, 12:61), in fitting circumstances a QDRO can be an alternate means of achieving a similar result. [ERISA § 205; Treas. Reg. § 1.401(a)-20/A-28]

Plan Administration Procedures

Q 13:29   Who decides whether a court order is a QDRO?

The plan administrator decides whether a court order is a QDRO. [ERISA § 206(d)(3)(G)(i)(II); I.R.C. § 414(p)(6)(A)(ii); Sippe v. Sippe, 398 S.E.2d 895 (N.C. App. 1990)]

Q 13:30   Who is the plan administrator?

A Section 403(b) plan's administrator is the person so named by the plan document. [I.R.C. § 414(g)(1); Treas. Reg. § 1.414(g)-1(a)] If there is no plan document, or if the plan document fails to name a plan administrator, the employer is the plan administrator. [I.R.C. § 414(g)(2)(A); Treas. Reg. § 1.414(g)-1(b)(1)]

Q 13:31   Why is it desirable for a plan administrator to adopt a written procedure?

ERISA requires a plan administrator to adopt written procedures to guide its determinations of whether each domestic relations order submitted to it is a QDRO. [ERISA § 206(d)(3)(G)(ii)] A prudent plan administrator may use its procedure to demonstrate to divorcing parties and their lawyers the correctness of the plan administrator's decisions. Since a failure to comply with ERISA's specific statutory command may be an abuse of discretion, the absence of a written procedure may make it difficult for a court to defer to the plan administrator's determination.

Further, a plan administrator might be liable to a disappointed alternate payee or person who sought to become an alternate payee if efforts to pursue a QDRO were frustrated by the plan administrator's lack of procedures. [*See, e.g.,* Stewart v. Thorpe Holding Co. Profit Sharing Plan, 207 F.3d 1143 (9th Cir. 2000)]

Q 13:32   Is the plan administrator's determination as to whether a court order is a QDRO a fiduciary activity?

Concerning an ERISA-governed plan, a determination concerning whether a court order is a QDRO is a plan administrator's decision governed by ERISA fiduciary standards. [ERISA § 206(d)(3)(I)] The plan administrator must act with the prudence, diligence, and skill of a person who is an expert in making such determinations. [ERISA §§ 206(d)(3)(I)(i), 404(a)(1); Marshall v. Snyder, 572 F.2d 894 (2d Cir. 1978)]

For a church plan that has not elected to be governed by ERISA or a governmental plan (which cannot be governed by ERISA), a decision whether a court order is a QDRO might be governed by state-law standards.

Q 13:33   How does a plan administrator decide whether a court order is a QDRO?

A plan (or its plan administrator) must establish reasonable procedures for deciding whether a court order submitted to the plan administrator is a QDRO, and for administering a distribution required following a QDRO. [ERISA § 206(d)(3)(G)(ii); I.R.C. § 414(p)(6)(B)] Those procedures must

(1) Be in writing;

(2) Provide for giving notice of the procedures to the participant and each alternate payee; and

(3) Permit an alternate payee to designate a representative (such as an attorney) to receive notices concerning a DRO.

[ERISA § 206(d)(3)(G)(ii)(I)–(III)]

Although it is not required, a plan administrator may include in the written procedure a provision that, while the plan administrator evaluates a court order proposed as a QDRO, the participant continues to have any investment-direction rights he or she ordinarily would have. [*See* Schoonmaker v. Employee Savings Plan of Amoco Corp., 987 F.2d 410 (7th Cir. 1993)]

In the DOL's view, a plan administrator need not evaluate the correctness of a state court's determination that an individual is or was a spouse under state domestic relations law. [D.O.L. Adv. Op. 92-17A]

Q 13:34   Does a plan administrator's failure to follow its QDRO procedures invalidate a QDRO?

No. A plan administrator's failure to follow its procedures, or procedures required by ERISA Sections 206(d)(3)(G) and 206(d)(3)(H), does not necessarily cause an otherwise valid order to fail to be a QDRO. [Brotman v. Molitch, 1989 WL 88998 (E.D. Pa. 1989) (*motion for reconsideration denied* Dec. 17, 1991)]

Q 13:35   Should a plan administrator consider whether an order complies with state law?

No. A plan administrator need not (and should not) consider whether a court order violates state law. That an order violates state law does not cause the order to fail to qualify as a QDRO. [Blue v. UAL Corp., 160 F.3d 383 (7th Cir. 1998)]

Courts have shown extraordinary deference to plan administrators' need for administrative certainty: "Pension plans are high-volume operations, which rely heavily on forms, such as designations of beneficiaries. Administrators are entitled to implement what the forms say, rather than what the signatories may have sought to convey." [Blue v. UAL Corp., 160 F.3d 383 (7th Cir. 1998) (*citing* Hightower v. Kirksey, 157 F.3d 528 (7th Cir. 1998))]

Q 13:36 Should a plan administrator furnish information to a prospective alternate payee?

No, a plan administrator has fiduciary duties to a participant and should not disclose the participant's confidential information until it receives the participant's written consent or an appropriate subpoena or other court order that binds the participant. To do otherwise risks liability to the participant. Conversely, a plan administrator has no fiduciary duty to a prospective alternate payee other than the duty to decide, following a proper QDRO determination procedure, whether an order submitted to the plan administrator is a QDRO. [ERISA §§ 206(d)(3)(G), 206(d)(3)(H)] A prudent plan administrator will adopt procedures that do not require it to disclose information without adequate protection.

Q 13:37 May a plan administrator or service provider give a participant or alternate payee legal advice about a QDRO?

No, if an employee of a plan administrator or service provider is not a lawyer, giving legal advice is the unauthorized practice of law, which is a crime in most states. A plan administrator has a duty to furnish plan documents, including the plan's QDRO procedure, on a proper request; however, the plan administrator has no duty to provide advice. [ERISA § 404(a)(1)] Although ERISA preempts many state laws, it does not preempt any generally applicable criminal law. [ERISA § 514(b)(4)]

In general, a lawyer must not give legal advice to a person who is not the lawyer's client. [Model Rules of Prof'l Conduct, R. 1.7 (ABA 2007)] If a participant or an alternate payee has retained a lawyer, any other lawyer (including an employee of a plan administrator or a service provider) must talk only with the represented person's lawyer. [Model Rules of Prof'l Conduct, R. 4.2 (ABA 2007)] If the participant or alternate payee does not have a lawyer, the plan's or service provider's lawyer must not give that unrepresented person any advice. [Model Rules of Prof'l Conduct, R. 1.7, 4.3 (ABA 2007)] The lawyer may (but is not required to) urge the individual to engage a lawyer.

Practice Pointer. A person who wants to speak to a lawyer other than his or her lawyer often will say that the inquirer dismissed his or her former lawyer and so is no longer represented. A lawyer is not free to accept such a statement "at face value." Instead, a lawyer must take reasonable steps, which include at least contacting the other lawyer to confirm whether the inquirer truly is unrepresented. [*See generally* ABA *Center for Prof'l Responsibility, Annotated Model Rules of Prof'l Conduct* at 396 (ABA 6th ed. 2007)]

Further, a careful lawyer might routinely refuse oral communications with a nonclient so that he or she might more easily defend against any potential assertions about his or her conduct by proving the absence of a conversation.

It might, however, be acceptable for either a lawyer or a nonlawyer employed by a plan administrator or service provider to give *information* to the participant's or alternate payee's lawyer. At least one advisory opinion recognizes that when "it furthers the interest of the [plan administrator] for [its lawyer] to assist *representatives* of [participants] or their spouses in the preparation of court orders acceptable to the [plan administrator]," the lawyer may (but is not obligated to) do so. [N.Y. County Lawyers Assoc. Comm. on Professional Ethics, Op. No. 713 (May 28, 1996)] If an employee of a plan administrator or service provider gives a lawyer information, the employee should remind the lawyer that any information is not legal advice.

Even when talking with a lawyer, a plan administrator or service provider should caution the lawyer not to rely on the administrator's or provider's assistance. At least one court has suggested that a lawyer may pursue a state law claim (for example, the tort of negligent communication) against a nonlawyer plan administrator who gave legal advice to the divorce lawyer. [Templeman v. Dahlgren, 1990 U.S. Dist LEXIS 10183 (D. Or. 1990)]

> **Practice Pointer.** If a plan administrator's or service provider's employee has a conversation with only one of the two lawyers engaged in a domestic relations matter, some practitioners recommend that the employee confirm the conversation in an even-handed letter delivered to both lawyers. Others suggest that information should be limited to furnishing (to whichever lawyer asks) a sample QDRO form, with no more than a written explanation of the assumptions used in drafting that sample form. In any communication to any divorce lawyer, a plan administrator or service provider should avoid suggesting that any information is for the benefit of either of the divorcing parties.

Q 13:38 Should a plan administrator provide a model QDRO?

Although there is no requirement that anyone do so, some plan administrators find it convenient to make available a model QDRO. Because many divorce lawyers are unfamiliar with QDRO rules or retirement plan provisions, making available a model QDRO might help avoid the expense of rejecting defective court orders and then reconsidering amended orders.

If a plan administrator makes available a model QDRO, it should furnish it only to a duly licensed lawyer. Because of the significant possibility that a nonlawyer might reasonably perceive a model QDRO as legal advice, furnishing it might constitute the practice of law. [*Cf.* Virginia Unauthorized Practice of Law Opinion 202 (June 18, 2002), published in *Virginia Lawyer Register* (August/September 2002) at page 3] Worse, if a person who has no lawyer relies on a model QDRO that is not suitable to that person's needs and circumstances and the plan administrator knew or should have known that an unadvised person might rely on the model QDRO as suitable for his or her use, the plan administrator might be liable to the person who relies on that communication. [ERISA § 404(a)(1); Restatement (Second) of Torts § 552 (1977)]

Q 13:39   Should a lawyer who advises an alternate payee rely on a sample QDRO?

No. While a lawyer (whether he or she advises a potential alternate payee or a participant) might consider the information in a sample QDRO, a lawyer should not rely on it, and instead must evaluate what form of court order would meet his or her client's purposes. If a plan administrator furnishes a sample QDRO (see Q 13:38), such a sample form likely will have been designed to support the plan administrator's convenience. A sample QDRO form might lack provisions that the lawyer's client wants, or might include provisions that the lawyer's client does not want. [*See* Marvin Snyder, *Value of Pensions in Divorce* at chapter 17 and § 17.6 (Aspen Publishers 3d ed. & 2007 Supp.)]

> **Practice Pointer:** A lawyer who represents an alternate payee should be especially careful to draft a court order that clearly specifies which rights are provided to the alternate payee if the participant dies before the QDRO distribution is paid. Further, a lawyer should be careful to draft a court order that clearly specifies the rights provided to the alternate payee's successors if the alternate payee dies before the QDRO distribution is paid.

Q 13:40   How does a Roth 403(b) account affect QDRO negotiations?

Before 2006, divorcing parties and their lawyers generally assumed that one federal income tax treatment applied concerning distributions from a Section 403(b) contract. After 2005, a participant and a potential alternate payee might consider that the tax treatment of a QDRO distribution could differ based on whether the distribution is attributable to Roth or non-Roth amounts. Along with this, divorcing parties and their lawyers should consider that a QDRO distribution to an alternate payee who is or was the participant's spouse is that alternate payee's income, but a QDRO distribution to a non-spouse alternate payee (such as, the participant's child) is the participant's income. (See Qs 13:47–13:50.)

Even without considering a choice of alternate payee and presuming that the alternate payee will be the participant's spouse or former spouse, using a QDRO to allocate Roth and non-Roth amounts between a participant and an alternate payee might lower the sum of the parties' income taxes.

> **Practice Pointer.** If a participant's Section 403(b) arrangement includes Roth and non-Roth amounts, a participant and a potential alternate payee could be affected by whether a QDRO distribution is drawn from Roth amounts or non-Roth amounts. [Treas. Reg. § 1.402A-1] To a spouse or former spouse, a distribution that is attributable to Roth amounts is more valuable than a distribution that is for the same amount but that is attributable to non-Roth amounts. Conversely, a participant might be more willing to agree to a QDRO distribution that will be attributable to non-Roth amounts than to a QDRO

distribution of the same amount to be drawn from Roth or blended amounts. If there is a helpful difference in the divorcing parties' marginal tax rates, negotiators who understand the tax treatment rules might find an opportunity to use differences to support a "win-win" negotiation that leads to a better outcome for both parties than the result that might have been negotiated had the parties not considered each party's taxes or tax preferences.

Caution. Nothing in the Code requires a Section 403(b) plan or contract to permit distributees to choose whether a distribution is attributable to Roth or non-Roth amounts. Before pursuing a negotiation strategy that depends on the parties' opportunity to control a QDRO distribution's contract-accounting and tax-reporting treatment, a negotiator or lawyer should carefully read the Section 403(b) contract to learn whether an allocation is permitted and what manner of instruction the insurer or custodian will accept.

Q 13:41   Should a plan administrator retain a lawyer to advise it concerning whether a court order is a QDRO?

In determining whether a court order is a QDRO, a plan administrator must act with the prudence, diligence, and skill of a person who is expert in making such a legal determination (see Q 13:32). If a plan administrator does not have the required expert skill, it has a fiduciary duty to obtain professional advice. [*See, e.g.,* Marshall v. Glass/Metal Ass'n and Glaziers and Glassworkers Pension Plan, 507 F. Supp. 378 (D. Haw. 1980)] A fiduciary that prudently relies on written legal advice should be protected against an allegation of breach of fiduciary duty.

Q 13:42   Can a plan administrator rely on its third-party administrator to decide whether a court order is a QDRO?

Although a recordkeeper or other third-party "administrator" might provide useful assistance in reviewing a court order, a nonlawyer cannot render advice about law. A plan administrator that seeks to defend its conduct by asserting that it was prudent to rely on the advice of an unlicensed person might find that it is very difficult to argue that view to a court that has inherent power to regulate the rendering of legal advice.

Q 13:43   Can a plan charge a participant for the expense of determining whether a court order is a QDRO?

When handling claims under a plan (including making a determination as to whether a court order is or is not a QDRO), a plan administrator has a fiduciary duty to make a correct legal determination so that the plan can avoid making an improper distribution (or improperly reducing the participant's benefit) or failing to make a proper distribution. [ERISA §§ 402, 404(a)(1)] Therefore, the expense, including the fees of a lawyer advising the plan administrator, incurred in making a determination on a particular court order is a plan administration expense. [ERISA § 404(a)(1)] Unless the plan's documents expressly obligate the employer to pay the plan's expenses, a plan administrator may charge a plan administration expense against plan assets.

A plan may provide that the expense incurred in making a determination on a particular court order is an expense chargeable to the participant's accrued benefit or account under the plan. To be effective, such a provision should be supported by explicit disclosure. If an ERISA-governed plan's documents do not state a provision for allocating an expense among individual accounts, the plan's administrator must decide the expense allocation in its discretion. ERISA provides general fiduciary principles, but generally does not state express rules, for how plan expenses may be allocated among an individual account retirement plan's participants and beneficiaries. Therefore, a plan administrator has considerable discretion to decide how plan expenses will be allocated among individual accounts. Obeying ERISA duties, a plan fiduciary must be prudent in selecting a method of allocation. Fiduciary duties of prudence and neutrality require a fiduciary to consider "the competing interests of various classes of the plan's participants and the effects of various allocation methods on those interests." A method of allocating expenses does not fail to meet prudence standards merely because the selected method happens to disfavor a class of participants, as long as there is some rational basis for the selected method. [See Allocation of Expenses in a Defined Contribution Plan, Field Assistance Bulletin 2003-3, DOL-EBSA (May 19, 2003)]

> **Note.** If a lawsuit asserts that a fiduciary's discretionary decision about allocating plan expenses was in breach of the fiduciary's standard of care, a court should review only whether the fiduciary acted capriciously or in an abuse of its discretion (assuming that the plan documents provided the administrator discretionary authority to decide the allocation). [Firestone Tire & Rubber Co. v. Bruch, 489 U.S. 101 (1989)]

For a non-ERISA 403(b) plan or contract, a plan or contract can effectively provide (when supported by explicit disclosure) that the expense incurred in making a determination on a particular court order is an expense chargeable to the participant's accrued benefit or account under the plan or contract.

In any case, a plan administrator that charges its lawyers' fees against a participant's account or against plan assets generally has a fiduciary duty to use a lawyer's time efficiently so as to not incur any more than "reasonably necessary" expense. [ERISA § 404(a)(1); accord Unif. Trust Code § 709, 7C U.L.A. 584–586 (2006), 2007 Supp. 49]

Q 13:44 Does a plan administrator have a duty to question a fraudulent divorce?

Maybe. According to the DOL, when faced with circumstances that strongly suggest the "divorcing" parties' perjury, a plan administrator *may* inquire about a court order to evaluate whether it is a domestic relations order (see Q 13:9) under state law; however, it is unclear whether a plan administrator *must* do so. [ERISA Adv. Op. 99-13A (Sept. 29, 1999)]

The ERISA Advisory Opinion describes a situation in which the plan administrator noticed information that suggested fraudulent domestic relations orders. The plan administrator received several domestic relations orders within a very short period, including several from the same lawyer. Each of these orders identically provided for an assignment to an alternate payee of *all* of the participant's benefit in an individual account plan, but made no division of any pension plan benefit. In each of the orders, the alternate payee and participant were shown as having the same address. The plan administrator was aware of the recent circulation of a pamphlet titled "Retirement Liberation Handbook." The pamphlet advocated, as a method of obtaining a retirement plan distribution before the participant's separation from service, that a participant and his or her spouse obtain a divorce for the sole purpose of entering a QDRO. Thereafter, the participant and his or her spouse might remarry. After reading the pamphlet, the plan administrator found that all of the questionable orders had significant similarities to the specific format promoted by the pamphlet, including an error repeated consistently in several of the orders. Further, all of the orders related to employees who resided in the same geographic area, were in related work groups, and had common atypical characteristics, including prompt remarriage and continued use of employer-provided fringe benefits for spouses.

ERISA requires a plan administrator to decide whether a DRO submitted to it is a QDRO. [ERISA § 206(d)(3)(G)] In doing so, a plan administrator must follow the plan's reasonable procedures and incur only reasonable expenses of administering the plan. [ERISA § 404(a)(1)(A)] Thus, the plan administrator should take prudent steps to ensure that the plan's QDRO procedure is cost-effective.

A plan administrator need not review the correctness of a court's decision on whether the parties are entitled to a judgment of divorce. [ERISA Adv. Op. 92-17A (Aug. 21, 1992)] However, the DOL suggests that the plan administrator's general fiduciary duty may require it to make some effort to avoid acquiescing in an obvious fraud:

> [I]f the plan administrator has received evidence calling into question the validity of an order relating to marital property rights under State domestic relations law, the plan administrator is not free to ignore that information. Information indicating that an order was fraudulently obtained calls into question whether the order was issued pursuant to State domestic relations law, and therefore whether the order is a "domestic relations order." . . . . When made aware of such evidence, the administrator must take reasonable steps to determine its credibility. If the administrator determines that the evidence is credible, the administrator must decide how best to resolve the question of the validity of the order without inappropriately spending plan assets or inappropriately involving the plan in the State domestic relations proceeding. The appropriate course of action will depend on the actual facts and circumstances of the particular case and may vary depending on the fiduciary's exercise of discretion. However, in these circumstances, . . . appropriate action could include relaying the evidence of invalidity to the State court or agency that issued the order and informing the court or agency that its resolution of the matter may affect the administrator's

determination of whether the order is a QDRO under ERISA. Appropriate action could take other forms, depending on the circumstances and the fiduciary's assessment of the relative costs and benefits, including actual intervention in or initiation of legal proceedings in State court. The plan administrator's ultimate treatment of the order could then be guided by the State court or agency's response as to the validity of the order under State law. If, however, the [plan] administrator is unable to obtain a response from the court or agency within a reasonable time, the [plan] administrator may not independently determine that the order is not valid under State law and therefore is not a "domestic relations order" . . . but should rather proceed with the determination of whether the order is a QDRO.

[ERISA Adv. Op. 99-13A (Sept. 29, 1999)]

Note. This Advisory Opinion is somewhat inconsistent with earlier guidance that a plan administrator need not (and should not) inquire into the correctness of an order under state law (see Q 13:35). Perhaps the DOL's dividing line was that a plan administrator should not "sit idly by" in the face of what seems an obvious falsehood that does not require significant legal reasoning.

Although it may seem strange to take action when the perjuring participant would harm no plan account but his or her own, the plan administrator must nevertheless administer the plan "in accordance with the [plan] documents" and "for the exclusive purpose of providing [retirement plan] benefits to participants and their beneficiaries." [ERISA §§ 404(a)(1)(A), (D)] Even for a non-ERISA plan, the common law requires a fiduciary to carry out the provisions of the document and not to acquiesce in the wishes of a participant or beneficiary. [Restatement (Third) of Trusts § 76 (2007)] However, a plan administrator does not have a duty to preserve a participant's retirement savings when doing so might require it to act in a manner contrary to ERISA or applicable law.

If the state court finds that the divorcing parties committed perjury, a plan administrator should consider whether it would be productive (or wasteful) for the plan to sue the participant and spouse for restoration of the expenses incurred in handling the fraud. [ERISA § 404(a)(1); Restatement (Third) of Trusts §§ 76, 88 (2007); Unif. Trust Code § 805, 7C U.L.A. 601–602 (2006), 2007 Supp. 52]

Also, a lawyer who observes the divorce lawyer's participation in the fraud might have a duty to report that lawyer to the state supreme court or other body that has disciplinary authority over the divorce lawyer. [Model Rules of Prof'l Conduct, R. 8.3 (ABA 2007)] However, in most cases, the lawyer's observation will be a client confidence that the lawyer is prohibited from disclosing without his or her client's informed consent. [Model Rules of Prof'l Conduct, R. 1.6 (ABA 2007); *see, e.g.*, Pa. Bar Op. 91-114 (a lawyer who knows that an alternate payee obtained a large QDRO distribution and knows that the alternate payee remarried the participant soon after the QDRO and *before* she received the QDRO distribution does not necessarily know that the divorce was fraudulent); *see generally,* ABA *Center for Prof'l Responsibility, Annotated Model Rules of Prof'l Conduct* at 574 (ABA 6th ed. 2007)]

Finally, the perjurers face criminal penalties and imprisonment. Under U.S. law, any person who makes a false statement to obtain any benefit from an employee benefit plan can be fined up to $10,000 and imprisoned for up to five years. [18 U.S.C. § 1027] Because perjury in a court proceeding is (in most states) a felony [*See generally,* Model Penal Code § 241.1, 10A U.L.A. 622–628 (2001), 2003 Supp. at 34; *see, e.g.,* 18 Pa. C.S.A. § 4902], each of the "divorcing" parties is subject to similar or additional punishment under state law. States' criminal laws are not preempted by ERISA. [ERISA § 514(b)(7)]

Q 13:45   Why should an ERISA plan administrator refuse to pay a nonparticipant based on an order that is not a QDRO?

A plan administrator should refuse to pay a nonparticipant based on a DRO that is not a QDRO because doing so is a fiduciary breach, for which the plan administrator is personally liable to the plan (and thereby the participant). [ERISA §§ 404(a)(1), 409(a)]

A Section 403(b) annuity contract (including an incidental life insurance contract) must provide that the participant's "rights under the contract are nonforfeitable," and the contract must be nontransferable. [I.R.C. §§ 401(g), 403(b)(1)(C)] A 403(b) custodial account must provide that "it is impossible . . . for any part of the corpus or income to be . . . used for, or diverted to," a purpose other than the participant's exclusive benefit, and that contract benefits may not be assigned or alienated. [I.R.C. §§ 401(a)(2), 401(a)(13)(A), 401(f)(2), 403(b)(7)(A)] ERISA requires that plan assets be held for the exclusive purpose[] of providing benefits to participants and that a plan provide that benefits may not be assigned or alienated. [ERISA §§ 206(d)(1), 403(c)(1)] Similar provisions usually apply to a church plan or governmental plan.

Both ERISA and the Code make clear that the anti-alienation provisions must preclude recognizing any domestic relations order unless the plan administrator has determined the order to be a QDRO. [ERISA § 206(d)(3)(A); I.R.C. § 401(a)(13)(B)] Further, the regulations (which apply for both ERISA and the Code) make clear that recognizing a court's order (other than a QDRO) or process will be an ERISA violation and will cause the Section 403(b) contract to fail to qualify for the tax treatment that would be provided by Code Section 403(b). [Treas. Reg. § 1.401(a)-13(b)(1)]

Making a payment that is contrary to the plan's provisions is a breach of the plan administrator's duty to administer the plan according to the plan documents. [ERISA § 404(a)(1)(D)] A fiduciary that breaches such a duty must restore to the plan the plan's losses resulting from the breach. [ERISA § 409(a)] This means that, following a payment under a non-QDRO, the plan administrator must restore the participant's plan account to the position it would be in if the payment had not occurred.

Note. An ERISA or non-ERISA plan's administrator has a fiduciary duty to defend the plan's provisions. [ERISA § 404(a)(1); Restatement (Third) of Trusts § 76 (2007)] If a plan's administrator fails to vigorously defend the plan, the administrator must restore to the plan the plan's losses resulting from the administrator's failure to defend the plan. [ERISA § 409(a); see also Restatement (Third) of Trusts § 76 (2007)]

If a plan's administrator acts to protect the plan's anti-alienation provision, it is entitled to pay or reimburse its attorneys' fees and other reasonable expenses from the plan's assets. [ERISA § 404(a)(1)(A)(ii); Restatement (Third) of Trusts § 88 (2007)]

Q 13:46   Why should an insurer or custodian of a Section 403(b) contract that is not held under an employer-administered plan refuse to pay a nonparticipant based on an order that is not a QDRO?

An insurer or custodian should refuse to pay a nonparticipant based on an order that is not a QDRO because doing so might be a breach of contract, for which the insurer or custodian might be liable to the participant.

A Section 403(b) annuity contract must provide that the participant's "rights under the contract are nonforfeitable," and the contract must be nontransferable. [I.R.C. §§ 401(g), 403(b)(1)(C)] A Section 403(b) custodial account must provide that "it is impossible . . . for any part of the corpus or income to be . . . used for, or diverted to," a purpose other than the participant's exclusive benefit, and that contract benefits "may not be assigned or alienated." [I.R.C. §§ 401(a)(2), 401(a)(13)(A), 401(f)(2), 403(b)(7)(A)]

The Code makes clear that the anti-alienation provision must preclude recognizing any domestic relations order unless the order is a QDRO. [I.R.C. § 401(a)(13)(B)] Further, the regulations make clear that recognizing a court's order (other than a QDRO) will cause the Section 403(b) contract to fail to qualify for the tax treatment that would be provided by Code Section 403(b). [Treas. Reg. § 1.401(a)-13(b)(1)]

Some states' laws are hostile to applying a spendthrift provision when reaching a trust interest is necessary to meet a spouse's rights to alimony and property division or a child's right to support. [*See generally* Restatement (Third) of Trusts § 59 (2003); Unif. Trust Code § 503(b), 7C U.L.A. 524–529 (2006), 2007 Supp. 45] Nevertheless, a court should enforce a Section 403(b) contract's anti-alienation provision for one or both of the following reasons. First, if the Section 403(b) contract is an annuity contract (or life insurance contract) and a state insurance regulator approved the form of the contract, there might be a presumption that the contract's provisions are legally enforceable. Further, because a Section 403(b) contract's anti-alienation provision is a necessary condition to the federal income tax treatment of Code Section 403(b), a failure to apply the provision might cause the contract to fail of its essential purpose.

An insurer or custodian that fails to perform its obligations under the Section 403(b) contract is responsible to the participant. However, because a typical anti-alienation provision is stated in the passive voice, whether the insurer or custodian, rather than the participant, must enforce the provision is a subject of contract interpretation.

Tax Treatment

Q 13:47   What is the tax effect of a QDRO?

If a court order is a QDRO, an alternate payee who is the spouse or former spouse of the participant is treated as a distributee for any distribution paid under the QDRO. [I.R.C. § 402(e)(1)(A)] The spouse or former spouse is taxed even if the court order states that the participant will be liable for the tax. [Clawson v. Comm'r, 72 TCM (CCH) 814, TCM 1996-446 (1996)] If a QDRO provides for an alternate payee other than a spouse or former spouse, that distribution is taxed to the participant. [Notice 89-25, 1989-1 C.B. 662]

If an alternate payee is treated as a distributee, the spouse/alternate payee who receives a distribution under a QDRO may make a rollover (including a direct rollover) to an eligible retirement plan. [I.R.C. §§ 402(c)(1), 402(e)(1)(B)]

If a distribution (including one provided by following a QDRO) is an eligible rollover distribution, the plan administrator must deliver to the distributee (such as an alternate payee who is or was the participant's spouse), within a reasonable time (at least 30 days) before paying the distribution, a written explanation of direct rollover provisions and the tax withholding that applies if the alternate payee does not elect a direct rollover. [I.R.C. § 402(f)(1); Treas. Reg. §§ 1.402(c)-2T, A-13; 1.402(f)-2T] Therefore, if the alternate payee desires to make a direct rollover (and thereby avoid mandatory federal income tax withholding), he or she should make sure the court order itself states the required explanation together with proof that the alternate payee received that explanation and waives the 30 days' time that the plan administrator or payer must give him or her to consider whether to make a rollover. [Treas. Reg. §§ 1.402(c)-2T, A-13; 1.411(a)-11; 1.417(e)-1]

A distribution to an alternate payee is not subject to the 10 percent penalty tax that generally applies to a distribution before a participant's age 59½. [I.R.C. § 72(t)(2)(D)]

Q 13:48   Can a QDRO apply to a distribution already made?

No. The special tax rule that treats a spouse alternate payee as the distributee for income tax purposes applies only if the distribution is made "pursuant to" a QDRO. If a distribution is made first and then a court order "ratifies" the distribution already made, QDRO tax treatment does not apply. [Karem v. Comm'r, 100 T.C. 521 (1993)]

Q 13:49   What is the tax effect of a court order that is not a QDRO?

If a plan administrator (or insurer or custodian) makes a payment pursuant to a court order that is not a QDRO, several undesirable tax consequences follow.

Unless the participant would have been entitled to a distribution because he or she reached age 59½ or separated from service, the payment to an alternate payee under a defective QDRO may be a violation of Section 403(b) withdrawal restrictions. [I.R.C. § 403(b)(11)]

Because the putative alternate payee is not treated as a distributee for any distribution paid under the defective QDRO, the participant will be taxed on the amount paid to the alternate payee. [I.R.C. § 402(e)(1)(A); Karem v Comm'r, 100 T.C. 521 (1993)] If the participant has not yet reached age 59½, the 10 percent early withdrawal penalty tax also will apply. [I.R.C. § 72(t)(2)(D)]

Further, because the putative alternate payee is not treated as a distributee for any distribution paid under the defective QDRO, the spouse/alternate payee who receives a distribution under a defective QDRO cannot make a rollover. [I.R.C. §§ 402(c)(1), 402(e)(1)(B)]

Q 13:50   Can an alternate payee assert that an order was not a QDRO for tax purposes?

Because the Code's definition of a QDRO is substantially identical to that of ERISA, a final federal court decision on whether an order is a QDRO might estop a taxpayer from taking a contrary position in his or her federal income tax return (as long as the taxpayer had a due-process opportunity to pursue that litigation). This is so even if that decision was wrong as a matter of law. When the underlying case litigated only whether an order was a QDRO, however, collateral estoppel would not preclude a taxpayer from litigating the issue of the "qualified" status of the plan. [Brotman v Comm'r, 105 T.C. 141 (1995)]

Bankruptcy

Q 13:51   Does a participant's bankruptcy affect an alternate payee's right to a Section 403(b) plan's payment?

No, usually. An alimony, maintenance, or support obligation that is a domestic support obligation is nondischargeable. [11 U.S.C. § 523(a)(5)] In addition, although a bankruptcy may impair a participant's obligation other than a domestic-support debt, a participant's bankruptcy does not affect a plan administrator's obligations. [*See, e.g., In re* Gendreau, 122 F.3d 815 (9th Cir. 1997), *cert. denied,* 523 U.S. 1005 (1998); *see also In re* McCafferty, 96 F.3d 192 (6th Cir. 1996)] However, a participant's bankruptcy might *discharge or impair* the participant's obligations other than a domestic support obligation. [*See, e.g., In re* Ellis, 72 F.3d 628 (8th Cir. 1995); Bush v. Taylor, 912 F.2d 989 (8th Cir.

1990), *vacating prior opinion* at 893 F.2d 962 (8th Cir. 1990)] Sometimes, it is unclear whether an obligation is a support obligation. [*See, e.g., In re* Barbaugh, 257 B.R. 485 (Bankr. E.D. Mich. 2001)]

Practice Pointer. The attorney for the nonparticipant should work promptly to have the QDRO completed. In the absence of a QDRO, the courts have discharged bankrupt participants from responsibility for meeting marital property expectations. [*See, e.g., In re* Varrone, 269 B.R. 475 (Bankr. D. Conn. 2001); *In re* King, 214 B.R. 69 (Bankr. D. Conn. 1997)]

Q 13:52   Does a participant's bankruptcy affect a plan administrator's duty to administer a QDRO?

No. Although a bankruptcy may impair a participant's obligation other than a domestic support obligation, a participant's bankruptcy does not affect a plan administrator's duties. [*See, e.g., In re* Gendreau, 122 F.3d 815 (9th Cir. 1997), *cert. denied*, 523 U.S. 1005 (1998); *see also In re* McCafferty, 96 F.3d 192 (6th Cir. 1996); *but see In re* King, 214 B.R. 69 (Bankr. D. Conn. 1997)]

Practice Pointer. If there is a significant risk that the participant might become bankrupt, his or her spouse or former spouse should prefer (in the absence of other factors) a QDRO over a personal obligation that might be discharged in bankruptcy.

State Courts' Purview

Q 13:53   Does a state court have power to determine whether an order is a QDRO?

No. For an ERISA plan, only a federal court has jurisdiction to review a plan administrator's determination on a domestic relations order. [ERISA §§ 502, 514] Nonetheless, at least one federal court held that state and federal courts have concurrent jurisdiction in determining whether an order is a QDRO. [Board of Trustees of Laborers Pension Trust Fund for N. Cal. V. Levingston, 816 F. Supp. 1496 (N.D. Cal. 1993); *see also In re* Marriage of Oddino, 16 Cal. 4th 67 (1997)] While the court in *Levingston* aptly recognized that Congress's unclear statutory language required it to imagine what Congress might have wanted, the better interpretation of ERISA requires exclusive federal jurisdiction for all plan claims.

Although referring to legislative history might not be a reliable guide for statutory interpretation, Congress said the following when enacting ERISA:

> [C]ivil actions may be brought by a participant or beneficiary to recover benefits due under the plan, to clarify rights to receive future benefits under the plan, and for relief from breach of fiduciary responsibility. The U.S. district courts are to have exclusive jurisdiction with respect to actions involving breach of fiduciary responsibility as well as *exclusive jurisdiction over other actions to enforce or clarify benefit rights provided*

under [ERISA] Title I. However, with respect to suits to enforce benefit rights under the plan or to recover benefits under the plan *which do not involve application of [ERISA] Title I provisions*, they may be brought not only in U.S. district courts but also in State courts of competent jurisdiction. [H.R. Conf. Rep. No. 1280, 93d Cong., 2d Sess. (1974), *reprinted in* 1974 U.S.C.C.A.N. 5038, 5107 (emphasis added)]

Yet, an alternate payee does not have benefit rights under a plan; the alternate payee's rights are provided by the statute. Further, even if it can be argued that an alternate payee obtains benefit rights under a plan, the plan will provide that an individual is not an alternate payee until the plan administrator has so determined. Also, even if it is assumed that a proposed alternate payee has benefit rights under a plan, it is difficult to imagine a suit to "recover" those benefits that does not involve application of ERISA.

For a plan or contract that is not governed by ERISA, a state court may in some circumstances have power to consider whether a domestic relations order must be given effect by a plan administrator, insurer, or custodian if the person that made the challenged decision is within the court's jurisdiction and has been properly made a party to an appropriate court proceeding. Of course, a state court's decision that an order must be given effect is not significant in determining whether the order is a QDRO for federal income tax purposes.

Q 13:54   Can a state court order an ERISA plan administrator to pay attorneys' fees arising from a QDRO matter?

No. ERISA preempts state laws (other than an order that the plan administrator has determined to be a QDRO). [ERISA § 514(b)(7)] A QDRO cannot order a payment of attorneys' fees (see Q 13:19). [ERISA § 206(d)(3)(B)(i)]

If a state court persists in making an order that purports to bind an ERISA plan or its plan administrator, a federal court will issue an injunction nullifying the acts of the state court. [AT&T Management Pension Plan v. Tucker, 902 F. Supp. 1168 (C.D. Cal. 1995)]

Chapter 14

Tax Aspects of Church Plans

Danny Miller, Esq.
Conner & Winters, LLP

David W. Powell, Esq.
Groom Law Group, Chartered

Church retirement plans described in Code Section 403(b) are generally retirement income account programs described in Code Section 403(b)(9), but they can also be characterized as Section 403(b)(1) or 403(b)(9) arrangements, if the vendors associated with the plan are insurance companies or mutual fund providers, respectively. This chapter discusses the requirements that must be met by a Section 403(b)(9) retirement income account plan or program. Because a church retirement income account plan will almost always want to be exempt from the requirements of ERISA, this chapter also discusses the requirements for being treated as an ERISA-exempt church plan. Finally, because the reader may wish to consider the advantages and disadvantages of a Section 403(b)(9) church retirement income account plan compared to a church Section 401(a) qualified plan, a general discussion of the requirements applicable to the latter type of plan has been provided (along with a discussion of a few miscellaneous church retirement plan issues).

Church Retirement Income Accounts

Q 14:1   What is a church retirement income account under Code Section 403(b)(9)?

A church may purchase an annuity contract or a custodial account treated as an annuity contract, as can any other Section 501(c)(3) entity under Code Section 403(b). However, a church, a convention or association of churches, or an organization described in Code Section 414(e)(3)(A) (such as a church pension board) may also establish and maintain a retirement program providing what are known as retirement income accounts under Code Section 403(b)(9), which will be treated as a Section 403(b) annuity contract even though it is not invested in insurance company annuities or regulated investment company stock. However, effective January 1, 2009, a church Section 403(b) plan will be treated as a Section 403(b)(9) retirement income account program only if it is specifically designated as such in the written plan document evidencing the plan.

Q 14:2   What requirements apply to a Section 403(b)(9) retirement income account?

Generally, the rules applicable to annuity contracts under Code Section 403(b) (discussed in chapter 6) are also applicable to retirement income accounts under Code Section 403(b)(9), but with some important exceptions and some special rules.

In the case of a retirement income account purchased by a church within the meaning of Code Section 3121(w)(3)(A) (note that this is a different use of the term *church* from that used for purposes of Code Section 414(e); see Q 14:20) or a qualified church-controlled organization (QCCO; see Q 14:4), the nondiscrimination rules otherwise applicable to Section 403(b) programs (e.g., Code Sections 401(a)(4), 401(a)(5), 401(a)(17), 401(a)(26), 401(m), 410(b)), including the special rule requiring (with some exceptions) universal availability of salary reduction agreements, do not apply. [I.R.C. § 403(b)(1)(D), (12)(A), (B)] In contrast, retirement income accounts purchased by a church-related organization that is not a QCCO must comply with the nondiscrimination rules listed above, effective January 1, 2009. Prior to such date, these nondiscrimination requirements are satisfied if a non-QCCO employer operates its Section 403(b) plan in accordance with a reasonable, good-faith interpretation of these rules. [Notices 89-23, 1989-1 C.B. 654; 96-64, 1996-2 C.B. 229]

Q 14:3   What is a church within the meaning of Code Section 3121(w)(3)(A)?

A church within the meaning of Code Section 3121(w)(3)(A) means a church, convention or association of churches, or an elementary or secondary school that is controlled, operated, or principally supported by a church or a convention or association of churches.

Q 14:4   What is a qualified church-controlled organization?

A qualified church-controlled organization (QCCO) means any church-controlled tax-exempt organization described in Code Section 501(c)(3) other than an organization that

1. Offers goods, services, or facilities for sale, other than on an incidental basis, to the general public, other than goods, services, or facilities that are sold at a nominal charge that is substantially less than the cost of providing such goods, services, or facilities; and

2. Normally receives more than 25 percent of its support from either (a) government sources or (b) receipts from admissions, sales of merchandise, performance of services, or furnishing of facilities, in activities that are not unrelated activities, or both.

[I.R.C. § 3121(w)(3)(B)]

As a result of the provisions of Code Section 3121(w)(3)(B), certain church-related organizations typically do not qualify as QCCOs, including colleges, universities, nursing homes, and hospitals. These organizations are commonly referred to as "non-QCCOs." Arguably, if such activities are carried on as part of the church itself (as opposed to being carried on through a separately incorporated organization), the QCCO test would not apply, subject to the constraint that, in the case of a Section 403(b) plan that desires to be treated as a church plan under ERISA and Code Section 414(e), the majority of the participants in a church plan may not be employed in connection with an unrelated trade or business (see Q 14:26).

Q 14:5   Can a retirement income account be a defined benefit plan?

Retirement income accounts must be defined contribution plans, although church Section 403(b) defined benefit plans that were in existence on August 12, 1982, are grandfathered. Presumably, a church plan may be treated as a defined benefit 403(b) annuity plan if it meets the requirements applicable to such an annuity, even if it does not meet the requirements of Code Section 403(b)(9). The final regulations under Code Section 415 indicate that a grandfathered Section 403(b)(9) defined benefit plan must satisfy both the Section 415(b) limitation applicable to defined benefit plans and the Section 415(c) limit applicable to defined contribution plans.

Q 14:6   Can retirement income account assets be commingled with other church assets?

The assets of a retirement income account may be commingled in a common fund with other church assets for investment purposes, but that part of any common fund that equitably belongs to any retirement income account must be separately accounted for and cannot be used for, or diverted to, any purposes other than the exclusive benefit of the employee and his or her beneficiaries. The other church assets with which retirement income account assets can be commingled are assets devoted exclusively to church purposes (e.g., a church endowment fund) and the assets of other church retirement and employee benefit programs (e.g., a Section 401(a) qualified plan). [TEFRA Comm. Rep.; *see* Ltr. Ruls. 19937052, 9645007, and 9123046. *See also* Ltr. Ruls. 200229050 (church permitted to commingle assets of Section 401(a) and Section 403(b) plans with church endowment funds), 200242047 (permitting commingling of assets of 403(b) plans, qualified plans, and IRAs)] The final Code Section 403(b) regulations indicate that, effective January 1, 2009, Section 403(b)(9) retirement income accounts held in trust are permitted to be commingled in a group trust with trust assets held under a Section 401(a) qualified plan, an individual retirement plan, or a Section 403(b)(7) custodial account. [Treas. Reg. § 1.403(b)-8(f)]

Q 14:7   Can IRS approval of a church retirement income account be obtained?

It is not uncommon for Section 403(b)(9) church retirement income accounts to be submitted to the IRS for a private letter ruling, which is generally a straightforward process of enumerating the applicable requirements and showing how they have been met. Such a private letter ruling, however, can be relied on only by the taxpayer to which it is issued. [Rev. Proc. 2000-4, 2000-1 I.R.B. 115] IRS determination letters are not available, unlike Section 401(a) qualified plans.

Special Definitions and Rules for Section 403(b) Church Plans

Q 14:8   Is there any special service rule that applies to church employees for purposes of Code Section 403(b)?

Code Section 415(c)(7)(B) provides that all years of service by a duly ordained, commissioned, or licensed minister or lay employee of a church or a convention or association of churches, including years of service with an organization controlled by or associated with the church, convention, or association, shall be considered as years of service for one employer. In addition, all amounts contributed for annuity contracts by each such church employer during these years of service are considered to have been contributed by one employer. [I.R.C. § 415(c)(7)(B)]

Following the elimination of the 403(b) maximum exclusion allowance limit by EGTRRA, the special years of service rule for church workers appears to have significance primarily for the special Section 403(b) catch-up contribution limit provided in Code Section 402(g)(7).

Q 14:9   Is there any special contribution rule available to church employees under Code Section 403(b)?

Under Code Section 415(c)(7)(C), a foreign missionary can contribute the greater of $3,000 or the missionary's includible compensation under Section 403(b)(3) to a Code Section 403(b) annuity contract or retirement income account [I.R.C. § 415(c)(7)(B)]

Q 14:10   Are there any special rules applicable to church employees participating in a Section 403(b) plan with respect to the contribution limits under Code Section 415(c)?

Church employees are entitled to make contributions of up to $10,000 per year, even if this amount is in excess of the 100 percent of compensation limitation on maximum annual additions otherwise applicable under Code Section 415(c). This special provision is limited to a $40,000 lifetime maximum. [I.R.C. § 415(c)(7)(A)]. Special foreign missionary contributions (see Q 14:9) are also treated as not exceeding the Code Section 415(c) limit.

Q 14:11   Are there any special minimum distribution rules applicable to a Section 403(b) church plan?

Yes. On April 17, 2002, the IRS issued final regulations relating to required minimum distributions (RMDs) from Section 403(b) plans. These final regulations included special provisions for church retirement income accounts. The final regulations provide that annuity payments from Section 403(b)(9) church retirement income accounts may satisfy the requirements applicable to annuity payments issued by insurance companies, even if the payments are not made through a commercial insurer. This rule permits church retirement income accounts that "self-annuitize" to provide annuity payments without the need to purchase annuity contracts from commercial insurers. [Treas. Reg. § 1.403(b)-3, A-1(c)(3)]

Q 14:12   Is there any special tax basis treatment for contributions made to a church plan on behalf of a foreign missionary?

Beginning in 1997, a church employer (including an employer controlled by or associated with a church) of a foreign missionary may make contributions directly to the missionary's denominational retirement plan and treat such contributions as though they had been made directly by the missionary on an after-tax basis for tax basis purposes. The employer contributions are therefore included in the missionary's "investment in the contract" under Code Section 72 to the extent the contributions would have been excludable from gross income if paid directly to the foreign missionary. [I.R.C. § 72(f)] It does not appear that the contributions paid directly by the employer have to be reflected on a Form W-2 or Form 1099 for the foreign missionary or, if nonelective, would be subject to FICA (or SECA, in the case of a minister).

Q 14:13 Can chaplains and self-employed clergy participate in their denomination's Section 403(b) plan?

For years beginning after December 31, 1996, the Small Business Job Protection Act of 1996 (SBJPA) has clarified that a self-employed minister can participate in a Section 403(b)(9) retirement income account program in a manner similar to ministers who are employees, and that a minister serving in a specialized ministry (e.g., chaplains) may also contribute (or the minister's employer may contribute) to the minister's denominational church plan (whether such plan is a Section 401(a) qualified plan or a Section 403(b)(9) retirement income account program). [I.R.C. § 414(e)(5)] Contributions made directly by a self-employed minister or chaplain to a Section 403(b)(9) retirement income account are deductible on the minister's individual income tax return. [I.R.C. § 404(a)(10)] The preamble to the final Code Section 403(b) regulations provides that, if a minister who is serving in specialized ministry ceases to perform services as a minister, but continues to work for the minister's employer, the minister is considered to have a severance from employment for purposes of Code Section 403(b).

Q 14:14 How does a minister's housing allowance affect contributions to a 403(b) plan?

A minister may be eligible to exclude all or a portion of his or her compensation from income to the extent that the compensation is eligible to be treated as a housing allowance under Code Section 107. Even though a minister's housing allowance may be excludable from income, it can still be counted as compensation for purposes of the plan's definition of that term used in determining retirement benefits. [Rev. Rul. 73-258, 1973-1 C.B. 194] The IRS there ruled that a minister's housing allowance can be counted as compensation for purposes of determining the amount of compensation on which contributions to a Section 401(a) qualified plan can be based. Although the IRS has not ruled on this issue in the context of a Section 403(b) plan, it is probable that the same conclusion would be reached with respect to determining the amount of compensation on which contributions to a Section 403(b) plan can be based.

However, although a 403(b) plan can include a minister's housing allowance in its plan definition of compensation, any such housing allowance that is excludable from income under Code Section 107 cannot be counted as compensation (or includible compensation) used for purposes of calculating contribution limits under Code Section 415. [Ltr. Rul. 200135045] Thus, in performing contribution limits testing, the excludable housing allowance will reduce the amount of a minister's includible compensation.

Final Code Section 403(b) Regulations Issues for Church Section 403(b) Arrangements

Q 14:15   Are church Section 403(b) plans subject to the written plan document requirement contained in the final Code Section 403(b) regulations?

Effective January 1, 2009, Section 403(b)(9) retirement income account arrangements must satisfy the written plan document requirement imposed under the final Code Section 403(b) regulations. However, if a church or a QCCO contributes to a Section 403(b)(1) annuity contract or a Section 403(b)(7) custodial account for its employees, the written plan document requirement is not applicable to such an arrangement. [Treas. Reg. § 1.403(b)-3(b)(3)(iii)] This exception is not available to non-QCCO employers contributing to a Section 403(b)(1) or Section 403(b)(7) arrangement. Some practitioners believe that a written plan document is nevertheless generally advisable and may be protective of the employer as well as the participants and beneficiaries.

Q 14:16   Must the assets of a Section 403(b)(9) retirement income account be held in trust?

Because a church plan is not subject to ERISA, the ERISA requirement that plan assets of an ERISA-covered plan be held in trust is inapplicable to such a plan, including a Section 403(b)(9) retirement income account arrangement. The final Code Section 403(b) regulations do not require that Section 403(b)(9) assets be held in trust unless the assets of the account are to be commingled in a group investment trust with the assets of Section 401(a) qualified plans, IRAs, or Section 403(b)(7) custodial accounts. However, the final Code Section 403(b) regulations provide that, if the assets of a Section 403(b)(9) retirement income account are held in trust, the trust is treated as tax-exempt under Code Section 501(a). [Treas. Reg. § 1.403(b)-9(a)(7)]

Q 14:17   Must employees who are affiliated with a religious order and who have taken a vow of poverty be taken into account for purposes of the universal availability nondiscrimination requirement applicable to Section 403(b) plans?

Under IRS Notice 89-23, employees who are affiliated with a religious order and who have taken a vow of poverty can be excluded from consideration for purposes of applying the universal availability nondiscrimination rule applicable to Section 403(b) elective deferrals. Effective January 1, 2009, this exclusion has been eliminated. However, the preamble to the final Code Section 403(b) regulations points out that Revenue Ruling 68-123 [1968-1 C.B. 35], as clarified by Revenue Ruling 83-127 [1983-2 C.B. 25] provides a basis for concluding that "vow of poverty" workers are not treated as employees of the entity maintaining the Section 403(b) plan, and thus can be excluded from the entity's Section 403(b) plan without violating the universal availability requirement.

Q 14:18   Is there a special effective date rule available to church Section 403(b) plans under the final Code Section 403(b) regulations?

If a Section 403(b) plan is maintained by a church or a convention or association of churches (including an organization described in Code Section 414(e)(3)(A), such as a church pension board), and if the authority to amend such a plan is held by a church convention (within the meaning of Code Section 414(e)), the final Code Section 403(b) regulations do not apply before January 1, 2010.

Church Plan Status for a Section 403(b) Church Plan

Q 14:19   What does the Internal Revenue Code require of a plan before it qualifies as a church plan?

A plan will qualify as a church plan if it establishes that

1. Substantially all of its covered employees are employees or "deemed" employees of a church or convention or association of churches under Code Section 414(e)(3)(B) [I.R.C. §§ 414(e)(1), 414(e)(2)];
2. It is not primarily for the benefit of employees (or their beneficiaries) who are employed in connection with one or more unrelated trades or businesses (within the meaning of Code Section 513) [I.R.C. § 414(e)(2)]; and
3. It is established or maintained for employees:
   a. by a church or a convention or association of churches that is exempt from tax under Code Section 501 [I.R.C. § 414(e)(1)], or
   b. by an organization described in Code Section 414(e)(3)(A). [I.R.C. § 414(e)(3)(A)]

Q 14:20   What is a church, as that term is used in Code Section 414(e)?

There is no definition of church in the Code, ERISA, or the regulations thereunder, but the IRS has published, in its Exempt Organizations Examination Guidelines Handbook, a list of characteristics it considers in evaluating whether an entity is a church. These include the following:

- A distinct legal existence
- A recognized creed and form of worship
- A definite and distinct ecclesiastical government
- A formal code of doctrine or discipline
- A distinct religious history
- A membership not associated with any other church or denomination
- A complete organization of ordained ministers ministering to their congregations

- Ordained ministers selected after completing prescribed courses of study
- A literature of its own
- An established place of worship
- Regular congregations
- Regular religious services
- Schools for the religious instruction of the young
- Schools for the preparation of its ministers
- Other facts and circumstances that may bear upon the organization's claim for church status

[IRS Publication 1828, Tax Guide for Churches and Religious Organizations]

For purposes of Code Section 414 only, the term *church* also includes a religious order or a religious organization if such order or organization is (1) an integral part of a church and (2) engaged in carrying out the functions of a church, whether it is a civil law corporation or otherwise. [Treas. Reg. § 1.414(e)-1(e); *see also* Rev. Proc. 91-20; Ltr. Rul. 9705020]

Q 14:21   Which individuals who are not employees of a church or a convention or association of churches may nevertheless be covered by a church plan as deemed employees?

Code Section 414(e)(3)(C) provides that a church that is exempt from tax under Code Section 501 shall be "deemed" the employer of any individual included as an employee under Code Section 414(e)(3)(B). That provision defines an employee as including a duly ordained, commissioned, or licensed minister of a church in the exercise of his or her ministry, regardless of the source of the minister's compensation, and an employee of an organization that is exempt from tax under Code Section 501 and that is "controlled by" or "associated with" a church or a convention or association of churches. This permits chaplains, regardless of their employer, and employees of church-related entities, such as church hospitals, universities, and publishing houses (provided that they are controlled by or associated with a church or a convention or association of churches), to participate in a church plan. The provisions just described relate to the definition of the term *church plan* in Code Section 414(e). In addition, the IRS has ruled that a church plan may cover an "insubstantial" number of employees who are employed by a for-profit subsidiary of a 501(c)(3) organization associated with the church. [*See* Ltr. Ruls. 9810034, 9810035] (See Q 14:27.)

Q 14:22   When is an organization "controlled by" a church or a convention or association of churches?

The regulations under Code Section 414(e) state that "an organization, a majority of whose officers or directors are appointed by a church's governing board or by officials of a church, is controlled by a church . . . ." [Treas. Reg. § 1.414(e)-1(d)(2)]

Q 14:23 When is an organization "associated with" a church or convention or association of churches?

In some cases, the IRS has recognized that an organization listed in a particular church directory is associated with the church. [*See, e.g.,* Ltr. Rul. 8824049; GCM 39832 (Oct. 12, 1990); GCM 39007 (July 1, 1983)]

Furthermore, an organization may be associated with a church within the meaning of Code Section 414(e)(3)(D) by reason of the common religious bonds and convictions it shares with that church. This may, for example, be evidenced by operating under church principles, by operating under articles of incorporation and bylaws that require the organization to incorporate in its policies and practices the moral teachings of the church, by maintaining a chapel where services are conducted, by employing chaplains, and by performing sacerdotal functions. One of the major reasons that church plans that cover employees of an "associated" organization request private letter rulings (or Department of Labor (DOL) opinions interpreting ERISA Section 3(33)) is to determine the applicability of the "associated with" criteria. For example, the sponsor of a pension plan that covered the employees of a nonprofit organization providing mental health and counseling services and psychotherapy that were "Christian in their vision" requested a letter ruling from the IRS that the plan was a church plan under Code Section 414(e). The IRS concluded that the organization was "associated with" a church or convention of churches primarily because it was listed in the official church directory. [Ltr. Rul. 9521038] The IRS has also ruled that a pension plan maintained by one church continued to be a church plan after the eligibility provisions were expanded to include other denominations holding similar beliefs. The IRS determined that holding similar beliefs meant that the other denominations were "associated with" the denomination maintaining the plan. [Ltr Rul 20042028] Plans may request determinations on church plan status from both the IRS and DOL for greatest certainty. [*See, e.g.,* Ltr. Rul. 9835028] However, for the past several years there has been an informal moratorium on the issuance of church-plan rulings by the IRS while it has had its church-plan rulings policies under study. The DOL and the Pension Benefit Guaranty Corporation (PBGC) are participating in discussions with IRS on these policies.

Q 14:24 May a church plan cover employees employed in an unrelated trade or business?

Yes, to an extent, but the plan may not be primarily for the benefit of employees who are employed in connection with one or more unrelated trades or businesses (within the meaning of Code Section 513).

Q 14:25 When is an employee employed in an unrelated trade or business?

An employee is employed in connection with one or more unrelated trades or businesses of a church if a majority of such employee's duties and responsibilities are directly or indirectly related to carrying on such trades or businesses.

Q 14:26   How is it determined that a plan is established or maintained primarily for employees of an unrelated trade or business?

A plan established after September 2, 1974, is established primarily for the benefit of employees who are not employed in connection with one or more unrelated trades or businesses if, on the date the plan is established, the number of employees employed in connection with the unrelated trades or businesses eligible to participate in the plan is less than 50 percent of the total number of employees of the church eligible to participate in the plan. [Treas. Reg. § 1.414(e)-1(b)(2)(i)(A)]

A plan in existence on September 2, 1974, is considered to be established primarily for the benefit of employees who are not employed in connection with one or more unrelated trades or businesses if, in either of its first two plan years ending after September 2, 1974, it meets the requirements described below for determining whether a plan is maintained primarily for the benefit of such employees. [Treas. Reg. § 1.414(e)-1(b)(2)(ii)(B)]

A plan will be considered maintained primarily for the benefit of employees of a church who are not employed in connection with one or more unrelated trades or businesses if, in four out of five of its most recently completed plan years, less than 50 percent of the persons participating in the plan (at any time during the plan year) consist of, and, in the same year, less than 50 percent of the total compensation paid by the employer during the plan year (if benefits or contributions are a function of compensation) to employees participating in the plan is paid to, employees employed in connection with an unrelated trade or business.

A determination that a plan is not a church plan will apply to the second year for which the plan fails to meet these two requirements and all plan years thereafter, unless, after taking into account all the facts and circumstances, the plan is still considered a church plan. Such facts and circumstances may include:

1. The margin by which the plan failed the 50 percent tests; and
2. Whether the failure was due to a reasonable mistake as to what constituted an unrelated trade or business or whether a particular person or group of persons were employed in connection with one or more unrelated trades or businesses.

[Treas. Reg. § 1.414(e)-(1)(b)(2)]

Q 14:27   How many nonchurch employees can participate in a church plan without jeopardizing its church-plan status?

Code Section 414(e)(2)(B) provides that the term *church plan* does not include a plan if less than substantially all of the individuals included in the plan are church employees or "deemed" church employees. [I.R.C. § 414(e)(2)(B)] Although the IRS has not published any guidelines on what number or percentage of employees will be considered "less than substantially all," it has issued a number of private letter rulings that address this issue. In these letter rulings, it has determined that plans in which less than 5 percent of the participants are nonchurch employees would still be considered church plans. [Ltr. Ruls. 9810034, 9441040, 9204034] One ruling issued by the IRS suggests that the 50 percent threshold used in connection with the presence of plan participants who are employed by unrelated trades or businesses can be used in testing the "substantially all" requirement. [Ltr. Rul. 8734045]

Q 14:28   When is a plan established and maintained by a church or a convention or association of churches or by an organization described in Code Section 414(e)(3)(A)?

Under the third test of Code Section 414(e), a church plan must be established and maintained for its employees and their beneficiaries by a church or a convention or association of churches exempt from taxes under Code Section 501(a) or an organization described in Code Section 414(e)(3)(A).

An organization described in Code Section 414(e)(3)(A) includes an organization the principal purpose or function of which is the administration or funding of a plan or program for the provision of retirement or welfare benefits for the employees (or deemed employees) of a church or convention or association of churches, if such organization is controlled by or associated with a church or convention or association.

Such an organization is commonly either a pension board of a religious denomination or, in the case of church hospitals, church universities, and other organizations controlled by or associated with a church or a convention or association of churches that maintain their own plans, a retirement plan committee appointed by the church or convention or association of churches, the sole purpose of which is to control and manage the operation and administration of the plan.

Q 14:29   Can nonchurch plans be merged into a parent entity's church plan?

In the health care area, the acquisition of unrelated tax-exempt and for-profit entities by health care providers that participate in church plans has raised the question of whether, after the acquisition of such entities, the church hospital may merge the subsidiaries' plans, which were previously not church plans, into the hospital's church plan. The IRS has, in rulings, indicated that such mergers will not adversely affect the status of the church hospital's church plans under Code Section 414(e), provided that the surviving plan meets the Section 414(e) requirements and that the number of covered employees of any for-profit subsidiary is insubstantial. [Ltr. Ruls. 9810036, 9717039] However, caution should be exercised in this area because the rulings do not address whether the monies originally contributed to nonchurch plans remain subject to such rules as the anticutback, QDRO, prohibited transaction, spousal consent, or cashout rules applicable to nonchurch plans. However, at least two rulings suggest that the anticutback rule does apply to benefits accrued during ERISA coverage. [Ltr. Ruls. 9733016, 9717039] More recently, the IRS issued a private letter ruling holding that, in the event of a merger of a church plan that had made a Section 410(d) election with a church plan that had not made such an election, the surviving plan would be treated as having made the election. [Ltr. Rul. 200350020] Note that the rulings are issued by the IRS and are not binding upon the DOL, which has not yet ruled on these issues, including the issue of whether such "old" monies may remain subject to ERISA protections. Also be aware that the IRS, the DOL, and the PBGC have been discussing church plan ruling policies for the last several years, and it may be that the area of church-plan mergers will be addressed in more detail following completion of those discussions.

Electing (or Not Electing) ERISA Coverage

Q 14:30 How does a church plan elect to be covered under ERISA and be subject to the same Section 401(a) plan qualification rules as secular employers?

An election under Code Section 410(d) may be made only by the plan administrator by attaching a statement to either (1) the annual return (Form 5500 series) or amended annual return that is filed for the first plan year for which the election is effective or (2) a written request for a determination letter relating to qualification of the plan. The statement must indicate (1) that the election is made under Code Section 410(d) and (2) the first plan year for which it is effective. [Treas, Reg, § 1.410(d)-1(c)] In practice, Section 410(d) elections are rare, probably due to the additional administrative burdens of being covered by ERISA and possible traps for related church entities under the prohibited transaction rules. Such an election results in PBGC insurance coverage for a defined benefit church plan, provided that the PBGC is notified, but at the cost, of course, of paying PBGC premiums.

Inadvertent elections of Section 410(d) coverage brought about by conforming to ERISA and Code requirements applicable to nonchurch plans should not normally occur, because Code Section 410(d)(1) and the legislative history of that section provide that such an election is to be made "in a form and manner to be prescribed in regulations." As noted above, the regulations provide only one form for such an election and only two ways to notify the IRS of the election. For example, in Private Letter Ruling 8536041, a church adopted a prototype plan for the benefit of its employees. Despite the fact that the prototype plan was apparently drafted to comply with all post-ERISA aspects of the Code and the plan received a favorable determination letter to this effect, the IRS concluded that the plan as adopted by the church for the benefit of its employees was a church plan within the meaning of Code Section 414(e). Similarly, in DOL Advisory Opinion 85-32 [Sept. 6, 1985], the DOL determined that a pension plan for a Catholic hospital qualified as a church plan under ERISA Section 4(b) despite the fact that a plan administrator had filed a Form 5500 for the 1982 plan year and had submitted premium payment forms and payments for plan years 1981 and 1982 to the PBGC.

Q 14:31 Can a church welfare plan make a Section 410(d) election?

The DOL has issued one Advisory Opinion indicating that only church pension plans may make the election under Code Section 410(d). [D.O.L. Adv. Op. 95-07A] However, at least one district court has opined that a church welfare plan may make such an election and thereby become subject to ERISA's preemption of state laws. [Catholic Charities of Maine, Inc. v. City of Portland, 304 F. Supp. 2d 77 (D. Maine Feb. 6, 2004)]

Rules Applicable to Nonelecting Church Qualified Plans

Q 14:32 Which provisions of Code Section 401(a) do not apply in the case of a nonelecting church plan?

Generally, the following rules are not applicable to a qualified nonelecting church plan (i.e., a Section 401(a) church plan that has not made a Section 410(d) election):

1. The participation and coverage rules of Code Section 410(b). Instead, the provisions of Code Section 401(a)(3), as in effect on September 1, 1974, apply (except that, under Code Section 414(q)(9), the pre-ERISA "prohibited group" concept used under the pre-ERISA nondiscriminatory classification coverage test has been replaced by the "highly compensated employee" definition set out in Code Section 414(q)).

2. The vesting requirements of Code Section 411, including the anticutback rules of Code Section 411(d)(6). Instead, the vesting requirements resulting from the application of Code Section 401(a)(4) and 401(a)(7), as in effect on September 1, 1974, apply. Under pre-ERISA law, qualified plans were required to vest participants upon attainment of normal retirement age, complete or partial plan termination, and complete discontinuance of contributions (see also Q 14:29). [Pre-ERISA I.R.C. § 401(a)(7); Rev. Rul. 66-11, 1966-1 I.R.B. 71]

3. The joint and survivor and preretirement survivor annuity requirements of Code Sections 401(a)(11) and 417 (although many church plans impose similar requirements voluntarily).

4. The rules regarding mergers and consolidations of plans and transfers of assets or liabilities to other plans set out in Code Section 401(a)(12) and the identical rule contained in Code Section 414(l). [Treas. Reg. § 1.414(l)-1(a)(1)]

5. The anti-assignment and anti-alienation rules of Code Section 401(a)(13). This exception means that the qualified domestic relations order (QDRO) rules of Code Section 414(p) are not applicable to a qualified nonelecting church plan. [I.R.C. § 414(p)(9)] Nevertheless, a church plan is permitted to make distributions pursuant to certain domestic relations orders [I.R.C. § 414(p)(11)] and many, if not most, do.

6. The provision in Code Section 401(a)(14) requiring distributions to a participant to begin not later than 60 days after the occurrence of certain events.

7. The provision of Code Section 401(a)(15) requiring that the benefits of a participant or beneficiary who is receiving benefits under the plan, or a participant who is separated from service with a nonforfeitable right to benefits, not be decreased by reason of any increase in Social Security benefits or wage base.

8. The provision in Code Section 401(a)(19) that prohibits making a participant's accrued benefit forfeitable solely because of the participant's withdrawal of his or her contributions.

9. The provision in Code Section 401(a)(20) permitting a pension plan to make a "qualified total distribution" described in Code Section 402(a)(5)(E)(i)(I).

10. The minimum funding rules of Code Section 412.

Q 14:33 Which rules under Code Section 401(a) remain applicable to a nonelecting church plan qualified under Code Section 401(a)?

The following post-ERISA rules apply to a qualified nonelecting church plan:

1. The exclusive benefit rule in Code Section 401(a)(2).

2. The portion of Code Section 401(a)(4) that prohibits discrimination in the level of contributions or benefits in favor of employees who are highly compensated employees as defined in Code Section 414(q).

3. The provisions of Code Section 401(a)(5) permitting certain eligibility classifications to be considered as nondiscriminatory for purposes of Code Section 401(a)(4).

4. The requirement that the participation and coverage rules of pre-ERISA Code Section 401(a)(3) be met (see Q 14:29).

5. The requirement in Code Section 401(a)(8) that, in a defined benefit setting, forfeitures cannot be applied to increase benefits to any employee.

6. The required distribution rules of Code Section 401(a)(9).

7. The top-heavy rules of Code Sections 401(a)(10)(B) and 416.

8. The benefit and contribution limits under Code Sections 401(a)(16) and 415.

9. The provision in Code Section 401(a)(17) capping the annual compensation of each employee to be taken into account under the plan at $200,000, as adjusted for cost of living.

10. The requirement in Code Section 401(a)(25) that a defined benefit plan specify actuarial assumptions in the plan in a way that precludes employer discretion (to meet the definitely determinable benefit requirement).

11. The additional participation requirements imposed under Code Section 401(a)(26). For years beginning after December 31, 1996, these requirements apply only to defined benefit plans, not defined contribution plans.

12. The permissive provision of Code Section 401(a)(27) that states that a profit-sharing plan may be established by a tax-exempt employer.

Q 14:34 When do the IRS nondiscrimination rules under Code Section 401(a)(4) and 401(a)(5) apply to qualified nonelecting church plans under Code Section 401(a)?

Under IRS Notice 2001-46, for nonelecting church plans qualified under Code Section 401(a), the regulations under Code Section 401(a)(4) and 401(a)(5) will not apply until subsequent IRS notice, but in no case earlier than the first plan year beginning on or after January 1, 2003. For all prior plan years, a nonelecting church plan must be operated in accordance with a reasonable, good-faith interpretation of those provisions. [Notice 96-64, 1996-2 C.B. 229, as modified by Notice 98-39, 1998-33 I.R.B. 11; Notice 2001-9, 2001-4 I.R.B. 375; Notice 2001-46, 2001-32 I.R.B. 122] The SBJPA authorizes the Secretary of the Treasury to design nondiscrimination and coverage safe harbors for church plans [SBJPA § 1462(b), Pub. L. No. 104-188], and Notice 98-39 [1998-33 I.R.B. 11] requests suggestions for such safe-harbor designs.

Q 14:35 Which rules under other provisions of the Code are applicable to nonelecting church plans qualified under Code Section 401(a)?

The provisions discussed in Questions 14:32 and 14:33 were drawn from an analysis of Code Section 401(a) (including the plan-related provisions of Code Sections 410 and 411). The following Code sections also have a potential impact on a Section 401(a) nonelecting church plan:

1. For plan years beginning after December 31, 1996, tax-exempt organizations (including churches) can now maintain 401(k) plans. (For a comparison of the rules applying to Section 401(k) and 403(b) plans, see Table 14-1.)

2. Code Section 401(l). The special integration rules of this subsection would seem to be applicable to nonelecting church plans because Code Section 401(a)(5) applies to them. However, the regulations under this subsection will not apply until notice from the IRS, and in no event earlier than the first plan year beginning on or after January 1, 2003. For all other years, a nonelecting church plan must be operated in accordance with a reasonable, good-faith interpretation of Code Section 401(l). [Notice 98-39, 1998-33 I.R.B. 11; Notice 2001-9, 2001-4 I.R.B. 375; Notice 2001-46, 2001-32 I.R.B. 1220]

3. Code Section 401(m). This subsection requires plans providing for matching contributions and after-tax employee contributions to meet

certain nondiscrimination requirements in order to satisfy Code Section 401(a)(4).

4. Code Section 414(a). This subsection provides that service for a predecessor employer must be taken into account in certain instances.

5. Code Section 414(b) and 414(c). These subsections provide for aggregating employees of controlled groups of corporations and certain organizations under common control. The IRS has issued final regulations under Code Section 414(c), effective January 1, 2009, for determining nonprofit employer controlled groups. (See Q 14:43 for a discussion of the impact of these regulations on church employers.) Until such date, church-plan sponsors may make a reasonable, good-faith determination of whether the employers participating in their plans constitute a single employer under the controlled group rules of Code Sections 414(b) and 414(c) for purposes of the nondiscrimination and coverage rules [Notice 96-64, 1996-2 C.B. 229]

6. Code Section 414(g). This subsection defines the term *plan administrator* for purposes of the employee benefit provisions of the Code.

7. Code Section 414(m). This subsection provides that employees of affiliated service groups are to be aggregated for purposes of certain Code rules.

8. Code Section 414(n). This subsection imposes certain requirements on any person or entity for whom a leased employee performs services.

9. Code Section 414(q). This subsection defines the term *highly compensated employee* for purposes of the employee benefit provisions of the Code. This definition is used in determining whether there has been impermissible coverage under Code Section 410(b) or any discrimination in the level of contributions or benefits under Code Section 401(a)(4). Prior to the enactment of SBJPA [Pub L No 104-188], the old "prohibited group" definition of pre-ERISA law was used in determining whether there was any impermissible discrimination under pre-ERISA Code Section 401(a)(3) or the vesting provisions of Code Section 401(a)(4) and Code Section 401(a)(7). For years beginning after December 31, 1996, however, generally only those church employees who have taxable compensation in excess of $80,000 (indexed for inflation to $105,000 in 2008) will be considered to be highly compensated employees, for purposes of the Code's nondiscrimination provisions. [I.R.C. § 414(q)(9)]

10. Code Section 414(r). This subsection establishes the "separate line of business" rules for purposes of Code Section 410(b).

11. Code Section 414(s). This subsection defines *compensation* for purposes of the employee benefit provisions of the Code. However, the regulations under this subsection apply only to plan years beginning no earlier than January 1, 2003. For all other years, a qualified nonelecting church plan must be operated in accordance with a reasonable, good-faith interpretation of Code Section 401(s). [Notice 98-39, 1998-33 I.R.B. 11; Notice 2001-9, 2001-4 I.R.B. 375; Notice 2001-46, 2001-32 I.R.B. 122]

12. Code Section 414(t). This subsection provides that the controlled group rules of Code Section 414(b), 414(c), or 414(m) are applicable for purposes of what might be called the welfare benefits sections of the Code.

13. Code Section 415. This section provides for limits on contributions or benefits under qualified plans and is applicable to qualified nonelecting church plans.

14. Code Section 416. This section contains the special rules applicable to top-heavy plans and, as noted earlier, is applicable to qualified nonelecting church plans, although not to government plans.

15. Code Sections 4975 and 503(a)(1)(B). Although electing church plans and other qualified plans are subject to the prohibited transaction excise tax provisions of Code Section 4975, qualified nonelecting church plans are not. However, it would appear that Code Section 503(a)(1)(B) would apply the prohibited transaction provisions of Code Section 503(b) to a qualified nonelecting church plan, and Code Section 503(a) would deny an exemption from taxation to such a church plan under Code Section 501(a) if it engaged in a Section 503 prohibited transaction after March 1, 1954.

Table 14-1. Comparison of Section 403(b) and 401(k) Plans

	403(b)	*401(k)*
Access	Available to churches	Now available to churches
Contribution Limits	• 415(c) limit ($46,000 in 2008) applies, but special $10,000/$40,000 lifetime contribution and foreign missionary rules are available)	• Limits are 402(g) ($15,500 in 2008) and 415(c) (and the cap—if any—effectively provided by the 401(k) ADP rule)
	• Age 50 catch-up contributions available	
	• 402(g) limit increase available ($3,000 per year up to $15,000 lifetime maximum)	
	• Two 415 limits apply for participant in both 403(b) and 401(a) plans under certain circumstances	
Nondiscrimination Rules	• No ADP testing	• Although ADP testing (and ACP, if employer match or after-tax contributions are made) is required, a plan with no HCEs passes automatically

Table 14-1. Comparison of Section 403(b) and 401(k) Plans (*cont'd*)

	403(b)	*401(k)*
	• Reasonable, good-faith interpretation standard available until January 1, 2009	• If HCEs do participate in plan, their contributions will likely be limited to less than the 402(g) limit
	• Notice 89-23 safe harbors are available until January 1, 2009	• If no HCEs, 401(a)(4) and 410(b) not a problem
	• Exempt from 401(a)(4), 410(b), etc. (unless a non-QCCO); ACP safe harbors available for non-QCCO matching contributions	• ADP and ACP safe harbors available
Top-Heavy Rules	Inapplicable	Applicable technically, but perhaps not practically
Salary Reduction Distribution Restrictions	Apply only to elective deferrals accumulated after 12/31/88 and earnings on deferrals; distribution permitted on plan termination effective January 1, 2009 (unless successor plan adopted)	Generally applicable; distribution available on plan termination (unless successor plan adopted)
Vesting Schedule	Permitted, can use pre-ERISA schedules (subject to nondiscrimination requirements); nonvested amounts are treated as Code Section 403(c) annuities	Permitted, can use pre-ERISA schedules (subject to nondiscrimination requirements)
401(a)(9) Distribution Requirements	Pre-1987 account balances are grandfathered (subject to age 75 rule)	Entire account balance subject to 401(a)(9)
Salary Reduction Agreement Rules	Multiple OK	Multiple OK
Transfer/Rollovers	Rollovers can be made to and received from other 403(b)s, and 401(a)s, IRAs, and governmental 457 plans; transfer from 403(b) to 403(b) only; transfers can be made by participants if plan permits; may promote transfers from other providers due to likelihood of use of 403(b) funding vehicle (due to absence of 401(k) option in the past)	Rollovers can be made to and received from other 401(a)s, 403(b)s, IRAs, or governmental 457(b) plans No participant level transfer permitted

Table 14-1. Comparison of Section 403(b) and 401(k) Plans (*cont'd*)

	403(b)	*401(k)*
ERISA Applicability	Exempt from ERISA	Exempt from ERISA
IRS Determinations on Plan Status	Only possible through National Office private letter ruling; no prototype submissions	Determination letters available; prototype submissions possible
IRS Audits	Have to consider whether IRS 403(b) audit activity makes an audit more likely	No specific focus on 401(k) plan audits
Plan Disqualification	415 excess only causes excess 415 amount to be taxed; only a few defects affect entire 403(b) plan	415 violation causes disqualification of plan; failures of other plan qualification requirements also affect entire plan
Correcting Plan Defects	VCP; SCP; Audit CAP	VCP; SCP; Audit CAP
Income Tax Considerations	• No income tax averaging • Some states (e.g., New Jersey and Pennsylvania) impose state income tax on 403(b) contributions	• 10-year averaging available to certain participants • States do not impose income tax on 401(k) contributions
Self-Employed Clergy and Chaplains	Eligible to participate	Eligible to participate
Section 503(b) Prohibited Transaction Rules	Inapplicable, but exclusive benefit rule is applicable	Applicable, if no 410(d) election made (*but* query as to practical difference between 503(b) rules and the exclusive benefit rule)
Protection from Creditors	Exempt under bankruptcy reform legislation	Exempt under bankruptcy reform legislation
Practical Considerations	• 403(b) annuities are not really understood as a 401(k) equivalent • Good 403(b) software not as available (but getting better) • Vendor understanding of 403(b) annuities more limited (but getting better)	• Overwhelming popularity makes 401(k) plans a recognizable commodity to most individuals • Good software and support materials are available • Better understanding in vendor community

Q 14:36   What were the Code Section 401(a)(3) requirements (as in effect on September 1, 1974) and other relevant pre-ERISA requirements for qualified plans?

IRS Publication 778, as it existed when it reflected pre-ERISA law, is one of the principal sources of rules for pre-ERISA Code Section 401(a)(3) and other pre-ERISA provisions applicable to nonelecting church plans. Among Publication 778's important provisions are the following:

- A plan must be a funded plan to be qualified. Publication 778 noted that a qualified plan may not provide for direct payments by an employer to its employees, as in the case of a pay-as-you-go pension plan.

- A Section 401(a) qualified plan contemplates a trust arrangement. Publication 778 noted that in the case of a trusteed plan, there must be a valid existing trust recognized as such under applicable local law. This trust is to be evidenced by an executed written document setting forth the terms of the trust.

- Publication 778 described certain rules applicable to investments by plans in securities of an employer. Publication 778 also indicated that the IRS is to be notified of trust funds invested in stock or securities of, or loaned to, the employer or related or controlled interests so that a determination may be made whether the trust serves any purpose other than constituting part of a plan for the exclusive benefit of employees.

- Because the anti-assignment and anti-alienation rules of Code Section 401(a)(13) are not applicable to a qualified nonelecting church plan, the statement in Publication 778 that it is permissible to use trust funds to repay indebtedness due the employer could presumably mean that a nonelecting church plan could offset such indebtedness in connection with distributions to a participant who is also a debtor to the employer.

- Publication 778 noted that under old Code Section 401(a)(3) it was permissible for an employer to designate several pension, stock bonus, profit-sharing, and annuity plans as constituting a part of a plan the employer intended to qualify under Code Section 401(a).

- For purposes of the percentage testing rules of old Code Section 401(a)(3), certain short-service, seasonal, and part-time employees could be excluded (i.e., those employees with fewer than five years of service or who work 20 hours or fewer per week, and those whose customary employment was for five months or less in any calendar year). These were the only permitted testing exclusions under old Code Section 401(a)(3).

- Publication 778 noted that pre-Code Section 401(a)(4) vesting schedules ranged from complete and immediate vesting, to graduated vesting, to no vesting until attainment of normal retirement age. However, Publication 778 made it clear that a vesting schedule must be analyzed based on the "facts in a particular case" to determine whether it would violate the general rule in Code Section 401(a)(4) that the schedule not provide for discriminatory benefits or contributions in favor of prohibited group members (now highly compensated employees).

- Under pre-ERISA law, Publication 778 noted that it was permissible to discontinue benefits for cause, where a discontinuance provision is specified in the plan. Publication 778 gave the example of discontinuing benefits because an employee worked for a competitor or divulged trade secrets as permissible restrictions.

- Publication 778 noted the so-called *termination rule,* under which the payment of benefits to the 25 highest-paid employees was restricted in certain circumstances.

- Publication 778 made note of the circumstances under which contributions can be suspended without creating a "discontinuance" of contributions requiring full vesting. This rule would seem to be of particular importance due to the inapplicability of Code Section 412 (and its contribution waiver provisions) to qualified nonelecting church plans. The rule in question provides that contributions can be suspended without creating a discontinuance if (1) benefits are not affected at any time by the suspension and (2) unfunded past service costs at any time do not exceed unfunded past service costs at the establishment of the plan.

Failure to Qualify as a Church Plan or a Church 403(b) or 401(a) Plan

Q 14:37 What happens if a plan fails to meet the requirements for being a church plan?

If a plan fails to meet the requirements of Code Section 414(e), a special remedial period will apply during which the plan may correct its faults and be deemed to meet the requirements of Code Section 414(e) for the year of correction and prior years. If a correction is not made during the correction period, the plan will fail to meet the requirements of Code Section 414(e) beginning with the date on which the earliest failure to meet one of the requirements occurred.

The correction period is the latest to end of

- The period ending 270 days after the date of mailing by the IRS of a notice of default with respect to the plan's failure to meet one or more of the Section 414(e) requirements;

- Any period set by a court of competent jurisdiction after a final determination that the plan fails to meet such requirements. If the court does not specify the period, any reasonable period may be determined by the IRS on the basis of the facts and circumstances, but no earlier than 270 days after the court determination becomes final; or

- Any additional period that the IRS determines is reasonable or necessary for the correction of the fault.

[I.R.C. § 414(e)(4); *see also* Ltr. Rul. 9652023]

Q 14:38   Can a church plan that fails to meet the requirements of Code Section 401(a) or 403(b) be amended retroactively to meet these requirements?

A church plan within the meaning of Code Section 414(e) has a special remedial amendment period and is not treated as not meeting the requirements of Code Section 401 or 403 if:

- By reason of any change in law, regulation, ruling, or otherwise, the plan is required to be amended to meet such requirements; and

- The plan is so amended at the next earliest church convention or such other time as the Secretary of the Treasury or his or her delegate may prescribe.

[Tax Equity and Fiscal Responsibility Act of 1982 (TEFRA) § 251(d), Pub. L. No. 97-248]

This section of TEFRA may permit retroactive amendment of a church plan so that a defect would not cause the plan to fail to meet the Section 401(a) or 403(b) requirements, so long as the plan is timely amended. The TVC program that the IRS opened on May 1, 1995 (now the Voluntary Correction Program (VCP)), does not address the application of this retroactive amendment rule in the context of the correction of defects in Section 403(b) church plans.

ERISA Coverage of Church Plans

Q 14:39   Does ERISA apply to church plans?

The pension provisions of Title I of ERISA (Sections 2 through 515) do not apply to a nonelecting church plan. [ERISA § 4(b)] Title IV of ERISA, regarding PBGC termination insurance, is also inapplicable to church plans unless the plan administrator makes the election under Code Section 410(d) and notifies the PBGC that it wishes those provisions to apply. [ERISA § 4021(b)(3)] The definition of *church plan* under ERISA is virtually identical to the Code Section 414(e) definition. [ERISA § 3(33)]

Occasionally, an employer such as a tax-exempt hospital or school may not have initially realized (because it is only associated with a church and is not a church itself) that its defined benefit plan qualified as a church plan under ERISA Section 3(33), and may have been paying premiums to the PBGC. In such a case, the plan typically first seeks a ruling on church plan status from the IRS or the DOL and then makes a claim for refund with the PBGC. Since February 15, 1994, the statute of limitations on such claims is six years from the date the claim arose. [PBGC Notice, 58 Fed. Reg. 6306 (Dec. 1, 1993)] For the past several years, the IRS, the DOL and the PBGC have been discussing IRS church plan ruling policies and procedures, and the ability to utilize IRS church-plan rulings in connection with PBGC premium refund applications has been a focus of those discussions.

Miscellaneous Church Plan Provisions

Q 14:40   When a nondenominational employer employs a minister, what is the effect on that employer's pension plan?

If a minister who participates in a church plan is employed by an employer not otherwise participating in a church plan and the services provided by such minister are "in the exercise of his or her ministry," the employer may exclude that minister from being treated as an employee of that employer for purposes of the nondiscrimination rules applicable to either a Section 401(a) qualified plan or a Section 403(b)(9) retirement income account program. [I.R.C. § 414(e)(5)(C)]

Q 14:41   Are nonelecting church plans (both Section 401(a) and 403(b)) required to file annual information returns?

Although nonelecting church plans are not subject to the reporting requirements of ERISA, there is no church plan exception under Code Section 6058 to the requirement of filing annual information returns with the IRS. However, the IRS has administratively relieved nonelecting church retirement plans (both Section 401(a) and 403(b)) from the requirement of filing the Form 5500 series. [Ann. 82-146, 1982-47 I.R.B. 53] Note that other types of plans that are not retirement plans, such as cafeteria plans, are not afforded relief from Code filing requirements, such as Code Section 6039D. [*But see* Notice 2002-24, which indicates that Section 6039D fringe benefit plans are not required to file Schedule F to Form 5500; the Notice is not clear as to whether Form 5500 still needs to be filed by such plans.]

Q 14:42   Are churches subject to Code Section 457?

Code Section 457 limits the ability of employees of tax-exempt "eligible employers" to defer compensation (see the discussion of Code Section 457 in chapter 15). The term *eligible employer* does not include a church (as defined in Code Section 3121(w)(3)(A)) or a QCCO (as defined in Section 3121(w)(3)(B); see Q 14:4). [I.R.C. § 457(e)(13)] Thus, in the case of those types of employers, the provisions of Code Section 457 will not apply. Note, however, that, as with the application of nondiscrimination rules under Code Section 403(b)(12) to retirement income accounts, these definitions are more limited than the definition of the term *church plan* under Code Section 414(e). Also note that, although nonqualified plans maintained by churches and QCCOs are not subject to Code Section 457, such plans are subject to the requirements of Code Section 409A.

Q 14:43   Are church plans subject to the securities laws?

Prior to the enactment of the National Securities Markets Improvements Act of 1996, there was some uncertainty about the scope of exemptions for church retirement plans from federal and state securities laws, particularly for church Section 403(b) retirement programs. The National Securities Markets Improvement Act provided the desired clarifications for church plans, and now such plans (and the investment pools maintained by church benefit programs in connection with such plans) are not subject to the Investment Company Act of 1940 or the Securities Act of 1933 (as well as certain requirements imposed under the Securities Exchange Act of 1934, the Investment Advisers Act of 1940, and the Trust Indenture Act of 1939). Significantly, state "blue sky" laws that require registration or qualification of securities have also been preempted in the case of church plans, as have been any state laws applicable to investmentcompanies or to brokers, dealers, investment advisors, or agents. However, the antifraud provisions of federal and state securities laws continue to apply, so church plan sponsors should consider what level of disclosure regarding plan investments should be given to participants to ensure compliance with such provisions.

Church plans utilizing these exemptions from federal and state securities laws are required to give plan participants notice of such exemptions and to inform them that they will therefore "not be afforded the protection of these provisions." This notice is to be given to new participants "as soon as practicable" after beginning participation, and to all participants annually. The Securities and Exchange Commission can also require church plans to file a notice with the Commission containing such information as the Commission may prescribe. It should be emphasized that these notices are only required (or can be required, in the case of notices to the Commission) for plans relying on the new exemption. Plans, such as Section 401(a) qualified plans, that can rely on another securities law exemption are not required to give these notices.

Q 14:44 Are retirement payments made to retired clergy considered to be compensation with respect to which a tax-excludable housing allowance can be claimed?

Retirement payments made from the national retirement program of a church or convention or association of churches are entitled to be treated as a tax-excludable housing allowance, subject to the requirements of Code Section 107. [Rev. Rul. 75-22, 1975-1 C.B. 49; Rev. Rul. 63-156, 1963-2 C.B. 79] The IRS has not ruled on whether retirement payments made to retired clergy outside of a national denominational retirement plan (e.g., made directly through a local church) are eligible for exclusion under Code Section 107, but the principle of Revenue Ruling 63-156 would seem to be applicable in such a case. Whether this principle would also be extended to payments made from IRAs is not clear.

In 2002, Congress passed legislation to clarify the amount of housing allowance that can be excluded from income under Code Section 107. The Clergy Housing Allowance Clarification Act of 2002 [Pub. L. No. 107-181, 116 Stat. 583] was signed into law on May 20, 2002, and provides that the amount of excludable clergy housing allowance is limited to the fair rental value of the clergy-person's housing. This clarification should also apply to any housing allowance with respect to retirement distributions to eligible clergy from a Section 403(b) plan.

Q 14:45   Are retirement payments made from a Section 414(e) church plan subject to SECA tax?

No. Such payments are not subject to Self-Employment Contributions Act (SECA) taxes, even if such payments are treated as a nontaxable housing allowance. [I.R.C. § 1402(a)(8); Rev. Rul. 58-359, 1958-2 C.B. 422]

Impact of New Tax-Exempt Controlled Group Rules on Church Section 403(b) Plans

Q 14:46   Do the new controlled group rules imposed on tax-exempt employers apply to churches and church-related employers?

The final Code Section 414(c) controlled group regulations applicable to tax-exempt employers do not apply to churches (as defined in Code Section 3121(w)(3)(A)) or QCCOs (as defined in Code Section 3121(w)(3)(B)). These regulations are, however, applicable to non-QCCO employers. However, the preamble to these regulations and Revenue Procedure 2007-71 [2007-51 I.R.B. 1184] indicate that churches and QCCOs are subject to a reasonable, good-faith standard in applying controlled group rules to their covered benefit plans, using the special controlled group rules applicable under IRS Notice 89-23. [1989-1 C.B. 654]

Q 14:47   To what types of benefit plans do these new Section 414(c) controlled group rules apply?

The new Section 414(c) controlled group rules applicable to tax-exempt employers apply to Section 401(a) qualified plans as well as to Section 403(b) plans. In addition, these new controlled group rules apply to a number of welfare benefit plans that cross-reference Code Section 414(c) (principally for the purpose of applying coverage and/or nondiscrimination rules to such welfare benefit plans).

Q 14:48   What are some of the important retirement plan requirements that could be affected by these new Section 414(c) controlled group rules?

The principal Section 401(a) and 403(b) requirements that could be affected by the new Section 414(c) controlled group rules are the coverage and nondiscrimination requirements, the Section 415 contribution limits, the special Section 403(b) catch-up contribution rules, and the Section 401(a)(9) minimum distribution requirements.

Q 14:49   In applying the new Section 414(c) controlled group regulations, do non-QCCO employers have to take into account the employees of churches and QCCOs, if all such entities are under "common control" (within the meaning of basic rule under such regulations)?

The final Section 414(c) controlled group regulations applicable to tax-exempt employers permit a non-QCCO employer to permissively disaggregate churches and QCCOs with which the non-QCCO employer would otherwise be aggregated in applying applicable Code requirements to the non-QCCO employer's benefit plans. [Treas. Reg. § 1.414(c)-5(d)] The IRS has not clearly indicated whether, if two or more non-QCCO employers are under the common control of a church, a convention or association of churches, or a QCCO, then such non-QCCO employers must be aggregated and treated as a single employer for purposes of applying the Code requirements to their respective benefit plans.

Chapter 15

Section 457 Plans

Henry A. Smith, III, Esq.
Smith & Downey

Internal Revenue Code Section 457 provides the rules on taxation of nonqualified deferred compensation arrangements between a state or local government or a nongovernmental, nonchurch tax-exempt organization and an individual who performs services for such an entity. This chapter examines both types of Section 457 plans: so-called eligible and ineligible plans. This chapter also examines which deferred compensation plans of governmental and tax-exempt entities are covered by Code Section 457 and the requirements that must be met by eligible plans under Code Section 457. The tax consequences to participants in eligible and ineligible plans under Code Section 457 are discussed, as well as the applicability of the Employee Retirement Income Security Act of 1974 (ERISA) to Section 457 plans. The IRS's final regulations under Code Section 457, which were issued in July 2003, are discussed in this chapter. The chapter discusses the impact on Section 457(f) plans of Code Section 409A, which was enacted as part of the American Jobs Creation Act of 2004, and the final regulations under Code Section 409A that were issued in April 2007. Finally, the chapter discusses IRS Notice 2007-62, in which the IRS announced its intention to issue guidance on certain Sections 457(f) and 457(e)(11) issues.

Overview

Q 15:1   To which deferred compensation plans does Code Section 457 apply?

Generally, Code Section 457 applies to any compensation that is deferred (plus income attributable to that deferred compensation) under an arrangement between a state or local government or a nonchurch (church being narrowly defined for this purpose), nongovernmental, tax-exempt organization and an individual employee or individual independent contractor who performs services for such an entity. [IRS Notice 87-13, 1987-1 C.B. 432, 444]

Q 15:2   Are there exceptions to the general rule of applicability of Code Section 457?

Yes. Code Section 457 does not apply to deferrals under any of the following:

1. A plan described in Code Section 401(a) that includes a trust exempt from tax under Code Section 501(a) (i.e., a tax-qualified retirement plan such as a defined benefit pension plan, a money purchase pension plan, a profit-sharing plan, or a 401(k) plan);

2. Any annuity plan or contract described in Code Section 403 (i.e., an employees' annuity plan or a tax-sheltered annuity plan);

3. That portion of any plan that consists of a property transfer described in Code Section 83 (e.g., certain life insurance arrangements between employers and employees, stock option plans);

4. That part of a plan that consists of a trust to which Code Section 402(b) applies (i.e., a nonqualified trust);

5. Any plan paying length-of-service awards to bona fide volunteers (or their beneficiaries) on account of fire fighting and prevention services, emergency medical services, and ambulance services if the aggregate amount accruing to the volunteer in any one year does not exceed $3,000 (this exception applies only to awards accruing after 1996) [Rev. Rul. 2003-47, 2003-1 C.B. 866 (May 1, 2003), contains a good overview of the rules applicable to length-of-service awards]; and

6. Any "qualified governmental excess benefit plan" described in Code Section 415(m).

Note. For years before 2002, contributions to some of the plans listed above may have an effect on contributions to an eligible Section 457 plan (see Q 15:18).

Q 15:3   What are the two types of Section 457 plans?

The first type of Section 457 plan is an *eligible deferred compensation plan.* Eligible plans must meet specific requirements contained in Code Section 457. If those requirements are met, participants may defer taxes on their elective deferrals and any employer contributions under the plan (and earnings on those deferrals and contributions) until amounts are paid or (with respect to eligible deferred compensation plans maintained by tax-exempt entities only) made available to them. (Prior to EGTRRA, this "or made available" rule applied both to governmental eligible plans and to eligible plans maintained by tax-exempt entities.) Although technically a nonqualified plan, an eligible plan resembles a tax-qualified plan in that as long as the plan meets the requirements of Code Section 457, plan participants are not taxed on their plan interests until they actually receive plan distributions, even if they are fully vested in those interests and even if, in the case of a governmental eligible deferred compensation plan, those interests are funded. In addition, like a qualified plan, an eligible deferred compensation plan is not subject to the Code Section 409A rules that are applicable to nonqualified plans.

The second type of Section 457 plan is an *ineligible deferred compensation plan.* Ineligible plans are deferred compensation plans of governmental and nonchurch tax-exempt employers that do not meet the Section 457 requirements for eligible plans and resemble, in some ways, the nonqualified plans of for-profit employers. Unlike participants in an eligible plan, participants in ineligible plans are taxed on their elective deferrals and any employer contributions under the plan when those amounts cease to be subject to a substantial risk of forfeiture. Earnings on ineligible plan contributions (defined by the IRS as earnings accruing after the vesting date for the contributions), like earnings on eligible plan contributions, are taxed when amounts are paid or made available under the plan. Ineligible deferred compensation plans are subject to the new Section 409A rules.

Before 1997, eligible plans typically were used to provide deferred compensation to employees only by governmental entities that could not, and still may not, sponsor tax-sheltered annuity programs under Code Section 403(b) (i.e., governmental entities other than certain educational organizations) and tax-exempt entities that could not, and still may not, sponsor those programs (i.e., tax-exempt entities other than Section 501(c)(3) entities), because, among other reasons, the dollar limit on annual deferrals under an eligible plan was (and still is for participants age 50 and over) less than the dollar limit on annual deferrals under more attractive Section 403(b) programs and was offset (through 2001), dollar for dollar, by deferrals under Section 403(b) programs.

Since 1997, under a change contained in SBJPA, tax-exempt employers have been able to sponsor 401(k) plans. Therefore, from 1997 through 2001, eligible plans typically were used only by governmental entities (which still may not sponsor 401(k) plans, except for certain grandfathered arrangements) that may not sponsor Section 403(b) programs, because, among other reasons, for those years the dollar limit on annual deferrals under an eligible plan was less than the dollar limit on annual deferrals for Section 401(k) and 403(b) plans and was offset, dollar for dollar, by deferrals under Section 401(k) and 403(b) plans.

Beginning in 2002, EGTRRA repealed the dollar-for-dollar offset of the Section 457(b) limit by deferrals under 401(k) and 403(b) plans. Therefore, beginning in 2002, most tax-exempt and governmental employers that did not previously maintain eligible plans established eligible plans in order to provide additional deferred compensation opportunities to their eligible employees. (It should be noted that although governmental and "ERISA church" employers may offer eligible plan participation to all their employees, employers governed by ERISA must limit participation in their eligible plans to top-hat group members.)

Furthermore, because of the relatively low dollar limit that applies to eligible plans, even after the EGTRRA increase, entities that use them as part of an executive's deferred compensation package usually supplement them with ineligible plans. Therefore, ineligible plans generally have a much broader application for executive deferred compensation planning than eligible plans.

Q 15:4   Is there any "grandfather" exception to the rule that amounts that are deferred under an ineligible Section 457 plan are included in the participant's income when they cease to be subject to a substantial risk of forfeiture?

Yes. The Tax Reform Act of 1986 (TRA '86) provided a special rule for participants in ineligible plans of nongovernment tax-exempt organizations. Under that rule, amounts that were deferred from taxable years beginning before January 1, 1987, were grandfathered and not subject to the income inclusion rules applicable to ineligible plans. Deferrals from taxable years beginning after December 31, 1986, were also grandfathered if they were made pursuant to an agreement that was in writing on August 16, 1986, and that provided for a deferral of either a fixed amount or an amount determined pursuant to a fixed formula for each taxable year covered by the agreement. The exception does not apply with respect to amounts deferred for any taxable year ending after the date on which the amount or formula is modified after August 16, 1986. A technical correction enacted under the Technical and Miscellaneous Revenue Act of 1986 (TAMRA) clarified that the relief afforded to amounts deferred after December 31, 1986, is limited to individuals covered under the plan or agreement on August 16, 1986. [TRA '86, Pub. L. No. 99-514, § 1107, 1986 U.S.C.C.A.N. (100 Stat.) 2426-2431; TAMRA § 1011(e)(6)(B); see Notice 87-13, 1987-1 C.B. 432; Ltr. Rul. 9018052]

A deferral with respect to an individual is treated as fixed on August 16, 1986, to the extent that a written plan on that date provided for the deferral for each taxable year of the plan and the deferral was determinable on that date under the written terms of the plan as a fixed dollar amount, a fixed percentage of a fixed base amount, or an amount to be determined under a fixed formula, or the deferral is the same as the deferral in effect with respect to the individual under the plan on August 16, 1986, even if on that date the written plan did not fix the amount of deferral. [Notice 87-13, 1987-1 C.B. 432, 445; Ltr. Rul. 8813026]

A deferral will not fail to be treated as fixed on August 16, 1986, merely because the written plan also provides for a deferral that is not fixed on that date. Further, a deferral will not fail to be treated as fixed on August 16, 1986, merely because the tax-exempt organization and the individual have the right, under the plan on that date, to renegotiate the plan and thus to alter the deferral (whether or not the plan is part of an employment contract between the organization and the individual) or merely because the individual has the right, under the plan, to vary the amount of the deferral in the future. If, at any time after August 16, 1986, however, those rights are exercised to modify the amount, percentage, or specified formula (whichever is applicable), deferrals after the effective date of that modification will fail to be treated as fixed on August 16, 1986, and thus will be subject to the income inclusion rules applicable to ineligible plans (unless the plan meets the requirements imposed on eligible plans). [Notice 87-13, 1987-1 C.B. 432, 445; Ltr. Ruls. 8813026, 9105011]

Q 15:5   What types of amendments has the IRS permitted to be made to grandfathered Section 457 plans without causing a loss of grandfather treatment?

Although TRA '86 is clear that any modification of a grandfathered plan's deferral percentage or dollar amount will cause the plan to lose its grandfathered status, the IRS has been relatively liberal in permitting changes to grandfathered plans without claiming that those changes modify the plans' deferral percentage or dollar amount and thereby affect the plans' enjoyment of grandfather treatment. For instance, at least informally, the IRS has approved of changes to the distribution options under grandfathered plans, the investment indices used to credit earnings under such plans, and so forth. In addition, the IRS has stated informally that a reduction of a deferral percentage or dollar amount to zero does not endanger grandfather treatment.

Letter Ruling 9549003 illustrated the rather liberal position of the IRS. In that ruling, two executives of an eligible employer were entitled to unfunded, nonqualified retirement benefits in a fixed amount. The arrangement had been in effect for more than 50 years. The employer proposed to amend the tax-qualified plan that it maintained for its rank-and-file employees to permit the two executives to participate in that plan and to offset the amounts due the two executives under the nonqualified plan by the amounts the executives would receive as a result of their eligibility to participate in the tax-qualified plan.

The IRS determined that the central question to be decided was whether the fixed formula under the nonqualified plan would be considered amended because of the proposed actions. It held that the total amount due the executives would not be changed by making the executives eligible for the tax-qualified plans and by offsetting the nonqualified benefits by the executives' tax-qualified benefits and that the use of the tax-qualified benefits to offset the amounts due under the nonqualified plan would not modify, either directly or indirectly, the defined benefit formula of the nonqualified plan. Therefore, the IRS concluded that the nonqualified plan would continue to enjoy grandfather-rule protection. The IRS also concluded that the use of the funded tax-qualified plan to provide a portion of the benefit that previously would have been provided through the unfunded nonqualified plan would not cause the executives to be taxed on any part of their previously unfunded nonqualified promise.

In Letter Ruling 9538021, the IRS considered a proposed amendment to a grandfathered plan that would prohibit additional salary deferrals under the plan and provide for certain distributions of existing plan account balances. The IRS concluded that although TRA '86 and its legislative history are silent on amendments to grandfathered plans that do not have the effect of increasing plan benefits, the amendment in question would not be treated as modifying the plan's fixed formula and therefore the plan would continue to enjoy grandfather treatment after the date of the amendment.

In a somewhat related ruling, Letter Ruling 9548006, the IRS held that the amendment of a grandfathered plan to include a spun-off employer as a participating employer, and to cover the employment with the spun-off employer of an executive previously employed with the original plan sponsor, would not cause the plan to lose its grandfathered status because the amendment would not have the effect of modifying the fixed formula under the plan.

In Letter Ruling 9822038, the IRS concluded that amendments to a grandfathered plan to add a participant-directed investment option and a distribution option (annual cash payments of 7 percent of the balance of the participant's account each year, until exhausted) would not cause the plan to lose its grandfathered status.

Q 15:6   Are church plans subject to the provisions of Code Section 457?

No. Plans of churches, as narrowly defined in Code Section 3121(w)(3)(A), and qualified church-controlled organizations, as narrowly defined in Code Section 3121(w)(3)(B), are not subject to Code Section 457. [I.R.C. § 457(e)(13)] Those definitions are extremely limited in nature, and many church entities do not qualify as churches for purposes of exemption from Code Section 457.

Q 15:7   Are vacation, sick leave, compensatory time, severance pay, disability pay, or death benefit plans subject to the provisions of Code Section 457?

No. Bona fide vacation leave, sick leave, compensatory time, severance pay, disability pay, and death benefit plans—whether elective or nonelective—are not deferred compensation plans subject to Code Section 457. Benefits under those plans generally are tax deferred until receipt. See Q 15:47 for a discussion of Notice 2007-62 that discusses the severance pay plan exemption from Code Section 457.

However, IRS regulations issued in July 2003 provide that an eligible plan may permit participants to elect to defer accumulated sick and vacation pay and back pay if an agreement providing for the deferral is entered into before the beginning of the month in which the amounts would otherwise be paid or made available and the participant is an employee in that month. The regulations also provide a special rule that allows an election for sick pay, vacation pay, or back pay that is not yet payable. Under this special rule, an employee who is having a severance from employment during a month may elect to defer, for example, his or her unused vacation pay after the beginning of the month if the vacation pay would otherwise have been payable before the employee has a severance from employment and the election is made before the date on which the vacation pay would otherwise have been payable. [Treas. Reg. § 1.457-4(d)]

> **Note.** The IRS has stated that equity split-dollar life insurance plans of governmental and nonchurch tax-exempt employers that are not taxed under the below market loan rules of Code Section 7872 (i.e., equity split-dollar life insurance plans of these employers that are taxed under the general rules of Code Section 61) are governed by the taxed-on-vesting rules of Code Section 457(f). Specifically, while official IRS guidance provides that any equity in pre-January 28, 2002 grandfathered split-dollar plans governed by the economic benefit tax regime is not taxed until the plan is terminated, the preamble to the split-dollar regulations suggests that, if there is no risk of forfeiture on receiving the equity cash value that may emerge, that equity is taxed under Code Section 457(f) in the year that it emerges and in each year thereafter on the growth in the equity during that year. If the IRS takes up this position that an equity split-dollar plan of a governmental or nonchurch tax-exempt employer is taxed when vested, then, if and when the equity is about to emerge, employers and executives may wish to amend their split-dollar agreements to impose a substantial risk of forfeiture so as to delay taxation of the equity.

Q 15:8 May a rabbi trust be used in connection with a Code Section 457 plan?

Yes. A rabbi trust may be used in connection with a plan created under Code Section 457 (see Q 15:30). [Ltr. Ruls. 9212011, 9211037] The existence of the rabbi trust does not cause the underlying Section 457 plan to be funded and does not alter the tax treatment of plan participants.

> **Note.** Governmental eligible deferred compensation plans must now have actual trusts, as discussed in Qs 15:15 and 15:30.

Q 15:9 Are arrangements providing for the transfer of property in return for the performance of services subject to the provisions of Code Section 457?

No. Property transfer arrangements governed by Code Section 83 are not deferred compensation plans subject to Code Section 457. Benefits under those plans are not taxed until the time provided in Code Section 83.

For example, a number of tax-exempt employers previously instituted stock option programs, using mutual fund stock in place of the more typical employer stock, to provide executives with a form of not-currently-taxed compensation that is not subject to the limitations on eligible deferred compensation plans or the onerous taxation-on-vesting rules applicable to ineligible deferred compensation plans. IRS final regulations under Code Section 457 issued in July 2003 state that vested options granted under these plans after May 8, 2002, will not result in deferral of taxation under Code Section 83, but rather will result in current taxation under Code Section 457(f). [Treas. Reg. § 1.457-12(d)]

Q 15:10   May an employer obtain an IRS ruling on its Section 457 plan?

Yes. The procedure for obtaining a ruling on the status of an eligible or ineligible Section 457 plan and the tax consequences to the plan's participants is similar to the procedure for obtaining a ruling on a secular trust. Although the IRS has indicated that no rulings will be issued with respect to the tax consequences to unidentified independent contractors in eligible state plans under Code Section 457, a ruling with respect to a specific independent contractor's participation in such a plan may be issued.

Q 15:11   Does Code Section 457 apply to elective and nonelective deferrals?

Yes. For taxable years beginning after 1987, Code Section 457 generally applies to nonelective deferrals as well as to elective deferrals. [IRS Notice 87-13, 1987-1 C.B. 432, 444; Notice 88-8, 1988-1 C.B. 477]. However, see Q 15:47 for a discussion of IRS Notice 2007-62 that discusses elective deferrals to Section 457(f) plans.

Q 15:12   Are nonelective deferred compensation plans that cover individuals who are not employees subject to Code Section 457?

Sometimes not. Code Section 457 does not apply to nonelective deferred compensation provided to individuals who are not employees if all individuals (who meet applicable initial service requirements) with the same relationship to the plan sponsor are covered under the same plan with no individual variations or options. The following example of the application of this rule is contained in the legislative history of TAMRA: If a doctor who is not an employee receives deferred compensation from a hospital, the deferred compensation is considered nonelective only if all doctors who are not employees (who have satisfied any applicable initial service requirements) are covered under the same plan with no individual variations or options. [I.R.C. § 457(e)(12); H.R. Conf. Rep. No. 1104, 100th Cong., 2d Sess. 155 (1988), reprinted in 1988 USCCAN 508, 5215]

Q 15:13   Are there transition rules under which the general application of Code Section 457 to nonelective deferrals may be avoided?

Yes. Under a union plan transition rule, Code Section 457 does not apply to compensation deferred under a written, nonelective deferred compensation plan that was in existence on December 31, 1987, and that was maintained pursuant to a collective bargaining agreement, until the effective date of any material modification to the plan after December 31, 1987. A modification is not treated as material unless it modifies the plan's benefit formula or expands the class of participants beyond those individuals who were participants under the plan on or before December 31, 1987, or beyond those individuals who would have become participants under the terms of the plan as it existed on that date. For purposes of this transition rule, a *nonelective plan* is defined as a plan that covers a broad group of employees who earn nonelective deferred compensation under a definite, fixed, and uniform benefit formula.

The union plan transition rule applies not only to union employees participating in nonelective plans maintained pursuant to collective bargaining agreements, but also to nonunion employee-participants under a plan if, on December 31, 1987, participation under the nonelective plan extended to a broad group of nonunion employees on the same terms as the participation provided to union employees, and provided that the union employees constituted at least 25 percent of the total participants in the plan.

In addition, under a government plan transition rule, Code Section 457 does not apply to amounts deferred under a nonelective deferred compensation plan maintained by a governmental entity if:

1. The amounts were deferred from periods before July 14, 1988; or

2. The amounts were deferred from periods on or after July 14, 1988, pursuant to an agreement that was in writing on that date and that provided for a deferral for each taxable year covered by the agreement of a fixed amount or of an amount determined pursuant to a fixed formula, and the individual with respect to whom the deferral is made was covered under the agreement on that date.

This rule does not apply to any taxable year ending after the date on which any modification of the amount or formula is effective; however, the rule does not cease to apply merely because of a modification to the agreement prior to January 1, 1989, that does not increase benefits for participants in the plan. [TAMRA 1988, Pub. L. No. 100-647, § 6064, 1988 USCCAN (102 Stat.) 3700-02; H.R. Conf. Rep. No. 1104, 2nd Sess. 153-55, reprinted in 1988 USCCAN 5213-5215; *see* TAM 9121004; Ltr. Rul. 9149032]

Q 15:14   How must nonqualified plans be reported by tax-exempt entities on their annual federal information returns?

Tax-exempt entities must report their nonqualified plans on their annual Form 990 federal information returns. The IRS issued final regulations, effective

June 8, 1999, that require tax-exempt entities to provide copies of their three most recently filed Forms 990 (including the portions thereof reporting details on their executive deferred compensation programs), their tax-exemption applications, and their IRS tax-exemption letters to anyone who requests them. Before these new rules, although the public could visit a tax-exempt entity and review copies of these documents, copies were not required to be provided on request.

These rules have resulted in regular requests to tax-exempt employers for Form 990 copies, and a particular focus on the portions of the Form 990 dealing with the compensation arrangements of executives. The final regulations contain details concerning how these requests must be responded to, items that can be excluded from disclosure, deadlines for responding to requests, restrictions on copy charges, and other relevant information.

Every tax-exempt employer should maintain and monitor procedures to ensure compliance with these disclosure rules (which carry a penalty of $5,000 per document per failure penalty). In addition, every tax-exempt employer should review regularly how it completes Form 990, in order to reflect most accurately and favorably its tax-exempt mission and the manner in which fairly compensating its executives advances that mission.

One particular problem occurs because the format of the Form 990 and its instructions require employers to aggregate a number of current and deferred compensation items, often causing the misleading appearance that executives' current compensation is higher than it actually is. Therefore, employers should carefully review these sections of the Form 990 and consider providing detailed answers to the questions involved that list individual compensation component values rather than simply answering the questions without explanation by providing a single, aggregate number that may tend to mislead.

Eligible Plans

Q 15:15   Does Code Section 457 impose special requirements on eligible plans?

Yes. Code Section 457 provides that an eligible plan must satisfy the following requirements:

1. The plan must be established and maintained by an eligible employer (see Q 15:16).
2. Only individuals who perform services for the plan sponsor may be participants (see Q 15:17).
3. The maximum amount that may be deferred by or on behalf of a participant for 2008 may not exceed the lesser of $15,500 or 100 percent of the participant's "includible compensation," subject to the rules under Code Section 457(b)(3) (see Qs 15:18–15:20).

4. Compensation may be deferred for any calendar month only if a deferral agreement has been entered into before the beginning of that month (see Q 15:21).

5. Distributions may not be made to a participant or beneficiary earlier than (a) the calendar year in which the participant reaches age 70½, (b) the date the participant separates from service with the employer, or (c) the date the participant incurs an unforeseeable emergency (see Q 15:22).

6. The plan must meet certain minimum distribution requirements (see Qs 15:27).

7. The plan must not be funded if maintained by a tax-exempt entity. If the plan is maintained by a governmental entity, under changes contained in SBJPA, amounts credited under the plan must be held in a trust, a custodial account, or an annuity contract (see Q 15:36).

[I.R.C. §§ 457(b), 457(d)]

Q 15:16   Who is an eligible employer?

An *eligible employer* under Code Section 457 is a state, a political subdivision of a state, an agency or instrumentality of a state or political subdivision, or any other organization that is exempt from tax under Subtitle A of the Code other than churches (as defined). It should be noted that, especially before the EGTRRA changes enhancing the Code Section 457 rules, being an eligible employer under Code Section 457 was not an advantageous designation, because it subjected the employer to the dollar-for-dollar offset rule, the Section 457(f) taxation-on-vesting rule, and other restrictions. There is still some controversy concerning whether a Native American tribe is an eligible employer as defined under Code Section 457. [*See, e.g.,* "American Indian Tribes and 401(k) Plans," 95 TNT 132-31]

> **Note.** Subtitle A of the Code includes all organizations exempt from tax under Code Section 501 (i.e., many more tax-exempt organizations than the religious, educational, and charitable organizations that are tax exempt under Code Section 501(c)(3)).

Q 15:17   Who may participate in an eligible plan?

Only individuals who perform services for the plan sponsor (including both employees and independent contractors) may participate in an eligible plan. Any or all of the employees of a government entity may be permitted to participate in an eligible plan; however, because of the impact of ERISA, only a select group of management or highly compensated employees of a nonchurch tax-exempt organization may so participate. This is a particularly important, and unfortunate, limitation in light of the EGTRRA changes which make eligible plans so much more attractive. [I.R.C. §§ 457(b)(1), 457(e)(2), 457(e)(3)]

Q 15:18   Is there a maximum amount that may be deferred by or on behalf of a participant under an eligible plan?

Yes. The maximum amount that may be deferred by or on behalf of a participant under an eligible plan for 2008 is the lesser of $15,500 or 100 percent of the participant's includible compensation, subject to rules under Code Section 457(b)(3), which provide for increased limits in certain limited circumstances (see Q 15:19). Before EGTRRA, this limit was the lesser of $8,500 or one-third of the participant's includible compensation.

The maximum amount of compensation that any individual participating in more than one eligible plan may defer under all of those plans during any taxable year may not exceed these limits (see Q 15:15). [I.R.C. §§ 457(b)(2), 457(c)]

For years before 2002, the maximum amount that a participant could defer under an eligible plan or plans also was required to be reduced by the following:

1. Amounts contributed by or on behalf of the participant under any tax-deferred annuity program for the taxable year (i.e., under a Section 403(b) plan);

2. Elective deferrals by the participant under any 401(k) plan for the taxable year (except a rural cooperative plan as defined in Code Section 401(k)(7));

3. Elective deferrals by the participant under any simplified employee pension (SEP) for the taxable year (except a rural cooperative plan as defined in Code Section 401(k)(7));

4. Amounts contributed by or on behalf of the individual under any savings incentive match plan for employees (SIMPLE) under Code Section 402(k) for the taxable year; and

5. Deductible contributions by the participant to a plan described in Code Section 501(c)(18), which involves certain trusts created before June 25, 1959, for the taxable year (except a rural cooperative plan as defined in Code Section 401(k)(7)).

The offset to the eligible plan limit for deferrals to other types of plans is repealed by EGTRRA, effective in 2002. [I.R.C. § 457(c)(2)]

The final regulation issued by the IRS in July 2003 addressed the situation of excess deferrals under an eligible plan of a tax-exempt employer. If this occurs, the plan may distribute any excess deferrals (and any income allocable to such amount) to a participant no later than the first April 15 following the close of the taxable year of the excess deferrals. The plan will continue to be treated as an eligible plan, but in accordance with Code Section 457(c), any excess deferral is included in the gross income of a participant for the taxable year of the excess deferral. If an excess deferral is not corrected by distribution, the plan is an ineligible plan under which benefits are taxable in accordance with ineligible plan rules. [Treas. Reg. § 1.457-4(e)]

For years before 2002, if a participant had amounts contributed under a Code Section 403(b) plan, a 401(k) plan, a SEP, or a Section 501(c)(18) trust for a year and had amounts deferred under an eligible plan in the same year, and the total amounts deferred exceed the eligible plan limits, the excess deferrals were considered made available to the participant in the year of the deferral and subject to taxation. (For those years, if an individual participated in both a Section 457 plan and a Section 403(b) or 401(k) plan, the maximum aggregate deferral was $7,500 (indexed to $8,500 for 2001) increased, if applicable, by the catch-up provision (see Q 15:19), but in no event in excess of the Section 403(b) or 401(k) limit, as applicable.) [Ltr. Rul. 9152026 (Sept. 27, 1991)]

Q 15:19   Are the maximum deferral amounts for eligible plans ever increased for a participant?

Yes. During each of the three taxable years ending before the participant reaches normal retirement age, the participant may defer up to the lesser of two times the regular dollar limit (i.e., two times $15,500 in 2008) or the sum of (1) the regular eligible plan limitation for the year (determined without regard to the special limit) and (2) as much of the maximum deferrals for prior years as have not been used previously (the catch-up provision).

This special catch-up limit is not available to a participant in a governmental eligible plan who takes advantage of the special "age 50 and older" catch-up provision made available under EGTRRA for those plans only. Specifically, EGTRRA permits a $5,000 special catch-up contribution, in addition to the regular eligible plan dollar limits, for participants age 50 and older in governmental eligible plans.

For purposes of the catch-up provision computation, unused deferrals for previous years may be included only for years after 1978 during which the individual was eligible to participate in the plan for all or any portion of the year.

A participant may elect the catch-up provision only once to apply to all or any portion of the three-year period. For example, if a participant elects to use the catch-up provision only for the one taxable year ending before normal retirement age, and, after retirement, the participant renders services for an eligible employer as an independent contractor, the eligible plan may not provide that the participant may use the catch-up provision for any of the taxable years subsequent to retirement. [I.R.C. §§ 457(b)(2), 457(b)(3); Treas. Reg. § 1.457-4(c)(2)(iii)]

For purposes of the catch-up provision, *normal retirement age* is the age specified in the plan. Under the IRS final regulations under Code Section 457 issued in July 2003, the plan must specify a normal retirement age under the plan which is no later than age 70½ and no earlier than the earlier of age 65 or the earliest age at which the participant has the right to retire under the eligible employer's basic pension plan and to receive immediate retirement benefits without an actuarial or similar reduction because of retirement before some later specified age in the eligible employer's basic pension plan. Alternatively, the plan may allow a participant to designate a normal retirement age which is within the permissible range of ages. [Treas. Reg. § 1.457-4(c)(3)(v)]

Q 15:20   What constitutes includible compensation eligible for deferral under an eligible plan?

Compensation eligible for deferral under an eligible plan means, with respect to a taxable year, the participant's compensation, as defined in Code Section 415(c)(3), for services performed for the eligible employer (determined without regard to any community property laws). This definition of includible compensation (effective for years beginning after Dec 31, 2001) was added by the Jobs Creation and Worker Assistance Act of 2002. [Pub. L. No. 107-147] For years beginning prior to Jan 1, 2002, includible compensation was defined as all compensation received by a participant for services performed for the eligible employer that currently is includible in the individual's gross income. That is, under the pre-2002 rules, includible compensation did not include amounts excludable under a Section 457 plan and did not include any other amount that was paid by the plan sponsor for services performed for the plan sponsor and that was excludible from gross income under the income tax rules of the Code. [I.R.C. §§ 457(e)(5), 457(e)(7); Treas. Reg. § 1.457-2(g)]

Q 15:21   When must an election to defer compensation under an eligible plan be made?

Generally, an agreement providing for deferral of compensation under an eligible plan must be entered into before the first day of the month in which the compensation is paid or made available. Nevertheless, an eligible plan may permit a new employee to defer compensation payable during the first calendar month of his or her employment if the employee enters into an agreement providing for the deferral on or before the first day of employment, even though that date may be after the first day of that month. In addition, under a change effected by SBJPA, an eligible plan may permit a participant to make a one-time election after a distribution event has occurred (e.g., termination of employment) and before commencement of distributions, to defer commencement of distributions. [I.R.C. § 457(b)(4); Treas. Reg. § 1.457-7(c)]

Q 15:22   When may benefits under an eligible plan be paid to participants or beneficiaries?

Amounts deferred under an eligible plan cannot generally be paid or made available to a participant or beneficiary before:

1. The calendar year in which the participant attains age $70\frac{1}{2}$;
2. The date the participant has a severance from employment with the employer; or
3. The date the participant is faced with an unforeseeable emergency.

Exceptions to this general rule exist for certain distributions of small accounts [Treas. Reg. § 1.457-6(e)], distributions relating to plan terminations [Treas. Reg. § 1.457-10(a)], and distributions relating to domestic relations orders [Treas. Reg. § 1.457-10(c)].

Prior to an EGTRRA change, the phrase *separation from service* was used in place of the phrase *severance from employment* in these rules. The use of the term *separation from service* created issues under the former "same desk rule" that were eliminated by this EGTRRA change. [I.R.C. § 457(d)(1)(A)]

Q 15:23   What did *separated from service* mean for purposes of these rules?

Under the pre-EGTRRA rules, an employee was *separated from service* if there was a separation from service within the meaning of Code Section 402(e)(4)(A)(iii) (relating to lump-sum distributions) or because of the employee's death or retirement. Separation from service was not further defined in the Code or the regulations. The Tax Court, however, consistently stated that a separation generally will not be found to have occurred "unless there is a change in the employment relationship in more than a formal or technical sense." Therefore, a reduction in work schedule or change in employment status that is anything less than a complete severance from the employer did not constitute a separation from service. Furthermore, a change in the employment relationship such as one caused by a merger, reorganization, liquidation, or other restructuring generally did not constitute a separation from service if the participant continues on the same job for the surviving employer. [*See* Rev. Rul. 81-26, 1981-1 C.B. 200; Edwards v. Comm'r, T.C. Memo. 1989-409 (1989); Reinhardt v. Comm'r, 85 T.C. 511 (1985)]

Q 15:24   When does an independent contractor experience a severance from employment for purposes of these rules?

Generally, an independent contractor experiences a "severance from employment" on the expiration of the contract (or all contracts if there is more than one contract) between the independent contractor and the plan sponsor if the contract expiration constitutes a good-faith and complete termination of the contractual relationship. If the sponsor anticipates a renewal of the contractual relationship or anticipates that the independent contractor will become an employee, the expiration will not constitute a good-faith and complete termination of the contractual relationship. Certain presumptions apply when determining whether a good-faith and complete termination of the relationship has occurred. The renewal of a contractual relationship is presumed to have been anticipated by the sponsor if the sponsor intends to contract again for the services provided under the expired contract, and the independent contractor has not been eliminated by either the sponsor or the independent contractor as a possible provider of services under the new contract. The sponsor will be presumed to intend to contract again for services provided under an expired contract if doing so is conditioned only upon the sponsor's incurring a need for the services, the availability of funds, or both.

The severance-from-employment requirement will be satisfied if, with respect to amounts payable to a participant who is an independent contractor, the plan provides that no amount is to be paid to the participant until at least 12 months after the expiration of the contract or, if there is more than one contract, all contracts under which services are performed for the sponsor, and no amount so payable is paid if the participant performs services for the sponsor as an independent contractor or an employee during that 12-month period. [Treas. Reg. § 1.457-6(b)(2)]

Q 15:25 What is an *unforeseeable emergency* for purposes of these rules?

The Treasury Regulations define an *unforeseeable emergency* as:

1. A severe financial hardship to the participant or beneficiary caused by an illness or accident of the participant or beneficiary, the participant's or beneficiary's spouse, or the participant's or beneficiary's dependent (as defined in Code Section 152(a));

2. A loss of the participant's or beneficiary's property as the result of casualty (including the need to rebuild a home following damage to a home not otherwise covered by homeowner's insurance, e.g., as a result of a natural disaster); or

3. Other similar extraordinary and unforeseeable circumstances caused by events beyond the participant's or beneficiary's control.

The circumstances that will constitute an unforeseeable emergency generally depend upon the facts and circumstances of each case. Payment may not be made to the extent the hardship may be relieved by insurance or other similar reimbursement or compensation, liquidation of assets (to the extent the liquidation would not itself cause severe financial hardship), or a cessation of deferrals under the plan. College tuition or the costs of purchasing a home are not considered unforeseeable emergencies. However, under final regulations issued by the IRS in July 2003, the need to pay for the funeral expenses of a family member may constitute an unforeseeable emergency. [Treas. Reg. § 1.457-6(c)]

Withdrawals on account of an unforeseeable emergency must be limited to the amount reasonably needed to satisfy the emergency requirement (which may include any amounts necessary to pay any federal, state, or local income taxes or penalties reasonably anticipated to result from the distribution). [Treas. Reg. § 1.457-6(c)(2)(iii)]

Q 15:26 When must distributions commence under an eligible plan?

To be an eligible plan, a plan must meet the distribution requirements of Code Section 457(d)(1) and (2). Under Code Section 457(d)(1), a plan must not distribute amounts earlier than: (i) the calendar year in which the participant attains age 70½, (ii) when the participant has severance from employment, or (iii) when the participant has an unforeseeable emergency. Under Section 457(d)(2), a plan must meet the minimum distribution requirements of Code Section 401(a)(9). (See Q 15:27.)

> **Note.** The IRS issued INFO 2001-0099, stating that the Code Section 72(t) penalty on premature distributions from qualified retirement plans and IRAs does not apply to Code Section 457 arrangements. However, distributions attributable to amounts rolled into a governmental eligible plan from an IRA, qualified plan, or Code Section 403(b) contract are subject to the Code Section 72(t) penalty on premature distributions. [I.R.C. § 72(t)(9)]

Q 15:27   Are there minimum distribution requirements that must be met under an eligible plan?

Yes. An eligible plan must meet the qualified plan distribution requirements of Code Section 401(a)(9). (Prior to January 1, 2002, there were also additional distribution requirements under Code Section 457, as described below.)

Generally, under Code Section 401(a)(9) as amended by SBJPA, distributions must begin no later than the later of the April 1 of the calendar year following the calendar year in which the individual attains age 70½ or the April 1 of the calendar year following the calendar year in which the individual retires. (Owners of 5 percent or more must begin receiving distributions no later than the April 1 of the calendar year following the calendar year in which the individual attains age 70½.) Code Section 401(a)(9) and regulations thereunder also require that certain minimum amounts be distributed to the participant each year over a certain limited period of time.

In addition, in the case of a distribution beginning before the participant's death, the plan must provide that the amounts payable must be paid at times that are not later than the time determined under Code Section 401(a)(9)(G) (relating to incidental death benefits). Amounts that have not been distributed to the participant during his or her life must be distributed after the participant's death at least as rapidly as under the method of distribution being used as of the date of the participant's death and must meet the Section 401(a)(9) death distribution rules.

On April 14, 2002, the IRS published final and temporary regulations modifying the Code Section 401(a)(9) minimum required distribution (MRD) rules. [Treas. Reg. § 1.401(a)(9)] The regulations are effective for determining MRDs in 2003 and thereafter. The regulations include a table for determining the MRD, permit the determination of the beneficiary as late as September 30 of the year following the employee's death, and allow the remaining benefit to be distributed following the employee's death using the employee's remaining life expectancy, among other changes.

Under the additional Code Section 457 distribution requirements that applied to distributions prior to January 1, 2002, a distribution that does not begin until after the death of the participant must be paid out in its entirety during a period of not more than 15 years, or the life expectancy of the beneficiary if the surviving spouse is the beneficiary. Also under the additional Code Section 457 distribution requirements that applied to distributions prior to January 1, 2002, a distribution payable over a period of more than one year must be made in substantially nonincreasing amounts in payments that are made at least annually. [I.R.C. §§ 457(d)(2); 401(a)(9); Treas. Reg. §§ 1.401(a)(9)-1, 1.401(a)(9)-2; Ltr. Rul. 8946019]

Q 15:28   May an eligible plan permit any elective withdrawals by a participant before the participant otherwise is entitled to a distribution?

Yes, it may, but only under limited circumstances. Under a change effected by SBJPA, if the total amount payable to a participant under an eligible plan (excluding, with respect to governmental eligible plans, rollover contributions) does not exceed $5,000, and no amount has been deferred by the participant under the plan during the two-year period ending on the date of the distribution, the participant may elect (or may be forced by the employer) to receive his or her account balance, even if the otherwise applicable distribution date has not arrived, so long as no prior similar distribution has been made from the plan to the participant. With respect to an eligible plan maintained by a tax-exempt entity, the Code provides that the mere availability of such an election right does not cause the participant's benefits to be treated as made available to and taxable to the participant. [I.R.C. § 457(e)(9); Treas. Reg. § 1.457-6(e)]

Q 15:29   Will amounts payable under an eligible plan maintained by a tax-exempt entity be considered made available to a participant or beneficiary if the participant or beneficiary has a right to elect to defer the payment of the amounts beyond the date on which the amounts otherwise would become payable?

No. Amounts deferred under an eligible plan maintained by a tax-exempt entity will not be considered made available to and therefore taxable to the participant or beneficiary if under the plan the participant or beneficiary may irrevocably elect, before the date on which the amounts become payable, to defer payment of some or all of the amounts to a fixed or determinable future date. [Treas. Reg. § 1.457-7(c)(11)] In addition, under SBJPA (see Q 15:21), a one-time election to defer distributions made after a distribution event but before commencement of distributions is available. [I.R.C. § 457(e)(9)(B); Treas. Reg. § 1.457-7(c)(2)(iii)]

Q 15:30   Can a participant direct the investment of amounts deferred under an eligible plan?

Yes. An eligible plan participant may be permitted to choose among various investment options under the plan. For the eligible plans of tax-exempt employers, any investment must be solely the property of the plan sponsor (or a rabbi trust established by the employer) and must be subject to the claims of its bankruptcy creditors. [Treas. Reg. § 1.457-8(b); *see* Ltr. Ruls. 9003021, 8946019] For the eligible plans of governmental employers, plan investments must be held in trust, or in custodial accounts or contracts described in section 401(f). [I.R.C. § 457(g); Treas. Reg. § 1.457-8(a)]

Q 15:31 Will amounts under an eligible plan maintained by a tax-exempt entity be considered made available to and taxable to a participant if the amounts are used to purchase life insurance contracts as an investment medium?

No. If the plan sponsor (1) retains all of the incidents of ownership of the contracts, (2) is the sole beneficiary under the contracts, and (3) is under no obligation to transfer the contracts or to pass through the proceeds of the contracts to any participant or beneficiary, the purchase of life insurance contracts as an investment medium will not cause the amounts used to purchase the contracts to be considered made available to and taxable to the participant. [*See, e.g.,* Treas. Reg. § 1.457-8(b)]

Q 15:32 Can a participant transfer deferred amounts between eligible plans?

Yes. Transfers of amounts from one governmental eligible plan to another governmental eligible plan (or from one eligible plan maintained by a tax-exempt entity to another eligible plan maintained by a tax-exempt entity) are permitted, without requiring the participant to include any portion of the amount transferred in the participant's gross income, as long as (1) the transferor plan provides for transfers, (2) the receiving plan provides for the receipt of transfers, (3) the amount deferred immediately after the transfer is at least equal to the amount deferred immediately before the transfer, and (4) in the case of a transfer for a participant, the participant incurred a severance from employment with the transferring employer and is performing services for the entity maintaining the receiving plan. [Treas. Reg. § 1.457-10(b)] A transfer from one eligible plan to another will not be treated as a distribution for any purposes under Code Section 457. [I.R.C. § 457(e)(10); Ltr. Rul. 8946019]

The July 2003 IRS final regulations provide that transfers are permitted among eligible governmental plans under three circumstances:

1. A person-by-person transfer is permitted for any beneficiary and for any participant who has had a severance from employment with the transferring employer and is performing services for the entity maintaining the receiving plan, whether or not the other plan is within the same state.

2. A transfer is permitted if the entire plan's assets for all participants and beneficiaries are transferred to another eligible governmental plan within the same state if there is a severance from employment.

3. A transfer is permitted if the transfer is from one eligible governmental plan to another eligible governmental plan of the same employer. No severance from employment is required in this type of transfer.

Furthermore, plan-to-plan transfers from an eligible governmental plan to a governmental defined benefit plan are allowed for permissive service credit, without regard to whether the defined benefit plan is maintained by a governmental entity that is in the same state.

Q 15:33   Can amounts deferred under an eligible plan be rolled over to an individual retirement account (IRA), a tax-qualified plan, or a tax-sheltered annuity?

Before EGTRRA, there was no provision that permitted a rollover to an IRA from an eligible plan. Under pre-EGTRRA law, such a transfer would constitute a taxable distribution and an impermissible IRA contribution. [I.R.C. § 457(a); Treas. Reg. § 1.457-1(a)(1); Rev. Rul. 86-103, 1986-2 C.B. 62; TAM 9121004] For example, the IRS noted in a 1991 ruling that a Section 457 plan is not an exempt trust, as described in Code Section 401(a), and is not treated as such an exempt trust; therefore, the Section 402(a)(6)(F) provision permitting tax-free rollovers of distributions required by a qualified domestic relations order (QDRO) from an exempt trust to an IRA does not apply to any distributions from a Section 457 plan made pursuant to a QDRO (see Q 15:39). [Ltr. Rul. 9145010]

Similarly, before EGTRRA, amounts deferred under an eligible plan could not be rolled over into a tax-qualified retirement plan (e.g., a 401(k) plan, a profit-sharing plan, a money purchase pension plan, or a defined benefit plan) or a Section 403(b) tax-sheltered annuity.

EGTRRA revised these rules to permit rollovers from governmental, but not tax-exempt, employer eligible plans to IRAs, Section 401(a) qualified plans, Section 403(b) plans, and other eligible plans, beginning in 2002.

(In addition, see Revenue Ruling 2004-12, holding that eligible retirement plans separately accounting for amounts attributable to rollover contributions may permit distribution of amounts rolled over at any time, pursuant to the individual's request.)

Q 15:34   Are lump-sum distributions from eligible plans eligible for income averaging treatment under Code Section 402?

No. To qualify for the income averaging treatment available under Code Section 402, the lump-sum distributions must be made (1) from a trust that forms a part of a plan described in Code Section 401(a) and that is exempt from tax under Code Section 501 (i.e., from a tax-qualified retirement plan) or (2) from an annuity plan described in Code Section 403(a). Section 457 plans are not plans under either Code Section 401(a) or Code Section 403(a). [Ltr. Rul. 8119020; Rheal v. Comm'r, 58 TCM 229 (1989)]

Note. Five-year averaging was repealed in any event by SBJPA for distributions after 1999.

Q 15:35 What are the consequences if a plan intended to be an eligible plan is administered in a manner inconsistent with the eligible plan requirements?

If a plan maintained by a governmental employer that is intended to be an eligible plan is not administered consistently with the requirements applicable to eligible plans, the plan will be deemed to be an ineligible plan as of the first plan year beginning more than 180 days after notice of the failure is given by the IRS to the sponsor, unless the sponsor corrects the inconsistency before the first day of that plan year. A plan maintained by a tax-exempt organization other than a governmental employer that is intended to be an eligible plan but that does not meet the eligible plan requirements will be treated as an ineligible plan, without notice from the IRS, immediately on its failure to meet the requirements. [I.R.C. § 457(b)]

Q 15:36 Can an individual participate in more than one eligible plan?

Yes. The maximum amount of compensation that an individual may defer for any taxable year under all eligible plans may not, however, exceed the general Section 457(b) limits discussed above. [I.R.C. § 457(c)(1)]

Q 15:37 Does a participant have any legal title rights in amounts deferred under an eligible plan?

No. All deferrals under an eligible plan sponsored by a tax-exempt entity, all property and rights purchased with those deferrals, and all income attributable to those deferrals, property, or rights must remain, until made available to participants or their beneficiaries, solely the property and rights of the plan sponsor (without being restricted to the provision of benefits under the plan) subject to the claims of its general creditors. [I.R.C. §§ 457(b)(6), 457(e)(8); Ltr. Rul. 8946019] A rabbi trust may be used in connection with an eligible plan, however (see Q 15:8).

Under a change effected by SBJPA (see Q 15:15), participants in government plans must have their plan interests funded in a trust, custodial account, or annuity maintained for their benefit, so those participants have a beneficial title interest, but not a legal title interest, in those assets. SBJPA provides that any such funding mechanism will be deemed to be tax exempt, and amounts will not be considered made available to, and therefore taxable to, participants merely because they are held in the trust or custodial account or annuity. (That SBJPA provision leaves open—unintentionally, apparently—the question of whether the funding of eligible plan interests raises tax issues under the economic benefit doctrine or Code Sections 83 and 402(b). Virtually all commentators take the position that no economic benefit doctrine taxation occurs by virtue of compliance with this governmental plan funding rule.)

Q 15:38   Are amounts deferred under an eligible plan and deposited in depositories insured by the Federal Deposit Insurance Corporation (FDIC) insured up to $100,000 per participant?

Yes. Section 311(b) of the FDIC Improvement Act of 1991, enacted December 19, 1991, provides, in pertinent part, that

> [e]xcept as provided in clause (ii), for the purpose of determining the amount of insurance due under subparagraph (B), the [FDIC] shall provide deposit insurance coverage with respect to deposits accepted by any insured depository institution on a pro rata or "pass-through" basis to a participant in or beneficiary of an employee benefit plan including any eligible deferred compensation plan described in section 457 of the Internal Revenue Code of 1986.

Subparagraph (B) provides, in general, that the net amount due any depositor at an insured depository institution may not exceed $100,000. The exception described in clause (ii) provides that after the end of the one-year period beginning on the date of the enactment of the FDIC Improvement Act of 1991, the FDIC will not provide insurance coverage on a pro rata or pass-through basis pursuant to clause (i) with respect to deposits accepted by any insured depository institution that, at the time the deposits are accepted, may not accept brokered deposits under Section 29 of the FDIC Act. (Section 29 prohibits institutions that do not meet minimum capital requirements from accepting brokered deposits.) This exception does not apply if the insured depository institution meets applicable capital standards and the depositor receives a written statement from the institution that the brokered deposits are eligible for insurance coverage on a pro rata or pass-through basis. [FDIC Improvement Act of 1991, Pub. L. No. 102-242, § 311(b)(1), USCCAN (105 Stat.) 2236, 2363-64; H.R. Rep. No. 330, 102d Cong., 1st Sess. 137 (1991), reprinted in 1991 USCCAN 1901, 1950-51]

Section 311(b)(2) of the FDIC Improvement Act of 1991 provides that deposits in an insured depository institution made in connection with

1. Any IRA described in Code Section 408(a);
2. Any eligible deferred compensation plan described in Code Section 457;
3. Any individual account plan defined in ERISA Section 3(34); and
4. Any plan described in Code Section 401(d), to the extent that participants and beneficiaries under the Section 401(d) plan have the right to direct the investment of assets held in individual accounts maintained on their behalf by the plan must be aggregated and insured in an amount not to exceed $100,000 per participant per insured depository institution. The amount aggregated for insurance coverage consists of the present vested and ascertainable interest of each participant under the plans, excluding any remainder interest created by, or as a result of, the plans. [FDIC Improvement Act of 1991, Pub. L. No. 102-242, § 311(b)(2), 1991 USCCAN (105 Stat.) 2236, 2364-65; H.R. 102d Cong., 1st Sess. Rep. No. 330, (1991), reprinted in 1991 USCCAN 1951]

Prior to the enactment of this law, FDIC regulations restricted deposit insurance for eligible Section 457 plans to $100,000 per plan, rather than $100,000 per participant. [55 Fed. Reg. 20111 (May 15, 1990); FDIC Improvement Act of 1991, Pub. L. No. 102-242, § 311, 1991 USCCAN (105 Stat.) 2236, 2363-67]

Q 15:39   May an eligible plan make distributions pursuant to a QDRO prior to the time distributions are permitted under Code Section 457(d)(1)(A)?

Yes. Code Section 414(p), as amended by EGTRRA, provides the QDRO rules for eligible plans for post-2001 QDROs. Prior to this EGTRRA change, this issue was less clear.

For example, in a 1991 ruling, the IRS responded to a request regarding whether an eligible plan may make distributions pursuant to a QDRO prior to the time distributions were permitted under Code Section 457(d)(1)(A). The IRS noted that an eligible plan is an unfunded, nonqualified deferred compensation plan in which the participant has only the plan sponsor's contractual promise that benefits will be paid, as provided in Code Section 457(b)(6). Therefore, the IRS concluded that, under Code Section 457(b)(6) and Treasury Regulations Section 1.457-2(j), the participant cannot have any interest in the plan sponsor's assets, and any funds used to pay benefits must be available to the plan sponsor's general creditors. The IRS stated that a Section 457 plan would violate these provisions of Code Section 457 and the regulations thereunder if the participant or anyone else received an interest in the plan sponsor's assets earlier than the earliest date established in Code Section 457(d)(1)(A).

The IRS also noted that under Code Section 457(d)(1)(A), payments under an eligible plan may not begin until the participant separates from service, attains age 70½, or has an unforeseeable emergency (see Q 15:25).

Because a divorce or separation generally does not give rise to an unforeseeable emergency within the meaning of these regulations, a participant who is working for the sponsor and who is under age 70½ cannot receive distributions from an eligible plan. The spouse or alternate payee likewise could not receive such distributions before the participant separates from service or attains age 70½. Therefore, an eligible plan must make any distribution pursuant to a QDRO only at or after the time permitted under Code Section 457(d)(1)(A) in order to remain an eligible plan. [Ltr. Rul. 9145010]

However, in Letter Ruling 200103017, the IRS held that an eligible plan that recognized the assignment of benefits under a QDRO did not lose its eligible plan status under Code Section 457. In that case, the plan was a governmental employer's eligible plan, the assets of which were held in a trust established under Code Section 457(g). The plan and trust provided that participants' benefits were not subject to assignment, but that the plan would recognize rights created under a domestic relations order so long as those rights did not require payment to the alternate payee prior to a date on which payments could be made under Code Section 457(d)(1)(A) (i.e., when the participant attains age 70½ or separates from service, or when the alternate payee experiences a hardship). The letter ruling also concluded that a separate account under the plan could be created for the alternate payee. The EGTRRA provision permitting eligible plans to recognize QDROs has eliminated this uncertainty.

Q 15:40 Has the IRS published any model language or recent regulations concerning eligible plans?

Yes. On July 27, 1998, the IRS published Revenue Procedure 98-41 [1998-32 I.R.B. 7], which provides model amendments that employers that sponsor eligible plans may use to bring their plans into compliance with the changes to Code Section 457 contained in SBJPA and the Tax Reform Act of 1997 (TRA '97). The model amendments contained in Revenue Procedure 98-41 are based on earlier guidance provided by the IRS in Notice 98-8 [1998-4 I.R.B. 6], which discussed the SBJPA and TRA '97 changes to Code Section 457. In August 2004, the IRS published similar model language to assist governmental employers in ensuring that their eligible plans comply with the changes contained in EGTRRA. [Rev. Rul. 2004-56]

In addition, in July 2003, the IRS published extensive final regulations under Code Section 457. [Treas. Reg. §§ 1.457-1–1.457-12] The regulations contained extensive guidance on the requirements for eligible plans and two provisions affecting ineligible plans.

Q 15:41 Will the IRS issue rulings on eligible plans that have been amended to comply with the requirements of SBJPA and TRA '97?

Yes. In Revenue Procedure 98-40 [1998-32 I.R.B. 6], issued by the IRS on July 27, 1998, the IRS stated that effective August 10, 1998, and subject to certain limitations outlined in the revenue procedure, it will consider requests for rulings on eligible plans that have been amended to comply with SBJPA and TRA '97. Requests for such rulings are to be made pursuant to the general ruling request requirements contained in the IRS's annual revenue procedure on this subject (e.g., Revenue Procedure 2002-1 [2002-1 I.R.B. 1]).

Q 15:42 Has the IRS issued any guidance on the withholding and reporting rules applicable to eligible deferred compensation plans?

Yes. On August 1, 2000, the IRS issued Notice 2000-38 [2000-33 I.R.B. 174] describing the withholding and reporting requirements applicable to eligible deferred compensation plans. Notice 2000-38 was updated in Notice 2003-20 [2003-19 C.B. 894] to reflect the EGTRRA changes to the Section 457(b) plan rules that permit direct rollovers of eligible rollover distributions from governmental—but not tax-exempt—employer 457(b) plans. Notice 2003-20 generally supersedes Notice 2000-38 for contributions and distributions made after December 31, 2001 (although, for deferrals and distributions made after December 31, 2001, and before January 1, 2004, the IRS will not assert that there has been a failure to comply with applicable reporting and withholding requirements if the applicable reporting and withholding requirements set forth in Notice 2000-38 have been satisfied). Described below are the reporting and withholding rules as set forth in Notice 2003-20.

The notice was aimed at addressing the following four points:

1. The income tax withholding and reporting requirements with respect to annual deferrals and distributions made to eligible deferred compensation plans;

2. FICA/Medicare/FUTA payment and reporting with respect to annual deferrals under eligible deferred compensation plans;

3. Employer identification numbers used in connection with trusts established under Code Section 457(b); and

4. The application of annual reporting requirements to Section 457(b) plan administrators and trustees holding plan assets in accordance with Code Section 457(g).

In general, the notice provides that annual deferrals under eligible deferred compensation plans are not subject to income tax withholding because amounts under such plans are not subject to income tax until those amounts are paid or (with respect to eligible plans of tax-exempt entities) made available. However, the notice provides that the amounts are required to be reported for informational purposes on the participants' Form W-2s.

The notice further provides that distributions from an eligible deferred compensation plan of a tax-exempt entity are wages under Code Section 3401(a) and therefore are subject to income tax withholding, with the party controlling the payment of the distributions being responsible for effecting the income tax withholding. Distributions from eligible plans maintained by tax-exempt entities are reported on Form W-2, and income tax withheld from such distributions is reported quarterly on Form 941. On the other hand, distributions from a governmental eligible deferred compensation plan are subject to income tax withholding in accordance with the income tax withholding requirements of Code Section 3405 applicable to distributions from qualified plans, annuities, and IRAs. Distributions from governmental eligible plans are reported on Form 1099-R, and income tax withheld from such distributions is reported annually on Form 945.

With respect to FICA/Medicare/FUTA issues, the notice provides that immediately vested deferrals under an eligible deferred compensation plan are subject to FICA/Medicare/FUTA taxes at the time of the deferral, with unvested deferrals generally subject to FICA/Medicare/FUTA taxes when they become vested.

The notice also provides that, where the sponsor of the eligible deferred compensation plan is a tax-exempt entity, annual deferrals and distributions under the plan must be reported on the entity's Form 990. Notice 2000-38 adds that, although Section 457(g) trusts are not required to file Form 990s and certain other forms, they may be required to file annual Form 990-Ts, if unrelated business taxable income is incurred.

Notice 2003-20 did not expressly address any withholding and reporting issues concerning independent contractor participants in eligible deferred compensation plans.

Q 15:43   Has the IRS issued any guidance on automatic salary reductions into eligible deferred compensation plans?

Yes. On July 18, 2000, the IRS issued Revenue Ruling 2000-33 [2000-31 I.R.B. 142] discussing automatic deferrals of a certain percentage of employees' compensation into their accounts in an eligible deferred compensation plan. The revenue ruling concluded that a provision in an eligible deferred compensation plan that provides for an automatic deferral of a specified percentage of an employee's pay into the plan each month, absent an affirmative election by the employee to have no deferrals or a different percentage deferral, will not cause the plan to fail to meet the Section 457(b) requirements for an eligible deferred compensation plan.

Revenue Ruling 2000-33 adds that, in keeping with the general rules of Code Section 457(b), the automatic deferral percentage, or the employee's affirmative election to change that percentage, must be made before the beginning of the month for which it will be effective.

Revenue Ruling 2000-33 follows earlier pronouncements from the IRS that state that similar types of automatic deferrals under 401(k) plans and 403(b) plans will not endanger those plans' qualified status. Although these IRS pronouncements do provide comfort to plan sponsors that automatic deferral provisions will not endanger the tax status of their voluntary deferral plans, the pronouncements do not deal with what is perhaps a larger issue; namely, do automatic deferral provisions in voluntary deferred compensation plans violate the criminal laws of many states that prohibit employers from withholding funds from employees' paychecks without written, signed, revocable consent from the employees. This question often turns on whether the employer in question is ERISA-governed and whether the state law in question is a "criminal law of general application" that survives ERISA preemption. Although the Pension Protection Act of 2006 (PPA) and guidance thereunder provide that ERISA preempts these state laws with respect to ERISA-governed plans, there is as yet no guidance providing that Section 457 plans are exempt from these state laws.

Therefore, Section 457 plan sponsors considering adding automatic deferral provisions to their plans should discuss these issues with their ERISA counsel before proceeding.

Ineligible Plans

Q 15:44 How does a participant in or beneficiary of an ineligible plan treat the compensation deferred under that plan?

Compensation deferred under an ineligible plan is included in the gross income of the participant or beneficiary in the first taxable year in which there is no substantial risk of forfeiture of the rights to the compensation. In other words, participants in ineligible plans are taxed on amounts deferred by them or on their behalf as soon as those amounts become vested, even if those amounts are not then distributed or made available (and even if those amounts are never, in fact, received).

Earnings on the compensation deferred under an ineligible plan are includible in gross income when amounts under the plan are paid or made available to the participant or beneficiary. However, the IRS's July 2003 final regulations under Code Section 457 suggest that "earnings" for this purpose include only earnings accruing on ineligible plan deferrals after the vesting date for those deferrals. [Treas. Reg. § 1.457-11(a)(2)] (It is unclear under the final regulations when fully vested earnings accruing before the deferrals' vesting date are taxable.) This position seems to contradict that of the prior regulation on this topic published in 1982. The prior regulation suggests that all earnings (regardless of when they accrue) are not taxed until distributions are made under the ineligible plan, and most ineligible plan sponsors have historically relied on the 1982 regulation. Sponsors of ineligible plans should consult with counsel about this technical, but operationally important, issue and should monitor carefully developments affecting this issue, especially if they need to transition from a position based on the 1982 regulations to a position based on the 2003 regulations.

The tax treatment of any amount made available to a participant or beneficiary under an ineligible plan is determined under the recovery-of-basis rules for annuities contained in Code Section 72. [I.R.C. §§ 457(f), 72; Ltr. Rul. 8946019]

The application of the ineligible plan rules can be illustrated by the following two IRS rulings. In the first, Letter Ruling 9212006, a school district permitted teachers to defer salary during a four-year period (the deferral period) and to take a paid leave of absence during the year following the deferral period. A teacher would agree to defer 20 percent of salary for each year in the deferral period, and he or she would receive 100 percent of salary during the leave of absence. If the teacher terminated employment during the four-year deferral period, he or she would forfeit any right to the deferred salary and would not be entitled to a leave of absence. If the teacher terminated employment during the leave of absence, he or she would forfeit the right to the remaining monthly payments of salary for the year. The teacher also was required to return to employment for at least one year following the leave of absence. If the teacher failed to return to employment for the full year after the leave of absence, he or she would be required to repay the salary received during the leave of absence.

The IRS determined that the school district was an eligible employer within the meaning of Code Section 457(e)(1) and that the plan was governed by Code Section 457. Because the plan did not limit the amount of deferrals and because it would pay out deferred amounts while the teachers were employed by the school district, however, the IRS determined that the plan was an ineligible plan subject to the rules of Code Section 457(f). Applying those rules, the IRS determined that, because the teacher would forfeit the deferred amounts unless the teacher worked for four years and for an additional year after the leave of absence, the deferred amounts were subject to a substantial risk of forfeiture until paid, for purposes of Code Section 457(f). When paid to the teacher in year five, however, the deferred amounts were includible in income in accordance with Code Section 72.

In the second ruling, Letter Ruling 9212011, a health care organization exempt from tax under Code Section 501(c)(3) entered into an agreement with an executive that created a supplemental account to which the employer credited 5 percent of the executive's monthly base salary. The executive was not able to make additional contributions to the account. The benefits would vest at the rate of 10 percent per year for 10 years, but if the executive terminated employment with the employer at any time within that 10-year period, the executive would forfeit the nonvested portion of his benefits. If the executive did not terminate employment with the employer within 10 years, payment of his benefits would commence within 60 days of the date of the executive's termination of employment and would be paid out in equal monthly installments over two years. The benefits could not be assigned, alienated, or encumbered by voluntary or involuntary action. The employer established a rabbi trust for the purpose of holding assets to fund the employer's obligations under the agreement.

The IRS determined that no plan contributions or benefits were taxable to the executive until the executive became vested in those benefits under the terms of the agreement, that the benefits would be includible in income at their value in the year when they were no longer subject to a substantial risk of forfeiture, and that the tax treatment of any amount made available under the agreement would be determined under Code Section 72.

Q 15:45   What have recent IRS private letter rulings concluded concerning the taxation of earnings in ineligible defined compensation plans?

On the issue of the timing of taxation of earnings in ineligible plans, there appears to be a conflict between the prior regulation issued in 1982 and the July 2003 final regulations. [Treas. Reg. § 1.457-11(a)(2)] In the past, the IRS has issued several letter rulings [see, e.g., Ltr. Rul. 9329010] that take the position reflected in the July 2003 final regulations that "earnings" that are taxed when distributions are made under the ineligible plan include only earnings accruing on ineligible plan deferrals after the vesting date for those deferrals. However, Letter Ruling 9444028 appears to confirm the position of those commentators who believe that the 1982 regulation stands for the proposition that earnings on amounts deferred under the plan, whether earned before or after the vesting date for the deferred amounts, are not taxed until amounts under the plan actually are paid or made available to the participants.

Sponsors of ineligible plans should consult with counsel about this technical, but operationally important, issue, especially because it is unclear under the final regulations when fully vested earnings accruing before the deferrals' vesting date are taxable.

Q 15:46   What is a *substantial risk of forfeiture* for purposes of Code Section 457?

Compensation is subject to a *substantial risk of forfeiture* if the right to the compensation is conditioned on the future performance of substantial services by any individual. Historically, the IRS indicated informally that it would be reasonable to look to the extensive interpretive regulations under Code Section 83 (e.g., Treasury Regulations Section 1.83-3(c), which defines situations involving a substantial risk of forfeiture) for guidance concerning the term *substantial risk of forfeiture* as used in Code Section 457. For example, under the Section 83 rules, the risk of a decline in value is not a substantial risk of forfeiture. Similarly, the fact that deferred amounts are subject to the claims of the employer's creditors does not constitute a substantial risk of forfeiture for purposes of Code Section 83. [I.R.C. § 457(f)(3)(B); Treas. Reg. § 1.83-3(c)(4); Ltr. Ruls. 9030028, 9030025]

In 1991, the IRS ruled that a substantial risk of forfeiture was considered to exist where an individual was required to complete a minimum of two years of service with the employer. [Ltr. Rul. 9211037]

In Letter Ruling 9215019, the IRS examined a deferred compensation plan established by a school district for its superintendent of schools. The superintendent's employment contract with the school district was for a three-year term and was renewed automatically each year so that the contract period would always be three years. The IRS ruled that because the plan did not limit the amount of deferrals, and because the school district could pay out deferred amounts while the superintendent was working for the school district, the plan was an ineligible plan, subject to Code Section 457(f). It also ruled that because the superintendent was required to work at least three years before benefits vested, the superintendent's rights to benefits under the plan were subject to a substantial risk of forfeiture during those three years.

The school district also could vest the superintendent in his benefits any time on or after three years from the effective date of the plan. The IRS refrained from expressing an opinion on whether a plan sponsor's retention of discretion to vest an otherwise unvested benefit eliminates the substantial risk of forfeiture.

Code Section 409A also utilizes the term *substantial risk of forfeiture* for certain purposes. In Notice 2005-1, the IRS specified that the definition of *substantial risk of forfeiture* for purposes of Code Section 409A is not necessarily the definition of substantial risk of forfeiture for purposes of Code

Sections 457(f) or 83. Although the Code Section 409A definition of substantial risk of forfeiture should not be applied to other Code Sections (e.g., to Code Section 457(f) to determine when amounts deferred by a service provider to a tax-exempt entity will be subject to inclusion in income), the date that deferred compensation is no longer subject to a substantial risk of forfeiture under Code Section 409A is the date that amounts that fail to meet the requirements of Code Section 409A must be included in income, and the date that is used to determine when short-term deferrals must be paid to avoid the application of Code Section 409A. Therefore, the Code Section 409A definition of substantial risk of forfeiture does have some application in the Code Section 457(f) context.

IRS Notice 2005-1 provides that any extension of the period during which compensation is subject to a substantial risk of forfeiture is disregarded for purposes of determining whether the compensation is subject to a substantial risk of forfeiture for Code Section 409A purposes, and a salary deferral generally may not be subject to a substantial risk of forfeiture for Code Section 409A purposes. The Code Section 409A proposed and final regulations restate these interpretations. However, although the preamble to the Code Section 409A proposed regulations included strong criticisms of the ability to extend, or roll, the risk of forfeiture (calling these elections "sufficiently suspect to question whether the parties ever intended that the right be subject to any true substantial risk"), risks of forfeiture tied to a noncompete agreement (stating that these risks can be "illusory"), and voluntary salary deferrals that are subject to forfeiture (stating that "a rational service provider normally would not agree to subject amounts that have already been earned, such as salary payments, to a condition that creates a real possibility of forfeiture"), these editorial comments were deleted from the Preamble to the final Code Section 409A regulations issued in April 2007. This deletion may have been in response to commentators' reactions to the preamble of the proposed regulations stating that the editorial comments were inappropriately placed in the Code Section 409A regulations preamble because of their potential impact on the currently very common Code Section 457(f) plan features that permit vesting renegotiation, utilize noncompete risks, and permit voluntary deferrals. These commentators suggested that, if the IRS and the Treasury Department wish to promulgate rules affecting the central taxation rule for Section 457(f) plans, they should do so in thoughtful and focused Section 457(f) guidance, and only after taking into account the actual facts and circumstances, and historical experience since 1986, with these common Section 457(f) plan provisions.

Perhaps in response to these comments, in July 2007 the IRS issued Notice 2007-62. [I.R.B. 2007-32] (See Q 15:47.)

Note. Notice 2005-1 is made obsolete by the final Code Section 409A regulations, except for its sections dealing with Section 457 plans, partnership plans, and reporting and withholding.

Q 15:47   What does IRS Notice 2007-62 say about Section 457(f) and Section 457(e)(11) severance pay plans?

On July 24, 2007, the IRS announced that it would issue, on August 6, 2007, Notice 2007-62 describing its "intent to issue guidance" on Code Section 457 issues affecting Section 457(f) and severance plans of tax-exempt and governmental employers.

The Notice contained the following statements:

1. *Defining the Section 457(e)(11) exemption.* Code Section 457(e)(11) provides that bona fide severance plans are exempt from the Section 457(f) taxation-on-vesting rules. Notice 2007-62 states that the IRS "anticipates issuing guidance" providing that plans will not qualify as bona fide severance plans under Code Section 457(e)(11), and therefore, will not be exempt from the taxation-on-vesting rules of Code Section 457(f) unless they:

(a) pay only on involuntary termination of employment (with exceptions for window programs, union plans, and certain reimbursement and in-kind programs);

(b) pay amounts that do not exceed two times "annual pay" (taking into account annual pay only up to the Code Section 401(a)(17) qualified plan compensation limit, $225,000 for 2007); and

(c) complete all payments by the end of the second calendar year after the year of the participant's separation from service.

Many executive severance plans do not satisfy these requirements, and therefore, vested amounts in these plans will become taxable under Code Section 457(f) if these proposed rules are implemented (absent any transitional relief that might be issued).

2. *Defining substantial risk of forfeiture under* Code Section 457(f). As noted above, amounts credited to a Section 457(f) plan are taxed when they vest (i.e., when they are no longer subject to a "substantial risk of forfeiture"). Notice 2007-62 provides that the IRS "anticipates issuing guidance" providing that the following will not qualify as "substantial risks of forfeiture" under Code Section 457(f) that are sufficient to postpone taxation of plan accounts:

(a) noncompete agreements; and/or

(b) extensions of initial vesting dates.

Participants with Section 457(f) plan accounts subject only to a noncompete risk, and/or subject only to an extension of an initial forfeiture risk period, would become taxable if these new rules were implemented (absent any transitional relief that might be issued).

3. *Prohibition of voluntary compensation deferrals.* Notice 2007-62 provides that voluntary compensation deferrals to Section 457(f) plans cannot be made subject to a substantial risk of forfeiture, and therefore, are taxable when made. Many Section 457(f) plans permit voluntary deferrals, which would become taxable when made if these new rules were implemented (absent any transitional relief that might be issued).

4. *Effective Date.* Notice 2007-62 provides that the IRS "anticipates that the guidance described in the Notice would be prospective," but that "no inference should be made from the [guidance]" with respect to the IRS's positions on these issues for periods before the Notice is issued. The IRS requests comments "as to the extent to which transition guidance . . . would be necessary and appropriate, and what such transition guidance would provide."

Although this effective date provision is certainly preferable to a statement that the guidance is retroactive, it fails to provide definitive guidance concerning what real-world employers with typical Section 457(e)(11) and Section 457(f) plans should do, if anything, before the Notice is supplemented with more formal guidance containing, or not containing, "necessary and appropriate transition guidance."

Employers with Section 457(e)(11) and/or Section 457(f) plans should consult with counsel to discuss the range of reasonable responses and the steps they should consider taking in light of Notice 2007-62.

Q 15:48   Has the IRS received comments on Notice 2007-62?

The IRS has received a number of comments in response to Notice 2007-62, including a number of comments suggesting appropriate transition rules to assist employers and plan participants in transitioning from the era prior to the issuance of the Notice to the era after definitive guidance is issued.

Q 15:49   Has the IRS issued any rulings concerning the various open issues affecting ineligible plans?

Yes. In Letter Ruling 9444028, the IRS discussed in detail the issues of participant investment direction, the definition of substantial risk of forfeiture, and the taxation of pre-vesting earnings as they apply to ineligible plans.

Under the facts of Letter Ruling 9444028, a tax-exempt employer established an ineligible plan and a related rabbi trust for members of its top-hat group. Under the plan, participants could elect to have their rabbi trust accounts invested among a group of investment options made available under the plan. The employer designated the vesting date for participants' accounts under the plan, and no deferred amounts were permitted to vest before the third January 1 after the calendar year in which the amounts were deferred. A participant's accounts also became vested on his or her death or disability.

The plan also provided that participants were entitled to distributions of their accounts on their vesting date and that nonvested amounts would be forfeited by a participant who terminated employment before his or her vesting date. The plan specifically provided, however, that a participant who forfeited all or a portion of his or her deferred compensation was nonetheless entitled to receive a distribution of the earnings related to the forfeited amount. That is, the plan provided that earnings credited to accounts, both before and after the account's vesting date, would be vested in the participant at all times.

The IRS concluded that the minimum vesting period provided under the plan (i.e., the third January 1 after the calendar year of the deferral) created a substantial risk of forfeiture under Code Section 457(f). It reached that conclusion by making reference to Treasury Regulations Section 1.83-3(c)(1), noting that Code Section 83 "includes the same definition of substantial risk of forfeiture as [Section 457(f)]." The IRS also concluded that no amount would be considered made available to a participant merely because that participant had a right to designate the deemed investment of that amount.

In addition, the IRS ruled that even though earnings on the deferred amounts were at all times vested—that is, a participant would not forfeit the earnings even if he or she terminated employment before his or her vesting date—the earnings would not be taxable to the participant until the taxable year in which the participant became entitled to receive the earnings.

In Letter Ruling 200302015, the IRS ruled on the effect on an employer's nonqualified plans of a conversion of the employer from a taxable entity to a tax-exempt entity. Before the conversion, the employer sponsored several nonqualified plans taxed under the Code Section 451 constructive receipt and economic benefit doctrines applicable to the nonqualified plans of for-profit employers. The employer was concerned that the continued maintenance of its nonqualified plans after its conversion to a tax-exempt entity would cause vested amounts in those plans to become immediately taxable to participants under the taxation-on-vesting rules of Code Section 457(f).

After noting that Congress had imposed the more restrictive taxation-on-vesting rules of Code Section 457(f) on tax-exempt employers' nonqualified plans as a substitute for the delayed deduction effect on for-profit employers' nonqualified plans, the IRS concluded that permitting the employer's nonqualified plans to continue to be taxed under the rules applicable to for-profit employers' plans was permissible, as long as the plans were frozen on the date of the conversion. That is, any post-conversion deferred compensation amounts would need to be taxed under the Code Section 457(f) rules.

Q 15:50   May a participant in an ineligible plan elect to defer his or her vesting date under the plan?

Nothing in Code Section 457(f) or the regulations under Code Section 457 addresses the subject of extensions of vesting dates under ineligible plans. In a private letter ruling concerning a Section 83 arrangement [Ltr. Rul. 9431021], however, the IRS held that an agreement between an employer and an employee to extend the period during which the employee was subject to a substantial risk of forfeiture of his rights to property transferred in connection with the performance of services for the employer would be given effect.

Because of the similarity between the language and structure of Code Sections 83 and 457(f), until further guidance is issued on this point, many taxpayers have taken the position that the conclusions reached in Letter Ruling 9431021 apply to ineligible plans as well as to Section 83 arrangements.

As discussed in Q 15:47, the IRS has announced its intent to issue guidance that would state that such deferrals of vesting/taxation dates are not effective to defer taxation beyond the initial, non-extended vesting date.

Q 15:51   What is the definition of a *bona fide severance plan* for purposes of Code Section 457(e)(11)?

No definition of *bona fide severance plan* is provided in Code Section 457(e)(11) or the regulations under Code Section 457; however, the phrase is defined in the regulations under ERISA Section 3. Generally, under this definition, an arrangement is a bona fide severance plan if:

1. Plan benefits are paid only on termination of employment and are not contingent, directly or indirectly, on the participant's retirement;
2. Plan benefits are limited to two times the participant's final year's cash plus noncash compensation; and
3. Plan benefits are paid only during the 24-month period following the participant's termination of employment.

In the absence of definitive guidance on the definition of a bona fide severance plan as used in Code Section 457(e)(11), most affected employers have used the ERISA definition of the phrase for purposes of Code Section 457(e)(11).

The IRS issued a private letter ruling, and the DOL recently issued an advisory opinion, that shed some light on this question. In each case, the guidance dealt with the concept that bona fide severance plan benefits cannot be contingent on retirement.

In Letter Ruling 199903032, the IRS examined an alleged bona fide severance pay plan that provided benefits to schoolteachers whose age plus years of service for the school system equaled 73. After conceding that "there is currently no interpretative guidance issued by the IRS, either in the form of regulations or otherwise, defining 'bona fide severance plan' for Code Section 457(e)(11) purposes," the IRS concluded that the school district plan was not a severance plan because, among other reasons, its benefits were "contingent on retirement," rather than true severance benefits.

Unfortunately, the IRS discussion in this letter ruling went beyond this seemingly dispositive issue and included statements such as "severance plans may provide for payment only on unanticipated sets of circumstances beyond the control of the employee," which are not reflective of the ERISA severance plan definition.

In DOL Advisory Opinion 99-01A, the DOL examined an alleged bona fide severance pay plan of a university that provided benefits to employees after attainment of age 60 with 20 or more years of continuous service. The DOL concluded, as did the IRS in the letter ruling, that the plan was not a bona fide severance plan because its benefits were "indirectly contingent on retirement."

In Notice 2007-62, the IRS announced that it intends to issue guidance providing a definitive definition of a severance pay plan for purposes of Code Section 457(e)(11). The IRS has not yet issued that guidance, nor any transition rules intended to assist employers in transitioning from the pre-Notice 2007-62 era to the post definitive guidance era, nor does Notice 2007-62 state whether the definition the IRS is considering issuing is merely a safe harbor, or is the exclusive definition to be used under Code Section 457(e)(11). (See Q 15:47 for a more complete discussion of this issue.)

Q 15:52   Is a bona fide severance plan maintained by a governmental or nonchurch tax-exempt employer subject to the ineligible plan rules?

No. Under Code Section 457(e)(11), a bona fide severance plan maintained by a governmental or nonchurch tax-exempt employer is not subject to the ineligible plan rules. Instead, such a plan presumably is subject to the rules of Code Section 451 and the constructive receipt and economic benefit doctrines. Therefore, a participant's interest in such a plan presumably is taxed when it is paid or made available to the participant or when it is first funded or assignable by the participant. In other words, a participant's interest in a bona fide severance plan maintained by a governmental or nonchurch tax-exempt employer is taxed in the same manner as a participant's interest in a deferred compensation plan of a taxable employer.

Q 15:53   Is a property transfer arrangement, such as a life-insurance-based plan or an option plan maintained by a governmental or nonchurch tax-exempt employer, subject to the ineligible plan rules?

No. Code Section 457 is not applicable to arrangements governed by Code Section 83 such as split-dollar life insurance plans or stock option plans. However, the July 2003 final regulations under Code Section 457 state that vested options issued by mutual fund stock option plans after May 8, 2002, are not effective to defer taxation under Code Section 83, but instead result in current taxation under Code Section 457. [*See* Treas. Reg. § 1.457-12]

ERISA Considerations

Q 15:54   Are Section 457 plans of governments subject to ERISA requirements?

No. Governmental deferred compensation plans, like all employee benefit plans of governmental employers, are exempt from the requirements of ERISA.

Q 15:55   Are Section 457 plans of nonchurch tax-exempt organizations subject to ERISA requirements?

Generally, yes. Unlike plans of state and local governments, plans of non-church tax-exempt organizations (as defined in ERISA rather than in the Code) are subject to ERISA. The IRS has noted that in the case of a Section 457 plan of a tax-exempt organization that is subject to Title I of ERISA, compliance with the exclusive purpose, trust, funding, and certain other rules of Title I of ERISA will cause the plan to fail to meet the requirements of Code Section 457(b)(6) and, therefore, will cause it to fail to be an eligible plan. Specifically, a Section 457 plan must be unfunded and all deferred amounts must remain solely the property and rights of the plan sponsor, subject only to the claims of the plan sponsor's general creditors. [I.R.C. § 457(b)(6); D.O.L. News Release 86-527 (Dec. 19, 1986); Notice 87-13, 1987-71 C.B. 432, 444; Ltr. Rul. 8950056; *but see* Foil v. Comm'r, 920 F.2d 1196 (5th Cir. 1990)]

Notwithstanding the foregoing, an unfunded ineligible plan maintained by an ERISA-governed tax-exempt organization primarily for the purpose of providing deferred compensation for a select group of management or highly compensated employees within the meaning of ERISA Sections 201(2), 301(a)(3), and 401(a)(1) (the top-hat plan exemption) may qualify for exemption from most of the provisions of Title I of ERISA because of its status as a top-hat plan.

Miscellaneous

Intermediate Sanctions Rules

Q 15:56   What are the intermediate sanctions rules?

In October 1995, Congress enacted the intermediate sanctions rules. Their purpose is to provide the IRS with a practical tool that could be used to help ensure that tax-exempt entities do not violate the private inurement rules applicable to those entities by providing unreasonable amounts of compensation to their executives.

Before the enactment of the intermediate sanctions rules, the only penalty the IRS could impose on a tax-exempt entity that provided unreasonable amounts of compensation to an executive was the revocation of the entity's tax-exempt status. Because of the severity of that penalty, and its blunt impact on many innocent constituencies, it was rarely used. Recognizing this problem, Congress enacted the intermediate sanctions rules, which permit the IRS to impose dollar penalties on tax-exempt entities, and excise taxes on executives, in cases in which tax-exempt entities and executives engage in so-called excess benefit transactions.

Practice Pointer. Most commentators expect that, armed with this relatively new enforcement tool, the IRS will begin to review much more carefully the compensation packages of executives of tax-exempt entities, including the deferred compensation elements of those packages. This is especially true because of the increased sensitivity to executive compensation issues in this post-Enron period. Therefore, a tax-exempt entity that is contemplating establishing a deferred compensation plan for one or more of its executives should consult with its advisors concerning the impact of the intermediate sanctions rules and the methods available under the rules for the proposed plan to enjoy a presumption of reasonableness.

Three-Party Nonqualified Arrangements

Q 15:57   Has the IRS ruled on any three-party nonqualified arrangements involving a tax-exempt entity, a taxable entity, and employees of the taxable entity?

Yes. In Letter Ruling 9810005, the IRS approved the following rather complex arrangement. A taxable entity contracted to provide physician services to a tax-exempt entity. The tax-exempt entity agreed to compensate the taxable entity for the services received by reimbursing it for its operating expenses, including those arising from its employee benefit plans. The taxable entity hired physician employees to provide the services to the tax-exempt entity and established a nonqualified plan for the physicians. The tax-exempt entity, under its agreement with the taxable entity, was obligated to reimburse the taxable entity for the expenses incurred in connection with the nonqualified plan. The tax-exempt entity proposed to establish an irrevocable funded trust to which it would contribute the amounts necessary to satisfy its reimbursement obligations relating to the taxable entity's nonqualified plan.

The IRS held that the trust would be treated as a grantor trust of the tax-exempt entity, with the result that the earnings of the trust would not be taxed. They would be treated, for tax purposes, as having been earned by the tax-exempt entity. The IRS then held that the taxable entity would not be taxable on amounts held in the trust until those amounts actually were paid to the taxable entity, that is, when they were paid to the taxable entity at the times at which payments were due under the nonqualified plan to the physician employees of the taxable entity.

Implicit in the IRS's holdings is the finding that the nonqualified plan is not to be treated as a funded plan and is not governed by Code Section 457(f), even though the amounts that ultimately will fund plan benefits are held, until benefits are paid, in an irrevocable trust maintained by a tax-exempt entity. In essence, the ruling permits the use of the tax-exempt status of the tax-exempt entity to accumulate assets, tax free and beyond the reach of bankruptcy creditors that will be used in connection with the nonqualified plan of a taxable employer.

Note. Sponsors of such arrangements would need to consider the impact on those arrangements of Section 409A, and Notice 2007-62.

Code Section 409A

Q 15:58 Has any recent legislation affected Code Section 457 Plans?

Yes. The American Jobs Creation Act of 2004, enacted on October 22, 2004, added Section 409A to the Code, which contains a number of new rules that apply to nonqualified plans. Although Section 409A rules do not apply to Section 457(b) eligible deferred compensation plans, they do apply to Section 457(f) ineligible deferred compensation plans.

Section 409A rules do not change the general tax treatment of amounts deferred under Section 457(f) plans, and do not alter the provisions of Section 457(f) itself. However, Section 409A rules impose new operational rules on Section 457(f) and other nonqualified plans that can result in substantial penalties if they are violated.

Code Section 409A applies to "amounts deferred after 2004," while pre-Section 409A law applies to pre-2005 deferrals (so long as the pre-2005 plan is not "materially modified" after October 3, 2004). The legislative history and IRS guidance to date state that a deferral (whether an employee or an employer contribution) is not a "pre-2005 deferral" unless it was both deferred and vested before 2005.

Generally, Section 409A requires the following:

A. *Deferral election deadlines.* Section 409A requires that participant deferral elections must be made by close of the calendar year prior to the calendar year in which the compensation to be deferred will be earned, and prohibits mid-year changes to these elections. Under an exception to this rule, newly eligible participants have 30 days from their eligibility date to make a prospective election to defer compensation not yet earned. Under another exception to this rule, elections to defer "performance-based compensation" measured over a period of at least 12 months must be made no later than six months prior to the end of the measurement period. For this purpose, "performance-based compensation" is defined by the IRS in the Section 409A proposed regulations.

B. *Limitations on distributions.* Code Section 409A limits the times at which distributions may be made from nonqualified plans to only the following:

1. *Separation from service (plus six months if the participant is a key employee of a public employer).* For this purpose, key employee is defined using the Code Section 416 definition, i.e., generally, officers making more than $145,000 (indexed) limited to 50 officers, 5 percent or greater owners, and 1 percent or greater owners making more than $150,000.

2. *Disability.* For this purpose, a participant is disabled if he or she is (i) unable to engage in any substantial gainful activity by reason of any medically determined physical or mental impairment that can be expected to result in death or can be expected to last for a continuous

period of not less than 12 months, or (ii) is, by reason of any medically determined physical or mental impairment that can be expected to result in death or can be expected to last for a continuous period of not less than 12 months, receiving income replacement benefits for a period of not less than three months under an accident or health policy covering employees of the employer.

3. *Death.*

4. *A "time" or fixed schedule specified at the date of deferral.* The legislative history and Notice 2005-1 make clear that Congress meant "date" when it said "time," and specifies that distributions may not be based on "occurrence of an event" such as when the participant's child begins college.

5. *Change of control.* This term is to be defined by the IRS, using a definition similar to, but more restrictive than, the Code Section 280G definition. The proposed regulations contain further guidance on this definition.

6. *Unforeseeable emergency.* This term is defined as a severe financial hardship to the participant resulting from illness or accident to the participant, the participant's spouse, or a dependent or loss of the participant property due to casualty or other similar extraordinary unforeseeable circumstances arising as a result of events beyond the control of the participant, and the distribution amount may not exceed the amount necessary to satisfy the emergency and pay taxes, after taking into account the extent to which the hardship is or may be relieved through reimbursement or compensation by insurance or by liquidation of the participant's assets.

   (Note that many nonqualified plan sponsors do not include an "unforeseeable emergency" distribution option in their plans because the standard it sets is so high that no participant is likely to meet it and including it may tend to suggest to participants that 401(k)-like "hardship" distributions are available under the plan.)

C. *Limitations on "downstream changes" to distribution elections.* Code Section 409A limits, substantially, a nonqualified plan participant's ability to make changes to previous distribution elections. Specifically, the new rules provide that changes to delay distributions or change a form of distribution may not take effect for 12 months, that the first payment under a changed election must be deferred for at least five years from the date it otherwise would have been made, and that changes to a time or schedule specified at the date of deferral must be made at least 12 months prior to the first scheduled payment.

The new rules confirm that a nonqualified plan may not permit the acceleration of the time or schedule of any payment, including changes in the form of distribution that accelerate payments. The legislative history states that IRS regulations are to permit accelerations for certain events beyond the participant's control such as distributions to comply with federal conflict of interest rules and court orders pursuant to divorce, withholding of employment taxes, distributions necessary to pay income taxes due a 457(f) plan vesting event, and, except for key employees, distributions of minimal amounts (e.g., $10,000 or less) for administrative convenience, and the proposed regulations provide further guidance on these exceptions. The proposed regulations also clarify that distribution elections of the "earlier of" or "later of" two or more of the permissible distribution dates are permissible.

D. *Rabbi trust limitations.* No rabbi trust (or similar arrangement under regulations to be issued) assets may be located outside the United States (unless substantially all of the services yielding the deferred compensation in question are performed in the applicable non-U.S. jurisdiction). Also, no trust provision may provide that amounts held in the trust will no longer be subject to bankruptcy creditors claims on a change in the employer's financial health.

E. *Reporting/withholding rules.* AJCA requires the reporting of amounts deferred under nonqualified plans on employees' Form W-2 and the Form 1099 of independent contractors. (The IRS "suspended" this requirement for tax year 2005 Form W-2 and Form 1099.) In addition, when these amounts become taxable, AJCA imposes Code Section 3401(a) wage withholding rules and Code Section 6041 reporting rules.

Q 15:59 What are the penalties for noncompliance with Code Section 409A?

Failure by a Code Section 457(f) ineligible deferred compensation plan to meet the requirements of Code Section 409A results in, with respect to the affected participant or participants, current income taxation, interest at the IRS underpayment rate plus 1 percent, and a flat 20 percent penalty. In cases in which state and local tax rules follow the new federal rules, failure to comply with the AJCA rules will, essentially, result in taxes, interest and penalties that easily could equal or exceed the participant's entire affected plan interest.

Q 15:60 Do the Code Section 409A regulations contain any Code Section 457 guidance?

In April 2007, the Treasury Department issued final regulations under Code Section 409A. These regulations contain detailed guidance on the operational rules applicable to all nonqualified plans under Code Section 409A (including Section 457(f) plans), and the following items of interest to Section 457 plan sponsors and participants (some of which also were contained in the proposed Code Section 409A regulations):

1. Guidance on the definitions of bona fide sick leave and vacation plans is not included in the Code Section 409A because of the impact that guidance might have on Section 457 plans.

2. Code Section 409A does not apply to Section 457(b) eligible plans or Section 457(e)(11)(A)(ii) bona fide volunteer service award plans, but does apply to Section 457(f) ineligible plans and other Section 457 plans.

3. For purposes of the 2½ month short-term deferral exception to the Code Section 409A rules, Section 457(f) plan amounts are treated as "paid" when they are included in income under Section 457(f)'s taxation-on-vesting rule, even if they are not actually or constructively received on that date. However, this rule applies only in cases in which the Section 457(f) plan amount is included in income at a time that is a lapse of a substantial risk of forfeiture under the Code Section 409A rules; that is, on the initial, non-renegotiated vesting date, without regard to noncompete risks, and with regard only to non-voluntary deferrals. The regulations also specify that the right to earnings on amounts that previously have been included as income under Code Section 457(f) will be treated as deferred compensation subject to Code Section 409A unless those earnings satisfy independently an applicable exclusion.

4. Section 457(f) plans do not violate Code Section 409A's anti-acceleration of payments rule if they distribute, prior to the otherwise applicable distribution date for the participant, amounts necessary to pay federal, state, local, and foreign income taxes, so long as the amount distributed does not exceed the amount of withholding that would have been remitted by the employer if the taxation-on-vesting amount under the Section 457(f) plan were ordinary wages paid to the participant by the employer.

Q 15:61   Does Code Section 409A present special problems for Code Section 457(f) plans?

Yes. As noted above, the legislative history to AJCA and Notice 2005-1 state that a deferral (whether an employee or an employer contribution) is not a "pre-2005 deferral" unless it was both deferred and vested before 2005. Therefore, "old money" that did not vest by December 31, 2004, is governed by the new rules.

Because Section 457(f) requires that deferred amounts be nonvested in order to achieve tax deferral, this rule results in essentially all amounts now held in Section 457(f) plans being governed by Code Section 409A rules (i.e., results in no grandfathering treatment under AJCA for Section 457(f) plans). (The exception would be 457(f) plan amounts that became vested (and taxed) before 2005—and earnings on those amounts—that were left in the plan beyond 2004 in order to enjoy the continued tax deferral on the post-vesting earnings.)

Therefore, to avoid subjecting their participants to the severe Section 409A penalties, it is especially important for Section 457(f) plan sponsors to:

1. Ensure their plans operate in compliance with Section 409A beginning January 1, 2005; and

2. Ensure their plan documents are amended to reflect the Section 409A rules by the December 31, 2006 deadline.

Chapter 16

Mergers and Acquisitions

David W. Powell, Esq.
Groom Law Group, Chartered

> Mergers and acquisitions are less common in the tax-exempt community than among for-profit corporations. In certain sectors (particularly health care), however, sponsors of Sections 403(b) and 457 plans are increasingly combining with or becoming part of other tax-exempt, governmental, and for-profit employers in a variety of arrangements, including mergers, acquisitions, and privatizations. The new configurations can give rise to many concerns—including plan terminations, severance pay, and distributions—that require unique responses. In addition, the Economic Growth and Tax Relief Reconciliation Act of 2001 (EGTRRA) added some flexibility to these arrangements but raised some new issues as well

Section 403(b) Plan Considerations

Q 16:1 What happens if a for-profit entity acquires a tax-exempt organization that maintains a Section 403(b) plan?

Prior to the issuance of final Code Section 403(b) regulations in 2007, there was little guidance on the consequences of a for-profit entity acquiring a tax-exempt organization that maintains a Section 403(b) plan. Many practitioners believed that plan termination or plan freeze was possible and the best solution, since for-profit entities are not employers eligible to maintain Section

403(b) plans. For this purpose, they generally followed, by analogy, the rules for terminations or freezes of defined benefit plans (see prior editions of this Answer Book).

Under the final Code Section 403(b) regulations, terminating or freezing the plan remains the appropriate option and the IRS has confirmed that it can be done. Contributions to the Section 403(b) plan must cease (see Q 16:2). [Treas. Reg. § 1.403(b)-10(a)(2)]

Q 16:2   How do you terminate or freeze a Section 403(b) plan?

Under the final Code Section 403(b) regulations, a Section 403(b) plan may contain provisions that provide for plan termination and that allow accumulated benefits to be distributed on plan termination. [Treas. Reg. § 1.403(b)-10(a)(1)] In order for a Section 403(b) plan to be considered terminated, all accumulated benefits under the plan must be distributed to all participants and beneficiaries as soon as administratively practicable after termination of the plan. For this purpose, delivery of a fully paid individual insurance annuity contract is treated as a distribution. [Treas. Reg. § 1.403(b)-10(a)(1)] The final regulations did not address group contracts, but presumably this would also include delivery of a fully paid certificate of insurance under a group annuity contract.

Under the plan termination and under the terms of the distributed contracts, amounts subject to the in-service distribution restrictions cannot be distributed if the employer (determined on a controlled group basis) makes any contributions to a another Section 403(b) contract that is not part of the plan during the period beginning on the date of plan termination and ending 12 months after distribution of all assets from the terminated plan, unless during the period beginning 12 months before the termination and ending 12 months after the distribution of all assets from the terminated plan, fewer than 2 percent of the employees who were eligible under the Section 403(b) plan as of the date of plan termination are eligible under the alternative Section 403(b) contract. [Treas. Reg. § 1.403(b)-10(a)(1)]

Thus, a plan may not allow distributions if there is a "successor plan" under a rule similar to the Section 401(k) plan rule. Notably, only Section 403(b) plans are treated as successor plans, so that if the employer establishes a Section 401(k) plan to replace the Section 403(b) plan, it will not be treated as a successor plan and distributions may be permitted.

Q 16:3   What happens if a tax-exempt organization eligible to maintain a Section 403(b) plan acquires another tax-exempt organization that maintains a Section 403(b) plan?

When a tax-exempt organization that sponsors a Section 403(b) plan is acquired by another tax-exempt organization, the acquiror should carefully review the acquiree's plan documents, Form 5500 filings, and other relevant information to determine whether the plan is in compliance with the Internal Revenue Code (Code) and, if applicable, ERISA. The acquiror should consider whether the design of the acquiree's plan is in accord with its own retirement plan objectives. Depending on the results of those examinations, the acquiror may choose to continue, correct, merge, freeze, or even terminate the acquiree's Section 403(b) plan (see Qs 16:2, 16:4, 16:5, 16:7). Whether the acquisition may result in a partial termination and vesting of accounts of affected participants under the acquiree's plan should also be considered.

If the acquiree becomes part of the same controlled group as the acquiror, careful attention should be paid to the impact of controlled group status on the application of nondiscrimination rules to the continued operation of the plans of either entity. The final Code Section 403(b) regulations were accompanied by a regulation under Code Section 414 on the application of the controlled group rules to tax-exempt entities. [Treas. Reg. § 1.414(c)-5] These provide a general rule that two organizations are under common control if at least 80 percent of the directors or trustees of one organization are either representatives of, or are directly or indirectly controlled by, the other organization. However, the new regulations also allow permissive aggregation such that multiple exempt organizations may treat themselves as under common control for purposes of Code Section 414(c) if each of the organizations regularly coordinates their day-to-day exempt activities. Examples include an exempt entity that provides a type of emergency relief within one geographic region and another exempt organization that proves that type of emergency relief within another geographic region, if they have a single plan covering employees of both entities and they regularly coordinate their day-to-day exempt activities. Another example is an exempt hospital and another exempt organization with which it coordinates the delivery of medical services or medical research. [Treas. Reg. § 1.414(c)-5(b)] The IRS reserves the right to treat multiple entities as under common control if the taxpayer's position is to avoid or evade any requirements under Code Sections 401(a), 403(b), or 457(b), however. [Treas. Reg. § 1.414(c)-5(f)] The new regulation does not apply to governmental and church plans, for which the controlled group rules remain unchanged except with respect to the application of the nondiscrimination rules to certain nonqualified church-controlled organizations (such as certain church-related hospitals, colleges, universities, and nursing homes) which are tested separately from their related churches and qualified church-controlled organizations. [Treas. Reg. §§ 1.414(c)-5(a), 1.414(c)-5(d), 1.414(c)-5(e), 1.414(c)-5(f)]

Where transactions involve church or governmental entities, careful attention must also be paid to whether the post-transaction plans will be or will continue to be church or governmental plans to be certain which Code or, if applicable, ERISA requirements must be met. [*See, e.g.,* Ltr. Rul. 9717039]

Where it is found that the acquiree's Section 403(b) plan has failed to satisfy the requirements of Code Section 403(b), it may be advisable for the plan to be frozen or terminated. Choosing either of those courses will depend on the degree of continuing responsibility that the acquiror wishes to have for the acquiree's plan. The acquiror may want for some reason (often, to meet employee expectations regarding the benefits that will continue to be available) to assume responsibility for the acquiree's Section 403(b) plan. Once the acquiree's

Section 403(b) plan is corrected to meet the requirements of Code Section 403(b) (e.g., through the Self-Correction Program (SCP) or the Voluntary Correction Program (VCP) under Revenue Procedure 2006-27 [2006-22 I.R.B. 945] (see Q 16:10)), the acquiror may either merge the acquiree's plan into its own Section 403(b) plan or simply assume operations of the plan.

In any event, any defects that would cause the acquiree's plan to fail to meet the requirements of Code Section 403(b), such as violations of the nondiscrimination requirements of Code Section 403(b)(12), must be given serious consideration. A merger of plans before appropriate correction that includes a plan that does not meet those requirements might cause the entire merged plan also to fail to satisfy Code Section 403(b). Other defects that may cause particular contracts not to satisfy Code Section 403(b) may be of concern if found in numerous contracts or in group contracts. [*See* Examination of 403(b) Plans, Guidelines Promulgated by the IRS, May 1999; Treas. Reg. § 1.403(b)-3(d)] Defects that merely cause an inclusion of excess amounts in taxable income, such as violations of the Section 415 limit, are presumably of lesser concern because they would not affect the status of the merged plan as a Section 403(b) plan. Nevertheless, they may, unless corrected, carry significant potential withholding tax or FICA tax liability for the acquiring employer.

Q 16:4   Can Section 403(b) plans be merged?

Yes. Though the final Code Section 403(b) regulations do not expressly address plan mergers, there is no provision that would not permit plans to be merged, and the transfer of assets and liabilities can be accomplished through the rules for contract exchanges within the same plan, if after the merger, or, if prior to the merger, through the provisions for plan-to-plan transfers. [Treas. Reg. § 1.403(b)-10(b)]

At a minimum, corporate resolutions should authorize the merger of the two plans, with the agreements, contracts, and other documents constituting the acquiror's plan serving as the surviving plan documents. Assuming that the Section 403(b) funding vehicle(s) of the acquiree's plan so permits, acquiree plan assets would then be directed by the acquiror to be transferred to the acquiror's Section 403(b) plan funding agent(s) (subject to the anti-cutback requirements) (see Q 16:8), together with all information necessary to carry over the accounts—provided that the terms of the applicable annuity contract(s) and custodial account(s) permit the employer to transfer account balances without participant consent. Otherwise, it may be necessary for each participant to direct his or her transfer.

All acquiree plan documents should be carefully reviewed as to the manner of making the transfer and any changes; plan documents may need to be amended. Presumably, Treasury Regulations Section 1.414(l)-1 will be satisfied because each participant will retain his or her full account balance in the merged plan; therefore, no Form 5310-A needs be filed. Any withdrawal restrictions on Section 403(b)(7) monies or salary reduction amounts, however, must be carried over to the new contract or plan in accordance with Revenue Ruling

90-24 [1990-1 C.B. 97] or the plan-to-plan transfer rule of the final regulations. [Treas. Reg. § 1.403(b)-10(b)(3)]

The acquiree's Section 403(b) plan should also be reviewed to determine whether there is a vesting schedule or there are any exclusions from participation that may be affected by the merger. In addition, Form 5500 must be filed (a merger is currently reflected in item 10 of the form, though that is not an item that must be completed by a Section 403(b) plan).

The equivalent of Code Section 414(l) would apply to ERISA-covered plans through the operation of ERISA Section 208. Further, if ERISA applies, ERISA Section 204(g) generally prohibits amending a plan to eliminate certain optional forms of benefit, though these rules were substantially liberalized in 2000. [See Treas. Reg. § 1.411(d)-4]

Prior to EGTRRA, after-tax monies could not be directly rolled over to another Section 403(b) plan in a direct rollover distribution (though they could be transferred in a plan merger or a plan-to-plan asset transfer) via a direct transfer pursuant to Revenue Ruling 90-24. [1990-1 C.B. 97] Effective in 2002, however, after-tax monies may be rolled over into another Section 403(b) plan [*see* IRS Notice 2002-3, 2002-2 I.R.B. 289] or to a Section 401(a) plan after 2006. [I.R.C. § 402(c)(A), as amended by the Pension Protection Act of 2006]

Q 16:5   Can a Section 403(b) plan be merged with a Section 401(a) plan?

No. Though some practitioners have made arguments that it should be permissible under some circumstances, the Service has uniformly rejected those arguments. [*See* Ltr. Rul. 200317022; Treas. Reg. § 1.403(b)-10(b)(3), and the Preamble to that regulation discussing "plan-to-plan transfers"]

Q 16:6   Can an acquiror refuse to accept responsibility for an acquiree's Section 403(b) plan?

Possibly. If an acquiree's Section 403(b) plan is a non-ERISA 403(b) plan, such as a salary-reduction-only plan under DOL Regulations Section 2510.3-2(f), the acquiror may be able to refuse to accept responsibility for the acquiree's plan and simply cease to deduct contributions from employees' salaries. If the acquiree's Section 403(b) plan is subject to ERISA, however, the duties of the plan administrator and other fiduciaries do not disappear when a plan sponsor ceases to exist. Those duties must devolve to other persons, and it is the responsibility of the fiduciaries of the terminating plan (one of which is usually the employer) to see that they are assumed. As a result, where the acquiree's obligations are generally assumed by the acquiror, as would be the case in a typical merger, any fiduciary obligations of the acquiree would also presumably transfer to the acquiror. [Where the plan sponsor can no longer be located, also see Labor Regulation Section 2578.1 for information on terminating an abandoned individual account plan.]

If the acquiree's Section 403(b) plan is terminated, the acquiror's responsibility to administer that plan should end with the final distribution and the filing of a final Form 5500, indicating that the plan has been terminated. The final Form 5500 is due on the last day of the seventh month (with an extension of 2½ months if Form 5558 is filed) after the date of the last distribution, which is also the close of the final plan year. [*See* Rev. Rul. 69-157, 1969-1 C.B. 115; Rev. Rul. 89-87, 1989-2 C.B. 81]

Q 16:7   Can an acquiror freeze an acquiree's Section 403(b) plan?

Yes, provided that no further contributions are made. [Treas. Reg. § 1.403(b)-10(a)(1)] Even if the acquiree's plan is frozen, however, the acquiror would assume the acquiree's responsibility for administering the acquiree's plan, including the obligation to continue to file Forms 5500 for as long as plan assets exist (see Q 16:6).

Q 16:8   Are there constraints on changes to an acquiree's Section 403(b) plan by the acquiror?

Very possibly. Promises made to participants in anticipation of a merger or contractual agreements under the merger agreement might constrain the successor employer's ability to alter a Section 403(b) plan that is subject to ERISA. Although the anticutback rule of Code Section 411(d)(6) does not apply to Section 403(b) plans, the parallel provision of ERISA Section 204(g) does apply to any Section 403(b) plan subject to ERISA. The provision does not permit an amendment that has the effect of eliminating or reducing an optional form of benefit with respect to benefits attributable to service before the amendment. If the acquiree's Section 403(b) plan was a money purchase pension plan, it should also be noted that a Section 204(h) notice must be provided to applicable individuals and employee organizations. Before EGTRRA, the notice had to be given after adoption—and at least 15 days before the effective date—of the resolution to cease or lower accruals. For plan amendments after the date EGTRRA was enacted (June 7, 2001), this notice period was changed by EGTRRA to be within a "reasonable time" before the effective date of the amendment, which is usually 45 days. [Treas. Reg. § 54.4980F-1]

Freezing a plan, as opposed to terminating it, will not normally result in immediate vesting of accounts of affected participants subject to the application of the partial termination rules or, in the case of profit-sharing plans, the rules regarding a complete discontinuance of contributions.

Q 16:9   Does the acquisition of a Section 403(b) plan constitute a separation from service or severance of employment that would permit distributions?

By itself, it probably does not. Generally, salary reduction contributions to a Section 403(b) plan and contributions to a Section 403(b)(7) custodial account cannot be distributed before one of the following: attainment of age 59½, separation from service (before 2002), death, disability, or hardship (and no income may be distributed on account of hardship). EGTRRA amended the Code to substitute the term "severance of employment" for "separation from service" after 2001. The legislative history indicates that the purpose of this change was to eliminate the "same desk" rule, regardless of when the severance of employment occurred, presumably by implying that it is a severance from common-law employment with a specific employer. [I.R.C. §§ 403(b)(7)(A)(ii), 403(b)(11)] Under the pre-EGTRRA rule, there was little authority on what constituted a separation from service for purposes of a Section 403(b) plan; however, the concept had been discussed by the IRS in other situations, such as the distribution rules applicable to Section 401(k) plans and the pre-1993 rules that applied to the rollover of in-service distributions. In rulings in those two contexts, the IRS has generally held that an employee would be considered separated from the service of his or her employer only upon death, retirement, resignation, or discharge, and not when he or she continued in the same position for a different employer as a result of a liquidation, merger, consolidation, change of form, or transfer of ownership of his or her former employer. [Rev. Rul. 77-336, 1977-2 C.B. 202; Rev. Rul. 80-129, 1980-1 C.B. 86; Rev. Rul. 81-141, 1981-1 C.B. 204; Ltr. Rul. 9443041] This stance was known as the "same desk rule." In at least one letter ruling, the IRS has applied its Section 401(a) plan rulings regarding the same desk rule to Section 403(b) plans. [Ltr. Rul. 8617125]

Thus, under the pre-EGTRRA rule, whether the acquisition of a Section 403(b) plan sponsor would constitute a separation from service that would permit a distribution depended on the facts of the situation, with particular emphasis on whether the employee under consideration was continuing in the same job. It was also important to consider how the acquisition was treated for other benefits purposes (e.g., under Consolidated Omnibus Budget Reconciliation Act of 1985 (COBRA) health care continuation coverage).

It may be noted that the rules permitting distribution upon separation from service in the context of Section 401(k) plans had been earlier amended by the Tax Reform Act of 1986 (TRA '86) specifically to permit distributions upon the disposition by a corporation of substantially all of its assets, upon the disposition by a corporation of its interest in a subsidiary, or upon plan termination, if certain additional requirements are met. [I.R.C. § 401(k)(10)] Similar provisions were not added to Code Section 403(b), however, and thus these exceptions to the distribution restrictions are not available to Section 403(b) plans.

After EGTRRA, a severance of employment with the common-law employer, such as in an asset acquisition, may be sufficient to permit distributions. This would make it possible for the affected participants to take eligible rollover distributions that might be rolled over to an acquiror's Section 401(k) plan, for example. However, distributions before age 59½ may still be subject to the 10 percent tax on early distributions under Code Section 72(t). In other cases, for example, where the acquiror may wish to take a transfer of a portion of the acquiror's Section 403(b) plan attributable to acquired participants into the acquiror's own Section 403(b) plan, it may be desirable to amend the Section 403(b) plan to not permit distributions upon severance of employment before age 59½.

Note, however, that the IRS has indicated that even though there may have been a severance of common-law employment, a distribution from the acquiree's plan may not be permitted when there is a transfer of assets and liabilities to a plan maintained by the new employer, or if the new employer assumes the acquiree's plan. [*See* Notice 2002-4, 2002-2 I.R.B. 298]

Under the final Code Section 403(b) regulations, *severance from employment* means when the employee ceases to be employed by the employer maintaining the plan, and the final regulations refer to Treasury Regulations Section 1.401(k)-1(d) for additional guidance on what that means. [Treas. Reg. § 1.403(b)-2(b)(19)] In addition, the regulations provide that a severance from employment will occur on the date on which an employee ceases to be an employee of an eligible employer, even though the employee may continue to be employed either by another entity that is treated as the same employer, where (1) the other entity is not an entity that can be an eligible employer (such as transferring from a Section 501(c)(3) organization to a for-profit subsidiary of the same Section 501(c)(3) organization), or (2) in a capacity that is not employment with an eligible employer (e.g., ceasing to be an employee performing services for a public school but continuing to work for the same state employer). The regulation indicates that the preceding rule does not apply if an employee transfers from one Section 501(c)(3) organization to another Section 501(c)(3) organization that is treated as the same employer or if an employee transfers from one public school to another public school of the same state employer. [Treas. Reg. § 1.403(b)-6(h)] This last provision appears to mean that transferring from one public school to another will only be a severance from employment if the schools are separate common law employers with separate plans.

Q 16:10 What happens if an acquiree's Section 403(b) plan is found to have defects?

Many defects of a Section 403(b) plan may be corrected under the VCP program. The VCP program, however, can require a time-consuming submission process. Further, under SCP, many operational defects can be corrected without involving the IRS. There is a requirement that corrections be completed by the end of the year after the year the violation occurred unless the defect was "insignificant." [Rev. Proc. 2006-27, 2006-22 I.R.B. 945] Generally, if the acquiror's Section 403(b) plan is not also defective, it will often be advisable to keep the acquiror's plan and the acquiree's plan separate until any deficiencies in the acquiree's Section 403(b) plan are resolved.

Q 16:11 If an acquiror maintains a Section 403(b) plan, should it count its new employees' service with the acquiree for plan purposes?

There is little authority regarding counting service with prior employers for Section 403(b) plan purposes. In the case of a corporate merger or acquisition, it appears that the surviving entity could count service with the predecessor employer for Section 403(b) plan purposes (e.g., for the pre-2002 MEA calculation). [*See* Ltr. Ruls. 9802043, 9451063, 9451082, 8617125] If, however, a prior entity (entity A) continues to exist separately, unrelated to the entity that acquired the employees (entity B), and B merely hired some of A's employees, it would appear that B may not count service with A for purposes of its Section 403(b) plan catch-up limitation of Code Section 402(g)(7) limit. Yet, counting prior service with A for vesting or eligibility might be permissible, subject to the nondiscrimination rules of Code Section 403(b)(12)(i).

Severance Pay and Section 403(b) Plans

Q 16:12   Can severance pay be deferred under a Section 403(b) plan as a salary reduction contribution?

Prior to the final Code Sections 403(b) and 415 regulations, the answer was unclear. (See prior editions of the *403(b) Answer Book*.)

The IRS finalized regulations under Code Section 415 on April 5, 2007. [T.D. 9319] These regulations generally provide that amounts paid after severance of employment may not be treated as Code Section 415 compensation unless the post-severance compensation is paid within the later of $2\frac{1}{2}$ months after severance from employment or the end of the limitation year in which the severance of employment occurs, and such amounts are one of the following types of compensation:

1. payments that, absent a severance from employment, would have been paid to the employee if the employee continued his or her employment, and are regular compensation for services (whether within or outside regular working hours), commissions, bonuses, or other similar compensation; or

2. payments for accrued bona fide sick, vacation, or other leave, but only if the employee would have been able to use the leave if employment had continued.

All other post-severance payments such as severance pay, unfunded nonqualified deferred compensation, and 280G parachute payments, are *not* Section 415 compensation under this rule.

Most importantly, the final regulations go on to indicate that compensation may not be contributed to a Section 401(k), 403(b), or 457(b) plan unless it is Section 415 compensation. Thus, while certain types of unused leave can be contributed to such a plan if paid within $2\frac{1}{2}$ months of termination, severance pay or nonqualified deferred payments cannot be deferred into a Section 401(k), 403(b), or 457(b) plan at all, even if paid within $2\frac{1}{2}$ months of termination or the end of the limitation year of termination. Governmental plans may use "calendar year" instead of "limitation year" for this purpose. [Treas. Reg. § 1.415(c)-2(e)(5)] It is clear that this prohibition applies to elective deferrals. The prohibition does not appear to be intended to apply to nonelective deferrals, which normally do not count as Section 415 compensation in any event. [Treas. Reg. § 1.403(b)-3(b)(4)]

Section 457 Plan Considerations

Q 16:13   What happens if an employer sponsoring a Section 457(b) plan is acquired by another tax-exempt or governmental employer?

When a tax-exempt organization such as a hospital is merged with another tax-exempt organization or a governmental employer, the acquiree's Section 457(b) plan may continue to be maintained (and expanded and modified favorably, in the case of a governmental acquiror), but it is advisable to review the terms of the plan to ensure that such terms will apply as intended under the post-merger entity.

Similarly, when a governmental employer maintaining a Section 457(b) plan is acquired by another governmental employer, the successor employer may continue to maintain the Section 457(b) plan. However, when a tax-exempt employer acquires a governmental employer's Section 457(b) plan, the differences between the Section 457 rules for governmental sponsors and tax-exempt sponsors in funding, distribution election, and rollover rules effectively preclude continued operation of the plan by a nongovernmental entity. In such cases, the regulations indicate that the governmental Section 457(b) plan may be frozen and transferred to continue to be maintained by another governmental entity, or the plan must be terminated, in which case all assets must be distributed as soon as practicable. If the plan is neither transferred nor terminated, the assets will be taxable under Code Section 402(b) or 403(c), and the trust will become a taxable trust. [Treas. Reg. § 1.457-10(a)(2)]

In the reverse situation, when a tax-exempt employer's Section 457(b) plan is acquired by a governmental employer, the proposed regulations indicate that Code Section 457(f) and Treasury Regulations Section 1.457-11 (i.e., the substantial risk of forfeiture rules) will apply. [Treas. Reg. § 1.457-10(a)(2)(i)] However, it is not clear that this cannot be corrected by commencing to comply with the special correction rules for governmental Section 457(b) plans. [See Treas. Reg. § 1.457-9]

Special attention should also be paid to whether the plans under the pre- or post-merger entities may be top-hat or church or governmental plans and whether they may gain or lose such status as a result of the merger or acquisition because retention of non-ERISA status is usually crucial to the compliance of such plans with the Code. In some types of business combinations, such as joint ventures, the status of a plan may not be at all clear, and the facts may require careful evaluation.

Q 16:14   What happens to an acquiree's Section 457(b) plan if the acquiror is not tax exempt or governmental?

When a tax-exempt organization is acquired by a for-profit organization, important issues arise. First, it should be noted that Code Section 457 does not in fact confer advantages to nonqualified plans of tax-exempt employers (other than perhaps to avoid constructive receipt upon making a payout election, and even that is questionable), but, rather, generally serves to restrict nonqualified deferrals. Thus, there is likely to be little advantage in deferring additional compensation in compliance with the terms of a Section 457(b) plan if the surviving entity is a for-profit corporation. The ordinary rules applicable to nonqualified arrangements not subject to Code Section 457 are likely to be much more beneficial with the exception of the distribution rules; therefore, the creation of a new nonqualified deferred compensation arrangement may be advisable. Treasury Regulations state that the acquired Section 457(b) plan will become subject to the constructive receipt rules of Code Section 451, but do not indicate what the result of that may be. [Treas. Reg. § 1.457-10(a)(2)(i)]

Where the acquiree's plan is a governmental plan, as noted above, the different rules for governmental Section 457(b) plans will preclude it from being maintained by a nongovernmental entity without violating numerous Code and ERISA requirements. Accordingly, the plan should be terminated or frozen or transferred to another governmental entity.

Q 16:15   What should be done with the acquiree's Section 457(b) plan if the acquiror is not tax exempt or governmental?

Treasury Regulations state that a Section 457(b) plan that is maintained by an employer who is not an eligible employer will become subject to (1) the constructive receipt rules of Code Section 451 if the employer is a for-profit entity, or (2) the "substantial risk of forfeiture" rules of Code Section 457(f) if the employer is a governmental entity. As a result, it is likely that most ineligible employers acquiring such plans will wish to terminate the plan and distribute the assets to participants and beneficiaries as soon as practicable. [*See* Treas. Reg. § 1.457-10(a)(2)] However, if a for-profit employer determines that the constructive receipt issues can be addressed, although the IRS has issued no guidance on the continued administration of a nongovernmental Section 457(b) plan when the sponsor is no longer tax exempt, presumably, continuation is permissible provided that the Section 457(b) plan must continue to operate in a manner exempt from ERISA. Again, it is not possible for a governmental Section 457(b) plan to be taken over by a nongovernmental sponsor. It will be necessary for the Section 457(b) plan to be terminated or frozen and transferred, to be maintained by another governmental entity.

Another issue not addressed by the IRS is the consequence of amending an eligible Section 457(b) plan so that it no longer meets the requirements of Code Section 457(b) (e.g., by deleting the minimum distribution rules or by providing a new, impermissible form of distribution election). Although arguably the plan may be viewed as no longer subject to Code Section 457, in the absence of a substantial risk of forfeiture, it is possible that the IRS might view such a change as giving rise to immediate taxation of the amounts previously deferred while the entity was subject to Code Section 457.

A different result may occur if the Section 457 plan sponsored by the tax-exempt sponsor was an ineligible plan. Presumably, additional deferrals of post-merger compensation under what had been a Section 457(f) plan (i.e., a plan not meeting the requirements of Code Section 457(b) and therefore either treating benefits as subject to a substantial risk of forfeiture or currently taxable) will operate to defer taxation pursuant to the ordinary nonqualified plan rules rather than the rules of Code Section 457(f). Of course, it will always be advisable to review the terms of the ineligible plan to determine whether any changes in plan design may be called for, such as changes in distribution elections. It is unclear whether the deferrals made while the plan was subject to Code Section 457(f) must remain subject to a substantial risk of forfeiture to defer taxation even if the plan is no longer subject to Code Section 457, although the prior and new regulations appear to suggest that this is so. [*See, e.g.,* former Treas. Reg. § 1.457-3(a) and final Treas. Reg. § 1.457-11(a)(1)]

Q 16:16   Can an acquiree's Section 457 plan be terminated?

If the terms of the plan so permit, an acquiree's Section 457 plan can be terminated after the acquisition, with distribution as soon as practicable and taxation of benefits to the participants and beneficiaries upon distribution as the result. [Treas. Reg. § 1.457-10(a)]

Q 16:17   Can Section 457(b) plans be merged?

Although there is no formal guidance, presumably, Section 457(b) plans may be merged, inasmuch as transfers from one Section 457(b) plan to another are permitted under the Code. [I.R.C. § 457(e)(10); Ltr. Rul. 9901014]

Q 16:18   Does the merger or acquisition of a Section 457(b) plan sponsor constitute a separation from service or severance of employment that would permit distributions?

Before June 7, 2001, probably not. As in the case of Section 403(b) plans, the same desk rule applied to the merger or acquisition of a Section 457 plan sponsor (see Q 16:9). A change in the tax-exempt status of the employer was apparently not a separation from service. [I.R.C. § 457(d)(1)(A)(ii); Ltr. Rul. 9901014] However, effective June 7, 2001, under EGTRRA, the reference to a "separation from service" to permit a distribution was amended to a "severance of employment" for the purpose of eliminating the same desk rule. Thus, upon a change in the common-law employer of the participant, a distribution may be permissible unless the plan terms themselves are more restrictive. [*See* Rev. Proc. 2002-47, 2002-29 I.R.B. 133]

Chapter 17

Designing Retirement Plans with Section 403(b) Components

Michael Footer, Esq.
Mike Footer & Associates, LLC

Glenn R. Poehler
Lori Z. Wright
Mercer

Although Section 403(b) plans evolved from *hands-off* payroll reduction arrangements, more employers than ever are using Section 403(b) plans as key components in their retirement programs. Section 403(b) plans play a strong role in an employer-sponsored retirement program that is customized to meet the organization's goals and objectives.

The issuance of comprehensive IRS regulations governing Section 403(b) plan operation and administration has heightened the need to take a serious look at the use of Section 403(b) retirement program arrangements.

One important aspect of plan design utilizing Section 403(b) arrangements is understanding how these arrangements interact with other defined contribution plan elements, including Code Sections 401(a), 401(k), and 457(b).

Finally, Section 403(b) plan design can both impact and be impacted by the employer's demographic profile, organizational objectives, cost parameters, and administrative resources.

Q 17:1 What are important considerations when designing or redesigning a defined contribution retirement plan?

The first and most important consideration is the organizational objectives the employer wants the plan to achieve. Is the plan simply a supplemental savings program for employees who choose to save? Is the plan a vehicle for employer-directed contributions in combination with or in lieu of a defined benefit plan? The identified objectives of the employer will drive the design as well as other plan components, such as administrative structure or investment types utilized, and, to the extent that more complex elements are utilized, will allow the employer to offer more sophisticated savings and investment opportunities.

A second key consideration is the organizational structure of the employer. If the employer is a public school system, public institution of higher education, or a governmental and Section 501(c)(3) employer, the decision to utilize a Section 403(b) plan has to be made in light of the other defined contribution vehicles available to such organizations, such as Sections 457(b) and 401(a) plans. Similarly, for a private not-for-profit employer, the decision to use a Section 403(b) arrangement has to be made after exploring Sections 401(k) and 401(a) options as well as Section 457(b) options for select highly compensated employees.

A third important point is to understand the employee relations issues. Are retirement benefits subject to collective bargaining? Has employee choice of a vendor been a historic circumstance that could be misunderstood if removed? Is a defined benefit plan being cut back, frozen or eliminated? All of these elements need to be taken into consideration to avoid alienating employees and to ensure that the elements of plan design come together to create a vital piece of the retirement puzzle for employees.

A fourth consideration revolves around governance issues. What level of oversight will the plan require? What level of staffing is available to monitor the plan and its investments? What internal procedures will need to be implemented or revised to accommodate the plan and its design? Many plan sponsors will need to work with a third-party expert, counsel, and/or vendors to establish appropriate governance procedures for the plan.

A fifth consideration is cost versus the adequacy of the retirement benefits being provided to employees, which is integral to the design of the plan. What level of benefits is affordable to the organization, both now and in the near future? If the plan is being redesigned, how will the level of benefits affect current participants? Should employer contributions be discretionary, so as to provide flexibility for budgeting? Specific costing of desired designs is critical to ensuring that the ultimate plan benefits are sufficient to attract and retain participants, while remaining affordable and sustainable for the plan sponsor.

Q 17:2 What are the types of retirement designs and defined contribution plans available to private not-for-profit employers? To governmental employers? To church employers?

All not-for-profit employers have similar defined contribution plan options available to them, although not all statutory plan types are available to all employers. Section 501(c)(3) organizations have the ability to offer Sections

401(k), 401(a), 403(b), and 457(b) plans. Governmental employers have the ability to offer Section 401(a) and 457(b) plans; for a public educational institution (either K-12 or higher education), a Section 403(b) plan is available. In addition, governmental organizations may maintain Section 401(k) plans, if they were implemented before 1986. Church employers can offer any of the above-mentioned plan types, as well as retirement income accounts under Code Section 403(b)(9).

When considering the types of contributions to include in the plan design, employers have the option of using a voluntary employee-contribution-only plan, an employer-contribution-only plan, or a combination plan. Employee contributions can include pre-tax deferrals, after-tax contributions, and/or Roth contributions. Employer contributions can include basic contributions (not contingent on employee contributions), matching contributions, or discretionary contributions. Employer basic contributions (e.g., 3 percent of pay to eligible employees) are often used in a defined contribution plan to replace the accruals under a prior defined benefit plan, which may have been reduced, frozen, or terminated by the employer. Employer-matching contributions (e.g., 50 percent of the first 6 percent of employee deferrals) are often used to encourage employee retirement savings by offering an incentive to participate.

Section 403(b) Plans

Section 403(b) plans are used by educational institutions and private not-for-profit organizations, including healthcare organizations, foundations, and service organizations, most typically as the savings vehicle for employee contributions. Some also include employer contributions under the Section 403(b) plan. However, another highly utilized design includes a Section 403(b) plan for employee contributions and a qualified Section 401(a) plan for employer contributions. This permits flexibility with regard to plan provisions and general testing options, while taking advantage of the universal availability nondiscrimination rules for employee deferrals, as many employers may have difficulty passing the more stringent ADP test under a Section 401(k) plan.

Church-related organizations (as defined in Treasury Regulations Section 1.403(b)-2) have the ability to offer retirement income accounts under Code Section 403(b)(9). These accounts are described in Qs 14:1–14:2.

401(k) Plans

Because not-for-profit organizations were permitted to offer Section 401(k) plans beginning in 1997, some employers have chosen to move in that direction. The rationale for utilizing Section 401(k) rather than Section 403(b) is often rooted in employee demographics or the overall employer profile. If an employer maintains significant for-profit operations or draws numerous personnel from the for-profit arena, then a single Section 401(k) plan could be considered in lieu of maintaining both a Section 403(b) plan and a Section 401(k) plan. With the issuance of the final Code Section 403(b) regulations in 2007, Section 401(k) and 403(b) plans are more similar than ever. However, there are still differences which directly impact plan design decisions.

Section 457(b) Plans

Governmental organizations (such as municipalities, states, and public schools) also have a tax-favored retirement plan available to them—the Section 457(b) plan. Section 457(b) plans as primary savings vehicles (known as *eligible* plans) have similar rules to Section 403(b) and 401(k) plans, but are not subject to the Code Section 402(g) contribution limits. This Code section limits the amount of elective contributions that can be made by an employee. Rather, Section 457(b) plans have their own limits under Code Section 457(e). The specific dollar amounts track the Section 402(g) limits that govern Section 403(b) and 401(k) employee deferral amounts. However, Section 457(b) plan contributions can be attributable to employee and/or employer contributions, but the Section 457(e) limit ($15,500 in 2008) is the total amount permitted for all contributions, regardless of source.

In addition to the governmental Section 457(b) plans described above, not-for-profit organizations are permitted to offer Section 457(b) plans to a select group of highly compensated or management employees. This provides an opportunity for those employees to effectively *double up* on deferrals or for the employer to provide an additional employer contribution to the group. These plans are considered subject to the Employee Retirement Income Security Act (ERISA), but are *top hat* plans that are subject to limited reporting and disclosure requirements and are exempt from ERISA's participation, vesting, funding, and fiduciary requirements.

Section 401(a) Plans

In addition to the employee contribution vehicles above, Section 401(a) plans are available for employer contributions. Section 401(a) plans can be designed as money purchase plans or profit-sharing plans to hold employer basic contributions, employer matching contributions, discretionary contributions, and/or rollover contributions.

Section 457(f) Plans

In addition to the above-described plans for large groups of employees, Code Section 457(f) (or *ineligible* 457 plans) provides the opportunity to offer nonqualified plans for select executives. The rules of Code Section 457(f) are fairly restrictive, and have been supplemented by the recent implementation of Code Section 409A. These plans are described in more detail in Q 15:44–15:53.

Combining Plan Types

The use of multiple plan types available to an organization can help to provide flexibility with regard to nondiscrimination testing, contribution types and amounts, and maximum deferral capability for employees.

- *Section 403(b)/401(a) Plan.* Permitting employee deferrals to be made to a Section 403(b) plan eliminates the need for 401(k) ADP testing, while maximizing contribution amounts through the use of separate Code Section 415 limits for Sections 403(b) and 401(a) plans. It may not, however, eliminate the need for ACP testing of the employer-matching contribution. Adding a Section 457(b) top hat plan maximizes deferral potential for a select group of employees. In determining whether to provide an employer contribution in the Section 403(b) plan or to maintain a separate Section 401(a) plan, a number of issues need to be considered, including:

  —The added administrative complexity of maintaining two plans, including the filing of two Form 5500s;

  —The need to utilize separate Section 415(c) limits for testing contributions; and,

  —Whether the employer contributions will be needed to test other plan benefits for nondiscrimination.

  Note. For a governmental plan wishing to use Code Section 415(m) for excess contributions, having two Section 415 limitations may not be advantageous to the administration of the plan.

- *Section 403(b)/401(k)/401(a) Plan.* Employers can combine the use of a Section 403(b) and a 401(k) vehicle for employee contributions in multiple ways to achieve plan goals. For example, a matching Section 401(k) plan could be implemented that permits a maximum percentage of employee deferrals (matched through the Section 401(a) portion of the plan), with additional deferrals over the maximum Section 401(k) percentage permitted into the Section 403(b) plan. This provides a greater opportunity to pass the Section 401(k) ADP test, thereby permitting full deferrals and matching contributions to highly compensated employees (HCE), and still permitting all employees to have the opportunity to defer the maximum amount during a year. A second combination would provide that highly compensated employees could only make deferrals to a Section 403(b) plan, while non-highly compensated employees (NHCE) could only defer to the Section 401(k) plan. If no HCEs are included in the Section 401(k) plan, then the plan is deemed to pass the ADP test. If HCE Section 403(b) deferrals are matched at the same rate as NHCE Section 401(k) deferrals, there may be adjustments necessary to pass the Section 401(m) ACP tests. Again, the addition of a Section 457(b) top hat plan for a select group of employees can assist in maximizing deferral opportunities.

- *457(b)/401(a) Plan.* For governmental organizations, the use of multiple plans provides needed flexibility from the contribution limits of Section 457(b) plans alone. Some governmental organizations provide employee deferrals in a Section 457(b) plan and employer contributions in a Section

401(a) plan to allow employees to defer the full amount available under Code Section 457(b). In addition, the exemption from nondiscrimination rules for a Section 401(a) plan permits governmental employers to set up multiple Section 401(a) plans or even use a Section 401(a) plan as a supplemental plan for a smaller group of employees or individual employees.

Safe-Harbor Designs

For employers with difficulty passing nondiscrimination tests, the IRS has provided safe-harbor designs that provide specific contribution formulas, eligibility, and vesting provisions that are deemed to meet specific Sections 401(k) and 401(m) nondiscrimination tests, thereby eliminating the need to test on an annual basis. While the use of a safe-harbor design precludes the flexibility to design a customized plan to meet organizational objectives, the safe harbor designs may be broad enough to meet the needs of many organizations. The addition of a safe harbor design with automatic enrollment by the Pension Protection Act of 2006 (PPA) increases the ability to utilize safe harbors to mitigate testing issues. (See chapter 4 for specific details on permissible safe-harbor designs.)

Application of ERISA

Section 403(b) plans, unlike qualified plans, have the opportunity to be exempt from ERISA, if they meet the requirements reiterated by the Department of Labor (DOL) in its Field Assistance Bulletin 2007-02, issued in July 2007. Although the exemption standards have not changed, when those standards are applied in context of the final Code Section 403(b) regulations issued by the Department of Treasury, the exemption has become significantly narrower. The ability to comply with the rules of Code Section 403(b) while maintaining the required *hands off* of the Section 403(b) program will be very difficult for many employers. Therefore, more employers may be opting to have their Section 403(b) programs become subject to ERISA and take control of them to ensure appropriate compliance with Code Section 403(b), achieve administrative, service, and cost efficiencies, and provide an employee savings vehicle that is coordinated with other retirement plans to provide maximum value for employees.

Sections 401(k) and 401(a) plans of private not-for-profit employers would be subject to ERISA under all circumstances. Governmental plans are not subject to ERISA, regardless of statutory plan type. Church plans are not subject to ERISA unless the organization specifically elects coverage by ERISA.

The impact of ERISA coverage also includes the fiduciary responsibility associated with the selection and availability of Section 403(b) vendors and investments. As long as the plan is not covered by ERISA, the employer assumes no such responsibility at the federal level; however, state and local codes may impose other fiduciary requirements with regard to contracts.

The ERISA fiduciary rules require an employer to act in a prudent manner when selecting vendors and investments. This is the standard of care that most employees would expect the plan sponsor to provide, as well. The selection and continued availability of both vendors and products, or individual investments, should be selected through an objective process to satisfy the due diligence requirements. Both vendors and investments should be monitored periodically to ensure continued acceptable performance when measured against industry benchmarks and performance guarantees included in the agreements between plan sponsor and vendor.

ERISA also mandates specific disclosure and reporting requirements, including a plan document, Summary Plan Description, and Summary of Material Modifications when plan changes occur. In addition, annual reporting is required through Form 5500 and a Summary Annual Report. Recent changes in DOL procedures have eliminated the simplified reporting required of Section 403(b) plans for years after 2009. After that time, Section 403(b) plans will be required to complete the full Form 5500 and attachments, including an auditor's report.

Plan Structure Options

The following chart summarizes the various plan structure options available to not-for-profit employers:

	403(b)	401(k)	401(a)	457(b)	457(f)
Eligible employer(s)	Public school systems Public colleges and universities 501(c)(3) organizations Church organizations	Private for-profit or not-for-profit organizations Private schools, colleges, and universities Church organizations Governmental organizations with plans established before 1986	All employers	Governmental organizations Private not-for-profit organizations (top hat plan only)	Private not-for-profit organizations Governmental organizations
Subject to ERISA	Exemptions permitted for certain voluntary deferral-only *plans*	Yes (unless governmental)	Yes (unless governmental or nonelecting church)	No (unless private employer top hat plan)	No

	403(b)	*401(k)*	*401(a)*	*457(b)*	*457(f)*
Types of contributions permitted	Employee pre-tax, employee after-tax, Roth, employer, rollover from 403(b), 401(k), 401(a), or governmental 457(b)	Employee pre-tax, employee after-tax, Roth, employer, rollover from 403(b), 401(k), 401(a), or governmental 457(b)	Employee after-tax, employer, rollover from 403(b), 401(k), 401(a) or governmental 457(b)	Employee pre-tax, employer, rollover from 403(b), 401(k), 401(a) or governmental 457(b)	Employee, employer, rollover from 457(f) plan
Catch-up contributions	15-year cap expansion under Code Section 402(g)(7) for eligible organizations Age 50 cap expansion under Code Section 414(v)	Age 50 cap expansion under Code Section 414(v)	None	3-year cap expansion under Code Section 457(b)(2) and (3)	None
Contribution limits (2008)	Employee deferral limit under Code Section 402(g): $15,500 15-year catch-up is least of $3,000 or difference between historical deferrals made and maximum available Age 50 catch-up limit under Code Section 414(v) limit: $5,000	Employee deferral limit under Code Section 402(g) limit: $15,500 Age 50 catch-up limit under Code Section 414(v): $5,000 Total contribution limit under Code Section 415 (aggregated with 401(a) plans): $46,000	Total contribution limit under Code Section 415 (aggregated with 401(k) plans): $46,000	Total contribution limit under Code Section 415(e): $15,500 Catch-up amounts permitted within last 3 years before normal retirement age limited to the lesser of twice regular contribution limit or the amount of unused prior years' limits (only available	None

	403(b)	401(k)	401(a)	457(b)	457(f)
	Total contribution limit under Code Section 415: $46,000 (applies separately for 403(b) plans)			to governmental plan participant if age 50 catch-up not utilized) Age 50 catch-up limit under Code Section 414(v): $5,000 (available to governmental plans)	
Qualified plan compensation limit under Code Section 401(a)(17) (2008)	$230,000 Applies only to employer contributions	$230,000 Applies to all contributions	$230,000 Applies to all contributions	Not applicable	Not applicable

Note: Some grandfathered compensation limits apply to governmental plans.

| Nondiscrimination testing | Universal availability for employee deferrals; 401(m) ACP test for employer matching contributions

None if governmental organization | 401(k) ADP test for employee deferrals

None if governmental organization

401(m) ACP test for employer matching contributions; 401(a) general test for employer basic contributions (not applicable to church plans)

None if governmental organization | 401(m) ACP test for employer matching contributions; 401(a) general test for employer basic contributions (not applicable to church plans)

None if governmental organization | None | None |

Q 17:3 What design considerations apply to pre-tax employee contributions?

The design considerations applicable to pre-tax employee deferrals fall into two categories: plan provisions and process-related issues. The plan provisions that need to be considered for pre-tax employee contributions generally relate to eligibility and participation. Although employee deferrals are, by statute, required to be 100 percent vested, the plan sponsor has some latitude regarding eligibility decisions. Qualified plans can generally include a service requirement before eligibility to make salary reduction contributions. The universal availability rules under Treasury Regulations Section 1.403(b)-5(b)(4), however, only permit certain exclusions of employee groups from the ability to make deferrals. These include employees who are eligible to make deferrals to another Section 403(b) plan or a governmental eligible Section 457 plan, employees who are eligible to make a cash or deferred election under a Section 401(k) plan of the employer, non-resident aliens with no U.S.-source income, students providing services described in Code Section 3121(b)(10), and employees who normally work fewer than 20 hours per week (with a requirement that the employee actually work less than 1,000 hours a year). In order to utilize the last exclusion, the employer must understand that if any employees are excluded under the fewer than 20 hours per week exclusion, all employees meeting that criterion must be excluded. In addition, the employer will have to track hours for the excluded employees to ensure that the employees are appropriately included or excluded.

The process-related issues include:

- Compliance with statutory contribution limitations (depending on plan type). The organization should be able to use its payroll system or payroll vendor to monitor pre-tax contributions to ensure few, if any, participants make excess deferrals to the plan. If a Section 457(b) plan with employer and employee contributions is utilized, the system will need to be able to monitor the combined contribution amounts to determine the maximum permissible contribution amounts.

- Whether contributions will be made as a percentage of pay, a flat dollar amount, or a combination thereof. Most plans today are requiring employees to elect a percentage of pay on an exclusive basis, as it keeps employee contributions on pace with pay increases, is easier to administer for employees with variable pay, and is easier to coordinate with a plan that provides an employer matching contribution. However, for employees who want to maximize their contribution amount, a flat dollar amount is easier to calculate and monitor. The employer should consider vendor capabilities, payroll capabilities, and its ability to communicate the deferral types effectively.

- The organization's ability to meet nondiscrimination testing around pre-tax deferrals. Whether a Section 401(k) or 403(b) plan is most effective may be determined around the organization's demographics and participation history. If passing the ADP test for Section 401(k) employee deferrals looks questionable, the organization may wish to eliminate the issue by utilizing a Section 403(b) plan for employee deferrals or all contributions.

In summary, when deciding whether to utilize a Section 403(b) plan or a Section 401(k) plan for employee deferrals, the plan sponsor should ultimately make the decision based on the following factors:

Plan Element	403(b)	401(k)
Vehicles for Plan Assets	Annuity contracts or custodial accounts	Trust, annuity contracts, or custodial accounts
ERISA Coverage	Safe harbor for ERISA exemption for certain deferral-only plans Governmental plans not subject to ERISA Church plans not subject to ERISA unless they elect coverage	All 401(k) plans are subject to ERISA, except church plans that do not elect ERISA coverage and government plans
Special Contributions	Roth contributions permitted 15-year catch-up permitted for eligible organizations Age 50 + catch-up permitted (after 15-year catch-up utilized)	Roth contributions permitted Age 50 + catch-up permitted
Limits	Compensation not subject to Code Section 401(a)(17) limit ($230,000 for 2008) for employee deferrals Employee deferrals coordinated with other 403(b) and 401(k) plans, but not 457(b) deferrals	Compensation subject to Code Section 401(a)(17) limit ($230,000 for 2008) for all contributions, including employee deferrals Employee deferrals coordinated with other 401(k) and 403(b) plans, but not 457(b) deferrals
Distribution Requirements	Elective deferrals allowed only upon severance from employment, hardship, disability, death, and age 59$\frac{1}{2}$	Elective deferrals allowed only upon death, age 59$\frac{1}{2}$, severance from employment, disability, or hardship

Plan Element	403(b)	401(k)
	Employer contributions from a custodial account allowed only upon severance from employment, disability, death, and age 59½	Employer contributions allowed only upon death, age 59,½, severance from employment, or disability
	Employer contributions from an annuity contract allowed only upon severance from employment or the prior occurrence of some event such as a fixed period of time, a stated age, or disability	Must meet Code Section 401(a)(9) minimum required distribution rules (except Roth contributions)
	Must meet Code Section 401(a)(9) minimum required distribution rules (except Roth contributions)	
Nondiscrimination and Minimum Coverage Rules	Minimum coverage and participation requirements and Code Section 401(m) (ACP test) apply for employer contributions (except for governmental and church plans); safe-harbor designs available to meet ACP tests	Subject to minimum coverage and participation rules, 401(k) (ADP) and 401(m) (ACP) tests (except for governmental and church plans)
	Universal availability rules apply to employee salary deferrals for all organizations	Safe-harbor designs available to meet ADP and ACP tests

Q 17:4   What design considerations apply to employer contributions?

The design considerations applicable to employer contributions relate to the types of contributions available to employers, the value of those contributions to the employer and the participant, and how the contributions will affect the administrative and benefits processes of the employer.

Employer contributions can generally be divided into two categories: matching contributions and basic contributions. Matching contributions are often used **as an incentive for** employees to participate in the defined contribution plan and partner with the employer in providing retirement amounts. Basic contributions are generally used as a replacement for a defined benefit plan accrual and are provided to participants regardless of whether they choose to save their own money through the plan. Each category of contribution has multiple permutations, which provide flexibility to employers to tailor the contributions to meet their individual objectives. And, of course, the two types of contributions can be used together to provide a comprehensive retirement plan design. However, matching contributions must meet the nondiscrimination rules under Code Section 401(m), the Actual Contribution Percentage Test, while basic contributions must meet the general nondiscrimination tests under Code Section 401(a)(4). Both types of contributions must meet the minimum participation and coverage rules under Code Sections 401(a)(26) and 410(b), respectively. However, there are several safe harbor designs incorporating some of these contribution types that appeal to many employers. (See Chapter 4 for more specifics on testing and safe-harbor formulas.)

Type of Contribution	Matching Contribution	Basic Contribution
Flat	A flat matching contribution is one that stays the same regardless of other variables	A flat basic contribution is one that does not change based on other factors
	Example: 100% of the first 6% of employee deferrals	Example: 3% of compensation
Tiered	A tiered matching contribution is one that has several components that, when taken together, constitute the employer contribution	Not applicable
	Example: 100% of the first 3% of employee deferrals plus 50% of the next 2% of employee deferrals	
Service-weighted	A service-weighted matching contribution would provide different matching levels for different lengths of service completed by the participant	A service-weighted basic contribution would provide different contribution levels for different lengths of service completed by the participant

Type of Contribution	Matching Contribution	Basic Contribution
	Example: During years 1–5 of service, matching contribution equals 50% of the first 6% of employee deferrals; during years 6–12 of service, matching contribution equals 75% of the first 6% of employee deferrals; and, after 12 years of service, matching contribution equals 100% of the first 6% of employee deferrals	Example: During years 1–5 of service, basic contribution equals 1% of pay; during years 6–12 of service, basic contribution equals 2% of pay; and, after 12 years of service, basic contribution equals 3% of pay

Note: Potential plan provisions should be reviewed carefully to determine their appropriateness under Code Section 403(b)'s nondiscrimination requirements.

Type of Contribution	Matching Contribution	Basic Contribution
Age-weighted	An age-weighted matching contribution would provide a different matching level at different ages of each participant	An age-weighted basic contribution would provide a different contribution level at different ages of each participant
	Example: while the participant is aged 21–35, the matching contribution is 50% on the first 6% of employee deferrals; while the participant is aged 36–50, the matching contribution is 75% on the first 6% of employee deferrals; and, once the participant reaches age 51, the matching contribution is 100% of the first 6% of employee deferrals	Example: while the participant is aged 21–35, the basic contribution is 1% of pay; while the participant is aged 36–50, the basic contribution is 2% of pay; and, once the participant reaches age 51, the basic contribution is 3% of pay

Note: Potential plan provisions should be reviewed carefully to determine their appropriateness under Code Section 403(b)'s nondiscrimination requirements

Type of Contribution	Matching Contribution	Basic Contribution
Integrated Contributions	Not Applicable	Basic contributions can be designed to provide higher contributions to participants with pay in excess of certain limits. While the rules around

Type of Contribution	Matching Contribution	Basic Contribution
		the design of these plans are fairly complicated, a typical design might be to have a contribution as much as 5.7% of pay higher on plan compensation above the Social Security taxable wage base. The design of the plan takes into consideration that an employer's contribution to Social Security (excluding Medicare) stops at the taxable wage base.

The core reasoning behind an employer-funded retirement plan is to provide a strong value proposition to employees. Attraction of new employees and retention of valued employees drive employer retirement plans in the not-for-profit sector, without the corporate attraction of a tax deduction for retirement plan contributions. Therefore, if the employer is providing contributions and benefits through a defined contribution plan, the following value-oriented issues should be considered:

- *Competitiveness with peers.* The plan sponsor should identify the organizations with which it competes for talent and design the plan to ensure competitiveness with similar benefits offered by its competitors. For some, the mere presence of an employer contribution (regardless of contribution type or level) may be enough. Others may need to conduct a benefits review to determine the competitive level in its market.

- *Value to employees.* The sponsor should understand the value that its employees place on the benefit, either through an informal or formal survey process. If a high value is placed on a matching contribution, then implementing a core contribution may not engender the same enthusiasm for the plan and participation on a voluntary basis may suffer. Conversely, if a high value is placed on a defined benefit retirement plan, but the organization cannot afford to maintain one, then a defined contribution core contribution may be perceived as more valuable to employees than a matching contribution.

- *Replacement of defined benefit plan.* For some plan sponsors, the defined contribution plan may be replacing a frozen or terminated defined benefit plan. In such cases, the plan sponsor needs to evaluate what level of contributions are needed to replace the defined benefit plan benefit, at least for some employees, and to what degree that contribution level is sustainable over time.

- *Viability of plan.* Regardless of the design chosen, the plan sponsor must have the resources to maintain the plan. Financial resources and budgets must incorporate the contribution amounts, and the sponsor's staff must have capacity to administer the plan. If either are in short supply, the plan should be designed with those constraints in mind. For example, if internal administrative resources are scarce, the plan should be designed to be as simple and standardized as possible. By reducing the complexity, the plan will use fewer internal resources and, in fact, be a better candidate for outsourcing to the plan's recordkeeper or bundled vendor.

Process-oriented issues include:

- *Compliance with statutory contribution and compensation limitations.* The organization should be able to use its payroll system or payroll vendor to monitor total contributions to comply with Section 415 limits and compensation to ensure that benefits are not provided on compensation in excess of the Section 401(a)(17) limitations.

- *Service tracking.* The plan sponsor must determine whether eligibility requirements and a vesting schedule will be associated with the employer contributions. Although a Section 403(b) plan cannot require an employee to complete a service requirement to make salary deferrals (other than the 20-hour per week restriction), eligibility requirements may be placed on employer contributions. In addition, although employee deferrals are always 100 percent vested, a vesting schedule may be appropriate for employer contributions. The effectiveness and value of such restrictions to a plan sponsor based on employee demographics and turnover should be weighed against the added complexity to communicate and administer the plan. If an eligibility waiting period and/or a vesting schedule is desired, appropriate resources need to be identified to handle the day-to-day administration of the plan provisions, whether it be internal or by a vendor.

- *Nondiscrimination testing issues.* Any plan with employer contributions, other than a governmental plan and true churches, will need to satisfy the appropriate nondiscrimination rules for the contribution and plan type. Church-related organizations deriving more the 25 percent of revenues from the sale of goods or services are subject to nondiscrimination testing. The plan sponsor should understand the potential participant base and design the plan to first meet the nondiscrimination rules to the extent possible, and then build in plan measures to correct the plan if nondiscrimination tests are not met. This can be done through the use of qualified non-elective contributions, refunds to highly compensated employees, or changes to design, such as implementing automatic enrollment and/or automated deferral increases.

Q 17:5 How should an organization consider accessibility to participant accounts when designing a defined contribution plan?

Under what circumstances should employees have access to their account balances attributable to employee deferrals? For Section 403(b) plans, deferral amounts are not available for distribution until severance from employment, death, hardship (see below), disability, or age 59½. [Treas. Reg. § 1.403(b)-6(d)]

With access to employee deferral amounts limited as above, employers must consider whether loans are a desired feature of the plan. If so, the employer must consider which party will be responsible for loan approvals, loan administration and whether its vendor(s) will be able to assist with appropriate information to ensure appropriate loan monitoring. In addition, the employer should consider vendor requirements for the form of the loan repayment (direct repayment, payroll deduction, or ACH debit) and whether the payroll system and staff are able to program and administer the payroll deduction repayment method. Direct repayment methods are utilized less frequently as vendors move toward more automated administrative processes, including loans.

The employer must also consider what parameters to put around hardship withdrawals. Many employers choose to follow the safe-harbor requirements provided in the Section 401(k) regulations [Treas. Reg. § 1.401(k)-1(d)(3)], as those are consistently administered by all vendors and easier to communicate.

Under what circumstances should employees have access to their account balances attributable to employer contributions? For Section 403(b) plans, the availability for distribution of account balances attributable to non-employee deferral amounts depends on the type of investment vehicle utilized. For amounts invested in annuity contracts, distribution is not permitted until the earlier of severance from employment or the prior occurrence of some event, such as after a fixed number of years, the attainment of a stated age, or disability. [Treas. Reg. § 1.403(b)-6(b)] For amounts invested in custodial accounts, distribution is not permitted until the participant has a severance from employment, dies, becomes disabled, or attains age 59½. [Treas. Reg. § 1.403(b)-6(c)] Many plan sponsors, especially those for which the defined contribution plan is the sole retirement plan, design the plan to offer little access to employer contributions, in order to preserve, to the extent possible, the participant's wealth accumulation opportunity for as long as possible. However, some employers feel it is important that employees have some access to employer contributions, as they may to employee deferrals, through loans or hardship distributions.

Q 17:6 How should an organization's vendor structure be taken into consideration when designing or redesigning a plan?

The vendor structure is a very important consideration when designing or redesigning a plan. Once the plan design has been finalized, the plan sponsor needs to determine what plan and participant services are needed to supplement (or replace) internal resources. This will then allow the plan sponsor to determine whether unbundled or bundled services are appropriate. If bundled services are desired, the plan sponsor must then determine whether multiple bundled vendors are feasible, or whether the plan is better served through working with an exclusive vendor. This will, in turn, determine the type and level of plan sponsor and participant services available.

Most plans in the small to large range tend to utilize bundled service providers in the tax-exempt market. Jumbo plans are the most likely to utilize an unbundled structure, as they have sufficient internal resources to administer the plan in-house, formalized governance frameworks that are designed to monitor the individual components of the plan and the vendors providing services for each component, and sufficient scale in terms of plan assets to make it cost-efficient. For the remaining majority of plan sponsors, the bundled service provider structure brings cost leverage, streamlined administration, and efficient interaction between internal resources and service provider contacts.

Another important factor in determining the appropriate vendor structure is the applicability of ERISA to the plan. For voluntary-only programs who can meet the exemption from ERISA under the DOL guidelines (see Qs 9:1–9:10), the use of multiple vendors has long been the standard. However, given the administrative requirements of the final Code Section 403(b) regulations effective January 1, 2009, with regard to loan monitoring, plan documentation, contract exchange requirements, and others, plan sponsors may find it difficult to reconcile the actions needed to satisfy those requirements with the "hands off" structure required to maintain the program's exemption from ERISA. Therefore, it seems logical that many programs that were formerly treated as non-ERISA may soon make (or accept) the determination that they are now subject to ERISA.

The use of multiple vendors in an ERISA environment requires extensive oversight by the plan sponsor to collect data and information from multiple sources, remit data and contributions to multiple recipients, and ensure that the plan is administered consistently among all vendors. Many plan sponsors are finding that the selection of multiple vendors may best be accomplished by the additional selection of a master administrator. A master administrator's role would be as the collection point for all data, information and contributions, so that it can assist the plan sponsor with administrative tasks, management reporting on a plan level, plan enrollment, dissemination of plan information, and provide links to and from the vendors receiving contributions and performing recordkeeping. This allows the plan sponsor to receive information on a level appropriate to satisfy its fiduciary responsibilities, while still maintaining the freedom of choice offered by a variety of vendors and investment vehicles.

However, other plan sponsors feel that the bundled service provider can bring sufficient investment choice to participants, and desire the opportunity to effectively outsource many of the compliance and administrative responsibilities to the exclusive vendor. Some of the services that can be delegated to these bundled service providers are:

- Loan approvals and monitoring
- Distribution approvals
- Minimum required distribution notification, calculation and processing
- Hardship distribution eligibility determination and processing
- Eligibility determination and service tracking
- Vesting determination and service tracking
- Qualification of domestic relations orders
- Calculation of employer contribution amounts
- Plan documents, Summary Plan Descriptions and other plan communications
- Form 5500 annual reporting

Q 17:7   What is a typical process to complete the plan design and implementation?

When undertaking a new plan design or a plan redesign, a plan sponsor should first put together a comprehensive workplan outlining the design tasks, responsibilities, and due dates. The first phase of the design process should include goals of the process and the ultimate objectives that the plan sponsor wants to achieve through the design process. This would include evaluating the impact of the addition of the new (or change to the existing) plan on the total employee benefit program and organizational budget and resources, evaluating the ultimate competitive advantage provided by the new design on employee attraction and retention, and determining available internal and external resources for the design and implementation process and, ultimately, the administration of the new design. In addition, the plan sponsor should plan through the completion of the process and contemplate ongoing monitoring of the plan to ensure it continues to meet the organizational and plan objectives for which it was designed. A typical plan design workplan is demonstrated below.

Task

Plan Design

1. Identify key stakeholders and solicit input on design objectives and organizational goals
2. Craft design objectives and governing principles
3. Develop potential new designs and model costs
4. Review potential designs, employee impact, costs and determine recommended option
5. Present high-level design for management approval
6. Determine recommended design details for new DC plan
7. Document rationale for design decisions
8. Prepare material for Board Meeting
9. Obtain Board approval of Resolution to adopt changes
10. Finalize design details for documentation and implementation

Task (cont'd)

Vendor Interface

1. If redesign, review plan changes in light of vendor relationship and determine viability of ongoing service provider
2. If continuing with current service provider, review changes with vendor and initiate document, administrative, service and investment updates
3. If new plan or open to exploring other potential service providers, initiate vendor search process

Investments

1. Review and select new funds
2. Manage implementation of new investments and coordinate with fiduciary/ governance activities (default fund selection and investment policy development/updates)

Documentation

1. Prepare DC plan draft specifications
2. Draft new DC Plan for review and approval by counsel
3. Finalize plan documents
4. Adopt plan documents
5. Draft custodial and service agreements
6. Review custodial and service agreements (plan sponsor and counsel)
7. Finalize and execute custodial/trust and service agreements
8. Prepare or update Summary Plan Description (SPD), if subject to ERISA
9. Distribute SPD to all participants

Compliance

1. Perform projected testing for new design and determine implications or validate initial design (if needed)
2. Develop and issue required notices to participants (204(h), safe harbor)
3. Final review of new procedures and system set up for compliance with new and amended plan provisions prior to go-live date
4. Develop timeline and strategy for filing new plans for determination letters, if qualified plans
5. File IRS Form 5300 for approval of plan changes, if qualified plan (determine filing cycle based on employer's EIN)

Communications and Advice

1. Develop strategy for communicating plan design changes
2. Develop/update web tools, intranet site and communications materials and delivery schedules
3. Deliver communications in accordance with agreed-upon schedule
4. Determine need for additional employee advice/investment support

Governance

1. Implement appropriate governance structure
2. Select default fund for DC plan
3. Develop / update documented Accountabilities Chart with detailed roles and responsibilities for all plans; update Committee Charter

Task (cont'd)

4. Fiduciary training to Administrative / Investment Fiduciaries relative to DC fiduciary risks
5. Update Investment Policies to reflect investment structures and updates for revised pension plan coverage

Plan Management

1. Quarterly review meetings with vendor to provide marketplace updates, vendor oversight, and analyses
2. Quarterly Investment Committee meetings to provide fund performance evaluation, marketplace updates, and analyses
3. Project manage design, compliance, administration and communication updates, implementation, and analyses
4. Update vendor contract and performance guarantees for new services and fees
5. Update Administration Manual and internal documented procedures (Payroll, Treasury, Audit, etc.)
6. Legislative and regulatory updates

Chapter 18

Roth 403(b) Contributions

Beverly J. Orth, Esq., FSA
Mercer

The Economic Growth and Tax Relief Reconciliation Act of 2001 (EGTRRA) added Section 402A to the Internal Revenue Code (Code), thereby allowing Section 401(k) and Section 403(b) plans to offer designated Roth contributions to their participants for taxable years beginning on or after January 1, 2006. Because Code Section 402A originally was scheduled to sunset in 2011, many plan sponsors postponed adding a Roth contribution feature to their plans. The Pension Protection Act of 2006 (PPA) removed the concern about the sunset provision by making Section 402A a permanent Code provision. As a result, Roth accounts in Section 403(b) plans are growing in popularity.

The tax rules governing Roth contributions are very complex. The IRS addressed the tax treatment of designated Roth contributions in final regulations issued in April 2007, effective for taxable years beginning on or after January 1, 2007.

This chapter outlines the requirements for setting up and maintaining Roth contribution accounts and the effect on routine plan transactions, including distributions, rollovers, loans, and hardship withdrawals. It also addresses plan design and communication considerations related to adding a Roth feature to a Section 403(b) program.

Introduction to Roth 403(b) Contributions

Q 18:1   What are *Roth 403(b) contributions*?

Roth 403(b) contributions are after-tax employee elective contributions to a Section 403(b) program. When distributed in a qualified distribution, the Roth 403(b) contributions and investment earnings are excluded from taxable income for federal income tax purposes. [I.R.C. § 402A(d)]

Q 18:2   How do Roth 403(b) contributions differ from pre-tax 403(b) contributions?

Pre-tax elective deferrals to a Section 403(b) program reduce the participant's taxable income for the year of contribution. Federal income taxes on investment gains are deferred while they remain in the Section 403(b) program. Upon distribution, the pre-tax deferrals and investment earnings are subject to federal income tax.

Roth 403(b) contributions are also elective but do not reduce the participant's taxable income. [I.R.C. § 402A(a)(1)] When distributed, the Roth contributions are not added to taxable income because they were taxed in the year contributed. Income taxes on investment gains are deferred while they remain in the program. The tax treatment of investment gains upon distribution depends on whether the distribution is *qualified*. If the distribution is *qualified*, the investment gains are distributed tax-free. [I.R.C. § 402A(d)] Otherwise, they are taxed as ordinary income. (See Q 18:19 for a discussion of qualified distributions.)

Q 18:3   Why might an employer decide to add a Roth contribution feature to a Section 403(b) program?

A Roth feature can benefit both low-income and high-income participants.

Low-income participants may expect their marginal tax rates to be higher in the future when they take distributions from a qualified Roth contribution 403(b) program. They will pay less in taxes now on their Roth contributions and no taxes on qualified distributions, compared to no taxes now on their pre-tax deferrals but higher taxes on future distributions.

High-income participants may be precluded from contributing to a Roth IRA due to limits on adjusted gross income that apply to Roth IRAs. Such limits do not apply to a Roth 403(b) feature.

All participants may benefit by *diversifying* their personal tax structure by using both pre-tax deferrals and Roth contributions. (See Q 18:31.)

Participants who desire to maximize bequests to heirs can avoid the minimum required distribution requirements of Code Section 401(a)(9) during their lifetime (i.e., before the participant's death) by using a direct rollover from a Roth 403(b) account to a Roth IRA.

A Roth 403(b) feature may appeal to employees who want to maximize their retirement savings. For example, assume an employee has a combined federal and state marginal tax rate of 40 percent and assume the same marginal tax rate applies at the time of distribution. For 2008, the most the employee can contribute on a pre-tax basis is $15,500 (if no catch-ups are used). The same limit applies to a Roth 403(b) contribution, but the employee's overall *investment* is $25,833: the $15,500 Roth contribution plus $10,333 in income taxes. If the Roth contribution and earnings are distributed in 20 years in a *qualified* distribution, the $15,500 Roth contribution produces the same after-tax benefit as a $25,833 pre-tax contribution.

> **Example. Assumptions:** 40% marginal tax rate (now and at retirement), investments triple in value between now and retirement.

	Pre-tax	Roth
(a) Total Initial Investment	$25,833	$25,833
(b) Tax on Initial Investment = (a) × 40%	0	10,333
(c) Contribution (a) − (b)	25,833	15,500
(d) Balance at Retirement = (c) × 3	77,500	46,500
(e) Tax at Retirement = (d) × 40%	31,000	0
(f) After-Tax Value at Retirement = (d)−(e)	$46,500	$46,500

Basic Requirements

Q 18:4 How does an employee make a Roth 403(b) contribution?

The employee must irrevocably designate the contribution as a Roth contribution. [I.R.C. § 402A(c)(1)] The administrative process is similar to that used to elect a pre-tax deferral. The employee signs a salary reduction agreement, but elects to have the contribution made as a Roth contribution. Alternatively, the plan administrator may have online or phone enrollment procedures in place for employees to elect to make Roth contributions.

The irrevocable designation means that the Roth contributions cannot be shifted to or commingled with pre-tax deferrals. [Treas. Reg. § 1.402A-1, Q&A-13(a)]

Q 18:5 What are the limits on Roth 403(b) contributions?

The sum of pre-tax Section 403(b) deferrals and Roth 403(b) contributions cannot exceed the Section 402(g) limit ($15,500 in 2008). [Treas. Reg. § 1.403(b)-4(c)(1)] The sum of pre-tax Section 403(b) deferrals, Roth 403(b) contributions, employee after-tax contributions, employer contributions, and reallocated forfeitures cannot exceed the Section 415(c) limit ($46,000 in 2008). [Treas. Reg. § 1.403(b)-4(b)(1)] (See Q 18:11 regarding limits on catch-up contributions.)

Q 18:6   Do income limits apply to Roth 403(b) contributions?

Unlike Roth IRA eligibility, there are no limits on adjusted gross income that apply to eligibility for making Roth 403(b) contributions.

Q 18:7   Does universal availability apply to the right to make designated Roth contributions?

Yes. The universal availability requirement of Code Section 403(b)(12) also applies to the right to make designated Roth contributions. [Treas. Reg. § 1.403(b)-5(b)(1)] Effective with the application of the final Code Section 403(b) regulations in 2009, this requirement will mean that employees must have an effective opportunity to make designated Roth contributions if the Roth feature is part of the Section 403(b) program. [Treas. Reg. § 1.403(b)-5(b)(2)]

Q 18:8   How do the limits on Roth 403(b) contributions coordinate with other limits?

For purposes of contribution limits, Roth contributions are treated like pre-tax elective deferrals in all respects. [I.R.C. § 402A(a)(1)]

The Section 402(g) limit ($15,500 in 2008) applies to the sum of pre-tax Section 403(b) and Section 401(k) contributions and Roth 403(b) and 401(k) contributions. [Treas. Reg. § 1.403(b)-4(c)(1)]

The Section 415(c) limit ($46,000 in 2008) applies to the sum of all employee contributions (pre-tax plus Roth plus after-tax) and all employer contributions combined. As noted in Q 3:25, the Section 415(c) limit applies separately to Section 403(b) and Section 401(a) plans, except in situations where the participant is in control of any employer during the limitation year. [Treas. Reg. § 1.415(f)-1(f)]

Q 18:9   How are refunds of excess deferrals handled?

Even though Roth contributions are made on an after-tax basis, they are treated as elective deferrals in applying the annual deferral limit under Code Section 402(g) ($15,500 in 2008). [I.R.C. § 402A(a)(1)] Consequently, the IRS made several changes to the existing Code Section 402(g) regulations in 2007, generally effective retroactively to 2006.

If a participant's total deferrals exceed the annual limit, the excess amount generally should be distributed by April 15 of the next year. [Treas. Reg. § 1.402(g)-1(e)(2)] Excess deferrals that are not timely corrected are taxed twice (as described below).

Plan procedures may permit participants to notify the plan of any excess deferrals and to what extent (if any) the excess is attributable to Roth contributions rather than traditional pre-tax deferrals. Under many plans, participants are deemed to have provided notice of excess deferrals—including the portion attributable to Roth contributions—to the extent the excess arose from deferrals to the employer's plans (as opposed to plans of unrelated employers). [Treas. Reg. § 1.402(g)-1(e)(3)(i)(A)]

Excess deferrals must be refunded with related earnings, including gains or losses for the "gap" period after the close of the taxable year and before the distribution. [Treas. Reg. § 1.402(g)-1(e)(5)] This requirement to distribute gap period earnings applies to excess deferrals for tax years beginning on or after January 1, 2007, which typically will be distributed in early 2008. However, the PPA technical corrections bills now pending before Congress [S. 1974/H.R. 3361] would eliminate the requirement to distribute the gap period earnings for refunds of excess deferrals.

Excess Roth amounts not distributed by April 15 must remain in the plan until a permissible distribution event (e.g., severance from employment) and are subject to double taxation—in the year contributed and again in the year of distribution. Distributions of excess deferrals and related earnings are not eligible for rollover. The regulations prescribe an ordering rule under which the first amounts distributed from a Roth account are treated as distributions of the excess until the full amount of the excess (and earnings) has been distributed. [Treas. Reg. § 1.402(g)-1(e)(8)(iv)] However, it is not clear how plan administrators can track excess amounts arising from deferrals to an unrelated employer's plan to determine whether they are subject to double taxation and ineligible for rollover. Plan administrators will have to rely on participants to notify them of such excess deferrals so that the excess plus earnings can be distributed by April 15.

Q 18:10   How does an automatic enrollment feature apply to Roth 403(b) contributions?

Plan sponsors adopting both auto-enrollment and a Roth 403(b) feature must determine whether the automatic feature applies to pre-tax elective deferrals or Roth 403(b) contributions or a combination. The five-year qualification period for determining a qualified Roth distribution does not start if an employee *unwinds* a Roth 403(b) contribution made under an automatic enrollment arrangement. [Treas. Reg. § 1.402A-1, Q&A-4(a)]

Q 18:11   Can catch-up contributions be designated as Roth contributions?

Yes. All or part of an age 50 catch-up contribution (up to $5,000 in 2008) under Code Section 414(v) can be designated as a Roth contribution. [Treas. Reg. § 1.403(b)-4(c)(2)]

In addition, all or part of a 15-year special Section 403(b) catch-up contribution can be designated as a Roth contribution (see Q 18:38). [Treas. Reg. § 1.402(g)-1(d)(2)]

Q 18:12   What recordkeeping procedures apply to designated Roth contributions?

The designated Roth contributions and their investment earnings must be maintained by the Section 403(b) program in a separate contract or account. The plan administrator must maintain a record of the employee's "investment in the contract" (see Q 18:18) in order to determine what amount of a distribution is taxable. [Treas. Reg. § 1.402A-2, Q&A-1]

Q 18:13   What are the payroll tax reporting rules for Roth contributions?

Unlike pre-tax Section 403(b) deferrals, Roth 403(b) contributions are subject to both income tax (federal, state, and local) and FICA taxes at the time of contribution. [I.R.C. § 402A(a)(1)] The employer must include the contribution in the employee's taxable income in Box 1 of IRS Form W-2, and also report them in Box 12, using code BB.

Q 18:14   May forfeitures be allocated to Roth contribution accounts?

No. Roth regulations prohibit forfeitures of nonvested employer contributions from being allocated to a designated Roth contribution account. [Treas. Reg. § 1.401(k)-1(f)(3)]

Q 18:15   What vesting rules apply to Roth contributions?

Roth 403(b) contributions must be 100 percent vested at all times. [I.R.C. § 411(a)(1)]

Q 18:16   When may Roth contributions be distributed?

Like pre-tax Section 403(b) deferrals, the designated Roth account may not be distributed until the participant has a distributable event under Code Section 403(b)(11): severance from employment, hardship, age 59½, a qualified reservist distribution, disability, or death.

Recordkeeping Requirements

Q 18:17   Why do Roth contributions and earnings need to be maintained in a separate account?

To apply requirements for *qualified* distributions and to properly report distributions for tax purposes, designated Roth contributions must be maintained separately from other contribution types: pre-tax deferrals, employer contributions, and regular after-tax contributions. The recordkeeper must also keep track of the employee's "investment in the contract" in order to determine what amount (if any) of a distribution is taxable. [Treas. Reg. § 1.402A-2, Q&A-1]

In applying the basis recovery rules, generally a plan can maintain only one separate contract for each participant's Roth contributions. Some plans maintain two Roth accounts for participants, one for designated Roth contributions under the plan and another for Roth rollovers received from another plan, so that participants can make withdrawals from the rollover account without the distribution restrictions that attach to the first account. Even in this case, the separate accounts are deemed one contract for purposes of applying the basis recovery rules to distributions from either account. [Treas. Reg. § 1.402A-1, Q&A-9]

The IRS is still evaluating the appropriate treatment of annuity contracts with combined investment return guarantees for both Roth and non-Roth accounts. The concern is that combined guarantees could violate the separate accounting rules for Roth accounts, which took effect in 2006 and prohibit any transfer of value to the Roth account from another account. The regulations under Code Section 402A authorize the IRS to provide additional guidance with respect to separate accounting under a single contract. [Preamble to Treas. Reg. § 1.402A-1]

Q 18:18   What is the employee's "investment in the contract?"

The employee's "investment in the contract" with respect to the Roth 403(b) account is the aggregate amount of the employee's after-tax Roth contributions, also known as "tax basis." Because the Roth 403(b) contributions are made from after-tax income, they are never subject to income tax when distributed. Tax basis is increased by contributions made and decreased by taxable distributions and by refunds of contributions (for example, when contributions exceed the Section 402(g) limit and the excess must be refunded). [Treas. Reg. § 1.402A-1, Q&A-3]

Distribution Requirements

Q 18:19   What is a "qualified" distribution?

For a distribution from a Roth 403(b) account to be "qualified," it must meet two conditions:

1. Payment must be made after age 59$\frac{1}{2}$, disability, or death, and
2. The Section 403(b) account must have been in existence at least five taxable years (i.e., calendar years). [Treas. Reg. § 1.402A-1, Q&A-2]

Termination of employment before age 59$\frac{1}{2}$, disability, or death does not trigger a *qualified* distribution. In such an event, to qualify for a tax-free distribution, the employee will either need to leave the Roth account in the Section 403(b) program until age 59$\frac{1}{2}$ or roll it over to a Roth IRA, a designated Roth 401(k) account, or another designated Roth 403(b) account.

Qualified distributions are completely free of federal income tax. This result means that the investment gains are never taxed. Many states follow the federal rules in the application of their income tax, as well.

Q 18:20   What special rules apply to the five-year qualification period?

The five-year period required for qualified distributions is measured as five consecutive taxable years beginning the first day of the first taxable year in which the employee makes a Roth contribution under the plan. [Treas. Reg. § 1.402A-1, Q&A-4(a)] If the entire contribution is returned as an excess deferral or excess contribution, or if the employee chooses to *unwind* contributions made under an automatic enrollment arrangement, the five-year period does not begin. [Treas. Reg. § 1.402A-1, Q&A-4(a)] Once the period does begin, it continues to run even if the employee makes no additional contributions. The regulations require plan administrators to assume the burden of tracking the five-year period. In the absence of information to the contrary, the plan administrator may assume that the participant's taxable year is the calendar year. [Treas. Reg. § 1.402A-2, Q&A-1]

Generally, the five-year period is determined once for each separate plan in which the employee participates (but see the special rules for rollovers, Q 18:25 and Q 18:27). It is not recalculated if the employee dies, a domestic relations order divides the account, or the employee withdraws the account during the five-year period but later makes additional Roth contributions under the plan. [Treas. Reg. § 1.402A-1, Q&A-4(c) and (d)]

The final rules under Code Section 402A add a special provision for reemployed veterans who performed qualified military service as defined by Code Section 414(u). Their Roth contributions generally are treated as made in the year of qualified military service to which the contributions relate (even if the contribution is actually made when the veteran later returns to full-time employment). Reemployed veterans may designate the year a contribution is made for other purposes, such as entitlement to a match, and that designation will determine the first year of the five-year Roth period. Where a veteran does not identify a year, by default the contribution is treated as made in the first year of military service for which the veteran could have made Roth contributions or, if later, the first taxable year in which Roth contributions could be made under the plan. [Treas. Reg. § 1.402A-1, Q&A-4(e)]

Q 18:21   Are there exceptions from the qualified distribution rules?

Certain amounts not eligible for rollover, such as hardship distributions, required minimum distributions, or periodic payments, can still be qualified distributions if they meet the conditions above. However, some payouts are not qualified distributions even if the conditions are met. These nonqualified distributions include:

- Refunds of contributions (and related earnings) that exceed the deferral limit under Code Section 402(g) ($15,500 in 2008) [Treas. Reg. § 1.402A-1, Q&A-2(c)] or the contribution limit under Code Section 415 ($46,000 in 2008), or refunds required to satisfy the ACP test [Treas. Reg. § 1.402A-1, Q&A-11; 1.402(c)-2, Q&A-4]; and

- Loans treated as *deemed* distributions under Code Section 72(p) (i.e., where a loan default occurs at a time when the participant is not yet eligible for a distribution). [Treas. Reg. § 1.402A-1, Q&A-11] (This should not be confused with actual distributions that occur when participants with outstanding loans terminate employment and their account balances are offset by the unpaid loan balance.)

Q 18:22   Do the minimum distribution rules apply to Roth 403(b) accounts?

Yes, the minimum distribution rules under Code Section 401(a)(9) apply to Roth 403(b) accounts. [I.R.C. § 403(b)(10)] Accordingly, distribution from the account must begin no later than the April 1 of the calendar year following the later of the calendar year in which the employee terminates employment or the calendar year in which the employee attains age 70½. [I.R.C. §§ 401(a)(9)(A), 401(a)(9)(C)] However, direct rollover of the Roth 403(b) account to a Roth IRA will allow the employee to avoid the minimum distribution rules during the employee's lifetime. As with all Roth IRAs, the post-death minimum distribution rules will apply. [I.R.C. § 408A(c)(5)]

Q 18:23   How do the basis recovery rules apply to Roth 403(b) accounts?

Nonqualified distributions from Roth accounts are treated partly as a tax-free return of contributions (the participants' "investment in the contract" or "basis" (see Q 18:18)) and partly as taxable investment earnings. The IRS does not allow Roth 403(b) accounts to use the special ordering rules for Roth IRAs that permit the tax-free recovery of contributions first, before any investment earnings are taken into account. [Preamble to Treas. Reg. § 1.402A-1] Instead, Roth accounts are subject to a pro rata basis recovery rule, as illustrated by this example:

Example. An employee's Roth 403(b) account holds $10,000, consisting of $9,400 in contributions and $600 in investment earnings. The employee terminates employment at age 40 and withdraws 50% of the account ($5,000). Because the employee is younger than age 59½, the amount received is a nonqualified distribution: it will be treated partly as a tax-free return of contributions ($4,700) and partly as taxable investment earnings ($300). (The Roth account is treated as a "separate contract" for this purpose—the employee's pre-tax deferral and employer contribution accounts are disregarded in applying the pro rata rule.) [Treas. Reg. § 1.402A-1, Q&A-3]

Similar rules apply for amounts received as annuities. The portion of an annuity payment attributable to Roth contributions is treated as recovery of basis and the amount attributable to investment income is treated as taxable earnings. [Treas. Reg. § 1.402A-1, Q&A-3]

Q 18:24   How is a distribution from a Roth 403(b) account reported on Form 1099R?

If the distribution is qualified, none of it is subject to income tax. The gross distribution should be reported in Box 1 and "zero" should be entered in Box 2a of the Form 1099R.

If the distribution is not qualified, the recordkeeper must apply the basis recovery rules (see Q 18:23) to determine how much of the distribution is subject to tax. The gross distribution should be reported in Box 1 of Form 1099R, and the taxable portion should be reported in Box 2a, using Code B in Box 7.

Q 18:25   What rollover rules apply to Roth 403(b) accounts?

Designated Roth 403(b) contributions and earnings may be rolled over only (1) to another Section 403(b) program that maintains designated Roth contribution accounts, (2) to a Section 401(k) plan that maintains designated Roth contribution accounts, or (3) to a Roth IRA. Participants whose adjusted gross income exceeds the $100,000 limit for converting a traditional IRA to a Roth IRA will not be able to do a direct rollover to a Roth IRA until 2010. If making a direct rollover before 2010, the participant must make the rollover to a traditional IRA, then convert it to a Roth IRA in 2010 or later. [I.R.C. § 408A(c)(3)(B)]

In a rollover to another designated Roth 403(b) account or to a designated Roth 401(k) account, the five-year qualification period transfers to the receiving Section 403(b) or 401(k) program, provided that the transferor program supplies the date of establishment of the Roth account to the receiving program's recordkeeper. In a rollover to a Roth IRA, the five-year qualification period does not transfer. If the Roth IRA was established prior to the rollover, its five-year qualification period also applies to the amount rolled over. [Treas. Reg. § 1.402A-2, Q&A-2]

Amounts held in a Roth IRA *cannot* be rolled over to a Roth 403(b) account even if all of the amounts in the Roth IRA can be traced to a rollover distribution from a Roth account in another 403(b) plan. [Treas. Reg. § 1.408A-10, Q&A-5]

Q 18:26   How do the automatic rollover rules for mandatory cashouts apply to the Roth 403(b) accounts?

Roth 403(b) accounts are treated separately from other accounts in applying the $1,000 minimum threshold for automatic rollovers of mandatory cashouts. However, the Roth regulations do *not* provide for separate treatment of Roth 403(b) accounts in applying the maximum threshold for mandatory cashouts. Instead, the plan administrator must consider the participant's entire plan balance. [Treas. Reg. § 1.401(k)-1(f)(4)(ii)]

Example. A plan provides for the mandatory distribution of balances up to $5,000 without participant consent. A participant with a $1,700 balance, $900 in a designated Roth account and $800 in other accounts, is entitled to a mandatory cashout upon termination of employment but fails to request a rollover or cash payment. The plan administrator is not required to execute an automatic rollover of $900 into a Roth IRA and $800 into a traditional IRA. The plan administrator may pay the $1,700 balance as a cash distribution. Alternatively, the plan could adopt a policy of executing two automatic rollovers ($900 to a Roth IRA and $800 to a traditional IRA), but the regulations do not require this approach.

Q 18:27   How is the five-year qualification period calculated after a rollover?

- For *direct* rollovers from one Roth account to another Roth account, participants receive credit in the recipient plan for their period of participation in the distributing plan. Thus, when distributions ultimately are made from the recipient plan, the five-year qualification period is measured from the earliest year in which the participant made contributions to either plan. [Treas. Reg. § 1.402A-2, Q&A-2(a)(1)]

- For *60-day* rollovers from one Roth account to another, participants do not receive credit in the recipient plan for their period of participation in the distributing plan. Instead, the recipient plan must use its own starting date for the five-year qualification period. However, if the participant already has a Roth account in the receiving plan, the starting date of that account is used. [Treas. Reg. § 1.402A-1, Q&A-5(c)]

- For rollovers to a Roth IRA, the period of participation in a Roth 403(b) account cannot be carried over. Under Code Section 408A, Roth IRAs are subject to a separate five-year qualification period beginning with the first taxable year for which the individual makes a contribution to any Roth IRA. For a direct rollover from a Roth 403(b) account to a Roth IRA, participation in the plan's Roth account does not count toward the Roth IRA's five-year qualification period. If an individual had already established a Roth IRA, the start of the five-year qualification period for the Roth IRA would apply to any distribution from that account, including any rollover amounts. [Treas. Reg. § 1.408A-10, Q&A-4] The new Roth regulations do not have special rules for rollovers from Roth accounts to Roth IRAs initiated by a spouse or nonspouse beneficiary.

- For a *direct* rollover from a participant's Roth 403(b) account to an alternate payee or spousal beneficiary's Roth account in a plan maintained by the alternate payee's employer, the five-year qualification period under the recipient plan begins on the earlier of the date the employee's period of participation began under the distributing plan or the date the alternate payee or beneficiary's Roth account began under the recipient plan. [Treas. Reg. § 1.402A-1, Q&A-9(b)] Regardless of whether a rollover is direct or 60-day, the alternate payee's or spousal beneficiary's age, disability, or death is used to determine whether a distribution from the recipient plan is qualified. [Treas. Reg. § 1.402A-1, Q&A-4(d)]

Q 18:28   What reporting requirements apply to rollovers?

The regulations impose new reporting requirements on plans that engage in rollovers. In some situations (e.g., direct rollovers between Section 403(b) plans), distributing plans have up to 30 days to report additional information to recipient plans about the nature of the rollover (i.e., whether the distribution is qualified); recipient plans are permitted to rely on these statements. In other cases (e.g., direct rollovers from Section 403(b) plans to Roth IRAs), distributing plans have 30 days to provide additional information to affected participants upon request. This requirement can be satisfied by providing a statement attached to the check issued to the employee. [Treas. Reg. § 1.402A-2, Q&A-2] Without this information, recipient plans will find it impossible to comply with their obligation to maintain separate Roth accounts and track each employee's tax basis.

In addition, recipient plans will have an obligation to notify the IRS when they accept 60-day rollovers from participants once the IRS issues Forms and Instructions. But until their release, no reporting is required. [Treas. Reg. § 1.402A-2, Q&A-3]

Q 18:29   Can Roth 403(b) accounts be transferred to other plans?

Generally, Roth 403(b) accounts can be transferred in a plan-to-plan transfer only to another Section 403(b) program that maintains designated Roth 403(b) accounts. They can never be transferred to Section 401(a), 401(k), or 457 plans, with one exception. They can be transferred to a governmental Section 401(a) pension plan for the purchase of service credit. In that event, they lose their Roth character. [Treas. Reg. §§ 1.403(b)-10(b)(3), 1.403(b)-10(b)(4)]

Q 18:30   How do the contract exchange rules apply to Roth 403(b) accounts?

Under the final Code Section 403(b) regulations, contract exchanges are considered a change of investment within a Section 403(b) program. Accordingly, they are not treated as distributions and the *qualified* distribution rules are not applicable. [Treas. Reg. § 1.402A-1, Q&A-13(a)] However, the receiving vendor must be able to maintain the designated Roth 403(b) account, including the basis recovery rules, and must receive the necessary historical information (e.g., the date the Roth 403(b) account was established and the current tax basis) from the sending vendor.

Plan Design and Communication Considerations

Q 18:31   Does a Roth 403(b) feature align with the employer's benefit objectives?

A Roth 403(b) feature adds considerable complexity to the Section 403(b) program. If the employer's objective is to maintain a very simple, no frills tax deferral program, a Roth feature may not be a good fit.

If the employer has a large population of high-paid or financially sophisticated employees, the Roth feature may be necessary to remain competitive with similar employers.

In the healthcare and higher education industries, many employees have adjusted gross incomes above the threshold for establishing a Roth IRA. These employees will find the Roth 403(b) feature to be very desirable and may expect their employer to offer it.

Prior to the Pension Protection Act of 2006 (PPA), many employers were reluctant to adopt a Roth 403(b) feature because the EGTRRA sunset provision was scheduled to terminate Roth 401(k) and 403(b) benefits in 2011. With the PPA's removal of the sunset provision, most employers indicate that they intend to add a Roth feature at some point in the future.

Employers who wish to provide the most flexibility possible to their employees will be more likely to add a Roth 403(b) feature. Many employees will want to *diversify* their personal tax structure by using both pre-tax 403(b) deferrals and Roth 403(b) contributions. Having both types of accounts will allow the employee to have more flexibility after retirement, taking taxable distributions from their pre-tax accounts in low-tax years and nontaxable qualified distributions from their Roth accounts in high-tax years.

Q 18:32   What impact will adding a Roth 403(b) feature have on the plan's actual contribution percentage (ACP) test?

Plan sponsors who offer an employer matching contribution will want to consider how a Roth 403(b) feature will affect results under the ACP test of Code Section 401(m). If lower-paid employees utilize Roth 403(b) contributions, but reduce their contribution levels in order to maintain their take-home pay, the average matching contributions made for nonhighly compensated employees (NHCEs) may go down and could make the ACP test more difficult to pass.

Currently, however, surveys show that fewer than 10 percent of employees who have Roth features available to them take advantage of the feature, so the impact on ACP test results generally is minimal.

Q 18:33 Can a Roth 403(b) feature be offered as a "stand-alone" program?

No, a Roth 403(b) feature may only be offered in a Section 403(b) program that also allows employees to make pre-tax 403(b) deferrals. [I.R.C. § 402A(b)(1)]

Q 18:34 Will adding a Roth feature to a Section 403(b) program affect employee communications?

Yes. Employee communications will generally be more complicated at all levels. Employees need to understand:

1. The differences between pre-tax deferrals and Roth contributions;
2. The effects of Roth contributions on the employee's take-home pay;
3. How distributions of Roth 403(b) accounts are taxed, including the rules for a distribution to be qualified;
4. How to determine which type of contribution will be better for the employee's individual situation; and
5. The effect of changes in individual marginal tax rates on the employee's analysis under item (4).

Written summaries of plan features should include examples to demonstrate items (2), (4) and (5). Online interactive calculators can be very helpful.

To avoid giving tax advice, however, employees should be cautioned to consult their personal tax advisors.

Q 18:35 What information will employees need in order to decide whether to make designated Roth contributions?

Employees should have a sense of their current marginal tax rate (federal and state combined) and how that rate will be different at the time of distribution. If they expect their marginal tax rate to be higher at distribution, the Roth contribution is the better choice if the employee expects the future distribution to be *qualified*. The greater the differential between current and future rates (e.g., a 10 percentage point differential or more), the larger the benefit from the Roth feature will be.

If the employees expect their marginal tax rate to be lower at the time of distribution, they will derive greater benefit from the immediate tax reduction of the pre-tax deferral. They will avoid higher taxes now and pay taxes on their entire distribution but at lower tax rates. Again, the differential between the tax rates makes considerable difference.

If the employee plans to take a distribution before meeting the rules for a qualified distribution (for example, a 58-year-old person who plans to retire at age 62), then the pre-tax deferral is better because of the immediate reduction in taxes.

EXAMPLES A AND B: NO CHANGE IN MARGINAL TAX RATES

Assumptions:

1. 40% marginal tax rates (now and at retirement)
2. Investments triple in value between now and retirement (i.e., 7.6% rate of return for 15 years)
3. 4.56% after-tax rate of return on separate taxable account in Example B (i.e., 7.6% × (1 − 40%))[1]

Example A: Employee with Limited Amount to Invest.

	Pre-Tax	Roth	Notes
Initial Investment	$ 5,000	$3,000	Roth participant pays $2,000 in current taxes, leaving only $3,000 for contribution.
Balance at Retirement	$15,000	$9,000	
Tax at Retirement	$ 6,000	$ 0	
Net Balance	**$ 9,000**	**$9,000**	

Example B: Employee Who Wants to Maximize Retirement Savings.

	Pre-Tax		Roth		
	Retirement Account	Separate Account	Retirement Account	Separate Account	Notes
Initial Investment	$15,500	$ 6,200	$15,500	$0	Pre-tax participant can invest tax savings in separate (taxable) account.
Balance at Retirement	$46,500	$12,103	$46,500	$0	
Tax at Retirement	$18,600	N/A	$ 0	$0	Taxes on earnings in separate account are paid annually.
Net Balance	$27,900	$12,103	$46,500	$0	
Total Net Balance		**$40,003**		**$46,500**	

---

[1] The taxable account generates 7.6% return annually. After paying a 40% tax on the returns, the after-tax rate of return is 7.6% × (1 − 40%) = 4.56%.

EXAMPLES C AND D: MARGINAL TAX RATES DECREASE

Assumptions:

1. 40% marginal tax rates now; 25% marginal tax rates at retirement
2. Investments triple in value between now and retirement (i.e., 7.6% rate of return for 15 years)
3. 4.56% after-tax rate of return for first 10 years and 5.7% (i.e., 7.6% × (1 –25%)) after-tax rate of return for next 5 years on separate taxable account in Example D

Example C: Employee with Limited Amount to Invest.

	Pre-Tax	Roth	Notes
Initial Investment	$ 5,000	$3,000	Roth participant pays $2,000 in current taxes, leaving only $3,000 in contributions.
Balance at Retirement	$15,000	$9,000	
Tax at Retirement	$ 3,750	$ 0	
Net Balance	**$11,250**	**$9,000**	

Example D: Employee Who Wants to Maximize Retirement Savings.

	Pre-Tax		Roth		
	Retirement Account	Separate Account	Retirement Account	Separate Account	Notes
Initial Investment	$15,500	$ 6,200	$15,500	$0	Pre-tax participant can invest tax savings in separate (taxable) account.
Balance at Retirement	$46,500	$12,777	$46,500	$0	
Tax at Retirement	$11,625	N/A	$ 0	$0	Taxes on earnings in separate account are paid annually.
Net Balance	$34,875	$12,777	$46,500	$0	
Total Net Balance		**$47,652**		**$46,500**	

EXAMPLES E AND F: MARGINAL TAX RATES INCREASE

Assumptions:

1. 40% marginal tax rates now; 50% marginal tax rates at retirement
2. Investments triple in value between now and retirement (i.e., 7.6% rate of return for 15 years)
3. 4.56% after-tax rate of return for first 10 years and 3.8% (i.e., 7.6% × (1–50%)) after-tax rate of return for next 5 years on separate taxable account in Example F

Example E: Employee with Limited Amount to Invest.

	Pre-Tax	Roth	Notes
Initial Investment	$ 5,000	$3,000	Roth participant pays $2,000 in current taxes, leaving only $3,000 in contributions.
Balance at Retirement	$15,000	$9,000	
Tax at Retirement	$ 7,500	$ 0	
Net Balance	**$ 7,500**	**$9,000**	

Example F: Employee Who Wants to Maximize Retirement Savings.

	Pre-Tax		Roth		Notes
	Retirement Account	Separate Account	Retirement Account	Separate Account	
Initial Investment	$15,500	$ 6,200	$15,500	$0	Pre-tax participant can invest tax savings in separate (taxable) account.
Balance at Retirement	$46,500	$11,669	$46,500	$0	
Tax at Retirement	$23,250	N/A	$ 0	$0	Taxes on earnings in separate account are paid annually.
Net Balance	$23,250	$11,669	$46,500	$0	
Total Net Balance		**$34,919**		**$46,500**	

Administrative Considerations

Q 18:36   What payroll system changes are needed to implement a Roth 403(b) feature?

The employer's payroll system must be able to track another deduction source (payroll *bucket*). The Roth 403(b) contributions are after-tax, so they must be included in taxable pay for FICA, FUTA, and federal and state income tax withholding purposes. The Roth 403(b) contributions also are included in Form W-2, Box 1 taxable income.

The payroll system also must be able to apply the Section 402(g) limit to the sum of pre-tax deferrals and Roth contributions.

Similarly, if the payroll system monitors the Section 415 limit, it must be able to apply the limit to the aggregate of pre-tax, Roth, after-tax and employer contributions (excluding age 50 catch-up contributions).

Q 18:37   What recordkeeping changes will be needed to implement a Roth 403(b) feature?

The recordkeeper must be able to accommodate and track the following information:

1. An additional contribution source;
2. The five-year qualification period for determining whether a distribution is qualified;
3. The Section 402(g) limit on combined pre-tax and Roth contributions;
4. The employee's "investment in the contract" (i.e., tax basis) in the Roth 403(b) account; and
5. The Section 415 limit on all contributions combined (excluding age 50 catch-up contributions).

Q 18:38   How do Roth contributions affect the 15-year special catch-up determination?

Prior Roth 403(b) contributions applied as a 15-year catch-up reduce the $15,000 limit in Code Section 402(g)(7)(A)(ii). Prior Roth 403(b) contributions that were not applied as a 15-year catch-up contribution and Roth IRA contributions do not affect the calculation. [I.R.C. § 402(g)(7)(A)(ii)(II)]

Q 18:39   Can participants borrow from their Roth 403(b) accounts?

Yes, the plan may allow participant loans from the Roth 403(b) account. The loan is treated as an investment option within the account and the interest on the loan is treated the same as other investment income within the account.

The same IRS requirements that apply to loans from pre-tax deferral accounts also apply to loans from the Roth 403(b) account. Additionally, the $50,000 limit on loans to avoid having a taxable distribution apply to the aggregate of all borrowing from the Section 403(b) program, across all vendors and all contribution types. If a loan is taken partly from the Roth 403(b) account and partly from other accounts, the repayments must be made proportionately to the Roth account to satisfy the level amortization requirement under Code Section 72(p). [Treas. Reg. § 1.402A-1, Q&A-12]

Q 18:40   Can participants take hardship distributions from their Roth 403(b) accounts?

Yes, the rules for hardship distributions apply equally to pre-tax deferral accounts and to Roth 403(b) accounts. If using the safe harbor deemed hardship rules, the plan administrator must suspend the participant's contributions (both pre-tax and Roth) for six months. [Treas. Reg. § 1.401(k)-1(d)(3)(iv)(E)(2)]

When a participant receives a nonqualified distribution from a Roth 403(b) account because of hardship, only a portion of the distribution is treated as a return of contributions for tax purposes. The final Code Section 402A regulations issued in April 2007 treat the *entire* amount of the Roth distribution as reducing the amount available for a subsequent hardship distribution, even though a pro rata portion of the distribution is treated as taxable investment earnings. [Treas. Reg. § 1.402A-1, Q&A-8]

> **Example.** An employee's Roth 403(b) account holds $23,000, consisting of $21,850 in contributions and $1,150 in investment earnings. The employee takes a hardship distribution of $12,000. If the employee is not yet age 59½ and is not disabled, this will be a nonqualified distribution. To determine the maximum amount available for a future hardship distribution, the employee's contributions ($21,850) are reduced by the entire amount of the hardship distribution ($12,000), leaving $9,850 available for future hardship withdrawals. This is true even though a pro rata portion of the $12,000, $600, is treated as taxable investment earnings at the time of the first hardship distribution.

Chapter 19

Retirement and Estate Planning for Section 403(b) Participants

John Curran, Esq.
Douglas Rothermich, Esq.
Teachers Insurance and Annuity Association-College Retirement
Equities Fund

> The estate and gift tax consequences of qualified and nonqualified annuities should also be considered in designing an estate plan for Section 403(b) participants. Retirement plan annuities can be used to fund trusts that are being established for planning purposes and to fund charitable gifts. However, the planner must take into account the complex rules that apply to distributions from retirement plans, particularly the minimum distribution rules and the rights that inure to spouses under certain plans.

Estate Tax Treatment

Q 19:1 Are annuities receivable under a Section 403(b) plan or other tax-favored retirement arrangements afforded any special estate tax treatment?

Generally, no. Under current law, there is no special treatment for annuities receivable under a Section 403(b) or other tax-favored arrangement. Before

1982, an amount receivable by a beneficiary under such retirement arrange- ments that qualified could be entirely excluded from the decedent's gross estate. [Former I.R.C. § 2039(c)] The Tax Equity and Responsibility Act of 1982 (TEFRA) reduced the exclusion to $100,000 in 1982 [Former I.R.C. § 2039(g)], and it was completely eliminated by the Deficit Reduction Act of 1984 (DEFRA) in 1984. [DEFRA § 525(a)]

Grandfather rules apply, however. The full exclusion is available to benefi- ciaries where the plan participants were in pay status on December 31, 1982, and irrevocably elected the form of benefit and beneficiary before January 1, 1983. The Tax Reform Act of 1986 (TRA '86) extended the full exclusion to those participants who separated from service before January 1, 1983, and who elected a form of benefit but did not change it before death. The $100,000 exclusion is available for beneficiaries where the plan participants were in pay status before January 1, 1985, and irrevocably elected the benefit before July 18, 1985. TRA '86 also extended the $100,000 exclusion to a participant who had separated from service before January 1, 1985, and who elected a form of benefit but did not change it before death. [TRA '86 § 1852(e)(3)]

Q 19:2   Is the death benefit payable from an annuity to a beneficiary, including a Section 403(b) annuity, includible in the decedent contract owner's gross estate?

Yes. The value of benefits payable to a beneficiary under a Section 403(b) arrangement will be includible in the employee's gross estate. In general, the value of payments from any annuity contract entered into after March 3, 1931, will be included in the decedent's gross estate if

1. There is a contract or agreement, including one with an employer;
2. The value of the payments is attributable to contributions made by the decedent or his or her employer;

   and

3. There is an amount receivable by a beneficiary by reason of surviving the decedent;

   and

1. The decedent at his or her death was being paid an annuity or other payment for his or her life, or for any period that could not be determined without reference to his or her death, or for any period that does not, in fact, end before the decedent's death;

   or

2. The decedent at his or her death had the right to receive an annuity or other payment for his or her life, or for any period not ascertainable without reference to his or her death, or for any period that does not, in fact, end before the decedent's death.

The payments, or right to payments, can be receivable either alone or in conjunction with another person or persons. [I.R.C. § 2039]

Thus, if the decedent was receiving a single life annuity whose payments ended at his or her death, no amount would be included in the gross estate. If, however, the annuity contract provides for payments to continue to a beneficiary after the contract owner's death, there may be an amount includible in the estate.

Q 19:3   If a decedent contract owner had not yet begun receiving payments from the annuity, is the death benefit includible in his or her gross estate?

Yes. The general rule is that if the decedent had the right at the time of his or her death to receive a payment for his or her life, or for any period not ascertainable without reference to the decedent's death, or for any period that does not, in fact, end before the decedent's death, the value of the amount payable to the beneficiary is included in the decedent contract owner's gross estate (see Q 19:2). Under a Section 403(b) arrangement, where the employee has a right to receive such a payment, the death benefit will be included in the gross estate.

Q 19:4   If the death benefit from a Section 403(b) arrangement is in the form of a lump sum, is it includible in the decedent contract owner's gross estate?

Yes. Section 2039 of the Internal Revenue Code (Code) states that the gross estate of a decedent will include the value of "an annuity or other payment." Treasury regulations explicitly provide that lump-sum distributions to a beneficiary are includible. [Treas. Reg. § 20.2039-1(b)(2)]

Q 19:5   Is the death benefit payable from an annuity to an estate includible in the gross estate of the decedent contract owner?

Yes. A payment to the estate is treated as property in which the decedent had an interest at the time of his or her death under Code Section 2033.

Q 19:6   What portion of the payment from an annuity to the beneficiary is included in the decedent contract owner's gross estate?

The amount of the payment from an annuity to the beneficiary that is included in the gross estate of the decedent contract owner is limited to the extent of the contribution of the decedent or his or her employer. Specifically, the amount to be included is the amount that bears the same ratio to the value of the annuity receivable by the beneficiary as the contribution to the contract made by the decedent and his or her employer bears to the total cost. [Treas. Reg. § 20.2039-1(c)] Therefore, the entire value of a Section 403(b) annuity contract will generally be included in the gross estate.

Q 19:7 What is a *commercial annuity*?

For purposes of estate tax valuation, a *commercial annuity* is defined as one issued by a company regularly engaged in the sale of annuities. [Treas. Reg. § 20.2031-7(b)] Annuity contracts used in Section 403(b) arrangements are commercial annuities.

Q 19:8 What valuation methods must be used to calculate the remaining interest in an annuity for estate tax purposes after the contract owner's death?

The value of a commercial annuity is established through the sale by that company of comparable contracts. [Treas. Reg. § 20.2031-8]

Example. Under the terms of the Section 403(b) annuity contract purchased by Roberto from a life insurance company, he was to receive payments of $1,200 annually for life, and, upon his death, his wife, Maria, was to receive the same amount for her life. Five years after the purchase, when Maria was 50 years of age, Roberto died. The value of the annuity contract at the date of Roberto's death is the amount that the company would charge for an annuity providing for the payment of $1,200 annually for the life of a female 50 years of age. [Treas. Reg. § 20.2031-8(b)]

Gift Tax Treatment

Q 19:9 Is there a gift for gift tax purposes when a joint and survivor annuity contract is purchased providing for payments during the life of the contract owner and the life of a second annuitant?

Yes. An individual who purchases a joint and survivor annuity on his or her life and the life of a second annuitant, and irrevocably names the second annuitant, has completed a gift for purposes of the gift tax. It is important to note, however, that it is not a gift if the owner reserves the right to change the second annuitant.

The same rule applies to the irrevocable designation of a second annuitant in a Section 403(b) annuity. If, however, the joint and survivor annuity is wholly subsidized by the employer—that is, there is no reduction in the amount payable to the employee by virtue of electing the joint and survivor option—it appears that the election does not constitute a taxable gift. [Treas. Reg. § 25.2511-1(h)(11)] It should be further noted that if the second annuitant is the individual's spouse (and he or she is the only joint annuitant), a marital deduction applies to eliminate any tax on the completed gift. [See I.R.C. § 2523(f)(6)]

Q 19:10   Is there a gift for gift tax purposes when the spouse of a participant in a 403(b) arrangement waives his or her statutory right to a survivor benefit?

No. Under Code Section 2503(f), a waiver of survivor rights pursuant to Code Sections 401(a) and 417 is not treated as a transfer of property by gift for purposes of the gift tax.

Q 19:11   How is the gift tax value of an annuity determined?

The value of a commercial annuity for gift tax purposes is determined by the cost of comparable contracts sold by the insurance company. Where the gift is made after the annuity has been in force for some years, the value is the amount that the company would charge for a single premium contract of the same amount on the life of a person who is the age of the donor at the time of the gift. In the case of a joint and survivor annuity, where the second annuitant is named irrevocably, the value is the difference between the cost of the joint and survivor annuity and the amount the insurance company would have charged for a single life annuity on the life of the donor. [Treas. Reg. § 25.2512-6]

Funding Trusts with Retirement Plan Annuities

Q 19:12   May retirement benefits be distributed to a trust?

Generally, yes. Nothing in the Code prevents distributions from a retirement annuity being paid following a contract owner's death to a trust he or she has established. If there is a restriction on who may receive the qualified or nonqualified retirement annuity following the contract owner's death, the restriction will be in the plan itself.

Caution. When income tax deferred retirement annuities are distributable to a trust, how those distributions are made can have a significant impact on the income tax that will be due on distribution (see Q 19:14).

Q 19:13   What distribution requirements apply if a trust is the beneficiary of retirement plan assets?

Retirement annuities, whether from a qualified or a nonqualified plan, may be distributed to a trust as an outright distribution following the contract owner's death. Such a form of distribution may be appropriate if income tax matters are not important (e.g., a distribution of a retirement annuity to a purely charitable trust, which is exempt from income tax). When the assets are distributed to a trust for the benefit of individual beneficiaries, however, income taxation of the distributions will have an impact. For qualified plan annuities, additional options exist to "stretch out" the payments—so that most of the assets remain in the tax-deferred account for a longer period, deferring further the income taxation of the annuity assets. Because the tax-deferred annuities will be subject to income tax only when distributed, stretching out the distributions can allow for greater tax-deferred buildup inside the retirement plan before distributions are made to the trust.

If the only designated beneficiary of a qualified retirement annuity is an individual, that individual can have the option to receive distributions following the contract owner's death over the beneficiary's life expectancy (i.e., he or she can "stretch out" the distributions over his or her life expectancy). Additional stretch-out options exist if the contract owner's designated beneficiary is his or her spouse. [I.R.C. § 401(a)(9)(B)(iv)]

If the contract owner's death occurs before his or her required beginning date, the general rule is that distributions to a trust must be made within five years from the date of the owner's death. [I.R.C. § 401(a)(9)(B)(ii)] Technically, the regulations allow the distributions to occur by December 31 of the year including the fifth anniversary of the contract owner's death. [Treas. Reg. § 1.401(a)(9)-3, A-2]

Q 19:14   What is look-through treatment of distributions to a trust from an annuity?

Distributions from a qualified retirement annuity to a trust (or another nonindividual; e.g., the decedent's estate) typically do not qualify for the stretch-out option described above (see Q 19:13). [Treas. Reg. § 1.401(a)(9)-4, Q&A 3] Treasury Regulations § 1.401(a)(9)-4, Q&A 5 provides an exception to the general rule for distributions to a trust, however. Under the regulation, if certain requirements are met, the trust can be "looked through," and the trust beneficiaries may be used as the designated beneficiaries. To qualify for such look-through treatment:

1. The trust must be valid under state law (or would be but for the fact that there is no corpus);
2. The trust must be irrevocable or become irrevocable, by its terms, upon the contract owner's death;
3. The trust must have identifiable beneficiaries from the trust instrument; and
4. A copy of the trust must be provided to the plan administrator (or alternative documentation requirements must be met).

If the contract owner's death occurs before his or her required beginning date and the owner's designated beneficiary is a trust meeting the requirements, look-through treatment could apply and distributions to the trust will be treated as distributed to the beneficiary—allowing the trust to stretch out distributions over the life expectancy of the trust beneficiary. If the trust has more than one beneficiary, the beneficiary with the shortest life expectancy will be used as the measuring life for purposes of calculating minimum distributions. [Treas. Reg. § 1.401(a)(9)-5, A-7]

If the contract owner is alive at his or her required beginning date and the owner's designated beneficiary is a trust meeting the requirements set forth above (see Q 19:13), minimum distributions during the owner's lifetime can be calculated using either the uniform table or the joint life expectancy of the contract owner and the spouse, if the spouse is more than 10 years younger than the owner, and is the sole beneficiary of the trust. Upon the contract owner's death following his or her required beginning date (again, with the trust designated as the owner's beneficiary), the beneficiaries of the trust will be treated as having been designated as the beneficiaries of the annuity (and distributions can continue based on the life expectancy of the oldest trust beneficiary).

The obvious benefit of look-through treatment is that annuity distributions may be made to the contract owner's trust but still be stretched out over the life expectancy of the oldest trust beneficiary (providing greater tax-deferred buildup inside the annuity). It should be noted, however, that the Final Regulations provide that "the separate account rules under A-2 of Section 1.401(a)(9)-8 are not available to beneficiaries of a trust with respect to the trust's interest in the employee's benefit." [Treas. Reg. § 1.401(a)(9)-4, A-5(c)] Based on this regulation, where there are multiple beneficiaries of a trust, it is not possible to establish separate accounts for each beneficiary and have them receive required minimum distributions over their respective life expectancies. All payments have to be calculated based upon the life expectancy of the oldest trust beneficiary.

It is important to note, however, that obtaining look-through treatment for a trust as the designated beneficiary of an individual's retirement annuity does not, by itself, ensure that the distributions may be stretched out over the life expectancy of the oldest beneficiary. Each of the trust beneficiaries must also qualify as designated beneficiaries. For instance, if a beneficiary of the trust is not an individual beneficiary (e.g., a charity or the contract owner's estate), the look-through treatment will not have accomplished the stretch-out that may have been sought. In such a case, if the contract owner's death occurred before his or her required beginning date, the look-through treatment would not apply, and the five-year rule (see Q 19:13) would have to be complied with for distributions to the trust.

Q 19:15   What issues, other than estate or income tax implications, should be considered when designating a trust as the beneficiary of retirement plan assets?

Aside from the estate or income tax implications associated with designating a trust as the beneficiary of retirement plan assets, there may be other issues to consider. A trust allows the individual who created it to determine when and how the assets funding the trust may be used. That benefit can give added control that would not be available with an outright distribution of the retirement annuity to a beneficiary.

On the other hand, using a trust can limit options for long-term distributions from a retirement annuity after the contract holder's death. This is particularly true for distributions to a surviving spouse. Distribution of a retirement annuity to a trust for the benefit of a surviving spouse can be structured to allow for minimum distributions during the contract owner's lifetime based on the uniform table, or over the joint life expectancy of the owner and his or her spouse if the spouse is more than 10 years younger than the owner, and is the sole beneficiary of the trust. Further, following the contract owner's death, the trustee of the trust can also continue to take distributions over the owner's spouse's remaining life expectancy. The option that is lost, however, with such a form of trust planning (that would be available if the contract owner distributed the retirement annuity to his or her spouse directly) is the opportunity for the owner's spouse to roll over the retirement annuity to an individual retirement account (IRA) in his or her own name. After rolling over the annuity to an IRA, the surviving spouse could then take minimum distributions (after reaching the required beginning date) using the uniform table or (if the surviving spouse has remarried by that time) the joint life expectancy of the surviving spouse and his or her new spouse, and then at the survivor's death, using the beneficiary's life expectancy.

Q 19:16 When should retirement annuities be considered for funding a credit shelter trust?

A *credit shelter (bypass) trust* is a trust established at death to be funded with the amount of assets that may be sheltered from estate tax by a decedent's applicable exclusion amount ($2.0 million for 2007-2008, and currently scheduled to increase to $3.5 million for 2009). This form of trust is typically used at the first spouse's death by a married couple with a taxable estate for estate tax purposes. The trust assets may be held for the benefit of the surviving spouse, if needed, but held in such a way that any unused assets be excluded from the survivor's estate for estate tax purposes.

When credit shelter trust planning is appropriate, it often makes sense to fund the trust at the first spouse's death with nonretirement plan assets equal to the deceased spouse's applicable exclusion amount. Retirement plan assets can then be given to the surviving spouse—and several options exist for deferring the income tax on the retirement plan assets until the surviving spouse actually withdraws the funds from the retirement plan (see above). Such a scenario allows a married couple to follow both an estate tax planning strategy that will fully use the deceased spouse's applicable exclusion amount at the first spouse's death and an income tax planning strategy of deferring the income tax on the retirement plan assets for as long as possible.

When there are not sufficient nonretirement plan assets available at the first spouse's death to fund the credit shelter trust, however, using retirement annuities to fund the trust may be necessary and appropriate. In such a situation, using retirement plan assets to "fill up" the trust may limit some of the options for income tax deferral otherwise available had those assets been given directly to the surviving spouse (see Q 19:15). On the other hand, if all of the retirement plan assets are transferred to the surviving spouse for income tax planning purposes, the credit shelter trust will not be fully funded. Under such circumstances, a couple's estate plan should consider how to balance the estate tax planning strategy of fully funding a credit shelter trust at the first spouse's death with the income tax planning strategy for income tax deferral on the retirement annuity. The decision to fully fund a credit shelter trust (at least in part) with retirement plan assets or to transfer all of the retirement plan assets to the surviving spouse to take full advantage of the income tax deferral may depend on a number of factors (e.g., the expected size of the surviving spouse's estate at his or her death, his or her life expectancy, and other factors).

If fully funding the credit shelter trust at the first spouse's death makes sense, two alternatives for using retirement plan assets to fund the credit shelter trust are as follows:

1. Designate the credit shelter trust directly as the primary beneficiary of that fraction of the retirement plan assets needed to "fill up" the credit shelter trust (after considering all other non-tax-deferred assets available); or

2. Arrange the retirement plan beneficiary designation in a manner that the same result could be attained through "disclaimer planning" (see below), if desired at the time of the first spouse's death.

Under the first alternative, designating the trustee of the credit shelter trust as the primary beneficiary for that fraction of the retirement plan assets necessary to fully fund the trust provides a means to fully use the applicable exclusion amount at the first spouse's death. (See Q 19:14 on the impact of designating a trust as beneficiary for distribution purposes.) The participant's spouse or other beneficiaries can remain the primary beneficiaries of retirement plan assets not needed to fully fund the credit shelter trust, allowing for the potential of further income tax deferral beyond the participant's death.

It also may be possible to structure the beneficiary designation using a "disclaimer" to provide greater flexibility to do post mortem estate planning following the first spouse's death. If a decedent's spouse or other beneficiaries "disclaim" property or an interest in property they would have received from the decedent, they will be treated as if they had never received the property or interest in property and had predeceased the decedent. Of course, the disclaimer rules under the Code must be followed to avoid any tax consequences for the beneficiary disclaiming (e.g., being treated as having made a taxable gift to the next beneficiary). [I.R.C. § 2518]

The disclaimer rules are quite technical. All the following requirements must be met for the disclaimer to be effective for tax purposes:

1. The disclaimer must be in writing and be irrevocable and unqualified;

2. The disclaimer must be made within nine months of when the interest in the disclaimed asset is created;

3. The disclaimer must be made before any benefit of the disclaimed asset is received; and

4. The disclaimed interest must pass without any direction from the disclaiming party.

A technique that contemplates the possible use of a disclaimer for an individual's retirement plan assets could be to name the individual's spouse as the primary beneficiary for all of the individual's retirement plan assets, but further provide that if any portion of the retirement plan assets are disclaimed, the credit shelter trust will receive the disclaimed assets as the contingent beneficiary. After the individual's death, his or her surviving spouse can then determine if there are enough nonretirement assets to fund the credit shelter trust. If there are not, the surviving spouse can decide whether it is more beneficial to continue the long-term income tax deferral on the retirement plan assets or if a portion should be used to fully fund the credit shelter trust. If funding the credit shelter trust with retirement plan assets makes sense at that time, then the surviving spouse can disclaim a portion of those assets necessary to fill up the credit shelter trust. The retirement plan assets then pass to the contingent beneficiary—the credit shelter trust. If the credit shelter trust qualifies for look-through treatment (see Q 19:14), and the decedent dies before his or her required beginning date, the life expectancy of the oldest beneficiary of the credit shelter trust can continue to be used to determine the minimum distributions from the retirement plan account to the trust. If the decedent's death occurs after his or her required beginning date, the surviving spouse's life expectancy can continue to be used to determine the minimum distributions for the retirement plan account to the credit shelter trust.

The form of disclaimer planning just outlined allows an individual to take a wait-and-see approach on how his or her retirement plan assets should be used. If full use of the deceased spouse's applicable exclusion amount will provide the best benefit for an individual's family or other beneficiaries, disclaiming may make sense. That may be the case, for example, if the surviving spouse's subsequent death is expected to occur in the near future and the estate tax savings from using both spouses' applicable exclusion amount outweighs the income tax benefit of slightly longer income tax deferral on the retirement plan assets.

Funding Charitable Gifts with Retirement Plan Annuities

Q 19:17   What benefits can be associated with funding charitable gifts with retirement plan assets?

Because retirement annuities are subject to income tax when distributed, if a decedent's estate consists of both retirement plan assets and nonretirement plan assets, his or her beneficiaries who receive retirement plan assets must pay income tax on the assets they receive. Such an outcome makes it worth planning that any charitable bequest to be made at an individual's death be funded from retirement annuities first.

Example. Joan's estate is worth $200,000, consisting of $100,000 of tax-deferred retirement annuities and $100,000 of other assets (e.g., securities). Joan wishes to leave one-half of her estate to a charity, Tortoise Aid, and the other half to an individual beneficiary, Henry. If Joan does not designate which beneficiary should receive which assets (and one-half of every asset is distributed to each beneficiary), the following results (assuming a 40 percent combined federal and state income tax rate for Henry):

Tortoise Aid Receives	*Henry Receives*
$50,000	$50,000 Securities
50,000 Retirement annuities	50,000 Retirement annuities
	(20,000) Income tax liability
$100,000 Net	$80,000 Net

Because Tortoise Aid, as a charity, is income-tax exempt, it will not pay any income tax on its gift from Joan. Henry, on the other hand, will pay income tax on the value of the retirement annuity when he receives it.

The following results if the charity's interest is funded first with the assets in Joan's retirement plan:

Tortoise Aid Receives	*Henry Receives*
$100,000 Retirement annuity	$100,000 Securities

The tax savings for Henry, the individual beneficiary, is $20,000.

Practice Pointer. There can be a significant advantage to a decedent's individual (or noncharitable) beneficiaries if the charity's interest is funded first from the decedent's retirement annuities.

Q 19:18   Which retirement assets should be used first to fund charitable gifts—nonqualified or qualified?

After considering the benefits to a decedent's individual beneficiaries from funding charitable gifts at his or her death first from income tax-deferred retirement annuities (see Q 19:17), the annuity contract owner should consider which form of retirement annuity should be used to fund the charitable gift if his or her estate will include both qualified and nonqualified retirement annuities.

Nonqualified tax-deferred plans do not contain many of the opportunities for a contract owner's individual beneficiaries to obtain further tax deferral after the owner's death; for example, the surviving spouse cannot roll over a nonqualified plan to his or her IRA. Therefore, because of the added tax-deferral opportunities that may be available to individual beneficiaries from qualified retirement plan assets, a contract owner should consider funding any charitable gifts that will be payable from tax-deferred assets at his or her death first from the owner's nonqualified plan assets.

Q 19:19   Can lifetime gifts to charity be funded with retirement plan assets?

Technically, yes, but (subject to the information described in the "Legislative Update" section below) it may not be desirable when other assets are available to fund the gift. Tax-deferred retirement plan assets that can be withdrawn during a participant's lifetime could be used to fund lifetime gifts to charity; however, the income tax consequences of accelerating a withdrawal from a retirement annuity to make charitable contributions during the contract owner's lifetime may be undesirable (see Practice Pointer below, concerning the Pension Protection Act of 2006 (PPA)). Under current law, except as noted below, any amount withdrawn from a tax-deferred retirement account will be subject to income tax when paid. [I.R.C. § 72] That is true whether the assets are distributed to the participant (as retirement income) or withdrawn to make a large charitable gift in a lump sum (if allowed under the plan's provisions).

If the withdrawn assets will be used to fund a gift to charity, the contribution may generate an offsetting income tax charitable deduction (depending on the amount of the withdrawal/gift)—effectively eliminating the income tax consequences of the large plan withdrawal. Code Section 170(a) provides that individual gifts to charity may be deducted for income tax purposes in the year of the gift; however, Code Section 170(b) limits the deductibility of charitable gifts to a percentage of the taxpayer's adjusted gross income (AGI) (e.g., cash gifts to public charities are deductible in the year of the gift to the extent they do not exceed 50 percent of the taxpayer's AGI). For very large gifts that an individual may want to fund from assets in his or her tax-deferred retirement annuities, such a limit on deductibility could result in that individual not being able to fully deduct the charitable gift in the year of the gift.

Example. Liam has an AGI of $100,000. He would like to use tax-deferred retirement assets to fund a gift of $500,000 to a favorite charity, Ever Eire. If his plan allows Liam to make a lump-sum withdrawal from the plan and he did so during his lifetime, the withdrawn assets would increase his AGI to $600,000 in the year of the withdrawal. If Liam makes a cash gift of the $500,000 in retirement plan assets, the gift will be deductible for income tax purposes to the extent that it does not exceed 50 percent of his AGI. Any excess amount will be deductible in future years as a carryover for up to five years. In the year of the gift, Liam's deduction will be limited to $300,000 (50 percent of his AGI ($600,000)), and the remaining $200,000 of the charitable gift will not be deductible until succeeding years. The obvious impact of such a limitation is that Liam will have a sizable income tax liability in the year of the gift—even though the full amount was given to charity.

Practice Pointer. Over the past several years, legislation has been introduced in Congress to allow withdrawals from some tax-deferred retirement plans to be given to charity (without the result illustrated in the above example). The PPA included provisions on a variety of topics, one of which allowed, in limited circumstances, an account owner to use IRA assets to be rolled over directly to charity without the implications described in the above example. The PPA provided that during 2006 and 2007 only, individuals who have reached age 70½ may give up to $100,000 per year from an IRA directly to charity. Such gifts, if meeting all of the qualifications within the PPA, were not includible in the taxpayer's gross income for the year as a "distribution" from an IRA, nor was the taxpayer allowed an income tax charitable deduction for the amount of the gift. It should be noted that the PPA only allows gifts from IRAs (not Section 403(b) or Section 401(k) accounts), and the gift could not be to a donor-advised fund, certain types of private foundations (non-operating) or a charity annuity trust, or unitrust. This provision of the PPA expired at the end of 2007 and has not (at the time of publication) been renewed. Many commentators speculate this provision could be renewed before the end of 2008, and there continues to be interest in Congress among many to do so. Based on this legislation (and the possibility Congress could take action to renew these or similar provisions), for qualified donors interested in using IRA assets to satisfy lifetime gifts to charity, they should now first consult with their tax advisors to determine if it is possible to (and wise to) use IRA assets within the PPA or other (after-tax) assets to satisfy those gifts.

Spousal Rollovers

Q 19:20   What distributions are eligible for spousal rollovers?

Distributions that are "eligible rollover distributions" as defined in Code Section 402(c)(4) but that are received by a participant's spouse after the participant's death are eligible "spousal" rollover distributions. [I.R.C. §§ 402(c)(4), 402(c)(9)]

Q 19:21   What types of plans may receive a spousal rollover distribution?

Spousal rollover distributions may be made to individual retirement accounts as defined in Code Section 408(a) and individual retirement annuities (other than endowment contracts) as defined in Code Section 408(b), as well as to a qualified trust or an annuity plan, as defined in Code Sections 401(a) and 403(a), respectively; a Code Section 403(b) annuity; or a Code Section 457(b) governmental plan in which the surviving spouse participates. [I.R.C. § 402(c)(8)(B)]

Q 19:22   What are the minimum distribution requirements for funds that have been rolled over by a surviving spouse?

The benefits that a surviving spouse rolls over into his or her own eligible retirement plan become subject to the minimum distribution requirements imposed on such contracts as though originally owned by the surviving spouse. That is true even if the deceased participant's accumulation was subject to minimum distribution at the participant's death. The rolled-over portion is net of any minimum distribution requirement owed by the participant's contract.

The surviving spouse can then elect the calculation beneficiary that would apply to the rolled-over funds. [I.R.C. § 403(b)(10); Treas. Reg. § 1.408-8, Q&A-7]

Retirement Equity Act of 1984

Q 19:23 What beneficiary designation requirements were imposed on qualified retirement plans by the Retirement Equity Act of 1984?

The Retirement Equity Act of 1984 (REA) amended Code Section 401(a)(11) and added Code Section 417 to require that, in order to remain qualified under Code Section 401(a) or 403(a), a plan had to provide the spouse of a plan participant with both a qualified preretirement survivor annuity (QPSA) (see Q 19:25) and a qualified joint and survivor annuity (QJSA) (see Q 19:26). [I.R.C. §§ 401(a)(11), 417]

Q 19:24 To what types of retirement plans does REA apply?

REA applies to any defined benefit plan and to any defined contribution plan that is subject to the minimum funding requirements of Code Section 412. [Treas. Reg. § 1.401(a)(11)-20, Q&A 3]

Q 19:25 What is a QPSA?

A QPSA is a benefit amount necessary to provide the surviving spouse with a single life annuity that is equal to at least 50 percent of such a benefit that would have been payable to the participant should the participant die before his or her annuity starting date. [I.R.C. § 417(c)]

Q 19:26 What is a QJSA?

A QJSA is a survivor annuity equal to at least 50 percent of the benefit being received by the participant should he or she die after his or her annuity starting date. [I.R.C. § 417(b)]

Q 19:27 May the REA requirement for a QPSA or a QJSA be waived?

Under certain circumstances, yes. The requirements for a QPSA or a QJSA may be waived by the participant if an informed consent to such a waiver is obtained from the participant's spouse. [Treas. Reg. § 1.401(a)(11)-20, Q&As 28, 29, 31]

The requirements for a spousal waiver and consent are as follows:

1. A waiver for both a QPSA and a QJSA must list the specific nonspouse beneficiary who will receive the benefit.

2. The waiver for a QJSA must specify the optional form of benefit being selected.

3. The consent is limited to the specific nonspouse beneficiary or optional form of benefit being selected, unless the plan allows for a general consent that acknowledges the existence of the right to limit the consent to a specific nonspouse beneficiary and optional form of benefit.

4. The waiver for the QJSA must be made no later than 180 days before the participant's annuity starting date in order to be effective.

Furthermore,

1. A waiver and consent contained in a premarital agreement is ineffective.

2. Consent to the waiver of QPSA or QJSA requirements made by one spouse is not binding on a subsequent spouse, except in the case of plan loans.

Q 19:28   Are there exceptions to the waiver and consent requirements for a QPSA or a QJSA?

Yes. Spousal consent to waive the QPSA or QJSA requirements is not required in the following circumstances:

1. It is established to the satisfaction of a plan representative that

   a. There is no spouse, or

   b. That the spouse cannot be located.

2. The spouse is legally incompetent to give consent (in which case the spouse's legal guardian, even if it is the participant, may give it).

3. The participant has an order of separation and a qualified domestic relations order (QDRO) does not exist that provides otherwise.

4. The participant has an order of abandonment and a QDRO does not exist that provides otherwise.

[Treas. Reg. § 1.401(a)(11)-20, Q&A 27]

Appendix A

Final Code Section 403(b) Regulations

DEPARTMENT OF THE TREASURY

Internal Revenue Service

26 CFR Parts 1, 31, 54 and 602

[TD 9340]

RIN 1545-BB64

Revised Regulations Concerning Section 403(b) Tax-Sheltered Annuity Contracts

AGENCY: Internal Revenue Service (IRS), Treasury.

ACTION: Final regulations.

SUMMARY: This document promulgates final regulations under section 403(b) of the Internal Revenue Code and under related provisions of sections 402(b), 402(g), 402A, and 414(c). The regulations provide updated guidance on section 403(b) contracts of public schools and tax-exempt organizations described in section 501(c)(3). These regulations will affect sponsors of section 403(b) contracts, administrators, participants, and beneficiaries.

DATES: Effective Date: July 26, 2007.

Applicability Date: These regulations generally apply for taxable years beginning after December 31, 2008. However, see the "Applicability date" section in this preamble for additional information regarding the applicability of these regulations.

FOR FURTHER INFORMATION CONTACT: Concerning the regulations, John Tolleris, (202) 622-6060; concerning the regulations as applied to church-related entities, Robert Architect (202) 283-9634 (not toll-free numbers).

SUPPLEMENTARY INFORMATION:

Paperwork Reduction Act

The collection of information in § 1.403(b)-10(b)(2)(i)(C) of these final regulations has been approved by the Office of Management and Budget in accordance with the Paperwork Reduction Act of 1995 (44 U.S.C. 3507(d)) under control number 1545-2068. Responses to this collection of information are required in order to provide certain benefits.

The estimated burden per respondent varies among the plan administrator/ payor/recordkeeper, depending upon individual respondents' circumstances, with an estimated average of 4.1 hours. Comments concerning the accuracy of this burden estimate and suggestions for reducing this burden should be sent to the Internal Revenue Service, Attn: IRS Reports Clearance Officer, SE:W:CAR: MP:T:T:SP, Washington, DC 20224, and to the Office of Management and Budget, Attn: Desk Officer for the Department of the Treasury, Office of Information and Regulatory Affairs, Washington, DC 20503.

The collection of information in § 1.403(b)-10(b)(2)(i)(C) of these final regulations was not contained in the prior notice of proposed rulemaking. For this reason, this additional collection of information has been reviewed and, pending receipt and evaluation of public comments, approved by the Office of Management and Budget in accordance with the Paperwork Reduction Act of 1995 (44 U.S.C. 3507(d)) under control number 1545-2068. Comments concerning this additional collection of information should be sent to the Internal Revenue Service, Attn: IRS Reports Clearance Officer, SE:W:CAR:MP:T:T:SP, Washington, DC 20224, and to the Office of Management and Budget, Attn: Desk Officer for the Department of the Treasury, Office of Information and Regulatory Affairs, Washington, DC 20503. Comments on the collection of information should be received by September 24, 2007. Comments are specifically requested concerning:

Whether the proposed collection of information is necessary for the proper performance of the functions of the Internal Revenue Service, including whether the information will have practical utility;

The accuracy of the estimated burden associated with the proposed collection of information (see above);

How the quality, utility, and clarity of the information to be collected may be enhanced;

How the burden of complying with the proposed collections of information may be minimized, including through the application of automated collection techniques or other forms of information technology; and

Estimates of capital or start-up costs and costs of operation, maintenance, and purchase of service to provide information.

An agency may not conduct or sponsor, and a person is not required to respond to, a collection of information unless it displays a valid control number assigned by the Office of Management and Budget.

The estimated burden per respondent varies among the plan administrator/payor/recordkeeper, depending upon individual respondents' circumstances, with an estimated average of 4.1 hours.

Books or records relating to a collection of information must be retained as long as their contents might become material in the administration of any internal revenue law. Generally, tax returns and tax return information are confidential, as required by 26 USC 6103.

Background

Regulations (TD 6783) under section 403(b) of the Internal Revenue Code (Code) were originally published in the Federal Register (29 FR 18356) on December 24, 1964 (1965-1 CB 180). Those regulations provided guidance for complying with section 403(b), which had been enacted in 1958 in section 23(a) of the Technical Amendments Act of 1958, Public Law 85-866 (1958), relating to tax-sheltered annuity arrangements established for employees by public schools and tax-exempt organizations described in section 501(c)(3). Since 1964, additional regulations were issued under section 403(b) to reflect rules relating to certain eligible rollover distributions[1] and required minimum distributions under section 401(a)(9).[2] See § 601.601(d)(2) relating to objectives and standards for publishing regulations, revenue rulings and revenue procedures in the Internal Revenue Bulletin.

On November 16, 2004, a notice of proposed rulemaking (REG-155608-02) was published in the Federal Register (69 FR 67075) that proposed a comprehensive update of the regulations under section 403(b) (2004 proposed regulations), including: amending the 1964 and subsequent regulations to conform them to the numerous amendments made to section 403(b) by subsequent legislation, including section 1022(e) of the Employee Retirement Income Security Act of 1974 (ERISA) (88 Stat. 829), Public Law 93-406; section 251 of the Tax Equity and Fiscal Responsibility Act of 1982 (TEFRA) (96 Stat. 324, 529), Public Law 97-248; section 1120 of the Tax Reform Act of 1986 (TRA '86) (100 Stat. 2085, 2463), Public Law 99-514; section 1450(a) of the Small Business Job Protection Act of 1996 (SBJPA) (110 Stat. 1755, 1814), Public Law 104-188; and sections 632, 646, and 647 of the Economic Growth and Tax Relief Reconciliation Act of 2001 (EGTRRA) (115 Stat. 38, 113, 126, 127), Public Law 107-16. The 2004 proposed regulations also included controlled group rules under section 414(c) for entities that are tax-exempt under section 501(a).

---

[1] See TD 8619, September 22, 1995 (60 FR 49199).

[2] See TD 8987, April 17, 2002 (67 FR 18987).

Following publication of the 2004 proposed regulations, comments were received and a public hearing was held on February 15, 2005. After consideration of the comments received, the 2004 proposed regulations are adopted by this Treasury decision, subject to a number of changes, some of which are summarized below in this preamble.

Section 403(b) was also amended by sections 811, 821, 822, 824, 826, and 829 of the Pension Protection Act of 2006 (PPA '06) (120 Stat. 780), Public Law 109-280. These final regulations reflect these amendments.

Sections 403(b) and 414(c) Statutory Provisions

Section 403(b) provides an exclusion from gross income for certain contributions made by specific types of employers for their employees and by certain ministers to specified types of funding arrangements. The employers are limited to public schools and section 501(c)(3) organizations. There are three categories of funding arrangements to which section 403(b) applies: (1) annuity contracts (as defined in section 401(g)) issued by an insurance company; (2) custodial accounts that are invested solely in mutual funds; and (3) retirement income accounts, which are only permitted for church employees and certain ministers. Except as otherwise indicated, an annuity contract, for purposes of these final regulations, includes a custodial account that is invested solely in mutual funds.

The exclusion applies to employer nonelective contributions (including matching contributions) and elective deferrals (other than designated Roth contributions) within the meaning of section 402(g)(3)(C) (which applies to section 403(b) contributions made pursuant to a salary reduction agreement). The exclusion applies only if certain requirements relating to availability, nondiscrimination, and distribution are satisfied. Section 403(b) arrangements may also include after-tax employee contributions.

Section 403(b)(1)(C) requires that the contract be nonforfeitable (except for the failure to pay future premiums), regardless of the type of contribution used to purchase the contract. Section 403(b)(1)(E) requires a section 403(b) contract purchased under a salary reduction agreement to satisfy the requirements of section 401(a)(30) relating to limitations on elective deferrals under section 402(g)(1). In addition, all contributions to a section 403(b) arrangement, when expressed as annual additions under section 415(c)(2), must not exceed the applicable limit of section 415.

Section 403(b)(5) provides that all section 403(b) contracts purchased for an individual by an employer are treated as purchased under a single contract for purposes of the requirements of section 403(b). Other aggregation rules apply both on an individual and aggregate basis. For example, the section 402(g) limitations on elective deferrals apply to all elective deferrals during the year with respect to an individual and the limitations of section 401(a)(30) apply to all elective deferrals made by an employer to that employer's plans with respect to an individual during the year. The contribution limitations of section 415 generally apply on an employer-by-employer basis.

Section 403(b)(12) requires a section 403(b) contract that provides for elective deferrals to make elective deferrals available to all employees (the universal availability rule) and requires other contributions to satisfy the general nondiscrimination requirements applicable to qualified plans. These rules are discussed further in this preamble under the heading "Section 403(b) Nondiscrimination and Universal Availability Rules."

A section 403(b) contract is also required to provide that it will satisfy the required minimum distribution requirements of section 401(a)(9), the incidental benefit requirements of section 401(a), and the rollover distribution rules of section 402(c).

Many section 403(b) arrangements of employers that are section 501(c)(3) organizations are subject to the Employee Retirement Income Security Act of 1974 (ERISA), which includes rules substantially identical to the rules for qualified plans, including rules parallel to the section 414(l) transfer rules, the section 401(a)(11) qualified joint and survivor annuity (QJSA) transferee plan rules, and the anti-cutback rules of section 411(d)(6) (which apply to transfers). See sections 204(g), 205, and 208 of ERISA. However, as discussed in this preamble under the heading "Interaction Between Title I of ERISA and Section 403(b) of the Code," Title I of ERISA does not apply to governmental plans, certain church plans, or a tax-exempt employer's section 403(b) program that is not considered to constitute the establishment or maintenance of an "employee pension benefit plan" under Title I of ERISA.

Section 414(c) authorizes the Secretary of the Treasury to issue regulations treating all employees of trades or businesses which are under common control as employed by a single employer.

Explanation of Provisions

Overview

Like the 2004 proposed regulations, these final regulations are a comprehensive update of the current regulations under section 403(b). These regulations replace the existing final regulations that were adopted in 1964 and reflect the numerous legal changes that have been made in section 403(b) since then and many of the positions that have been taken in interpretive guidance that has been issued under section 403(b).

As was noted in the preamble to the 2004 proposed regulations, the effect of the various amendments made to section 403(b) within the past 40 years has been to diminish the extent to which the rules governing section 403(b) plans differ from the rules governing other tax-favored employer-based retirement plans, including arrangements that include salary reduction contributions, such as section 401(k) plans and section 457(b) plans for state and local governmental entities. However, there remain significant differences between section 403(b) plans and section 401(a) and governmental section 457(b) plans For example, section 403(b) is limited to certain specific employers and employees (namely, employees of a public school, employees of a section 501(c)(3) organization, and certain ministers) and to certain funding arrangements (namely, an insurance annuity contract, a custodial account that is limited to mutual fund shares, or a church retirement income account). Also, section 403(b) contains the universal availability requirement for section 403(b) elective deferrals and provides consequences for failing to satisfy certain of the section 403(b) rules (described in this preamble under the heading "Effect of a Failure to Satisfy Section 403(b)")[3] that differ in significant respects from the consequences applicable to qualified plans.

The final regulations, as did the 2004 proposed regulations, require the section 403(b) contract to satisfy both in form and operation the applicable requirements for exclusion. The final regulations also require that the contract be maintained pursuant to a written plan as described in the next section.

The final regulations, like the proposed regulations, provide rules under which tax-exempt entities are aggregated and treated as a single employer under section 414(c). These rules apply to plans referenced in section 414(b), (c), (m), (o), and (t), such as plans qualified under section 401(a) or 403(a), as well as section 403(b) plans.

Comments on the 2004 proposed regulations raised a number of questions and concerns about:

- The requirement in the 2004 proposed regulations under which a section 403(b) contract would be required to be maintained pursuant to a written plan;
- The elimination of certain non-statutory exclusions that a section 403(b) plan was permitted to have under Notice 89-23 (1989-1 CB 654) for purposes of the universal availability rule;
- The elimination of Rev. Rul. 90-24 (1990-1 CB 97), which allowed a section 403(b) contract to be exchanged for another contract; and
- The controlled group rules under section 414(c) for entities that are tax-exempt under section 501(a).

These final regulations include a number of revisions to reflect the comments received, as described further in this preamble.

Written Plan Requirement

These regulations retain the requirement from the 2004 proposed regulations that a section 403(b) contract be issued pursuant to a written plan which, in both form and operation, satisfies the requirements of section 403(b) and these

---

[3] Other differences between the rules applicable to section 403(b) plans and qualified plans include the following: the definition of compensation (including the five-year rule) in section 403(b)(3); the special section 403(b) catch-up elective deferral in section 402(g)(7); and the section 415 aggregation rules. An additional difference relates to when a severance from employment occurs for purposes of section 403(b) plans maintained by State and local government employers. See § 1.403(b)-6(h) of these regulations.

regulations. This requirement implements the statutory requirements of section 403(b)(1)(D), which provides that the contract must be purchased "under a plan" that satisfies the nondiscrimination requirements delineated in section 403(b)(12).

The existence of a written plan facilitates the allocation of plan responsibilities among the employer, the issuer of the contract, and any other parties involved in implementing the plan. Without such a central document for a comprehensive summary of responsibilities, there is a risk that many of the important responsibilities required under the statute and final regulations may not be allocated to any party. While a section 403(b) contract issued to an employee can provide for the issuer to perform many of these functions by itself, the contract cannot satisfy the function of setting forth the eligibility criteria for other employees, nor can the issuer by itself coordinate those Code requirements that depend on other contracts, such as the loan limitations under section 72(p). The issuer must rely on information or representations provided by either the employer or the employee for employment-based information that is essential for compliance with section 403(b) provisions, such as the limitations on elective deferrals in section 402(g) and the requirements of section 72(p)(2) for a plan loan that is not a taxable deemed distribution. In addition to providing a central locus to coordinate those functions, the maintenance of a written plan also benefits participants by providing a central document setting forth their rights and enables government agencies to determine whether the arrangements satisfy applicable law and, in particular, for determining which employees are eligible to participate in the plan.

The 2004 proposed regulations would have required that the section 403(b) plan include all of the material provisions regarding eligibility, benefits, applicable limitations, the contracts available under the plan, and the time and form under which benefit distributions would be made. The proposed regulations would not have required that there be a single plan document. However, under the proposed regulations, the written plan requirement would be satisfied by complying with the plan document rules applicable to qualified plans.

Some comments raised concerns that the written plan requirement would impose additional administrative burdens. In response, the final regulations make a number of clarifications, including that the plan is permitted to allocate to the employer or another person the responsibility for performing functions to administer the plan, including functions to comply with section 403(b). Any such allocation must identify who is responsible for compliance with the requirements of the Code that apply based on the aggregated contracts issued to a participant, including loans under section 72(p) and the requirements for obtaining a hardship withdrawal under § 1.403(b)-6 of these regulations.

Additional comments recommended that certain responsibilities be permitted to be allocated to employees. The IRS and Treasury Department have concluded that it is generally inappropriate to allocate these responsibilities to employees for a number of reasons. First, employees often lack the expertise to systematically meet these responsibilities and may not recognize the importance of performing these actions (including not fully appreciating the tax consequences of failing to perform the responsibility). Second, an individual employee may have a self-interest in a particular transaction. In addition, while there are various factors that will often cause an employer or issuer to have an interest in procedures that ensure that the requirements of section 403(b) are satisfied (including income tax withholding requirements), an employee generally bears the income tax exposure and other risks of failing to comply with rules set forth in the plan. The IRS and Treasury Department believe it is important to prevent failures in advance so as to minimize the cases in which the adverse effects of a failure fall on the employee. See the discussion in this preamble under the heading "Contract Exchanges."

In response to comments, the final regulations clarify the requirement that the plan include all of the material provisions by permitting the plan to incorporate by reference other documents, including the insurance policy or custodial account, which as a result of such reference would become part of the plan. As a result, a plan may include a wide variety of documents, but it is important for the employer that adopts the plan to ensure that there is no conflict with other documents that are incorporated by reference. If a plan does incorporate other documents by reference, then, in the event of a conflict with another document, except in rare and unusual cases, the plan would govern. In the case of a plan that is funded through multiple issuers, it is expected that an employer would adopt a single plan document to coordinate administration among the issuers, rather than having a separate document for each issuer.

Finally, comments also indicated that, while section 403(b) contracts that are subject to ERISA are maintained pursuant to written plans, there may be a potential cost associated with satisfying the written plan requirement for those employers that do not have existing plan documents, such as public schools. To address this concern, the IRS and Treasury Department expect to publish guidance which includes model plan provisions that may be used by public school employers for this purpose. Because the requirement for a written plan will not go into effect until 2009 (see the discussion under the heading "Applicability date"), employers would be expected to adopt a written plan (including applicable amendments) no later than the applicability date of these regulations.

Contract Exchanges, Plan-to-Plan Transfers, and Purchases of Permissive Service Credit

The final regulations, like the 2004 proposed regulations, provide for three specific kinds of non-taxable exchanges or transfers of amounts in section 403(b) contracts. Specifically, under the final regulations, a non-taxable exchange or transfer is permitted for a section 403(b) contract if either: (1) it is a mere change of investment within the same plan (contract exchange); (2) it constitutes a plan-to-plan transfer, so that there is another employer plan receiving the exchange; or (3) it is a transfer to purchase permissive service credit (or a repayment to a defined benefit governmental plan). If an exchange or transfer does not constitute a change of investment within the plan, a plan-to-plan transfer, or a purchase of permissive service credit, the exchange or transfer would be treated as a taxable distribution of benefits in the form of property if the exchange occurs after a distributable event (assuming the distribution is not rolled over to an eligible retirement plan) or as a taxable conversion to a section 403(c) nonqualified annuity contract if a distributable event has not occurred. See the "Effect of a Failure to Satisfy Section 403(b)" section in this preamble for discussion of section 403(c) nonqualified annuity contracts. In any case in which a distributable event has occurred, a participant in a section 403(b) plan can always change the investment through a distribution and non-taxable rollover from a section 403(b) contract to an IRA annuity, as long as the distribution is an eligible rollover distribution. Note, however, that an IRA annuity cannot include provisions permitting participant loans. See section 408(e)(3) and (4) and §§ 1.408-1(c)(5) and 1.408-3(c).

Any contract exchange, plan-to-plan transfer, or purchase of permissive service credit that is permitted under the final regulations is not treated as a distribution for purposes of the section 403(b) distribution restrictions (so that such an exchange or transfer may be made before severance from employment or another distribution event).

Contract Exchanges

Rev. Rul. 73-124 (1973-1 CB 200) and Rev. Rul. 90-24 (1990-1 CB 97) dealt with contract exchanges. Rev. Rul. 73-124 had allowed section 403(b) contracts to be exchanged, without income inclusion, if, pursuant to an agreement with the employer, the employee cashed in the first contract and immediately transmitted the cash proceeds for contribution to the successor contract to which all subsequent employer contributions would be made. This ruling was replaced by Rev. Rul. 90-24 which does not provide for the first contract to be cashed in but allows section 403(b) contracts to be exchanged, without income inclusion, so long as the successor contract includes distribution restrictions that are the same or more stringent than the distribution restrictions in the contract that is being exchanged.

The 2004 proposed regulations would have imposed additional restrictions on contract exchanges by limiting tax-free contract exchanges to situations in which the new contract is provided under the plan. The proposal was intended to improve compliance with the Code requirements that apply on an aggregated basis because, without coordination, it is difficult, if not impossible, for a plan to comply with those tax requirements. These requirements include certain distribution restrictions, including the rule that requires the suspension of deferrals for a plan that uses the hardship withdrawal suspension safe harbor rules for elective deferrals, and the section 72(p) rules for loans. In addition, these changes make it easier for employers to respond to an IRS inquiry or audit. For example, where assets have been transferred to an insurance carrier or mutual fund that has no subsequent connection to the plan or the employer, IRS audits and related investigations have revealed that employers encounter substantial difficulty in demonstrating compliance with hardship withdrawal and loan rules. These problems are particularly acute when an individual's benefits are held by numerous carriers. Such multiple contract issuers are commonly associated with plans in which Rev. Rul. 90-24 exchanges have occurred.

Commentators generally objected to the proposal to limit exchanges allowed under Rev. Rul. 90-24. They argued that such exchanges enable participants to change funding arrangements and claimed that these exchanges have generally been responsible for improved efficiency and lower cost in the section 403(b) market. Comments often included specific suggestions, such as limiting any restrictions on exchanges to active employees and effectuating compliance with loan restrictions by alternative methods, such as having the issuer report loans on, for example, a Form 1099-R (Distributions From Pensions, Annuities, Retirement or Profit-Sharing Plans, IRA, Insurance Contracts), or notify the employer about loans. Other comments included a recommendation that the employer be involved to ensure that the exchange is within the plan. Comments also suggested that a grandfather may be necessary for exchanges made before the applicability date of the restrictions imposed by the final regulations.

These final regulations include a number of changes to reflect these comments. The regulations allow contract exchanges with certain characteristics associated with Rev. Rul. 90-24, but under rules that are generally similar to those applicable to qualified plans.

Unlike the 2004 proposed regulations, these regulations permit an exchange of one contract for another to constitute a mere change of investment within the same plan, but only if certain conditions are satisfied in order to facilitate compliance with tax requirements. Specifically, the other contract must include distribution restrictions that are not less stringent than those imposed on the contract being exchanged and the employer must enter into an agreement with the issuer of the other contract under which the employer and the issuer will from time to time in the future provide each other with certain information. This includes information concerning the participant's employment and information that takes into account other section 403(b) contracts or qualified employer plans, such as whether a severance from employment has occurred for purposes of the distribution restrictions and whether the hardship withdrawal rules in the regulations are satisfied. Additional information that is required is information necessary for the resulting contract or any other contract to which contributions have been made by the employer to satisfy other tax requirements, such as whether a plan loan constitutes a deemed distribution under section 72(p).

These regulations also authorize the IRS to issue guidance of general applicability allowing exchanges in other cases. This authority is limited to cases in which the resulting contract has procedures that the IRS determines are reasonably designed to ensure compliance with those requirements of section 403(b) or other tax provisions that depend on either information concerning the participant's employment or information that takes into account other section 403(b) contracts or qualified employer plans. For example, the procedures must be reasonably designed to determine whether a severance from employment has occurred for purposes of the distribution restrictions, whether the hardship withdrawal rules are satisfied, and whether a plan loan constitutes a deemed distribution under section 72(p). By contrast, procedures that rely on an employee certification, such as whether a severance from employment has occurred or whether the participant has other outstanding loans, would generally not be adequate to meet this standard, because such a certification is not disinterested, and also because of the lack of employer oversight in the certification process to ensure accuracy.

Plan-to-Plan Transfers

The final regulations expand the rules in the 2004 proposed regulations under which plan-to-plan transfers would have been permitted only if the participant was an employee of the employer maintaining the receiving plan. Under the final regulations, plan-to-plan transfers are permitted if the participant whose assets are being transferred is an employee or former employee of the employer (or business of the employer) that maintains the receiving plan and certain additional requirements are met. However, the final regulations retain the rules that were in the 2004 proposed regulations prohibiting a plan-to-plan transfer to a qualified plan, an eligible plan under section 457(b), or any other type of plan that is not a section 403(b) plan, except as described in the next paragraph. Similarly, a section 403(b) plan is not permitted to accept a transfer from a qualified plan, an eligible plan under section 457(b), or any other type of plan that is not a section 403(b) plan.

Purchases of Permissive Service Credit and Certain Repayments

The final regulations, like the 2004 proposed regulations, include an exception permitting a section 403(b) plan to provide for the transfer of its assets to a qualified plan under section 401(a) to purchase permissive service credit under a defined benefit governmental plan or to make a repayment to a defined benefit governmental plan.

Limitations on Contributions

The final regulations, like the 2004 proposed regulations, provide that the section 403(b) exclusion applies only to the extent that all amounts contributed by the employer for the purchase of an annuity contract for the participant do not exceed the applicable limits under section 415. The final regulations retain the rule in the 2004 proposed regulations that if an excess annual addition is made to a contract that otherwise satisfies the requirements of section 403(b), then the portion of the contract that includes the excess will fail to be a section 403(b) contract (and instead will be a contract to which section 403(c), relating to nonqualified annuity contracts, applies) and the remaining portion of the contract that includes the contribution that is not in excess of the section 415 limitations is a section 403(b) contract. This rule under which only the excess annual addition is subject to section 403(c) does not apply unless, for the year of the excess and each year thereafter, the issuer of the contract maintains separate accounts for the portion that includes the excess and for the section 403(b) portion (which is the portion that includes the amount that is not in excess of the section 415 limitations).

With respect to section 403(b) elective deferrals, section 403(b) applies only if the contract is purchased under a plan that includes the elective deferral limits under section 402(g), including aggregation of all plans, contracts, or arrangements of the employer that are subject to the limits of section 402(g). As in the 2004 proposed regulations, the final regulations require a section 403(b) contract to include this limit on section 403(b) elective deferrals, as imposed under sections 401(a)(30) and 402(g). For purposes of the final regulations, the term "elective deferral" includes a designated Roth contribution as well as a pre-tax elective contribution. These rules are generally the same as the rules for qualified cash or deferred arrangements (CODAs) under section 401(k).

Any contribution made for a participant to a section 403(b) contract for a taxable year that exceeds either the section 415 maximum annual contribution limits or the section 402(g) elective deferral limit constitutes an excess contribution that is included in gross income for that taxable year (or, if later, the taxable year in which the contract becomes nonforfeitable). The final regulations, like the 2004 proposed regulations, provide that the section 403(b) plan (including contracts under the plan) may provide that any excess deferral as a result of a failure to comply with the section 402(g) elective deferral limit for the taxable year with respect to any section 403(b) elective deferral made for a participant by the employer will be distributed to the participant, with allocable net income, no later than April 15 or otherwise in accordance with section 402(g).

Catch-up Contributions

A section 403(b) plan may provide for additional catch-up contributions for a participant who is age 50 by the end of the year, provided that those age 50 catch-up contributions do not exceed the catch-up limit under section 414(v) for the taxable year ($5,000 for 2007). In addition, a section 403(b) plan may provide that an employee of a qualified organization who has at least 15 years of service (disregarding any period during which an individual is not an employee of the eligible employer) is entitled to a special section 403(b) catch-up limit. Under the special section 403(b) catch-up limit, the section 402(g) limit is increased by the lowest of the following three amounts: (i) $3,000; (ii) the excess of $15,000 over the amount not included in gross income for prior taxable years by reason of the special section 403(b) catch-up rules, plus elective deferrals that are designated Roth contributions;[4] or (iii) the excess of (A) $5,000 multiplied by

---

[4] A technical correction was made to section 402(g)(7)(A)(ii) by section 407(a) the Gulf Opportunity Zone Act of 2005 (119 Stat. 2577), P.L 109-135, to clarify that the aggregate $15,000 limit on such contributions was reduced not only by pre-tax elective deferrals made pursuant to the special section 403(b) catch-up rules, but also by designated Roth contributions. Treasury has recommended that this language be further changed to reflect the intent that the reduction for designated Roth contributions at section 402(g)(7)(A)(ii)(II) be limited to designated Roth contributions that have been made pursuant to the special section 403(b) catch-up rules.

the number of years of service of the employee with the qualified organization, over (B) the total elective deferrals made for the employee by the qualified organization for prior taxable years. For this purpose, a qualified organization is an eligible employer that is a school, hospital, health and welfare service agency (including a home health service agency), or a church-related organization.

The 2004 proposed regulations defined a health and welfare service agency as either an organization whose primary activity is to provide medical care as defined in section 213(d)(1) (such as a hospice), or a section 501(c)(3) organization whose primary activity is the prevention of cruelty to individuals or animals or which provides substantial personal services to the needy as part of its primary activity (such as a section 501(c)(3) organization that provides meals to needy individuals). In response to several commentators' requests, the final regulations expand this definition to include an adoption agency and an agency that provides either home health services or assistance to individuals with substance abuse problems or that provides help to the disabled.

Like the 2004 proposed regulations, the final regulations provide that any catch-up contribution for an employee who is eligible for both an age 50 catch-up and the special section 403(b) catch-up is treated first as a special section 403(b) catch-up to the extent a special section 403(b) catch-up is permitted, and then as an amount contributed as an age 50 catch-up (to the extent the age 50 catch-up amount exceeds the maximum special section 403(b) catch-up).

Timing of Distributions and Benefits

The final regulations, like the 2004 proposed regulations, contain provisions reflecting the statutory rules regarding when distributions can be made from a section 403(b) plan. Distributions of amounts attributable to section 403(b) elective deferrals may not be paid to a participant earlier than when the participant has a severance from employment, has a hardship, becomes disabled (within the meaning of section 72(m)(7)), or attains age 59½. Hardship is generally defined under regulations issued under section 401(k). In addition, amounts held in a custodial account attributable to employer contributions (that are not section 403(b) elective deferrals) may not be paid to a participant before the participant has a severance from employment, becomes disabled (within the meaning of section 72(m)(7)), or attains age 59½. This rule also applies to amounts transferred out of a custodial account to an annuity contract or retirement income account, including earnings thereon.

The final regulations, as did the 2004 proposed regulations, include a number of exceptions to the timing restrictions. For example, the rule for elective deferrals does not apply to distributions of section 403(b) elective deferrals (not including earnings thereon) that were contributed before January 1, 1989.

The final regulations, as did the 2004 proposed regulations, reflect the direct rollover rules of section 401(a)(31) and the related requirements of section 402(f) concerning the written explanation requirement for distributions that qualify as eligible rollover distributions, including conforming the timing rule to the rule for qualified plans.

In addition to the restrictions described in this preamble, the final regulations generally retain, with certain modifications, the additional rules from the 2004 proposed regulations relating to when distributions are permitted to be made from a section 403(b) plan, including the restrictions described in this preamble imposed by section 403(b)(7)(A)(ii) and (11) on distribution of amounts held in custodial accounts and elective deferrals, and the tax treatment of distributions from section 403(b) plans. Comments raised no objections to the various rules that were proposed in 2004, other than concerning the general rule requiring the occurrence of a stated event. The 2004 proposed regulations generally would have required the occurrence of a stated event in order to commence distributions of amounts attributable to employer contributions to section 403(b) plans other than elective deferrals or distributions from custodial accounts. The stated event rule is substantially the same as the rule applicable to qualified defined contribution plans that are not money purchase pension plans (under § 1.401-1(b)(1)(ii)), so that a plan is permitted to provide for a distribution upon completion of a fixed number of years (such as five years of participation), the attainment of a stated age, or upon the occurrence of some other identified event (such as the occurrence of a financial need,[5] including a need to buy a home).

However, the final regulations make a number of changes relating to distributions. First, the final regulations clarify that after-tax employee contributions are not subject to any in-service distribution restrictions. Second, the regulations address comments that were made regarding certain disability arrangements by clarifying that, if an insurance contract includes provisions under which contributions will be continued in the event a participant becomes disabled, then that benefit is treated as an incidental benefit that must satisfy the incidental benefit requirement applicable to qualified plans (at § 1.401-1(b)(1)(ii)). Third, changes were made to reflect elective deferrals that are designated Roth contributions, discussed further later in this preamble under the heading, "Requirement of Certain Separate Accounts Under Section 403(b)." Fourth, § 1.403(b)-7(b)(5) has been added referencing the automatic rollover rules of section 401(a)(31), in accordance with section 403(b)(10). See Notice 2005-5, 2005-1 CB 337, for rules interpreting this requirement. Fifth, a cross-reference to certain employment tax rules was added, discussed under the heading "Employment Taxes." Sixth, in response to comments, the final regulations provide that the general rule requiring the occurrence of a stated event in order for distributions to commence does not apply to insurance contracts issued before January 1, 2009, and a special rule has been added allowing conforming amendments to be adopted by plans that are subject to ERISA. Section 1.403(b)-10(c) has been clarified to indicate that in order to be treated as a distribution under this section, the distribution must be pursuant to a QDRO as described in section 206(d)(3) of ERISA and the Department of Labor's guidance.

---

[5] See, for example, Rev. Rul. 56-693 (1956-2 CB 282).

Severance From Employment

The final regulations, like the 2004 proposed regulations, define severance from employment in a manner that is generally the same as the regulations under section 401(k) (see § 1.401(k)-1(d)(2)), but provide that, for purposes of distributions from a section 403(b) plan, a severance from employment occurs on any date on which the employee ceases to be employed by an eligible employer that maintains the section 403(b) plan. Thus, a severance from employment would occur when an employee ceases to be employed by an eligible employer, even though the employee may continue to be employed by an entity that is part of the same controlled group but that is not an eligible employer, or on any date on which the employee works in a capacity that is not employment with an eligible employer. Examples of the situations that constitute a severance from employment include: an employee transferring from a section 501(c)(3) organization to a for-profit subsidiary of the section 501(c)(3) organization; an employee ceasing to work for a public school, but continuing to be employed by the same State; and an individual employed as a minister for an entity that is neither a State nor a section 501(c)(3) organization ceasing to perform services as a minister, but continuing to be employed by the same entity.

Section 401(a)(9)

The final regulations, like the 2004 proposed regulations, require section 403(b) plans to comply with rules similar to those in the existing regulations relating to the required minimum distribution requirements of section 401(a)(9), but with some minor changes (for example, omitting the special rules for 5-percent owners). Thus, section 403(b) contracts must satisfy the incidental benefit rules. Guidance concerning the application of the incidental benefit requirements to permissible nonretirement benefits such as life, accident, or health benefits is contained in revenue rulings.[6]

Loans

The final regulations adopt the provisions in the 2004 proposed regulations relating to loans to participants from a section 403(b) contract.

QDROs

The final regulations also adopt the 2004 proposed regulations' limited rules relating to QDROs under section 414(p). Section 414(p)(9) provides that the QDRO rules only apply to plans that are subject to the anti-alienation provisions of section 401(a)(13), except that section 414(p)(9) also provides that the

---

[6] See, for example, Rev. Rul. 61-121 (1961-2 CB 65); Rev. Rul. 68-304 (1968-1 CB 179); Rev. Rul. 72-240 (1972-1 CB 108); Rev. Rul. 72-241 (1972-1 CB 108); Rev. Rul. 73-239 (1973-1 CB 201); and Rev. Rul. 74-115 (1974-1 CB 100).

section 414(p) QDRO rules apply to a section 403(b) contract. The final regulations, like the proposed regulations, clarify that the QDRO rules under section 414(p) apply to section 403(b) plans. The Secretary of Labor has authority to interpret the QDRO provisions, section 206(d)(3), and its parallel provision at section 414(p) of the Code, and to issue QDRO regulations in consultation with the Secretary of the Treasury. 29 USC 1056(d)(3)(N). Under section 401(n) of the Internal Revenue Code, the Secretary of the Treasury has authority to issue rules and regulations necessary to coordinate the requirements of section 414(p) (and the regulations issued by the Secretary of Labor thereunder) with the other provisions of Chapter I of Subtitle A of the Code.

Taxation of Distributions and Benefits From a Section 403(b) Contract

The final regulations, like the 2004 proposed regulations, reflect the statutory provisions regarding the taxation of distributions and benefits from section 403(b) contracts, including the provision that generally only amounts actually distributed from a section 403(b) contract are includible in the gross income of the recipient under section 72 for the year in which distributed. The final regulations also reflect the rule that any payment that constitutes an eligible rollover distribution is not taxed in the year distributed to the extent the payment is rolled over to an eligible retirement plan. The payor must withhold 20 percent Federal income tax, however, if an eligible rollover distribution is not rolled over in a direct rollover. Another provision requires the payor to give proper written notice to the section 403(b) participant or beneficiary concerning the eligible rollover distribution provision.

Section 403(b) Nondiscrimination and Universal Availability Rules

Nondiscrimination

Section 403(b)(12)(A)(i) requires that employer contributions, other than elective deferrals, and after-tax employee contributions made under a section 403(b) contract satisfy a specified series of requirements (the nondiscrimination requirements) in the same manner as a qualified plan under section 401(a). These nondiscrimination requirements include rules relating to nondiscrimination in contributions, benefits, and coverage (sections 401(a)(4) and 410(b)), a limitation on the amount of compensation that can be taken into account (section 401(a)(17)), and the average contribution percentage rules of section 401(m) (relating to matching and after-tax employee contributions).

Notice 89-23 discusses these requirements and provides a good faith reasonable standard for satisfying these requirements. The 2004 proposed regulations would have eliminated the good faith reasonable standard for satisfying the nondiscrimination requirements of section 403(b)(12)(A)(i) for non-governmental plans. Comments acknowledged the need for and the IRS's authority to make this change. Accordingly, these final regulations do not include the Notice 89-23 good faith reasonable standard.

However, as discussed in this preamble under the heading "Treatment of Controlled Groups that Include Certain Entities," the Notice 89-23 good faith reasonable standard will continue to apply to State and local public schools (and certain church entities) for determining the controlled group. Although the general nondiscrimination requirements do not apply to governmental plans (within the meaning of section 414(d)), these plans are required to limit the amount of compensation to the amount permitted under section 401(a)(17) for all purposes under the plan, including, for example the amount of compensation taken into account for employer contributions, and are required to satisfy the universal availability rule (described in this preamble under the heading "Universal Availability for Elective Deferrals"). A non-governmental section 403(b) plan that provides for nonelective employer contributions must satisfy the coverage requirements of section 410(b) and the nondiscrimination requirements of section 401(a)(4) with respect to such contributions.

These final regulations, like the 2004 proposed regulations, require a section 403(b) plan to comply with the nondiscrimination requirements for matching contributions in the same manner as a qualified plan. Thus, a non-governmental section 403(b) plan that provides for matching contribution must satisfy the nondiscrimination requirements of section 401(m). The nondiscrimination requirements are generally tested using compensation as defined in section 414(s) and are applied on an aggregated basis taking into account all plans of the employer. See the discussion under the heading "Treatment of Controlled Groups that Include Certain Entities."

The nondiscrimination requirements do not apply to section 403(b) elective deferrals. Instead, a universal availability requirement, discussed further in the next section, applies to all section 403(b) elective deferrals (including elective deferrals made under a governmental section 403(b) plan).

Universal Availability for Elective Deferrals

The universal availability requirement of section 403(b)(12)(A)(ii) provides that all employees of the eligible employer must be permitted to elect to have section 403(b) elective deferrals contributed on their behalf if any employee of the eligible employer may elect to have the organization make section 403(b) elective deferrals. Under the 2004 proposed regulations, the universal availability requirement would not have been satisfied unless the contributions were made pursuant to a section 403(b) plan and the plan permitted all employees of an employer an opportunity to make elective deferrals if any employee of that employer has the right to make elective deferrals.

The rules in the final regulations relating to the universal availability requirement are substantially similar to those in the 2004 proposed regulations. The final regulations clarify that the employee's right to make elective deferrals also includes the right to designate section 403(b) elective deferrals as designated Roth contributions (if any employee of the eligible employer may elect to have the organization make section 403(b) elective deferrals as designated Roth contributions).

The preamble to the 2004 proposed regulations requested comments regarding certain exclusions that have been permitted under transitional guidance issued in 1989. Specifically, Notice 89-23 had allowed, pending issuance of regulatory guidance, the exclusion of the following classes of employees for purposes of the universal availability rule: employees who are covered by a collective bargaining agreement; employees who make a one-time election to participate in a governmental plan described in section 414(d), instead of a section 403(b) plan; professors who are providing services on a temporary basis to another public school for up to one year and for whom section 403(b) contributions are being made at a rate no greater than the rate each such professor would receive under the section 403(b) plan of the original public school; and employees who are affiliated with a religious order and who have taken a vow of poverty where the religious order provides for the support of such employees in their retirement.

The comments submitted in response to the request generally requested to have these exclusions continue to be allowed. However, after consideration of the comments received, the IRS and Treasury Department have concluded that these exclusions are inconsistent with the statute and, accordingly, they are not permitted under these regulations. Nonetheless, as described further in the following paragraphs, other rules may provide relief with respect to individuals who are under a vow of poverty and to certain university professors affected.

Rev. Rul. 68-123 (1968-1 CB 35), as clarified by Rev. Rul. 83-127 (1983-2 CB 25), generally excludes from gross income, and from wage withholding, income of an individual working under a vow of poverty for an employer controlled by a church and the individual is treated as working as an agent of the church, not as an employee. While these regulations do not provide an exclusion from the universal availability requirement for individuals working under a vow of poverty, individuals who work for an institution that is controlled by the church organization and whose compensation from the employer is not treated as wages for purposes of income tax withholding under Rev. Rul. 68-123 may be excluded from the section 403(b) plan without violating the universal availability requirement because they are not treated as employees of the entity maintaining the section 403(b) plan.

With respect to an exclusion relating to visiting professors, if an individual is rendering services to a university as a visiting professor, but continues to receive his or her compensation from his or her home university and elective deferrals on his or her behalf are made under the home university's section 403(b) plan, the final regulations do not, for purposes of section 403(b) and in any case in which such treatment is appropriate, preclude the plan maintained by the home university from treating the visiting professor as an eligible employee of the home university.

The discussion in this preamble under the heading "Applicability date" describes transition relief for any existing plan that excludes, in accordance with Notice 89-23, collective bargaining employees, visiting professors, government employees who make a one-time election, or employees who work under a vow of poverty.

Rules Relating to Funding Arrangements

These regulations retain, with certain modifications, the rules in the 2004 proposed regulations relating to the permitted investments for a section 403(b) contract. In general, a section 403(b) plan must be funded either by an annuity contract issued by an insurance company qualified to issue annuities in a State or a custodial account held by a bank (or a person who satisfies the conditions in section 401(f)(2)) where all of the amounts in the account are held for the exclusive benefit of plan participants or their beneficiaries in regulated investment companies (mutual funds) and certain other conditions are satisfied (including restrictions on distributions). Additional rules apply with respect to retirement income accounts for plans of a church or a convention or association of churches as discussed in the next section.

Special Rules for Church Plans' Retirement Income Accounts

The final regulations, like the 2004 proposed regulations, include a number of special rules for church plans. Under section 403(b)(9), a retirement income account for employees of a church-related organization is treated as an annuity contract for purposes of section 403(b). Under these regulations, the rules for a retirement income account are based largely on the provisions of section 403(b)(9) and the legislative history of TEFRA. The regulations define a retirement income account as a defined contribution program established or maintained by a church-related organization under which (i) there is separate accounting for the retirement income account's interest in the underlying assets (namely, it must be possible at all times to determine the retirement income account's interest in the underlying assets and to distinguish that interest from any interest that is not part of the retirement income account), (ii) investment performance is based on gains and losses on those assets, and (iii) the assets held in the account cannot be used for, or diverted to, purposes other than for the exclusive benefit of plan participants or their beneficiaries. For this purpose, assets are treated as diverted to the employer if the employer borrows assets from the account. A retirement income account must be maintained pursuant to a program which is a plan and the plan document must state (or otherwise evidence in a similarly clear manner) the intent to constitute a retirement income account.

If any asset of a retirement income account is owned or used by a participant or beneficiary, then that ownership or use is treated as a distribution to that participant or beneficiary. The regulations also provide that a retirement income account that is treated as an annuity contract is not a custodial account (even if it is invested in stock of a regulated investment company).

A life annuity can generally only be provided from an individual account by the purchase of an insurance annuity contract. However, in light of the special rules applicable to church retirement income accounts, the final regulations, like the 2004 proposed regulations, permit a life annuity to be paid from such an account if certain conditions are satisfied. The conditions are that the distribution from the account has an actuarial present value, at the annuity starting date, that is equal to the participant's or beneficiary's accumulated benefit, based on reasonable actuarial assumptions, including assumptions regarding interest and mortality, and that the plan sponsor guarantee benefits in the event that a payment is due that exceeds the participant's or beneficiary's accumulated benefit.

Termination of a Section 403(b) Plan

The final regulations adopt the provisions of the 2004 proposed regulations permitting an employer to amend its section 403(b) plan to eliminate future contributions for existing participants, and allowing plan provisions that permit plan termination and a resulting distribution of accumulated benefits, with the associated right to roll over eligible rollover distributions to an eligible retirement plan, such as an individual retirement account or annuity (IRA). Comments on the rules in the 2004 proposed regulations regarding plan termination were favorable. In general, the distribution of accumulated benefits is permitted under these regulations only if the employer (taking into account all entities that are treated as a single employer under section 414 on the date of the termination) does not make contributions to any section 403(b) contract that is not part of the plan during the period beginning on the date of plan termination and ending 12 months after distribution of all assets from the terminated plan. However, if at all times during the period beginning 12 months before the termination and ending 12 months after distribution of all assets from the terminated plan, fewer than 2 percent of the employees who were eligible under the section 403(b) plan as of the date of plan termination are eligible under the alternative section 403(b) contract, the other section 403(b) contract is disregarded. In order for a section 403(b) plan to be considered terminated, all accumulated benefits under the plan must be distributed to all participants and beneficiaries as soon as administratively practicable after termination of the plan. A distribution for this purpose includes delivery of a fully paid individual insurance annuity contract.

Effect of a Failure to Satisfy Section 403(b)

These regulations include revisions to the 2004 proposed regulations that address the effects of a failure to satisfy section 403(b). Section 403(b)(5) provides for all of the contracts purchased for an employee by an employer to be treated as a single contract for purposes of section 403(b). Thus, if a contract fails to satisfy any of the section 403(b) requirements, then not only that contract but also any other contract purchased for that individual by that employer would fail to be a contract that qualifies for tax-deferral under section 403(b).

Under these regulations, as under the 2004 proposed regulations, if a contract includes any amount that fails to satisfy the requirements of these regulations, then, except for special rules relating to vesting conditions and excess contributions (under section 415 or section 402(g)), that contract and any other contract purchased for that individual by that employer does not constitute a section 403(b) contract. In addition, if a contract is not established pursuant to a written plan, then the contract does not satisfy section 403(b). Thus, if an employer fails to have a written plan, any contract purchased by that employer would not be a section 403(b) contract. Similarly, if an employer is not an eligible employer for purposes of section 403(b), none of the contracts purchased by that employer is a section 403(b) contract. If a plan fails to satisfy the nondiscrimination rules (including a failure to operate the plan in accordance with its coverage provisions or a failure to operate the plan in a manner that satisfies the nondiscrimination rules), none of the contracts issued under the plan would be section 403(b) contracts.

However, under these regulations, any operational failure, other than those described in the preceding paragraph, that is solely within a specific contract generally will not adversely affect the contracts issued to other employees that qualify in form and operation with section 403(b). Thus, for example, if an employee's elective deferrals under a contract, when aggregated with any other contract, plan, or arrangement of the employer for that employee during a calendar year, exceed the maximum deferral amount permitted under section 402(g)(1)(A) (as made applicable by section 403(b)(1)(E)), the failure would adversely affect the contracts issued to the employee by that employer, but would not adversely affect any other employee's contracts.

Requirement of Certain Separate Accounts Under Section 403(b)

The final regulations, like the 2004 proposed regulations, include technical provisions addressing certain situations in which a separate account[7] is necessary under section 403(b). For example, a separate bookkeeping account is required for any contract in which only a portion of the employee's interest is vested because, in such a case, separate accounting for each type of contribution (and earnings thereon) that is subject to a different vesting schedule is necessary to determine which vested contributions, including earnings thereon, are treated as held under a section 403(b) contract. In addition, the final regulations also clarify that if the section 403(b) plan fails to establish a separate account for contributions in excess of the section 415(c) limitation under section 403(c) (relating to nonqualified annuity contracts whose present values are generally subject to current taxation), so that such excess contributions are commingled in a single insurance contract with contributions intended to qualify under section 403(b) without maintaining a separate account for each amount, then none of the amounts held under the insurance contract qualify for tax deferral under section 403(b). Any such separate account must be established by the time the excess contribution is made to the plan. The separate account for excess contributions under section 415(c) is necessary to effectuate differences in the tax treatment of distributions (for example, because of the need to properly allocate basis under section 72 and separately identify amounts that can be rolled over). Similarly, a separate account is required for elective deferrals to be

---

[7] These rules are not related to segregated asset accounts under section 817(h).

treated as held in a designated Roth account, as described in the following paragraph.

Designated Roth Accounts

These regulations also include final regulations relating to elective deferrals that are designated Roth contributions under a section 403(b) plan. These regulations, however, do not address the taxation of a distribution of designated Roth contributions from a section 403(b) plan. See § 1.402A-1 for those rules. The final regulations relating to elective deferrals under a section 403(b) plan that are designated Roth contributions are substantially unchanged from the proposed regulations that were issued in January of 2006 regarding designated Roth accounts under a section 403(b) plan.[8]

Interaction Between Title I of ERISA and Section 403(b) of the Code

The Treasury Department and the IRS consulted with the Department of Labor in connection with both the 2004 proposed regulations and these final regulations concerning the interaction between Title I of ERISA and section 403(b) of the Internal Revenue Code. In particular, the consultation focused on whether the requirements imposed on employers in these regulations would exceed the scope of the Department of Labor's safe harbor regulation at 29 CFR § 2510.3-2(f) and result in all section 403(b) programs sponsored by tax-exempt employers (other than governmental plans and certain church plans) falling under the purview of ERISA.

According to the Department of Labor, Title I of ERISA generally applies to "any plan, fund, or program . . . established or maintained by an employer or by an employee organization, or by both, to the extent that . . . such plan, fund, or program . . . provides retirement income to employees, or . . . results in a deferral of income by employees for periods extending to the termination of covered employment or beyond." ERISA section 3(2)(A). However, governmental plans and church plans are generally excluded from coverage under Title I of ERISA. ERISA section 4(b)(1) and (2). Therefore, contracts purchased or provided under a program that is either a "governmental plan" under section 3(32) of ERISA or a "church plan" under section 3(33) of ERISA are not generally covered under Title I. However, section 403(b) of the Internal Revenue Code is also available with respect to contracts purchased or provided by employers for employees of a section 501(c)(3) organization, and many programs for the purchase of section 403(b) contracts offered by such employers are covered under Title I of ERISA as part of an "employee pension benefit plan" within the meaning of section 3(2)(A) of ERISA. The Department of Labor promulgated a regulation in 1975, 29 CFR § 2510.3-2(f), describing circumstances under which an employer's program for the purchase of section 403(b) contracts for its employees, which is not otherwise excluded from coverage under Title I, will

---

[8] REG-146459-05, published in the **Federal Register** (71 FR 4320) on January 26, 2006.

not be considered to constitute the establishment or maintenance of an "employee pension benefit plan" under Title I of ERISA.

As described in the preamble to the 2004 proposed regulations, the Department of Labor advised the Treasury Department and the IRS that the proposed regulations did not appear to require, but left open the possibility that an employer may undertake, responsibilities in connection with a section 403(b) program that would exceed the limits in the safe harbor and constitute establishing and maintaining an ERISA-covered plan. Comments submitted on the proposal supported the continued availability of non-Title I section 403(b) programs to employees of tax-exempt employers and asked for additional guidance for employers who offer their employees access to such programs.

According to the Department of Labor, review of the final section 403(b) regulations has not led the Department of Labor to change its view on the principles that apply in determining whether any given section 403(b) program is covered by Title I of ERISA. Even though the differences between the tax rules for section 403(b) programs and those governing other ERISA-covered pension plans may have diminished as a result of the final section 403(b) regulations, the Department of Labor continues to be of the view that tax-exempt employers can comply with the requirements in the section 403(b) regulations and remain within the Department of Labor's safe harbor for tax-sheltered annuity programs funded solely by salary deferrals. The Department of Labor notes, however, that the new section 403(b) regulations offer employers considerable flexibility in shaping the extent and nature of their involvement. The question of whether any particular employer, in complying with the section 403(b) regulations, has established or maintained a plan covered under Title I of ERISA must be analyzed on a case-by-case basis applying the criteria set forth in 29 CFR § 2510.3-2(f) and section 3(2) of ERISA. To assist employers interested in offering their employees access to a tax sheltered annuity program that would not be an ERISA-covered plan, the Department of Labor is issuing, in conjunction with the final publication of this regulation, a Field Assistance Bulletin to provide additional guidance on the interaction of the safe harbor and the requirements in these final regulations. The Field Assistance Bulletin can be found at www.dol.gov/ebsa.

Treatment of Controlled Groups that Include Tax-Exempt Entities

The final regulations retain the basic rules in the 2004 proposed regulations regarding controlled groups for entities that are tax-exempt under section 501(a), but with a number of modifications to reflect the comments that were made. As in the 2004 proposed regulations, these rules are not limited to section 403(b) plans, but apply more broadly for purposes of determining when tax-exempt entities are treated as a single employer under section 414(b), (c), (m), and (o). Thus, for example, these rules apply for purposes of plans maintained by a tax-exempt entity that are intended to be qualified under section 401(a). These rules can apply to treat two section 501(c) organizations as a single employer, or a section 501(c) organization and a non-section 501(c) organization as a single employer, if the organizations are under common control. For a section 501(c)(3) organization that makes contributions to a section 403(b) plan, these rules would be generally relevant for purposes of the nondiscrimination requirements, as well as for the section 415 contribution limitations, the special section 403(b) catch-up contributions, and the section 401(a)(9) minimum distribution rules.

Under the rules in the 2004 proposed regulations, the employer for a plan maintained by a section 501(c) organization would include not only the organization whose employees participate in the plan, but also any other organization that is under common control with the tax-exempt organization. Under the 2004 proposed regulations, the existence of control would be determined based on the facts and circumstances. For this purpose, common control would exist between a tax-exempt organization and another organization if at least 80 percent of the directors or trustees of one organization were either representatives of, or directly or indirectly controlled by, the other organization.[9] The 2004 proposed regulations permitted tax-exempt organizations to choose to be aggregated (permissive aggregation) if they maintained a single plan covering one or more employees from each organization and the organizations regularly coordinated their day-to-day exempt activities. These rules were subject to an overall anti-abuse rule. The final regulations retain the basic rules in the 2004 proposed regulations and the anti-abuse rule, and add an example to illustrate when the anti-abuse rule might apply.

Comments on the 2004 proposed regulations generally approved of the proposed controlled group rules, but some comments argued for expanding the category of entities that can use the permissive aggregation rules. These comments typically did not recommend an overall standard for when permissive aggregation should be permitted, but identified certain specific practices which would be facilitated by permissive aggregation. In response, these regulations authorize the IRS to issue published guidance permitting other types of combinations of entities that include tax-exempt entities to elect to be treated as under common control for one or more specified purposes. This authority is limited to situations in which there are substantial business reasons for maintaining each entity in a separate trust, corporation, or other form, and under which common control treatment would be consistent with the anti-abuse standards in the regulations. It is expected that this authority would not be exercised unless the IRS determines that the organizations are so integrated in their operations as to effectively constitute a single coordinated employer for purposes of sections 414(b), (c), (m), and (o), including common employee benefit plans.

A comment was also received stating that a legally required trusteeship for a labor union that has been imposed in order to correct corruption or financial malpractice[10] should not constitute control. In response, a change was made to the regulations to reflect the intent that whether a person has the power to

---

[9] Treas. Reg. § 1.512(b)-1(l)(4)(i)(b) uses a similar test to determine control of a non-stock organization. Note that those regulations do not reflect amendments that were made in section 512(b)(13) by section 1041(a) of the Taxpayer Relief Act of 1997 (111 Stat. 788).

[10] See 29 USC 462.

appoint and replace a trustee or director is based on facts and circumstances. For example, that power would generally not exist if that power was extremely limited due to the application of other laws, such as where a labor union was put under trusteeship pursuant to a court order, the trusteeship is for the sole purpose of correcting corruption, financial malpractice, or similar circumstances, and the replacement trustees were permitted to serve only for the time necessary for that purpose.

These controlled group rules for tax-exempt entities generally do not apply to certain church entities under section 3121(w)(3). These rules also do not apply to a State or local government or a federal government entity. Until further guidance is issued, church entities under section 3121(w)(3)(A) and (B) and State or local government public schools that sponsor section 403(b) plans can continue to rely on the rules in Notice 89-23 for determining the controlled group.

Employment Taxes

These regulations include several new cross-references to certain rules concerning the application of employment taxes. For example, the definition of an elective deferral at § 1.403(b)-2(a)(7) of these regulations refers to § 1.402(g)(3)-1 of these regulations, which in turn refers to section 3121(a)(5)(D). See § 31.3121(a)(5)-2T of the temporary regulations for additional guidance on section 3121(a)(5)(D) (defining salary reduction agreement for purposes of the Federal Insurance Contributions Act (FICA)).

As another example, § 1.403(b)-7(f) of these regulations generally references the special income tax withholding rules under section 3405 for purposes of income tax withholding on distributions from section 403(b) contracts and also references the special rules at § 1.72(p)-l, Q&A-15, and § 35.3405(c)-1, Q&A-11, relating to income tax withholding for loans deemed distributed from qualified employer plans, including section 403(b) contracts. However, the general income tax withholding rules apply for purposes of income tax withholding for annuity contracts or custodial accounts that are not section 403(b) contracts, as well as for cases in which an annuity contract or custodial account ceases to qualify as a section 403(b) contract. See section 3401 and §§ 1.83-8(a) and 35.3405-1T, Q&A-18.

Effect of These Regulations on Other Guidance

Since the existing regulations were issued in 1964, a number of revenue rulings and other items of guidance under section 403(b) have become outdated as a result of changes in law. In addition, as a result of the inclusion in these regulations of much of the guidance that the IRS has issued regarding section 403(b), these regulations effectively supersede or substantially modify a number of revenue rulings and notices that have been issued under section 403(b). Thus, as indicated in the preamble to the 2004 proposed regulations, the IRS anticipates taking action in the future to obsolete many revenue rulings, notices, and other guidance under section 403(b).[11]

However, the positions taken in certain rulings and other outstanding guidance are expected to be retained. For example, it is intended that the existing rules[12] for determining when employees are performing services for a public school will continue to apply. Further, as discussed above in the preamble under the heading, "Treatment of Controlled Groups that Include Tax-Exempt Entities," church entities under section 3121(w)(3)(A) and (B) and public schools that sponsor section 403(b) plans can continue to rely on the rules in Notice 89-23 for determining the controlled group. In addition, certain positions taken in prior guidance are expected to be reevaluated in light of these regulations, such as Rev. Rul. 2004-67 (2004-28 IRB 28), which revised the group trust rules of Rev. Rul. 81-100 (1981-1 CB 326). With the issuance of these regulations, a number of conforming changes will be considered for the compliance programs maintained by the IRS, as most recently published in Rev. Proc. 2006-27 (2006-22 IRB 945) (EPCRS), including, for example, to reflect the written plan requirement and the positions described above in this preamble under the heading, "Effect of a Failure to Satisfy Section 403(b)."

The prior regulations under section 403(b) had included certain rules for determining the amount of the contributions made for an employee under a defined benefit plan, based on the employee's pension under the plan. These rules are generally no longer applicable for section 403(b) because the limitations on contributions to a section 403(b) contract under section 415(c) are no longer coordinated with accruals under a defined benefit plan.[13] However, the rules for determining the amount of contributions made for an employee under a defined benefit plan in the prior regulations under section 403(b) had also been used for purposes of section 402(b) (relating to nonqualified plans funded through trusts). These regulations replace those rules with regulations under section 402(b) that provide for the same rules (those in the section 403(b) regulations that were in effect prior to these regulations) to continue to apply for purposes of section 402(b). However, these section 402(b) regulations also

---

[11] When these regulations go into effect, the following guidance will be outdated or superseded by these regulations and it is expected that guidance will be issued in the future to formally supersede these items: Rev. Rul. 64-333 (1964-2 CB 114); Rev. Rul. 65-200 (1965-2 CB 141); Rev. Rul. 66-254 (1966-2 CB. 125); Rev. Rul. 66-312 (1966-2 CB 127); Rev. Rul. 67-78 (1967-1 CB 94); Rev. Rul. 67-69 (1967-1 CB 93); Rev. Rul. 67-361 (1967-2 CB 153); Rev. Rul. 67-387 (1967-2 CB 153); Rev. Rul. 67-388 (1967-2 CB 153); Rev. Rul. 68-179 (1968-1 CB 179); Rev. Rul. 68-482 (1968-2 CB 186); Rev. Rul. 68-487 (1968-2 CB 187); Rev.Rul. 68-488 (1968-2 CB 188); Rev. Rul. 69-629 (1969-2 CB 101); Rev. Rul. 70-243 (1970-1 CB 107); Rev. Rul. 87-114 (1987-2 CB 116); Rev. Rul. 90-24 (1990-1 CB 97); Notice 90-73 (1990-2 CB 353); Notice 92-36 (1992-2 CB 364); and Announcement 95-48 (1995-23 IRB 13). In addition, Notice 89-23 (1989-1 CB 654) is likewise superseded as a result of these regulations, except to the extent described above under the heading "Treatment of Controlled Groups that Include Tax-Exempt Entities." It is expected that the following guidance will not be superseded when these regulations are issued in final form: Rev. Rul. 66-254 (1966-2 CB 125); Rev. Rul. 68-33 (1968-1 CB 175); Rev. Rul 68-58 (1968-1 CB 176); Rev. Rul. 68-116 (1968-1 CB 177); Rev. Rul. 68-648 (1968-2 CB 49); Rev. Rul. 68-488 (1968-2 CB 188); and Rev. Rul. 69-146 (1969-1 CB 132).

[12] Rev. Rul. 73-607 (1973-2 CB 145) and Rev. Rul. 80-139 (1980-1 CB 88).

[13] However, see § 1.403(b)-10(f)(2) of these regulations for a special rule applicable to certain church defined benefit plans that were in effect on September 3, 1982.

authorize the Commissioner to issue guidance for determining the amount of the contributions made for an employee under a defined benefit plan under section 402(b).

Applicability Date

These regulations are generally applicable for taxable years beginning after December 31, 2008. Thus, because individuals will almost uniformly be on a calendar taxable year, these regulations will generally apply on January 1, 2009. However, these regulations include a number of explicit transition rules.

For a section 403(b) plan maintained pursuant to one or more collective bargaining agreements that have been ratified and are in effect on July 26, 2007, the regulations do not apply until the earlier of: (1) the date on which the last of such collective bargaining agreements terminates (determined without regard to any extension thereof after July 26, 2007; or (2) July 26, 2010. For a section 403(b) plan maintained by a church-related organization for which the authority to amend the plan is held by a church convention (within the meaning of section 414(e)), the regulations do not apply before the beginning of the first plan year following December 31, 2009.

There are also special applicability dates for several of the specific provisions in these regulations. First, special rules apply to plans which may have included one or more of the exclusions that Notice 89-23 permitted for the universal availability rule, but which are no longer permitted under these regulations. Specifically, a special rule applies if a plan has eligibility conditions for elective deferrals relating to employees who make a one-time election to participate in a governmental plan described in section 414(d) instead of a section 403(b) plan, professors who are providing services on a temporary basis to another school for up to one year and for whom section 403(b) contributions are being made at a rate no greater than the rate each such professor would receive under the section 403(b) plan of the original school, or employees who are affiliated with a religious order and who have taken a vow of poverty where the religious order provides for the support of such employees in their retirement. If, as permitted by Notice 89-23, a plan excludes any of these three classes of employees from eligibility to make elective deferrals on July 26, 2007, the plan is permitted to continue that exclusion until taxable years beginning on or after January 1, 2010. In addition, if a plan excludes employees covered by a collective bargaining agreement from eligibility to make elective deferrals on July 26, 2007, the plan is permitted to continue that exclusion until the later of (i) the first day of the first taxable year that begins after December 31, 2008, or (ii) the earlier of (I) the date that such agreement terminates (determined without regard to any extension thereof after July 26, 2007) or (II) July 26, 2010. In the case of a governmental plan (as defined in section 414(d)) for which the authority to amend the plan is held by a legislative body that meets in legislative session, the plan is permitted to continue the exclusion until the earlier of: (i) the close of the first regular legislative session of the legislative body with the authority to amend the plan that begins on or after January 1, 2009; or (ii) January 1, 2011.

These regulations (at § 1.403(b)-6(b)) also provide that a section 403(b) contract is permitted to distribute retirement benefits to the participant no earlier than the earliest of the participant's severance from employment or upon the prior occurrence of some event, subject to a number of exceptions (relating to distributions from custodial accounts, distributions attributable to section 403(b) elective deferrals, correction of excess deferrals, distributions at plan termination, and payment of after-tax employee contributions). This rule does not apply for contracts issued before January 1, 2009. In addition, in order to permit plans to comply with the rules relating to in-service distributions for contracts issued before January 1, 2009, the regulations provide that an amendment adopted before January 1, 2009, to comply with these rules does not violate the anti-cutback rules of section 204(g) of ERISA.

These regulations (at § 1.403(b)-8(c)(2)) also do not permit a life insurance contract, an endowment contract, a health or accident insurance contract, or a property, casualty, or liability insurance contract to constitute an annuity contract for purposes of section 403(b). This rule does not apply for contracts issued before September 24, 2007.

These regulations also include specific rules relating to contract exchanges that were permitted under Rev. Rul. 90-24. These new rules do not apply to contracts received in an exchange that occurred on or before September 24, 2007, assuming that the exchange (including the contract received in the exchange) satisfies applicable pre-existing legal requirements (including Rev. Rul. 90-24).

Finally, these regulations include special applicability date rules to coordinate with recently issued regulations under sections 402A and 415.

For periods following July 26, 2007, and before the applicable date, taxpayers can rely on these regulations, except that (1) such reliance must be on a consistent and reasonable basis and (2) the special rule at § 1.403(b)-10(a) of these regulations permitting accumulated benefits to be distributed on plan termination can be relied upon only if all of the contracts issued under the plan at that time satisfy all of the applicable requirements of these regulations (other than the requirement at § 1.403(b)-3(b)(3)(i) of these regulations that there be a written plan).

Special Analyses

It has been determined that this Treasury decision is not a significant regulatory action as defined in Executive Order 12866. Therefore, a regulatory assessment is not required. It also has been determined that section 553(b) of the Administrative Procedure Act (5 U.S.C. chapter 5) does not apply to these regulations. It is hereby certified that the collection of information in these regulations will not have a significant economic impact on a substantial number of small entities. This certification is based upon the determination that respondents will need to spend minimal time (an average of 4.1 hours per year) complying with the contract exchange requirements in these regulations, and small entities are generally expected to spend much less time. Thus, the cost of complying with this statutory requirement is small, even for small entities. Therefore, a Regulatory Flexibility Analysis is not required under the Regulatory Flexibility Act (5 U.S.C. chapter 6).

Pursuant to section 7805(f) of the Code, the notice of proposed rulemaking preceding these regulations was submitted to the Chief Counsel for Advocacy of the Small Business Administration for comment on its impact on small businesses.

Drafting Information

The principal authors of these regulations are R. Lisa Mojiri-Azad and John Tolleris, Office of the Division Counsel/Associate Chief Counsel (Tax Exempt and Government Entities), IRS. However, other personnel from the IRS and the Treasury Department participated in their development.

List of Subjects

26 CFR Part 1

Income taxes, Reporting and recordkeeping requirements.

26 CFR Part 31

Employment taxes, Income taxes, Penalties, Pensions, Railroad retirement, Reporting and recordkeeping requirements, Social security, Unemployment compensation.

26 CFR Part 54

Excise taxes. Pensions, Reporting and recordkeeping requirements.

26 CFR Part 602

Reporting and recordkeeping requirements.

Adoption of Amendments to the Regulations

Accordingly, 26 CFR parts 1, 31, 54 and 602 are amended as follows:

PART 1—INCOME TAXES

Paragraph 1. The authority citation for part 1 is amended by removing the entry for § 1.403(b)-3 and adding entries in numerical order to read in part as follows:

Authority: 26 U.S.C. 7805 * * *

§ 1.403(b)-6 also issued under 26 U.S.C. 403(b)(10). * * *

§ 1.414(c)-5 also issued under 26 U.S.C. 414(b), (c), and (o). * * *

Par. 2. Section 1.402(b)-1 is amended by revising paragraphs (a)(2) and (b)(2)(ii) to read as follows:

§ 1.402(b)-1 Treatment of beneficiary of a trust not exempt under section 501(a).

(a) * * *

(2) Determination of amount of employer contributions. If, for an employee, the actual amount of employer contributions referred to in paragraph (a)(1) of this section for any taxable year of the employee is not determinable or for any other reason is not known, then, except as set forth in rules prescribed by the Commissioner in revenue rulings, notices, or other guidance published in the Internal Revenue Bulletin (see § 601.601(d)(2)(ii)(b) of this chapter), such amount shall be either—

(i) The excess of—

(A) The amount determined as of the end of such taxable year in accordance with the formula described in § 1.403(b)-1(d)(4), as it appeared in the April 1, 2006, edition of 26 CFR Part 1; over

(B) The amount determined as of the end of the prior taxable year in accordance with the formula described in paragraph (a)(2)(i)(A) of this section; or

(ii) The amount determined under any other method utilizing recognized actuarial principles that are consistent with the provisions of the plan under which such contributions are made and the method adopted by the employer for funding the benefits under the plan.

(b) * * *

(2) * * *

(ii) If a separate account in a trust for the benefit of two or more employees is not maintained for each employee, the value of the employee's interest in such trust is determined in accordance with rules prescribed by the Commissioner under the authority in paragraph (a)(2) of this section.

* * * * *

Par. 3. Section 1.402(g)(3)-1 is added to read as follows:

§ 1.402(g)(3)-1 Employer contributions to purchase a section 403(b) contract under a salary reduction agreement.

(a) General rule. With respect to an annuity contract under section 403(b), except as provided in paragraph (b) of this section, an elective deferral means an employer contribution to purchase an annuity contract under section 403(b) under a salary reduction agreement within the meaning of section 3121(a)(5)(D).

(b) Special rule. Notwithstanding paragraph (a) of this section, for purposes of section 403(b), an elective deferral only includes a contribution that is made pursuant to a cash or deferred election (as defined at § 1.401(k)-1(a)(3)). Thus, for purposes of section 402(g)(3)(C), an elective deferral does not include a contribution that is made pursuant to an employee's one-time irrevocable election made on or before the employee's first becoming eligible to participate under the employer's plans or a contribution made as a condition of employment that reduces the employee's compensation.

(c) Applicable date. This section is applicable for taxable years beginning after December 31, 2008.

Par. 4. Section 1.402A-1, A-1 is revised to read as follows:

§ 1.402A-1 Designated Roth Accounts.

* * * * *

A-1. A designated Roth account is a separate account under a qualified cash or deferred arrangement under a section 401(a) plan, or under a section 403(b) plan, to which designated Roth contributions are permitted to be made in lieu of elective contributions and that satisfies the requirements of § 1.401(k)-1(f) (in the case of a section 401(a) plan) or § 1.403(b)-3(c) (in the case of a section 403(b) plan).

* * * * *

Par. 5. Section 1.403(b)-0 is added to read as follows:

§ 1.403(b)-0 Taxability under an annuity purchased by a section 501(c)(3) organization or a public school

This section lists the headings that appear in §§ 1.403(b)-1 through 1.403(b)-11.

§ 1.403(b)-1 General overview of taxability under an annuity contract purchased by a section 501(c)(3) organization or a public school.

§ 1.403(b)-2 Definitions.

(a) Application of definitions.

(b) Definitions.

§ 1.403(b)-3 Exclusion for contributions to purchase section 403(b) contracts.

(a) Exclusion for section 403(b) contracts.

(b) Application of requirements.

(c) Special rules for designated Roth section 403(b) contributions.

(d) Effect of failure.

§ 1.403(b)-4 Contribution limitations.

(a) Treatment of contributions in excess of limitations.

(b) Maximum annual contribution.

(c) Section 403(b) elective deferrals.

(d) Employer contributions for former employees.

(e) Special rules for determining years of service.

(f) Excess contributions of deferrals.

§ 1.403(b)-5 Nondiscrimination rules.

(a) Nondiscrimination rules for contributions other than section 403(b) elective deferrals.

(b) Universal availability required for section 403(b) elective deferrals.

(c) Plan required.

(d) Church plans exception.

(e) Other rules.

§ 1.403(b)-6 Timing of distributions and benefits.

(a) Distributions generally.

(b) Distributions from contracts other than custodial accounts or amounts attributable to section 403(b) elective deferrals.

(c) Distributions from custodial accounts that are not attributable to section 403(b) elective deferrals.

(d) Distribution of section 403(b) elective deferrals.

(e) Minimum required distributions for eligible plans.

(f) Loans.

(g) Death benefits and other incidental benefits.

(h) Special rule regarding severance from employment.

§ 1.403(b)-7 Taxation of distributions and benefits.

(a) General rules for when amounts are included in gross income.

(b) Rollovers to individual retirement arrangements and other eligible retirement plans.

(c) Special rules for certain corrective distributions.

(d) Amounts taxable under section 72(p)(1).

(e) Special rules relating to distributions from a designated Roth account.

(f) Certain rules relating to employment taxes.

§ 1.403(b)-8 Funding.

(a) Investments.

(b) Contributions to the plan.

(c) Annuity contracts.

(d) Custodial accounts.

(e) Retirement income accounts.

(f) Combining assets.

§ 1.403(b)-9 Special rules for church plans.

(a) Retirement income accounts.

(b) Retirement income account defined.

(c) Special deduction rule for self-employed ministers.

§ 1.403(b)-10 Miscellaneous provisions.

(a) Plan terminations and frozen plans.

(b) Contract exchanges and plan-to-plan transfers.

(c) Qualified domestic relations orders.

(d) Rollovers to a section 403(b) contract.

(e) Deemed IRAs.

(f) Defined benefit plans.

(g) Other rules relating to section 501(c)(3) organizations.

§ 1.403(b)-11 Applicable date.

(a) General rule.

(b) Collective bargaining agreements.

(c) Church conventions.

(d) Special rules for plans that exclude certain types of employees from elective deferrals.

(e) Special rules for plans that permit in-service distributions.

(f) Special rule for life insurance contracts.

(g) Special rule for contracts received in an exchange.

Par. 6. Sections 1.403(b)-1, 1.403(b)-2, and 1.403(b)-3 are revised to read as follows:

§ 1.403(b)-1 General overview of taxability under an annuity contract purchased by a section 501(c)(3) organization or a public school.

Section 403(b) and §§ 1.403(b)-2 through 1.403(b)-10 provide rules for the Federal income tax treatment of an annuity purchased for an employee by an employer that is either a tax-exempt entity under section 501(c)(3) (relating to certain religious, charitable, scientific, or other types of organizations) or a public school, or for a minister described in section 414(e)(5)(A). See section 403(a) (relating to qualified annuities) for rules regarding the taxation of an annuity purchased under a qualified annuity plan that meets the requirements of section 404(a)(2), and see section 403(c) (relating to nonqualified annuities) for rules regarding the taxation of other types of annuities.

§ 1.403(b)-2 Definitions.

(a) Application of definitions. The definitions set forth in this section are applicable for purposes of § 1.403(b)-1, this section and §§ 1.403(b)-3 through 1.403(b)-11.

(b) Definitions—(1) Accumulated benefit means the total benefit to which a participant or beneficiary is entitled under a section 403(b) contract, including all contributions made to the contract and all earnings thereon.

(2) Annuity contract means a contract that is issued by an insurance company qualified to issue annuities in a State and that includes payment in the form of an annuity. See § 1.401(f)-1(d)(2) and (e) for the definition of an annuity, and see § 1.403(b)-8(c)(3) for a special rule for certain State plans. See also §§ 1.403(b)-8(d) and 1.403(b)-9(a) for additional rules regarding the treatment of custodial accounts and retirement income accounts as annuity contracts.

(3) Beneficiary means a person who is entitled to benefits in respect of a participant following the participant's death or an alternate payee pursuant to a qualified domestic relations order, as described in § 1.403(b)-10(c).

(4) Catch-up amount or catch-up limitation for a participant for a taxable year means a section 403(b) elective deferral permitted under section 414(v) (as described in § 1.403(b)-4(c)(2)) or section 402(g)(7) (as described in § 1.403(b)-4(c)(3)).

(5) Church means a church as defined in section 3121(w)(3)(A) and a qualified church-controlled organization as defined in section 3121(w)(3)(B).

(6) Church-related organization means a church or a convention or association of churches, including an organization described in section 414(e)(3)(A).

(7) Elective deferral means an elective deferral under § 1.402(g)-1 (with respect to an employer contribution to a section 403(b) contract) and any other amount that constitutes an elective deferral under section 402(g)(3).

(8) (i) Eligible employer means—

(A) A State, but only with respect to an employee of the state performing services for a public school;

(B) A section 501(c)(3) organization with respect to any employee of the section 501(c)(3) organization;

(C) Any employer of a minister described in section 414(e)(5)(A), but only with respect to the minister; or

(D) A minister described in section 414(e)(5)(A), but only with respect to a retirement income account established for the minister.

(ii) An entity is not an eligible employer under paragraph (a)(8)(i)(A) of this section if it treats itself as not being a State for any other purpose of the Internal Revenue Code, and a subsidiary or other affiliate of an eligible employer is not an eligible employer under paragraph (a)(8)(i) of this section if the subsidiary or other affiliate is not an entity described in paragraph (a)(8)(i) of this section.

(9) Employee means a common-law employee performing services for the employer, and does not include a former employee or an independent contractor. Subject to any rules in § 1.403(b)-1, this section and §§ 1.403(b)-3 through 1.403(b)-11 that are specifically applicable to ministers, an employee also includes a minister described in section 414(e)(5)(A) when performing services in the exercise of his or her ministry.

(10) Employee performing services for a public school means an employee performing services as an employee for a public school of a State. This definition is not applicable unless the employee's compensation for performing services for a public school is paid by the State. Further, a person occupying an elective or appointive public office is not an employee performing services for a public school unless such office is one to which an individual is elected or appointed only if the individual has received training, or is experienced, in the field of education. The term public office includes any elective or appointive office of a State.

(11) Includible compensation means the employee's compensation received from an eligible employer that is includible in the participant's gross income for Federal income tax purposes (computed without regard to section 911) for the most recent period that is a year of service. Includible compensation for a minister who is self-employed means the minister's earned income as defined in section 401(c)(2) (computed without regard to section 911) for the most recent

period that is a year of service. Includible compensation does not include any compensation received during a period when the employer is not an eligible employer. Includible compensation also includes any elective deferral or other amount contributed or deferred by the eligible employer at the election of the employee that would be includible in the gross income of the employee but for the rules of section 125, 132(f)(4), 402(e)(2), 402(h)(1)(B), 402(k), or 457(b). The amount of includible compensation is determined without regard to any community property laws. See section 415(c)(3)(A) through (D) for additional rules, and see § 1.403(b)-4(d) for a special rule regarding former employees.

(12) Participant means an employee for whom a section 403(b) contract is currently being purchased, or an employee or former employee for whom a section 403(b) contract has previously been purchased and who has not received a distribution of his or her entire accumulated benefit under the contract.

(13) Plan means a plan as described in § 1.403(b)-3(b)(3).

(14) Public school means a State-sponsored educational organization described in section 170(b)(1)(A)(ii) (relating to educational organizations that normally maintain a regular faculty and curriculum and normally have a regularly enrolled body of pupils or students in attendance at the place where educational activities are regularly carried on).

(15) Retirement income account means a defined contribution program established or maintained by a church-related organization to provide benefits under section 403(b) for its employees or their beneficiaries as described in § 1.403(b)-9.

(16) Section 403(b) contract; section 403(b) plan—(i) Section 403(b) contract means a contract that satisfies the requirements of § 1.403(b)-3. If for any taxable year an employer contributes to more than one section 403(b) contract for a participant or beneficiary, then, under section 403(b)(5), all such contracts are treated as one contract for purposes of section 403(b) and § 1.403(b)-1, this section, and §§ 1.403(b)-3 through 1.403(b)-11. See also § 1.403(b)-3(b)(1).

(ii) Section 403(b) plan means the plan of the employer under which the section 403(b) contracts for its employees are maintained.

(17) Section 403(b) elective deferral; designated Roth contribution—(i) Section 403(b) elective deferral means an elective deferral that is an employer contribution to a section 403(b) plan for an employee. See § 1.403(b)-5(b) for additional rules with respect to a section 403(b) elective deferral.

(ii) Designated Roth contribution under a section 403(b) plan means a section 403(b) elective deferral that satisfies § 1.403(b)-3(c).

(18) Section 501(c)(3) organization means an organization that is described in section 501(c)(3) (relating to certain religious, charitable, scientific, or other types of organizations) and exempt from tax under section 501(a).

(19) Severance from employment means that the employee ceases to be employed by the employer maintaining the plan. See § 1.401(k)-1(d) for additional guidance concerning severance from employment. See also § 1.403(b)-6(h) for a special rule under which severance from employment is determined by reference to employment with the eligible employer.

(20) State means a State, a political subdivision of a State, or any agency or instrumentality of a State. For this purpose, the District of Columbia is treated as a State. In addition, for purposes of determining whether an individual is an employee performing services for a public school, an Indian tribal government is treated as a State, as provided under section 7871(a)(6)(B). See also section 1450(b) of the Small Business Job Protection Act of 1996 (110 Stat. 1755, 1814) for special rules treating certain contracts purchased in a plan year beginning before January 1, 1995, that include contributions by an Indian tribal government as section 403(b) contracts, whether or not those contributions are for employees performing services for a public school.

(21) Year of service means each full year during which an individual is a full-time employee of an eligible employer, plus fractional credit for each part of a year during which the individual is either a full-time employee of an eligible employer for a part of the year or a part-time employee of an eligible employer. See § 1.403(b)-4(e) for rules for determining years of service.

§ 1.403(b)-3 Exclusion for contributions to purchase section 403(b) contracts.

(a) Exclusion for section 403(b) contracts. Amounts contributed by an eligible employer for the purchase of an annuity contract for an employee are excluded from the gross income of the employee under section 403(b) only if each of the requirements in paragraphs (a)(1) through (9) of this section is satisfied. In addition, amounts contributed by an eligible employer for the purchase of an annuity contract for an employee pursuant to a cash or deferred election (as defined at § 1.401(k)-1(a)(3)) are not includible in an employee's gross income at the time the cash would have been includible in the employee's gross income (but for the cash or deferred election) if each of the requirements in paragraphs (a)(1) through (9) of this section is satisfied. However, the preceding two sentences generally do not apply to designated Roth contributions; see paragraph (c) of this section and § 1.403(b)-7(e) for special taxation rules that apply with respect to designated Roth contributions under a section 403(b) plan.

(1) Not a contract issued under qualified plan or eligible governmental plan. The annuity contract is not purchased under a qualified plan (under section 401(a) or 403(a)) or an eligible governmental plan under section 457(b).

(2) Nonforfeitability. The rights of the employee under the annuity contract (disregarding rights to future premiums) are nonforfeitable. An employee's rights under a contract fail to be nonforfeitable unless the employee for whom the contract is purchased has at all times a fully vested and nonforfeitable right (as defined in regulations under section 411) to all benefits provided under the

contract. See paragraph (d)(2) of this section for additional rules regarding the nonforfeitability requirement of this paragraph (a)(2).

(3) Nondiscrimination. In the case of an annuity contract purchased by an eligible employer other than a church, the contract is purchased under a plan that satisfies section 403(b)(12) (relating to nondiscrimination requirements, including universal availability). See § 1.403(b)-5.

(4) Limitations on elective deferrals. In the case of an elective deferral, the contract satisfies section 401(a)(30) (relating to limitations on elective deferrals). A contract does not satisfy section 401(a)(30) as required under this paragraph (a)(4) unless the contract requires that all elective deferrals for an employee not exceed the limits of section 402(g)(1), including elective deferrals for the employee under the contract and any other elective deferrals under the plan under which the contract is purchased and under all other plans, contracts, or arrangements of the employer. See § 1.401(a)-30.

(5) Nontransferability. The contract is not transferable. This paragraph (a)(5) does not apply to a contract issued before January 1, 1963. See section 401(g).

(6) Minimum required distributions. The contract satisfies the requirements of section 401(a)(9) (relating to minimum required distributions). See § 1.403(b)-6(e).

(7) Rollover distributions. The contract provides that, if the distributee of an eligible rollover distribution elects to have the distribution paid directly to an eligible retirement plan, as defined in section 402(c)(8)(B), and specifies the eligible retirement plan to which the distribution is to be paid, then the distribution will be paid to that eligible retirement plan in a direct rollover. See § 1.403(b)-7(b)(2).

(8) Limitation on incidental benefits. The contract satisfies the incidental benefit requirements of section 401(a). See § 1.403(b)-6(g).

(9) Maximum annual additions. The annual additions to the contract do not exceed the applicable limitations of section 415(c) (treating contributions and other additions as annual additions). See paragraph (b) of this section and § 1.403(b)-4(b) and (f).

(b) Application of requirements—(1) Aggregation of contracts. In accordance with section 403(b)(5), for purposes of determining whether this section is satisfied, all section 403(b) contracts purchased for an individual by an employer are treated as purchased under a single contract. Additional aggregation rules apply under section 402(g) for purposes of satisfying paragraph (a)(4) of this section and under section 415 for purposes of satisfying paragraph (a)(9) of this section.

(2) Disaggregation for excess annual additions. In accordance with the last sentence of section 415(a)(2), if an excess annual addition is made to a contract that otherwise satisfies the requirements of this section, then the portion of the contract that includes such excess annual addition fails to be a section 403(b) contract (as further described in paragraph (d)(1) of this section) and the

remaining portion of the contract is a section 403(b) contract. This paragraph (b)(2) is not satisfied unless, for the year of the excess and each year thereafter, the issuer of the contract maintains separate accounts for each such portion. Thus, the entire contract fails to be a section 403(b) contract if an excess annual addition is made and a separate account is not maintained with respect to the excess.

(3) Plan in form and operation. (i) A contract does not satisfy paragraph (a) of this section unless it is maintained pursuant to a plan. For this purpose, a plan is a written defined contribution plan, which, in both form and operation, satisfies the requirements of § 1.403(b)-1, § 1.403(b)-2, this section, and §§ 1.403(b)-4 through 1.403(b)-11. For purposes of § 1.403(b)-1, § 1.403(b)-2, this section, and §§ 1.403(b)-4 through 1.403(b)-11, the plan must contain all the material terms and conditions for eligibility, benefits, applicable limitations, the contracts available under the plan, and the time and form under which benefit distributions would be made. For purposes of § 1.403(b)-1, § 1.403(b)-2, this section, and §§ 1.403(b)-4 through 1.403(b)-11, a plan may contain certain optional features that are consistent with but not required under section 403(b), such as hardship withdrawal distributions, loans, plan-to-plan or annuity contract-to-annuity contract transfers, and acceptance of rollovers to the plan. However, if a plan contains any optional provisions, the optional provisions must meet, in both form and operation, the relevant requirements under section 403(b), this section and §§ 1.403(b)-4 through 1.403(b)-11.

(ii) The plan may allocate responsibility for performing administrative functions, including functions to comply with the requirements of section 403(b) and other tax requirements. Any such allocation must identify responsibility for compliance with the requirements of the Internal Revenue Code that apply on the basis of the aggregated contracts issued to a participant under a plan, including loans under section 72(p) and the conditions for obtaining a hardship withdrawal under § 1.403(b)-6. A plan is permitted to assign such responsibilities to parties other than the eligible employer, but not to participants (other than employees of the employer a substantial portion of whose duties are administration of the plan), and may incorporate by reference other documents, including the insurance policy or custodial account, which thereupon become part of the plan.

(iii) This paragraph (b)(3) applies to contributions to an annuity contract by a church only if the annuity is part of a retirement income account, as defined in § 1.403(b)-9.

(4) Exclusion limited for former employees—(i) General rule. Except as provided in paragraph (b)(4)(ii) of this section and in § 1.403(b)-4(d), the exclusion from gross income provided by section 403(b) does not apply to contributions made for former employees. For this purpose, a contribution is not made for a former employee if the contribution is with respect to compensation that would otherwise be paid for a payroll period that begins before severance from employment.

(ii) Exceptions. The exclusion from gross income provided by section 403(b) applies to contributions made for former employees with respect to compensation described in § 1.415(c)-2(e)(3)(i) (relating to certain compensation paid by the later of 2½ months after severance from employment or the end of the limitation year that includes the date of severance from employment), and compensation described in § 1.415(c)-2(e)(4), § 1.415(c)-2(g)(4), or § 1.415(c)-2(g)(7) (relating to compensation paid to participants who are permanently and totally disabled or relating to qualified military service under section 414(u)).

(c) Special rules for designated Roth section 403(b) contributions. (1) The rules of § 1.401(k)-1(f)(1) and (2) for designated Roth contributions under a qualified cash or deferred arrangement apply to designated Roth contributions under a section 403(b) plan. Thus, a designated Roth contribution under a section 403(b) plan is a section 403(b) elective deferral that is designated irrevocably by the employee at the time of the cash or deferred election as a designated Roth contribution that is being made in lieu of all or a portion of the section 403(b) elective deferrals the employee is otherwise eligible to make under the plan; that is treated by the employer as includible in the employee's gross income at the time the employee would have received the amount in cash if the employee had not made the cash or deferred election (such as by treating the contributions as wages subject to applicable withholding requirements); and that is maintained in a separate account (within the meaning of § 1.401(k)-1(f)(2)).

(2) A designated Roth contribution under a section 403(b) plan must satisfy the requirements applicable to section 403(b) elective deferrals. Thus, for example, designated Roth contributions under a section 403(b) plan must satisfy the requirements of § 1.403(b)-6(d). Similarly, a designated Roth account under a section 403(b) plan is subject to the rules of section 401(a)(9)(A) and (B) and § 1.403(b)-6(e).

(d) Effect of failure—(1) General rules. (i) If a contract includes any amount that fails to satisfy the requirements of section 403(b), § 1.403(b)-1, § 1.403(b)-2, this section, or §§ 1.403(b)-4 through 1.403(b)-11, then, except as otherwise provided in paragraph (d)(2) of this section (relating to failure to satisfy nonforfeitability requirements) or § 1.403(b)-4(f) (relating to excess contributions under section 415 and excess deferrals under section 402(g)), the contract is not a section 403(b) contract. In addition, section 403(b)(5) and paragraph (b)(1) of this section provide that, for purposes of determining whether a contract satisfies section 403(b), all section 403(b) contracts purchased for an individual by an employer are treated as purchased under a single contract. Thus, except as provided in paragraph (b)(2) of this section or as otherwise provided in this paragraph (d), a failure to satisfy section 403(b) with respect to any contract issued to an individual by an employer adversely affects all contracts issued to that individual by that employer.

(ii) In accordance with paragraph (b)(3) of this section, a failure to operate in accordance with the terms of a plan adversely affects all of the contracts issued by the employer to the employee or employees with respect to whom the operational failure occurred. Such a failure does not adversely affect any other contract if the failure is neither a failure to satisfy the nondiscrimination requirements of § 1.403(b)-5 (a nondiscrimination failure) nor a failure of the employer to be an eligible employer as defined in § 1.403(b)-2 (an employer eligibility failure). However, any failure that is not an operational failure adversely affects all contracts issued under the plan, including: a failure to have contracts issued pursuant to a written defined contribution plan which, in form, satisfies the requirements of § 1.403(b)-1, § 1.403(b)-2, this section and §§ 1.403(b)-4 through 1.403(b)-11 (a written plan failure); a nondiscrimination failure; or an employer eligibility failure.

(iii) See other applicable Internal Revenue Code provisions for the treatment of a contract that is not a section 403(b) contract, such as sections 61, 83, 402(b), and 403(c). Thus, for example, section 403(c) (relating to nonqualified annuities) applies if any annuity contract issued by an insurance company fails to satisfy section 403(b), based on the value of the contract at the time of the failure. However, see paragraph (d)(2) of this section for special rules with respect to the nonforfeitability requirement of paragraph (a)(2) of this section.

(2) Failure to satisfy nonforfeitability requirement—(i) Treatment before contract becomes nonforfeitable. If an annuity contract issued by an insurance company would qualify as a section 403(b) contract but for the failure to satisfy the nonforfeitability requirement of paragraph (a)(2) of this section, then the contract is treated as a contract to which section 403(c) applies. See § 1.403(b)-8(d)(4) for a rule under which a custodial account that fails to satisfy the nonforfeitability requirement of paragraph (a)(2) of this section is treated as a section 401(a) qualified plan for certain purposes.

(ii) Treatment when contract becomes nonforfeitable—(A) In general. Notwithstanding paragraph (d)(2)(i) of this section, on or after the date on which the participant's interest in a contract described in paragraph (d)(2)(i) of this section becomes nonforfeitable, the contract may be treated as a section 403(b) contract if no election has been made under section 83(b) with respect to the contract, the participant's interest in the contract has been subject to a substantial risk of forfeiture (as defined in section 83) before becoming nonforfeitable, each contribution under the contract that is subject to a different vesting schedule is maintained in a separate account, and the contract has at all times satisfied the requirements of paragraph (a) of this section other than the nonforfeitability requirement of paragraph (a)(2) of this section. Thus, for example, for the current year and each prior year, no contribution can have been made to the contract that would cause the contract to fail to be a section 403(b) contract as a result of contributions exceeding the limitations of section 415 (except to the extent permitted under paragraph (b)(2) of this section) or to fail to satisfy the nondiscrimination rules described in § 1.403(b)-5. See also § 1.403(b)-10(a)(1) for a special rule in connection with termination of a section 403(b) plan.

(B) Partial vesting. For purposes of applying this paragraph (d), if only a portion of a participant's interest in a contract becomes nonforfeitable in a year, then the portion that is nonforfeitable and the portion that fails to be nonforfeitable are each treated as separate contracts. In addition, for purposes of applying this paragraph (d), if a contribution is made to an annuity contract in excess of the limitations of section 415(c) and the excess is maintained in a separate account, then the portion of the contract that includes the excess contributions account and the remainder are each treated as separate contracts. Thus, if an annuity contract that includes an excess contributions account changes from forfeitable to nonforfeitable during a year, then the portion that is not attributable to the excess contributions account constitutes a section 403(b) contract (assuming it otherwise satisfies the requirements to be a section 403(b) contract) and is not included in gross income, and the portion that is attributable to the excess contributions account is included in gross income in accordance with section 403(c). See § 1.403(b)-4(f) for additional rules.

Par. 7. Sections 1.403(b)-4, 1.403(b)-5, 1.403(b)-6, 1.403(b)-7, 1.403(b)-8, 1.403(b)-9, 1.403(b)-10, and 1.403(b)-11 are added to read as follows:

§ 1.403(b)-4 Contribution limitations.

(a) Treatment of contributions in excess of limitations. The exclusion provided under § 1.403(b)-3(a) applies to a participant only if the amounts contributed by the employer for the purchase of an annuity contract for the participant do not exceed the applicable limit under sections 415 and 402(g), as described in this section. Under § 1.403(b)-3(a)(4), a section 403(b) contract is required to include the limits on elective deferrals imposed by section 402(g), as described in paragraph (c) of this section. See paragraph (f) of this section for special rules concerning excess contributions and deferrals. Rollover contributions made to a section 403(b) contract, as described in § 1.403(b)-10(d), are not taken into account for purposes of the limits imposed by section 415, § 1.403(b)-3(a)(9), section 402(g), § 1.403(b)-3(a)(4), and this section, but after-tax employee contributions are taken into account under section 415, § 1.403(b)-3(a)(9), and paragraph (b) of this section.

(b) Maximum annual contribution—(1) General rule. In accordance with section 415(a)(2) and § 1.403(b)-3(a)(9), the contributions for any participant under a section 403(b) contract (namely, employer nonelective contributions (including matching contributions), section 403(b) elective deferrals, and after-tax employee contributions) are not permitted to exceed the limitations imposed by section 415. Under section 415(c), contributions are permitted to be made for participants in a defined contribution plan, subject to the limitations set forth therein (which are generally the lesser of a dollar limit for a year or the participant's compensation for the year). For purposes of section 415, contributions made for a participant are aggregated to the extent applicable under section 414(b), (c), (m), (n), and (o). For purposes of section 415(a)(2), §§ 1.403(b)-1 through 1.403(b)-3, this section, and §§ 1.403(b)-5 through 1.403(b)-11, a contribution means any annual addition, as defined in section 415(c).

(2) Special rules. See section 415(k)(4) for a special rule under which contributions to section 403(b) contracts are generally aggregated with contributions under other arrangements in applying section 415. For purposes of applying section 415(c)(1)(B) (relating to compensation) with respect to a

section 403(b) contract, except as provided in section 415(c)(3)(C), a participant's includible compensation (as defined in § 1.403(b)-2) is substituted for the participant's compensation, as described in section 415(c)(3)(E). Any age 50 catch-up contributions under paragraph (c)(2) of this section are disregarded in applying section 415.

(c) Section 403(b) elective deferrals—(1) Basic limit under section 402(g)(1). In accordance with section 402(g)(1)(A), the section 403(b) elective deferrals for any individual are included in the individual's gross income to the extent the amount of such deferrals, plus all other elective deferrals for the individual, for the taxable year exceeds the applicable dollar amount under section 402(g)(1)(B). The applicable annual dollar amount under section 402(g)(1)(B) is $15,000, adjusted for cost-of-living after 2006 in the manner described in section 402(g)(4). See § 1.403(b)-5(b) for a universal availability rule that applies if any employee is permitted to have any section 403(b) elective deferrals made on his or her behalf.

(2) Age 50 catch-up—(i) In general. In accordance with section 414(v) and the regulations thereunder, a section 403(b) contract may provide for catch-up contributions for a participant who is age 50 by the end of the year, provided that such age 50 catch-up contributions do not exceed the catch-up limit under section 414(v)(2) for the taxable year. The maximum amount of additional age 50 catch-up contributions for a taxable year under section 414(v) is $5,000, adjusted for cost-of-living after 2006 in the manner described in section 414(v)(2)(C). For additional requirements, see regulations under section 414(v).

(ii) Coordination with special section 403(b) catch-up. In accordance with sections 414(v)(6)(A)(ii) and 402(g)(7)(A), the age 50 catch-up described in this paragraph (c)(2) may apply for any taxable year in which a participant also qualifies for the special section 403(b) catch-up under paragraph (c)(3) of this section.

(3) Special section 403(b) catch-up for certain organizations—(i) Amount of the special section 403(b) catch-up. In the case of a qualified employee of a qualified organization for whom the basic section 403(b) elective deferrals for any year are not less than the applicable dollar amount under section 402(g)(1)(B), the section 403(b) elective deferral limitation of section 402(g)(1) for the taxable year of the qualified employee is increased by the least of—

(A) $3,000;

(B) The excess of—

(1) $15,000, over

(2) The total elective deferrals described in section 402(g)(7)(A)(ii) made for the qualified employee by the qualified organization for prior years, or

(C) The excess of—

(1) $5,000 multiplied by the number of years of service of the employee with the qualified organization, over

(2) The total elective deferrals (as defined at § 1.403(b)-2) made for the employee by the qualified organization for prior years.

(ii) Qualified organization. (A) For purposes of this paragraph (c)(3), qualified organization means an eligible employer that is—

(1) An educational organization described in section 170(b)(1)(A)(ii);

(2) A hospital;

(3) A health and welfare service agency (including a home health service agency);

(4) A church-related organization; or

(5) Any organization described in section 414(e)(3)(B)(ii).

(B) All entities that are in a church-related organization or an organization controlled by a church-related organization under section 414(e)(3)(B)(ii) are treated as a single qualified organization (so that years of service and any special section 403(b) catch-up elective deferrals previously made for a qualified employee for a church or other entity within a church-related organization or an organization controlled by the church-related organization are taken into account for purposes of applying this paragraph (c)(3) to the employee with respect to any other entity within the same church-related organization or organization controlled by a church-related organization).

(C) For purposes of this paragraph (c)(3)(ii), a health and welfare service agency means—

(1) An organization whose primary activity is to provide services that constitute medical care as defined in section 213(d)(1) (such as a hospice);

(2) A section 501(c)(3) organization whose primary activity is the prevention of cruelty to individuals or animals;

(3) An adoption agency; or

(4) An agency that provides substantial personal services to the needy as part of its primary activity (such as a section 501(c)(3) organization that either provides meals to needy individuals, is a home health service agency, provides services to help individuals who have substance abuse, or provides help to the disabled).

(iii) Qualified employee. For purposes of this paragraph (c)(3), qualified employee means an employee who has completed at least 15 years of service (as defined under paragraph (e) of this section) taking into account only employment with the qualified organization. Thus, an employee who has not completed at least 15 years of service (as defined under paragraph (e) of this section) taking into account only employment with the qualified organization is not a qualified employee.

(iv) Coordination with age 50 catch-up. In accordance with sections 402(g)(1)(C) and 402(g)(7), any catch-up amount contributed by an employee who is eligible for both an age 50 catch-up and a special section 403(b) catch-up is treated first as an amount contributed as a special section 403(b) catch-up to the extent a special section 403(b) catch-up is permitted, and then as an amount contributed as an age 50 catch-up (to the extent the catch-up amount exceeds the maximum special section 403(b) catch-up after taking into account sections 402(g) and 415(c), this paragraph (c)(3), and any limitations on the special section 403(b) catch-up that are imposed by the terms of the plan).

(4) Coordination with designated Roth contributions. See regulations under section 402A for rules for determining whether an elective deferral is a pre-tax elective deferral or a designated Roth contribution.

(5) Examples. The provisions of this paragraph (c) are illustrated by the following examples:

Example 1. (i) Facts illustrating application of the basic dollar limit. Participant B, who is 45, is eligible to participate in a State university section 403(b) plan in 2006. B is not a qualified employee, as defined in paragraph (c)(3)(iii) of this section. The plan permits section 403(b) elective deferrals, but no other employer contributions are made under the plan. The plan provides limitations on section 403(b) elective deferrals up to the maximum permitted under paragraphs (c)(1) and (3) of this section and the additional age 50 catch-up amount described in paragraph (c)(2) of this section. For 2006, B will receive includible compensation of $42,000 from the eligible employer. B desires to elect to have the maximum section 403(b) elective deferral possible contributed in 2006. For 2006, the basic dollar limit for section 403(b) elective deferrals under paragraph (c)(1) of this section is $15,000 and the additional dollar amount permitted under the age 50 catch-up is $5,000.

(ii) Conclusion. B is not eligible for the age 50 catch-up in 2006 because B is 45 in 2006. B is also not eligible for the special section 403(b) catch-up under paragraph (c)(3) of this section because B is not a qualified employee. Accordingly, the maximum section 403(b) elective deferral that B may elect for 2006 is $15,000.

Example 2. (i) Facts illustrating application of the includible compensation limitation. The facts are the same as in Example 1, except B's includible compensation is $14,000.

(ii) Conclusion. Under section 415(c), contributions may not exceed 100 percent of includible compensation. Accordingly, the maximum section 403(b) elective deferral that B may elect for 2006 is $14,000.

Example 3. (i) Facts illustrating application of the age 50 catch-up. Participant C, who is 55, is eligible to participate in a State university section 403(b) plan in 2006. The plan permits section 403(b) elective deferrals, but no other employer contributions are made under the plan. The plan provides limitations on section 403(b) elective deferrals up to the maximum permitted under paragraphs (c)(1) and (c)(3) of this section and the additional age 50 catch-up amount described in paragraph (c)(2) of this section. For 2006, C will receive includible compensation of $48,000 from the eligible employer. C desires to elect to have the maximum section 403(b) elective deferral possible contributed in

2006. For 2006, the basic dollar limit for section 403(b) elective deferrals under paragraph (c)(1) of this section is $15,000 and the additional dollar amount permitted under the age 50 catch-up is $5,000. C does not have 15 years of service and thus is not a qualified employee, as defined in paragraph (c)(3)(iii) of this section.

(ii) Conclusion. C is eligible for the age 50 catch-up in 2006 because C is 55 in 2006. C is not eligible for the special section 403(b) catch-up under paragraph (c)(3) of this section because C is not a qualified employee (as defined in paragraph (c)(3)(iii) of this section). Accordingly, the maximum section 403(b) elective deferral that C may elect for 2006 is $20,000 ($15,000 plus $5,000).

Example 4. (i) Facts illustrating application of both the age 50 and the special section 403(b) catch-up. The facts are the same as in Example 3, except that C is a qualified employee for purposes of the special section 403(b) catch-up provisions in paragraph (c)(3) of this section. For 2006, the maximum additional section 403(b) elective deferral for which C qualifies under the special section 403(b) catch-up under paragraph (c)(3) of this section is $3,000.

(ii) Conclusion. The maximum section 403(b) elective deferrals that C may elect for 2006 is $23,000. This is the sum of the basic limit on section 403(b) elective deferrals under paragraph (c)(1) of this section equal to $15,000, plus the $3,000 additional special section 403(b) catch-up amount for which C qualifies under paragraph (c)(3) of this section, plus the additional age 50 catch-up amount of $5,000.

Example 5. (i) Facts illustrating calculation of years of service with a predecessor organization for purposes of the special section 403(b) catch-up. Participant A is an employee of hospital H and is eligible to participate in a section 403(b) plan of H in 2006. A does not have 15 years of service with H, but A has previously made special section 403(b) catch-up deferrals to a section 403(b) plan maintained by hospital P which has since been acquired by H.

(ii) Conclusion. The special section 403(b) catch-up amount for which A qualifies under paragraph (c)(3) of this section must be calculated taking into account A's prior years of service and section 403(b) elective deferrals with the predecessor hospital if and only if A did not have any severance from service in connection with the acquisition.

Example 6. (i) Facts illustrating application of the age 50 catch-up and the section 415(c) dollar limitation. The facts are the same as in Example 4, except that the employer makes a nonelective contribution for each employee equal to 20 percent of C's compensation (which is $48,000). Thus, the employer makes a nonelective contribution for C for 2006 equal to $9,600. The plan provides that a participant is not permitted to make section 403(b) elective deferrals to the extent the section 403(b) elective deferrals would result in contributions in excess of the maximum permitted under section 415 and provides that contributions are reduced in the following order: the special section 403(b) catch-up elective deferrals under paragraph (c)(3) of this section are reduced first; the age 50 catch-up elective deferrals under paragraph (c)(2) of this section are reduced second; and then the basic section 403(b) elective deferrals under paragraph (c)(1) of this section are reduced. For 2006, the applicable dollar limit under section 415(c)(1)(A) is $44,000.

(ii) Conclusion. The maximum section 403(b) elective deferral that C may elect for 2006 is $23,000. This is the sum of the basic limit on section 403(b) elective deferrals under paragraph (c)(1) of this section equal to $15,000, plus the $3,000 additional special section 403(b) catch-up amount for which C qualifies under paragraph (c)(3) of this section; plus the additional age 50 catch-up amount of $5,000. The limit in paragraph (b) of this section would not be exceeded because the sum of the $9,600 nonelective contribution and the $23,000 section 403(b) elective deferrals does not exceed the lesser of $49,000 (which is the sum of $44,000 plus the $5,000 additional age 50 catch-up amount) or $53,000 (which is the sum of C's includible compensation for 2006 ($48,000) plus the $5,000 additional age 50 catch-up amount).

Example 7. (i) Facts further illustrating application of the age 50 catch-up and the section 415(c) dollar limitation. The facts are the same as in Example 6, except that C's includible compensation for 2006 is $58,000 and the plan provides for a nonelective contribution equal to 50 percent of includible compensation, so that the employer nonelective contribution for C for 2006 is $29,000 (50 percent of $58,000).

(ii) Conclusion. The maximum section 403(b) elective deferral that C may elect for 2006 is $20,000. A section 403(b) elective deferral in excess of this amount would exceed the sum of the limit in section 415(c)(1)(A) plus the additional age 50 catch-up amount, because the sum of the employer's nonelective contribution of $29,000 plus a section 403(b) elective deferral in excess of $20,000 would exceed $49,000 (the sum of the $44,000 limit in section 415(c)(1)(A) plus the $5,000 additional age 50 catch-up amount). (Note that a section 403(b) elective deferral in excess of $20,000 would also exceed the limitations of section 402(g) unless a special section 403(b) catch-up were permitted.)

Example 8. (i) Facts further illustrating application of the age 50 catch-up and the section 415(c) dollar limitation. The facts are the same as in Example 7, except that the plan provides for a nonelective contribution for C equal to $44,000 (which is the limit in section 415(c)(1)(A)).

(ii) Conclusion. The maximum section 403(b) elective deferral that C may elect for 2006 is $5,000. A section 403(b) elective deferral in excess of this amount would exceed the sum of the limit in section 415(c)(1)(A) plus the additional age 50 catch-up amount ($5,000), because the sum of the employer's nonelective contribution of $44,000 plus a section 403(b) elective deferral in excess of $5,000 would exceed $49,000 (the sum of the $44,000 limit in section 415(c)(1)(A) plus the $5,000 additional age 50 catch-up amount).

Example 9. (i) Facts illustrating application of the age 50 catch-up and the section 415(c) includible compensation limitation. The facts are the same as in Example 7, except that C's includible compensation for 2006 is $28,000, so that the employer nonelective contribution for C for 2006 is $14,000 (50 percent of $28,000).

(ii) Conclusion. The maximum section 403(b) elective deferral that C may elect for 2006 is $19,000. A section 403(b) elective deferral in excess of this amount would exceed the sum of the limit in section 415(c)(1)(B) plus the additional age 50 catch-up amount, because C's includible compensation is $28,000 and the sum of the employer's nonelective contribution of $14,000 plus a section 403(b) elective deferral in excess of $19,000 would exceed $33,000 (which is the sum of 100 percent of C's includible compensation plus the $5,000 additional age 50 catch-up amount).

Example 10. (i) Facts illustrating that section 403(b) elective deferrals cannot exceed compensation otherwise payable. Employee D is age 60, has includible compensation of $14,000, and wishes to contribute section 403(b) elective deferrals of $20,000 for the year. No nonelective contributions are made for Employee D.

(ii) Conclusion. Because a contribution is a section 403(b) elective deferral only if it relates to an amount that would otherwise be included in the participant's compensation, the effective limitation on section 403(b) elective deferrals for a participant whose compensation is less than the basic dollar limit for section 403(b) elective deferrals is the participant's compensation. Thus, D cannot make section 403(b) elective deferrals in excess of D's actual compensation, which is $14,000, even though the basic dollar limit exceeds that amount.

Example 11. (i) Facts illustrating calculation of the special section 403(b) catch-up. For 2006, employee E, who is age 53, is eligible to participate in a section 403(b) plan of hospital H, which is a section 501(c)(3) organization. H's plan permits section 403(b) elective deferrals and provides for an employer contribution of 10 percent of a participant's compensation. The plan provides limitations on section 403(b) elective deferrals up to the maximum permitted under paragraphs (c)(1), (2), and (3) of this section. For 2006, E's includible compensation is $50,000. E wishes to elect to have the maximum section 403(b) elective deferral possible contributed in 2006. E has previously made $62,000 of section 403(b) elective deferrals under the plan, but has never made an election for a special section 403(b) catch-up elective deferral. for 2006, the basic dollar limit for section 403(b) elective deferrals under paragraph (c)(1) of this section is $15,000, the additional dollar amount permitted under the age 50 catch-up is $5,000, E's employer will make a nonelective contribution of $5,000 (10% of $50,000 compensation), and E is a qualified employee of a qualified employer as defined in paragraph (c)(3) of this section.

(ii) Conclusion. The maximum section 403(b) elective deferrals that E may elect under H's section 403(b) plan for 2006 is $23,000. This is the sum of the basic limit on section 403(b) elective deferrals for 2006 under paragraph (c)(1) of this section equal to $15,000, plus the $3,000 maximum additional special section 403(b) catch-up amount for which D qualifies in 2006 under paragraph (c)(3) of this section, plus the additional age 50 catch-up amount of $5,000. The limitation on the additional special section 403(b) catch-up amount is not less than $3,000 because the limitation at paragraph (c)(3)(i)(B) of this section is $15,000 ($15,000 minus zero) and the limitation at paragraph (c)(3)(i)(C) of this section is $13,000 ($5,000 times 15, minus $62,000 of total deferrals in prior years). These conclusions would be unaffected if H were an eligible governmental employer under section 457(b) that has a section 457(b) eligible governmental plan and E were in the past to have made annual deferrals to that plan, because contributions to a section 457(b) eligible governmental plan do not constitute elective deferrals; and these conclusions would also be the same if H had a section 401(k) plan and E were in the past to have made elective deferrals to that plan, assuming that those elective deferrals did not exceed $10,000 ($5,000 times 15, minus the sum of $62,000 plus $10,000, equals $3,000), so as to result in the limitation at paragraph (c)(3)(i)(C) of this section being less than $3,000.

Example 12. (i) Facts illustrating calculation of the special section 403(b) catch-up in the next calendar year. The facts are the same as in Example 11, except that, for 2007, E has includible compensation of $60,000. For 2007, E now has previously made $85,000 of section 403(b) elective deferrals ($62,000 deferred before 2006, plus the $15,000 in basic section 403(b) elective deferrals in 2006, the $3,000 maximum additional special section 403(b) catch-up amount in 2006, plus the $5,000 age 50 catch-up amount in 2006). However, the $5,000 age 50 catch-up amount deferred in 2006 is disregarded for purposes of applying the limitation at paragraph (c)(3)(i)(B) of this section to determine the special section 403(b) catch-up amount. Thus, for 2007, only $80,000 of section 403(b) elective deferrals are taken into account in applying the limitation at paragraph (c)(3)(i)(B) of this section. For 2007, the basic dollar limit for section 403(b) elective deferrals under paragraph (c)(1) of this section is assumed to be $16,000, the additional dollar amount permitted under the age 50 catch-up is assumed to be $5,000, and E's employer contributes $6,000 (10% of $60,000) as a non-elective contribution.

(ii) Conclusion. The maximum section 403(b) elective deferral that D may elect under H's section 403(b) plan for 2007 is $21,000. This is the sum of the basic limit on section 403(b) elective deferrals under paragraph (c)(1) of this section equal to $16,000, plus the additional age 50 catch-up amount of $5,000. E is not entitled to any additional special section 403(b) catch-up amount for 2007 under paragraph (c)(3) of this section due to the limitation at paragraph (c)(3)(i)(C) of this section (16 times $5,000 equals $80,000, minus D's total prior section 403(b) elective deferrals of $80,000 equals zero).

(d) Employer contributions for former employees—(1) Includible compensation deemed to continue for nonelective contributions. For purposes of applying paragraph (b) of this section, a former employee is deemed to have monthly includible compensation for the period through the end of the taxable year of the employee in which he or she ceases to be an employee and through the end of each of the next five taxable years. The amount of the monthly includible compensation is equal to one twelfth of the former employee's includible compensation during the former employee's most recent year of service. Accordingly, nonelective employer contributions for a former employee must not exceed the limitation of section 415(c)(1) up to the lesser of the dollar amount in section 415(c)(1)(A) or the former employee's annual includible compensation based on the former employee's average monthly compensation during his or her most recent year of service.

(2) Examples. The provisions of paragraph (d)(1) of this section are illustrated by the following examples:

Example 1. (i) Facts. Private college M is a section 501(c)(3) organization operated on the basis of a June 30 fiscal year that maintains a section 403(b) plan for its employees. In 2004, M amends the plan to provide for a temporary early retirement incentive under which the college will make a nonelective contribution for any participant who satisfies certain minimum age and service conditions and who retires before June 30, 2006. The contribution will equal 110 percent of the participant's rate of pay for one year and will be payable over a period ending no later than the end of the fifth fiscal year that begins after retirement. It is assumed for purposes of this Example 1 that, in accordance with § 1.401(a)(4)-10(b) and under the facts and circumstances, the post-retirement contributions made for participants who satisfy the minimum age and service conditions and retire before June 30, 2006, do not discriminate in favor of former employees who are highly compensated employees. Employee A retires under the early retirement incentive on March 12, 2006, and A's annual includible compensation for the period from March 1, 2005, through February 28, 2006 (which is A's most recent one year of service) is $30,000. The applicable dollar limit under section 415(c)(1)(A) is assumed to be $44,000 for 2006 and $45,000 for 2007. The college contributes $30,000 for A for 2006 and $3,000 for A for 2007 (totaling $33,000 or 110 percent of $30,000). No other contributions are made to a section 403(b) contract for A for those years.

(ii) Conclusion. The contributions made for A do not exceed A's includible compensation for 2006 or 2007.

Example 2. (i) Facts. Private college N is a section 501(c)(3) organization that maintains a section 403(b) plan for its employees. The plan provides for N to make monthly nonelective contributions equal to 20 percent of the monthly includible compensation for each eligible employee. In addition, the plan provides for contributions to continue for 5 years following the retirement of any employee after age 64 and completion of at least 20 years of service (based on the employee's average annual rate of base salary in the preceding 3 calendar years ended before the date of retirement). It is assumed for purposes of this Example 2 that, in accordance with § 1.401(a)(4)-10(b) and under the facts and circumstances, the post-retirement contributions made for participants who satisfy the minimum age and service conditions do not discriminate in favor of former employees who are highly compensated employees. Employee B retires on July 1, 2006, at age 64 after completion of 20 or more years of service. At that date, B's annual includible compensation for the most recently ended fiscal year of N is $72,000 and B's average monthly rate of base salary for 2003 through 2005 is $5,000. N contributes $1,200 per month (20 percent of 1/12th of $72,000) from January of 2006 through June of 2006 and contributes $1,000 (20 percent of $5,000) per month for B from July of 2006 through June of 2011. The applicable dollar limit under section 415(c)(1)(A) is $44,000 for 2006 through

2011. No other contributions are made to a section 403(b) contract for B for those years.

(ii) Conclusion. The contributions made for B do not exceed B's includible compensation for any of the years from 2006 through 2010.

Example 3. (i) Facts. A public university maintains a section 403(b) under which it contributes annually 10% of compensation for participants, including for the first 5 calendar years following the date on which the participant ceases to be an employee. The plan provides that if a participant who is a former employee dies during the first 5 calendar years following the date on which the participant ceases to be an employee, a contribution is made that is equal to the lesser of —

(A) The excess of the individual's includible compensation for that year over the contributions previously made for the individual for that year; or

(B) The total contributions that would have been made on the individual's behalf thereafter if he or she had survived to the end of the 5-year period.

(ii) Individual C's annual includible compensation is $72,000 (so that C's monthly includible compensation is $6,000). A $600 contribution is made for C for January of the first taxable year following retirement (10% of individual C's monthly includible compensation of $6,000). Individual C dies during February of that year. The university makes a contribution for individual C for February equal to $11,400 (C's monthly includible compensation for January and February, reduced by $600).

(iii) Conclusion. The contribution does not exceed the amount of individual C's includible compensation for the taxable year for purposes of section 415(c), but any additional contributions would exceed C's includible compensation for purposes of section 415(c).

(3) Disabled employees. See also section 415(c)(3)(C) which sets forth a special rule under which compensation may be treated as continuing for purposes of section 415 for certain former employees who are disabled.

(e) Special rules for determining years of service—(1) In general. For purposes of determining a participant's includible compensation under paragraph (b)(2) of this section and a participant's years of service under paragraphs (c)(3) (special section 403(b) catch-up for qualified employees of certain organizations) and (d) (employer contributions for former employees) of this section, an employee must be credited with a full year of service for each year during which the individual is a full-time employee of the eligible employer for the entire work period, and a fraction of a year for each part of a work period during which the individual is a full-time or part-time employee of the eligible employer. An individual's number of years of service equals the aggregate of the annual work periods during which the individual is employed by the eligible employer.

(2) Work period. A year of service is based on the employer's annual work period, not the employee's taxable year. For example, in determining whether a

university professor is employed full time, the annual work period is the school's academic year. However, in no case may an employee accumulate more than one year of service in a twelve-month period.

(3) Service with more than one eligible employer—(i) General rule. With respect to any section 403(b) contract of an eligible employer, except as provided in paragraph (e)(3)(ii) of this section, any period during which an individual is not an employee of that eligible employer is disregarded for purposes of this paragraph (e).

(ii) Special rule for church employees. With respect to any section 403(b) contract of an eligible employer that is a church-related organization, any period during which an individual is an employee of that eligible employer and any other eligible employer that is a church-related organization that has an association (as defined in section 414(e)(3)(D)) with that eligible employer is taken into account on an aggregated basis, but any period during which an individual is not an employee of a church-related organization or is an employee of a church-related organization that does not have an association with that eligible employer is disregarded for purposes of this paragraph (e).

(4) Full-time employee for full year. Each annual work period during which an individual is employed full time by the eligible employer constitutes one year of service. In determining whether an individual is employed full-time, the amount of work which he or she actually performs is compared with the amount of work that is normally required of individuals performing similar services from which substantially all of their annual compensation is derived.

(5) Other employees. (i) An individual is treated as performing a fraction of a year of service for each annual work period during which he or she is a full-time employee for part of the annual work period and for each annual work period during which he or she is a part-time employee either for the entire annual work period or for a part of the annual work period.

(ii) In determining the fraction that represents the fractional year of service for an individual employed full time for part of an annual work period, the numerator is the period of time (such as weeks or months) during which the individual is a full-time employee during that annual work period, and the denominator is the period of time that is the annual work period.

(iii) In determining the fraction that represents the fractional year of service of an individual who is employed part time for the entire annual work period, the numerator is the amount of work performed by the individual, and the denominator is the amount of work normally required of individuals who perform similar services and who are employed full time for the entire annual work period.

(iv) In determining the fraction representing the fractional year of service of an individual who is employed part time for part of an annual work period, the fractional year of service that would apply if the individual were a part-time employee for a full annual work period is multiplied by the fractional year of service that would apply if the individual were a full-time employee for the part of an annual work period.

(6) Work performed. For purposes of this paragraph (e), in measuring the amount of work of an individual performing particular services, the work performed is determined based on the individual's hours of service (as defined under section 410(a)(3)(C)), except that a plan may use a different measure of work if appropriate under the facts and circumstances. For example, a plan may provide for a university professor's work to be measured by the number of courses taught during an annual work period in any case in which that individual's work assignment is generally based on a specified number of courses to be taught.

(7) Most recent one-year period of service. For purposes of paragraph (d) of this section, in the case of a part-time employee or a full-time employee who is employed for only part of the year determined on the basis of the employer's annual work period, the employee's most recent periods of service are aggregated to determine his or her most recent one-year period of service. In such a case, there is first taken into account his or her service during the annual work period for which the last year of service's includible compensation is being determined; then there is taken into account his or her service during his next preceding annual work period based on whole months; and so forth, until the employee's service equals, in the aggregate, one year of service.

(8) Less than one year of service considered as one year. If, at the close of a taxable year, an employee has, after application of all of the other rules in this paragraph (e), some portion of one year of service (but has accumulated less than one year of service), the employee is deemed to have one year of service. Except as provided in the previous sentence, fractional years of service are not rounded up.

(9) Examples. The provisions of this paragraph (e) are illustrated by the following examples:

Example 1. (i) Facts. Individual G is employed half-time in 2004 and 2005 as a clerk by H, a hospital which is a section 501(c)(3) organization. G earns $20,000 from H in each of those years, and retires on December 31, 2005.

(ii) Conclusion. For purposes of determining G's includible compensation during G's last year of service under paragraph (d) of this section, G's most recent periods of service are aggregated to determine G's most recent one-year period of service. In this case, since D worked half-time in 2004 and 2005, the compensation D earned in those two years are aggregated to produce D's includible compensation for D's last full year in service. Thus, in this case, the $20,000 that D earned in 2004 and 2005 for D's half-time work are aggregated, so that D has $40,000 of includible compensation for D's most recent one-year of service for purposes of applying paragraphs (b)(2), (c)(3), and (d) of this section.

Example 2. (i) Facts. Individual H is employed as a part-time professor by public University U during the first semester of its two-semester 2004-2005 academic year. While H teaches one course generally for 3 hours a week during the first semester of the academic year, U's full-time faculty members generally teach for 9 hours a week during the full academic year.

(ii) Conclusion. For purposes of calculating how much of a year of service H performs in the 2004-2005 academic year (before application of the special rules of paragraphs (e)(7) and (8) of this section concerning less than one year of service), paragraph (e)(5)(iv) of this section is applied as follows: since H teaches one course at U for 3 hours per week for 1 semester and other faculty members at U teach 9 hours per week for 2 semesters, H is considered to have completed 3/18 or 1/6 of a year of service during the 2004-2005 academic year, determined as follows:

(A) The fractional year of service if H were a part-time employee for a full year is 3/9 (number of hours employed divided by the usual number of hours of work required for that position).

(B) The fractional year of service if H were a full-time employee for half of a year is ½ (one semester, divided by the usual 2-semester annual work period).

(C) These fractions are multiplied to obtain the fractional year of service: 3/9 times ½, or 3/18, equals 1/6 of a year of service.

(f) Excess contributions or deferrals—(1) Inclusion in gross income. Any contribution made for a participant to a section 403(b) contract for the taxable year that exceeds either the maximum annual contribution limit set forth in paragraph (b) of this section or the maximum annual section 403(b) elective deferral limit set forth in paragraph (c) of this section constitutes an excess contribution that is included in gross income for that taxable year. See § 1.403(b)-3(d)(1)(iii) and (2)(i) for additional rules, including special rules relating to contracts that fail to be nonforfeitable. See also section 4973 for an excise tax applicable with respect to excess contributions to a custodial account and section 4979(f)(2)(B) for a special rule applicable if excess matching contributions, excess after-tax employee contributions, and excess section 403(b) elective deferrals do not exceed $100.

(2) Separate account required for certain excess contributions; distribution of excess elective deferrals. A contract to which a contribution is made that exceeds the maximum annual contribution limit set forth in paragraph (b) of this section is not a section 403(b) contract unless the excess contribution is held in a separate account which constitutes a separate account for purposes of section 72. See also § 1.403(b)-3(a)(4) and paragraph (f)(4) of this section for additional rules with respect to the requirements of section 401(a)(30) and any excess deferral.

(3) Ability to distribute excess contributions. A contract does not fail to satisfy the requirements of § 1.403(b)-3, the distribution rules of § 1.403(b)-6 or 1.403(b)-9, or the funding rules of § 1.403(b)-8 solely by reason of a distribution made from a separate account under paragraph (f)(2) of this section or made under paragraph (f)(4) of this section.

(4) Excess section 403(b) elective deferrals. A section 403(b) contract may provide that any excess deferral as a result of a failure to comply with the limitation under paragraph (c) of this section for a taxable year with respect to any section 403(b) elective deferral made for a participant by the employer will be distributed to the participant, with allocable net income, no later than April 15 of the following taxable year or otherwise in accordance with section 402(g). See section 402(g)(2)(A) for rules permitting the participant to allocate excess deferrals among the plans in which the participant has made elective deferrals, and see section 402(g)(2)(C) for special rules to determine the tax treatment of such a distribution.

(5) Examples. The provisions of this paragraph (f) are illustrated by the following examples:

Example 1. (i) Facts. Individual D's employer makes a $46,000 contribution for 2006 to an individual annuity insurance policy for Individual D that would otherwise be a section 403(b) contract. The contribution does not include any elective deferrals and the applicable limit under section 415(c) is $44,000 for 2006. The $2,000 section 415(c) excess is put into a separate account under the policy. Employer includes $2,000 in D's gross income as wages for 2006 and, to the extent of the amount held in the separate account for the section 415(c) excess contribution, does not treat the account as a contract to which section 403(b) applies.

(ii) Conclusion. The separate account for the section 415(c) excess contribution is a contract to which section 403(c) applies, but the excess contribution does not cause the rest of the contract to fail section 403(b).

Example 2. (i) Facts. Same facts as Example 1, except that the contribution is made to purchase mutual funds that are held in a custodial account, instead of an individual annuity insurance policy.

(ii) Conclusion. The conclusion is the same as in Example 1, except that the purchase constitutes a transfer described in section 83.

Example 3. (i) Facts. Same facts as Example 1, except that the amount held in the separate account for the section 415(c) excess contribution is subsequently distributed to D.

(ii) Conclusion. The distribution is included in gross income to the extent provided under section 72 relating to distributions from a section 403(c) contract.

Example 4. (i) Facts. Individual E makes section 403(b) elective deferrals totaling $15,500 for 2006, when E is age 45 and the applicable limit on section 403(b) elective deferrals is $15,000. On April 14, 2007, the plan refunds the $500 excess along with applicable earnings of $65.

(ii) Conclusion. The $565 payment constitutes a distribution of an excess deferral under paragraph (f)(4) of this section. Under section 402(g), the $500 excess deferral is included in E's gross income for 2006. The additional $65 is included in E's gross income for 2007 and, because the distribution is made by

April 15, 2007 (as provided in section 402(g)(2)), the $65 is not subject to the additional 10 percent income tax on early distributions under section 72(t).

§ 1.403(b)-5 Nondiscrimination rules.

(a) Nondiscrimination rules for contributions other than section 403(b) elective deferrals—(1) General rule. Under section 403(b)(12)(A)(i), employer contributions and after-tax employee contributions to a section 403(b) plan must satisfy all of the following requirements (the nondiscrimination requirements) in the same manner as a qualified plan under section 401(a):

(i) Section 401(a)(4) (relating to nondiscrimination in contributions and benefits), taking section 401(a)(5) into account.

(ii) Section 401(a)(17) (limiting the amount of compensation that can be taken into account).

(iii) Section 401(m) (relating to matching and after-tax employee contributions).

(iv) Section 410(b) (relating to minimum coverage).

(2) Nonapplication to section 403(b) elective deferrals. The requirements of this paragraph (a) do not apply to section 403(b) elective deferrals.

(3) Compensation for testing. Except as may otherwise be specifically permitted under the provisions referenced in paragraph (a)(1) of this section, compliance with those provisions is tested using compensation as defined in section 414(s) (and without regard to section 415(c)(3)(E)). In addition, for purposes of paragraph (a)(1) of this section, there may be excluded employees who are permitted to be excluded under paragraph (b)(4)(ii)(D) and (E) of this section. However, as provided in paragraph (b)(4)(i) of this section, the exclusion of any employee listed in paragraph (b)(4)(ii)(D) or (E) of this section is subject to the conditions applicable under section 410(b)(4).

(4) Employer aggregation rules. See regulations under section 414(b), (c), (m), and (o) for rules treating entities as a single employer for purposes of the nondiscrimination requirements.

(5) Special rules for governmental plans. Paragraphs (a)(1)(i), (iii), and (iv) of this section do not apply to a governmental plan as defined in section 414(d) (but contributions to a governmental plan must comply with paragraphs (a)(1)(ii) and (b) of this section).

(b) Universal availability required for section 403(b) elective deferrals—(1) General rule. Under section 403(b)(12)(A)(ii), all employees of the eligible employer must be permitted to have section 403(b) elective deferrals contributed on their behalf if any employee of the eligible employer may elect to have the organization make section 403(b) elective deferrals. Further, the employee's right to make elective deferrals also includes the right to designate section 403(b) elective deferrals as designated Roth contributions.

(2) Effective opportunity required. For purposes of paragraph (b)(1) of this section, an employee is not treated as being permitted to have section 403(b) elective deferrals contributed on the employee's behalf unless the employee is provided an effective opportunity that satisfies the requirements of this paragraph (b)(2). Whether an employee has an effective opportunity is determined based on all the relevant facts and circumstances, including notice of the availability of the election, the period of time during which an election may be made, and any other conditions on elections. A section 403(b) plan satisfies the effective opportunity requirement of this paragraph (b)(2) only if, at least once during each plan year, the plan provides an employee with an effective opportunity to make (or change) a cash or deferred election (as defined at § 1.401(k)-1(a)(3)) between cash or a contribution to the plan. Further, an effective opportunity includes the right to have section 403(b) elective deferrals made on his or her behalf up to the lesser of the applicable limits in § 1.403(b)-4(c) (including any permissible catch-up elective deferrals under § 1.403(b)-4(c)(2) and (3)) or the applicable limits under the contract with the largest limitation, and applies to part-time employees as well as full-time employees. An effective opportunity is not considered to exist if there are any other rights or benefits (other than rights or benefits listed in § 1.401(k)-1(e)(6)(i)(A), (B), or (D)) that are conditioned (directly or indirectly) upon a participant making or failing to make a cash or deferred election with respect to a contribution to a section 403(b) contract.

(3) Special rules. (i) In the case of a section 403(b) plan that covers the employees of more than one section 501(c)(3) organization, the universal availability requirement of this paragraph (b) applies separately to each common law entity (that is, applies separately to each section 501(c)(3) organization). In the case of a section 403(b) plan that covers the employees of more than one State entity, this requirement applies separately to each entity that is not part of a common payroll. An eligible employer may condition the employee's right to have section 403(b) elective deferrals made on his or her behalf on the employee electing a section 403(b) elective deferral of more than $200 for a year.

(ii) For purposes of this paragraph (b)(3), an employer that historically has treated one or more of its various geographically distinct units as separate for employee benefit purposes may treat each unit as a separate organization if the unit is operated independently on a day-to-day basis. Units are not geographically distinct if such units are located within the same Standard Metropolitan Statistical Area (SMSA).

(4) Exclusions—(i) Exclusions for special types of employees. A plan does not fail to satisfy the universal availability requirement of this paragraph (b) merely because it excludes one or more of the types of employees listed in paragraph (b)(4)(ii) of this section. However, the exclusion of any employee listed in paragraph (b)(4)(ii)(D) or (E) of this section is subject to the conditions applicable under section 410(b)(4). Thus, if any employee listed in paragraph (b)(4)(ii)(D) of this section has the right to have section 403(b) elective deferrals made on his or her behalf, then no employee listed in that paragraph

(b)(4)(ii)(D) of this section may be excluded under this paragraph (b)(4) and, if any employee listed in paragraph (b)(4)(ii)(E) of this section has the right to have section 403(b) elective deferrals made on his or her behalf, then no employee listed in that paragraph (b)(4)(ii)(E) of this section may be excluded under this paragraph (b)(4).

(ii) List of special types of excludible employees. The following types of employees are listed in this paragraph (b)(4)(ii):

(A) Employees who are eligible under another section 403(b) plan, or a section 457(b) eligible governmental plan, of the employer which permits an amount to be contributed or deferred at the election of the employee.

(B) Employees who are eligible to make a cash or deferred election (as defined at § 1.401(k)-1(a)(3)) under a section 401(k) plan of the employer.

(C) Employees who are non-resident aliens described in section 410(b)(3)(C).

(D) Subject to the conditions applicable under section 410(b)(4) (including section 410(b)(4)(B) permitting separate testing for employees not meeting minimum age and service requirements), employees who are students performing services described in section 3121(b)(10).

(E) Subject to the conditions applicable under section 410(b)(4), employees who normally work fewer than 20 hours per week (or such lower number of hours per week as may be set forth in the plan).

(iii) Special rules. (A) A section 403(b) plan is permitted to take into account coverage under another plan, as permitted in paragraphs (b)(4)(ii)(A) and (B) of this section, only if the rights to make elective deferrals with respect to that coverage would satisfy paragraphs (b)(2) and (4)(i) of this section if that coverage were provided under the section 403(b) plan.

(B) For purposes of paragraph (b)(4)(ii)(E) of this section, an employee normally works fewer than 20 hours per week if and only if—

(1) For the 12-month period beginning on the date the employee's employment commenced, the employer reasonably expects the employee to work fewer than 1,000 hours of service (as defined in section 410(a)(3)(C)) in such period; and

(2) For each plan year ending after the close of the 12-month period beginning on the date the employee's employment commenced (or, if the plan so provides, each subsequent 12-month period), the employee worked fewer than 1,000 hours of service in the preceding 12-month period. (See, however, section 202(a)(1) of the Employee Retirement Income Security Act of 1974 (ERISA) (88 Stat. 829) Public Law 93-406, and regulations under section 410(a) of the Internal Revenue Code applicable with respect to plans that are subject to Title I of ERISA.)

(c) Plan required. Contributions to an annuity contract do not satisfy the requirements of this section unless the contributions are made pursuant to a plan, as defined in § 1.403(b)-3(b)(3), and the terms of the plan satisfy this section.

(d) Church plans exception. This section does not apply to a section 403(b) contract purchased by a church (as defined in § 1.403(b)-2).

(e) Other rules. This section only reflects requirements of the Internal Revenue Code applicable for purposes of section 403(b) and does not include other requirements. Specifically, this section does not reflect the requirements of ERISA that may apply with respect to section 403(b) arrangements, such as the vesting requirements at 29 U.S.C. 1053.

§ 1.403(b)-6 Timing of distributions and benefits.

(a) Distributions generally. This section provides special rules regarding the timing of distributions from, and the benefits that may be provided under, a section 403(b) contract, including limitations on when early distributions can be made (in paragraphs (b) through (d) of this section), required minimum distributions (in paragraph (e) of this section), and special rules relating to loans (in paragraph (f) of this section) and incidental benefits (in paragraph (g) of this section).

(b) Distributions from contracts other than custodial accounts or amounts attributable to section 403(b) elective deferrals. Except as provided in paragraph (c) of this section relating to distributions from custodial accounts, paragraph (d) of this section relating to distributions attributable to section 403(b) elective deferrals, § 1.403(b)-4(f) (relating to correction of excess deferrals), or § 1.403(b)-10(a) (relating to plan termination), a section 403(b) contract is permitted to distribute retirement benefits to the participant no earlier than upon the earlier of the participant's severance from employment or upon the prior occurrence of some event, such as after a fixed number of years, the attainment of a stated age, or disability. See § 1.401-1(b)(1)(ii) for additional guidance. This paragraph (b) does not apply to after-tax employee contributions or earnings thereon.

(c) Distributions from custodial accounts that are not attributable to section 403(b) elective deferrals. Except as provided in § 1.403(b)-4(f) (relating to correction of excess deferrals) or § 1.403(b)-10(a) (relating to plan termination), distributions from a custodial account, as defined in § 1.403(b)-8(d)(2), may not be paid to a participant before the participant has a severance from employment, dies, becomes disabled (within the meaning of section 72(m)(7)), or attains age 59½. Any amounts transferred out of a custodial account to an annuity contract or retirement income account, including earnings thereon, continue to be subject to this paragraph (c). This paragraph (c) does not apply to distributions that are attributable to section 403(b) elective deferrals.

(d) Distribution of section 403(b) elective deferrals—(1) Limitation on distributions —(i) General rule. Except as provided in § 1.403(b)-4(f) (relating to correction of excess deferrals) or § 1.403(b)-10(a) (relating to plan termination), distributions of amounts attributable to section 403(b) elective deferrals may not be paid to a participant earlier than the earliest of the date on which the participant has a severance from employment, dies, has a hardship, becomes disabled (within the meaning of section 72(m)(7)), or attains age 59½.

(ii) Special rule for pre-1989 section 403(b) elective deferrals. For special rules relating to amounts held as of the close of the taxable year beginning before January 1, 1989 (which does not apply to earnings thereon), see section 1123(e)(3) of the Tax Reform Act of 1986 (100 Stat. 2085, 2475) Public Law 99-514, and section 1011A(c)(11) of the Technical and Miscellaneous Revenue Act of 1988 (102 Stat. 3342, 3476) Public Law 100-647.

(2) Hardship rules. A hardship distribution under this paragraph (d) has the same meaning as a distribution on account of hardship under § 1.401(k)-1(d)(3) and is subject to the rules and restrictions set forth in § 1.401(k)-1(d)(3) (including limiting the amount of a distribution in the case of hardship to the amount necessary to satisfy the hardship). In addition, a hardship distribution is limited to the aggregate dollar amount of the participant's section 403(b) elective deferrals under the contract (and may not include any income thereon), reduced by the aggregate dollar amount of the distributions previously made to the participant from the contract.

(3) Failure to keep separate accounts. If a section 403(b) contract includes both section 403(b) elective deferrals and other contributions and the section 403(b) elective deferrals are not maintained in a separate account, then distributions may not be made earlier than the later of—

(i) Any date permitted under paragraph (d)(1) of this section; and

(ii) Any date permitted under paragraph (b) or (c) of this section with respect to contributions that are not section 403(b) elective deferrals (whichever applies to the contributions that are not section 403(b) elective deferrals).

(e) Minimum required distributions for eligible plans—(1) In general. Under section 403(b)(10), a section 403(b) contract must meet the minimum distribution requirements of section 401(a)(9) (in both form and operation). See section 401(a)(9) for these requirements.

(2) Treatment as IRAs. For purposes of applying the distribution rules of section 401(a)(9) to section 403(b) contracts, the minimum distribution rules applicable to individual retirement annuities described in section 408(b) and individual retirement accounts described in section 408(a) apply to section 403(b) contracts. Consequently, except as otherwise provided in paragraphs (e)(3) through (e)(5) of this section, the distribution rules in section 401(a)(9) are applied to section 403(b) contracts in accordance with the provisions in § 1.408-8 for purposes of determining required minimum distributions.

(3) Required beginning date. The required beginning date for purposes of section 403(b)(10) is April 1 of the calendar year following the later of the calendar year in which the employee attains 70½ or the calendar year in which the employee retires from employment with the employer maintaining the plan. However, for any section 403(b) contract that is not part of a governmental plan or church plan, the required beginning date for a 5-percent owner is April 1 of

the calendar year following the calendar year in which the employee attains 70½.

(4) Surviving spouse rule does not apply. The special rule in § 1.408-8, A-5 (relating to spousal beneficiaries), does not apply to a section 403(b) contract. Thus, the surviving spouse of a participant is not permitted to treat a section 403(b) contract as the spouse's own section 403(b) contract, even if the spouse is the sole beneficiary.

(5) Retirement income accounts. For purposes of § 1.401(a)(9)-6, A-4 (relating to annuity contracts), annuity payments provided with respect to retirement income accounts do not fail to satisfy the requirements of section 401(a)(9) merely because the payments are not made under an annuity contract purchased from an insurance company, provided that the relationship between the annuity payments and the retirement income accounts is not inconsistent with any rules prescribed by the Commissioner in revenue rulings, notices, or other guidance published in the Internal Revenue Bulletin (see § 601.601(d)(2)(ii)(b) of this chapter). See also § 1.403(b)-9(a)(5 for additional rules relating to annuities payable from a retirement income account).

(6) Special rules for benefits accruing before December 31, 1986. (i) The distribution rules provided in section 401(a)(9) do not apply to the undistributed portion of the account balance under the section 403(b) contract valued as of December 31, 1986, exclusive of subsequent earnings (pre-'87 account balance). The distribution rules provided in section 401(a)(9) apply to all benefits under section 403(b) contracts accruing after December 31, 1986 (post-'86 account balance), including earnings after December 31, 1986. Consequently, the post-'86 account balance includes earnings after December 31, 1986, on contributions made before January 1, 1987, in addition to the contributions made after December 31, 1986, and earnings thereon.

(ii) The issuer or custodian of the section 403(b) contract must keep records that enable it to identify the pre-'87 account balance and subsequent changes as set forth in paragraph (d)(6)(iii) of this section and provide such information upon request to the relevant employee or beneficiaries with respect to the contract. If the issuer or custodian does not keep such records, the entire account balance is treated as subject to section 401(a)(9).

(iii) In applying the distribution rules in section 401(a)(9), only the post-'86 account balance is used to calculate the required minimum distribution for a calendar year. The amount of any distribution from a contract is treated as being paid from the post-'86 account balance to the extent the distribution is required to satisfy the minimum distribution requirement with respect to that contract for a calendar year. Any amount distributed in a calendar year from a contract in excess of the required minimum distribution for a calendar year with respect to that contract is treated as paid from the pre-'87 account balance, if any, of that contract.

(iv) If an amount is distributed from the pre-'87 account balance and rolled over to another section 403(b) contract, the amount is treated as part of the post-'86 account balance in that second contract. However, if the pre-'87 account balance under a section 403(b) contract is directly transferred to another section 403(b) contract (as permitted under § 1.403(b)-10(b)), the amount transferred retains its character as a pre '87 account balance, provided the issuer of the transferee contract satisfies the recordkeeping requirements of paragraph (e)(6)(ii) of this section.

(v) The distinction between the pre-'87 account balance and the post-'86 account balance provided for under this paragraph (e)(6) of this section has no relevance for purposes of determining the portion of a distribution that is includible in income under section 72.

(vi) The pre-'87 account balance must be distributed in accordance with the incidental benefit requirement of § 1.401-1(b)(1)(i). Distributions attributable to the pre-'87 account balance are treated as satisfying this requirement if all distributions from the section 403(b) contract (including distributions attributable to the post-'86 account balance) satisfy the requirements of § 1.401-1(b)(1)(i) without regard to this section, and distributions attributable to the post-'86 account balance satisfy the rules of this paragraph (e) (without regard to this paragraph (e)(6)). Distributions attributable to the pre-'87 account balance are treated as satisfying the incidental benefit requirement if all distributions from the section 403(b) contract (including distributions attributable to both the pre-'87 account balance and the post-'86 account balance) satisfy the rules of this paragraph (e) (without regard to this paragraph (e)(6)).

(7) Application to multiple contracts for an employee. The required minimum distribution must be separately determined for each section 403(b) contract of an employee. However, because, as provided in paragraph (e)(2) of this section, the distribution rules in section 401(a)(9) apply to section 403(b) contracts in accordance with the provisions in § 1.408-8, the required minimum distribution from one section 403(b) contract of an employee is permitted to be distributed from another section 403(b) contract in order to satisfy section 401(a)(9). Thus, as provided in § 1.408-8, A-9, with respect to IRAs, the required minimum distribution amount from each contract is then totaled and the total minimum distribution taken from any one or more of the individual section 403(b) contracts. However, consistent with the rules in § 1.408-8, A-9, only amounts in section 403(b) contracts that an individual holds as an employee may be aggregated. Amounts in section 403(b) contracts that an individual holds as a beneficiary of the same decedent may be aggregated, but such amounts may not be aggregated with amounts held in section 403(b) contracts that the individual holds as the employee or as the beneficiary of another decedent. Distributions from section 403(b) contracts do not satisfy the minimum distribution requirements for IRAs, nor do distributions from IRAs satisfy the minimum distribution requirements for section 403(b) contracts.

(f) Loans. The determination of whether the availability of a loan, the making of a loan, or a failure to repay a loan made from an issuer of a section 403(b) contract to a participant or beneficiary is treated as a distribution (directly or indirectly) for purposes of this section, and the determination of whether the availability of the loan, the making of the loan, or a failure to repay the loan is in any other respect a violation of the requirements of section 403(b) and

§§ 1.403(b)-1 through 1.403(b)-5, this section and §§ 1.403(b)-7 through 1.403(b)-11 depends on the facts and circumstances. Among the facts and circumstances are whether the loan has a fixed repayment schedule and bears a reasonable rate of interest, and whether there are repayment safeguards to which a prudent lender would adhere. Thus, for example, a loan must bear a reasonable rate of interest in order to be treated as not being a distribution. However, a plan loan offset is a distribution for purposes of this section. See § 1.72(p)-1, Q&A-13. See also § 1.403(b)-7(d) relating to the application of section 72(p) with respect to the taxation of a loan made under a section 403(b) contract. (Further, see section 408(b)(1) of Title I of ERISA and 29 CFR 2550.408b-1 of the Department of Labor regulations concerning additional requirements applicable with respect to plans that are subject to Title I of ERISA.)

(g) Death benefits and other incidental benefits. An annuity is not a section 403(b) contract if it fails to satisfy the incidental benefit requirement of § 1.401-1(b)(1)(ii) (in form or in operation). For purposes of this paragraph (g), to the extent the incidental benefit requirement of § 1.401-1(b)(1)(ii) requires a distribution of the participant's or beneficiary's accumulated benefit, that requirement is deemed to be satisfied if distributions satisfy the minimum distribution requirements of section 401(a)(9). In addition, if a contract issued by an insurance company qualified to issue annuities in a State includes provisions under which, in the event a participant becomes disabled, benefits will be provided by the insurance carrier as if employer contributions were continued until benefit distribution commences, then that benefit is treated as an incidental benefit (as insurance for a deferred annuity benefit in the event of disability) that must satisfy the incidental benefit requirement of § 1.401-1(b)(1)(ii) (taking into account any other incidental benefits provided under the plan).

(h) Special rule regarding severance from employment. For purposes of this section, severance from employment occurs on any date on which an employee ceases to be an employee of an eligible employer, even though the employee may continue to be employed either by another entity that is treated as the same employer where either that other entity is not an entity that can be an eligible employer (such as transferring from a section 501(c)(3) organization to a for-profit subsidiary of the section 501(c)(3) organization) or in a capacity that is not employment with an eligible employer (for example, ceasing to be an employee performing services for a public school but continuing to work for the same State employer). Thus, this paragraph (h) does not apply if an employee transfers from one section 501(c)(3) organization to another section 501(c)(3) organization that is treated as the same employer or if an employee transfers from one public school to another public school of the same State employer.

(i) Certain limitations do not apply to rollover contributions. The limitations on distributions in paragraphs (b) through (d) of this section do not apply to amounts held in a separate account for eligible rollover distributions as described in § 1.403(b)-10(d).

§ 1.403(b)-7 Taxation of distributions and benefits.

(a) General rules for when amounts are included in gross income. Except as provided in this section (or in § 1.403(b)-10(c) relating to payments pursuant to a qualified domestic relations order), amounts actually distributed from a section 403(b) contract are includible in the gross income of the recipient participant or beneficiary (in the year in which so distributed) under section 72 (relating to annuities). For an additional income tax that may apply to certain early distributions that are includible in gross income, see section 72(t).

(b) Rollovers to individual retirement arrangements and other eligible retirement plans—(1) Timing of taxation of rollovers. In accordance with sections 402(c), 403(b)(8), and 403(b)(10), a direct rollover in accordance with section 401(a)(31) is not includible in the gross income of a participant or beneficiary in the year rolled over. In addition, any payment made in the form of an eligible rollover distribution (as defined in section 402(c)(4)) is not includible in gross income in the year paid to the extent the payment is contributed to an eligible retirement plan (as defined in section 402(c)(8)(B)) within 60 days, including the contribution to the eligible retirement plan of any property distributed. For this purpose, the rules of section 402(c)(2) through (7) and (c)(9) apply. Thus, to the extent that a portion of a distribution (including a distribution from a designated Roth account) would be excluded from gross income if it were not rolled over, if that portion of the distribution is to be rolled over into an eligible retirement plan that is not an IRA, the rollover must be accomplished through a direct rollover of the entire distribution to a plan qualified under section 401(a) or section 403(b) plan and that plan must agree to separately account for the amount not includible in income (so that a 60-day rollover to a plan qualified under section 401(a) or another section 403(b) plan is not available for this portion of the distribution). Any direct rollover under this paragraph (b)(1) is a distribution that is subject to the distribution requirements of § 1.403(b)-6.

(2) Requirement that contract provide rollover options for eligible rollover distributions. As required in § 1.403(b)-3(a)(7), an annuity contract is not a section 403(b) contract unless the contract provides that if the distributee of an eligible rollover distribution elects to have the distribution paid directly to an eligible retirement plan (as defined in section 402(c)(8)(B)) and specifies the eligible retirement plan to which the distribution is to be paid, then the distribution will be paid to that eligible retirement plan in a direct rollover. For purposes of determining whether a contract satisfies this requirement, the provisions of section 401(a)(31) apply to the annuity as though it were a plan qualified under section 401(a) unless otherwise provided in section 401(a)(31). Thus, the special rule in § 1.401(k)-1(f)(3)(ii) with respect to distributions from a designated Roth account that are expected to total less than $200 during a year applies to designated Roth accounts under a section 403(b) plan. In applying the provisions of this paragraph (b)(2), the payor of the eligible rollover distribution from the contract is treated as the plan administrator.

(3) Requirement that contract payor provide notice of rollover option to distributees. To ensure that the distributee of an eligible rollover distribution from a section 403(b) contract has a meaningful right to elect a direct rollover,

section 402(f) requires that the distributee be informed of the option. Thus, within a reasonable time period before making the initial eligible rollover distribution, the payor must provide an explanation to the distributee of his or her right to elect a direct rollover and the income tax withholding consequences of not electing a direct rollover. For purposes of satisfying the reasonable time period requirement, the plan timing rule provided in section 402(f)(1) and § 1.402(f)-1 applies to section 403(b) contracts.

(4) Mandatory withholding upon certain eligible rollover distributions from contracts. If a distributee of an eligible rollover distribution from a section 403(b) contract does not elect to have the eligible rollover distribution paid directly to an eligible retirement plan in a direct rollover, the eligible rollover distribution is subject to 20 percent income tax withholding imposed under section 3405(c). See section 3405(c) and § 31.3405(c)-1 of this chapter for provisions regarding the withholding requirements relating to eligible rollover distributions.

(5) Automatic rollover for certain mandatory distributions under section 401(a)(31). In accordance with section 403(b)(10), a section 403(b) plan is required to comply with section 401(a)(31) (including automatic rollover for certain mandatory distributions) in the same manner as a qualified plan.

(c) Special rules. See section 402(g)(2)(C) for special rules to determine the tax treatment of a distribution of excess deferrals, and see § 1.401(m)-1(e)(3)(v) for the tax treatment of corrective distributions of after-tax employee contributions and matching contributions to comply with section 401(m). See sections 402(l) and 403(b)(2) for a special rule regarding distributions for certain retired public safety officers made from a governmental plan for the direct payment of certain premiums.

(d) Amounts taxable under section 72(p)(1). In accordance with section 72(p), the amount of any loan from a section 403(b) contract to a participant or beneficiary (including any pledge or assignment treated as a loan under section 72(p)(1)(B)) is treated as having been received as a distribution from the contract under section 72(p)(1), except to the extent set forth in section 72(p)(2) (relating to loans that do not exceed a maximum amount and that are repayable in accordance with certain terms) and § 1.72(p)-1. See generally § 1.72(p)-1. Thus, except to the extent a loan satisfies section 72(p)(2), any amount loaned from a section 403(b) contract to a participant or beneficiary (including any pledge or assignment treated as a loan under section 72(p)(1)(B)) is includible in the gross income of the participant or beneficiary for the taxable year in which the loan is made. A deemed distribution is not an actual distribution for purposes of § 1.403(b)-6, as provided at § 1.72(p)-1, Q&A-12 and Q&A-13. (Further, see section 408(b)(1) of Title I of ERISA concerning the effect of noncompliance with Title I loan requirements for plans that are subject to Title I of ERISA.)

(e) Special rules relating to distributions from a designated Roth account. If an amount is distributed from a designated Roth account under a section 403(b) plan, the amount, if any, that is includible in gross income and the amount, if any, that may be rolled over to another section 403(b) plan is determined under § 1.402A-1. Thus, the designated Roth account is treated as a separate contract for purposes of section 72. For example, the rules of section 72(b) must be applied separately to annuity payments with respect to a designated Roth account under a section 403(b) plan and separately to annuity payments with respect to amounts attributable to any other contributions to the section 403(b) plan.

(f) Aggregation of contracts. In accordance with section 403(b)(5), the rules of this section are applied as if all annuity contracts for the employee by the employer are treated as a single contract.

(g) Certain rules relating to employment taxes. With respect to contributions under the Federal Insurance Contributions Act (FICA) under Chapter 21, see section 3121(a)(5)(D) for a special rule relating to section 403(b) contracts. With respect to income tax withholding on distributions from section 403(b) contracts, see section 3405 generally. However, see section 3401 for income tax withholding applicable to annuity contracts or custodial accounts that are not section 403(b) contracts or for cases in which an annuity contract or custodial account ceases to be a section 403(b) contract. See also § 1.72(p)-1, Q&A-15, and § 35.3405(c)-1, Q&A-11 of this chapter, for special rules relating to income tax withholding for loans made from certain employer plans, including section 403(b) contracts.

§ 1.403(b)-8 Funding.

(a) Investments. Section 403(b) and § 1.403(b)-3(a) only apply to amounts held in an annuity contract (as defined in § 1.403(b)-2), including a custodial account that is treated as an annuity contract under paragraph (d) of this section, or a retirement income account that is treated as an annuity contract under § 1.403(b)-9.

(b) Contributions to the plan. Contributions to a section 403(b) plan must be transferred to the insurance company issuing the annuity contract (or the entity holding assets of any custodial or retirement income account that is treated as an annuity contract) within a period that is not longer than is reasonable for the proper administration of the plan. For purposes of this requirement, the plan may provide for section 403(b) elective deferrals for a participant under the plan to be transferred to the annuity contract within a specified period after the date the amounts would otherwise have been paid to the participant. For example, the plan could provide for section 403(b) elective deferrals under the plan to be contributed within 15 business days following the month in which these amounts would otherwise have been paid to the participant.

(c) Annuity contracts—(1) Generally. As defined in § 1.403(b)-2, and except as otherwise permitted under this section, an annuity contract means a contract that is issued by an insurance company qualified to issue annuities in a State and that includes payment in the form of an annuity. This paragraph (c) sets forth additional rules regarding annuity contracts.

(2) Certain insurance contracts. Neither a life insurance contract, as defined in section 7702, an endowment contract, a health or accident insurance contract, nor a property, casualty, or liability insurance contract meets the definition of an annuity contract. See § 1.401(f)-4(e). If a contract issued by an insurance company qualified to issue annuities in a State provides death benefits as part of the contract, then that coverage is permitted, assuming that those death benefits do not cause the contract to fail to satisfy any requirement applicable to section 403(b) contracts, for example, assuming that those benefits satisfy the incidental benefit requirement of § 1.401-1(b)(1)(i), as required by § 1.403(b)-6(g).

(3) Special rule for certain contracts. This paragraph (c)(3) applies in the case of a contract issued under a State section 403(b) plan established on or before May 17, 1982, or for an employee who becomes covered for the first time under the plan after May 17, 1982, unless the Commissioner had before that date issued any written communication (either to the employer or financial institution) to the effect that the arrangement under which the contract was issued did not meet the requirements of section 403(b). The requirement that the contract be issued by an insurance company qualified to issue annuities in a State does not apply to a contract described in the preceding sentence if one of the following two conditions is satisfied and that condition has been satisfied continuously since May 17, 1982—

(i) Benefits under the contract are provided from a separately funded retirement reserve that is subject to supervision of the State insurance department; or

(ii) Benefits under the contract are provided from a fund that is separate from the fund used to provide statutory benefits payable under a state retirement system and that is part of a State teachers retirement system (including a state university retirement system) to purchase benefits that are unrelated to the basic benefits provided under the retirement system, and the death benefit provided under the contract does not at any time exceed the larger of the reserve or the contribution made for the employee.

(d) Custodial accounts—(1) Treatment as a section 403(b) contract. Under section 403(b)(7), a custodial account is treated as an annuity contract for purposes of §§ 1.403(b)-1 through 1.403(b)-7, this section and §§ 1.403(b)-9 through 1.403(b)-11. See section 403(b)(7)(B) for special rules regarding the tax treatment of custodial accounts and section 4973(c) for an excise tax that applies to excess contributions to a custodial account.

(2) Custodial account defined. A custodial account means a plan, or a separate account under a plan, in which an amount attributable to section 403(b) contributions (or amounts rolled over to a section 403(b) contract, as described in § 1.403(b)-10(d)) is held by a bank or a person who satisfies the conditions in section 401(f)(2), if—

(i) All of the amounts held in the account are invested in stock of a regulated investment company (as defined in section 851(a) relating to mutual funds);

(ii) The requirements of § 1.403(b)-6(c) (imposing restrictions on distributions with respect to a custodial account) are satisfied with respect to the amounts held in the account;

(iii) The assets held in the account cannot be used for, or diverted to, purposes other than for the exclusive benefit of plan participants or their beneficiaries (for which purpose, assets are treated as diverted to the employer if the employer borrows assets from the account); and

(iv) The account is not part of a retirement income account.

(3) Effect of definition. The requirement in paragraph (d)(2)(i) of this section is not satisfied if the account includes any assets other than stock of a regulated investment company.

(4) Treatment of custodial account. A custodial account is treated as a section 401 qualified plan solely for purposes of subchapter F of subtitle A and subtitle F of the Internal Revenue Code with respect to amounts received by it (and income from investment thereof). This treatment only applies to a custodial account that constitutes a section 403(b) contract under §§ 1.403(b)-1 through 1.403(b)-7, this section and §§ 1.403(b)-9 through 1.403(b)-11 or that would constitute a section 403(b) contract under §§ 1.403(b)-1 through 1.403(b)-7, this section and §§ 1.403(b)-9 through 1.403(b)-11 if the amounts held in the account were to satisfy the nonforfeitability requirement of § 1.403(b)-3(a)(2).

(e) Retirement income accounts. See § 1.403(b)-9 for special rules under which a retirement income account for employees of a church-related organization is treated as a section 403(b) contract for purposes of §§ 1.403(b)-1 through 1.403(b)-7, this section and §§ 1.403(b)-9 through 1.403(b)-11.

(f) Combining assets. To the extent permitted by the Commissioner in revenue rulings, notices, or other guidance published in the Internal Revenue Bulletin (see § 601.601(d)(2)(ii)(b) of this chapter), trust assets held under a custodial account and trust assets held under a retirement income account, as described in § 1.403(b)-9(a)(6), may be invested in a group trust with trust assets held under a qualified plan or individual retirement plan. For this purpose, a trust includes a custodial account that is treated as a trust under section 401(f).

§ 1.403(b)-9 Special rules for church plans.

(a) Retirement income accounts—(1) Treatment as a section 403(b) contract. Under section 403(b)(9), a retirement income account for employees of a church-related organization (as defined in § 1.403(b)-2) is treated as an annuity contract for purposes of §§ 1.403(b)-1 through 1.403(b)-8, this section, § 1.403(b)-10 and § 1.403(b)-11.

(2) Retirement income account defined—(i) In general. A retirement income account means a defined contribution program established or maintained by a church-related organization under which—

(A) There is separate accounting for the retirement income account's interest in the underlying assets (namely, there must be sufficient separate accounting in order for it to be possible at all times to determine the retirement income account's interest in the underlying assets and to distinguish that interest from any interest that is not part of the retirement income account);

(B) Investment performance is based on gains and losses on those assets; and

(C) The assets held in the account cannot be used for, or diverted to, purposes other than for the exclusive benefit of plan participants or their beneficiaries (and for this purpose, assets are treated as diverted to the employer if there is a loan or other extension of credit from assets in the account to the employer).

(ii) Plan required. A retirement income account must be maintained pursuant to a program which is a plan (as defined in § 1.403(b)-3(b)(3)) and the plan document must state (or otherwise evidence in a similarly clear manner) the intent to constitute a retirement income account.

(3) Ownership or use constitutes distribution. Any asset of a retirement income account that is owned or used by a participant or beneficiary is treated as having been distributed to that participant or beneficiary. See §§ 1.403(b)-6 and 1.403(b)-7 for rules relating to distributions.

(4) Coordination of retirement income account with custodial account rules. A retirement income account that is treated as an annuity contract is not a custodial account (as defined in § 1.403(b)-8(d)(2)), even if it is invested solely in stock of a regulated investment company.

(5) Life annuities. A retirement income account may distribute benefits in a form that includes a life annuity only if—

(i) The amount of the distribution form has an actuarial present value, at the annuity starting date, equal to the participant's or beneficiary's accumulated benefit, based on reasonable actuarial assumptions, including regarding interest and mortality; and

(ii) The plan sponsor guarantees benefits in the event that a payment is due that exceeds the participant's or beneficiary's accumulated benefit.

(6) Combining retirement income account assets with other assets. For purposes of § 1.403(b)-8(f) relating to combining assets, retirement income account assets held in trust (including a custodial account that is treated as a trust under section 401(f)) are subject to the same rules regarding combining of assets as custodial account assets. In addition, retirement income account assets are permitted to be commingled in a common fund with amounts devoted exclusively to church purposes (such as a fund from which unfunded pension payments are made to former employees of the church). However, unless otherwise permitted by the Commissioner, no assets of the plan sponsor, other than retirement income account assets, may be combined with custodial account assets or any other assets permitted to be combined under § 1.403(b)-8(f). This paragraph (a)(6) is subject to any additional rules issued by the

Commissioner in revenue rulings, notices, or other guidance published in the Internal Revenue Bulletin (see § 601.601(d)(2)(ii)(b) of this chapter).

(7) Trust treated as tax exempt. A trust (including a custodial account that is treated as a trust under section 401(f)) that includes no assets other than assets of a retirement income account is treated as an organization that is exempt from taxation under section 501(a).

(b) No compensation limitation up to $10,000. See section 415(c)(7) for special rules regarding certain annual additions not exceeding $10,000.

(c) Special deduction rule for self-employed ministers. See section 404(a)(10) for a special rule regarding the deductibility of a contribution made by a self-employed minister.

§ 1.403(b)-10 Miscellaneous provisions.

(a) Plan terminations and frozen plans—(1) In general. An employer is permitted to amend its section 403(b) plan to eliminate future contributions for existing participants or to limit participation to existing participants and employees (to the extent consistent with § 1.403(b)-5). A section 403(b) plan is permitted to contain provisions that provide for plan termination and that allow accumulated benefits to be distributed on termination. However, in the case of a section 403(b) contract that is subject to the distribution restrictions in § 1.403(b)-6(c) or (d) (relating to custodial accounts and section 403(b) elective deferrals), termination of the plan and the distribution of accumulated benefits is permitted only if the employer (taking into account all entities that are treated as the same employer under section 414(b), (c), (m), or (o) on the date of the termination) does not make contributions to any section 403(b) contract that is not part of the plan during the period beginning on the date of plan termination and ending 12 months after distribution of all assets from the terminated plan. However, if at all times during the period beginning 12 months before the termination and ending 12 months after distribution of all assets from the terminated plan, fewer than 2 percent of the employees who were eligible under the section 403(b) plan as of the date of plan termination are eligible under the alternative section 403(b) contract, the alternative section 403(b) contract is disregarded. To the extent a contract fails to satisfy the nonforfeitability requirement of § 1.403(b)-3(a)(2) at the date of plan termination, the contact is not, and cannot later become, a section 403(b) contract. In order for a section 403(b) plan to be considered terminated, all accumulated benefits under the plan must be distributed to all participants and beneficiaries as soon as administratively practicable after termination of the plan. For this purpose, delivery of a fully paid individual insurance annuity contract is treated as a distribution. The mere provision for, and making of, distributions to participants or beneficiaries upon plan termination does not cause a contract to cease to be a section 403(b) contract. See § 1.403(b)-7 for rules regarding the tax treatment of distributions, including § 1.403(b)-7(b)(1) under which an eligible rollover distribution is not included in gross income if paid in a direct rollover to an eligible retirement plan or if transferred to an eligible retirement plan within 60 days.

(2) Employers that cease to be eligible employers. An employer that ceases to be an eligible employer may no longer contribute to a section 403(b) contract for any subsequent period, and the contract will fail to satisfy § 1.403(b)-3(a) if any further contributions are made with respect to a period after the employer ceases to be an eligible employer.

(b) Contract exchanges and plan-to-plan transfers—(1) Contract exchanges and transfers—(i) General rule. If the conditions in paragraph (b)(2) of this section are met, a section 403(b) contract held under a section 403(b) plan is permitted to be exchanged for another section 403(b) contract held under that section 403(b) plan. Further, if the conditions in paragraph (b)(3) of this section are met, a section 403(b) plan is permitted to provide for the transfer of its assets (including any assets held in a custodial account or retirement income account that are treated as section 403(b) contracts) to another section 403(b) plan. In addition, if the conditions in paragraph (b)(4) of this section (relating to permissive service credit and repayments under section 415) are met, a section 403(b) plan is permitted to provide for the transfer of its assets to a qualified plan under section 401(a). However, neither a qualified plan nor an eligible governmental plan under section 457(b) may transfer assets to a section 403(b) plan, and a section 403(b) plan may not accept such a transfer. In addition, a section 403(b) contract may not be exchanged for an annuity contract that is not a section 403(b) contract. Neither a plan-to-plan transfer nor a contract exchange permitted under this paragraph (b) is treated as a distribution for purposes of the distribution restrictions at § 1.403(b)-6. Therefore, such a transfer or exchange may be made before severance from employment or another distribution event. Further, no amount is includible in gross income by reason of such a transfer or exchange.

(ii) ERISA rules. See § 1.414(l)-1 for other rules that are applicable to section 403(b) plans that are subject to section 208 of the Employee Retirement Income Security Act of 1974 (88 Stat. 829, 865).

(2) Requirements for contract exchange within the same plan—(i) General rule. A section 403(b) contract of a participant or beneficiary may be exchanged under paragraph (b)(1) of this section for another section 403(b) contract of that participant or beneficiary under the same section 403(b) plan if each of the following conditions are met:

(A) The plan under which the contract is issued provides for the exchange.

(B) The participant or beneficiary has an accumulated benefit immediately after the exchange that is at least equal to the accumulated benefit of that participant or beneficiary immediately before the exchange (taking into account the accumulated benefit of that participant or beneficiary under both section 403(b) contracts immediately before the exchange).

(C) The other contract is subject to distribution restrictions with respect to the participant that are not less stringent than those imposed on the contract being exchanged, and the employer enters into an agreement with the issuer of the other contract under which the employer and the issuer will from time to time in the future provide each other with the following information:

(1) Information necessary for the resulting contract, or any other contract to which contributions have been made by the employer, to satisfy section 403(b), including information concerning the participant's employment and information that takes into account other section 403(b) contracts or qualified employer plans (such as whether a severance from employment has occurred for purposes of the distribution restrictions in § 1.403(b)-6 and whether the hardship withdrawal rules of § 1.403(b)-6(d)(2) are satisfied).

(2) Information necessary for the resulting contract, or any other contract to which contributions have been made by the employer, to satisfy other tax requirements (such as whether a plan loan satisfies the conditions in section 72(p)(2) so that the loan is not a deemed distribution under section 72(p)(1)).

(ii) Accumulated benefit. The condition in paragraph (b)(2)(i)(B) of this section is satisfied if the exchange would satisfy section 414(l)(1) if the exchange were a transfer of assets.

(iii) Authority for future guidance. Subject to such conditions as the Commissioner determines to be appropriate, the Commissioner may issue rules of general applicability, in revenue rulings, notices, or other guidance published in the Internal Revenue Bulletin (see § 601.601(d)(2)(ii)(b) of this chapter), permitting an exchange of one section 403(b) contract for another section 403(b) contract for an exchange that does not satisfy paragraph (b)(2)(i)(C) of this section. Any such rules must require the resulting contract to set forth procedures that the Commissioner determines are reasonably designed to ensure compliance with those requirements of section 403(b) or other tax provisions that depend on either information concerning the participant's employment or information that takes into account other section 403(b) contracts or other employer plans (such as whether a severance from employment has occurred for purposes of the distribution restrictions in § 1.403(b)-6, whether the hardship withdrawal rules of § 1.403(b)-6(d)(2) are satisfied, and whether a plan loan constitutes a deemed distribution under section 72(p)).

(3) Requirements for plan-to-plan transfers. (i) A plan-to-plan transfer under paragraph (b)(1) of this section from a section 403(b) plan to another section 403(b) plan is permitted if each of the following conditions are met—

(A) In the case of a transfer for a participant, the participant is an employee or former employee of the employer (or the business of the employer) for the receiving plan.

(B) In the case of a transfer for a beneficiary of a deceased participant, the participant was an employee or former employee of the employer (or business of the employer) for the receiving plan.

(C) The transferor plan provides for transfers.

(D) The receiving plan provides for the receipt of transfers.

(E) The participant or beneficiary whose assets are being transferred has an accumulated benefit immediately after the transfer that is at least equal to the accumulated benefit of that participant or beneficiary immediately before the transfer.

(F) The receiving plan provides that, to the extent any amount transferred is subject to any distribution restrictions under § 1.403(b)-6, the receiving plan imposes restrictions on distributions to the participant or beneficiary whose assets are being transferred that are not less stringent than those imposed on the transferor plan.

(G) If a plan-to-plan transfer does not constitute a complete transfer of the participant's or beneficiary's interest in the section 403(b) plan, the transferee plan treats the amount transferred as a continuation of a pro rata portion of the participant's or beneficiary's interest in the section 403(b) plan (for example, a pro rata portion of the participant's or beneficiary's interest in any after-tax employee contributions).

(ii) Accumulated benefit. The condition in paragraph (b)(3)(i)(D) of this section is satisfied if the transfer would satisfy section 414(l)(1).

(4) Purchases of permissive service credit by contract-to-plan transfers from a section 403(b) contract to a qualified plan—(i) General rule. If the conditions in paragraph (b)(4)(ii) of this section are met, a section 403(b) plan may provide for the transfer of assets held in the plan to a qualified defined benefit plan that is a governmental plan (as defined in section 414(d)).

(ii) Conditions for plan-to-plan transfers. A transfer may be made under this paragraph (b)(4) only if the transfer is either—

(A) For the purchase of permissive service credit (as defined in section 415(n)(3)(A)) under the receiving defined benefit plan; or

(B) A repayment to which section 415 does not apply by reason of section 415(k)(3).

(c) Qualified domestic relations orders. In accordance with the second sentence of section 414(p)(9), any distribution from an annuity contract under section 403(b) (including a distribution from a custodial account or retirement income account that is treated as a section 403(b) contract) pursuant to a qualified domestic relations order is treated in the same manner as a distribution from a plan to which section 401(a)(13) applies. Thus, for example, a section 403(b) plan does not fail to satisfy the distribution restrictions set forth in § 1.403(b)-6(b), (c), or (d) merely as a result of distribution made pursuant to a qualified domestic relations order under section 414(p), so that such a distribution is permitted without regard to whether the employee from whose contract the distribution is made has had a severance from employment or another event permitting a distribution to be made under section 403(b). In the case of a plan that is subject to Title I of ERISA, see also section 206(d)(3) of ERISA under which the prohibition against assignment or alienation of plan benefits under section 206(d)(1) of ERISA does not apply to an order that is determined to be a qualified domestic relations order.

(d) Rollovers to a section 403(b) contract—(1) General rule. A section 403(b) contract may accept a contribution that is an eligible rollover distribution (as defined in section 402(c)(4)) made from another eligible retirement plan (as defined in section 402(c)(8)(B)). Any amount contributed to a section 403(b) contract as an eligible rollover distribution is not taken into account for purposes of the limits in § 1.403(b)-4, but, except as otherwise specifically provided (for example, at § 1.403(b)-6(i)), is otherwise treated in the same manner as an amount held under a section 403(b) contract for purposes of §§ 1.403(b)-3 through 1.403(b)-9 and this section.

(2) Special rules relating to after-tax employee contributions and designated Roth contributions. A section 403(b) plan that receives an eligible rollover distribution that includes after-tax employee contributions or designated Roth contributions is required to obtain information regarding the employee's section 72 basis in the amount rolled over. A section 403(b) plan is permitted to receive an eligible rollover distribution that includes designated Roth contributions only if the plan permits employees to make elective deferrals that are designated Roth contributions.

(e) Deemed IRAs. See regulations under section 408(q) for special rules relating to deemed IRAs.

(f) Defined benefit plans—(1) Defined benefit plans generally. Except for a TEFRA church defined benefit plan as defined in paragraph (f)(2) of this section, section 403(b) does not apply to any contributions or accrual under a defined benefit plan.

(2) TEFRA church defined benefit plans. See section 251(e)(5) of the Tax Equity and Fiscal Responsibility Act of 1982, Public Law 97-248, for a provision permitting certain arrangements established by a church-related organization and in effect on September 3, 1982 (a TEFRA church defined benefit plan) to be treated as section 403(b) contract even though it is a defined benefit arrangement. In accordance with section 403(b)(1), for purposes of applying section 415 to a TEFRA church defined benefit plan, the accruals under the plan are limited to the maximum amount permitted under section 415(c) when expressed as an annual addition, and, for this purpose, the rules at § 1.402(b)-1(a)(2) for determining the present value of an accrual under a nonqualified defined benefit plan also apply for purposes of converting the accrual under a TEFRA church defined benefit plan to an annual addition. See section 415(b) for additional limits applicable to TEFRA church defined benefit plans.

(g) Other rules relating to section 501(c)(3) organizations. See section 501(c)(3) and regulations thereunder for the substantive standards for tax-exemption under that section, including the requirement that no part of the organization's net earnings inure to the benefit of any private shareholder or individual. See also sections 4941 (self dealing), 4945 (taxable expenditures), and 4958 (excess benefit transactions), and the regulations thereunder, for rules relating to excise taxes imposed on certain transactions involving organizations described in section 501(c)(3).

§ 1.403(b)-11 Applicable dates.

(a) General rule. Except as otherwise provided in this section, §§ 1.403(b)-1 through 1.403(b)-10 apply for taxable years beginning after December 31, 2008.

(b) Collective bargaining agreements. In the case of a section 403(b) plan maintained pursuant to one or more collective bargaining agreements that have been ratified and in effect on July 26, 2007, §§ 1.403(b)-1 through 1.403(b)-10 do not apply before the earlier of—

(1) The date on which the last of the collective bargaining agreements terminates (determined without regard to any extension thereof after July 26, 2007); or

(2) July 26, 2010.

(c) Church conventions; retirement income account. (1) In the case of a section 403(b) plan maintained by a church-related organization for which the authority to amend the plan is held by a church convention (within the meaning of section 414(e)), §§ 1.403(b)-1 through 1.403(b)-10 do not apply before the first day of the first plan year that begins after December 31, 2009.

(2) In the case of a loan or other extension of credit to the employer that was entered into under a retirement income account before July 26, 2007, the plan does not fail to satisfy § 1.403(b)-9(a)(2)(C) on account of the loan or other extension of credit if the plan takes reasonable steps to eliminate the loan or other extension of credit to the employer before the applicable date for § 1.403(b)-9(a)(2) or as promptly as practical thereafter (including taking steps after July 26, 2007 and before the applicable date).

(d) Special rules for plans that exclude certain types of employees from elective deferrals. (1) If, on July 26, 2007, a plan excludes any of the following categories of employees, then the plan does not fail to satisfy § 1.403(b)-5(b) as a result of that exclusion before the first day of the first taxable year that begins after December 31, 2009:

(i) Employees who make a one-time election to participate in a governmental plan described in section 414(d) that is not a section 403(b) plan.

(ii) Professors who are providing services on a temporary basis to another educational organization (as defined under section 170(b)(1)(A)(ii)) for up to one year and for whom section 403(b) contributions are being made at a rate no greater than the rate each such professor would receive under the section 403(b) plan of the original educational organization.

(iii) Employees who are affiliated with a religious order and who have taken a vow of poverty where the religious order provides for the support of such employees in their retirement from eligibility to make elective deferrals.

(2) If, on July 26, 2007, a plan excludes employees who are covered by a collective bargaining agreement from eligibility to make elective deferrals, the plan does not fail to satisfy § 1.403(b)-5(b) (relating to universal availability) as a result of that exclusion before the later of—

(i) The first day of the first taxable year that begins after December 31, 2008; or

(ii) The earlier of—

(A) The date on which the related collective bargaining agreement terminates (determined without regard to any extension thereof after July 26, 2007); or

(B) July 26, 2010.

(3) In the case of a governmental plan (as defined in section 414(d)) for which the authority to amend the plan is held by a legislative body that meets in legislative session, the plan does not fail to satisfy § 1.403(b)-5(b) as a result of any exclusion in paragraph (d)(1)(i), (d)(1)(ii),(d)(1)(iii), or (d)(2) of this section before the earlier of —

(i) The close of the first regular legislative session of the legislative body with the authority to amend the plan that begins on or after January 1, 2009; or

(ii) January 1, 2011.

(e) Special rules for plans that permit in-service distributions. (1) Section 1.403(b)-6(b) does not apply to a contract issued by an insurance company before January 1, 2009.

(2) Any amendment to comply with the requirements of § 1.403(b)-6 (disregarding paragraph (e)(1) of this section) that is adopted before January 1, 2009,or such later date as may be permitted under guidance issued by the Commissioner in revenue rulings, notices, or other guidance published in the Internal Revenue Bulletin (see § 601.601(d)(2)(ii)(b) of this chapter), does not violate section 204(g) of the Employee Retirement Income Security Act of 1974 to the extent the amendment eliminates or reduces a right to receive benefit distributions during employment.

(f) Special rule for life insurance contracts. Section 1.403(b)-8(c)(2) does not apply to a contract issued before September 24, 2007.

(g) Special rule for contracts received in an exchange. Section 1.403(b)-10(b)(2) does not apply to a contract received in an exchange that occurred on or before September 24, 2007 if the exchange (including the contract received in the exchange) satisfies such rules as the Commissioner has prescribed in guidance of general applicability at the time of the exchange.

(h) Special rule for coordination with regulations under section 415. Section 1.403(b)-3(b)(4)(ii) is applicable for taxable years beginning on or after July 1, 2007.

(i) Special rule for coordination with regulations under section 402A. Sections 1.403(b)-3(c), 1.403(b)-7(e), and 1.403(b)-10(d)(2) are applicable with respect to taxable years beginning on or after January 1, 2007.

§ 1.403(d)-1 [Removed]

Par. 8. Section 1.403(d)-1 is removed.

Par. 9. Section 1.414(c)-5 is redesignated as § 1.414(c)-6 and new § 1. 414(c)-5 is added to read as follows:

§ 1.414(c)-5 Certain tax-exempt organizations.

(a) Application. This section applies to an organization that is exempt from tax under section 501(a). The rules of this section only apply for purposes of determining when entities are treated as the same employer for purposes of section 414(b), (c), (m), and (o) (including the sections referred to in section 414(b), (c), (m), (o), and (t)), and are in addition to the rules otherwise applicable under section 414(b), (c), (m), and (o) for determining when entities are treated as the same employer. Except to the extent set forth in paragraphs (d), (e), and (f) of this section, this section does not apply to any church, as defined in section 3121(w)(3)(A), or any qualified church-controlled organization, as defined in section 3121(w)(3)(B).

(b) General rule. In the case of an organization that is exempt from tax under section 501(a) (an exempt organization) whose employees participate in a plan, the employer with respect to that plan includes the exempt organization whose employees participate in the plan and any other organization that is under common control with that exempt organization. For this purpose, common control exists between an exempt organization and another organization if at least 80 percent of the directors or trustees of one organization are either representatives of, or directly or indirectly controlled by, the other organization. A trustee or director is treated as a representative of another exempt organization if he or she also is a trustee, director, agent, or employee of the other exempt organization. A trustee or director is controlled by another organization if the other organization has the general power to remove such trustee or director and designate a new trustee or director. Whether a person has the power to remove or designate a trustee or director is based on facts and circumstances. To illustrate the rules of this paragraph (b), if exempt organization A has the power to appoint at least 80 percent of the trustees of exempt organization B (which is the owner of the outstanding shares of corporation C, which is not an exempt organization) and to control at least 80 percent of the directors of exempt organization D, then, under this paragraph (b) and § 1.414(b)-1, entities A, B, C, and D are treated as the same employer with respect to any plan maintained by A, B, C, or D for purposes of the sections referenced in section 414(b), (c), (m), (o), and (t).

(c) Permissive aggregation with entities having a common exempt purpose—(1) General rule. For purposes of this section, exempt organizations that maintain a plan to which section 414(c) applies that covers one or more employees from each organization may treat themselves as under common control for purposes of section 414(c) (and, thus, as a single employer for all purposes for which section 414(c) applies) if each of the organizations regularly coordinates their day-to-day exempt activities. For example, an entity that provides a type of emergency relief within one geographic region and another exempt organization that provides that type of emergency relief within another geographic region may treat themselves as under common control if they have a single plan covering employees of both entities and regularly coordinate their day-to-day exempt activities. Similarly, a hospital that is an exempt organization and another exempt organization with which it coordinates the delivery of medical services or medical research may treat themselves as under common control if there is a single plan covering employees of the hospital and employees of the other exempt organization and the coordination is a regular part of their day-to-day exempt activities.

(2) Authority to permit aggregation. (i) For determining when entities are treated as the same employer under section 414(b), (c), (m), and (o), the Commissioner may issue rules of general applicability, in revenue rulings, notices, or other guidance published in the Internal Revenue Bulletin (see § 601.601(d)(2)(ii)(b) of this chapter), permitting other types of combinations of entities that include exempt organizations to elect to be treated as under common control for one or more specified purposes if—

(A) There are substantial business reasons for maintaining each entity in a separate trust, corporation, or other form; and

(B) Such treatment would be consistent with the anti-abuse standards in paragraph (f) of this section.

(ii) For example, this authority might be exercised in any situation in which the organizations are so integrated in their operations as to effectively constitute a single coordinated employer for purposes of section 414(b), (c), (m), and (o), including common employee benefit plans.

(d) Permissive disaggregation between qualified church controlled organizations and other entities. In the case of a church plan (as defined in section 414(e)) to which contributions are made by more than one common law entity, any employer may apply paragraphs (b) and (c) of this section to those entities that are not a church (as defined in section 403(b)(12)(B) and § 1.403(b)-2) separately from those entities that are churches. For example, in the case of a group of entities consisting of a church (as defined in section 3121(w)(3)(A)), a secondary school (that is treated as a church under § 1.403(b)-2), and several nursing homes each of which receives more than 25 percent of its support from fees paid by residents (so that none of them is a qualified church-controlled organization under § 1.403(b)-2 and section 3121(w)(3)(B)), the nursing homes may treat themselves as being under common control with each other, but not as being under common control with the church and the school, even though the nursing homes would be under common control with the school and the church under paragraph (b) of this section.

(e) Application to certain church entities under section 3121(w)(3). [Reserved].

(f) Anti-abuse rule. In any case in which the Commissioner determines that the structure of one or more exempt organizations (which may include an exempt organization and an entity that is not exempt from income tax) or the positions taken by those organizations has the effect of avoiding or evading any requirements imposed under section 401(a), 403(b), or 457(b), or any applicable section (as defined in section 414(t)), or any other provision for which section 414(c) applies, the Commissioner may treat an entity as under common control with the exempt organization.

(g) Examples. The provisions of this section are illustrated by the following examples:

Example 1. (i) Facts. Organization A is a tax-exempt organization under section 501(c)(3) which owns 80% or more of the total value of all classes of stock of corporation B, which is a for profit organization.

(ii) Conclusion. Under paragraph (a) of this section, this section does not alter the rules of section 414(b) and (c), so that organization A and corporation B are under common control under § 1.414(c)-2(b).

Example 2. (i) Facts. Organization M is a hospital which is a tax-exempt organization under section 501(c)(3) and organization N is a medical clinic which is also a tax-exempt organization under section 501(c)(3). N is located in a city and M is located in a nearby suburb. There is a history of regular coordination of day-to-day activities between M and N, including periodic transfers of staff, coordination of staff training, common sources of income, and coordination of budget and operational goals. A single section 403(b) plan covers professional and staff employees of both the hospital and the medical clinic. While a number of members of the board of directors of M are also on the board of directors of N, there is less than 80% overlap in board membership. Both organizations have approximately the same percentage of employees who are highly compensated and have appropriate business reasons for being maintained in separate entities.

(ii) Conclusion. M and N are not under common control under this section, but, under paragraph (c) of this section, may chose to treat themselves as under common control, assuming both of them act in a manner that is consistent with that choice for purposes of § 1.403(b)-5(a), sections 401(a), 403(b), and 457(b), and any other applicable section (as defined in section 414(t)), or any other provision for which section 414(c) applies.

Example 3. (i) Facts. Organization O and P are each tax-exempt organizations under section 501(c)(3). Each organization maintains a qualified plan for it employees, but one of the plans would not satisfy section 410(b) (or section 401(a)(4)) if the organizations were under common control. The two organizations are closely related and, while the organizations have several trustees in common, the common trustees constitute fewer than 80 percent of the trustees of either organization. Organization O has the power to remove any of the trustees of P and to select the slate of replacement nominees.

(ii) Conclusion. Under these facts, pursuant to paragraphs (b) and (f) of this section, the Commissioner treats the entities as under common control.

(h) Applicable date. This section applies for plan years beginning after December 31, 2008.

Par. 10. For each entry listed in the "Location" column, remove the language in the "Remove" column and add the language in the "Add" column in its place.

Location	Remove	Add
§ 1.101-1(a)(2)(ii)	paragraph (a) or (b) of § 1.403(b)-1	§ 1.403(b)-3
§ 1.101-1(a)(2)(ii)	paragraph (c)(3) of § 1.403(b)-1	§ 1.403(b)-7
§ 1.401(a)(9)-1, A-1	§ 1.403(b)-3	§ 1.403(b)-6(e)
§ 1.401(a)(31)-1, introductory text	§ 1.403(b)-2	§ 1.403(b)-7(b)
§ 1.401(a)(31)-1, A-1(b)(3)	§ 1.403(b)-2	§ 1.403(b)-7(b)
§ 1.402(c)-2, introductory text	§ 1.403(b)-2	§ 1.403(b)-7(b)
§ 1.402(c)-2, A-1(b)(4)	§ 1.403(b)-2	§ 1.403(b)-7(b)
§ 1.402(f)-1, introductory text	§ 1.403(b)-2	§ 1.403(b)-7(b)
§ 1.403(a)-1(a)	§ 1.403(b)-1	§§ 1.403(b)-1 through 1.403(b)-10
§ 1.403(c)-1, all locations	§ 1.403(b)-1(b)	§ 1.403(b)-3
§ 1.403(c)-1, all locations	§ 1.403(b)-1(b)(2)	§ 1.403(b)-3(c)

PART 31—EMPLOYMENT TAXES, INCOME TAXES, PENALTIES, PENSIONS, RAILROAD RETIREMENT, REPORTING AND RECORDKEEPING REQUIREMENTS, SOCIAL SECURITY, UNEMPLOYMENT COMPENSATION

Par. 11. The authority citation for part 31 continues to read in part as follows:

Authority: 26 U.S.C. 7805 * * *

Par. 12. For each entry listed in the "Location" column, remove the language in the "Remove" column and add the language in the "Add" column in its place.

Location	Remove	Add
§ 31.3405(c)-1, all locations	§ 1.403(b)-2, Q&A-1	§ 1.403(b)-7(b)
§ 31.3405(c)-1, A-1(b)	§ 1.403(b)-2, Q&A-3	§ 1.403(b)-7(b)

§ 31.3405(c)-1, A-1(b)	§ 1.403(b)-2, Q&A-1 and Q&A-2	§ 1.403(b)-7(b)
§ 31.3405(c)-1, A-2	§ 1.403(b)-2, Q&A-2	§ 1.403(b)-7(b)

PART 54—EXCISE TAXES. PENSIONS, REPORTING AND RECORDKEEPING REQUIREMENTS

Par. 13. The authority citation for part 54 continues to read in part as follows:

Authority: 26 U.S.C. 7805 * * *

Par. 14. For the entry listed in the "Location" column, remove the language in the "Remove" column and add the language in the "Add" column in its place.

Location	Remove	Add
§ 54.4974-2, A-3(a)(2)	§ 1.403(b)-3	§ 1.403(b)-6(e)

PART 602—OMB CONTROL NUMBERS UNDER THE PAPERWORK REDUCTION ACT

Par 15. The authority citation for part 602 continues to read in part as follows:

Authority: 26 U.S.C. 7805.

Par 16. In § 602.101, paragraph (b) is amended by removing the entry for § 1.403(b)-2 and adding entries to the table for §§ 1.403(b)-7 and 1.402(b)-10 to read as follows:

§ 602.101 OMB Control numbers.

* * * * *

(b) * * *

CFR part or section where identified and described	Current OMB control no.
* * * * *	
1.403(b)-7...	1545-1341
1.403(b)-10	1545-2068
* * * * *	

/s/ Kevin M. Brown

Deputy Commissioner for Services and Enforcement

Approved: July 2, 2007

/s/ Eric Solomon

Assistant Secretary of Treasury (Tax Policy)

Appendix B

Revenue Procedure 2007-71

Part III—Administrative, Procedural, and Miscellaneous

26 CFR 601.201: Rulings and determination letters. (Also, Part I, § 403; § 1.403(b)-3.)

Rev. Proc. 2007-71

SECTION 1. PURPOSE

This revenue procedure provides model plan language that may be used by public schools either to adopt a written plan to reflect the requirements of § 403(b) and the regulations thereunder or to amend its § 403(b) plan to reflect the requirements of § 403(b) and the regulations thereunder. This revenue procedure also provides rules for when plan amendments or a written plan are required to be adopted by public schools or other eligible employers to comply with the recently published final regulations under § 403(b) (72 FR 41128; TD 9340). This revenue procedure also provides guidance relating to the application of § 403(b) to certain contracts issued before 2009.

SECTION 2. BACKGROUND AND GENERAL INFORMATION

.01 Section 403(b) applies to contributions made for employees who are performing services for a public school of a State or a local government or for employees of employers that are tax-exempt organizations under § 501(c)(3). Section 403(b) also applies to contributions made for certain ministers. Under § 403(b), contributions are excluded from gross income only if made to certain funding arrangements: (1) contracts issued by an insurance company qualified to issue annuities in a State that includes payment in the form of an annuity; (2) custodial accounts that are exclusively invested in stock of a regulated investment company (as defined in § 851(a) relating to mutual funds); or (3) a retirement income account for employees of a church-related organization (as defined in § 1.403(b)-2 of the Income Tax Regulations).

.02 Final regulations under § 403(b) (TD 9340) were published in the Federal Register (72 FR 41128) on July 26, 2007 (2007 regulations). The 2007 regulations replaced existing regulations that were published in the Federal Register (29 FR 18356) on December 24, 1964,1965-1 C.B. 180, that provided guidance for complying with § 403(b), as well as certain provisions of regulations that were published in the **Federal Register** (60 FR 49199) on September 22, 1995, relating to eligible rollover distributions and regulations that were published in the **Federal Register** (67 FR 18987) on April 17, 2002, relating to minimum distributions under § 401(a)(9). The 2007 regulations reflected the numerous amendments made to § 403(b) by legislation enacted since 1964. Subject to a number of special effective date rules, the 2007 regulations are generally effective for taxable years beginning after December 31, 2008.

.03 The 2007 regulations include comprehensive guidance relating to § 403(b), including the requirement that § 403(b) contracts must be maintained pursuant to a written plan. (References in this revenue procedure to a contract or an issuer include a custodial account under § 403(b)(7) and an issuer of such an account, respectively.) As indicated in the preamble to the regulations, while § 403(b) contracts that are subject to the Employee Retirement Income Security Act of 1974 (ERISA) are already maintained pursuant to written plans, there may be a potential cost associated with satisfying the written plan requirement for those employers that do not have existing plan documents, such as public schools. This revenue procedure is intended to address this concern by providing model plan language that may be used for this purpose by public schools.

.04 Section 1.403(b)-3(b)(3) of the 2007 regulations requires that contracts be issued under a plan, which, in both form and operation, satisfies the requirements of the 2007 regulations and which contains all the material terms and conditions for eligibility, benefits, applicable limitations, the contracts available under the plan, and the time and form under which benefit distributions would be made. Section 1.403(b)-10(b) of the 2007 regulations includes a special rule for situations in which a contract has been exchanged for another contract, under which the successor contract (an "exchange contract") is treated as part of the plan if certain conditions are satisfied, including an information sharing agreement between the employer and the issuer. Section 1.403(b)-11(g) of the 2007 regulations provides that those conditions are not imposed with respect to a contract if the exchange occurred before September 25, 2007, and the exchange satisfied applicable requirements at that time (a "grandfathered exchange contract").

SECTION 3. USE OF MODEL PLAN LANGUAGE BY PUBLIC SCHOOLS

.01 Any public school employer with respect to its employees performing services for it, to the extent provided, may comply with the written plan requirements of the 2007 regulations by adopting the model provision(s) contained in the Appendix to this revenue procedure. The model language has been prepared to take into account the general requirement that a § 403(b) plan include all the material terms and conditions for benefits under the plan. For example, the model language does not incorporate the applicable legal requirements by reference, but instead describes them in a manner intended to enable the plan administrator to implement the plan provisions on the basis of the model language to the extent feasible.

.02 The 2007 regulations provide that a § 403(b) plan, including one established by a public school employer, may contain certain optional features not required to satisfy § 403(b), such as in-service distributions from rollover accounts, distributions for financial hardships, loans, contract exchanges, and plan to plan transfers. If optional provisions are used, the optional provisions must meet, in both form and operation, the relevant requirements under the Code and the 2007 regulations, as well as operate in accordance with the terms of the plan. If a public school employer adopts one or more of these optional model plan language provisions for its § 403(b) plan, the form of the plan will be treated as meeting the requirements under § 403(b) with respect to those provisions.

SECTION 4. RELIANCE BY PUBLIC SCHOOL EMPLOYERS ON MODEL PLAN LANGUAGE

.01 Amendments. (a) Reliance. If a public school employer amends its plan language to include any portion of the model language, the form of the written plan will be treated as meeting the requirements of § 403(b), to the extent covered by the model plan language that is adopted. This reliance applies only if the employer adopts the model language on a word-for-word basis or adopts an amendment that is substantially similar in all material respects.

(b) Effect on public schools. If a public school employer adopts any portion of the model plan language, the written plan must also be operated in accordance with the amendment, from and after the effective date of the amendment, and the § 403(b) plan must continue to satisfy, in both form and operation, all other requirements of § 403(b) in order to maintain § 403(b) status. To the extent a public school employer's § 403(b) plan does not include the model plan language or an amendment that is substantially similar in all respects, a public school that requests a private letter ruling from the Internal Revenue Service (IRS) with respect to the qualification of its § 403(b) written plan must clearly highlight and describe in the written request how its plan provisions differ from the model language.

.02 Adoption of written plan. The model language is also designed for use by a public school that does not have a written § 403(b) plan. Thus, adoption of the entire model language (on a word-for-word basis or using language that is substantially similar in all material respects) by a public school has the same status as a private letter ruling which provides that the written form of the plan satisfies § 403(b). However, if a public school employer adopts the entire model plan language, the § 403(b) written plan must also be operated in accordance with that language, from and after the effective date of adoption, and must continue to satisfy in both form and operation all other requirements of § 403(b) in order for the plan to maintain its § 403(b) status.

SECTION 5. USE OF THE MODEL PLAN LANGUAGE BY EMPLOYERS THAT ARE NOT PUBLIC SCHOOLS

.01 The model plan language in the Appendix to this revenue procedure is designed for use by a public school employer with respect to its employees. The model language is intended for a basic plan under which contributions are limited to pre-tax elective deferrals (without any designated Roth, employer matching, or other employer nonelective contributions). An eligible employer that is not a public school may use the provisions of the Appendix as sample language to comply with one or more of the requirements imposed by the 2007 regulations issued under § 403(b).

.02 Because the model plan language in the Appendix has been designed for a State or local government with respect to its employees performing services for a public school, a § 501(c)(3) organization must determine the extent to which the model language is appropriate for use in connection with its § 403(b) plan to comply with one or more of the requirements imposed by the regulations issued under § 403(b). Notes in the Appendix identify the principal provisions which require modification for use by an eligible employer that is not a public school maintaining a § 403(b) arrangement. Moreover, if an eligible employer that is not a public school uses the model language in the Appendix, additional or revised provisions may be necessary or appropriate in order to comply with the 2007 regulations and, if applicable, ERISA, especially if either (i) the plan is not limited to elective deferrals, (ii) the plan is designed to not be an employee pension benefit plan under ERISA in accordance with 29 CFR 2510.3-2(f) of the Department of Labor Regulations, or (iii) the plan is maintained by a church (or a church-related organization described in § 414(e)(3)(A) or a qualified church-controlled organization under § 3121(w)(3)(B)) or applies with respect to one or more ministers.[1]

.03 Adoption of the model plan language contained in the Appendix by an eligible employer that is not a public school does not have the same status as a private letter ruling with respect to the adopted language. However, if an eligible employer that is not a public school has received from the IRS a favorable private letter ruling under § 403(b), then, except as provided in section 5.02 of this revenue procedure, the eligible employer's adoption of appropriate plan model language contained in the Appendix will not result in the loss of its reliance on the private letter ruling for periods prior to the effective date of the 2007 regulations.

SECTION 6. DATE AMENDMENTS ARE ADOPTED

Pursuant to this revenue procedure, a § 403(b) plan will be treated as having been amended timely to reflect a requirement of the 2007 regulations if an amendment that satisfies that requirement (such as the model language in the Appendix of this revenue procedure that reflects that requirement) is adopted no later than the first day of the first taxable year beginning after December 31, 2008, the amendment is effective as of the applicable effective date of the requirement under the 2007 regulations, and the written plan is operated as if that amendment is in effect. This section 6 applies to the requirement to have a written plan. However, for a special rule with respect to amendments made pursuant to the Pension Protection Act of 2006, Public Law 109-280 (PPA '06), see section 1107 of the PPA '06.

---

[1] See United States Department of Labor Field Assistance Bulletin No. 2007-02.

SECTION 7. AREAS NOT COVERED BY SECTIONS 3 AND 4 OF THIS REVENUE PROCEDURE

Except as provided in section 5 of this revenue procedure, the model plan language referenced in sections 3 and 4 of this revenue procedure is not designed to apply to any employer other than a State or local government with respect to its employees performing services for a public school.

SECTION 8. GUIDANCE REGARDING CERTAIN CONTRACTS ISSUED BEFORE 2009

.01 Contracts issued before 2009 as part of employer's plan. In the case of a contract issued after December 31, 2004 and before January 1, 2009 by an issuer that does not receive contributions under the plan in a year after the contract was issued (e.g., due to the issuer having been discontinued as an issuer under the plan or the issuer having become an issuer under the plan due to the contract having been issued in a post-September 24, 2007 exchange permitted under Rev. Rul. 90-24, 1990-1 CB 97), the contract will not fail to satisfy § 403(b) for the year merely because the contract is not part of a written plan that satisfies § 1.403(b)-3(b)(3) of the 2007 regulations if the employer makes a reasonable, good faith effort to include the contract as part of the employer's plan that satisfies § 1.403(b)-3(b)(3) of the 2007 regulations. For this purpose, a reasonable, good faith effort to include those contracts as part of the employer's plan includes collecting available information concerning those issuers (for which purpose, the information is not required to be collected for issuers that ceased to receive contributions before January 1, 2005) and notifying them of the name and contact information for the person in charge of administering the employer's plan for the purpose of coordinating information necessary to satisfy § 403(b). As an alternative to the actions described in the preceding sentence, a reasonable, good faith effort to include that contract as part of the employer's plan also includes the issuer taking action before making any distribution or loan to the participant or beneficiary which constitutes a reasonable, good faith effort to contact the employer and exchange any information that may be needed in order to satisfy § 403(b) with the person in charge of administering the employer's plan.

.02 Contracts issued before 2009 held for former employees or beneficiaries. In the case of an issuer that holds § 403(b) contracts under a § 403(b) plan, but which ceases to receive contributions before January 1, 2009 (e.g., due to the issuer having been discontinued as an issuer under the plan, the employer having ceased to exist, or the issuer having become an issuer under the plan due to the contract having been issued in a post-September 24, 2007 exchange permitted under Rev. Rul. 90-24, 1990-1 CB 97), those contracts continue to be subject to the requirements of § 403(b) and the 2007 regulations to the extent applicable. However, pursuant to this revenue procedure, a § 403(b) plan will not be treated as failing to satisfy the requirements of § 1.403(b)-3(b)(3) if the plan does not include terms relating to those contracts. If the participant or beneficiary requests a loan from the contract in accordance with § 72(p)(2), this relief applies only if the issuer makes such a loan only after the issuer has made reasonable efforts to determine: (1) whether the participant or beneficiary has in the prior 12 months had any other outstanding loans from qualified employer plans of the employer (taking into account §§ 72(p)(2)(D) and 72(p)(5)); and (2) if the participant or beneficiary has had any such loans, the highest outstanding balance of such loans during that period. For this purpose, assuming the employer is still in existence at the time of the loan, mere reliance on information from the participant or beneficiary about outstanding loans does not constitute reasonable efforts to determine whether the participant or beneficiary has other outstanding loans from plans of the employer.

The special rules in this section 8.02 apply only with respect to a contract that has been issued before January 1, 2009, under a § 403(b) plan that is held on behalf of a participant who, on January 1, 2009, is a former employee of the employer or for a beneficiary. For this purpose, the issuer can rely on information from the participant as to whether the participant is a former employee, assuming that reliance on that information is not unreasonable under the facts and circumstances.

8.03. Re-exchange back into plan. If, after September 24, 2007 and before January 1, 2009, a contract is issued in an exchange permitted under Rev. Rul. 90-24 (an "intermediate contract") and, before July 1, 2009, the contract is exchanged in accordance with Rev. Rul. 90-24 for a contract issued by an issuer which is either receiving contributions as part of the plan or has an information sharing agreement as set forth in § 1.403(b)-10(b)(2)(i)(C)(1) and (2) of the 2007 regulations, then the information sharing conditions in § 1.403(b)-10(b)(2)(i)(C)(1) and (2) of the 2007 regulations do not apply to the intermediate contract.

8.04. Information sharing agreements. The model plan in this revenue procedure includes optional provisions in Section 6.4(a) through (d) to allow contract exchanges with an issuer that is not receiving contributions. See Section 6.4(d) of the model language for the type of information that would satisfy the information sharing agreement conditions in § 1.403(b)-10(b)(2)(i)(C)(1) and (2) of the 2007 regulations.

SECTION 9. COMMENTS REQUESTED

Treasury and IRS are interested in receiving comments on the model language contained in this revenue procedure and any other model language that interested parties believe should be added to this revenue procedure. Comments are specifically requested on the following questions. While the model language has generally been prepared for use by employers based on provisions commonly found in defined contribution retirement plans, are there additional provisions which should be added to reflect features that are widely used? Are there changes that should especially be made to reflect the circumstances applicable to public schools, including not only revised versions of the model language, but also whether additional provisions are necessary or appropriate for them? Should the provisions found in section 7.3 of the model language, which have been prepared to satisfy the 2007 final regulations requirements for the plan document to reflect the available vendors, be expanded, including changes to reflect the special relief in section 8 of this revenue procedure?

Comments should be sent to the following address: Internal Revenue Service, Attn: CC:PA:LPD:PR (Rev. Proc. 2007-71), Room 5203, P. O. Box 7604, Ben Franklin Station, Washington, DC 20044. Written comments may be hand delivered Monday through Friday between 8 a.m. and 4 p.m. to: Internal Revenue Service, Courier's Desk, Attn: CC:PA:RU (Section 403(b) Plans), 1111 Constitution Avenue, NW., Washington, DC 20224. Alternatively, written comments may be submitted electronically via the Internet to notice. comments@irscounsel.treas.gov (Rev. Proc. 2007-71). Comments should be received by March 16, 2008.

SECTION 10. EFFECTIVE DATE

This revenue procedure is effective December 17, 2007.

DRAFTING INFORMATION

The principal author of this revenue procedure is Robert Architect of the Employee Plans, Tax Exempt and Government Entities Division. For further information regarding this revenue procedure, please contact the Employee Plans taxpayer assistance telephone service at (877) 829-5500 (a toll-free number) between the hours of 8:30 am and 4:30 pm Eastern Time, Monday through Friday. Mr. Architect may be e-mailed at Retirement Plan Questions@irs.gov.

APPENDIX FOR REVENUE PROCEDURE 2007-71
MODEL PLAN LANGUAGE

Note to sponsors: *The model language in this Appendix is designed primarily for use by a public school in order for it to offer its employees the ability to elect to make pre-tax elective deferrals in accordance with § 403(b) of the Internal Revenue Code. (See section 5 of the revenue procedure for use of the model language by an organization that is a tax-exempt organization under § 501(c)(3) or for a church entity.) In addition, the contributions permitted under the model language are limited to pre-tax elective deferrals, and it is assumed that the plan is maintained on the basis of the calendar year. This model language is not designed for a plan that provides for matching contributions or other employer nonelective contributions, or for adoption by any other type of employer. The model language also includes certain optional alternatives, including an alternative under which the plan may automatically enroll employees for elective deferrals (or alternatively to enroll only employees who file an affirmative election) and an alternative under which the plan may permit a contract issued under the plan by a vendor to whom contributions are made to be exchanged for a contract issued by vendors to whom contributions are not made under the plan.*

The portions of this Appendix printed in italics are explanatory notes for the benefit of the public school plan sponsor and thus are not to be included in the model plan document. In addition, certain items indicated by brackets can be filled in by the plan sponsor as appropriate.

Section 403(b) Model Plan Language for a Public School

Section 1
Definition of Terms Used

The following words and terms, when used in the Plan, have the meaning set forth below.

1.1 **"Account"**: The account or accumulation maintained for the benefit of any Participant or Beneficiary under an Annuity Contract or a Custodial Account.

1.2 **"Account Balance"**: The bookkeeping account maintained for each Participant which reflects the aggregate amount credited to the Participant's Account under all Accounts, including the Participant's Elective Deferrals, the earnings or loss of each Annuity Contract or a Custodial Account (net of expenses) allocable to the Participant, any transfers for the Participant's benefit, and any distribution made to the Participant or the Participant's Beneficiary. If a Participant has more than one Beneficiary at the time of the Participant's death, then a separate Account Balance shall be maintained for each Beneficiary. The Account Balance includes any account established under Section 6 for rollover contributions and plan-to-plan transfers made for a Participant, the account established for a Beneficiary after a Participant's death, and any account or accounts established for an alternate payee (as defined in section 414(p)(8) of the Code).

Note: A vendor is not required to maintain a separate account for each beneficiary in order to satisfy § 401(a)(9), but this sample plan language provides for such separate accounts so that installment payments are permitted to be made over each beneficiary's life expectancy as permitted under § 1.401(a)(9)-8, A-2(a)(2) of the Income Tax Regulations. However, because, under the sample plan language, each separate account is permitted to have only a single beneficiary, certain beneficiary designations are not permitted under the sample plan language, such as a death benefit in the form of a fixed dollar payment that is not determined as of the date of death and that is not to be maintained in a separate account to which gains and losses are credited.

1.3 **"Administrator"**: [INSERT IDENTITY OF PERSON, COMMITTEE, OR ORGANIZATION APPOINTED TO ADMINISTER THE PLAN].

1.4 **"Annuity Contract"**: A nontransferable contract as defined in section 403(b)(1) of the Code, established for each Participant by the Employer, or by each Participant individually, that is issued by an insurance company qualified to issue annuities in [Insert name of State] and that includes payment in the form of an annuity.

1.5 **"Beneficiary"**: The designated person who is entitled to receive benefits under the Plan after the death of a Participant, subject to such additional rules as may be set forth in the Individual Agreements.

1.6 **"Custodial Account"**: The group or individual custodial account or accounts, as defined in section 403(b)(7) of the Code, established for each Participant by the Employer, or by each Participant individually, to hold assets of the Plan.

1.7 **"Code"**: The Internal Revenue Code of 1986, as now in effect or as hereafter amended. All citations to sections of the Code are to such sections as they may from time to time be amended or renumbered.

1.8 **"Compensation"**: All cash compensation for services to the Employer, including salary, wages, fees, commissions, bonuses, and overtime pay, that is includible in the Employee's gross income for the calendar year, plus amounts that would be cash compensation for services to the Employer includible in the Employee's gross income for the calendar year but for a compensation reduction election under section 125, 132(f), 401(k), 403(b), or 457(b) of the Code (including an election under Section 2 made to reduce compensation in order to have Elective Deferrals under the Plan).

1.9 **"Disabled"**: The definition of disability provided in the applicable Individual Agreement.

1.10 **"Elective Deferral"**: The Employer contributions made to the Plan at the election of the Participant in lieu of receiving cash compensation. Elective Deferrals are limited to pre-tax salary reduction contributions.

1.11 **"Employee"**: Each individual, whether appointed or elected, who is a common law employee of the Employer performing services for a public school as an employee of the Employer. This definition is not applicable unless the employee's compensation for performing services for a public school is paid by the Employer. Further, a person occupying an elective or appointive public office is not an employee performing services for a public school unless such office is one to which an individual is elected or appointed only if the individual has received training, or is experienced, in the field of education. A public office includes any elective or appointive office of a State or local government.

1.12 **"Employer"**: [NAME OF PUBLIC SCHOOL].

Note: The definitions of "Employee" and "Employer" are specifically tailored for use by a State or local government maintaining a § 403(b) plan for its employees who perform services for a public school and must be modified for use by any other employer.

1.13 **"Funding Vehicles"**: The Annuity Contracts or Custodial Accounts issued for funding amounts held under the Plan and specifically approved by Employer for use under the Plan.

1.14 **"Includible Compensation"**: An Employee's actual wages in box 1 of Form W-2 for a year for services to the Employer, but subject to a maximum of $200,000 (or such higher maximum as may apply under section 401(a)(17) of the Code) and increased (up to the dollar maximum) by any compensation reduction election under section 125, 132(f), 401(k), 403(b), or 457(b) of the Code (including any Elective Deferral under the Plan). The amount of Includible Compensation is determined without regard to any community property laws.

1.15 "**Individual Agreement**": The agreements between a Vendor and the Employer or a Participant that constitutes or governs a Custodial Account or an Annuity Contract.

1.16 "**Participant**": An individual for whom Elective Deferrals are currently being made, or for whom Elective Deferrals have previously been made, under the Plan and who has not received a distribution of his or her entire benefit under the Plan.

1.17 "**Plan**": [INSERT NAME OF PLAN].

1.18 "**Plan year**": The calendar year.

1.19 "**Related Employer**": The Employer and any other entity which is under common control with the Employer under section 414(b) or (c) of the Code. For this purpose, the Employer shall determine which entities are Related Employers based on a reasonable, good faith standard and taking into account the special rules applicable under Notice 89-23, 1989-1 C.B. 654.

Note: The definition of "Related Employer" is specifically tailored for use by a State or local government maintaining a § 403(b) plan for its employees who perform services for a public school and must be modified for use by any other employer by deleting the sentence in Section 1.19 that begins "For this purpose . . ." because Notice 89-23 only applies to employers that are State or local public schools and churches. See § 1.414(c)-5 of the Income Tax Regulations (and the related discussion at pages 41137 and 41138 of the **Federal Register** *(72 FR 41128) in the preamble to those regulations).*

1.20 "**Severance from Employment**": For purpose of the Plan, Severance from Employment means Severance from Employment with the Employer and any Related Entity. However, a Severance from Employment also occurs on any date on which an Employee ceases to be an employee of a public school, even though the Employee may continue to be employed by a Related Employer that is another unit of the State or local government that is not a public school or in a capacity that is not employment with a public school (e.g., ceasing to be an employee performing services for a public school but continuing to work for the same State or local government employer).

Note: The definition of "Severance from Employment" is specifically tailored for use by a State or local government maintaining a § 403(b) plan for its employees who perform services for a public school and must be modified for use by any other employer.

1.21 "**Vendor**": The provider of an Annuity Contract or Custodial Account.

1.22 "**Valuation Date**": [Each business day/The last day of the calendar month/The last day of the calendar quarter/Each December 31].

Section 2
Participation and Contributions

2.1 **Eligibility.** Each Employee shall be eligible to participate in the Plan and elect to have Elective Deferrals made on his or her behalf hereunder immediately upon becoming employed by the Employer. However, an Employee who is a student-teacher (i.e., a person providing service as a teacher's aid on a temporary basis while attending aschool, college or university) or who normally works fewer than 20 hours per week is not eligible to participate in the Plan. An Employee normally works fewer than 20 hours per week if, for the 12-month period beginning on the date the employee's employment commenced, the Employer reasonably expects the Employee to work fewer than 1,000 hours of service (as defined under section 410(a)(3)(C) of the Code) and, for each plan year ending after the close of that 12-month period, the Employee has worked fewer than 1,000 hours of service.

Note: *This model language assumes that the plan has immediate eligibility, that the plan is limited to pre-tax elective deferrals, and that the plan has no matching or other employer non-elective contributions.*

The model language in Section 2.1 also assumes that employees who normally work fewer than 20 hours per week or who are student-teachers are not eligible. Either of these exclusions may be deleted on a uniform basis for all employees. If this model language is used by a § 501(c)(3) employer that is not a public school and the plan is subject to ERISA, the plan should delete the exclusion for employees who normally work fewer than 20 hours per week.

2.2 **Compensation Reduction Election.** (a) **General Rule.** An Employee elects to become a Participant by executing an election to reduce his or her Compensation (and have that amount contributed as an Elective Deferral on his or her behalf) and filing it with the Administrator. This Compensation reduction election shall be made on the agreement provided by the Administrator under which the Employee agrees to be bound by all the terms and conditions of the Plan. The Administrator may establish an annual minimum deferral amount no higher than $200, and may change such minimum to a lower amount from time to time. The participation election shall also include designation of the Funding Vehicles and Accounts therein to which Elective Deferrals are to be made and a designation of Beneficiary. Any such election shall remain in effect until a new election is filed. Only an individual who performs services for the Employer as an Employee may reduce his or her Compensation under the Plan. Each Employee will become a Participant in accordance with the terms and conditions of the Individual Agreements. All Elective Deferrals shall be made on a pre-tax basis. An Employee shall become a Participant as soon as administratively practicable following the date applicable under the employee's election.

(b) **Special Rule for New Employees.** (1) **Automatic Enrollment for New Employees.** For purposes of applying this Section 2.2, a new Employee is deemed to have elected to become a Participant and to have his or her Compensation reduced by [5%] (and have that amount contributed as an Elective Deferral on his or her behalf), at the time the Employee is hired, and to have agreed to be bound by all the terms and conditions of the Plan. Contributions made under this automatic participation provision shall be made to the Funding Vehicle or Vehicles selected for this purpose for all new Employees by the Administrator. Any Employee who automatically becomes a Participant under this Section 2.2(b) shall file a designation of Beneficiary with the Funding Vehicle or Vehicles to which contributions are made.

(2) **Right to File a Different Election; Notice to Employee.** This Section 2.2(b) shall not apply to the extent an Employee files an election for a different percentage reduction or elects to have no Compensation reduction, or designates a different Funding Vehicle to receive contributions made on his or her behalf. Any new Employee shall receive a statement at the time he or she is hired that describes the Employee's rights and obligations under this Section 2.2(b) (including the information in this Section 2.2(b) and identification of how the Employee can file an election or make a designation as described in the preceding sentence, and the refund right under Section 2.2(b)(3), including the specific name and location of the person to whom any such election or designation may be filed), and how the contributions under this Section 2.2(b) will be invested.

(3) **Refund of Contributions.** An Employee for whom contributions have been automatically made under Section 2.2(b)(1) may elect to withdraw all of the contributions made on his or her behalf under Section 2.2(b)(1), including earnings thereon to the date of the withdrawal. This withdrawal right is available only if the withdrawal election is made within 90 days after the date of the first contribution made under Section 2.2(b)(1).

Note: Section 2.2(b) is an optional provision that provides for any new employee to be automatically enrolled in the Plan, with 5% of Compensation to be contributed to the Plan, unless the employee elects otherwise. See §§ 414(w) and 4979(f) of the Code for special relief that applies to a plan that uses automatic enrollment, as provided in Section 2.2(b). Plan sponsors should make any revisions in this optional provision that may be necessary in order to take into account any additional guidance that may be provided by the Treasury Department or the IRS regarding automatic enrollment under §§ 414(w) and 4979(f) of the Code.

2.3 **Information Provided by the Employee.** Each Employee enrolling in the Plan should provide to the Administrator at the time of initial enrollment, and later if there are any changes, any information necessary or advisable for the Administrator to administer the Plan, including any information required under the Individual Agreements.

2.4 **Change in Elective Deferrals Election.** Subject to the provisions of the applicable Individual Agreements, an Employee may at any time revise his or her participation election, including a change of the amount of his or her Elective Deferrals, his or her investment direction, and his or her designated Beneficiary. A change in the investment direction shall take effect as of the date provided by the Administrator on a uniform basis for all Employees. A change in the Beneficiary designation shall take effect when the election is accepted by the Vendor.

2.5 **Contributions Made Promptly.** Elective Deferrals under the Plan shall be transferred to the applicable Funding Vehicle within 15 business days following the end of the month in which the amount would otherwise have been paid to the Participant.

2.6 **Leave of Absence**. Unless an election is otherwise revised, if an Employee is absent from work by leave of absence, Elective Deferrals under the Plan shall continue to the extent that Compensation continues.

Note: If this Section 2 is adopted separately, the following definitions from Section 1 should also be adopted: Account, Administrator, Beneficiary, Compensation, Elective Deferral, Employee, Employer, Funding Vehicles, Individual Agreement, Participant, Plan, and Vendor.

Section 3
Limitations on Amounts Deferred

3.1 **Basic Annual Limitation.** Except as provided in Sections 3.2 and 3.3, the maximum amount of the Elective Deferral under the Plan for any calendar year shall not exceed the lesser of (a) the applicable dollar amount or (b) the Participant's Includible Compensation for the calendar year. The applicable dollar amount is the amount established under section 402(g)(1)(B) of the Code, which is $15,500 for 2007, and is adjusted for cost-of-living after 2007 to the extent provided under section 415(d) of the Code.

3.2 **Special Section 403(b) Catch-up Limitation for Employees With 15 Years of Service**. Because the Employer is a qualified organization (within the meaning of § 1.403(b)-4(c)(3)(ii) of the Income Tax Regulations), the applicable dollar amount under Section 3.1(a) for any "qualified employee" is increased (to the extent provided in the Individual Agreements) by the least of:

(a) $3,000;

(b) The excess of:

    (1) $15,000, over

    (2) The total special 403(b) catch-up elective deferrals made for the qualified employee by the qualified organization for prior years; or

(c) The excess of:

    (1) $5,000 multiplied by the number of years of service of the employee with the qualified organization, over

    (2) The total Elective Deferrals made for the employee by the qualified organization for prior years.

For purposes of this Section 3.2, a "qualified employee" means an employee who has completed at least 15 years of service taking into account only employment with the Employer.

Note: Section 3.2 is specifically written for use by a State or local government maintaining a § 403(b) plan for its employees who perform services for a public school and, if used by a § 501(c)(3) employer, must be limited to cases in which the Employer is a "qualified organization" under § 1.403(b)-4(c)(3)(iii) of the Income Tax Regulations.

    3.3 **Age 50 Catch-up Elective Deferral Contributions.** An Employee who is a Participant who will attain age 50 or more by the end of the calendar year is permitted to elect an additional amount of Elective Deferrals, up to the maximum age 50 catch-up Elective Deferrals for the year. The maximum dollar amount of the age 50 catch-up Elective Deferrals for a year is $5,000 for 2007, and is adjusted for cost-of-living after 2007 to the extent provided under the Code.

    3.4 **Coordination**. Amounts in excess of the limitation set forth in Section 3.1 shall be allocated first to the special 403(b) catch-up under Section 3.2 and next as an age 50 catch-up contribution under Section 3.3. However, in no event can the amount of the Elective Deferrals for a year be more than the Participant's Compensation for the year.

    3.5 **Special Rule for a Participant Covered by Another Section 403(b) Plan.** For purposes of this Section 3, if the Participant is or has been a participant in one or more other plans under section 403(b) of the Code (and any other plan that permits elective deferrals under section 402(g) of the Code), then this Plan and all such other plans shall be considered as one plan for purposes of applying the foregoing limitations of this Section 3. For this purpose, the Administrator shall take into account any other such plan maintained by any Related Employer and shall also take into account any other such plan for which the Administrator receives from the Participant sufficient information concerning his or her participation in such other plan. Notwithstanding the foregoing, another plan maintained by a Related Entity shall be taken into account for purposes of Section 3.2 only if the other plan is a § 403(b) plan.

    3.6 **Correction of Excess Elective Deferrals.** If the Elective Deferral on behalf of a Participant for any calendar year exceeds the limitations described above, or the Elective Deferral on behalf of a Participant for any calendar year exceeds the limitations described above when combined with other amounts deferred by the Participant under another plan of the employer under section 403(b) of the Code (and any other plan that permits elective deferrals under section 402(g) of the Code for which the Participant provides information that is accepted by the Administrator), then the Elective Deferral, to the extent in excess of the applicable limitation (adjusted for any income or loss in value, if any, allocable thereto), shall be distributed to the Participant.

    Note: *Corrective distributions are generally required to be made within 2½ months after the end of the calendar year, but can be made within 6 months after the end of the calendar year if the plan uses the optional provision at Section 2.2(b) and otherwise constitutes an eligible automatic contribution arrangement. See §§ 414(w)(3) and 4979(f) of the Code.*

    3.7 **Protection of Persons Who Serve in a Uniformed Service.** An Employee whose employment is interrupted by qualified military service under section 414(u) of the Code or who is on a leave of absence for qualified military service under section 414(u) of the Code may elect to make additional Elective Deferrals upon resumption of employment with the Employer equal to the maximum Elective Deferrals that the Employee could have elected during that period if the Employee's employment with the Employer had continued (at the same level of Compensation) without the interruption or leave, reduced by the Elective Deferrals, if any, actually made for the Employee during the period of the interruption or leave. Except to the extent provided under section 414(u) of the Code, this right applies for five years following the resumption of employment (or, if sooner, for a period equal to three times the period of the interruption or leave).

Note: *If this Section 3 is adopted separately, the following definitions from Section 1 should also be adopted: Administrator, Code, Compensation, Elective Deferral, Employee, Employer, Includible Compensation, Participant, Plan, and Related Employer.*

Section 4
Loans

4.1 **Loans**. Loans shall be permitted under the Plan to the extent permitted by the Individual Agreements controlling the Account assets from which the loan is made and by which the loan will be secured.

4.2 **Information Coordination Concerning Loans.** Each Vendor is responsible for all information reporting and tax withholding required by applicable federal and state law in connection with distributions and loans. To minimize the instances in which Particpants have taxable income as a result of loans from the Plan, the Administrator shall take such steps as may be appropriate to coordinate the limitations on loans set forth in Section 4.3, including the collection of information from Vendors, and transmission of information requested by any Vendor, concerning the outstanding balance of any loans made to a Participant under the Plan or any other plan of the Employer. The Administrator shall also take such steps as may be appropriate to collect information from Vendors, and transmission of information to any Vendor, concerning any failure by a Participant to repay timely any loans made to a Participant under the Plan or any other plan of the Employer.

4.3 **Maximum Loan Amount.** No loan to a Participant under the Plan may exceed the lesser of:

(a) $50,000, reduced by the greater of (i) the outstanding balance on any loan from the Plan to the Participant on the date the loan is made or (ii) the highest outstanding balance on loans from the Plan to the Participant during the one-year period ending on the day before the date the loan is approved by the Administrator (not taking into account any payments made during such one-year period); or

(b) one half of the value of the Participant's vested Account Balance (as of the valuation date immediately preceding the date on which such loan is approved by the Administrator).

For purposes of this Section 4.3, any loan from any other plan maintained by the Employer and any Related Employer shall be treated as if it were a loan made from the Plan, and the Participant's vested interest under any such other plan shall be considered a vested interest under this Plan; provided, however, that the provisions of this paragraph shall not be applied so as to allow the amount of a loan to exceed the amount that would otherwise be permitted in the absence of this paragraph.

Note: Loans are included in taxable income under certain conditions, including: if the loan, when combined with the balance of all other loans from plans of the employer, exceeds the limitations described in Section 4.3; or if there is a failure to repay the loan in accordance with the repayment schedule. Because the tax treatment of a loan depends on information concerning aggregate loan balances under all annuity contracts and custodial accounts within the Plan (and under all plans of the employer), information about loan balances under the contracts and accounts of other vendors is needed before making a loan. That information may be obtained from the participant, but this sample language provides for the Administrator also to collect and coordinate that information in order to decrease the instances in which participants have taxable income from plan loans.

Note: See § 1.72(p)-1 of the Income Tax Regulations for the federal income tax treatment of loans generally.

Note: If this Section 4 is adopted separately, the following definitions from Section 1 should also be adopted: Account, Administrator, Account Balance, Employer, Individual Agreement, Participant, Plan, Related Employer, Valuation Date, and Vendor.

Section 5
Benefit Distributions

5.1 **Benefit Distributions At Severance from Employment or Other Distribution Event**. Except as permitted under Section 3.6 (relating to excess Elective Deferrals), Section 5.4 (relating to withdrawals of amounts rolled over into the Plan), Section 5.5 (relating to hardship), or Section 8.3 (relating to termination of the Plan), distributions from a Participant's Account may not be made earlier than the earliest of the date on which the Participation has a Severance from Employment, dies, becomes Disabled, or attains age 59½. Distributions shall otherwise be made in accordance with the terms of the Individual Agreements.

5.2 **Small Account Balances**. The terms of the Individual Agreement may permit distributions to be made in the form of a lump-sum payment, without the consent of the Participant or Beneficiary, but no such payment may be made without the consent of the Participant or Beneficiary unless the Account Balance does not exceed $5,000 (determined without regard to any separate account that holds rollover contributions under Section 6.1) and any such distribution shall comply with the requirements of section 401(a)(31)(B) of the Code (relating to automatic distribution as a direct rollover to an individual retirement plan for distributions in excess of $1,000).

5.3 **Minimum Distributions**. Each Individual Agreement shall comply with the minimum distribution requirements of section 401(a)(9) of the Code and the regulations thereunder. For purposes of applying the distribution rules of section 401(a)(9) of the Code, each Individual Agreement is treated as an individual retirement account (IRA) and distributions shall be made in accordance with the provisions of § 1.408-8 of the Income Tax Regulations, except as provided in § 1.403(b)-6(e) of the Income Tax Regulations.

Note: This Section 5.3 assumes that each individual agreement with a vendor complies with the minimum distribution requirements of § 401(a)(9) of the Code. See section 5 of the Appendix for Rev. Proc. 2004-56, 2004-2 C.B. 37, for model language that may be used to set forth the minimum distribution requirements of § 401(a)(9) of the Code.

5.4 **In-Service Distributions From Rollover Account.** If a Participant has a separate account attributable to rollover contributions to the plan, to the extent permitted by the applicable Individual Agreement, the Participant may at any time elect to receive a distribution of all or any portion of the amount held in the rollover account.

Note: A plan is not required to permit in-service distribution from a rollover account. See Rev. Rul. 2004-12, 2004-1 C.B. 478.

5.5 **Hardship Withdrawals**. (a) Hardship withdrawals shall be permitted under the Plan to the extent permitted by the Individual Agreements controlling the Account assets to be withdrawn to satisfy the hardship. If applicable under an Individual Agreement, no Elective Deferrals shall be allowed under the Plan during the 6-month period beginning on the date the Participant receives a distribution on account of hardship.

(b) The Individual Agreements shall provide for the exchange of information among the Employer and the Vendors to the extent necessary to implement the Individual Agreements, including, in the case of a hardship withdrawal that is automatically deemed to be necessary to satisfy the Participant's financial need (pursuant to § 1.401(k)-1(d)(3)(iv)(E) of the Income Tax Regulations), the Vendor notifying the Employer of the withdrawal in order for the Employer to implement the resulting 6-month suspension of the Participant's right to make Elective Deferrals under the Plan. In addition, in the case of a hardship withdrawal that is not automatically deemed to be necessary to satisfy the financial need (pursuant to § 1.401(k)-1(d)(3)(iii)(B) of the Income Tax Regulations), the Vendor shall obtain information from the Employer or other Vendors to determine the amount of any plan loans and rollover accounts that are available to the Participant under the Plan to satisfy the financial need.

5.6 **Rollover Distributions**. (a) A Participant or the Beneficiary of a deceased Participant (or a Participant's spouse or former spouse who is an alternate payee under a domestic relations order, as defined in section 414(p) of the Code) who is entitled to an eligible rollover distribution may elect to have any portion of an eligible rollover distribution (as defined in section 402(c)(4) of the Code) from the Plan paid directly to an eligible retirement plan (as defined in section 402(c)(8)(B) of the Code) specified by the Participant in a direct rollover. In the case of a distribution to a Beneficiary who at the time of the Participant's death was neither the spouse of the Participant nor the spouse or former spouse of the participant who is an alternate payee under a domestic relations order, a direct rollover is payable only to an individual retirement account or individual retirement annuity (IRA) that has been established on behalf of the Beneficiary as an inherited IRA (within the meaning of section 408(d)(3)(C) of the Code).

(b) Each Vendor shall be separately responsible for providing, within a reasonable time period before making an initial eligible rollover distribution, an explanation to the Participant of his or her right to elect a direct rollover and the income tax withholding consequences of not electing a direct rollover.

Note: Section 402(f) of the Code requires a plan administrator to provide a written explanation to any recipient of an eligible rollover distribution. The written explanation must cover the direct rollover rules, the mandatory income tax withholding on distributions not directly rolled over, the tax treatment of distributions not rolled over (including the special tax treatment available for certain lump sum distributions), and when distributions may be subject to different restrictions and tax consequences after being rolled over. Section 402(f) provides that this explanation must be given within a reasonable period of time before the plan makes an eligible rollover distribution. See Notice 2002-3, 2002-1 C.B. 289, that contains a Safe Harbor Explanation that plan administrators may provide to recipients of eligible rollover distributions from employer plans in order to satisfy the notice requirement.

Note: See generally § 1.403(b)-6 of the Income Tax Regulations for rules relating to restrictions on distributions.

Note: If this Section 5 is adopted separately, the following definitions from Section 1 should also be adopted: Account, Account Balance, Beneficiary, Code, Disabled, Elective Deferral, Employer, Individual Agreement, Participant, Plan, Severance from Employment, and Vendor.

Section 6
Rollovers to the Plan and Transfers

6.1 Eligible Rollover Contributions to the Plan.

(a) **Eligible Rollover Contributions**. To the extent provided in the Individual Agreements, an Employee who is a Participant who is entitled to receive an eligible rollover distribution from another eligible retirement plan may request to have all or a portion of the eligible rollover distribution paid to the Plan. Such rollover contributions shall be made in the form of cash only. The Vendor may require such documentation from the distributing plan as it deems necessary to effectuate the rollover in accordance with section 402 of the Code and to confirm that such plan is an eligible retirement plan within the meaning of section 402(c)(8)(B) of the Code. However, in no event does the Plan accept a rollover contribution from a Roth elective deferral account under an applicable retirement plan described in section 402A(e)(1) of the Code or a Roth IRA described in section 408A of the Code.

Note: This provision does not permit rollovers to be accepted from a Roth elective deferral account or a Roth IRA because the Plan does not provide for designated Roth contributions.

(b) **Eligible Rollover Distribution**. For purposes of Section 6.1(a), an eligible rollover distribution means any distribution of all or any portion of a Participant's benefit under another eligible retirement plan, except that an eligible rollover distribution does not include (1) any installment payment for a period of 10 years or more, (2) any distribution made as a result of an unforeseeable emergency or other distribution which is made upon hardship of the employee, or (3) for any other distribution, the portion, if any, of the distribution that is a required minimum distribution under section 401(a)(9) of the Code. In addition, an eligible retirement plan means an individual retirement account described in section 408(a) of the Code, an individual retirement annuity described in section 408(b) of the Code, a qualified trust described in section 401(a) of the Code, an annuity plan described in section 403(a) or 403(b) of the Code, or an eligible governmental plan described in section 457(b) of the Code, that accepts the eligible rollover distribution.

(c) **Separate Accounts**. The Vendor shall establish and maintain for the Participant a separate account for any eligible rollover distribution paid to the Plan.

6.2 **Plan-to-Plan Transfers to the Plan**. (a) At the direction of the Employer, for a class of Employees who are participants or beneficiaries in another plan under section 403(b) of the Code, the Administrator may permit a transfer of assets to the Plan as provided in this Section 6.2. Such a transfer is permitted only if the other plan provides for the direct transfer of each person's entire interest therein to the Plan and the participant is an employee or former employee of the Employer. The Administrator and any Vendor accepting such transferred amounts may require that the transfer be in cash or other property acceptable to it. The Administrator or any Vendor accepting such transferred amounts may require such documentation from the other plan as it deems necessary to effectuate the transfer in accordance with § 1.403(b)-10(b)(3) of the Income Tax Regulations and to confirm that the other plan is a plan that satisfies section 403(b) of the Code.

(b) The amount so transferred shall be credited to the Participant's Account Balance, so that the Participant or Beneficiary whose assets are being transferred has an accumulated benefit immediately after the transfer at least equal to the accumulated benefit with respect to that Participant or Beneficiary immediately before the transfer.

(c) To the extent provided in the Individual Agreements holding such transferred amounts, the amount transferred shall be held, accounted for, administered and otherwise treated in the same manner as an Elective Deferral by the Participant under the Plan, except that (1) the Individual Agreement which holds any amount transferred to the Plan must provide that, to the extent any amount transferred is subject to any distribution restrictions required under section 403(b) of the Code, the Individual Agreement must impose restrictions on distributions to the Participant or Beneficiary whose assets are being transferred that are not less stringent than those imposed on the transferor plan and (2) the transferred amount shall not be considered an Elective Deferral under the Plan in determining the maximum deferral under Section 3.

Note: This provision limits transfer to the plan to cases involving a class of participants whose entire benefit is being transferred, such as where employees are being transferred from another employer to employment with the employer maintaining this plan and the portion of the other plan held on their behalf is being merged into this plan. Plan-to-plan transfers are not required to be limited to such situations. See § 1.403(b)-10(b)(3) of the Income Tax Regulations for rules relating to plan-to-plan transfers among § 403(b) plans and, in the case of plans that are subject to ERISA, see also § 1.414(l)-1 of the Income Tax Regulations.

6.3 **Plan-to-Plan Transfers from the Plan.**

(a) At the direction of the Employer, the Administrator may permit a class of Participants and Beneficiaries to elect to have all or any portion of their Account Balance transferred to another plan that satisfies section 403(b) of the Code in accordance with § 1.403(b)-10(b)(3) of the Income Tax Regulations. A transfer is permitted under this Section 6.3(a) only if the Participants or Beneficiaries are employees or former employees of the employer (or the business of the employer) under the receiving plan and the other plan provides for the acceptance of plan-to-plan transfers with respect to the Participants and Beneficiaries and for each Participant and Beneficiary to have an amount deferred under the other plan immediately after the transfer at least equal to the amount transferred.

(b) The other plan must provide that, to the extent any amount transferred is subject to any distribution restrictions required under section 403(b) of the Code, the other plan shall impose restrictions on distributions to the Participant or Beneficiary whose assets are transferred that are not less stringent than those imposed under the Plan. In addition, if the transfer does not constitute a complete transfer of the Participant's or Beneficiary's interest in the Plan, the other plan shall treat the amount transferred as a continuation of a pro rata portion of the Participant's or Beneficiary's interest in the transferor plan (e.g., a pro rata portion of the Participant's or Beneficiary's interest in any after-tax employee contributions).

(c) Upon the transfer of assets under this Section 6.3, the Plan's liability to pay benefits to the Participant or Beneficiary under this Plan shall be discharged to the extent of the amount so transferred for the Participant or Beneficiary. The Administrator may require such documentation from the receiving plan as it deems appropriate or necessary to comply with this Section 6.3 (for example, to confirm that the receiving plan satisfies section 403(b) of the Code and to assure that the transfer is permitted under the receiving plan) or to effectuate the transfer pursuant to § 1.403(b)-10(b)(3) of the Income Tax Regulations.

Note: This provision limits transfer from the plan to cases involving a class of participants whose entire benefit is being transferred, such as where employees are being transferred from employment with the employer maintaining this plan to another employer and the portion of the plan held on their behalf is being merged into another plan. Plan-to-plan transfers are not required to be limited to such situations. See § 1.403(b)-10(b)(3) of the Income Tax Regulations for rules relating to plan-to-plan transfers among § 403(b) plans and, in the case of plans that are subject to ERISA, see also § 1.414(l)-1 of the Income Tax Regulations.

6.4 **Contract and Custodial Account Exchanges**. (a) A Participant or Beneficiary is permitted to change the investment of his or her Account Balance among the Vendors under the Plan, subject to the terms of the Individual Agreements. However, an investment change that includes an investment with a Vendor that is not eligible to receive contributions under Section 2 (referred to below as an exchange) is not permitted unless the conditions in paragraphs (b) through (d) of this Section 6.4 are satisfied.

(b) The Participant or Beneficiary must have an Account Balance immediately after the exchange that is at least equal to the Account Balance of that Participant or Beneficiary immediately before the exchange (taking into account the Account Balance of that Participant or Beneficiary under both section 403(b) contracts or custodial accounts immediately before the exchange).

(c) The Individual Agreement with the receiving Vendor has distribution restrictions with respect to the Participant that are not less stringent than those imposed on the investment being exchanged.

(d) The Employer enters into an agreement with the receiving Vendor for the other contract or custodial account under which the Employer and the Vendor will from time to time in the future provide each other with the following information:

(1) Information necessary for the resulting contract or custodial account, or any other contract or custodial accounts to which contributions have been made by the Employer, to satisfy section 403(b) of the Code, including the following: (i) the Employer providing information as to whether the Participant's employment with the Employer is continuing, and notifying the Vendor when the Participant has had a Severance from Employment (for purposes of the distribution restrictions in Section 5.1); (ii) the Vendor notifying the Employer of any hardship withdrawal under Section 5.5 if the withdrawal results in a 6-month suspension of the Participant's right to make Elective Deferrals under the Plan; and (iii) the Vendor providing information to the Employer or other Vendors concerning the Participant's or Beneficiary's section 403(b) contracts or custodial accounts or qualified employer plan benefits (to enable a Vendor to determine the amount of any plan loans and any rollover accounts that are available to the Participant under the Plan in order to satisfy the financial need under the hardship withdrawal rules of Section 5.5); and

(2) Information necessary in order for the resulting contract or custodial account and any other contract or custodial account to which contributions have been made for the Participant by the Employer to satisfy other tax requirements, including the following: (i) the amount of any plan loan that is outstanding to the Participant in order for a Vendor to determine whether an additional plan

loan satisfies the loan limitations of Section 4.3, so that any such additional loan is not a deemed distribution under section 72(p)(1); and (ii) information concerning the Participant's or Beneficiary's after-tax employee contributions in order for a Vendor to determine the extent to which a distribution is includible in gross income.

(e) If any Vendor ceases to be eligible to receive Elective Deferrals under the Plan, the Employer will enter into an information sharing agreement as described in Section 6.4(d) to the extent the Employer's contract with the Vendor does not provide for the exchange of information described in Section 6.4(d)(1) and (2).

Note: Section 6.4(a) through (d) are optional provisions for a plan that chooses to allow participants to exchange all or a portion of their account balance with vendors with respect to which the plan has no regular contact, i.e., insurance companies or mutual funds that do not receive regular contributions made for participants. Note also that additional information would be necessary in the case of an exchange involving a designated Roth account. See generally § 1.403(b)-10(b)(2) of the Income Tax Regulations for rules relating to exchanges of contracts.

6.5 Permissive Service Credit Transfers.

(a) If a Participant is also a participant in a tax-qualified defined benefit governmental plan (as defined in section 414(d) of the Code) that provides for the acceptance of plan-to-plan transfers with respect to the Participant, then the Participant may elect to have any portion of the Participant's Account Balance transferred to the defined benefit governmental plan. A transfer under this Section 6.5(a) may be made before the Participant has had a Severance from Employment.

(b) A transfer may be made under Section 6.5(a) only if the transfer is either for the purchase of permissive service credit (as defined in section 415(n)(3)(A) of the Code) under the receiving defined benefit governmental plan or a repayment to which section 415 of the Code does not apply by reason of section 415(k)(3) of the Code.

(c) In addition, if a plan-to-plan transfer does not constitute a complete transfer of the Participant's or Beneficiary's interest in the transferor plan, the Plan shall treat the amount transferred as a continuation of a pro rata portion of the Participant's or Beneficiary's interest in the transferor plan (e.g., a pro rata portion of the Participant's or Beneficiary's interest in any after-tax employee contributions).

Note: See § 1.403(b)-10(b)(4) of the Income Tax Regulations for rules relating to transfers for permissive service credit.

Note: If this Section 6 is adopted separately, the following definitions from Section 1 should also be adopted: Administrator, Account Balance, Beneficiary, Code, Elective Deferral, Employee, Employer, Individual Agreement, Participant, Plan, Severance from Employment, and Vendor.

Section 7
Investment of Contributions

7.1 **Manner of Investment**. All Elective Deferrals or other amounts contributed to the Plan, all property and rights purchased with such amounts under the Funding Vehicles, and all income attributable to such amounts, property, or rights shall be held and invested in one or more Annuity Contracts or Custodial Accounts. Each Custodial Account shall provide for it to be impossible, prior to the satisfaction of all liabilities with respect to Participants and their Beneficiaries, for any part of the assets and income of the Custodial Account to be used for, or diverted to, purposes other than for the exclusive benefit of Participants and their Beneficiaries.

7.2 **Investment of Contributions**. Each Participant or Beneficiary shall direct the investment of his or her Account among the investment options available under the Annuity Contract or Custodial Account in accordance with the terms of the Individual Agreements. Transfers among Annuity Contracts and Custodial Accounts may be made to the extent provided in the Individual Agreements and permitted under applicable Income Tax Regulations.

Note: See generally § 1.403(b)-8 of the Income Tax Regulations for rules relating to funding.

Note: If this Section 7 is adopted separately, the following definitions from Section 1 should also be adopted: Annuity Contract, Beneficiary, Custodial Account, Individual Agreement, Elective Deferral, Participant, and Plan.

7.3 **Current and Former Vendors**. The Administrator shall maintain a list of all Vendors under the Plan. Such list is hereby incorporated as part of the Plan. Each Vendor and the Administrator shall exchange such information as may be necessary to satisfy section 403(b) of the Code or other requirements of applicable law. In the case of a Vendor which is not eligible to receive Elective Deferrals under the Plan (including a Vendor which has ceased to be a Vendor eligible to receive Elective Deferrals under the Plan and a Vendor holding assets under the Plan in accordance with Section 6.2 or 6.4), the Employer shall keep the Vendor informed of the name and contact information of the Administrator in order to coordinate information necessary to satisfy section 403(b) of the Code or other requirements of applicable law.

Section 8
Amendment and Plan Termination

8.1 **Termination of Contributions**. The Employer has adopted the Plan with the intention and expectation that contributions will be continued indefinitely. However, the Employer has no obligation or liability whatsoever to maintain the Plan for any length of time and may discontinue contributions under the Plan at any time without any liability hereunder for any such discontinuance.

8.2 **Amendment and Termination**. The Employer reserves the authority to amend or terminate this Plan at any time.

8.3 **Distribution upon Termination of the Plan**. The Employer may provide that, in connection with a termination of the Plan and subject to any restrictions contained in the Individual Agreements, all Accounts will be distributed, provided that the Employer and any Related Employer on the date of termination do not make contributions to an alternative section 403(b) contract that is not part of the Plan during the period beginning on the date of plan termination and ending 12 months after the distribution of all assets from the Plan, except as permitted by the Income Tax Regulations.

Note: See generally § 1.403(b)-10(a) of the Income Tax Regulations for rules relating to discontinuance of contributions and plan termination.

Note: If this Section 8 is adopted separately, the following definitions from Section 1 should also be adopted: Account, Employer, Individual Agreement, Plan, and Related Employer.

Section 9
Miscellaneous

9.1 **Non-Assignability**. Except as provided in Sections 9.2 and 9.3, the interests of each Participant or Beneficiary under the Plan are not subject to the claims of the Participant's or Beneficiary's creditors; and neither the Participant nor any Beneficiary shall have any right to sell, assign, transfer, or otherwise convey the right to receive any payments hereunder or any interest under the Plan, which payments and interest are expressly declared to be non-assignable and non-transferable.

Note: The anti-alienation rules of section 401(a)(13) of the Code generally do not apply to § 403(b) plans of public schools, but the parallel rule at section 206(d) of ERISA applies to plans that are subject to ERISA.

9.2 **Domestic Relation Orders**. Notwithstanding Section 9.1, if a judgment, decree or order (including approval of a property settlement agreement) that relates to the provision of child support, alimony payments, or the marital property rights of a spouse or former spouse, child, or other dependent of a Participant is made pursuant to the domestic relations law of any State ("domestic relations order"), then the amount of the Participant's Account Balance shall be paid in the manner and to the person or persons so directed in the domestic relations order. Such payment shall be made without regard to whether the Participant is eligible for a distribution of benefits under the Plan. The Administrator shall establish reasonable procedures for determining the status of any such decree or order and for effectuating distribution pursuant to the domestic relations order.

Note: Section 9.2 is specifically written for use by a State or local government maintaining a § 403(b) plan for its employees who perform services for a public school and, if used by a § 501(c)(3) employer, must be revised to be limited to cases in which the domestic relations order is "qualified" under § 414(p) of the Code.

Note: See generally § 414(p) of the Code and § 1.403(b)-10(c) of the Income Tax Regulations for rules regarding domestic relations orders.

9.3 **IRS Levy.** Notwithstanding Section 9.1, the Administrator may pay from a Participant's or Beneficiary's Account Balance the amount that the Administrator finds is lawfully demanded under a levy issued by the Internal Revenue Service with respect to that Participant or Beneficiary or is sought to be collected by the United States Government under a judgment resulting from an unpaid tax assessment against the Participant or Beneficiary.

9.4 **Tax Withholding**. Contributions to the Plan are subject to applicable employment taxes (including, if applicable, Federal Insurance Contributions Act (FICA) taxes with respect to Elective Deferrals, which constitute wages under section 3121 of the Code). Any benefit payment made under the Plan is subject to applicable income tax withholding requirements (including section 3401 of the Code and the Employment Tax Regulations thereunder). A payee shall provide such information as the Administrator may need to satisfy income tax withholding obligations, and any other information that may be required by guidance issued under the Code.

9.5 **Payments to Minors and Incompetents.** If a Participant or Beneficiary entitled to receive any benefits hereunder is a minor or is adjudged to be legally incapable of giving valid receipt and discharge for such benefits, or is deemed so by the Administrator, benefits will be paid to such person as the Administrator may designate for the benefit of such Participant or Beneficiary. Such payments shall be considered a payment to such Participant or Beneficiary and shall, to the extent made, be deemed a complete discharge of any liability for such payments under the Plan.

9.6 **Mistaken Contributions.** If any contribution (or any portion of a contribution) is made to the Plan by a good faith mistake of fact, then within one year after the payment of the contribution, and upon receipt in good order of a proper request approved by the Administrator, the amount of the mistaken contribution (adjusted for any income or loss in value, if any, allocable thereto) shall be returned directly to the Participant or, to the extent required or permitted by the Administrator, to the Employer.

9.7 **Procedure When Distributee Cannot Be Located.** The Administrator shall make all reasonable attempts to determine the identity and address of a Participant or a Participant's Beneficiary entitled to benefits under the Plan. For this purpose, a reasonable attempt means (a) the mailing by certified mail of a notice to the last known address shown on [INSERT NAME OF THE EMPLOYER]'s or the Administrator's records, (b) notification sent to the Social Security Administration or the Pension Benefit Guaranty Corporation (under their program to identify payees under retirement plans), and (c) the payee has not responded within 6 months. If the Administrator is unable to locate such a person entitled to benefits hereunder, or if there has been no claim made for such benefits, the funding vehicle shall continue to hold the benefits due such person.

9.8 **Incorporation of Individual Agreements**. The Plan, together with the Individual Agreements, is intended to satisfy the requirements of section 403(b) of the Code and the Income Tax Regulations thereunder. Terms and conditions of the Individual Agreements are hereby incorporated by reference into the Plan, excluding those terms that are inconsistent with the Plan or section 403(b) of the Code.

9.9 **Governing Law**. The Plan will be construed, administered and enforced according to the Code and the laws of the State in which the Employer has its principal place of business.

9.10 **Headings**. Headings of the Plan have been inserted for convenience of reference only and are to be ignored in any construction of the provisions hereof.

9.11 **Gender**. Pronouns used in the Plan in the masculine or feminine gender include both genders unless the context clearly indicates otherwise.

IN WITNESS WHEREOF, the Employer has caused this Plan to be executed this ＿＿ day of ＿＿, ＿＿.

Employer: ＿＿＿＿＿＿＿＿＿＿＿＿＿＿＿＿＿＿＿＿

By: ＿＿＿＿＿＿＿＿＿＿＿＿＿＿＿＿＿＿＿＿

Title: ＿＿＿＿＿＿＿＿＿＿＿＿＿＿＿＿＿＿＿＿

Date signed: ＿＿＿＿＿＿＿＿＿＿＿＿＿＿＿＿＿＿＿＿

Effective
Date of the Plan: ＿＿＿＿＿＿＿＿＿＿＿＿＿＿＿＿＿＿＿＿

Note: *The provisions in Section 9 are optional provisions that are not required to be adopted.*

Note: *If this Section 9 is adopted separately, the following definitions from Section 1 should also be adopted: Administrator, Account Balance, Beneficiary, Employer, Individual Agreement, Participant, and Plan.*

Appendix C

Table for Determining Distribution Period

Table for determining distribution period—(i) General rule. The following table is used for determining the distribution period for lifetime distributions to an employee.

Uniform Lifetime Table	
Age of employee	*Distribution period*
70	27.4
71	26.5
72	25.6
73	24.7
74	23.8
75	22.9
76	22.0
77	21.2
78	20.3
79	19.5
80	18.7
81	17.9
82	17.1
83	16.3
84	15.5
85	14.8
86	14.1

Uniform Lifetime Table

Age of employee	Distribution period
87	13.4
88	12.7
89	12.0
90	11.4
91	10.8
92	10.2
93	9.6
94	9.1
95	8.6
96	8.1
97	7.6
98	7.1
99	6.7
100	6.3
101	5.9
102	5.5
103	5.2
104	4.9
105	4.5
106	4.2
107	3.9
108	3.7
109	3.4
110	3.1
111	2.9
112	2.6
113	2.4
114	2.1
115 and older	1.9

The Role of the Tax or Employee Benefits Professional in the 403(b) Arena

Janet M. Anderson-Briggs, Esq.
Michael Footer, Esq.

Since the early 1990s, two forces have been affecting Section 403(b) programs: the IRS forcing stricter compliance with the rules and competitive pressures bringing about changes in Section 403(b) products. These concerns have led employers who sponsor Section 403(b) programs to seek the assistance of outside consultants or other tax professionals. Appendix D answers some common questions about the role of the tax or employee benefits professional in the Section 403(b) environment and provides employers who are eligible to offer Section 403(b) programs with helpful information concerning the selection and engagement of consultants and other tax professionals.

Q D:1 What are some reasons prompting employers who sponsor Section 403(b) programs to seek the advice of a tax or employee benefits professional?

Most employers hire tax or employee benefits professionals for two important reasons. First, they do not have the internal expertise to complete a necessary task, or second, the task is of such duration that it would be impractical to employ the talent in-house on a long-term basis. Both of these reasons are usually present in finding a Section 403(b) product. Where a Code Section 403(b) plan is subject to ERISA, often the plan fiduciary does not have sufficient expertise to evaluate the merits of the products underwriting the plan. Since most tax-exempt employers are conducting businesses such as running hospitals and other nonprofit organizations and are not in the business of evaluating such products, these employers should be turning to qualified professionals to evaluate the merits of the available Section 403(b) products.

Employers are also seeking the advice of consultants and other tax professionals in ensuring that their Section 403(b) programs are (and remain) in compliance with the Section 403(b) rules.

Additionally, with the implementation of the Pension Protection Act of 2006 (PPA) and the final Code Section 403(b) regulations, there are new rules and concepts employers have to handle. This will include not only the legal requirements but the practical issues as well.

Q D:2 What assistance can a tax or employee benefits professional provide?

A tax or employee benefits professional can provide services such as, but not limited to, plan design, evaluation of tax-sheltered annuity (TSA) providers' products and recordkeepers, compliance assistance associated with the TSA program, and employee educational assistance associated with the TSA program. Consultants and other tax professionals often find it necessary to provide assistance in the area of deferred compensation in an effort to achieve equity for the highly compensated due to the limits on compensation and contributions.

A particularly difficult area comes about for those employers who have multiple vendors. With the requirement that there be a plan document, questions will arise regarding the construction of the document, whether it will be embodied in one writing or a series of writings. If it is made up of a series of documents, it is essential there be no inconsistencies in the aggregation of documents that make up the plan.

Q D:3 Where should an employer look to find a "403(b) professional"?

Because Section 403(b) programs and nonprofit organizations involve very specialized technical and legal issues, to ensure that one finds a true "403(b) professional," an employer might want to investigate consulting firms with proven expertise in the area of Section 403(b) programs.

There seem to be two types of consultants who work in this area: those who are truly independent and do not sell a product in conjunction with their services and those who are essentially brokers selling products. At first glance, one might assume that an independent consultant is always preferable to a broker. Picking a consultant, however, like picking a doctor or a lawyer, starts with trust. If there is any question that a particular broker-consultant might be giving his or her commission or fee priority over providing objective advice, an independent consultant should instead be retained. However, it is also possible that establishing a relationship of trust with a broker-consultant will be sufficient to cause that consultant to set aside personal compensation issues in order to provide sound objective advice.

The final Code Section 403(b) regulations touch on what plans will or will not be covered by ERISA. Although it is still not completely clear what an employer may do and still avoid ERISA, what is clear is that it may become harder to avoid

ERISA coverage. An important consequence of this is ERISA's fiduciary requirement. Picking an independent consultant versus a broker may have to be measured within the context of whether the employer used the requisite prudence in the selection process.

Q D:4   What level of experience should an employer expect from a consultant or other Section 403(b) professional?

The key knowledge bases and skills that a consultant or other Section 403(b) professional (such as an attorney or accountant) should have include insurance expertise, investment expertise, a broad knowledge of the services that are available in the marketplace, and a sense of the costs of investments and services. In addition to requiring that the Section 403(b) professional be experienced with the technical issues associated with all types of retirement plans of nonprofit employers, the employer should expect this individual to be very experienced with the culture associated with retirement programs of nonprofit organizations. This is especially true now that private, nonprofit organizations can sponsor Section 401(k) plans. The level of service and administration traditionally associated with TSA programs leads to a different level of expectation than that associated with the "for-profit" 401(k) marketplace.

Q D:5   Should an employer issue a request for proposal (RFP) when seeking to engage a Section 403(b) professional?

It is not always necessary to issue an RFP when seeking to engage the services of a consultant or other Section 403(b) professional. Most governmental organizations have procurement requirements that necessitate the issuance of RFPs. At the very least, employers should request a proposal letter from a prospective Section 403(b) professional that sets out the scope of the project, the fees and expenses, the project team and its expertise, and a timeline associated with the project.

The employer should always ask for references from the consultant and check those references.

Q D:6   If an employer issues an RFP seeking a Section 403(b) professional, what issues should be addressed in it?

The employer should carefully spell out the nature of the assistance it is seeking in as much detail as possible, when it expects the project to start and finish, and any other time constraints associated with the project. It should also indicate whether and when it expects to conduct finalist interviews of prospective candidates. Finally, whenever possible, the employer should give the candidate adequate time to respond to the RFP.

The more precise the employer can be in defining the scope of work requested, the stronger the employer's position will be when asking for a "not-to-exceed" fee quotation on the work to be performed. Rarely will a consultant provide a "not-to-exceed" fee quotation when the consultant is not sure of the scope of the project.

Q D:7   What type of disclosure should an employer expect from a Section 403(b) professional before engaging the professional's services?

An employer should expect a Section 403(b) professional to disclose any conflicts it may have in providing services. Examples of such conflicts include the following: acting as a broker for a TSA vendor company while acting as a Section 403(b) consultant conducting a vendor evaluation, or being affiliated with a company (such as a parent company or a sister subsidiary) employed by a TSA vendor company that is being scrutinized by the consultant during a vendor evaluation or compliance review.

If the Section 403(b) professional's services are being paid for by the plan, an employer should have such an arrangement reviewed by its ERISA counsel to ensure that these are permissible plan fees and that they are reasonable in amount. Oftentimes, such Section 403(b) professional will be paid on the basis of a percentage of plan assets (for example, 45 basis points on the assets in the plan). In some instances, the Section 403(b) vendor will be asked to pay the Section 403(b) professional up front and then deduct the Section 403(b) professional's fees from each participant's account. Although the plan sponsor is not paying for the Section 403(b) professional's fees from its own operating funds, it may not realize how costly it is to the participants to pay for the Section 403(b) professional's fees on an asset based basis. It is important that the plan sponsor negotiate "break points" if the Section 403(b) professional is paid on a percentage of assets basis. When the plan assets grow larger, the Section 403(b) professional's percentage of the assets should be decreasing or the Section 403(b) professional's services should increase. A fee of 45 basis points on a $5 million plan is a lot less than a fee of 45 basis points on a $10 million plan. The plan sponsor should always be aware that any of these fees will operate to reduce the employees' ultimate retirement benefits.

Q D:8   How large a factor should the cost of services be in choosing a consultant or other Section 403(b) professional?

Cost is always an issue in the purchase of any goods or services. As such, the cost should be one of the determining factors when selecting professional services, but not the primary factor. Although budgetary constraints may be in force, quality should not be sacrificed in the rush to cut costs. The cost of consulting services should be measured by the following:

1. The number of participants who will benefit from the services;
2. The total plan assets involved; or
3. The frequency with which such projects need to occur.

For example, a relatively large fee may become more reasonable if 5,000 employees, instead of just 50, will benefit from the services, or if plan assets will grow from $20 million to $30 million, or if the project need only be done once every five years, rather than every year.

Q D:9 How do the services of a Section 403(b) professional compare to those of a TSA provider?

A TSA provider is selling an employer a "product," and usually all of the offerings of the TSA provider are associated with that product. A Section 403(b) professional, on the other hand, is engaged by the employer to provide particular services; therefore, these services should meet the employer's needs as closely as possible. The Section 403(b) professional should understand the various providers' products and should assist the employer in plan-related issues.

In the TSA market, the provider's fees are often included in the product being sold and with a consultant, the fees are often outside of the product. In the former case the fees are paid by participants; and in the latter case, the fees are paid by the employer.

Q D:10 What should a TSA provider expect from a Section 403(b) professional?

A TSA provider should expect to be dealt with fairly and impartially by the professional hired by a Section 403(b) employer in connection with the employer's Section 403(b) program. Section 403(b) professionals often ask probing questions related to the provider's products and tax compliance obligations. The provider needs to trust the Section 403(b) professional not to share confidential information with competing providers. Often, a truly independent Section 403(b) professional can introduce a provider to a situation where even the provider had no knowledge the opportunity existed.

Appendix E

Field Assistance Bulletin No. 2007-02

U.S. Department of Labor   **Employee Benefits Security Administration**
Washington, D.C. 20210

FIELD ASSISTANCE BULLETIN NO. **2007-02**

DATE: JULY 24, 2007

MEMORANDUM FOR: VIRGINIA C. SMITH, DIRECTOR OF ENFORCEMENT
                      REGIONAL DIRECTORS

FROM: ROBERT J. DOYLE
                      DIRECTOR OF REGULATIONS AND INTERPRETATIONS

SUBJECT: ERISA COVERAGE OF IRC § 403(b) TAX-SHELTERED ANNUITY
                      PROGRAMS

ISSUE: How do the Department of the Treasury/ Internal Revenue Service regulations governing Internal Revenue Code § 403(b) tax-sheltered annuity programs affect the status of such programs under the Department of Labor's safe harbor regulation at 29 C.F.R. § 2510.3-2(f)?

BACKGROUND:

A tax-sheltered annuity (TSA) program under section 403(b) of the Internal Revenue Code (Code), also known as a "403(b) plan," is a retirement plan for employees of public schools, employees of certain tax-exempt organizations, and certain ministers. Under a 403(b) plan, employers may purchase for their eligible employees annuity contracts or establish custodial accounts invested only in mutual funds for the purpose of providing retirement income. Annuity contracts must be purchased from a state licensed insurance company, and the custodial accounts must be held by a custodian bank or IRS approved non-bank trustee/custodian. The annuity contracts and custodial accounts may be funded by employee salary deferrals, employer contributions, or both. Although not subject to the qualification requirements of section 401 of the Code, some of the requirements that apply to qualified plans also apply, with modifications, to 403(b) plans.

These TSA programs, if established or maintained by an employer engaged in commerce or in any industry or activity affecting commerce, generally are "pension plans" within the meaning of section 3(2) of ERISA and covered by Title I pursuant to section 4(a) of ERISA.[1] The terms "establish" or "maintain" are not defined in ERISA, and uncertainty as to the application of ERISA to TSA programs funded entirely with employee contributions prompted the Department of Labor in 1979 to issue a "safe harbor" regulation at 29 C.F.R. § 2510.3-2(f).

The safe harbor at § 2510.3-2(f) states that a program for the purchase of annuity contracts or custodial accounts in accordance with provisions set forth in section 403(b) of the Code and funded solely through salary reduction agreements or agreements to forego an increase in salary, are not "established or maintained" by an employer under section 3(2) of the Act, and, therefore, are not employee pension benefit plans subject to Title I, provided that certain factors are present. These factors are: (1) that participation of employees is completely voluntary, (2) that all rights under the annuity contract or custodial account are enforceable solely by the employee or beneficiary of such employee, or by an authorized representative of such employee or beneficiary, (3) that the involvement of the employer is limited to certain optional specified activities, and (4) that the employer receive no direct or indirect consideration or compensation in cash or otherwise other than reasonable reimbursement to cover expenses properly and actually incurred in performing the employer's duties pursuant to the salary reduction agreements. In this latter regard, if an employer, or a person acting in the interest of an employer, receives, for example, other consideration from an annuity contractor, the employer could be deemed to have "established or maintained" a plan.

The safe harbor allows the employer to engage in a range of activities to facilitate the operation of the program. The employer may permit annuity contractors—including agents or brokers who offer annuity contracts or make available custodial accounts—to publicize their products, may request information concerning proposed funding media, products, or annuity contractors, and may compile such information to facilitate review and analysis by the employees. The employer may enter into salary reduction agreements and collect annuity or custodial account considerations required by the agreements, remit them to annuity contractors, and maintain records of such collections. The employer may hold one or more group annuity contracts in the employer's name covering its employees and exercise rights as representative of its employees under the contract, at least with respect to amendments of the contract. The employer may also limit funding media or products available to employees, or annuity contractors who may approach the employees, to a number and selection designed to afford employees a reasonable choice in light of all relevant circumstances.[2]

The Department of the Treasury/Internal Revenue Service has issued final regulations at 26 C.F.R. 1.403(b)-0 et seq. (July 2007) reflecting legislative changes made to § 403(b) since the existing regulations were adopted in 1964. The § 403(b) regulations also incorporate interpretive positions that the Department of the Treasury/Internal Revenue Service have taken in other guidance on § 403(b). This Bulletin is intended to provide guidance to EBSA's national and regional offices concerning the extent to which compliance with the updated regulations would cause employers to exceed the limitations on employer involvement permitted under the Department of Labor's safe harbor for tax-sheltered annuity programs at 29 C.F.R. § 2510.3-2(f).

---

[1] Under ERISA § 4(b)(1) and (2), "governmental plans" and "church plans" generally are excluded from coverage under Title I of ERISA. Therefore, § 403(b) contracts and custodial accounts purchased or provided under a program that is either a "governmental plan" under § 3(32) of ERISA or a non-electing "church plan" under § 3(33) of ERISA are not subject to Tide I.

[2] The regulation at 29 C.F.R. § 2510.3-2(f) provides a "safe harbor" for TSA programs that conform to its provisions. The safe harbor does not preclude the possibility that programs that do not fully conform with the regulation may nevertheless not be "established or maintained" by an employer for purposes of Tide I of ERISA.

ANALYSIS:

The new § 403(b) regulations have not led the Department of Labor to change its view on the principles that apply in determining whether any given TSA program is covered by Title I of ERISA. Even though the differences between the tax rules for TSA programs and those governing other ERISA-covered pension plans may have diminished, the Department's safe harbor regulation at 29 C.F.R. § 2510.3-2(f) remains operative. The new § 403(b) regulations allow significant flexibility regarding the employer's functions in the structure and operation of the arrangement. Thus, compliance with the new § 403(b) regulations will not necessarily cause a TSA program to become covered by Title I of ERISA.

The Department has acknowledged that employers have an interest separate from acting as their employees' authorized representatives in ensuring that the annuity contracts and custodial accounts in TSA programs are tax compliant. The Code's qualification requirements impose obligations directly on employers in connection with the employees' annuity contracts and custodial accounts. If individual contracts or accounts fail to satisfy the tax qualification requirements, even if due to actions or errors of an employee or annuity contractor, the employer can be liable to the IRS for potentially substantial penalty taxes, correction fees, and employment taxes on employee salary deferrals. Accordingly, in the Department's view, the safe harbor at section 2510.3-2(f) subsumes certain employer activities designed to ensure that a TSA program continues to be tax compliant under section 403(b) of the Code.

The Department of Labor has issued advisory opinions and other guidance on whether specific employer functions are compatible with the safe harbor. The Department believes that the safe harbor allows an employer to conduct administrative reviews of the program structure and operation for tax compliance defects. Such reviews may include discrimination testing and compliance with maximum contribution limitations under the Treasury regulations. As noted in previous guidance issued by the Department, the employer may also fashion and propose corrections; develop improvements to the plan's administrative processes that will obviate the recurrence of tax defects; obtain the cooperation of independent entities involved in the program needed to correct tax defects; and keep records of its activities.[3]

A program could fit within the section 2510.3-2(f) safe harbor and include terms that require employers to certify to an annuity provider a state of facts within the employer's knowledge as employer, such as employee addresses, attendance records or compensation levels. The employer may also transmit to the annuity provider another party's certification as to other facts, such as a doctor's certification of the employee's physical condition. The employer could not, however, consistent with the safe harbor, have responsibility for, or make, discretionary determinations in administering the program. Examples of such discretionary determinations are authorizing plan-to-plan transfers, processing distributions, satisfying applicable qualified joint and survivor annuity requirements, and making determinations regarding hardship distributions, qualified domestic relations orders (QDROs), and eligibility for or enforcement of loans.[4]

An important requirement in the Treasury regulations is that a TSA program must be maintained pursuant to a "written defined contribution plan" that satisfies the Code's regulatory requirements and contains all the material terms and conditions for benefits under the plan. An employer, by adopting such a written plan, does not automatically establish a Tide I plan. Compiling the benefit terms of the contracts and the responsibilities of the employer, annuity providers and participants is a function similar to the information collection and compilation activities expressly permitted under the Department's TSA safe

---

[3] *See* DOL Information Letter to Siegel Benefit Consultants (Feb. 27, 1996).
[4] *See* Advisory Opinion Nos. 94-30A, 83-23A, and 80-11A.

harbor. Indeed, the preamble to the final Treasury regulations makes clear that the "plan" required to satisfy the Code does not have to be a single document, but may incorporate by reference other documents, including insurance policies and custodial account agreements and other documents governing the contracts and accounts prepared by the annuity providers. 26 C.F.R. § 1.403(b)-3(b)(3).

The Department of Labor expects that the written plan for a TSA program that complies with the safe harbor would consist largely of the separate contracts and related documents supplied by the annuity providers and account trustees or custodians. An employer's development and adoption of a single document to coordinate administration among different issuers, and to address tax matters that apply, such as the universal availability requirement in Code section 403(b)(12)(A)(ii), without reference to a particular contract or account, would not put the TSA program out of compliance with the safe harbor.

Because the Treasury regulations allow a plan to allocate responsibility for performing administrative functions to persons other than the employer, the relevant documents should identify the parties that are responsible for administrative functions, including those related to tax compliance. The documents should correctly describe the employer's limited role and allocate discretionary determinations to the annuity provider or participant or other third party selected by the provider or participant.

In addition, an employer seeking to take advantage of the safe harbor may periodically review the documents making up the plan for conflicting provisions and for compliance with the Code and the Treasury regulations. Negotiating with annuity providers or account custodians to change the terms of their products for other purposes, such as setting conditions for hardship withdrawals, would be a form of employer involvement outside the safe harbor.

A tax-sheltered annuity program will not, in the Department's view, become covered by Title I of ERISA merely because the written plan conforms to the new § 403(b) regulations by limiting employees to exchanges of contract funds only among providers who have adopted the written plan, or transfers from the program of a former employer to that of the current employer. Under the safe harbor, the employer may limit funding media or products available to employees, or annuity providers who may approach the employee, to a number designed to afford employees a reasonable choice in light of all relevant circumstances. The Code-mandated restrictions on transfers of funds may, however, require the employer to allow providers to offer a wider variety of products in order to afford employees a reasonable choice in light of all relevant circumstances for purposes of the safe harbor. Alternately, an employer may limit the number of providers to which it will forward salary reduction contributions as long as employees may transfer all or a part of their funds to any provider whose annuity contract or custodial account complies with the Code requirements and who agrees to the plan's division of tax compliance responsibilities among the employer, provider and participant.

Finally, in the event an employer decides that it does not want to continue to perform the ministerial and administrative functions required under the § 403(b) regulations, the Department does not believe that the employer's determination to terminate a TSA program in compliance with the Treasury regulations will cause a program not otherwise covered by Title I of ERISA to become covered.

CONCLUSION:

The Department is of the view that tax-exempt employers will be able to comply with the requirements in the new § 403(b) regulations and remain within the Department's safe harbor for TSA programs funded solely by salary deferrals. We note, however, that the new § 403(b) regulations offer employers considerable flexibility in shaping the extent and nature of their involvement under a tax-sheltered annuity program. The question of whether any particular employer, in complying with the § 403(b) regulations, has established or maintained a plan covered under Title I of ERISA must be analyzed on a case-by-case basis applying the criteria set forth in 29 C.F.R. § 2510.3-2(f) and section 3(2) of ERISA.

Questions concerning the information contained in this Bulletin may be directed to the Division of Coverage, Reporting and Disclosure, Office of Regulations and Interpretations, 202.693.8523.

Internal Revenue Code

[References are to question numbers.]

IRC §

IRC §

IRC §

IRC §

IRC §

Treasury Regulations

[References are to question numbers.]

Treas. Reg. §

Treas. Reg. §

Treas. Reg. §

Temp. Treas. Reg. §

Prop. Treas. Reg. §

Internal Revenue Service Announcements, Notices, Memoranda, Rulings, and Procedures

[*References are to question numbers.*]

IRS Announcements

IRS Notices

IRS Notices

Private Letter Rulings

Revenue Rulings

Revenue Rulings

Revenue Procedures

ERISA

[References are to question numbers.]

United States Code

[References are to question numbers.]

Department of Labor Regulations and Opinions

[References are to question numbers.]

Table of Cases

[References are to question numbers.]

Index

References are to question numbers.

S

T